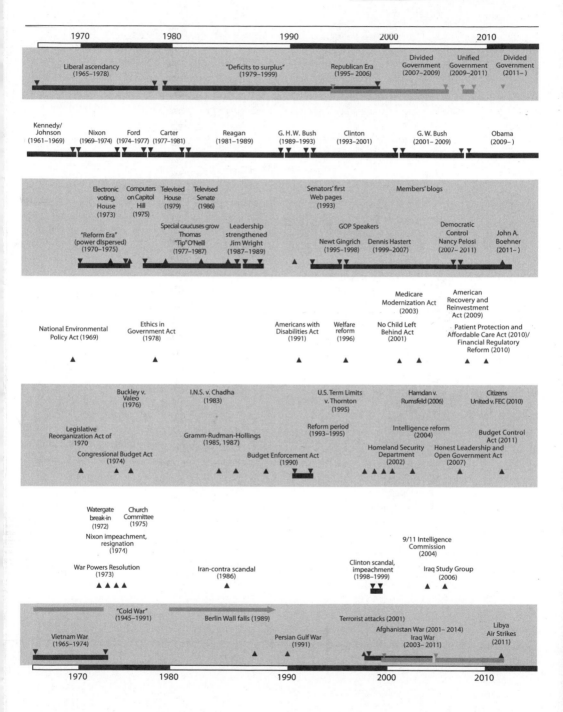

Congress and Its Members

14th Edition

Roger H. Davidson

University of Maryland

Walter J. Oleszek

Congressional Research Service

Frances E. Lee

University of Maryland

Eric Schickler

University of California, Berkeley

Los Angeles | London | New Delhi
Singapore | Washington DC

Los Angeles | London | New Delhi
Singapore | Washington DC

FOR INFORMATION:

CQ Press

An Imprint of SAGE Publications, Inc.

2455 Teller Road

Thousand Oaks, California 91320

E-mail: order@sagepub.com

SAGE Publications Ltd.

1 Oliver's Yard

55 City Road

London EC1Y 1SP

United Kingdom

SAGE Publications India Pvt. Ltd.

B 1/I 1 Mohan Cooperative Industrial Area

Mathura Road, New Delhi 110 044

India

SAGE Publications Asia-Pacific Pte. Ltd.

3 Church Street

#10-04 Samsung Hub

Singapore 049483

This book is printed on acid-free paper.

Publisher: Charisse Kiino

Editorial Assistant: Davia Grant

Production Editor: Olivia Weber-Stenis

Copy Editor: Talia Greenberg

Typesetter: C&M Digitals (P) Ltd

Proofreader: Kate Macomber Stern

Indexer: Will Ragsdale

Cover Designer: Auburn Associates Inc.

Marketing Manager: Erica DeLuca

Permissions Editor: Jennifer Barron

13 14 15 16 17 10 9 8 7 6 5 4 3 2 1

BRIEF CONTENTS

CONTENTS

PART III A Deliberative Assembly of One Nation

**PART IV   Policy Making and Change
in the Two Congresses**

Reference Materials

TABLES, FIGURES, AND BOXES

Boxes

F *our Pivotal Events in Congressional History.* British troops burn the Capitol and capture Washington, D.C., in 1814 (top left). Inflamed sectional passions caused violence on the Senate floor in 1856 (top right): An enraged Rep. Preston Brooks (S.C.), right, raises his cane against an unsuspecting Sen. Charles Sumner (Mass.). Laurence M. Keitt, a fellow South Carolinian (center), raises his cane and holds a pistol behind his back to keep other northerners from interfering. In the televised Army-McCarthy hearings of 1954 (bottom), Sen. Joseph McCarthy (R-Wis.) is chastened by U.S. Army counsel Joseph Welsh (left) during the Senate inquiry into McCarthy's reckless charges about communists in government. "At long last, sir, have you no sense of decency?" Welsh exclaimed after McCarthy attacked one of the lawyer's young aides. The dramatic exchange was a turning point in McCarthy's career; eventually he was censured by his Senate colleagues. Finally (center), Senate Majority Leader Lyndon B. Johnson (D-Texas) gives "the treatment"—prolonged persuasion at very close range—to Sen. Theodore Francis Green (D-R.I.).

As authors of the fourteenth edition of a book that first appeared in 1981, we are perforce believers in the maxim that in politics six months is a long time and four years practically a lifetime. Events of recent years surely bear out this wisdom. The roller-coaster reversals of government and politics require frequent updates of any text on the U.S. Congress that aims to be both current and comprehensive.

Presidents typically suffer steep declines in public support during their tenures in office. Three postwar presidents—Gerald R. Ford, Jimmy Carter, and George H. W. Bush—were denied a second term. A fourth, Lyndon Johnson, withdrew from his reelection race after losing the support of critical factions in his own party. George W. Bush holds the record for some of the highest approval ratings ever recorded for any president, as well as some of the lowest. Entering office during a financial crisis and the worst recession since the Great Depression, Barack Obama has never enjoyed particularly high approval ratings. Even so, he saw his public support drop sharply during his first term. Six months before election day, it appeared quite possible that both George W. Bush and Barack Obama would lose their reelection bids. In the end, each survived to grapple with second terms even more difficult than their first.

Nearly every president since World War II has faced a Congress controlled wholly or in part by the opposition party. Each of the last three presidents has endured midterm backlashes that cost their party control of Congress. After an exceptionally productive Congress under unified government in his first two years of office, Obama received what he termed a "shellacking" in the 2010 elections. Republicans gained a historic sixty-three seats to retake control of the House of Representatives, the greatest gain of House seats for a party since 1938. Republicans also narrowed Democratic margins in the Senate. For the next two years, the president's relations with Congress lurched from crisis to crisis, with impasses threatening to halt federal agency operations or send the government into default.

Toward the end of a Congress widely described as dysfunctional and gridlocked, and with a president at barely 50 percent approval, American voters returned most of the same players to Washington in the 2012 elections. Republicans retained their House majority, the Democrats their Senate majority, and the president was reelected. The new Congress, still mired in the depths of public disapproval, was asked to resolve the multitude of difficult issues left outstanding from previous years.

The precarious fortunes of recent presidents and congressional majorities are a reminder of the pervasive pluralism of the American political system, with its diverse viewpoints and interests. Presidents and congressional leaders see their mandates sooner or later bump against the founders' intricate "auxiliary precautions" for preventing majorities from winning quick or total victories. Not the least of the system's attributes is what we call the "two Congresses": Congress is both a conduit for localized interests and a maker of national policy.

In this edition, we discuss new developments and fresh research findings on nearly every aspect of Congress. When the first edition of this book came out, political scientists were still seeking to explain the decline of party unity in Congress. Today, the strength of partisanship and party leaders is the most salient reality of Capitol Hill. Congress is a vortex of so-called permanent campaigns, in which electioneering is interlocked with the process and content of lawmaking. We record shifts in party leaders, the committee system, floor procedures, and the Capitol Hill community. Complex, interdependent relationships with presidents, bureaucrats, and the courts put Congress at the center of the entire federal government.

In the midst of fundamental political change, there remain underlying constants in Congress's character and behavior. Most important is the dual nature of Congress as a collection of career-minded politicians, and also as a forum for shaping national policy. We employ the two-Congresses theme to explain the details of congressional life as well as the scholarly findings about legislators' behavior. Colorful personalities and interesting events are never in short supply when examining Capitol Hill. We strive to describe recent developments and trends precisely and perceptively; more important, we try to place them in broader historical and conceptual context.

These are troubling times for those of us who believe in representative democracy. True, Congress has, with varying levels of success, absorbed astonishing changes in its membership, partisan control, structural and procedural arrangements, and policy agendas. Yet Congress has all too often retreated from its constitutional mandate to initiate national policy and oversee government operations. Its prerogatives are under siege from executive decision makers, federal judges, and elite opinion makers, who constantly belittle its capacities, ignore its authority, and evade its scrutiny. Yet lawmakers themselves are to blame for failing to address pressing policy problems, for reinforcing disdain of the institution, and for substituting partisan allegiance for independent judgment and critical thinking. Yes, today's Congress all too often falls short of the founders' vision as the "first branch of government"—for reasons that this book explains.

This edition, like its predecessors, is written for general readers seeking an introduction to the modern Congress as well as for college or university students taking courses on the legislative process or national policy making. We try to present accurate, timely, and readable information, along with insights from scholars and practitioners. Although wrapped around our core theme, the book's chapters are long on analysis. We make no apologies for this. Lawmaking is an arduous, complicated business; those who would understand it must master its details and nuances. At the same time, we hope to convey the energy and excitement of the place. After all, our journalist friends are right: Capitol Hill is the best beat in town.

ACKNOWLEDGMENTS

We have incurred more debts to friends and fellow scholars than we could ever recount. We thank especially our colleagues at the Congressional Research Service and elsewhere: Richard Beth, Ida Brudnick, Maeve Carey, Royce Crocker, Christopher Davis, C. Lawrence Evans, Louis Fisher, Sam Garrett, Valerie Heitshusen, William Heniff Jr., Henry Hogue, Michael Koempel, Emery Lee, Mindy Levit, Megan Lynch, Jennifer Manning, Elizabeth Rybicki, James Saturno, Judy Schneider, Barbara Schwemle, Stephen W. Stathis, Jacob Strauss, Michele Swers, Kenneth Thomas, Jim Thurber, Jessica Tollestrup, and Donald Wolfensberger. The views and interpretations expressed in this book are in no way attributable to the Congressional Research Service. Kelsey Hinchliffe and Heather Creek provided valuable research assistance. We wish to thank our reviewers: Robert Locander, Lone Star College; Jonathan McKenzie, Northern Kentucky University; Brian Newman, Pepperdine University; and Linda Trautman, Ohio University. The comments of these valued colleagues prompted us to consider new questions and undertake improvements for the current edition. We gratefully welcome our new co-author, Eric Schickler, who has contributed substantially to this edition, broadening our vision and enriching the book's content. He will play a fully equal role as co-author of subsequent editions.

Our friends at CQ Press deserve special appreciation. Brenda Carter, executive editorial director of the college division, has inspired and prodded us over the last nine editions. Charisse Kiino, our editor, capably reviewed the book's overall structure and helped us tighten this edition. Talia Greenberg offered skilled and probing editorial assistance. Olivia Weber-Stenis supervised the book's production. And we thank Davia Grant for providing photo research.

Our deep appreciation for our families, for their love and support, cannot be fully expressed in words. As a measure of our affection, this book is dedicated to them.

—Roger H. Davidson
Santa Barbara, California

—Walter J. Oleszek
Fairfax, Virginia

—Frances E. Lee
Washington, D.C.

—Eric Schickler
Berkeley, California

June 2013

Roger H. Davidson is professor emeritus of government and politics at the University of Maryland, and has served as visiting professor of political science at the University of California, Santa Barbara. He is a Senior Fellow of the National Academy of Public Administration. During the 1970s, he served on the staffs of reform efforts in both the House (Bolling-Martin Committee) and the Senate (Stevenson-Brock Committee). For the 2001–2002 academic year, he served as the John Marshall Chair in political science at the University of Debrecen, Hungary. His books include *Remaking Congress: Change and Stability in the 1990s,* co-edited with James A. Thurber (1995), and *Understanding the Presidency,* 7th ed., co-edited with James P. Pfiffner (2013). Davidson is co-editor with Donald C. Bacon and Morton Keller of *The Encyclopedia of the United States Congress* (1995).

Walter J. Oleszek is a senior specialist in the legislative process at the Congressional Research Service. He has served as either a full-time professional staff aide or consultant to every major House and Senate congressional reorganization effort beginning with passage of the Legislative Reorganization Act of 1970. In 1993 he served as Policy Director of the Joint Committee on the Organization of Congress. A longtime adjunct faculty member at American University, Oleszek is a frequent lecturer to various academic, governmental, and business groups. He is the author or co-author of several books, including *Congressional Procedures and the Policy Process,* 9th ed. (2014), and *Congress under Fire: Reform Politics and the Republican Majority,* with C. Lawrence Evans (1997).

Frances E. Lee is professor of government and politics at the University of Maryland. She has been a Research Fellow at the Brookings Institution and an APSA Congressional Fellow. She is the author of *Beyond Ideology: Politics, Principles, and Partisanship in the U.S. Senate* (2009), which received the Richard F. Fenno Jr. Prize for the best book on legislative politics in 2010 and the D. B. Hardeman Prize for the best book on the U.S. Congress published in 2009. She is also co-author, with Bruce I. Oppenheimer, of *Sizing Up the Senate: The Unequal Consequences of Equal Representation* (1999). Her articles have appeared in the *American Political Science Review, Journal of Politics, Legislative Studies Quarterly,* and *American Journal of Political Science,* among others.

Eric Schickler is Jeffrey & Ashley McDermott Professor of Political Science at the University of California, Berkeley. He is the author of *Disjointed Pluralism: Institutional Innovation and the Development of the U.S. Congress* (2001) which won the Richard F. Fenno Jr. Prize for the best book on legislative politics in 2002. He is the co-author, with Donald Green and Bradley Palmquist, of *Partisan Hearts and Minds* (2002) and, with Gregory Wawro, of *Filibuster: Obstruction and Lawmaking in the U.S. Senate* (2006), which won the Fenno Prize in 2007. His articles have appeared in the *American Political Science Review, American Journal of Political Science, Legislative Studies Quarterly,* and *Studies in American Political Development,* among others.

Congress and Its Members

The Two Congresses clash. A pair of liberal Democratic allies became foes after being tossed into the same district by California's reform districting scheme in 2012. Legislative policy leader Rep. Howard Berman (below), ranking Democrat on the House Foreign Affairs Committee, speaks on war powers and the Libyan uprising. He and his rival, Rep. Brad Sherman —famous for his constituency work—engaged in a contentious debate at a candidate forum in Reseda (above) in the last month of the campaign. Victor in both the primary and general election (featuring the top two contenders), Sherman and his fans celebrate at a Ventura Boulevard restaurant (right).

The Two Congresses

"How does it feel to topple an icon?" a reporter asked Rep. Brad Sherman, D-Calif., on election night 2012.[1] In one of the most expensive and hardest-fought congressional races in the country, Sherman had defeated veteran lawmaker Rep. Howard Berman, D-Calif. Over a long and bitter campaign, Sherman's opponent had lined up endorsements from nearly the whole Democratic Party establishment in California, including both of the state's U.S. senators, its Democratic governor, and most of its House delegation. The region's leading newspaper, the *Los Angeles Times*, also endorsed Berman, praising him for his leadership on foreign affairs, immigration, and free trade.[2] "Howard Berman is a highly respected member of the House on both sides of the aisle," said Rep. Henry A. Waxman, another Los Angeles Democrat. "Brad Sherman is a member of Congress who is not taken seriously by most of his colleagues."[3]

The two rivals were congressional long-termers, Berman since 1983 and Sherman since 1997. Until California's 2012 redistricting, they had represented neighboring districts in the San Fernando Valley. Both liberal Democrats, they took similar positions on most political issues, including abortion, gay rights, Israel, and the environment. The main differences between them were stylistic. On this dimension, they were a study in contrasts. "On the one hand, you get a congressman (Sherman) who is visible and present in the district, and totally keyed in on the local concerns and issues," observed a Los Angeles Democratic Party official. "And on the other hand, you get a highly respected congressman (Berman) who is on the national and international stage, and who is a leader in Washington and on foreign affairs."[4]

Over the course of his career, Sherman had dedicated himself to staying in close touch with his constituents. Nearly every weekend, Sherman thrived on interacting with voters, shaking hands, and attending community events. During the campaign, he touted his work getting funding for a new lane on the 405 Freeway and for Topanga State Park. He had held more than 150 town hall events in his district. As a self-deprecating joke, the balding lawmaker often passed out plastic combs printed with his name and phone number.[5] In Washington, Sherman was noted for his opposition to the 2008 Wall Street bailout—which continued even when his party's president, Barack Obama, sought support for his own Wall Street initiatives. "Sherman is seen by the

Democratic leadership as a pesky loner who will only sponsor legislation that looks good back home," one political pundit remarked.[6]

Berman, by contrast, was known as a highly effective lawmaker, though not one who won a lot of publicity.[7] As chair or ranking member of the House Foreign Affairs Committee, he had taken more than 150 trips abroad over his thirty-year career. He was best known in Washington for taking on difficult, complex issues, such as immigration, intellectual property, and patent law. But he was less known in the San Fernando Valley.

California's game-changing 2012 redistricting created more competitive districts, discarded old-fashioned gerrymandering, and installed a new "top-two" primary system—in which the two leading candidates from an open primary face each other in the general election. In this system, candidates of the same party may be forced to run against one another—something that rarely occurs in American politics outside of nominating primaries. In this case, both Democrats were tossed into the same district—forcing them to reintroduce themselves to San Fernando Valley's voters all over again. Despite the consensus preference of party elites, Sherman won. The result wasn't even close, with Sherman's vote share nearly 20 percentage points greater than Berman's.

The Berman-Sherman race of 2012 illustrates the themes of this book. In some respects, of course, this race was highly unusual. But the contrasts between Berman and Sherman highlight basic truths about political representation. The work of Congress is conducted not only on Capitol Hill but also in states and districts hundreds or thousands of miles away. No matter how much members of Congress distinguish themselves as lawmakers or Beltway insiders, they also have to distinguish themselves in the eyes of local constituents. To do this, constituents must have some sense of connection with their representatives. Members must build and maintain personal relationships and open lines of communication. Constituents may not always understand the details of national policy debates, but they know when members make themselves accessible and open to local input. One of Sherman's voters summed up his decision this way: "[H]e has done a lot for the Valley. He does a lot of town halls and listens to people. I don't see a lot of congressmen doing that."[8]

THE DUAL NATURE OF CONGRESS

Brad Sherman's political experiences underscore the dual nature of Congress. Like all members, Sherman inhabits two very different but closely linked worlds. There is the world of the San Fernando Valley, where Sherman lives and cultivates his "Valley guy" persona.[9] Then there is the world of Washington policy making, where Sherman has sought to build a reputation as a liberal Democrat with an independent streak. These two worlds are intertwined in complex ways. After defeating Berman, for example, Sherman sought to move up to the ranking minority leadership of the Foreign Affairs Committee, a position he would have been expected to win given his seniority. But fallout from the bitter contest with the highly respected Berman led his fellow committee Democrats to prefer someone else.[10] Such interconnections highlight the dual character of the national legislature—Congress as a lawmaking institution and Congress as an assembly of local representatives.

In this sense, there are two Congresses. One is the Congress of textbooks, of "how a bill becomes a law." It is Congress acting as a collegial body, performing constitutional duties, and debating legislative issues that affect the entire nation. This Congress is a fascinating arena in which all the forces of American political life converge—presidents, cabinet members, career bureaucrats, activists, lobbyists, policy wonks, military leaders, and ambitious political entrepreneurs of every stripe. This Congress is more than a collection of its members at any given time. It is a mature institution with a complex network of rules, organizations, and traditions. Norms mark the boundaries of the legislative playing field and define the rules of the game. Individual members generally must accept Congress on its own terms and conform to its established ways of doing things.

A second Congress exists as well, and it is every bit as important as the Congress portrayed in textbooks. This is the representative assembly of 541 individuals (100 senators, 435 representatives, 5 delegates, and 1 resident commissioner). This Congress includes men and women of many different ages, backgrounds, and routes to office, all doing what is necessary to maintain political support in their local constituencies. Their electoral fortunes depend less on what Congress produces as a national institution than on the policy positions they take individually and the local ties they build and maintain. "As locally elected officials who make national policy," observes Paul S. Herrnson, "members of Congress almost lead double lives."[11]

The two Congresses are in many ways separated by a wide gulf. The complex, often insular world of Capitol Hill is far removed from most constituencies, in perspective and outlook, as well as in miles. Lawmaking and representing are separate tasks, and members of Congress recognize them as such. Yet these two Congresses are bound together. What affects one affects the other—sooner or later.

Legislators' Tasks

The duality between institutional and individual duties permeates legislators' daily activities and roles. As Speaker Sam Rayburn, D-Texas, once remarked: "A congressman has two constituencies—he has his constituents at home, and his colleagues here in the House. To serve his constituents at home, he must also serve his colleagues here in the House."[12]

No problem vexes members more than that of juggling constituency and legislative tasks. The pull of constituency business is relentless. To maintain their local connections, Congress schedules lengthy recesses, termed "district work periods," and many short Tuesday-to-Thursday legislative weeks. "I can tell you based on my experience that the number of days Congress spends in Washington should not be correlated with the quality of the work that is accomplished. . . . I can also tell you that time spent in our districts is not 'time off,' " observed Rep. Rob Bishop, R-Utah. "There is much more to effective representation than just voting in Washington."[13] On average, between 2000 and 2011, Congress was in session for less than 40 percent of the calendar year. Members spend much of the rest of their time at home in their constituencies.

Reelection is the paramount operational goal of members of Congress. As a former representative put it, "All members of Congress have a primary interest in getting reelected. Some members have no other interest."[14] After all, politicians must win elections before they can achieve any long-range political goals. "[Reelection] has to be the *proximate* goal of everyone, the goal that must be achieved over and over if other ends are to be entertained," David R. Mayhew observed in *Congress: The Electoral Connection.*[15]

Individual legislators vary in how they balance the twin roles of legislator and representative. Some legislators devote more time and resources to lawmaking, while others focus almost entirely on constituency tending. With their longer terms, some senators stress voter outreach and fence mending during the year or two before reelection and focus on legislative activities at other times. Yet senatorial contests normally are more competitive and costlier than House races, and many senators now run for reelection all the time—like most of their House colleagues.[16] Most senators and representatives would like to devote more time to lawmaking and other Capitol Hill duties, but the press of constituency business is relentless.[17]

Popular Images

The notion of two Congresses also conforms to the average citizen's perceptions. The public views the U.S. Congress differently from the way it sees individual senators and representatives. Congress as an institution is perceived primarily as a lawmaking body. It is judged mainly on the basis of citizens' overall attitudes toward politics, policy processes, and the state of the Union. Do people like the way things are going or not? Do they feel that Congress is carrying out its duties equitably and efficiently? Are they optimistic or pessimistic about the nation's future? Do they subscribe to Mark Twain's cynical view of Congress as a "native criminal class"?

In contrast with their expectations of Congress as a whole, citizens view their own legislators largely as agents of local concerns. People judge individual legislators by yardsticks such as service to the district, communication with constituents, and home style (the way officeholders present themselves in their districts or states). In judging their senators or representatives, voters ponder questions such as: Is the legislator trustworthy? Does the legislator communicate well with the state (or district) by answering mail promptly and offering timely help to constituents? Does the legislator listen to the state (or district) and its concerns?[18]

The public's divergent expectations of Congress and its members send conflicting signals to senators and representatives. Congress as a whole is judged by the processes it uses and the policies it adopts (or fails to adopt), however vaguely voters understand them.[19] But individual legislators are regularly elected and returned to office because of their personal qualities, the positions they take, and their constituency service. In response to this incongruity, officeholders adopt a strategy of opening as much space as possible between themselves and those other politicians back in Washington.

The Constitutional Basis

Congress's dual nature—the dichotomy between its lawmaking and representative functions—is dictated by the U.S. Constitution. Congress's mandate to write the nation's laws is found in Article I of the Constitution. By contrast, Congress's representational functions are not specified in the Constitution, although these duties flow from the constitutional provisions for electing senators and House members.

It is no accident that the Constitution's drafters devoted the first article to establishing the legislature and enumerating most of the government's powers. Familiar with the British Parliament's prolonged struggles with the Crown, the authors assumed the legislature would be the chief policy-making body and the bulwark against arbitrary executives. "In republican government, the legislative authority necessarily predominates," observed James Madison in *The Federalist Papers.*[20]

Although in the ensuing years the initiative for policy making has shifted many times between the legislative and executive branches, the U.S. Congress remains virtually the only national assembly in the world that drafts in detail the laws it passes instead of simply debating and ratifying measures prepared by the government in power.

The House of Representatives was intended to be the most representative element of the U.S. government. House members are elected directly by the people for two-year terms to ensure that they do not stray too far from popular opinion. As Madison explained, the House should have "an immediate dependence on, and an intimate sympathy with, the people."[21] For most representatives, this two-year cycle means nonstop campaigning, visiting, and looking after constituents.

The Senate was initially one step removed from popular voting. Some of the Constitution's framers hoped the Senate would temper the popular passions expressed in the House, so under the original Constitution, state legislatures selected senators. But this original vision was ultimately overruled in favor of a Senate that, like the House, directly expresses the people's voice. In 1913 the Seventeenth Amendment to the Constitution was adopted, providing for direct popular election of senators. Although elected for six-year terms, senators must stay in close touch with the electorate. Like their House colleagues, senators typically regard themselves as constituency servants. Most have transformed their office staffs into veritable cottage industries for generating publicity and handling constituents' inquiries.

Thus the Constitution and subsequent historical developments affirm Congress's dual functions of lawmaker and representative assembly. Although the roles are tightly bound together, they nonetheless impose separate duties and functions.

Back to Burke

On November 3, 1774, in Bristol, England, the British statesman and philosopher Edmund Burke set forth in a speech the dual character of a national legislature. The constituent-oriented parliament, or Congress, he described as

> a Congress of ambassadors from different and hostile interests, which interests each must maintain, as an agent and advocate, against other agents and advocates.

The parliament of substantive lawmaking he portrayed in different terms. It was

> a deliberative assembly of one nation, with one interest, that of the whole—where not local purposes, not local prejudices, ought to guide, but the general good, resulting from the general reason of the whole.[22]

Burke preferred the second concept and did not hesitate to let his voters know it. He would give local opinion a hearing, but his judgment and conscience would prevail in all cases. "Your faithful friend, your devoted servant, I shall be to the end of my life," he declared; "a flatterer you do not wish for."[23]

Burke's Bristol speech is an enduring statement of the dilemma legislators face in balancing their two roles. Burke was a brilliant lawmaker. (He even sympathized with the cause of the American colonists.) But, as might be said today, he suffered from an inept home style. His candor earned him no thanks from his constituents, who turned him out of office at the first opportunity.

Burke's dilemma applies equally on this side of the Atlantic. American voters tend to prefer their lawmakers to be delegates who listen carefully to constituents and follow their guidance. During an encounter in Borger, Texas, an irate Baptist minister shouted at then-representative Bill Sarpalius, D-Texas, "We didn't send you to Washington to make intelligent decisions. We sent you to represent us."[24] Sarpalius was later defeated for reelection.

Representing local constituents is not the whole story, of course. Burke's idea that legislators are trustees of the nation's common good is still extolled. In a 1995 decision, U.S. Supreme Court justice John Paul Stevens noted that, once elected, members of Congress become "servants of the people of the United States. They are not merely delegates appointed by separate, sovereign states; they occupy offices that are integral and essential components of a single national Government."[25]

Many talented individuals seek public office, often forgoing more lucrative opportunities in the private sector, precisely because they believe strongly in a vision of what government should do and how it should do it. For such legislators, winning office is simply a means to a larger end. It is reasonable to assume that elected officials "make an honest effort to achieve good public policy."[26]

Burke posed the tension between the two Congresses so vividly that we have adopted his language to describe the conceptual distinction that forms the crux of this book. From Burke, we have also drawn the titles for Part II, "A Congress of Ambassadors," and Part III, "A Deliberative Assembly of One Nation." Every member of Congress sooner or later must come to terms with Burke's dichotomy; citizens and voters will have to form their own answers.

THE TWO CONGRESSES IN COMPARATIVE CONTEXT

A look around the world reveals that most democracies differ from the United States in how they elect legislators. Members of Congress are selected by means of the oldest form of elected democratic representation: a plurality vote within geographic constituencies. By contrast, most other advanced democracies elect legislative representatives under systems of proportional representation (PR), a more recent innovation in democratic institutions. Many varieties of PR are in use, but compared with the U.S. electoral system, these systems tend to tie legislators more closely to their political parties than to local constituencies. In this way, PR systems somewhat alleviate the difficult trade-offs that members of Congress face as they attempt to balance national lawmaking with attention to local constituencies.

PR systems rest on the basic principle that the number of seats a political party wins in the legislature should be proportional to the level of support it receives from voters. If a political party wins 40 percent of the vote overall, then it should receive about 40 percent of the seats. In other words, these systems explicitly assume that political parties are more important than geographic locales to voters' values and political interests.[27] Most commonly in these systems, the parties put lists of candidates before the electorate. The number of a party's candidates to be seated in the legislature from those lists then depends on the percentage of voters supporting that party in legislative elections. To a greater extent than is true of members of the U.S. Congress, candidates elected in PR systems thus serve as representatives of their party's policy goals and ideological commitments.

Legislators in PR systems face fewer dilemmas about how to balance local constituency politics with national party platforms. Indeed, some PR systems, such as those in Israel and the Netherlands, do not tie representatives to local geographic constituencies at all; legislators represent the entire nation. Other countries, such as Austria and Sweden, elect multiple representatives from regional districts. Such districts are not captured by a single party on a winner-take-all basis (this is the system used in the United States—each constituency has only one representative). Districts in which more than one political party enjoys a meaningful level of voter support will elect representatives from more than one party, with each legislator representing those voters who supported his or her party. Some countries, such as Germany, Italy, and New Zealand, use a mixed system, with some representatives elected in individual geographic constituencies and others drawn from party lists to ensure proportionality. In all cases, citizens and legislators alike recognize that the system is primarily designed to ensure that voters' party preferences are proportionally represented.

Members of the U.S. Congress, by contrast, officially represent all residents of their geographic constituency—a difficult task. The constituents grouped together within congressional districts often have little in common. Indeed, constituencies can be very diverse in terms of race, class, ethnicity, religion, economic interests, and urbanization. The largest states are microcosms of the nation. Some constituencies are narrowly divided in terms of partisanship and ideology, forcing representatives to cope with continual local controversy about their stances on national issues. Some constituencies even present a member with the challenge of representing constituents who lean toward the opposing party.

In attempting to represent their whole state or district, some senators and House members attempt a "lowest common denominator" form of representation, de-emphasizing their party affiliation and their opinions on controversial national issues. Instead, they advertise their personal accessibility to constituents, focus on narrow, localized concerns, and dodge hot-button questions whenever they can.[28] This strategy is most appealing to members representing swing or cross-pressured districts. But, to an important extent, the U.S. system of representation encourages a focus on parochial matters among lawmakers generally. Members see themselves, at least to some degree, as attorneys for their constituencies.

Even though the U.S. system of representation does not recognize the importance of political parties in the way that PR systems do, members of Congress have nevertheless become more closely tied to their parties since the 1970s. Lawmakers vote with their parties far more reliably than they did in the 1950s and 1960s. The sources of this increased partisanship are many, but it has corresponded with an increasing partisan-ideological polarization in the activist base of both political parties. "The American public has become more consistent and polarized in its policy preferences over the past several decades," writes Alan I. Abramowitz, "and this increase in consistency and polarization has been concentrated among the most politically engaged citizens."[29] At the same time, the politically engaged public has also sorted itself into more ideologically coherent political parties, with fewer liberals identifying with the Republican Party and fewer conservatives identifying with the Democratic Party.[30] Consequently, relatively few voters split their tickets today by voting for one party's presidential candidate and another party's congressional candidate. These trends have reduced the cross-pressures that members face as they attempt to balance their roles as constituency representatives and national policy makers. More members are able to cooperate with their national party leaders without endangering the support of an electoral majority in their constituency. At the same time, a body of members responding to this more polarized activist base may have a harder time engaging in genuine deliberation and crafting workable legislative compromises.

All members must constantly cultivate the local roots of their power as national legislators. Yet Congress is one body, not two. The same members who attempt to forge national legislation in committee and on the floor must rush to catch planes back to their districts, where they are plunged into a different world of local problems and personalities. The same candidates who sell themselves at shopping centers also shape the federal budget or military weapons systems in the nation's capital. The unique character of Congress arises directly from its dual role as a representative assembly and a lawmaking body.

DIVERGENT VIEWS OF CONGRESS

Congress is subject to intense scrutiny, as the huge array of books, monographs, blogs, and articles devoted to it attest. Many of its features make Congress a favorite object of scholarly attention. For one thing, it is relatively open and accessible, so it can be approached by traditional means—journalistic stories, case studies, normative assessments, and historical accounts. It is also amenable to the analytic techniques of social science. Indeed, the availability of quantitative indicators of congressional work (floor votes, for example) permits elaborate statistical analyses. Its rule-governed processes allow it to be studied with increasingly sophisticated formal models. And Congress is, above all, a fascinating place—the very best location from which to view the varied actors in the American political drama.

Writers of an interpretive book on the U.S. Congress thus can draw on a multitude of sources, an embarrassment of riches. In fact, studies of Congress constitute a vast literature. This is a mixed blessing because all this information must be integrated into a coherent whole. Moreover, the scholarly writing is often highly detailed, technical, and theoretical. We have tried to put such material in perspective, make it accessible to all interested readers, and use illustrative examples wherever possible.

Meanwhile, a gaping chasm exists between this rich scholarly literature and the caricature of Congress prevalent in the popular culture. Humorists from Mark Twain and Will Rogers to Jay Leno, Bill Maher, Stephen Colbert, and Jon Stewart have found Congress an inexhaustible source of raw material. Citizens tend to share this disdain toward the legislative branch—especially at moments of furor over, say, ethics scandals or difficult legislative fights. When legislators are at home with constituents, they themselves often reinforce Congress's poor image by portraying themselves as escapees from the funny farm on Capitol Hill. As Richard F. Fenno puts it, members "run *for* Congress by running *against* Congress."[31]

The picture of Congress conveyed by the media is scarcely more flattering. Journalistic hit-and-run specialists perpetuate a cartoon-like stereotype of Congress as "a place where good ideas go to die in a maelstrom of bureaucratic hedging and rank favor-trading."[32] News magazines, editorial writers, comedians, and nightly news broadcasts regularly portray Congress as an irresponsible and somewhat disreputable gang, reminiscent of Woodrow Wilson's caustic description of the House as "a disintegrated mass of jarring elements."[33]

To comprehend how the two Congresses function—both the institution and individual members—popular stereotypes must be abandoned and the complex realities examined. Citizens' ambivalence toward the popular branch of government—which goes back to the beginnings of the Republic—says something about the milieu in which public policy is made. We believe we know our subject well enough to appreciate Congress's foibles and understand why it works the way it does, yet we try to maintain a professional, scholarly distance from it.

According to an old saying, two things should never be viewed up close: making sausages and making laws. Despite this warning, we urge readers to take a serious look at the workings of Congress and form their own opinions about Congress's effectiveness. Some may recoil from what they discover. Numerous flaws can be identified in members' personal or public behavior, in their priorities and incentive structures, and in lawmaking processes generally. Recent Congresses especially have displayed troubling tendencies, including rushed legislation, extreme partisanship, minimal executive oversight, and abdication of legislative power to the executive branch.[34]

Yet careful observers will also discover much behavior in Congress that is purposeful and principled, many policies that are reasonable and workable. We invite students and colleagues to examine with us what Congress does, and why, and ponder its values and its prospects.

Changing Gender Demography on Capitol Hill. Former Speaker "Uncle Joe" Cannon, last of the post–Civil War House leaders (1903–1911), gets a shave from his House barber (top). Challenging male domination on Capitol Hill, the seven women of the 71st Congress (1929–1931) pose on the Capitol steps (center). In 2013 (bottom), the 59 Democratic women in the 113th House—the first caucus in either chamber not to have a majority of white males—gather with Minority Leader Nancy Pelosi (sixth from right). Twenty of the hundred senators are women (16 D, 4 R), which means waiting lines for the tiny women's restroom.

chapter 2

Evolution of the Modern Congress

T
he first Congress met in New York City in the spring of 1789. Business couldn't begin until April 1, when a majority of the fifty-nine House members finally arrived to make a quorum. Members then chose Frederick A. C. Muhlenberg of Pennsylvania as Speaker of the House. Five days later, the Senate achieved its first quorum, although its presiding officer, Vice President John Adams, did not arrive for another two weeks.

New York City, the seat of government, was then a bustling port on the southern tip of Manhattan Island. Congress met in Federal Hall at the corner of Broad and Wall Streets. The House of Representatives occupied a large chamber on the first floor and the Senate a more intimate chamber upstairs. The new chief executive, George Washington, was still en route from Mount Vernon, his plantation in Virginia; his trip had become a triumphal procession with crowds and celebrations at every stop. To most of his countrymen, Washington—austere, dignified, the soul of propriety—embodied a government that otherwise was no more than a plan on paper.

The two houses of Congress did not wait for Washington's arrival. The House began debating tariffs, a perennial legislative topic. In the Senate, Vice President Adams, a brilliant but self-important man, prodded his colleagues to decide on proper titles for addressing the president and himself. Adams was dubbed "His Rotundity" by a colleague who thought the whole discussion absurd.

On inaugural day, April 30, Adams was still worrying about how to address the president when the representatives, led by Speaker Muhlenberg, burst into the Senate chamber and seated themselves. Meanwhile, a special committee was dispatched to escort Washington to the chamber for the ceremony. The swearing-in was conducted on an outside balcony in front of thousands of assembled citizens.[1] Then the nervous Washington reentered the Senate chamber and haltingly read his inaugural address. After the speech, everyone adjourned to nearby St. Paul's Chapel for a special prayer service. Thus the U.S. Congress became part of a functioning government.[2]

ANTECEDENTS OF CONGRESS

The legislative branch of the new government was untried and unknown, searching for procedures and precedents. And yet it grew out of a rich history of development—stretching back more than five hundred years in Great Britain and no less than a century and a half in North America. If the architects of the U.S. Constitution of 1787 were unsure of how well their new design would work, they had firm ideas about what they intended.

The English Heritage

The evolution of representative institutions on a national scale began in medieval Europe. Monarchs gained power over large territories where inhabitants were divided into social groupings, called "estates of the realm"— among them, the nobility, clergy, landed gentry, and town officials. The monarchs brought together the leaders of these estates, not to create representative government but to fill the royal coffers.

These assemblies later came to be called parliaments, from the French *parler*, "to speak." Historians and political scientists have identified four distinct stages in the evolution of the assemblies of estates into the representative legislatures of today. The first stage saw the assemblies representing the various estates gathering merely to vote taxes for the royal treasury; they engaged in little discussion. During the second stage, these tax-voting bodies evolved into bodies that presented the king with petitions for redressing grievances. In the third stage, by a gradual process that culminated in the revolutions of the seventeenth and eighteenth centuries, parliaments wrested lawmaking and tax-levying powers from the king. In the fourth and final stage, during the nineteenth and twentieth centuries, parliamentary representation expanded beyond the older privileged groups to embrace all adult men and women.[3]

By the time the New World colonies were founded in the 1600s, the struggle for parliamentary rights was well advanced into the third stage, at least in England. Bloody conflicts, culminating in the beheading of Charles I in 1649 and the dethroning of James II in the Glorious Revolution of 1688, established parliamentary influence over the Crown.

Out of the struggles between the Crown and Parliament flowed a remarkable body of political and philosophic writings. By the eighteenth century, works by James Harrington (1611–1677), John Locke (1632–1704), William Blackstone (1723–1780), and the Frenchman Baron de Montesquieu (1689–1755) were the common heritage of educated leaders in North America as well as in Europe.

The Colonial Experience

European settlers in the New World brought this tradition of representative government with them. As early as 1619, the thousand or so Virginia colonists elected twenty-two burgesses, or delegates, to a general assembly. In 1630 the Massachusetts Bay Company established itself as the governing body for the Bay Colony, subject to annual elections. The other colonies followed suit.

Representative government took firm root in the colonies. The broad expanse of ocean shielding America from its European masters fostered autonomy on the part of the colonial assemblies. Claiming prerogatives similar to those of the British House of Commons, these assemblies exercised the full range of lawmaking powers—levying taxes, issuing money, and providing for colonial defense. Legislation could be vetoed by colonial governors (appointed by the Crown in the eight royal colonies); but the governors, cut off from the home government and dependent on local assemblies for revenues and even for their own salaries, usually preferred to reach agreement with the locals. Royal vetoes could emanate from London, but these took time and were infrequent.[4]

Other elements nourished the growth of democratic institutions. Many of the colonists were free-spirited dissidents set on resisting traditional forms of authority, especially that of the Crown. Their self-confidence was bolstered by the readily available land, the harsh frontier life, and—by the eighteenth century—a robust economy. The town meeting form of government in New England and the separatists' church assemblies helped cultivate habits of self-government. Newspapers, unfettered by royal licenses or government taxes, stimulated lively exchanges of opinions.

When Britain decided in the 1760s, following the ruinous French and Indian War, to tighten its rein on the American colonies, it met with stubborn opposition. Colonists asked: Why don't we enjoy the same rights as Englishmen? Why aren't our colonial assemblies legitimate governments, with authority derived from popular elections? As British enactments grew increasingly unpopular, along with the governors who tried to enforce them, the locally based legislatures took up the cause of their constituents.

The colonists especially resented the Stamp Act of 1765, which provoked delegates from nine colonies to meet in New York City. There, the Stamp Act Congress adopted a fourteen-point *Declaration of Rights and Grievances*. The Stamp Act was later repealed. But new import duties levied in 1767 brought inflated customs receipts that enabled the Crown to begin directly paying the salaries of royal governors and other officials, thereby freeing those officials from the influence of colonial assemblies. The crisis worsened in the winter of 1773–1774, when a group of colonists staged a revolt, the Boston Tea Party, to protest the taxes imposed by the Tea Act. In retaliation, the House of Commons closed the port of Boston and passed a series of so-called Intolerable Acts, further tightening royal control.

National representative assemblies in America were born on September 5, 1774, when the First Continental Congress convened in Philadelphia. Every colony except Georgia sent delegates—a varied group that included peaceable souls loyal to the Crown, moderates such as Pennsylvania's John Dickinson, and firebrands such as Samuel Adams and Paul Revere. Gradually, anti-British sentiment congealed, and Congress passed a series of declarations and resolutions (each colony casting one vote) amounting to a declaration of war against the mother country.[5] After Congress adjourned on October 22, King George III declared that the colonies were "now in a state of rebellion; blows must decide whether they are to be subject to this country or independent."[6]

If the First Continental Congress gave colonists a taste of collective decision making, the Second Continental Congress proclaimed their independence from Britain. When this second Congress convened on May 10, 1775, many colonists still believed war might be avoided. A petition to King George asking for "happy and permanent reconciliation" was even approved. The British responded by proclaiming a state of rebellion and launching efforts to crush it. Sentiment in the colonies swung increasingly toward independence, and by the middle of 1776 Congress was debating Thomas Jefferson's draft resolution that "these united colonies are, and of right ought to be, free and independent states."[7]

The two Continental Congresses gave birth to national politics in America. Riding the wave of patriotism unleashed by the British actions of 1773–1774, the Congresses succeeded in pushing the sentiments of leaders and much of the general public toward confrontation and away from reconciliation with the mother country. They did so by defining issues one by one and by reaching compromises acceptable to both moderates and radicals—no small accomplishment. Shared legislative experience, in other words, moved the delegates to the threshold of independence. Their achievement was all the more remarkable in light of what historian Jack N. Rakove describes as the "peculiar status" of the Continental Congress, "an extra-legal body whose authority would obviously depend on its ability to maintain a broad range of support."[8]

More than five years of bloody conflict ensued before the colonies won their independence. Meanwhile, the former colonies hastened to form new governments and draft constitutions. Unlike the English constitution, these charters were written documents. All included some sort of bill of rights, and all paid lip service to the doctrine of separating powers among legislative, executive, and judicial branches of government. But past conflicts with the Crown and the royal governors had instilled a fear of all forms of executive authority. So nearly all the constitutions gave the bulk of powers to their legislatures, effectively creating what one historian termed "legislative omnipotence."[9]

The national government was likewise, as James Sterling Young put it, "born with a legislative body and no head."[10] Strictly speaking, no national executive existed between 1776 and 1789—the years of the Revolutionary War and the Articles of Confederation (adopted in 1781). On its own, Congress struggled to wage war against the world's most powerful nation, enlist diplomatic allies, and manage internal affairs. As the war progressed and legislative direction proved unwieldy, Congress tended to delegate authority to its own committees and to permanent (executive) agencies. Strictly military affairs were placed in the hands of Commander in Chief George Washington, who at the war's end returned his commission to Congress in a public ceremony. Considering the obstacles it faced, congressional government was far from a failure. Yet the mounting inability of the all-powerful legislative bodies, state and national, to deal with the postwar problems spurred demands for change.

At the state level, Massachusetts and New York rewrote their constitutions, adding provisions for stronger executives. At the national level, the Confederation's frailty led many to advocate what Alexander Hamilton called a more "energetic" government—one with enough authority to implement laws, control currency, levy taxes, dispose of war debts, and, if necessary, put down rebellion. Legislative prerogatives, Hamilton and others argued, should be counterbalanced with a vigorous, independent executive.

In this spirit, delegates from the states convened in Philadelphia on May 25, 1787, intending to strengthen the Articles of Confederation. Instead, they drew up a wholly new governmental charter.

CONGRESS IN THE CONSTITUTION

The structure and powers of Congress formed the core of the Constitutional Convention's deliberations. The delegates broadly agreed that a stronger central government was needed.[11] But the fifty-five delegates who met in the summer of 1787 in Philadelphia were deeply divided on issues of representation, and more than three months passed before they completed their work. The plan, agreed on and signed on September 17, 1787, was a bundle of compromises. In structuring the representational system, divergent interests—those of large and small states, land-locked states and those with ports, northern and southern (that is, slave-holding) states—had to be placated. The final result was an energetic central government that could function independently of the states, but with limited, enumerated powers divided among three branches.

Powers of Congress

The federal government's powers are shared by three separate branches: legislative, executive, and judicial. Separation of powers was not a new idea. Philosophers admired by the framers of the Constitution, including Harrington, Locke, and especially Montesquieu, had advocated the principle. But the U.S. Constitution's elaborate system of checks and balances is considered one of its most innovative features. The failure of the Articles of Confederation to separate governmental functions was widely regarded as a serious defect, as were the all-powerful legislatures created by the first state constitutions. Thus the framers sought to create a federal government that would avoid the excesses and instabilities that had marked policy making at both the national and state levels.

Article I of the Constitution embraces many provisions to buttress congressional authority and independence. Legislators have unfettered authority to organize the chambers as they see fit and are accorded latitude in performing their duties. To prevent intimidation, they cannot be arrested during sessions or while traveling to and from sessions (except for treason, felony, or breach of the peace). In their deliberations, members enjoy immunity from any punitive action; for their speech and debate, "they shall not be questioned in any other place" (Article I, section 6).

Despite their worries over all-powerful legislatures, the framers laid down an expansive mandate for the new Congress. Mindful of the achievements of New World assemblies, not to mention the British Parliament's struggles with the Crown, the framers viewed the legislature as the chief repository of the government's powers. Locke had observed that "the legislative is not only the supreme power, but is sacred and unalterable in the hands where the community have placed it."[12] Locke's doctrine found expression in Article I, section 8, which enumerates Congress's impressive array of powers and sets out virtually the entire scope of governmental authority as the eighteenth-century founders understood it. This portion of the Constitution clearly envisions a vigorous legislature as the engine of a powerful government.

Raising and spending money for governmental purposes stand at the heart of Congress's prerogatives. The "power of the purse" was historically the lever by which parliaments gained bargaining advantages over kings and queens. The Constitution's authors, well aware of this lever, gave Congress full powers over taxing and spending.

Financing the government is carried out under Congress's broad mandate to "lay and collect taxes, duties, imposts and excises, to pay the debts and provide for the common defense and general welfare of the United States" (Article I, section 8). Although this wording covered almost all known forms of taxation, there were limitations. Taxes had to be uniform throughout the country; duties could not be levied on goods traveling between states; and "capitation or other direct" taxes were prohibited, unless levied according to population (Article I, section 9). This last provision proved troublesome when the U.S. Supreme Court held in 1895 (*Pollock v. Farmers' Loan and Trust Co.*) that it precluded taxes on incomes. To overcome this obstacle, the Sixteenth Amendment, ratified eighteen years later, explicitly conferred on Congress the power to levy income taxes.

Congressional power over government spending is no less sweeping. Congress is to provide for the "common defense and general welfare" of the country (Article I, section 8). Furthermore, "No money shall be drawn from the Treasury, but in consequence of appropriations made by law" (Article I, section 9). This funding provision is one of the legislature's most potent weapons in overseeing the executive branch.

Congress possesses broad powers to promote the nation's economic well-being and political security. It has the power to regulate interstate and foreign commerce, which it has used to regulate not only trade, but also transportation, communications, and such disparate subjects as civil rights and violent crime. The exact limits of the commerce power have been the subject of numerous political and legal battles. In 2012, this issue was at the center of the dispute over the constitutionality of the individual mandate, a key provision of the Patient Protection and Affordable Care Act ("Obamacare"). The individual mandate requires every person to obtain health insurance or suffer a (relatively minor) sanction. Five justices agreed that the individual mandate exceeded Congress's commerce power because it was a regulation of commercial *inactivity*, as opposed to commercial activity. Chief Justice John Roberts wrote: "Construing the Commerce Clause to permit Congress to regulate individuals precisely *because* they are doing nothing would open a new and potentially vast domain to congressional authority."[13] Roberts and four other justices upheld the individual mandate, however, as a valid exercise of Congress's power to tax. Congress may also coin money, incur debts, establish post offices, build post roads, issue patents and copyrights, provide for the armed forces, and call forth the militia to repel invasions or suppress rebellions.

Although the three branches supposedly are coequal, the legislature is empowered to define the structure and duties of the other two. The Constitution mentions executive departments and officers, but it does not specify their organization or functions, aside from those of the president. Thus the design of the executive branch, including cabinet departments and other agencies, is spelled out in laws passed by Congress and signed by the president.

The judiciary, too, is a statutory creation. The Constitution provides for a federal judicial system consisting of "one supreme Court, and . . . such inferior courts as the Congress may from time to time ordain and establish" (Article III, section 1). Congress determines the number of justices on the Supreme Court, and the number and types of lower federal courts. The outer limits of the federal courts' jurisdiction are delineated in Article III, but Congress must also define their jurisdictions through statute. (It is worth noting that Congress has never extended the federal courts' jurisdiction as far as the Constitution would presumably allow.) Moreover, the Supreme Court's appellate jurisdiction is subject to "such exceptions" and "such regulations as the Congress shall make" (Article III, section 2).

Congress can also limit the federal courts' discretion in ways other than altering their jurisdiction. Mandatory minimum sentences imposed by statute, for example, limit judges' discretion in imposing prison sentences.

Congress's powers within the federal system were greatly enlarged by the Civil War constitutional amendments—the Thirteenth (ratified in 1865), Fourteenth (ratified in 1868), and Fifteenth (ratified in 1870). The Radical Republicans, who had supported the war and controlled Congress in its aftermath, feared that former Confederate states would ignore the rights of former slaves—the cause over which the war had ultimately been waged. The Civil War amendments were primarily intended to ensure that former slaves would have the rights to vote, to be accorded due process, and to receive equal protection of the laws. Nevertheless, the language of the Fourteenth Amendment was cast broadly, referring to "all persons" rather than only to "former slaves." These amendments also authorized Congress to enforce these rights with "appropriate legislation." As a result, these amendments (and subsequent legislation) greatly expanded the federal government's role relative to the states. Over time, the Civil War amendments effectively nationalized the key rights of citizenship throughout the United States. Through a long series of Court rulings, state governments were eventually required to respect many of the Bill of Rights guarantees that originally applied only to the federal government.

Congress can also be an active partner in foreign relations and national defense. It has the power to declare war, ratify treaties, raise and support armies, provide and maintain a navy, and make rules governing the military forces— including those governing "captures on land and water." Finally, Congress is vested with the power "to make all laws which shall be necessary and proper for carrying into execution the foregoing powers" (Article I, section 8).

Limits on Legislative Power

The very act of enumerating these powers was intended to limit government, for by implication those powers not listed were prohibited. The Tenth Amendment reserves to the states or to the people all those powers neither delegated nor prohibited by the Constitution. This guarantee has long been a rallying point for those who take exception to particular federal policies or who wish broadly to curtail federal powers.

Eight specific limitations on Congress's powers are noted in Article I, section 9. The most important bans are against bills of attainder, which pronounce a particular individual guilty of a crime without trial or conviction and impose a sentence, and ex post facto laws, which make an action a crime after it has been committed or otherwise alter the legal consequences of some past action. Such laws are traditional tools of authoritarian regimes.

The original Constitution contained no bill of rights. Pressed by opponents during the ratification debate, supporters of the Constitution promised early enactment of amendments to remedy this omission. The resulting ten amendments, drawn up by the First Congress (James Madison was their main author) and ratified December 15, 1791, are a basic charter of liberties that limit the reach of government. The First Amendment prohibits Congress from establishing a national religion, preventing the free exercise of religion, or abridging the freedoms of speech, press, peaceable assembly, and petition. Other amendments secure the rights of personal property and fair trials and prohibit arbitrary arrest, questioning, or punishment.

Rights not enumerated in the Bill of Rights are not necessarily denied (Ninth Amendment). In fact, subsequent amendments, legislative enactments, judicial rulings, and states' actions have enlarged citizens' rights to include the rights of citizenship, of voting, of privacy, and of "equal protection of the laws."

It should also be noted that the political process itself is a significant limit on the use of government powers, even those clearly granted in Article I, section 8. As Madison noted in *Federalist* No. 51, "A dependence on the people is, no doubt, the primary control on the government."[14]

Separate Branches, Shared Powers

The Constitution not only lists Congress's powers but also sets them apart from those of the other two branches. Senators and representatives, while in office, are prohibited from serving in other federal posts; those who serve in such posts are, in turn, forbidden from serving in Congress (Article I, section 6). This restriction forecloses any form of parliamentary government in which leading members of the dominant party or coalition form a cabinet to direct the ministries and other executive agencies.

Because the branches are separated, some people presume that their powers should be isolated as well. In practice, however, governmental powers are interwoven. Madison explained that the Constitution created not a system of separate institutions performing separate functions but separate institutions that share functions, so that "these departments be so far connected and blended as to give each a constitutional control over the others."[15]

Historically, presidents, Congress, and the courts have reached accommodations to exercise the powers they share. As Justice Joseph Story once wrote, the authors of the Constitution sought to "prove that rigid adherence to [separation of powers] in all cases would be subversive to the efficiency of government and result in the destruction of the public liberties." Justice Robert Jackson noted in 1952 that "while the Constitution diffuses power the better to secure liberty, it also contemplates that practice will integrate the dispersed powers into a workable government."[16]

Legislative-Executive Interdependence. Each branch of American government needs cooperation from its counterparts. Although the Constitution vests Congress with "all legislative powers," these powers cannot be exercised without the involvement of the president and the courts. This same interdependency applies to executive and judicial powers.

The president is a key figure in lawmaking. According to Article II, the president "shall from time to time give to the Congress information on the state of the Union, and recommend to their consideration such measures as he shall judge necessary and expedient." Although Congress is not required to consider the president's legislative initiatives, the president's State of the Union address profoundly shapes the nation's political agenda. In the modern era, Congress has "enacted in some form roughly six in ten presidential initiatives."[17] The Constitution also grants the president the power to convene one or both houses of Congress in a special session.

The president's ability to veto congressional enactments influences both the outcome and content of legislation. After a bill or resolution has passed both houses of Congress and has been delivered to the White House, the president must sign it or return it within ten days (excluding Sundays). Overruling a presidential veto requires a two-thirds vote in each house. Presidential review might seem to be an all-or-nothing affair. In the words of George Washington, a president "must approve all the parts of a bill, or reject it in toto." Veto messages, however, often suggest revisions that would make the measure more likely to win the president's approval. Furthermore, veto threats allow the president to intervene earlier in the legislative process by letting members of Congress know in advance what measures or provisions will or will not receive presidential support. Considering the extreme difficulty of overriding a president's veto, members of Congress know that White House support for legislation is almost always necessary and so will often incorporate presidential preferences into early drafts of legislation.

Carrying out laws is the duty of the president, who is directed by the Constitution to "take care that the laws be faithfully executed" (Article II, section 3). To this end, as chief executive the president has the power to appoint "officers of the United States." However, the president's appointment power is limited by the requirement to obtain the Senate's advice and consent for nominees, which has been interpreted as requiring a majority vote in the Senate.[18] The president's executive power is further constrained by Congress's role in establishing and overseeing executive departments and agencies. Because these agencies are subject to Congress's broad-ranging influence, modern presidents have struggled to force them to march to a common cadence.

Even in the realms of diplomacy and national defense—the traditional domains of royal prerogative—the Constitution apportions powers between the executive and legislative branches. Following tradition, presidents are given wide discretion in such matters. They appoint ambassadors and other envoys, negotiate treaties, and command the country's armed forces. However, like other high-ranking presidential appointees, ambassadors and envoys must be approved by the Senate. Treaties do not become the law of the land until they are ratified by a two-thirds vote of the Senate. Although the president may dispatch troops by means of executive order, only Congress may formally declare war. Even in time of war, Congress still wields formidable powers if it chooses to employ them. Congress can refuse to provide continued funding for military actions, engage in vigorous oversight of the executive branch's military operations, and influence public opinion regarding the president's leadership.[19]

Impeachment. Congress has the power to impeach and remove the president, the vice president, and other "civil officers of the United States" for serious breaches of the public trust: treason, bribery, or "other high crimes and misdemeanors." The House of Representatives has the sole authority to draw up and adopt (by majority vote) articles of impeachment, which are specific charges that the individual has engaged in one of the named forms of misconduct. The Senate is the final judge of whether to convict on any of the articles of impeachment. A two-thirds majority is required to remove the individual from office, or to remove and also bar the individual from any future "offices of public trust."

Three attributes of impeachment fix it within the separation of powers framework. First, it is exclusively the domain of Congress. (The chief justice of the United States presides over Senate trials of the president, but rulings by the chief justice may be overturned by majority vote.) The two chambers are also free to devise their own procedures for reaching their decisions.[20]

Second, impeachment is essentially political in character. The structure may appear judicial—with the House resembling a grand jury and the Senate a trial court—but lawmakers decide whether and how to proceed, which evidence to consider, and even what constitutes an impeachable offense. Treason is defined by the Constitution and bribery is defined by statute, but the words "high crimes and misdemeanors" are open to interpretation. They are usually defined (in Alexander Hamilton's words) as "abuse or violation of some public trust"—on-the-job offenses against the state, the political order, or the society at large.[21] According to this definition, they could be either more or less than garden variety criminal offenses. Both presidential impeachment trials (Andrew Johnson, 1868; Bill Clinton, 1998–1999) were fiercely partisan affairs, in which combatants disputed not only the facts but also the appropriate grounds for impeachment.

Finally, impeachment is a clumsy instrument for punishing officials for the gravest of offenses. Congress has many lesser ways of reining in wayward officials. As for presidents and vice presidents, their terms are already limited. Although impeachments are often threatened, only sixteen Senate trials have taken place, and only eight individuals have been convicted. Significantly, all eight who were removed from office were judges—who, unlike executive officers, enjoy open-ended terms of office.[22]

Interbranch "No-Fly Zones." Although the constitutional system requires that the separate branches share powers, each branch normally honors the integrity of the others' internal operations. Communications between the president and his advisers are mostly (though not entirely) exempt from legislative or judicial review under the doctrine of "executive privilege." Similarly, Article I places congressional organization and procedures beyond the scrutiny of the other branches. This provision was given new meaning in 2007 when the courts determined that an FBI search of the office of Rep. William J. Jefferson, D.-La., who was under investigation for bribery, had been unconstitutional under the Constitution's speech and debate clause.[23] The case established a precedent that members of Congress be provided advance notice and the right to review materials before the execution of a search warrant on their congressional offices.

Judicial Review

The third branch, the judiciary, interprets and applies laws in particular cases, when called upon to resolve disputes. In rare instances, this requires the judiciary to adjudicate a claim that a particular law or regulation violates the Constitution. This is called "judicial review." Whether the framers anticipated judicial review is open to question. Perhaps they expected each branch to reach its own judgments on constitutional questions, especially those pertaining to its own powers. Whatever the original intent, Chief Justice John Marshall soon preempted the other two branches with his Supreme Court's unanimous assertion of judicial review in *Marbury v. Madison* (1803). Judicial review involves both interpretation and judgment. First, "It is emphatically the province and duty of the judicial department to say what the law is." Second, the Supreme Court has the duty of weighing laws against the Constitution, the "supreme law of the land," and invalidating those that are inconsistent—in *Marbury*, a minor provision of the Judiciary Act of 1789.[24]

Despite the *Marbury* precedent, Congress—not the Court—was the primary forum for weighty constitutional debates until the Civil War. Before 1860, only one other law (the Missouri Compromise of 1820) had been declared unconstitutional by the Court (in *Dred Scott v. Sandford,* 1857). Since the Civil War, the Court has been more aggressive in interpreting and judging congressional handiwork. For the record, the Supreme Court has invalidated 173 congressional statutes in whole or in part—the vast majority of these during the twentieth century.[25] This count does not include lower-court holdings that have not been reviewed by the Supreme Court. Nor does it include laws whose validity has been impaired because a similar law was struck down.

Who Is the Final Arbiter? Congress's two most common reactions to judicial review of its enactments are not responding at all (in 38 percent of cases, 1954–1997) or amending the statute to comply with the Court's holding (in 36 percent of cases).[26] Other responses are repealing the law, repealing the law to pass new legislation, or even seeking a constitutional amendment.

Reconstruction laws and constitutional amendments after the Civil War explicitly nullified the Court's 1857 holding in *Dred Scott v. Sandford*.[27] More recently, a great deal of legislative ferment has followed the Supreme Court's ruling in *Citizens United v. Federal Election Commission* (2010),[28] a 5–4 decision that held that the First Amendment protects corporate, union, and nonprofit funding of independent political speech. Even though legislation has not yet been passed in response to *Citizens United,* many members of Congress want to find ways to undo or mitigate the Court's holding in this case.

In some cases, Congress reacts to Supreme Court rulings by simply ignoring them. For example, even though legislative veto provisions were largely outlawed by the Court's decision in *Immigration and Naturalization Service v. Chadha* (1983),[29] Congress continues to enact them, and administrators nevertheless feel obliged to honor them out of political prudence.

The Supreme Court does not necessarily have the last word in saying what the law is. Its interpretations of laws may be questioned and even reversed. One study found that 121 of the Court's interpretive decisions were overridden between 1967 and 1990, an average of 10 per Congress. The author of the study concluded that "congressional committees in fact carefully monitor Supreme Court decisions." Congress was most apt to override decisions of a closely divided Court; decisions that relied on the law's plain meaning; and decisions that clashed with positions taken by federal, state, and local governments.[30]

Nor are the courts the sole judges of what is or is not constitutional. Courts routinely accept customs and practices developed by the other two branches. Likewise, they usually decline to decide sensitive political questions within the province of Congress and the executive.

In summary, the courts play a leading but not exclusive role in interpreting laws and the regulations implementing them. When Congress passes a law, the policy-making process has just begun. Courts and administrative agencies then assume the task of refining the policy, but they do so under Congress's watchful eye. "What is 'final' at one stage of our political development," Louis Fisher observes, "may be reopened at some later date, leading to revisions, fresh interpretations, and reversals of Court doctrines."[31]

Bicameralism

Although "the Congress" is discussed as if it were a single entity, Congress is divided internally into two very different, virtually autonomous chambers—that is, it is bicameral. Following the pattern that originated with the British Parliament and was then imitated by most of the states, the Constitution created a bicameral legislature. If tradition recommended the two-house formula, the politics of the early Republic commanded it. The larger states preferred population-based representation, but the smaller states insisted on retaining the equal representation they enjoyed under the Articles of Confederation.

The first branch—as the House was called by framers James Madison and Gouverneur Morris, among others—rests on the idea that the legislature should represent "the many," the people of the United States. As George Mason, another framer, put it, the House "was to be the grand depository of the democratic principles of the government."[32]

By contrast, the composition of the Senate reflected the framers' concerns about controlling excessive popular pressures. Senators were chosen by the state legislatures and not by popular vote. This, in theory, would curb the excesses of popular government. "The use of the Senate," explained Madison, "is to consist in its proceeding with more coolness, with more system, and with more wisdom, than the popular branch."[33]

Senate behavior did not necessarily match up with the framers' theories, however. Even though senators were chosen by state legislatures, they were not insulated from democratic pressures. To be selected, Senate candidates "had to cultivate local party officials in different parts of the state and appeal directly to constituents in order to bolster their electoral chances."[34] Once in office, senators voiced their state's dominant economic interests. They also sponsored private bills for pensions and other relief for individual constituents, doled out federal patronage, and sought committee assignments that would enable them to bring home their state's share of federal money. Recent research has shown that senators selected by state legislators were not substantially different from modern, directly elected senators.[35]

Historical evolution finally overran the framers' intentions. Direct election of senators was ushered in with the Seventeenth Amendment, ratified in 1913. A by-product of the Progressive movement, the new arrangement was designed to broaden citizens' participation and blunt the power of shadowy special interests such as party bosses and business trusts. Thus the Senate became directly subject to popular will.

Bicameralism is the most obvious organizational feature of the U.S. Congress. Each chamber has distinct processes for handling legislation. According to the Constitution, each house sets its own rules, keeps a journal of its proceedings, and serves as final judge of its members' elections and qualifications. In addition, the Constitution assigns unique duties to each of the two chambers. The Senate ratifies treaties and approves presidential appointments. The House must originate all revenue measures; by tradition, it also originates appropriations bills.

The two houses jealously guard their prerogatives and resist intrusions by the other body. Despite claims that one or the other chamber is more important—for example, that the Senate has more prestige or that the House pays more attention to legislative details—the two houses staunchly defend their equal places. On Capitol Hill, there is no "upper" or "lower" chamber.

INSTITUTIONAL EVOLUTION

Written constitutions go only a short way toward explaining how real-life governmental institutions work. On many questions such documents are inevitably silent or ambiguous. Important issues of both power and process emerge and develop only in the course of later events. Political institutions continually change under pressures from public demands, shifting political contexts, and the needs and goals of officeholders.

Congress has evolved dramatically over time. "Reconstitutive change" is what Elaine K. Swift calls instances of "rapid, marked, and enduring shift[s] in the fundamental dimensions of the institution."[36] During one such period—1809–1829—Swift argues, the Senate was transformed from an elitist, insulated "American House of Lords" into an active, powerful institution whose debates stirred the public and attracted the most talented politicians of the time. Major reform efforts in Congress have also periodically resulted in bold new departures in process and structure.

Yet much of Congress's institutional development has occurred gradually. Early on, Congress had little formal structure. When the first Congress convened, there were no standing committees. Deliberation about policy issues occurred directly on the floors of the House and Senate, where any interested members could participate. After chamber-wide debate had taken place on a broad issue, members would create temporary ad hoc committees to draft bills. The early Congress also had no formal party leadership organization.[37] Prior to the 1830s, the Federalist and Republican coalitions that existed in Congress were "no more than proto-parties."[38]

Today's Congress is a mature institution characterized by complex internal structures and procedures. It is led by a well-defined party apparatus, with each party organized according to its established rules and headed by a hierarchy of leaders and whips, elected and appointed. Party organization extends to policy committees, campaign committees, research committees, and numerous task forces. Minority and majority party leaders command considerable resources in terms of budgets and staff. Taken together, they employ some four hundred staff aides, and the various party committees employ about an equal number.[39]

The contemporary Congress also has an elaborate committee system bolstered by a vast body of rules and precedents regulating committee jurisdictions and operations.[40] In the 113th Congress (2013–2015), the Senate has sixteen standing committees and the House has twenty. But these committees are only the tip of the iceberg. House committees have about one hundred subcommittees; Senate committees, nearly seventy subcommittees. Four joint House-Senate committees have been retained. All this adds up to some two hundred work groups, plus an abundance of informal caucuses.

A basic concept scholars use to analyze the development of Congress's growth and adaptation is *institutionalization*. Political scientist Nelson W. Polsby applied this concept to track the institution's professionalization of the legislative career; its increasing organizational complexity—the growth of more component parts (committees, subcommittees, caucuses, leadership organizations) within the institution; and its elaboration and observance of formal rules governing its internal business.[41] Scholars have identified some important factors that have driven institutional development. Among these are legislative workload, institutional size, conflict with the executive branch, and members' partisan interests.

Workload

Congress's workload—once limited in scope, small in volume, and simple in content—has burgeoned since 1789. Today's Congress grapples with many issues that were once considered entirely outside the purview of governmental activity or were left to states or localities. From eight to ten thousand bills and joint resolutions are introduced in the span of each two-year Congress; from four to eight hundred of them are enacted into law. By most measures—hours in session, committee meetings, floor votes—the congressional workload doubled between the 1950s and the late 1970s. Legislative business expanded in scope and complexity as well as in sheer volume. The average public bill of the late 1940s was two-and-a-half pages long; by the first decade of the 2000s it ran to more than fifteen pages.[42]

Changes in workload have been an important driver of institutional change over the course of congressional history. Many of the earliest committees were established to help Congress manage a growing volume of constituent requests. When the nineteenth-century Congress was deluged with petitions requesting benefits, members created committees such as Claims, Pensions, and Public Lands to process requests.[43] Similarly, the creation and, occasionally, the abolition of committees parallel shifting perceptions of public problems. As novel policy problems arose, new committees were added.[44] The House, for example, established Commerce and Manufactures in 1795, Public Lands in 1805, Freedmen's Affairs in 1866, Roads in 1913, Science and Astronautics in 1958, Standards of Official Conduct in 1967, Small Business in 1975, and Homeland Security in 2005. An extensive system of committees allows the contemporary Congress to benefit from a division of labor as it strives to manage a far-reaching governmental agenda and the press of public business.

Congress's growing workload does not come only from outside the institution. From the earliest days to the present, members themselves have contributed to their collective burden. Seeking to make names for themselves, members champion causes, deliver speeches on various subjects, offer floor amendments, refer matters to committees for consideration, and engage in much policy entrepreneurship. All these activities raise the congressional workload.

At regular intervals over congressional history, the crush of business, combined with a widespread sense that Congress is unable to manage its responsibilities, prompts members to experiment with institutional reforms.[45] In 2010, for example, Congress created a short-lived institutional mechanism to negotiate an agreement on the pressing problem of long-term deficit reduction: a joint select committee, known generally as the "Super Committee." If the Super Committee had been able to produce an agreement, its recommendation would have come up for a vote in Congress under special, streamlined procedures permitting no amendments or obstruction.[46] In the end, the committee could not break the partisan deadlock on fiscal policy. Under workload pressure, Congress has repeatedly adopted measures to streamline procedures and to limit the participation of individual members. Like the Super Committee, many such reforms are not successful. Nevertheless, pressure for change is ongoing, with congressional innovators devising new "unorthodox" procedures to cope with the workload challenges of today.[47]

The Size of Congress

Like workload, the size of a legislative institution profoundly affects its organization. Legislatures with more members face greater problems of agenda control and time management, unless they adopt mechanisms to manage the participation of their members. [48] The U.S. Congress has grown dramatically over time, and this growth has created pressure for institutional adaptation.

Looking at the government of 1789 through modern lenses, one is struck by the relatively small circles of people involved. The House of Representatives, that "impetuous council," was composed of sixty-five members—when all of them showed up. The aristocratic Senate boasted only twenty-six members, two from each of the thirteen original states.

As new states were added, the Senate grew, from thirty-two senators in 1800 to sixty-two in 1850, ninety by 1900, and, since 1959, one hundred.

For much of the nation's history, the House grew alongside the nation's population. The House membership was raised to 104 after the first census, and it steadily enlarged throughout the nineteenth century. The 1910 census, which counted 92 million people, led to an expansion to 435 members. After the 1920 census, Congress declined to enlarge the House further. And that is the way things stand to this day.

Growth impelled House members to empower strong leaders, to rely on committees, to impose strict limits on floor debate, and to devise elaborate ways of channeling the flow of floor business. It is no accident that strong leaders emerged during the periods the House experienced the most rapid growth. After the initial growth spurt in the first two decades of the Republic, vigorous leadership appeared in the person of Henry Clay (1811–1814, 1815–1820, and 1823–1825). Similarly, the post–Civil War expansion of the House was met with an era of forceful Speakers that lasted from the 1870s until 1910.

In the smaller and more intimate Senate, vigorous leadership has been the exception rather than the rule. The relative informality of Senate procedures and the long-cherished right of unlimited debate testify to the looser reins of leadership. Compared with the House's complex rules and voluminous precedents, the Senate's rules are relatively brief and simple. Informal negotiations among senators interested in a given measure prevail on most matters.

Conflict with the Executive Branch

Conflict with the president is a perennial impetus for institutional reform. When Congress cannot collaborate on policy with the executive branch, members seek out ways to increase their capacity for independent action. During such confrontations, Congress creates new institutions and procedures that often endure long beyond the specific contexts that gave rise to them.

One of the most important standing House committees, Ways and Means, was first established to provide a source of financial information independent of the controversial and divisive Treasury secretary at the time, Alexander Hamilton.[49] Similarly, the landmark Legislative Reorganization Act of 1946 was adopted amidst members' growing concerns about congressional power. Following the massive growth of the administrative state during the New Deal and World War II, members feared that Congress could simply no longer compete with the executive branch. Reformers saw "a reorganized Congress as a way to redress the imbalance of power that had developed between the branches."[50] The act streamlined the legislative process by dramatically reducing the number of committees and regularizing their jurisdictions. Sen. Owen Brewster, R-Maine, argued at the time that the reforms were necessary "to retain any semblance of the ancient division of functions under our constitution."[51] The act was adopted by a sizable bipartisan majority, with both Republicans and Democrats expressing hope that reform would strengthen Congress's power and prestige.

Another major institutional innovation, Congress's budget process, was fashioned in an environment of intense interbranch warfare between President Richard Nixon and a Democratic Congress.[52] President Nixon's unprecedented assertion of authority to withhold funds that Congress had appropriated was a major stimulus for passage of the Congressional Budget and Impoundment Control Act of 1974. Without the power of the purse, Sen. John Tunney, D-Calif., remarked, "we may as well go out of business."[53] However, the act addressed an array of structural issues that went far beyond the particulars of the dispute over the president's impoundment powers. It established a new internal congressional budget process; new budget committees in both chambers; and a new congressional agency, the nonpartisan Congressional Budget Office (CBO). The goal was to allow Congress to formulate a comprehensive national budget on its own, backed by appropriate estimates and forecasts, without relying on the president's budget or the executive branch's Office of Management and Budget.

In *Federalist* No. 51 Madison justified the Constitution as a system to "divide and arrange the several offices in such a manner as that each may be a check on the other." Congress's institutional development bears the indelible stamp of this checking and balancing, as Congress has repeatedly reformed itself to meet challenges from the executive branch.

Partisan Interests

Political parties had no place in the original constitutional blueprint. However, no account of institutional development in Congress can ignore their vital role.

Everything about the organization and operation of Congress is shaped by political parties. Indeed, the first thing a visitor to the House or Senate chamber notices is that the seats or desks are divided along partisan lines—Democrats to the left facing the dais, Republicans to the right. Although today's congressional parties are remarkably cohesive and energetic, the goals and capacities of the political parties have been a major engine of change throughout congressional history.

Parties began to develop in Congress during the first presidential administration. When Treasury secretary Alexander Hamilton unveiled his financial program in 1790, a genuine partisan spirit swept the capital. The Federalists, with Hamilton as their intellectual leader, espoused energetic government to deal forcefully with national problems and foster economic growth. The rival Republicans, who looked to Thomas Jefferson and James Madison for leadership, rallied opponents of Federalist policies and championed local autonomy, a weaker national government, and programs favoring agricultural or debtor interests. By 1794 Sen. John Taylor of Virginia could write:

> The existence of two parties in Congress is apparent. The fact is disclosed almost upon every important question. Whether the subject be foreign or domestic—relative to war or peace—navigation or commerce—the magnetism of opposite views draws them wide as the poles asunder.[54]

Parties also flourished throughout the nineteenth century. Regional conflicts, along with economic upheavals produced by rapid industrialization, nurtured partisan differences. At the grassroots level, the parties were differentiated along class, occupational, and regional lines. Grassroots party organizations were massive and militant. In the context of this vibrant nineteenth-century party system, the majority party gained organizational control over the House of Representatives. Ever since the Civil War, the leader of the House majority party has served as Speaker.[55] By the end of the nineteenth century, strong Speakers had tamed the unruly House, and a coterie of state party bosses dominated the Senate.

Even though parties were weaker during the Progressive era and throughout the middle of the twentieth century, they never became irrelevant. Despite the demise of the strong Speakership (1910), the direct election of senators (1913), and profound divisions in the Democratic majority party between the late 1930s and the 1970s, the parties continued to organize Congress down to the present day.[56] All contemporary House and Senate members receive and retain their committee assignments through their parties. Likewise, members of the majority party chair all the standing committees of Congress.

Party politics has impelled the development of floor procedure, members' parliamentary rights, leaders' prerogatives, and agenda-control devices. The rules of the legislative process at any given time are, in Sarah A. Binder's words, a "result of hard-nosed partisan battles—fought, of course, under a particular set of inherited institutional rules."[57]

A watershed moment in the development of the House of Representatives, the adoption of Reed's Rules in 1890, offers one of the clearest examples of partisan influence on institutional procedure. Prior to 1890, the minority party in the House of Representatives possessed an arsenal of dilatory tactics to obstruct the majority party's agenda.[58] Reed's Rules, named for then–House Speaker Thomas Brackett Reed, R-Maine, revolutionized House procedure by granting the Speaker secure control over the order of business and strictly curbing the minority party's ability to obstruct the majority party's floor agenda. Republicans, the majority party, fought for the adoption of Reed's Rules over strong opposition from the Democrats. At that time, Republicans had just won unified party control of the government for the first time in nearly a decade, and they had an ambitious and controversial agenda. Knowing that Democrats would use their resources to obstruct their agenda, Republicans changed the rules of the House to permit majority party control over the institution, a fact of life in the House of Representatives since. In procedural terms, Reed's Rules permanently transformed the House of Representatives.

The circumstances surrounding the adoption of Reed's Rules offers a blueprint for many partisan rules changes over the course of House history. Based on a study of all procedural rules changes that benefited the majority party at the expense of the minority party between 1789 and 1990, Binder finds that "crucial procedural choices have been shaped not by members' collective concerns about the institution, but by calculations of partisan advantage."[59] When necessary to overcome minority party obstruction, unified majority parties have repeatedly shown themselves willing to alter the institution's rules to ensure the passage of their agenda.

Members' Individual Interests

Institutional development has been driven by more than members' partisan and institutional goals; members also have individual goals. As individuals, members want to build a reputation as effective lawmakers and representatives. To do so, they must be able to point to achievements of their own. When congressional rules or structures inhibit their ability to do so, pressure builds for institutional reform.

In addition to its value as an institutional division of labor, the elaborate committee system in Congress serves members' individual political needs and policy goals. Because of the multitude of leadership positions created by the numerous committees and subcommittees, nearly every member has an opportunity to make an individual contribution. "Whatever else it may be, the quest for specialization in Congress is a quest for credit," observes David R. Mayhew. "Every member can aspire to occupy a part of at least one piece of policy turf small enough that he can claim personal responsibility for some of the things that happen on it."[60]

The congressional reforms of the 1970s are one example of the ways in which members' individual goals have affected institutional development. Over that decade, the two chambers revamped their committee systems through a series of measures designed to allow more input from rank-and-file members. The streamlined committee systems that had been put in place after the Legislative Reorganization Act of 1946 offered relatively few committee leadership positions, and those were gained on the basis of seniority. Every committee was led by its longest-serving members, who retained their positions until death, defeat, or retirement. The large classes of new members elected in the 1970s, feeling thwarted by this system, began to press for change.[61] Out of this ferment emerged a variety of reforms that opened up new opportunities for junior members. Among these reforms, the seniority system was weakened as committee chairs were forced to stand for election in their party caucus, making them accountable to the party's rank and file.

The persistence of Senate rules that permit unlimited debate is another example of the ways in which individual goals shape institutional rules.[62] Despite the many frustrations unlimited debate has caused for Senate majority parties over the years, senators have been unwilling to embrace changes that would allow for simple majority rule. Senators realize that a great part of their own institutional power derives from their ability to take advantage of unlimited debate to block votes on matters that have majority support. Senate leaders are forced to negotiate with senators who threaten to obstruct Senate action via unlimited debate.

Reforms that would make it possible for a Senate majority to force a vote have long been in the interest of the Senate's majority party. But such reforms come at a direct, substantial cost to senators' individual power. Not surprisingly, senators have proven very reluctant to trade off so much of their individual influence in favor of collective party goals.

Like everything else about Congress, the institution's rules and procedures can only be fully understood in the context of the two Congresses. Members want rules and processes to serve them as individual lawmakers and representatives, as well as to facilitate the functioning of the legislature as a whole.

Changing pressure on the institution, congressional-executive conflicts, partisan agendas, and members' individual goals have all been important drivers of Congress's institutional development. Indeed, significant reforms are almost always the result of several of these forces simultaneously buffeting the institution. One broad-ranging study of forty-two major institutional innovations concludes that institutional reforms are typically brought about through "common carriers," reform initiatives that are at once supported by several different groups of legislators for different sets of reasons.[63] The Legislative Reorganization Act of 1946, for example, was espoused by many legislators who wanted to enhance the power and effectiveness of the legislative branch, but it was also supported by members who valued the new pay and pension benefits included in the legislation.[64] Similarly, many members favored the 1970s reforms reducing the power of committee chairs because they wanted access to more policy turf of their own. Many liberal members backed the reforms because they wanted to reduce the influence of the disproportionately conservative committee chairs.[65]

Because the same reforms are so often backed for several different reasons, no single theory can explain congressional change. Legislative institutions incorporate internal tensions and contradictions, rather than maximize the attainment of any particular goal.[66] Furthermore, reforms inevitably fall short of their sponsors' objectives. Instead of achieving stable, effective arrangements, reforms frequently produce "a set of institutions that often work at cross-purposes."[67] At the same time, innovations usually have unanticipated consequences, which may lead to yet another round of reform.

EVOLUTION OF THE LEGISLATOR'S JOB

What is it like to be a member of Congress? The legislator's job, like the institution of Congress, has evolved since 1789. During the early Congresses, being a senator or representative was a part-time occupation. Few members regarded congressional service as a career, and according to most accounts the rewards were slim. Since then, lawmakers' exposure to constituents' demands and their career expectations have changed dramatically. Electoral units, too, have grown very large. With the nation's population estimated at some 309 million citizens, the average House constituency since the 2010 reapportionment consists of more than 710,000 people, and the average state of more than 6 million.

The Congressional Career

During its early years, Congress was an institution composed of transients. The nation's capital was an unsightly place, and its culture was provincial. Members remained in Washington only a few months, spending their unpleasant sojourns in boardinghouses. "While there were a few for whom the Hill was more than a way station in the pursuit of a career," notes James Sterling Young, "affiliation with the congressional community tended to be brief."[68]

The early Congresses failed to command the loyalty needed to keep members in office. Congressional service was regarded more as odious duty than as rewarding work. "My dear friend," wrote a North Carolina representative to his constituents in 1796, "there is nothing in this service, exclusive of the confidence and gratitude of my constituents, worth the sacrifice."[69] Of the ninety-four senators who served between 1789 and 1801, thirty-three resigned before completing their terms, only six to take other federal posts.[70] In the House, almost 6 percent of all early-nineteenth-century members resigned during each Congress.

Careerism mounted toward the end of the nineteenth century. As late as the 1870s, more than half the House members at any given time were freshmen, and the mean length of service was barely two terms. By the end of the century, however, the proportion of newcomers had fallen to 30 percent, and average

House tenure had reached three terms, or six years. About the same time, senators' mean term of service topped seven years, in excess of one full term.[71]

Today, the average senator has served more than eleven years, the average House member nearly ten. Table 2-1 shows changes since 1789 in the percentages of new and veteran members and the mean number of terms claimed by incumbents. In both the House and Senate, members' average length of service has increased over time, and the proportion of first-termers is substantially lower than it was during the first two hundred years of the nation's history.

Rising careerism has a number of causes. The increase in one-party states and districts following the Civil War, and especially after 1896, enabled repeated reelection of a dominant party's candidates—Democrats in the South, Republicans in the Midwest and the rural Northeast. Members themselves also began to find congressional service more rewarding. The growth of national government during the twentieth century enhanced the

TABLE 2-1 Length of Service in House and Senate, 1789–2015

Chamber and terms	Congress			
	1st–56th (1789–1901)	57th–103d (1901–1995)	104th–112th (1995–2013)	113th (2013–2015)
House				
One (up to 2 years)	44.0%	23.3%	13.8%	19.2%
Two to six (3–12 years)	53.4	49.7	52.6	33.7
Seven or more (12+ years)	2.6	27.0	33.6	47.1
Mean number of terms[1]	2.1	4.8	5.2	4.9
Senate				
One (up to 6 years)	65.6%	45.6%	33.4%	29.0%
Two (7–12 years)	23.4	22.4	26.8	25.0
Three or more (12+ years)	11.0	32.0	40.2	46.0
Mean number of terms[1]	1.5	2.2	2.3	1.9

Sources: Adapted from David C. Huckabee, *Length of Service for Representatives and Senators: 1st–103d Congresses,* Congressional Research Service Report No. 95-426GOV, March 27, 1995. Authors' calculations for the 104th through 113th Congresses. See also Mildred Amer, *Average Years of Service for Members of the Senate and House of Representatives, First–109th Congresses,* Congressional Research Service Report RL32648, November 9, 2005.

[1]Figures are derived from the total number of terms claimed by members whether or not those terms were served out. For example, members in their initial year of service are counted as having one full term, and so on. Thus the figures cannot be equated precisely with years of service.

excitement and glamour of the Washington political scene, especially when compared with state or local renown.

The prerogatives accorded to seniority further rewarded lengthy service. Beginning in the late nineteenth century in the Senate and in the early twentieth century in the House, members with the longest tenure in office began to dominate positions of power in Congress. However, seniority norms have been considerably eroded since the 1990s. After taking over the House in 1995, Republican leaders passed over several senior members in naming committee chairs. At the same time, the GOP Conference also limited chairs' terms to six years—a provision again enforced when Republicans selected committee chairs after reclaiming a House majority in the 2010 elections.[72] Although seniority is no longer the unquestioned norm it once was, extended service generally remains a prerequisite for top party and committee posts. The benefits accruing to seniority continue to compound the returns on long service in the contemporary Congress.

Professionalization

During the Republic's early days, lawmaking was not a full-time occupation. As President John F. Kennedy was fond of remarking, the Clays, Calhouns, and Websters of the nineteenth century could afford to devote a whole generation or more to debating and refining the few great controversies at hand. Rep. Joseph W. Martin, R-Mass., who entered the House in 1925 and went on to become Speaker (1947–1949, 1953–1955), described the leisurely atmosphere of earlier days and the workload changes during his service:

> From one end of a session to another Congress would scarcely have three or four issues of consequence besides appropriations bills. And the issues themselves were fundamentally simpler than those that surge in upon us today in such a torrent that the individual member cannot analyze all of them adequately before he is compelled to vote. In my early years in Congress the main issues were few enough so that almost any conscientious member could with application make himself a quasi-expert at least. In the complexity and volume of today's legislation, however, most members have to trust somebody else's word or the recommendation of a committee. Nowadays bills, which thirty years ago would have been thrashed out for hours or days, go through in ten minutes.[73]

In recent decades, legislative business has kept the House and Senate almost perpetually in session—punctuated by constituency work periods. Members of the contemporary Congress are—and must be—full-time professional politicians.

Congress has also professionalized in that members now direct a large staff of aides. Until recent decades, members of Congress had access to very limited staff. In the 1890s, only 142 clerks (62 for the House and 80 for the Senate) were on hand to serve members of Congress. Many senators and all representatives handled their own correspondence. It was not until 1946 that Congress began to develop professional staffing. Every member now has employees to handle mail and phone calls, appointments, policy research, speechwriting, and constituent service. With each member directing his or her own staff "enterprise," Congress now sustains a distinct Washington subculture.[74] All told, the legislative branch employs more than thirty thousand people housed in nearly a dozen Capitol Hill buildings.[75]

Constituency Demands

Since the beginning, American legislators have been expected to remain close to voters. Early representatives reported to their constituents through circular letters, communications passed around throughout their districts.[76] But the volume of those demands has increased many times over. Before the Civil War, a member's business on behalf of constituents was confined mainly to awarding rural mail routes, arranging for Mexican War pensions, sending out free seed, and only occasionally explaining legislation. This unhurried pace has long since vanished.

Reflecting on his forty years of congressional service concluding in 1967, Representative Martin remarked on the dramatic upsurge of constituent awareness:

> Today the federal government is far more complex, as is every phase of national life. People have to turn to their Representative for aid. I used to think ten letters a day was a big batch; now I get several hundred a day. In earlier times, constituents didn't know their Congressman's views. With better communications, their knowledge has increased along with their expectations of what he must know.[77]

People of Martin's era would be astonished at the volume of constituency work now handled by House and Senate offices. The advent of new communications technologies has increased the volume of congressional mail by an order of magnitude. In 1997, the last year before e-mail use became widespread, members of Congress received 30.5 million pieces of posted mail; by 2007 the volume of mail, e-mail included, had surged to 491 million pieces.[78] Not only are constituents more numerous than ever before, but they are also better educated, served by faster communication and transportation, and mobilized by lobby organizations. Public opinion surveys reveal that voters expect legislators to dispense federal services and to communicate frequently with the home folks. Even though the more flagrant forms of pork-barrel politics are denounced, constituents' demands are unlikely to ebb in the future.

CONCLUSION

While the founders understood the guiding principles of representative assemblies, they could not have foreseen what sort of institution they had created. They wrote into the Constitution legislative powers as they understood them and left the details to future generations.

Just as physical anthropologists believe the Earth's history is marked by periods of intense, even cataclysmic, change—punctuated equilibrium—so historians of Congress have identified several eras of intensive institutional change, such as the advent of Reed's Rules or the early-nineteenth-century transformation of the Senate described by Elaine Swift. But institutional change is not necessarily dramatic. Incremental changes of one kind or another are also always unfolding.

Over time, as a result of changes large and small, Congress became the mature institution of today. The contemporary Congress abounds with norms and traditions, rules and procedures, committees and subcommittees. In short, the modern Congress is highly institutionalized. How different it is from the First Congress, personified by fussy John Adams worrying about what forms of address to use.

This institutionalization has a number of important consequences, some good and some bad. It enables Congress to cope with its extensive workload. A division of labor, primarily through standing committees, permits the two houses to process a wide variety of issues simultaneously. Careerism encourages legislators to develop skills and expertise in specific areas. In tandem with staff resources, this specialization allows Congress to compete with the executive branch in absorbing information and applying expertise to public issues. The danger of institutionalization is organizational rigidity. Institutions that are too rigid can frustrate policy making, especially in periods of rapid social or political change. Structures that are too complex can tie people in knots, producing inaction, delays, and confusion.

The institutionalization of the contemporary Congress must be taken into account by anyone who seeks to understand it today. Capitol Hill newcomers—even those who vow to shake things up—confront not an unformed, pliable institution but an established, traditional one that must be approached largely on its own terms.

E*lectoral Process.* A Census Bureau worker conducts a personal interview, 2010 (top left). A long line of citizens wait in the rain to cast their vote in St. Petersburg, FL (center)—a 2012 problem so acute that the president mentioned it in his victory speech and Florida promised overhaul of its electoral procedures. Ted Cruz, R-Tex, celebrates his upset 2012 Senate primary victory (top right), while Elizabeth Warren, D-Mass., celebrates her hard-fought victory (bottom left). Five-term Rep. G. K. Butterfield (bottom right), an African American, holds the gerrymandered "majority-minority" First District in North Carolina.

chapter 3

Going for It:
Recruitment and Candidacy

At the start of the 113th Congress in January 2013, one of the largest freshman classes in recent decades assembled to take the oath of office. Among the fourteen new senators (9D, 1 IND, 4R) were a law professor, two former governors, a state senator, and six former U.S. House members. Among the 84 new House members (49D, 35R) were a veterinarian, a reindeer farmer, an air force officer, a physicist, a surgeon, a TV anchor, a plumber, and numerous state lawmakers and city council members. Nine House freshmen are former House members.

How did these people get to Congress? This question has no simple answer. In the broadest sense, all legislators are products of recruitment—the social and political process through which people achieve leadership posts. Recruitment is a key to the effective performance of all institutions, including legislatures. Ideally, the recruitment process should secure the ablest individuals to lead their community, a subject addressed in the first great book about politics, Plato's *Republic*. Sociologists have long observed, however, that recruitment reflects a society's class structure: The most privileged classes are overrepresented in the power structure. Contemporary political scientists, whatever their normative concerns, have charted the paths that individuals travel to gain positions in Congress and other institutions of government.

Any recruitment process has both formal and informal elements. For Congress, the formal elements include the Constitution and state and federal laws governing nominations and elections. Equally important are the informal, often unwritten, rules of the game. Ambitions, skills, and resources favor certain aspirants over others; popular moods and attitudes—which are changeable—induce citizens to support some candidates and reject others. Taken together, such elements add up to a series of filters or screens. The recruitment process is a mix of rules, probabilities, chance events, and timing. Its biases, both overt and hidden, affect the quality of representation and decision making in the House and Senate.

FORMAL RULES OF THE GAME

The formal gateways to congressional office are wide. There are only three constitutional qualifications for holding congressional office: age (twenty-five years of age for the House, thirty for the Senate); citizenship (seven years for the House, nine years for the Senate); and residency (in the state from which the officeholder is elected).

These qualifications cannot be augmented by the states or by Congress. For example, the Supreme Court has held that states cannot limit the number of terms their members of Congress can serve. A change of this kind can only be made through constitutional amendment.[1] Notably, the drafters of the Constitution considered but rejected term limits. According to *The Federalist Papers*, officeholders' desire for reelection was thought a powerful incentive for faithful service. In addition, the framers valued the expertise that experienced lawmakers—people like themselves—could bring to legislative deliberations.

The residency requirement is traditionally stricter in practice than the Constitution prescribes. Voters tend to prefer candidates with long-standing ties to their states or districts and to shun outsiders who move into a state primarily to seek public office (so-called carpetbaggers). Nevertheless, Americans' geographical mobility has swollen the "carpetbagger caucus" on Capitol Hill. About a third of the members of both chambers in recent Congresses were born outside the states they represent. Especially in the more populous, faster-growing areas, shrewd candidates can overcome objections to their outsider status. Barely a year after he settled in Arizona, Republican John McCain, a career navy officer and six-year prisoner of war in North Vietnam, beat three established politicians for a congressional nomination. He stifled carpetbagging charges by explaining that, as the son of a navy officer and one himself, he had never been able to put down roots: "The longest place I ever lived was Hanoi."

Senate Apportionment

At the 1789 Constitutional Convention, delegates from small states demanded equal representation in the Senate as the price for their support of the Constitution. This arrangement is virtually unamendable, because Article V assures that no state can be deprived of its equal voice in the Senate without its own consent. As a result, the Senate is the one legislative body in the nation in which "one person, one vote" emphatically does not apply. By this standard, the Senate is one of the most malapportioned legislatures in the democratic world.[2] As one scholar has noted, "The nine largest states are home to 51 percent of the population but elect only 18 percent of the Senate; the twenty-six smallest states control 52 percent of the Senate but hold only 18 percent of the population.[3]

Over time, the Senate's representative character was eroded by widening disparities in state population. After the first census in 1790, the spread between the most populous state (Virginia) and the least populous (Delaware) was nineteen to one. Today, the spread between the most populous state (California) and the least populous (Wyoming) is sixty-six to one.

Populous states complain that they are shortchanged in the federal bargain. Compared with lightly populated states, they contribute more revenue and receive fewer benefits.[4] A recent study using survey, electoral, and demographic data concludes that the Senate's malapportionment "has increasingly come to underweight the preferences of liberals, Democrats, African Americans, and Latinos."[5]

House Apportionment

The 435 House seats are apportioned among the states by population, with districts averaging more than 710,000 people each. This apportionment process excludes the five delegates (American Samoa, the District of Columbia, Guam, the Virgin Islands, and the Northern Mariana Islands) and one resident commissioner (Puerto Rico). These nonapportioned seats represent populations ranging from 55,519 (American Samoa) to 3.7 million (Puerto Rico).

Role of the Census. To allocate House seats among the states, the Constitution requires a census of the population every ten years. Once the figures are gathered by the Commerce Department's Census Bureau, House apportionment is derived by a mathematical formula called the method of equal proportions.[6] However, reapportionment does not fully guarantee equality of district population because of two additional requirements: (1) every state must receive one House member, and (2) congressional districts cannot cross state lines.[7] After the 2010 apportionment, for example, the entire state of Montana, with one representative-at-large for nearly a million people, was the nation's most populous district. Neighboring Wyoming, with slightly over half a million represented by its single seat, was the least populous.

Because the size of the House has remained unchanged since 1911, one state's gain now means another state's loss.[8] This reality provoked sharp controversy in the aftermath of the 1920 census. For the first time ever, the results indicated that more Americans lived in urban than in rural areas. With the nation's cities and rural towns sharply at odds over the burning issue of the enforcement of Prohibition, the power struggle over representation was so intractable that Congress failed to pass a reapportionment bill after the 1920 census.[9] Finally, in 1929 a law was enacted that "established a permanent system for apportioning the 435 House seats following each census."[10] Thus the reapportionment of House seats occurred after the 1930 census and every census since (Figure 3-1).

For some decades now, older industrial and farm states of the Northeast and Midwest have lost ground to fast growing states in the South and West—the declining Rust Belt versus the booming Sun Belt. After the 1940 census, states in the East and Midwest commanded 58 percent of all House seats, compared with 42 percent for states in the South and West. With the 2000 census, the ratio was exactly reversed. Over two generations, then, "a huge shift in political power" occurred between the geographic regions.[11] The trend continued with the results of the 2010 census, after which the northeastern and midwestern states once again lost seats to the Sun Belt. Most dramatically, Texas and Florida increased their congressional representation by four and two seats, respectively, while Ohio and New York each lost two seats.

FIGURE 3-1 House Apportionment in the 113th Congress

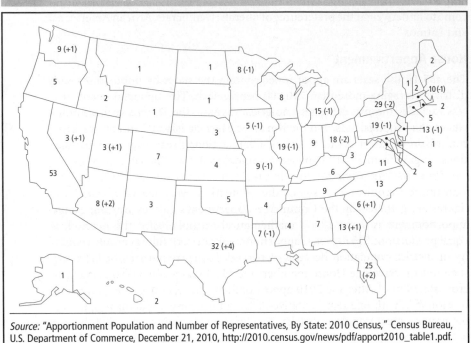

Source: "Apportionment Population and Number of Representatives, By State: 2010 Census," Census Bureau, U.S. Department of Commerce, December 21, 2010, http://2010.census.gov/news/pdf/apport2010_table1.pdf.

Note: Entries show the total number of House seats held by each state. Numbers in parentheses show the seats each state gained or lost after the post-2010 reapportionment.

Census Politics. The Constitution describes the decennial census as an "actual enumeration" of persons (Article I, section 2). The Fourteenth Amendment adds: "Representatives shall be apportioned among the several States according to their respective numbers, counting the whole number of persons in each State, excluding Indians not taxed." Because population figures determine seats and affect power, including each state's share of the Electoral College vote for president and vice president, controversy surrounds nearly every aspect of apportionment and districting.

First, counting such a large and diverse population is logistically and methodologically daunting. Certain hard-to-contact groups—transients, the homeless, renters, immigrants (legal or not), children, and poorer people generally—elude census takers and are undercounted. College students or others temporarily living away from home are sometimes double-counted (an overcount, in effect).[12] The so-called "tri-caucus" in the House—the Black Caucus, the Hispanic Caucus, and the Asian Caucus—has long been concerned about getting accurate counts of hard-to-reach minorities.[13]

Second, the issue of statistical sampling has been a subject of considerable controversy. For the 2000 census, the Census Bureau had planned to use statistical sampling to augment its traditional methods for counting people to minimize the undercount of minority populations. But, because minorities tend to vote Democratic, congressional Republicans feared "that sampling would overestimate minority populations and thereby cause Republicans to lose seats to Democrats."[14] Legal challenges to the sampling plan eventually ended up in the Supreme Court, which held that sampling could not be used to apportion seats among the states, but kept open the possibility that it could be used for other purposes, such as the redistricting of House seats within a state.[15]

Third, the immigration issue adds yet another dimension to census politics. Because the Fourteenth Amendment refers to "persons" rather than "citizens," states with large numbers of undocumented immigrants (such as Arizona, California, and Texas) gain House seats at the expense of states with fewer undocumented immigrants (such as Michigan and Pennsylvania). "It's one thing if we lose seats simply because of population loss," complained Rep. Candice Miller, R-Mich., "but it's another thing if we lose this seat because of illegal immigration, and that's exactly what is happening."[16] However, the Supreme Court in 2013 declined to review lower court rulings on an Irving, Texas, case—in which the complainants argued that any count that included noncitizens diluted their votes and deprived them of the Fourteenth Amendment's guarantee of equal protection of the laws. Thus the census embraces all residents—whether they are citizens or noncitizens, or whether or not they are qualified to vote.[17]

DISTRICTING IN THE HOUSE

Redistricting is fundamentally a state responsibility, but the federal courts increasingly govern the process. Congressional districting is regulated by two federal statutes. The first is a 1967 statute that mandates that all states entitled to more than one seat create districts, each represented by a single member. At-large or multimember districts are prohibited. The second statute is the Voting Rights Act of 1965, which requires that districts not dilute the representation of racial minorities. In addition to interpreting these statutes, the courts have construed the Constitution to require that districts be nearly equal in population, a standard that they rigorously enforce.

Redistricting is a fiercely political process that affects the fortunes of many people—state legislators, governors, incumbent House members, the congressional leadership, lobbyists, and the leaders of racial and ethnic groups.[18] To insulate the process from politics, a handful of states have turned the job over to some form of independent commission.[19] In most states, however, redistricting is carried out by the legislature, with the governor able to approve or veto the plan. If a state's politicians become deadlocked on redistricting, or if they fail to observe legal guidelines, judges may finish the job—sometimes awarding victory to parties that lost out earlier in the political fracas.

In the redistricting wars no weapons are left sheathed. Both political parties pour money into state legislative and gubernatorial elections and into post-census lobbying efforts so they can control the mapmaking process. The shift of only a few seats in a state legislature can thereby determine not only which party dominates its congressional delegation, but potentially which party achieves majority control of the House itself. As a GOP consultant said about his role in drawing House seats, "As a mapmaker, I can have more of an impact on an election than a campaign, than a candidate."[20]

Because congressional seats are political prizes, districting is a tool by which politicians seek partisan, factional, and even personal advantage. Two perennial problems of districting are malapportionment and gerrymandering.

Malapportionment

Before 1964, districts of grossly unequal populations often existed side by side in the same state. As metropolitan areas grew in population, rurally dominated legislatures simply refused to redistrict, holding on to power regardless of population movements and demographic trends—the "silent gerrymander." The courts were slow to venture into this "political thicket." By the 1960s, however, the problem of unequal representation was crying out for resolution.[21]

In a series of landmark rulings in the 1960s, the Supreme Court held that districting schemes that fell short of standards of population equality violated the Constitution. In *Reynolds v. Sims* (1964), the Court ruled that the Fourteenth Amendment's equal protection clause requires that all state legislative seats be apportioned "substantially on population." That same year, the Court also applied the "one person, one vote" principle to the U.S. House of Representatives. In *Wesberry v. Sanders* (1964) the Court based its decision not on the Fourteenth Amendment but on Article I, section 2, of the Constitution, which directs that House representatives be apportioned among the states according to their respective numbers and chosen by the people of the several states. This language, argued Justice Hugo Black, means that "as nearly as is practicable, one person's vote in a congressional election is to be worth as much as another's."

How much equality of population is "practicable" within the states? The Supreme Court has adopted rigid mathematical equality as the underlying standard. In a 1983 case (*Karcher v. Daggett*), a 5–4 majority voided a New Jersey plan in which districts varied by no more than one-seventh of 1 percent. "Adopting any standard other than population equality would subtly erode the Constitution's ideal of equal representation," wrote Justice William J. Brennan for the majority.[22]

Other goals must sometimes be sacrificed to achieve population equality. It is often not feasible to follow other economic, social, or geographic boundaries in drawing districts of equal population in more populous states. The congressional district, therefore, tends to be an artificial creation, often bearing little relationship to real communities of interest—economic, geographic, or political. "The main casualty of the tortuous redistricting process now under way," remarked journalist Alan Ehrenhalt, "is the erosion of geographical community—of place—as the basis of political representation."[23]

Gerrymandering

The term *gerrymander* refers to district line-drawing that purposefully maximizes seats for one party or voting bloc. The gerrymander takes its name from Gov. Elbridge Gerry of Massachusetts, who in 1812 created a peculiar salamander-shaped district north of Boston to benefit his Democratic Party (see Box 3-1). Gerrymandering is used not only to gain partisan advantage but also to shape the political prospects of incumbents, particular aspiring politicians, or racial or ethnic groups. For most of its history, Congress has regarded gerrymandering as part of the spoils of partisan warfare.

Two common gerrymandering techniques are cracking and packing.[24] Cracking splits a party's or a grouping's strength between two or more districts, thereby diluting its voting leverage. A Republican cracking strategy, for example, might call for dividing a Democratic-leaning university town across two districts, combining each with the surrounding Republican-leaning rural areas, ensuring that Democrats will have difficulty winning either seat. A packing strategy draws districts dominated by voters of one party or group. Obviously, packing will likely make a district safe for a particular party, group, or incumbent. But it is also a way to waste votes. If a party's or ethnic group's voters are systematically concentrated in a small number of districts, it will win those seats with more votes than it needs, reducing its chances of winning nearby seats.

Today, gerrymandering is much more easily carried out than in the past. With computer technology and software, knowledgeable individuals and groups can use census and other data to match people's voting patterns where they live, even street by street. Political leaders are able to consider various alternative plans until they identify a redistricting map that achieves their objectives.

Partisan Gerrymandering. The most common form of gerrymandering is aimed at partisan advantage. This type of gerrymandering occurs in states in which one political party controls the process. A noteworthy and unusual example involved the Texas legislature after the 2002 elections. Texas Republicans—controlling both legislative chambers and the state house for the first time since Reconstruction—pushed through a new districting plan even though an earlier post-census districting scheme was already in place. When the plan—masterminded by then–U.S. House majority leader Tom DeLay of Texas—was used for the 2004 balloting, the GOP gained five seats, four of them from defeated Democratic incumbents. Subsequently, the U.S. Supreme Court upheld the 2003 Texas redistricting scheme by a 7–2 margin (*League of United Latin American Citizens v. Perry*, 2006).[25] Despite finding that the Texas GOP appeared to have acted "with the sole purpose of achieving a Republican majority," Justice Anthony M. Kennedy—speaking for the Court—found that the case did not provide a "workable test" for deciding "how much partisan dominance is too much."

On the issue of partisan gerrymandering, the Supreme Court, like Congress, has largely chosen to look the other way. In a 1986 case involving Indiana state legislative districts, a Court majority held that gerrymandering

BOX 3-1   Origins of the Gerrymander

The practice of "gerrymandering"—the excessive manipulation of the shape of a legislative district to benefit certain persons or groups—is probably as old as the Republic, but the name for the practice originated in 1812.

In that year, the Massachusetts legislature carved out of Essex County a district that historian John Fiske described as having a "dragon-like contour." When the painter Gilbert Stuart saw the misshapen district, he penciled in a head, wings, and claws and exclaimed, "That will do for a salamander!" to which editor Benjamin Russell replied, "Better say a Gerrymander"—after Elbridge Gerry, then-governor of Massachusetts.

By the 1990s, the term had broadened to include the modern-day practice of drawing maps to benefit racial and ethnic groups. In the past, the term was applied largely to districts drawn to benefit incumbents or political parties.

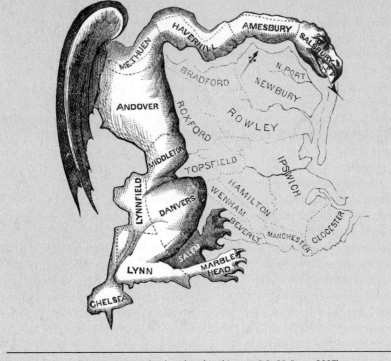

Source: CQ's Guide to Congress, 5th ed., vol. III (Washington, DC: CQ Press, 2007).

was a justiciable issue—that is, it could be properly raised in court (*Davis v. Bandemer*).[26] If the gerrymandering were substantial, long-standing, and truly harmful to a political minority, it could violate the Constitution's equal protection clause. At the same time, the Court's majority was not convinced that the Indiana gerrymander met those tests. Indeed, the Court has never overturned a districting scheme on the grounds of partisan gerrymandering. Despite a number of cases dealing with the issue, the Court has neglected to set out any standard for distinguishing permissible from impermissible partisan gerrymandering.[27]

Because of their large gains in state legislatures and gubernatorial seats in the 2010 elections, Republicans enjoyed substantial advantages over Democrats in redrawing House district boundaries after the most recent reapportionment. Republicans held the governor's mansion and both chambers of the state legislature in seventeen states, which allowed them to redistrict four times as many seats as Democrats.[28] Favorable district lines helped Republicans retain their House majority in 2012, even though Democrats won 1.1 million more votes than Republicans in House elections nationally.[29] District lines undoubtedly affect party fortunes. According to a Brennan Center analysis of the 2012 elections, in states where Republicans had controlled the redistricting process, Republican candidates won 53 percent of the vote and 72 percent of the seats. By comparison, in the states where Democrats were in control, Democratic candidates won around 56 percent of the vote and 71 percent of the seats.[30]

Many pundits and politicians complain that the prevalence of partisan gerrymandering inhibits the construction of cross-party coalitions. As former representative John Tanner, D-Tenn., stated:

> When Members come here from these [partisan] districts that have been gerrymandered, they have little incentive really to work across party lines in order to reach solutions. As a matter of fact, they have a disincentive because if their district is skewed so heavily one way or the other, then the election is really in the party primaries, where . . . the highly charged partisans, either Democrat or Republican, [dominate]. And so if one comes here wanting to work across the aisle, one has to watch one's back, because the highly charged partisans don't like that.[31]

Scholarly research, however, provides little support for the claim that gerrymandering is an important cause of party polarization in Congress. Political scientist Sean M. Theriault reports that redistricting is responsible for between 10 and 20 percent of the party polarization that has occurred.[32] Other scholars dispute even this relatively modest effect. A study by Nolan McCarty, Keith T. Poole, and Howard Rosenthal concludes that gerrymandering has not contributed to the rise of partisanship to any meaningful extent: "Polarization is not primarily a phenomenon of how voters are sorted into districts. It is mainly the consequence of the different ways Democrats and Republicans would represent the same districts."[33] Changes in congressional districts over time simply cannot account for party polarization in Congress. Republicans who represent swing districts are little different in their voting behavior than Republicans who represent seats that are safe for their party. The same is true for Democrats.

Pro-Incumbent Gerrymandering. Bipartisan or "sweetheart" gerrymanders are those with lines drawn to protect incumbents. These gerrymanders are often by-products of divided party control—either between the two chambers of the legislature or between the legislature and the governor. In the wake of the 2000 census, the dominant parties in several populous states—California, Illinois, Michigan, and New York—chose to hoard their existing assets. In New York, which lost two seats in the reapportionment, two pairs of incumbents (one from each party) were thrown into the same districts, and the remaining twenty-seven districts were drawn for incumbents. "Neither party [wanted] to lose its hard-won gains," election analyst Rhodes Cook explained.[34]

The case of California, home of 12 percent of all House members, illustrates how districting affects the fate of incumbents. After the 2000 census California's ascendant Democrats opted to play it safe and adopted an incumbent-friendly districting plan. Under this map, only one California congressional incumbent was defeated over the course of the five election cycles between 2002 and 2010.[35] All this changed after California voters took the job of redistricting away from the state legislature and gave it to a bipartisan citizens' commission. After the 2010 census, the commission drew contiguous and compact districts without regard for the fate of incumbents or political parties. In conjunction with California's new primary system, in which the top two vote getters advance to the general election regardless of party affiliation, there was considerable turnover in California's congressional delegation in 2012. House campaigns broke spending records, many races were hotly contested, eight House members opted not to run for reelection, and seven incumbents lost their seats.

Some commentators blame incumbent-protective line-drawing for producing noncompetitive elections.[36] However, the prevalence of partisan gerrymandering (parties' efforts to boost their number of seats) tends to counteract the effect on competition. When parties seek to maximize the number of seats they can win, they cannot afford to create many entirely "safe" seats without wasting votes.[37] Parties expose their incumbents to greater electoral competition when they spread out their party's voters across more districts in an effort to win more seats. In Florida's post-2010 redistricting, for example, Republicans sought to pad their large majority of the state's House seats. Their goal was to craft a plan that would allow Republicans to win both of the new seats Florida received as a result of reapportionment, as well as to hold onto their current seats. With Florida a swing state, they could not do so without endangering some of their incumbents.[38] In the end, Florida Republicans lost House seats in 2012, going from controlling 76 percent of the state's House delegation in 2011 to only 62 percent in 2013.

The competitiveness of congressional elections is almost certainly shaped as much by demography as by gerrymandering. "The problem is not who draws the legislative lines, it's where people live," notes one observer.[39] As Bruce Oppenheimer of Vanderbilt University explains, "Democrats tend to live next to Democrats. Republicans tend to live next to Republicans."[40] In the case of urban Democrats, they may be victims of what political scientists Jowei Chen and Jonathan Rodden call "unintentional gerrymandering": natural geographic patterns that lead Democrats to live in "dense, urban areas with very high concentrations of Democrats, effectively packing themselves into fewer districts."[41]

Combating partisan and incumbent-friendly districting could nevertheless become the next big voting reform cause. "The reason that people push for taking this out of the hands of the Legislature is there is really an inherent conflict of interest here where politicians are getting to custom-design which voters they want in their districts," one reform advocate explained.[42] A number of reform initiatives were considered in the lead-up to the post-2010 redistricting, with California reformers having the most success. Whether such remedies will sufficiently address the root causes of safe districts is another matter.

Majority-Minority Districts

Another form of gerrymandering involves the districting of racial minorities. After the Fifteenth Amendment was ratified to grant former slaves the right to vote, southern states adopted a variety of measures to thwart implementation of the law. One of those was the racial gerrymander—that is, "the deliberate and arbitrary distortion of district boundaries for racial purposes."[43] In the 1870s, for example, Mississippi opponents of Reconstruction concentrated the bulk of their state's black population in a long, narrow congressional district running along the Mississippi River, leaving five other districts with white majorities. Meanwhile, Alabama lawmakers scattered black voters over six different congressional districts to dilute their influence.[44] In other words, blacks were systematically "packed" into or "cracked" across congressional districts in order to weaken their electoral influence. In addition to racial gerrymandering, a variety of tools, such as literacy tests and poll taxes, were employed over time to disenfranchise black voters across the South, largely denying them the right to participate in elections until the civil rights reforms of the 1960s.

The Voting Rights Act (VRA) of 1965 is arguably the most effective civil rights law ever enacted. It did away with the whole panoply of legal impediments erected to limit minority electoral participation. Section 2 of the VRA abolished all voting qualifications or prerequisites that had stood in the way of the franchise. In addition, sixteen states (mainly southern) that historically had discriminated against minorities were required (under the VRA's Section 5) to "pre-clear" with either the U.S. District Court for the District of Columbia or the U.S. attorney general any changes in election rules to ensure that those changes would not deny or abridge the right to vote on account of race or color. Officials announced that changes to election rules would only be pre-cleared if they would not lead to "a retrogression in the position of racial minorities."[45] For districting, this requirement means that changes must not lessen the likelihood that minorities will be elected. Amendments to the VRA in 1982 strengthened the legislation, establishing that a state's redistricting plan or other changes to its electoral laws could be overturned if they had racially discriminatory effects, even if it was impossible to prove that state officials had intended to discriminate.

As states and the Department of Justice attempted to implement the amended VRA after the 1990 census, congressional district lines were drawn to help minorities elect candidates of their choice, unlike in previous eras when districts had been manipulated to limit minority influence. Indeed, states began to deliberately create "majority-minority" districts to enhance the probability that minorities would be elected to Congress. A National Conference of State Legislatures report describes the effect:

> As states drew the [post-1990] plans, they discovered that the Justice Department had little concern that majority-minority districts be compact. In some cases, the department refused to pre-clear a plan unless the state "maximized" the number of majority-minority districts by drawing them wherever pockets of minority population could be strung together. As the plans were redrawn to obtain pre-clearance, some districts took on bizarre shapes that caused them to be labeled "racial gerrymanders."[46]

During this time, fifteen new majority African American districts were created, thirteen of them in the South, along with nine new majority Latino districts. Many of these districts were so oddly shaped they made Governor Gerry's 1812 creation look amateurish by comparison.

The Supreme Court Enters the Quagmire. Some of these newly created majority-minority districts were later attacked in federal court. Plaintiffs charged that the districts violated white voters' Fourteenth Amendment right to equal protection of the law. The legal battles that resulted progressively deepened the Court's involvement in congressional districting. In a long series of complex, sometimes contradictory cases in this area, the Court has attempted to balance two competing values: first, the Fourteenth Amendment's requirement that states not discriminate on the basis of race, and second, the VRA's protection against racial discrimination in the electoral process.

At the center of the controversy was North Carolina's shoestring Twelfth District, which remained under a legal cloud after four remappings (see Figure 3-2). As first drawn, this district was 160 miles long, in many places no wider than a two-lane highway, winding back and forth to capture pockets of black voters. Examining the North Carolina map, Justice Sandra Day O'Connor questioned "districting so highly irregular that, on its face, it rationally cannot be understood as anything other than an effort to segregate voters . . . on the basis of race."[47] In the 1993 case reviewing the North Carolina districting scheme (*Shaw v. Reno*), a narrowly divided Supreme Court recognized a claim of "racial gerrymandering" and held that districts could be challenged under the Fourteenth Amendment's equal protection clause.

In cases dealing with racial gerrymandering, the Court has indicated that it will apply a standard of "strict scrutiny" to any district in which race was the "predominant factor" in its creation.[48] To prove racial predominance, it must be shown that "the legislature subordinated to racial considerations traditional race-neutral districting principles, including but not limited to compactness, contiguity, and respect for political subdivisions of communities defined by actual shared interests."[49]

"Strict scrutiny" sets a very high bar that requires a state to demonstrate that its districting plan is, in the language of the legal test, "narrowly tailored to achieve a compelling state interest." For a districting scheme to survive this test, states must show that the challenged districts were drawn specifically to satisfy the requirements of Sections 2 or 5 of the VRA. According to the Court's reading of Section 2, a districting scheme is not narrowly tailored to avoid discrimination when there is not a population of minority voters "sufficiently large and geographically compact to constitute a majority in a single-member district."[50] As a consequence, majority-minority districts that are not "reasonably compact" have been unable to withstand strict scrutiny.[51] According to the Court's reading of Section 5 of the VRA, the requirement is "non-retrogression," meaning that a new districting scheme must not cause fewer minority representatives to be elected than before.[52] Most districting schemes subjected to the strict scrutiny standard have been overturned.[53]

Subsequent cases have clarified the law, although considerable uncertainty remains about precisely what majority-minority districting schemes will stand or fall upon judicial review. One important clarification is that racial gerrymandering claims will fail unless race was the "predominant factor" in the creation of the district.[54] Writing for the Court in *Easley v. Cromartie* (2001), Justice Clarence Thomas declared:

> A jurisdiction may engage in constitutional political gerrymandering, even if it so happens that the most loyal Democrats happen to be black Democrats and even if the state were conscious of that fact.[55]

A racial gerrymandering challenge will not be upheld even if race was a factor in the districting if it was not the predominant factor.[56]

In the end, the key question is whether the Supreme Court will provide clear guidelines as to what racial (even partisan) redistricting the Constitution will permit. In the quest for a workable standard, the justices have adopted a version of Justice Potter Stewart's 1964 test for defining obscenity: "I know it when I see it." And in view of the closeness of its past decisions on majority-minority districts—nearly every major case on this question has turned on a 5–4 vote—the Court could again shift its direction as its membership changes. Race-conscious districting will surely be contested well beyond the 2010 remaps. As a North Carolina state senator quipped, "If the Lord God Almighty threw down lightning bolts and carved plans into the side of Mount Mitchell, and we adopted them, there would still be challenges to redistricting under every legal theory devised."[57]

FIGURE 3-2 **Racial Gerrymandering in the 1990s and 2000s: North Carolina's First and Twelfth Congressional Districts**

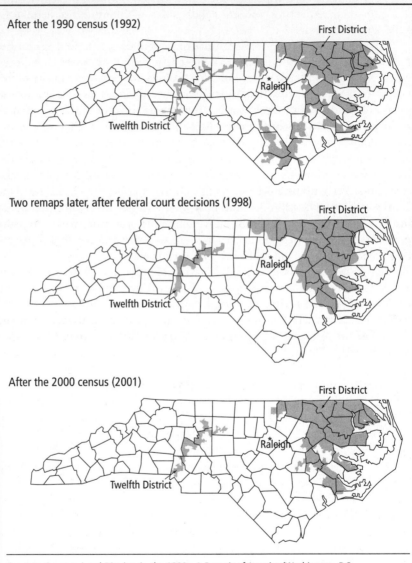

After the 1990 census (1992)

First District

Raleigh

Twelfth District

Two remaps later, after federal court decisions (1998)

First District

Raleigh

Twelfth District

After the 2000 census (2001)

First District

Raleigh

Twelfth District

Sources: Congressional Districts in the 1990s: A Portrait of America (Washington, DC: Congressional Quarterly, 1993), 548; Congressional Districts in the 2000s: A Portrait of America (Washington, DC: CQ Press, 2003), 673.

Note: North Carolina's First and Twelfth Congressional Districts were drawn to give the state its first black representatives in ninety-three years. First elected in 1992, the two African American representatives were subsequently reelected. Twenty years later, these two geographically equivalent districts were still electing blacks by overwhelming majorities.

Consequences of Majority-Minority Districts. Proponents of majority-minority districts view them as "the political equivalent to the ethnically homogeneous neighborhood," in the words of law professor Lani Guinier. "They are a safe haven for members of that group, a bit of turf that one ethnic grouping controls, a place where their voice is pre-eminent."[58] The growing numbers of majority-minority districts have unquestionably made the House of Representatives more racially and ethnically diverse. Most minority legislators are elected in districts where minority groups make up the majority of the population. Indeed, a recent study confirms that a district's racial composition is by far the most important factor in determining the race of the representative it elects: "Race-conscious redistricting and the creation of effective minority districts remain the basis upon which most African American and Latino officials gain election."[59] Over time, representatives of majority-minority districts have built up a great deal of seniority and institutional clout within the Democratic Party in the House.

Nevertheless, the creation of majority-minority districts comes at some cost to minority voters. Concentrating minorities into districts where they constitute a majority wastes their votes by producing outsized electoral majorities for the winning candidates. Relatedly, the way districting plans pack minority voters together has arguably slowed the diversification of Congress. Minority populations have grown faster than the share of House districts that elect minority representatives. A *National Journal* analysis after the 2010 redistricting determined that minority voters were more concentrated in fewer House districts than they were after the 2000 redistricting: "In the 33 states that made new district demographics available, minority influence has been packed into a greater number of more heavily nonwhite districts, and the number of more heavily white House seats has also grown."[60] Latino groups were particularly disappointed by the latest rounds of redistricting in Texas and California.

Packing minority voters into districts simultaneously "bleaches" surrounding nonminority districts, along with whatever leverage minority voters might wield. Even if the share of minority officeholders rises, "the number of white legislators who have any political need to respond to minority concerns goes down as their minority constituents are peeled off to form the new black and Hispanic districts."[61]

There is evidence that racial redistricting has contributed to the Democratic Party's southern meltdown since the 1990s.[62] Concentrating minority (mostly Democratic) voters in safe (mainly urban) districts strengthened the GOP in outlying suburban and rural areas. The combination of African Americans, who wanted more representation in the House, and Republicans, who supported that goal because it served their political purposes, has been dubbed an "unholy alliance."[63] Scholar David Lublin has described the outcome as a "paradox of representation" in which packed districts yielded more minority lawmakers but also led to a more conservative House that reduced minorities' leverage and influence over legislative outcomes.[64]

Many doubt that packing districts is the best way to advance minorities' interests. Another strategy for enhancing the political influence of minorities is to maintain substantial minorities of racial and ethnic voters—say, 40 percent or so—in a larger number of districts (so-called influence districts) to expand the ranks of officeholders responsive to minority needs.[65] In the wake of the 2000 census, many Democrats concluded that racial gerrymandering had hurt their party and set about unpacking some of the minority districts. "For 20 years I've been arguing against the stacking of black voters in districts that has the overall effect of diluting the voting strength of black people," said Rep. James E. Clyburn, D-S.C. "It's better to maintain a 35 to 40 percent black district where [blacks] would have a tremendous influence on elections. I don't think you need 75 percent in order for a black to be elected. That's kind of insulting to me."[66]

BECOMING A CANDIDATE

Very few of those who are eligible for Congress vie for a seat. Candidates who meet the legal qualifications must weigh a variety of considerations—some practical and rational, others personal and emotional. Candidacy decisions are often the pivotal moments in the entire recruitment process, although students of politics have only recently given them the attention they deserve. "The decision to run obviously structures everything else that goes on in the primary process," writes political scientist L. Sandy Maisel. "Who runs, who does not run, how many candidates run. These questions set the stage for the campaigns themselves."[67]

Called or Chosen?

From their Jacksonian heyday in the 1830s to the decline of big-city machines in the 1960s, local party organizations customarily enlisted and sponsored candidates. When these organizations withered, the initiative passed to the candidates themselves: self-starters who pulled their own bandwagons. "The boys in the back room aren't going to decide who stays in this race," one representative remarked. "There are no boys anymore."[68] "The skills that work in American politics at this point in history," writes Alan Ehrenhalt, "are those of entrepreneurship. . . . People nominate themselves."[69]

Congressional aspirants, however, quickly encounter national networks of party committees and their allied interest groups. At the heart of these networks are the two major parties' House and Senate campaign committees, now active in nearly all phases of congressional elections.[70] They seek out and encourage promising candidates at the local level, sometimes even taking sides to help ensure their nomination. They assist promising candidates with filing deadlines, lining up supporters, and handling finances. In fact, recent research reveals that "recruitment from party leaders, elected officials, and political activists is one of the most important predictors" of who will consider a candidacy for political office.[71]

During the recruiting season (beginning in early 2013 for the 2014 contests, for example), the leaders and campaign committee staffs of the two major parties "reach out across the country in search of political talent. Like college football coaching staffs in hot pursuit of high-school prospects, they are putting together the lineups of the future."[72] Prospects can expect calls from the president, former presidents, governors, high-profile financial backers, and other notables. The run-ups to recent elections all began with fierce recruiting seasons, as both parties sought lineups that could win House and Senate majorities.

Not all recruiting takes place on the road. Open seats—those in newly created districts or those in which incumbents have died or retired—are less secure. So, to the extent they can, party leaders try to discourage their incumbent colleagues from retiring. If members are going to retire, however, party leaders encourage them to announce their retirement early so that they have time to make preparations to hold the seat.[73]

A few nonparty groups also sponsor congressional candidates. The leading small-business lobby, the National Federation of Independent Business (NFIB), has been a major contributor to the GOP cause. In the mid-1990s, the NFIB began to pick potential candidates from its own membership, train them, and help them run for office. "We're trying to develop a farm team for down the road," explained the federation's national political director, "so we can work in more of a proactive instead of a reactive way"—fielding, not just endorsing, candidates who support the small-business agenda.[74] Other organizations with strong grassroots networks now pursue a similar course.

Most would-be officeholders seek advancement within the two major parties, which boast not only the brand loyalties of a huge majority of voters but also extensive financial and logistical resources. Still, independents and minor-party candidates enter congressional contests. Seldom do these contenders win a sizable number of votes, but they do provide alternatives where only one major party fields a candidate. Only two independents served in Congress in 2013: Vermont senator Bernard Sanders, a self-styled "democratic socialist," and Maine senator Angus King.

Amateurs and Professionals

How do would-be candidates, whether self-starters or recruited by party leaders, make up their minds to run? The answer often depends on whether the individual is a political amateur or a professional.

Amateurs. Amateur candidates are defined by their lack of previous political experience. Despite inexperience and nonexistent name recognition, many amateurs run for Congress. A few run to bring a specific issue to public attention and are less interested in winning than in advancing their cause. Most amateurs are what David T. Canon calls "hopeless amateurs"—people with little or no chance of winning.[75] Nevertheless, political amateurs regularly compete, and almost every congressional election brings a few amateurs to Capitol Hill. Indeed, the freshman class of 2010 had the largest number of political amateurs of any class since 1944.[76]

Amateurs are more willing than experienced politicians to make a long-shot bid for office. They are frequently the only candidates who will take on seemingly invulnerable incumbents. Amateurs often find that an uncompetitive primary offers their only chance to win a major-party nomination. More attractive political opportunities will generally entice more politically experienced competitors. "I think his chances have gone from absolutely out of the question to extremely remote," remarked the wife of one hopeless contender. "But he's learning a lot, and I think he has enjoyed it."[77] Many such amateurs nevertheless indulge in self-delusion about their prospects. Maisel, a political scientist who wrote candidly about his own unsuccessful congressional primary campaign, described politicians as possessing an "incredible ability to delude themselves about their own chances."[78]

One group of amateurs, however, sometimes proves to be the exception—those with highly visible nonpolitical careers. Astronauts, war heroes, entertainers, and athletes are in big demand as candidates. Local or statewide television personalities also make attractive contenders. Al Franken's status as a nationally known comedian, writer, and commentator helped to launch his political career as a candidate in 2008 for Minnesota's U.S. Senate seat. Once in office, though, Franken stressed his seriousness.

Professionals. Professionals are more cautious than amateurs about the races they enter. Those who seek to make a career in politics must consider carefully not just whether to run for a particular political office but when to do so. Political careerists often have more to lose than amateurs from an unsuccessful bid for office, because entering one race often means forgoing the office they already hold. An experienced state legislator is unlikely to gamble a safe seat in the state house or senate on a remote chance that he or she might defeat a popular congressional incumbent. Such a candidate will wait for a better opening, when an incumbent retires or is clearly vulnerable. Similarly, a sitting House member will usually wait for an open seat or an exceptional opportunity before attempting to move up to the Senate. In the end, such decisions hinge on "the not-so-simple calculus of winning."[79]

Strategic contenders weigh the chances of getting the party's nomination in view of the party's ideological bent, leadership, and nominating procedures. They also consider what it will cost to succeed. If there is an incumbent, they identify the incumbent's weaknesses. And they take a look at the broader political environment, including the condition of the economy, the president's standing, and public dissatisfaction with the status quo. They then evaluate their own personal strengths and weaknesses in campaigning, voter appeal, and fund-raising,

Most successful congressional candidates are professionals—seasoned politicians—before they run for Congress. Grassroots organizations and movements are a breeding ground for candidates—for example, environmental activists in the 1970s, religious conservatives in the 1990s, antiwar activists during the George W. Bush presidency, and Tea Party activists after 2008. But more often, elective office is the immediate springboard: mayors, district attorneys, or state legislators for the House; governors, lieutenant governors, and attorneys general—who have already faced a statewide electorate—for the Senate. House members, especially from smaller states, are also strategically positioned to run for the Senate. A majority of senators in the 113th Congress had "moved up" from the House.

The circle of people pondering a candidacy (the challenger pool) may be large or small, depending on the office and the circumstances.[80] Any number of elected officials—state legislators (especially if subject to term limits), county officers, mayors, city council members, even governors—are weighing a race for Congress at any given time. "The people who have been successful in the political world are people who know when to strike at the right time," remarked one veteran state legislator contemplating a run against a House incumbent.[81]

Finding Quality Candidates

Candidate quality and campaign strength are critical factors in many battles for congressional seats.[82] A party's success in November hinges on its efforts during the recruitment season. Often races turn on bids that are not made. An election outcome frequently becomes a *fait accompli* when a strong potential candidate chooses whether to run.

According to Maisel and his colleagues, candidate quality is measured in strategic resources and personal attributes.[83] Quality candidates are skilled in presenting themselves as candidates and are attractive to voters. Previous experience in public office—and the accompanying visibility and credibility—is one of the most important attributes of a quality candidate. Simply having a familiar political name can also be a ticket to candidacy. In particular, candidates from famous political families have a "brand-name" advantage.[84] Fame or notoriety can sometimes overcome lack of relevant background or experience. Other characteristics of quality candidates include physical appearance, personality, speaking ability, and a talent for organizing or motivating others. Fund-raising ability or potential is essential as well. Overall, likely candidates have ambition and a keen desire for public life, both of which will help them to succeed in their attempt to gain public office.[85]

Stamina is also important. No matter how talented, principled, or well funded, aspirants for public office must be ready, physically and emotionally, to face the rigors of campaigning. They must be willing to hit the road nonstop, meet new people, attend gatherings, sell themselves, ask for money, and endure verbal abuse—all the while appearing to enjoy it. "People who do not like to knock on strangers' doors or who find it tedious to repeat the same 30-second introduction thousands of times," explains Alan Ehrenhalt, "are at a severe disadvantage in running for office."[86]

The Incumbency Factor. Of all the inducements for launching a candidacy, the odds of winning stand at the top. A clearly winnable seat seldom lacks for eager quality candidates. Open seats—those without an incumbent running—are especially attractive. As a result, open-seat races are more likely to be competitive and to shift party control than those with an incumbent. Party strategists thus concentrate on these races.

In most House and Senate contests, however, incumbents will be running, and most of them will be reelected. As Gary C. Jacobson writes, "Nearly everything pertaining to candidates and campaigns for Congress is profoundly influenced by whether the candidate is an incumbent, challenging an incumbent, or pursuing an open seat."[87] Perhaps less forcibly, the same could be said of the Senate. Since World War II, on average 93.3 percent of all incumbent representatives and 81.5 percent of all incumbent senators running for reelection have been returned to office. In 2012, 90 percent of House members and 91 percent of senators seeking reelection were returned to Congress.

Because any savvy politician contemplating a bid for Congress recognizes the difficulty of defeating an incumbent, incumbents often face only low-quality opponents. Challengers are often weak fund-raisers, poorly qualified, and unknown to voters. Party leaders sometimes struggle to rouse any candidate at all willing to run against an incumbent. In 2012 ten incumbent House members ran for reelection unopposed. Similarly, Democrats in 2012 had so much difficulty finding a challenger for Sen. Bob Corker, R-Tenn., that the state's Democratic primary victor, Mark Clayton, prevailed despite raising no money, having no website, and being a member of a known hate group.[88]

An incumbent's most effective electoral strategy is to scare off serious opposition. "If an incumbent can convince potentially formidable opponents and people who control campaign resources that he or she is invincible," says Jacobson, "he or she is very likely to avoid a serious challenge and so will be invincible—as long as the impression lasts."[89] Any sign of weakness is likely to encourage opponents in the next election.[90] For that reason, incumbents try to sustain wide electoral margins, show unbroken strength, keep up constituency ties, and build giant war chests of reelection money.

Incumbents are not invincible, however, even if their high reelection rates make them seem so. Indeed, in view of the prevalence of strategic retirement—the tendency of incumbents to retire when they perceive themselves to be politically vulnerable—reelection rates are a somewhat misleading indicator of incumbent safety. Incumbents keep close tabs on political developments in their constituencies, and many would prefer to retire rather than suffer the rebuke of voters. These strategic considerations lurk behind many incumbents' retirements, even when they cite other reasons for their decisions. In 2012, for example, Democratic senators Ben Nelson of Nebraska and Kent Conrad of North Dakota both opted to retire rather than face the voters of their Republican-leaning states in an unfavorable political climate. In short, the chances of success are equally important for incumbents as for challengers when considering future career options.[91]

No-Shows. High-caliber potential candidates apparently abound in America's communities—even in minority party circles within noncompetitive districts.[92] But all too often these individuals prefer to remain on the sidelines. The road to public office is increasingly arduous and costly. And the odds are often long, especially when running against a dominant party or an entrenched incumbent. Therefore, quality challengers often fail to step forward. Poor-quality challengers raise less money and are less successful than the handful of blue-ribbon contenders. This dynamic depresses competition in congressional elections across the board.

Raising the money needed to run an effective race is a major deterrent to would-be candidates. Twenty-five percent of potential candidates in one survey designated fund-raising as a major obstacle to running; they described the prospect of soliciting campaign funds with words such as "daunting," "petrifying," "disgusting," "off-putting," and "more painful than a root canal without anesthesia."[93] Other candidates reject campaigns because of the high costs for their personal lives, incomes, careers, and families. The benefits side of the ledger may not outweigh the costs of gaining and holding public office. All too often, prospective candidates decide that their destinies lie elsewhere—in state or local politics, in nonprofit community service, or in family and profession.

Women are especially likely to forgo opportunities to run for political office, even when they have been highly successful in the professions that usually precede public office. Research by political scientists Jennifer L. Lawless and Richard L. Fox reports that prominent female lawyers, business people, educators, and political activists are less likely than similarly situated males to see themselves as good candidates for political office.[94] U.S. political institutions are more male-dominated than those in most other advanced democracies, but the cause appears to lie more with the calculations of prospective candidates than with voters. Women are not less likely than men to win races they enter, but they are less likely to consider a candidacy in the first place. In part, this difference reflects the fact that party leaders, elected officials, and advocacy groups are less likely to recruit women to run. But it also reflects broader societal norms and socialization processes that make it more difficult for women to promote themselves and seek political leadership positions.

NOMINATING POLITICS

Nominating procedures, set forth in state laws and conditioned by party customs, further shape the potential pool of candidates. Historically, these procedures have expanded to ever wider circles of participants—a development that has diminished the power of party leaders and thrust more initiative upon the candidates themselves. In most states, the direct primary—allowing party voters to choose their party's nominees—is the formal mechanism for selecting congressional candidates.

Rules of the Nominating Game

Every state has election laws that provide for primary elections for House and Senate candidates, but these laws vary widely.[95] The critical question is who should be permitted to vote in a party's primary. The states have adopted varying answers. Party leaders naturally prefer strict rules that reward party loyalty, discourage outsider candidates, and maximize their own influence on the outcome. States with strong party traditions therefore tend to have closed primaries. This arrangement, found in twenty-three states, requires voters to declare party affiliation in order to vote in the primary. (Their affiliation is considered permanent until they take steps to change it.) In open primaries, conducted in twenty states, voters can vote in the primary of either party (but not in both) simply by requesting the party's ballot at the polling place.

Few primaries are competitive races. Primary winners typically prevail in lopsided victories, and incumbents are almost always renominated. According to a recent study, only about 1 percent of incumbents in the postwar period were defeated in a primary.[96] Nominations for open-seat races, however, are virtually certain to feature contested primaries. "If a district party is without an incumbent, and has a fighting chance in November," Harvey L. Schantz writes, "there is a strong possibility of a public contest for the U.S. House nomination."[97] But even including primaries for open seats, the typical primary winner's share is more than 60 percent of the vote.[98]

Parties and Nominations

Despite the prevalence of primaries, party organizations at all levels are hardly without leverage in nominations. Although party organizations play no formal role in the primary process in the majority of states, in nine states parties have conventions that influence candidates' access to the primary ballot.[99] More important, party organizations influence nominations indirectly—by contacting promising prospects, linking them with campaign contributors, endorsing them, and assisting in other ways.

Parties are centrally involved in candidate recruitment. Parties are most active in districts regarded as winnable, and the people they seek out are the "usual suspects"—officeholders, prominent figures, and the wealthy.[100] The obvious candidate also may be someone who has run for the seat before. For example, at least a dozen House races in 2012 were rematches of the same candidates from a previous election.[101]

Party leaders tend to be pragmatists—above all, bent on finding winners. Democrats deliberately seek to recruit anti-abortion, pro–gun rights candidates in conservative areas such as the South. Republicans have historically recruited moderates for swing states and districts, though the strategy has been more difficult to execute since the emergence of the Tea Party movement, which has successfully resisted the nomination of moderate Republicans in many cases.

Intraparty rivalries often mark nominating contests. In 2010 intraparty conflicts led to primary or convention defeats for three sitting senators and four incumbent House members. The Tea Party movement, in particular, fueled an unusually high level of internal contention within the Republican Party between 2009 and 2013. In 2010, for example, candidates endorsed by the Tea Party unseated eighteen-year veteran senator Bob Bennett, R-Utah, and declined to renominate Sen. Lisa Murkowski, R-Alaska—who, remarkably, retained her seat as a write-in candidate. In 2012 a Tea Party favorite, Richard Mourdock, defeated longtime senator Richard G. Lugar, R-Ind., for the Republican nomination. Mourdock then went on to lose the seat to Democratic senator Joe Donnelly in a year when the Republican nominee for president carried Indiana by 10 percentage points.

Sizing Up the Primary System

The direct primary was one of the reforms adopted early in the twentieth century to overcome corrupt, boss-dominated nominating conventions. It has permitted more participation in selecting candidates, and yet primaries normally attract a narrower segment of voters than do general elections (except in one-party areas, where primaries dictate the outcomes). Primary contests in recent years have drawn less than 25 percent of eligible voters—or less than half the number who voted in the general elections. Less publicized than general elections, primaries tend to attract voters who are somewhat older, wealthier, better educated, more politically aware, and more ideologically committed than the electorate as a whole.[102]

Primaries also have hampered the political parties by encouraging would-be officeholders to appeal directly to the public and construct support networks apart from the party machinery. Still, leaders strive to influence who enters their primaries and who wins them. Displaying impressive resilience and adaptability, party organizations at all levels have recast themselves into organizations "'in service' to [their] candidates and officeholders but not in control of them."[103]

Finally, primaries are a costly way of choosing candidates. Unless candidates begin with overwhelming advantages (such as incumbency), they must mount virtually the same kind of campaign in the primary that they will repeat later in the general election.

CONCLUSION

The rules of the game that narrow the potential field of congressional contenders can be thought of as a series of gates, each narrower than the one before. First are the constitutional qualifications for holding office. Far more restrictive are the personal attributes associated with a successful public career. Next are the complex rules of apportionment and districting. Beyond these are the nominating procedures (usually primaries). These successive gates sharply reduce the number of people who are likely to become real contenders.

Equally important, individuals must make up their own minds about running for the House or Senate. Such choices embrace a range of considerations—many personal and emotional but all based on some estimate of the likely benefits and costs of the candidacy. This winnowing process presents voters with a limited choice on election day: two, occasionally more, preselected (or self-selected) candidates. From this tiny circle, senators and representatives are chosen.

W*inners and losers.* Sen.-elect Heidi Heitkamp, D-N.D., holds up the *Fargo Forum's* erroneous headline proclaiming her defeat (top). A disappointed campaigner (center) mourns Missouri's GOP Senate candidate, Rep. Todd Aikin, who lost a hotly contested 2012 race to Democratic Sen. Clare McCaskill. New senator Rand Paul, R-Ky., takes his oath of office in the Old Senate Chamber in 2010 as his wife and family look on. Vice President Joe Biden, Jr., officiates (bottom).

chapter 4

Making It: The Electoral Game

The 2012 Senate race in North Dakota was not expected to be close. North Dakota is a deeply conservative, overwhelmingly Republican state. When longtime senator Kent Conrad, D-N.D., announced his retirement in 2011, Republicans saw the race as a prime opportunity to pick up a seat. After all, Democrats held no other statewide office in North Dakota at the time. Republicans also enjoyed supermajorities in both houses of the state legislature. Only one Democratic presidential candidate had won the state during the preceding forty-eight years: Lyndon B. Johnson in 1964. President Barack Obama lost the state by nearly 20 percentage points. Any credible Republican running for a North Dakota Senate seat in 2012 would surely be considered the heavy favorite.

On paper, the two Senate candidates also looked poorly matched. Republican nominee Rick Berg was an experienced politician who represented the state in the U.S. House. Previously he had served as a majority leader and Speaker in the state's House. The Democratic candidate, Heidi Heitkamp, had been out of elective office for more than a decade. A veteran of North Dakota politics, she was a former state attorney general, but she had left her last statewide campaign in 2000 due to illness. Nevertheless, despite the state's partisan tilt, Democrat Heitkamp won the state's Senate seat in 2012.

Stylistically, the two candidates were a study in contrasts. Warm and personable, Heitkamp connected easily with voters. "She's as much at ease with grizzled, mostly male energy producers as she is touring a health care clinic staffed by young females—shaking hands, cracking one-liners, and doling out hugs," observed one journalist.[1] She "hugs her way through a room," noted another.[2] In a state with fewer than 700,000 people, she related to voters on the basis of personal ties and mutual friends. Everyone seemed to call her "Heidi." Meanwhile, Berg appeared much more comfortable addressing voters from behind a podium. An affluent businessman, he struggled to master the art of chit-chat. "He's not very personable," remarked a dishwasher at a Minot café.[3] Explaining why the race was a contest at all, one Republican statewide official took note of Heitkamp's strengths: "I like her very much. Decent person, got a great sense of humor. That's why it's competitive. It's the people's goodwill toward her."[4]

Heitkamp's appeal went beyond personal style. She also conveyed broad knowledge of political issues important to North Dakota. She focused on the state's special needs for improved airline service and flood control. She understood its reliance upon federal agricultural assistance. She stressed the problem of soaring home prices in the western part of the state—where a booming energy industry attracted newcomers from all over the country. She took a moderate stance on energy and gun issues, distinct from the national Democratic Party. Not mincing words, she criticized the Obama administration for being "hostile" to the coal industry.[5] At a time of frustration with Washington gridlock, she underscored the need for constructive engagement across party lines: "I fundamentally believe we need to get partisanship out of government if we're going to get anything done."[6]

Idiosyncratic in so many respects, the 2012 North Dakota Senate battle illustrates several elements of congressional elections. It highlights the importance of candidates' personal skills and campaign message. Even in an era when relatively few voters split their tickets, Americans' party preferences are not so rigid that skilled candidates cannot sometimes overcome them.

A candidate's media persona is not the only image that matters—especially in constituencies the size of congressional districts, North Dakota, or even the typical state. A "retail" politician who can reach voters one on one can still reap dividends. Heitkamp's kindness and rapport with ordinary voters built ties and positive word of mouth that enhanced their trust of her, even among constituents who did not share her views on specific policy questions. The race also illuminates the freedom candidates have to distance themselves from their national parties, when it is useful for them to do so. Running in a state where the typical voter often disagrees with the Democratic Party, Heitkamp successfully projected her image of independence and pragmatism. Finally, the race reminds us of the continued unpredictability of politics, even as the science of targeting voters becomes increasingly sophisticated.

CAMPAIGN STRATEGIES

Campaigns are volatile mixtures of personal contacts, fund-raising, speechmaking, advertising, and symbolic appeals. As acts of communication, campaigns are designed to convey messages to potential voters. The goal is to win over a plurality of those who cast ballots on election day.

Asking the Right Questions

Whether incumbents or challengers, candidates for Congress strive to map out a successful campaign strategy. To that end, each potential candidate must consider the following questions: What sort of constituency do I seek to represent? Are my name, face, and career familiar to voters? What resources—money, group support, volunteers—can I attract? What leaders and groups are pivotal to a winning campaign? What issues are uppermost in potential voters' minds? How can I reach those voters most effectively? When should my campaign begin, and how should it be paced? And, perhaps most important, what are my chances for victory? The answers to such questions define the campaign strategy.

The constituency itself shapes a candidate's campaign strategy. In populous states, Senate aspirants must appeal to diverse economic and social groups scattered over wide areas and many media markets. In fast-growing states, even Senate incumbents must introduce themselves to new voters who have arrived since the last election. Only small-state Senate candidates are able to know their constituents as well as House candidates know theirs. But unlike states, House districts often fit within no natural geographic community, media market, or existing political division.[7] In such situations, candidates and their managers must find the most suitable forums, media outlets, and organizations to reach voters who may have little in common other than being enclosed within the same district boundaries.

Because incumbents are typically hard to defeat, the incumbent's decision to seek reelection colors the entire electoral undertaking. The partisan leanings of the electorate are also critical. The dominant party's candidates stress party loyalty, underscore long-standing partisan values, and sponsor get-out-the-vote (GOTV) drives, because high voter turnout usually aids their cause. Minority party campaigns highlight personalities, downplay partisan differences, and exploit factional splits within the majority party, perhaps by invoking "wedge issues" designed to pry voters away from their usual party home.

Finally, the perceptions and attitudes of voters must be reflected in campaign planning. Through surveys, focus groups, or old-fashioned informal pulse taking, strategists take account of what is on voters' minds and what, if anything, they know or think about the candidate. Well-known candidates try to capitalize on their visibility; lesser-known ones run ads that repeat their names over and over again. Candidates with a reputation for openness and geniality highlight those qualities in ads. Those who are more introverted (yes, there are such politicians) stress experience and competence. Candidates who are young emphasize their vigor, energy, new ideas, and independence. Candidates who have made tough, unpopular decisions are touted as courageous leaders. In the wake of scandals, honesty and openness are on display.

Choosing the Message

The average citizen is barraged with media messages of all kinds—an hour of television commercials per day, among other things. The candidate's overarching challenge is to project an image through this cacophony of media appeals, including those from other candidates. "The only way to cut through this communication clutter," a political marketing executive points out, "is to adopt the strategy proven effective by successful businesses. Create a brand. And manage the message with discipline and impact."[8] In other words, forge a message that will stand out from all the competing messages in the media marketplace.

A candidate's message is usually distilled into a single theme or slogan that is repeated on radio, TV, billboards, websites, and in campaign literature. "A good message . . . is a credible statement that can be summed up in a few sentences and frequently ends with a kicker slogan."[9]

Strategists use these messages to frame the campaign: to set the election's agenda—not by changing people's attitudes, but by shifting their attention to issues that favor their candidate or diminish the opponent. "There's only three or four plots," explained Carter Eskew, a Democratic consultant. "Plots for incumbents are Representative X is different from the rest; X can deliver; X stands with you. And the perennial plot for challengers is (fill in the blank) years are long enough; it's time for a change."[10]

As challengers seek lines of attack, officeholders often find that incumbency has its liabilities. An extensive public record gives enterprising opponents many potential openings to exploit. Past votes or positions may be highlighted to discredit the officeholder, sometimes fairly and sometimes unfairly. Incumbents may be shackled to unpopular issues, such as a growing federal deficit, Medicare premium hikes, ongoing wars, economic crises, or unpopular presidents. Sometimes incumbents become complacent and take voters' support for granted, a major political mistake. One campaign consultant summed up the lesson of such races: "You have to earn that support every two years. A lot of members of Congress forget how to run."[11]

CAMPAIGN RESOURCES

Even the best campaign strategy will fail if the candidate cannot muster the resources necessary to implement it. The chief resources in congressiwonal elections are money and organization.

"Money is the mother's milk of politics," declared California's legendary Assembly Speaker Jess Unruh. Money is not everything in politics, but many candidates falter for lack of it, and nearly all expend valuable time and energy struggling to get it. Every candidate, writes Paul S. Herrnson, wages not one but two campaigns—a campaign for resources (the so-called money primary) that precedes, and underwrites, the more visible campaign for votes.[12]

Campaigns in the United States are very costly. In the 2011–2012 electoral cycle, congressional candidates raised $1.8 billion and spent most of it. The average Senate race cost $2.8 million. The average House contest cost $652,000.[13] When modern record-keeping began some forty years ago, no House candidate spent half that much.[14] Even controlling for inflation, expenditures for congressional campaigns have nearly tripled over the last forty years.

No mystery surrounds these skyrocketing costs. Population growth and new campaign technologies—electronic media, polling, and consultants of all kinds—account for much of the increase. To be sure, old-fashioned campaigns based on armies of volunteers canvassing door to door can be effective in some contests. But candidates raise as much money as they can for good reason.

FIGURE 4-1   **The Democratic Congressional Campaign Committee's Recommended Daily Schedule for New Members, 2013**

☑   **4 hours**   **Call Time**

☑   **1-2 hours**   **Constituent Visits**

☑   **2 hours**   **Committee/Floor**

☑   **1 hour**   **Strategic Outreach**
                     Breakfasts, Meet & Greets, Press

☑   **1 hour**   **Recharge Time**

Source: Ryan Grim and Sabrina Siddiqui, "Call Time for Congress Shows How Fundraising Dominates Bleak Work," *Huffington Post*, politics blog, January 8, 2013, www.huffingtonpost.com/2013/01/08/call-time-con-gressional-fudraising_n_2427291.html?ncid=edlinkusaolp00000003.

Fund-raising consumes tremendous amounts of time. In January 2013, the Democratic Congressional Campaign Committee (DCCC) gave a presentation for incoming frweshmen about the time they should expect to dedicate to raising money. Figure 4-1 displays a slide from the PowerPoint presentation these new members received. The DCCC prescribed a ten-hour day for members while they are in Washington, D.C. Out of each day, four hours should be spent on "call time" and another hour set aside for "strategic outreach," which includes fund-raising as well as media relations. By comparison, three to four hours are set aside for doing the regular work of Congress, including hearings, votes, and meetings with constituents. A subsequent slide specified that members should expect to devote three hours for fund-raising out of every eight-hour work day while they are in their districts during congressional recesses. Former representative Tom Periello, D-Va., commented that the time the DCCC recommended for fund-raising may even be "low balling the figure so as not to scare the new members too much."[15] To be sure, fund-raising practices vary; members from safe districts often raise less money than their party committees request. There is no question, however, that fund-raising puts intense year-round pressure on members' daily schedules.

Campaign Finance Regulations

The regulation of campaign finance in the United States is a dauntingly complicated subject. Congress's regulatory efforts have led to a proliferation of entities, many with the sole purpose of raising and spending money in political campaigns, each with its own rules and regulations. In addition, campaign finance law in the United States has been greatly complicated by a variety of Supreme Court rulings. In the landmark case of *Buckley v. Valeo* (1976),[16] the Supreme Court held that campaign contributions and spending are free speech protected by the First Amendment of the Constitution. The Court ruled that Congress may legitimately regulate campaign contributions—to prevent corruption or the appearance of corruption. But they held that most campaign spending could not be regulated. Other recent Supreme Court cases have had far-reaching effects on the state of the law in this area.

We must distinguish between (1) the rules governing how candidates can raise money for their own campaigns, and (2) the rules governing the electioneering activities of organized entities not controlled by candidates. So-called "outside money"—campaign expenditures made by party committees and other organized groups not under candidates' control—has become a much more important feature of campaign financing.

Candidates' Campaigns. Congressional candidates may raise funds from four sources: individual contributors, political action committees (PACs), party committees, and themselves and their families. More than half of the money raised by House and Senate candidates comes from individuals. In the 2011–2012 election cycle, congressional candidates (or their campaign committees) could receive up to $2,500 from each individual contributor for each election (primary, general, run-off). Individual contributions of more than $200 must identify the contributor's name and employer—information reported to the Federal Election Commission (FEC), the federal agency charged with regulating campaign finance. An individual contributor's overall contribution to federal candidates for the entire cycle was capped at $46,200.

PACs may also contribute directly to congressional candidates. Under current regulations, multicandidate PACs are defined as those registered for more than six months, having fifty or more contributors, and making contributions to five or more candidates for federal office. In the 2011–2012 election cycle, multicandidate PACs could contribute up to $5,000 to a congressional candidate (or the candidate's campaign committee) for each election. For PACs not meeting the definition of multicandidate PACs, contributions to congressional candidates were capped at $2,400 per election. Neither type of PAC is subject to an overall cap on contributions for the election cycle. In the 2011–2012 election cycle, PAC contributions topped $350 million. PACs are key players in House races: They accounted for almost a third of House candidates' campaign receipts in 2012 and just slightly more than 10 percent for Senate candidates.

In the 2011–2012 election cycle, party committees—national, state, congressional, and local—could contribute up to $5,000 per election to congressional candidates. National party committees could not exceed a total of $43,100 to any Senate candidate per campaign. As these amounts make clear, party funds cannot begin to cover the costs of today's campaigns. Party organizations of all types account for a relatively small portion of individual candidates' funding, even though in recent years they have greatly increased their efforts and fund-raising capacities. Parties may also use additional funds to pay for services requested by a candidate such as polling, advertisements, and media time. But these "coordinated expenditures" are also subject to limits set by the FEC.

Another source of campaign money for congressional candidates is the candidate's own funds. Candidates and their families may spend as much of their own money in a campaign as they wish. Self-financing is no guarantee of success, however. In the 2012 elections, extraordinary sums were personally spent by Senate candidates Linda McMahon in Connecticut ($48.8 million), David Dewhurst in Texas ($20.4 million), and Tom Smith in Pennsylvania ($16.8 million)—and they all lost.

Independent Expenditures. Parties and organized groups also seek to influence elections, separate from candidates' own campaigns. They develop campaigns, run media ads, and support get-out-the-vote drives—that is, underwriting independent activities formally unconnected to candidates' own efforts. Such independent expenditures are not subject to any limits.

There are several types of organized groups, each typically identified by the sections of the Internal Revenue Code that govern their structure and activities. Tax-exempt 527s, for example, must register with the Internal Revenue Service (IRS) and disclose expenses and contributors. Subject to those requirements, they may raise unlimited funds from individuals, labor unions, and corporations. In the 2011–2012 election cycle, for example, 527s raised about $460 million.

A wide array of new organized groups operating outside the control of federal candidates have emerged in the wake of two 2010 court rulings, *Citizens United v. FEC*[17] and *Speechnow.org v. Federal Election Commission*.[18] Exploiting the opportunities opened up by these cases, hundreds of new, big-spending organizations known as "Super PACs" have been formed. Super PACs are defined by the FEC as "non-connected political action committees." Such PACs cannot contribute directly to federal candidates' campaigns and cannot spend money in coordination with their campaigns. But they are permitted to make unlimited expenditures to influence the outcome of elections. Before 2010, corporations, nonprofits, and labor unions could not spend funds out of their general treasuries for pro-candidate advertisements. In *Citizens United*, the Supreme Court struck down that limitation as a form of censorship of protected political speech.

The Court expected, however, that such independent expenditures would be subject to the disclaimer and disclosure requirements imposed by existing campaign finance law. In the Court's opinion, Justice Anthony Kennedy wrote, "A campaign finance system that pairs corporate independent expenditures with effective disclosure has not existed before today.... With the advent of the Internet, prompt disclosure of expenditures can provide shareholders and citizens with the information needed to hold corporations and elected officials accountable."[19]

The disclosure requirements in the Bipartisan Campaign Reform Act of 2002 (BCRA), however, did not afford information that Justice Kennedy assumed would be available. Under the current FEC interpretation, a contribution of $1,000 or more to a group making an electioneering communication—that is, a pro-candidate advertisement in close proximity to an election—is reportable only if the contributor designated it to be used for a particular electioneering communication.[20] In other words, a contributor may avoid disclosure merely by not directing the contribution toward any particular advertisement.

Certain types of groups are wholly exempted from disclosure laws. The 2010 midterm elections saw the emergence of groups organized under section 501(c)(4) of the Internal Revenue Code.[21] These groups are generally civic organizations, with no more than half of their activities classed as political. Organized as a 501(c)(4), Karl Rove's Crossroads Grassroots Policy Strategies, for example, is not required to disclose its funders. American Crossroads/Crossroads GPS spent $17.1 million in the 2010 midterm election and $104.7 million in the 2012 election. The U.S. Chamber of Commerce, which is organized as a 501(c)(6), does not identify its donors, even though it spent $36 million in 2011–2012, largely to assist Republican candidates.

The upshot of these developments is that the fund-raising efforts of outside groups are far less stringently regulated than those of both candidates and political parties. "Super PACs can raise and spend money relatively easily," writes campaign finance expert Ray LaRaja. "For example, a Super PAC called 'Winning Our Future' in support of GOP presidential candidate Newt Gingrich, received most of its $17 million financing from one mega-donor."[22] Thus expenditures by outside groups have surged since 2010. These groups went from being a negligible factor in congressional elections as recently as 2004 to paying for fully 19 percent of all House campaign ads in 2012. Similarly, outside groups funded nearly 30 percent of the total ads run in the 2012 Senate races, up from less than 5 percent as recently as 2006.[23]

Unlike contributions to Super PACs, contributions to the parties are subject to caps, though higher ones than permitted as direct contributions to the candidates themselves.[24] In the 2011–2012 election cycle, the national parties' entities, including the House and Senate campaign committees, raised and spent more than $3.4 billion. This is a staggering figure, considering that the parties face an array of contribution limits that don't apply to outside groups.

As one former FEC commissioner put it, then, "the money's flowing."[25] When the last major campaign finance reform law (BCRA) was enacted in 2002, skeptics argued that the new law would do little to halt the overall flow of money into political campaigns. "This law will not remove one dime from politics," predicted Sen. Mitch McConnell, R-Ky., the measure's leading GOP foe. McConnell's skepticism has certainly been borne out, both by innovations in campaign finance and by Supreme Court rulings limiting the scope of regulatory restrictions. In the end, campaign finance laws have failed to limit the influence of money in politics. Big money is alive and well in U.S. elections.

Incumbents versus Challengers

Although incumbents need less money than do challengers, they receive more—a double-barreled financial advantage (see Figure 4-2). Incumbents are both better known than challengers and enjoy government-subsidized ways of reaching constituents. Nevertheless, incumbents are able to raise substantially more money. In 2012 House incumbents raised $1.6 million on average to defend their seats—more than six times what their opponents could muster. Senate incumbents outpaced their challengers by an even wider margin in 2012, raising on average 8.6 times more than their opponents.[26]

Challengers' first hurdle is to raise enough money to make their names and faces known to voters. Because most of them start from a low baseline of name recognition, their campaign dollars tend to be more cost-effective than those of incumbents. Nevertheless, they must raise a great deal of money to defeat an incumbent. As Gary C. Jacobson points out, "The minimum price tag for a competitive House campaign under average conditions today is probably [around] $800,000; 125 of the 136 challengers who defeated incumbents from 1996 through 2010 spent more than that amount."[27]

Incumbents of both parties are able to raise money far more easily than challengers because contributors see them as better investments. Most donors to congressional campaigns seek to cultivate closer relationships with people in positions of power. Donors know that incumbents usually win reelection, so they do not usually waste their money on challengers, even when those challengers might be more appealing in their policy stances or party affiliation. Indeed, "access-oriented" giving follows the shifts in party control of Congress, as donors curry favor with committee chairs and other leaders regardless of party.[28] Challengers obviously cannot attract this type of campaign donation, which gives incumbents a substantial fund-raising advantage.

Challengers have a difficult time convincing donors that they have any reasonable chance of winning. In this arena, as in so many others, nothing succeeds like success. "Failure to raise enough money creates a vicious spiral," explains political analyst Thomas B. Edsall. "Some donors become reluctant to invest their cash, and then state and national parties are less likely to target . . . party building and get out the vote drives in those races."[29]

When challengers are successful in raising money, they typically find that the funds make a significant difference in their electoral chances. Generally speaking, the more challengers spend, the more votes they are likely to attract.[30] The same is not true of incumbents. In fact, for incumbents there is

FIGURE 4-2 **Average Campaign Expenditures for Incumbents, Challengers, and Open-Seat Candidates: House and Senate, 1974–2012**

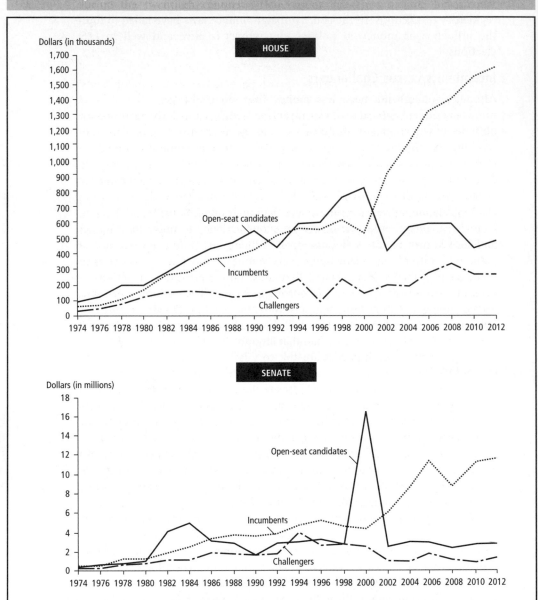

Sources: Federal Election Commission (FEC) figures for campaigns through 2000 are compiled in Norman J. Ornstein, Thomas E. Mann, and Michael J. Malbin, *Vital Statistics on Congress 2001–2002* (Washington, DC: AEI Press, 2002), 87–98. Figures through 2012, also derived from the FEC, are found at Center for Responsive Politics, "Election Overview, Incumbent Advantage," www.opensecrets.org.

actually a negative correlation between campaign expenditures and electoral success. Vulnerable incumbents tend to speed up their fund-raising. As Jacobson points out, "Incumbents can raise whatever they think they need."[31] Endangered incumbents thus raise prodigious sums as they seek to hold onto their seats. Meanwhile, safe incumbents—especially senior members who infrequently face significant electoral challenges—raise and spend much less. Despite the negative correlation, incumbents are unquestionably better off with more campaign money than less. But compared to challengers, incumbents' success or failure is much less tied to their fund-raising totals.

Many incumbents raise and spend far more than is necessary. Incumbents' overspending is frequently motivated by a sense of uncertainty and risk. "Because of uncertainty," Jacobson explains, "members tend to exaggerate electoral threats and overreact to them. They are inspired by worst-case scenarios—what would they have to do to win if everything went wrong?— rather than objective probabilities."[32]

Not all incumbent fund-raising is actually aimed at the race at hand. Incumbents often have strategic purposes for fund-raising beyond campaign finance. Preemptive fund-raising is aimed at dissuading serious opponents. "If you look like a 900-pound gorilla, people won't want to take you on," remarked a GOP campaign aide.[33] Some members, especially those with party leadership ambitions, raise money so they can impress colleagues by distributing funds to needier candidates. Sometimes established incumbents deliberately overspend in pursuit of decisive electoral victories that might establish their claims for higher office.

Allocating Resources

As exercises in communication, campaigns are driven by the need to find a cost-effective way of reaching citizens and getting them to vote. Candidates and their managers face many different trade-offs as they make decisions about allocating resources, depending on the context.

As a rule, statewide Senate races are mass media contests with messages conveyed mainly through radio and television. Costs are especially high in densely populated states with large metropolitan media markets. Senate candidates typically spend far more on media advertising and fund-raising than do their House counterparts, who spend more on traditional means of voter contact.

Despite its astronomical costs, television advertising is popular because candidates believe it works. Almost all households in the United States own at least one television, and the average adult watches five hours of television a day.[34] The 2012 congressional elections saw unprecedented expenditures for television advertising. Between January 1, 2012, and election day, over 1.6 million election-related spots aired on television for House and Senate candidates, at a total estimated cost of $973 million.[35] This level of spending on television advertisements was more than double the amount spent for 2008 congressional races.

Candidates tailor their use of media to their political circumstances. Confident incumbents can channel their money into telephone, Internet and e-mail, or door-to-door appeals that direct their messages to activists, partisans, and supporters. Lesser-known candidates must turn to broad-scale media, such as television, radio, newsletters, and billboards, to promote name recognition.

Candidates also have to make decisions about their pace of spending. Especially useful is early money—that is, having funds on hand to organize a campaign at the outset. EMILY's List—Early Money Is Like Yeast ("It makes the 'dough' rise")—a group begun in 1985, was formed on this premise. This group collects (bundles) individuals' donations for Democratic women candidates who support abortion rights. The Republican counterpart is Women in the Senate and House (WISH).

Late blitz money also can turn the tide, although money alone rarely makes the difference at the end of a race. In the final weeks of a hard-fought race, both sides are trying to reach undecided voters. "You've got to move that 10 or 15 percent, many of whom are not paying much attention," a Democratic consultant explained. "Unfortunately, the way to do that is with negative or comparative ads."[36] Late in a competitive race, opponents frantically attack and—despite the scant time—counterattack.

Another question of timing involves candidates facing tough contests in both the primary and general elections. In this situation, candidates lacking personal wealth find themselves in an especially vexing dilemma. Should they ration their outflow of funds and risk losing the primary, or should they wage an expensive primary campaign and risk running out of money later on?

Organizing the Campaign

Implementing a campaign strategy is the job of the candidates and their organizations. Waging a campaign is not for the fainthearted. Take the case of psychology professor Brian Baird, a Democrat who won Washington's Third District (comprising Olympia and southwest Washington State) seat in 1998. Having lost to the incumbent by a mere 887 votes two years earlier, Baird vowed to run full tilt the second time. As a result, he spent almost all of his waking hours campaigning during the peak months (July–October)—more than ten hours a day for 123 days. Travel alone consumed many hours in his average-sized district.[37]

Few localities today boast tight party organizations. In some strong party areas, voter contact is the job of ward, precinct, and block captains. Candidates in some such areas still dispense "walking-around money" to encourage precinct captains to get out the vote and provide small financial rewards for voting. But in most places today the traditional local parties have been replaced by hybrid organizations that partner with state and national parties and their allied interest groups.

When they can pay the price, today's candidates purchase campaign services from political consulting firms, most of them operating within partisan networks. Consulting firms took in an estimated $3 billion during the

2012 cycle—more than a third of total campaign spending.[38] Some firms offer a wide array of services; others specialize in polling, direct mail, phone banks, advertising, purchasing media time, coordinating volunteer efforts, fundraising, or financial management and accounting. Despite the hype they often receive, consultants by themselves rarely turn a campaign around. At best, they can make the most of a candidate's resources and help combat opponents' attacks. They cannot compensate for an unskilled or lazy candidate or for a candidate's staff which does not follow through on details.

CAMPAIGN TECHNIQUES

Campaigns are designed to convey the candidate's messages to people who will lend support and vote in the election. Campaigns are not necessarily directed at all voters. Often narrower groups are targeted—most notably, the political party's core supporters.

The Air War: Media and Other Mass Appeals

Candidates reach the largest numbers of voters by running broadcast ads and making televised appearances. Television is the broadest spectrum medium, and its costs eat up the bulk of most campaign budgets.

Candidates obviously cannot fully control their media coverage. Some of the most effective appeals—news coverage and endorsements, for example— are determined by persons other than the candidate. Because journalists can raise unwanted or hostile questions, many politicians seek out the friendlier environments of talk shows hosted by nonjournalists. Even more congenial are appeals the candidates themselves buy and pay for—newsletters, websites, media ads, and direct mail. The drawback is that self-promotion is seen as less credible than information from independent sources.

Nearly half of all voters rely primarily on television for their campaign news—network, cable, or local. About a quarter turn to the Internet as their primary campaign news source, and 8 percent rely on newspapers.[39] And yet local news programming largely ignores congressional campaign coverage. In the weeks preceding the 2004 elections, for example, 92 percent of the scheduled half-hour local news programs in eleven select media markets offered no coverage at all of local candidates' races, including those for the U.S. House. In the ten markets with statewide Senate races, the "blackout rate" was 94 percent.[40] Most candidates must therefore pay to reach the voters.

Positive Themes. Most campaign themes call for promotions that evoke positive responses from citizens. Positive ads present candidates in warm, human terms to which citizens can relate. Skillfully done, TV ads can be very effective in bringing home the candidate's themes. A case in point was the series of brilliant, funny—and inexpensive—television ads that helped a little-known Wisconsin state legislator, Russ Feingold, win the Democratic primary, defeat a two-term incumbent senator, and then go on to serve three terms in the U.S. Senate (1993–2011). As his opponents battered each other with negative ads,

Feingold ran clever, personal spots describing himself as the "underdog candidate." One showed Elvis, alive and endorsing Feingold. Another showed Feingold walking through his modest home, opening up a closet and saying, "No skeletons."

One of the best positive ads in 2012 was run by Senate candidate Heidi Heitkamp, D-N.D. In this ad, Heitkamp was shown wearing a baseball pullover and helmet while hitting line drives in a batting cage. In voice-over, she narrates that her political opponents "try to hit me with all sorts of stuff." Rather than respond to those "negative ads that aren't true," she pivots to highlighting her own priorities of "Medicare" and "jobs." In the last frame, she turns to the camera, winks, smiles broadly, and says, "I'm just getting warmed up."

Negative Themes. Candidates also deploy campaign resources against their opponents. Contrast ads distinguish the candidate from the opponent on the grounds of policy and experience, and attack ads strike at the opponent's record or personal character. Republican representative Leonard Lance's 2008 winning bid for an open seat in New Jersey's Seventh District offers an example of an effective contrast ad. The ad featured a series of "man on the street"–style shots, showing male and female voters of different ages and races, each saying "Linda Stender is a Spender." The ad's tone was high-spirited, with bright colors and punctuated by a cash register sound. One voter is even shown cracking up in laughter as he attempts the line. The repetition, combined with the rhyme on his opponent's name, memorably conveyed the central contrast Lance sought to draw in his campaign. Because challengers are usually less known than incumbents, they are more vulnerable to attacks and unflattering personal revelations.

Negative campaign themes are often the result of opposition research (called "oppo" by campaigners). Its purpose is "to get the skinny on the client's opponents and, if all goes well, expose them as hypocrites, liars, thieves, or just plain unsavory characters."[41] Both national parties and many campaigns invest in opposition research. The Republican National Committee's 2013 self-evaluation (the "Autopsy" report) called for an "allied group dedicated solely to research to establish a private archive and public website that does nothing but post inappropriate Democratic utterances."[42]

Though not technically a campaign ad, the "push poll" is another negative campaign technique. These are not actual polls designed to elicit public attitudes, but instead are biased phone calls with questions aimed at changing voters' opinions. The caller divulges negative information—often false or misleading—in the hope of pulling the voter away from the opponent and toward the candidate paying for the call.

Negative ads are common in modern campaigning because politicians believe they work. This strategy was forcefully described by Rep. Tom Cole, R-Okla., in a memo to his House colleagues: "Define your opponent immediately and unrelentingly. Do not let up—keep the tough ads running right up to election day. Don't make the mistake of pulling your ads in favor of a positive rotation the last weekend."[43]

Recent experiments by two noted communications researchers tend to confirm the power of negative ads. Such ads, these scholars found, lift voters' information levels, even if the information conveyed is distorted or trivial. Although neither positive nor negative ads have much effect on strong partisans, negative ads can work powerfully on citizens who have little information to begin with and on those with little or no party allegiance.[44] "We should not necessarily see negative ads as a harmful part of our electoral system," argues Kenneth Goldstein, head of the University of Wisconsin's political advertising project. "They are much more likely [than positive ads] to be about policy, to use supporting information, and to be reliable. Few negative ads are on personal issues."[45]

Like other forms of product promotion, political ads often stretch or distort the truth. Sometimes the disinformation is so blatant that the term *dirty tricks* applies. This tactic includes not only spreading falsehoods but also using doctored photographs or faking news reports or news headlines.

One of the most controversial attack ads in the 2010 campaign was aired by Democratic candidate Jack Conway in his unsuccessful attempt to defeat Republican Rand Paul for the open Senate seat in Kentucky. The ad asserted that when Paul was a student at Baylor University he was "a member of a secret society that called the Holy Bible 'a hoax,'" and the society "was banned for mocking Christianity and Christ."[46] The subject matter of the ad was obviously inflammatory, particularly in Kentucky, one of the most religious states in the country.[47]

Victims of such tactics have some means of defense, even when attacks are leveled close to election day. The campaign can promptly air response ads or accuse the offender of mudslinging. During a candidate debate, for example, Paul repeatedly called on Conway to apologize. In the end, many analysts felt that Conway's ad backfired, undermining his support among independents and even among Democrats. "Backlash [over the ad] may have sunk Conway's campaign for good," reported PPP, a Democratic-leaning polling firm.[48]

Formal complaints can sometimes persuade opponents to disavow attack ads or local broadcasters to pull them off the air. Media outlets sometimes find themselves in the unwanted role of arbiter, when candidates demand that opponents' ads be discontinued.[49] As one deterrent to smear tactics, the BCRA of 2002 requires that candidates personally appear and vouch for their advertisements.

Evolving Mass Media. The old-fashioned media—newspapers, radio, and television networks—are on the decline. The newspaper business in the United States, in particular, appears to be in crisis. Even before the 2007–2009 recession, newspapers around the country had cut staff and closed bureaus in an effort to remain economically viable. The proportion of people who read newspapers continues to fall. According to a 2012 poll, just 23 percent reported that they read a print newspaper the day before, a decline of about half since 2000.[50] Changing media pose a threat even to television, in that young people rely far less on television news than they did in earlier years. By contrast, the Internet is an increasingly important news source. A study by the Pew Research Center reported a 300 percent increase in Internet usage for campaign news between 2000 and 2012, with the shift most pronounced among young people.[51]

Web outlets are thus far unregulated. In 2006 the Federal Elections Commission (FEC) decided to treat the Internet "as a unique and evolving mode of mass communication and political speech that warrants a restrained regulatory approach."[52] Critics of the hands-off approach point out that Web political messages can be costly to produce and are sometimes far edgier than would be permitted in traditional media outlets. At the least, the public has an interest in learning who instigates these messages, who prepares them, and who pays for them.[53]

Still, the variety and seeming spontaneity of the Web intrigue many political analysts. One observer of the Web scene calls it "word of mouth on steroids." Although campaign organizations use the medium, the knowledge and skill to make compelling videos—like those unleashed on YouTube and other outlets—have "moved out of campaign headquarters" and into the hands of private citizens.

The Ground War: Pressing the Flesh and Other Forms of Close Contact

Direct appeals to voters through personal appearances by candidates or their surrogates—at shopping centers, factory gates, or even door to door—are part of every campaign. In his successful 1948 Senate campaign, Lyndon B. Johnson swooped out of the sky in a helicopter to visit small Texas towns, grandly pitching his Stetson from the chopper for a bold entrance; an aide was assigned to retrieve the hat for use at the next stop.[54] Other candidates, preferring to stay closer to the ground, stage walking tours or other events to attract attention. Few elected officials get by without doing a great deal of what is inelegantly called "pressing the flesh."

Recent social science research has demonstrated the importance of retail, as opposed to wholesale, campaigning. TV ads, direct mail, and phone banks are less effective than old-fashioned ways of getting out the vote. An array of experiments has shown that personalized messages delivered face to face or in conversational manner over the phone are far superior to impersonal methods of reaching potential voters.[55] According to Yale political scientists Donald P. Green and Alan S. Gerber, face-to-face canvassing raises turnout by 7 to 12 percentage points.[56]

One-on-one campaigning is physically and emotionally challenging. But an obvious advantage of so-called shoe-leather campaigning is cost, at least when compared with mass media appeals. "Door-to-door canvassing is the tactic of choice among candidates and campaigns that are short on cash," explain Green and Gerber. "Precinct walking is often described as the weapon of underdogs."[57] Former representative Dan Glickman, D-Kan. (1977–1995), describes his first House campaign as a thirty-one-year-old challenger facing a long-term incumbent:

I walked door-to-door to 35,000 homes over an eight-month period. I walked from 10:30 a.m. to 2 p.m. and again from 5:30 to 8 p.m. I lost 35 pounds and learned to be very realistic about dogs. I met a woman my father had lent $100 or $150 to 30 years before. She embraced me and said, "You saved us." I won by three percentage points.[58]

Face-to-face campaigning is obligatory in smaller communities, where people expect politicians to show up at festivals, parades, or annual county fairs. "If you ain't seen at the county fair, you're preached about on Sunday," remarked a politician as he led his party's Senate candidate around the hog and sheep barns in Ada, Oklahoma.[59] In small states, first-name relationships are often valued. "They want to know you," political scientist Garrison Nelson remarked about Vermont voters. The state's Independent senator, Bernard Sanders, distributes bumper stickers that simply say, "Bernie."[60] In Bristol, on Rhode Island's coast, the Fourth of July parade—the oldest in the country—is "the first and perhaps biggest event of the campaign season."[61]

Getting Out the Vote. GOTV drives are focused on making sure constituents are registered and getting voters to the polls. Recognizing the importance of personalized voter contact, both parties have developed sophisticated GOTV operations. Each now relies on "micro-targeting" to reach sympathetic voters. This approach employs computer models to exploit a wide array of data, such as the groups to which people belong or the magazines they read, to identify potential voters and the issues that are important to them. "Micro-targeting has become so widespread that it is now used by all House and Senate candidates, on both sides, in state legislative races, and in some cases, all the way down the ballot to local school board elections," concludes one journalist.[62]

In addition, many groups are prepared to finance their own field operations in support of favored candidates. In this sense, the parties' GOTV efforts are just part of a broader campaign waged by their allied groups. For example, "in most states union members will be contacted between fourteen and twenty-four times by other union members in some fashion," the AFL-CIO's political director reported in 2002.[63] For their part, Republicans depend on a wide array of pro-life, evangelical, and socially conservative organizations to undertake GOTV drives for their candidates.

The Parallel Campaigns

The scene is a hospital operating room; the patient is surrounded by surgeons and nurses. One surgeon in a voice of astonished concern exclaims, "Oh my." A nurse asks, "Colitis?" Another nurse asks, "Hepatitis?" A third, "Diverticulitis?" The surgeon replies, "No, I'm afraid it's Dina Titus. Taxes up the yingyang. Her tax policy is killing us." The target of this television ad was 2008 Democratic House challenger Dina Titus, a former political science professor at University of Nevada–Las Vegas and current representative for Nevada's First Congressional District. The ad was paid for by Freedom's Watch, a lobbying group bankrolled by wealthy conservatives, notably billionaire casino developer Sheldon Adelson.

An important development in recent congressional campaigns is the role played by outside groups, big spenders in congressional elections that are not formally affiliated with either the candidates or the parties. Campaigns no longer resemble boxing matches between two combatants. They have become free-for-alls in which multiple combatants throw punches and land roundhouse kicks. Candidates compete not only against their opponents and their parties but also against scores of groups that join the fray.

Hundreds of such organizations engage in congressional campaigning, most of them favoring one or the other major political party. As allies of a national party, these organizations contribute to the "nationalization" of congressional elections. The ads these organizations run tend to reinforce existing stereotypes about the parties. "To watch the advertisements blanketing the airwaves, every Democrat is an Obamacare-loving big spender," observes journalist Reid Wilson. "Every Republican is a Medicare-slashing tea partier."[64] Such ads undercut the candidates' ability to control their own political image. As outside-group spending becomes a paramount element of campaign finance, it becomes harder for candidates to differentiate themselves from their national parties. Candidates in swing states or districts attempting to carve out distinctive profiles run up against their opponents' Super PAC–funded ads painting with a broad brush, lumping them in with the rest of their party's team.

WHO VOTES?

Although Congress is supposed to be the people's branch of government, only around half of voting-age citizens normally take part in House elections. In the 2010 House elections just 40.7 percent of the voting-age population, or VAP (all eligible residents age eighteen and over), participated.[65] In 2012, turnout was 58.7 percent—slightly below the 61.6 percent turnout of 2008.[66]

As Figure 4-3 indicates, turnout varies according to whether the election is held in a presidential or a midterm year. Midterm races lack the intense publicity and stimulus to vote provided by presidential contests. Since the 1930s, turnout in midterm congressional elections has averaged about 12 percent below that of the preceding presidential election. Midterm electorates include more people who are interested in politics, and—not unrelated—who are also more affluent and better educated.[67] Voter turnout in congressional races fails to match that of presidential elections—even in presidential election years.

Reasons for Not Voting

Political analysts disagree over the reasons for the anemic voting levels in the United States, which are near the bottom among established democratic countries. Several explanations—not all of them compatible—have been suggested.[68]

One explanation for nonvoting is simply demographic. Groups with low voting rates, such as young people, African Americans, and Latinos, have been

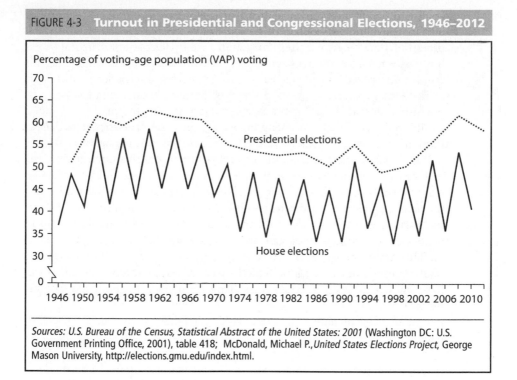

FIGURE 4-3 **Turnout in Presidential and Congressional Elections, 1946–2012**

Percentage of voting-age population (VAP) voting

Presidential elections

House elections

Sources: U.S. Bureau of the Census, Statistical Abstract of the United States: 2001 (Washington DC: U.S. Government Printing Office, 2001), table 418; McDonald, Michael P.,*United States Elections Project,* George Mason University, http://elections.gmu.edu/index.html.

growing as a share of the U.S. population. Young people (ages eighteen through twenty-nine) are traditional no-shows, perhaps because they have fewer of the life experiences (mortgages, taxes, school-age children, community ties) that propel older people toward activism. Four out of ten young people have not registered to vote (three times greater than those aged fifty and older).[69] Turnout among young Americans in the 2010 midterms was estimated at 20.4 percent.[70]

A second explanation stresses legal barriers to voting. Only about 70 percent of the VAP are registered to vote. Many democracies automatically register all adults; some even require that people vote. By contrast, U.S. citizens must take the initiative to register and vote. The National Voter Registration Act of 1993 (the so-called Motor Voter law) aimed to increase citizens' access to voter registration by, among other things, requiring states to offer voter registration as an option when citizens apply for a driver's license. Registration of eligible voters soon rose about 3.8 percent nationwide, but voting levels failed to climb—especially among the young and the poor, the targets of the measure.[71]

Other disincentives can be blamed on electoral arrangements. U.S. citizens are asked to vote far more often than voters in parliamentary regimes; and elections are held on weekdays, not on weekends or national holidays. A number of states and localities have modernized their election procedures, making it easier to register and vote. Absentee balloting and vote by mail have become more common. Some states permit ballots to be submitted over a period of time. Oregon citizens may even vote by telephone. In recent years, however, lawmakers in many states have raised new barriers through voter ID requirements—such as photo IDs or proof-of-citizenship papers.[72] Although passed under the pretext of combating "voter fraud," these are in fact partisan measures intended "to depress voter turnout in minority and poor communities."[73] In 2008 the Supreme Court upheld the strictest such law, Indiana's 2005 statute that requires all voters to present a valid government ID.[74]

Biased or careless election administration can also turn away voters or lead to a miscount of their ballots, as uncovered in voting scandals in Florida (2000) and Ohio (2004). Local election practices often weigh most heavily on minority or socioeconomically disadvantaged citizens, who are more likely to encounter insufficient numbers of poll workers, antiquated or badly designed voting machines, and longer lines. Limited voting hours and inadequate polling facilities, for example, led to extremely long lines in a number of urban Florida communities in 2012. An Ohio State University researcher estimated that the long lines that year turned away as many as 49,000 voters across Central Florida.[75]

A third explanation for low voter turnout is citizen disaffection. Noncompetitive elections, poor candidates, and contentious or negative campaigning are thought to keep people away from the polling booths. To be sure, apathy and cynicism are part of the picture. Surveys sponsored by Harvard University's "Vanishing Voters" project found that four out of ten nonvoters in 2000 claimed to care little about politics and public affairs. A quarter were dismayed or confused by the barrage of campaign messages. And another quarter were simply angry or cynical about politics.[76]

Finally, even conceding all these disincentives, the level of nonvoting is frequently exaggerated. In calculating turnout, many scholars fail to take into account the large number of voting-age residents who are not eligible to vote. Three sizable and growing segments of the population are not entitled to vote and must be excluded when properly calculating turnout: (1) jailed felons (1.5 million) are barred from voting in all but two states; (2) ex-felons (5.8 million) are barred from voting in fourteen states; and (3) undocumented aliens (11.5 million or more) may not vote anywhere. Failure to take account of these ineligible residents artificially depresses the turnout rate. Recalculating the VAP for elections between World War II and 2000, Samuel L. Popkin and Michael P. McDonald estimated turnout ranging from 52.7 to 60.6 percent—still nothing to be proud of, but "a lot less dismal than is generally believed."[77]

Biases of Voting

Although voting is the simplest and most accessible form of political involvement, it is still biased in favor of people at the higher rungs of the social and generational ladders—those who are older, more affluent, better educated, and more in touch with political events. Eight in ten people whose annual incomes exceed $50,000 vote in a typical election. This is twice the voting rate of the poor, defined as people with annual incomes of less than $15,000.

Alternative forms of political participation are even more sharply biased. For example, giving money is mainly an elite activity. According to a study by Sidney Verba and his colleagues, 35 percent of all political money flowed from the 4 percent of people making more than $125,000 a year. Poor people, who were 19 percent of the sample, made only 2 percent of political donations.[78]

HOW VOTERS DECIDE

What induces voters to cast their ballots for one candidate and not another? As a general rule, voters reach their decisions on the basis of party loyalty. But candidate assessments and salient issues also figure into voters' decisions. The relative strength of these elements varies over time and among specific races.

Although American voters are often uninformed or indifferent about political issues and candidates, they employ what is called low-information rationality, or gut reasoning, to make voting booth decisions. As Samuel L. Popkin explains, people "triangulate and validate their opinions in conversations with people they trust and according to the opinions of national figures whose judgments and positions they have come to know."[79] Thus voters work through imperfect information to make choices that will often roughly approximate the choices they would have made with more perfect information.

Party Loyalties

Party identification is the single most powerful factor in determining voters' choices. And it remains the strongest single correlate of voting in congressional elections. In recent elections, at least nine in every ten Democrats and Republicans voted for their parties' nominees. Independents tend to split their votes more evenly between the parties. In 2006 they veered toward Democratic candidates by a three-to-two margin.[80] But in 2010 independents preferred Republican to Democratic candidates by 19 percentage points.[81]

According to surveys, most people who claim to be independents are in fact closet partisans who lean toward one party or the other. These independent leaners—about a quarter of the total electorate—hold attitudes similar to those of partisans. Not only do they favor one party over the other, but they also share many (though not necessarily all) of the party's values and will vote for the party's candidates—if they vote at all.

Only a small percentage of citizens (5–10 percent) are true independents; they are unpredictable, however, and have dismal turnout rates. "I would encourage candidates not to play to them," advises David Magleby of Brigham Young University, "because they tend to jump on bandwagons, to follow tides. You're better off [working] on getting your weak partisans and your leaners."[82]

Partisan Resurgence. Today's voters are as loyal to their professed party identification as they have ever been.[83] Few voters who identify as either Republican or Democrat defect from their party when they cast votes in particular congressional races. However, today's high level of party loyalty is a notable shift from the 1970s and 1980s.

Between 1950 and 1980, partisan loyalty declined among the American electorate, with voters identifying with one party and often supporting candidates from the other party. These weakened party ties led to an epidemic of split-ticket voting—that is, voters supporting one party's presidential candidate and the opposition party's congressional candidate. Between 1952 and 1988, the number of voters who reported in surveys that they split their ticket between presidential and House candidates rose from 12 percent to 25 percent. Those who split their ballots between different parties' House and Senate candidates grew from 9 percent to 27 percent.[84]

Most of these ticket-splitters, it turned out, were in the throes of moving from one party to another. White southern conservatives made up a large share of ticket-splitters during this era. Targeted by the GOP's so-called southern strategy, these voters were attracted to presidential candidates such as Barry Goldwater, Richard Nixon, and Ronald Reagan. At the same time, southern conservatives continued to back Democrats in congressional and state races as strong Republican candidates often failed to challenge entrenched incumbents—because the Democratic Party put up conservative candidates, and because long-serving Democrats won the "personal vote" of constituents by delivering more benefits back home through their party's control of legislative chambers. The same phenomenon occurred to a lesser degree in the Northeast, where voters were drawn to the Democrats' national policies and candidates but continued to support moderate to liberal Republican representatives or senators.[85]

Recent party realignment has brought party affiliation into sync with policy and ideological preferences. Although the process extended over many years, the long Republican courtship of southern conservatives was consummated in 1994. Merle Black of Emory University estimates that more than 80 percent of white conservatives in the South are Republicans; only 10 percent are Democrats.[86] A parallel trend, no less dramatic, has been the Democratic Party's absorption of GOP moderates and liberals. Finding acceptable candidates up and down the ballot, these voters have less need to pick and choose—hence revived partisanship and dwindling split tickets.

In short, the bulge in split-ticket voting was a by-product of gradual partisan realignment. Over the last six presidential elections, ticket-splitting has plummeted to less than 10 percent—exactly the same level it was fifty years ago. The number of congressional districts voting for one party's presidential candidate and the other party's House candidate fell as well. In 2012 only around 11 percent of districts voted for one party for the House and the other party for president. Just fifteen House Republicans won in districts that were carried by President Obama.

Midterm and Presidential Election Years. Politicians have long talked about "coattails": how House and Senate candidates could be pulled into office by the strength of a popular presidential candidate. The idea is that successful presidential candidates will entice new voters not just for themselves but for their whole party.

In presidential election years, the party that wins the presidency typically does increase its numbers in Congress. As shown in Table 4-1, the winning presidential candidate's party gains on average 15.1 seats in the House and 2.1 seats in the Senate. Boosts for the president's congressional party were considerably more modest in recent election years than they were in the 1930s and 1940s. George H. W. Bush, Bill Clinton, and George W. Bush all began their presidencies with some congressional seat losses for their party. Nevertheless, political scientists who have analyzed the influence of presidential candidates on the outcome of congressional elections have found that "nontrivial coattail effects have been discernible in recent elections."[87] President Ronald Reagan, for example, boosted his party's congressional votes by 2–3 percent in 1980 and 5 percent in 1984. In 1996 President Clinton's reelection added about 2.6 percentage points to Democrats' House and Senate totals. [88]President Obama began his presidency with the largest increases in his party's numbers in Congress for any president since Reagan in 1980.

The president's party normally suffers significant reversals in the midterm congressional elections. In fact, the president's party has lost seats in thirty-two of the thirty-five midterm elections since 1860. "This is not quite the certainty of 'death and taxes,' but it is about as dependable as things get in politics," observes political scientist James E. Campbell.[89] As evident in Table 4-2, since 1934 the presidential party has lost an average of 28 House seats and 3.6 Senate seats in midterm elections.

The "midterm law" was broken on only three occasions. Democrats gained four seats in the House and held their own in the Senate in 1998, in the midst of President Clinton's impeachment proceedings. Although voters deplored Clinton's personal behavior, his job ratings remained robust; Republicans were rebuked for insisting on impeaching him. Four years later, President Geroge W. Bush's GOP gained eight House seats and one Senate seat, no doubt because of the post-9/11 rally effect. The only other anomaly occurred in 1934, when President Franklin D. Roosevelt's popularity strengthened the Democrats' grip on both chambers. Set in historical context, the 2010 election results were remarkable only in that the loss by the president's party was so huge. It was the largest seat gain by an out-party in a midterm since 1938.

One theory that endeavors to explain this pattern is known as "surge and decline." This theory posits that the visibility and excitement of a winning presidential campaign attracts intermittent voters who tend to support the president's party in down-ticket races. When these presidential candidates are not on the ballot, the shrunken electorate of midterm years contains fewer supporters of the president's party—that is, a presidential surge, swollen by less motivated voters attracted by presidential campaigns, is followed two years later by a decline as intermittent voters drop out of the electorate. But other studies suggest that midterm voters are no more or less partisan than those in presidential years and share most of their demographic characteristics.[90] Another problem with the theory is that, no matter the circumstances, the president's party typically loses more seats at the midterm than it gains during a presidential year.

TABLE 4-1 **Seats in Congress Gained or Lost by the President's Party in Presidential Election Years, 1932–2012**

Year	President	Seats gained or lost	
		House	Senate
1932	Franklin D. Roosevelt (D)	+90	+9
1936	Roosevelt (D)	+12	+7
1940	Roosevelt (D)	+7	−3
1944	Roosevelt (D)	+24	−2
1948	Harry S. Truman (D)	+75	+9
1952	Dwight D. Eisenhower (R)	+22	+1
1956	Eisenhower (R)	−2	−1
1960	John F. Kennedy (D)	−22	+2
1964	Lyndon B. Johnson (D)	+37	+1
1968	Richard M. Nixon (R)	+5	+6
1972	Nixon (R)	+12	−2
1976	Jimmy Carter (D)	+1	0
1980	Ronald Reagan (R)	+34	+12
1984	Reagan (R)	+14	−2
1988	George H. W. Bush (R)	−2	0
1992	Bill Clinton (D)	−10	0
1996	Clinton (D)	−9	−2
2000	George W. Bush (R)	−3	−4
2004	Bush (R)	+3	+4
2008	Barack Obama (D)	+21	+8
2012	Obama (D)	+8	+2
Average seats gained (21 elections)		+15.1	+2.1

Source: Compiled by the authors.

A second theory argues that midterm elections serve in part as a referendum on the president's popularity and performance in office during the previous two years.[91] Voters may hold the president's party responsible for economic reverses, unpopular policies, or military ventures. The 2010 midterm elections were seen as a referendum on President Obama's first two years: although Obama wasn't on the ballot, his Democratic legislators were, and they bore the brunt of voter dissatisfaction.

A third theory emphasizes voters' preferences for "balance." By favoring the out-party at midterm, voters can pull policy back toward the ideological center.[92] Voter behavior may not be driven so much by dissatisfaction with the president as by the desire to check potential presidential excesses. This may seem like an overly sophisticated calculation for the average voter, but even if only a relatively small portion of the electorate follows this logic it can have a sizable impact on electoral outcomes. Balance theory helps explain why the shift against the president's party in midterm elections is typically larger than one would expect based on presidents' (usually favorable) approval ratings or based on the "surge and decline" thesis.[93]

All three schools of thought—"surge and decline," referendum theory, and balance theory—can shed light on such dramatic midterm outcomes as the Democrats' 1974 post-Watergate bonus of forty-eight representatives and five senators, the Democrats' retaking of House and Senate majorities in 2006, and the Republicans' gain of sixty-three representatives and six senators in 2010.

The Appeal of Candidates

"My theory on politics is ultimately that people vote for the person they like most," declared former senator David Pryor, D-Ark. (1979–1997).[94] Apart from partisan loyalties, the appeal of given candidates is the strongest force in congressional voting. Not surprisingly, candidate appeal normally tilts toward incumbents. When voters abandon their party to vote for House or Senate candidates, they usually vote for incumbents.

Incumbency Advantage. Incumbents rarely lose their bids for reelection, as is evident in Table 4-3. Incumbent reelection rates have always been robust. Even in the 2010 watershed election, incumbent winners still included 85 percent of all representatives and 83 percent of all senators who ran for reelection. Comparable percentages from 2006, a year when Democrats retook control of Congress from the Republicans, were 94 percent and 79 percent. Changes in party control of seats are attributable as much to winning seats opened up by retirements as to defeating incumbents.

Defeating a House incumbent is an uphill struggle, absent a scandal or misstep. Senate challengers—more often than not, well known and generously financed—have a stronger chance of unseating incumbents than do those seeking House seats. Nevertheless, more than four out of five Senate incumbents win the contests they enter.

Why are incumbents so formidable? Incumbents' success rates go beyond what one should expect based on the partisan character of their constituencies. In other words, incumbents often win by solid margins in constituencies that are closely divided between Republicans and Democrats. This phenomenon has led scholars to ask whether the sheer fact of incumbency itself offers advantages: Do candidates fare better running as incumbents than they would running as nonincumbents?[95]

To measure this advantage, scholars often look to the "sophomore surge" and the "retirement slump." The sophomore surge refers to the average gain in vote share by candidates running for reelection for the first time, compared with their performance in their first election. The retirement slump is the average drop in a party's vote share when an incumbent retires and the seat opens up.

| TABLE 4-2 | **Midterm Fortunes of Presidential Parties, 1934–2010** | | |

		Seats gained or lost	
Year	President	House	Senate
1934	Franklin D. Roosevelt (D)	+9	+10
1938	Roosevelt (D)	−71	−6
1942	Roosevelt (D)	−45	−9
1946	Roosevelt and Harry S. Truman (D)	−55	−12
1950	Truman (D)	−29	−6
1954	Dwight D. Eisenhower (R)	−18	−1
1958	Eisenhower (R)	−47	−13
1962	John F. Kennedy (D)	−5	+3
1966	Lyndon B. Johnson (D)	−47	−4
1970	Richard M. Nixon (R)	−12	+3
1974	Nixon and Gerald R. Ford (R)	−48	−5
1978	Jimmy Carter (D)	−15	−3
1982	Ronald Reagan (R)	−26	+1
1986	Reagan (R)	−5	−8
1990	George H. W. Bush (R)	−7	−1
1994	Bill Clinton (D)	−54	−10
1998	Clinton (D)	+4	0
2002	George W. Bush (R)	+8	+1
2006	Bush (R)	−31	−6
2010	Obama (D)	−63	−6
Average seats lost (20 elections)		−27.8	−3.6

Sources: CQ Press Electronic Library, *Vital Statistics on American Politics Online Edition*, table 1-17. Originally published in Harold W. Stanley and Richard G. Niemi, eds., *Vital Statistics on American Politics, 2009–2010* (Washington, DC: CQ Press, 2009). Each entry is the difference between the number of seats held by the president's party at the start of Congress after the midterm election and the number of seats held by that party at the start of Congress after the preceding general election. Special elections that shifted partisan seat totals between elections are not noted.

Scholars then average these two calculations into a single index, known as the "slurge," which is often used to measure the overall incumbency advantage. According to this measure, contemporary incumbents enjoy about a 5.5 percent boost in their share of the vote simply by virtue of being incumbents.[96]

Political scientists have launched a veritable cottage industry to explain incumbency advantage. Certainly, one key factor is incumbents' campaign fund-raising advantages, which were described earlier (see "Incumbents versus Challengers"). It is also no secret that incumbents have many methods of gathering support—through speeches, press coverage, newsletters, staff assistance, and constituent service. Incumbents' popularity depends in large part on their success in shaping information that constituents receive about them and their performance—through advertising, credit claiming, and position taking.[97]

The unequal visibility of candidates is thus an important source of incumbency advantage. In National Election Study (NES) surveys spanning almost thirty years, nearly all respondents were able to recognize the names of, and offer opinions about, their Senate and House incumbents running for reelection (means of 97 percent and 92 percent, respectively). Senate challengers were recognized and rated by 77 percent of the respondents, House challengers by only 53 percent.[98]

Voters also report having high levels of contact with House and Senate incumbents. The more contact voters have with their legislators, the more positive their evaluations are likely to be. According to NES surveys, at least nine out of ten voters said they had some form of contact with their representative. A fifth of them reported having met the lawmaker in person. Many constituents receive mail from their representatives or read about them in newspapers. Virtually all voters reported some contacts with their senators, mostly through mailings, TV appearances, or other media coverage.

Incumbents achieve these high levels of visibility and constituency contact in part because of their perquisites of office. The typical House member receives staff, office, and travel allocations valued at between $2 and $3 million over a two-year term; senators, with six-year terms, command between $17 and $27 million in resources. Everyone concedes the value of incumbents' perquisites, but scholars differ on how much they affect electoral success. One view is that incumbents exploit their resources to ensure reelection, seizing on their ability to assist constituents in dealing with the bureaucracy to build electoral credit. Others counter that legislators are simply responding to constituents' demands, aided by advances in communication technology. Still others question whether incumbents' resources are directly translatable into votes.[99]

Senate and House. The factors contributing to incumbency advantage help explain why senators are more vulnerable at the polls than their House counterparts. First, Senate challengers are far more conspicuous than House challengers. Senate contests are more widely reported by the media, and challengers can gain almost as much exposure as incumbents. Media coverage of House races is more fragmentary than that of Senate races, throwing more weight to incumbents' techniques of contacting voters.

Second, senators cannot manipulate voter contacts as much as representatives do. Voters get their information about Senate races largely through the organized media, which senators do not control. Representatives gain exposure through focused means—personal appearances, mailings, and newsletters—which they fashion to their own advantage. "Somewhat ironically," observes Michael J. Robinson, "powerful senators are less able to control their images than 'invisible' House members."[100]

TABLE 4-3 **Reelection Rates in the House and Senate, by Decade, 1950s–2000s, plus 2012**

Decade	House					Senate				
	Sought reelection	Faced no opponent	Lost primary	General election	Percent reelected	Sought reelection	Faced no opponent	Lost primary	General election	Percent reelected
1950s	402	85	6	25	93.2%	30	4	1	6	77.3%
1960s	404	52	8	26	91.5	32	1	2	4	80.8
1970s	389	57	2	23	92.3	27	1	2	6	67.7
1980s	403	67	13	15	95.7	29	1	0	3	88.0
1990s	385	36	8	18	93.6	26	0	0	3	87.4
2000s	395	40	3	24	93.2	28	1	1	4	87.9
2012	393	10	13	26	90.0	23	0	1	1	91.0

Sources: CQ Weekly Report, April 5, 1980, 908; November 8, 1980, 3302, 3320–3321; July 31, 1982, 1870; November 6, 1982, 2781; November 10, 1984, 2897, 2901; November 12, 1988, 3264, 3270; November 10, 1990, 3796–3805; November 7, 1992, 3557–3564, 3570–3576; November 12, 1994, 329ff; February 15, 1997, 447–455; November 7, 1998, 3027–3035; November 11, 2000, 2694–2706; December 14, 2002, 2694–2706; December 14, 2002, 3289–3297; November 6, 2004, 2653–2660; November 13, 2006, 3068–3075; November 10, 2008, 3043–3052; November 8, 2010, 2618–1627; November 12, 2012, 2284–2293.

Note: Statistics for each decade are election-year averages for the five elections conducted under that decade's apportionment of House districts. For example, the 1950s include the five elections 1952 through 1960. "Percent reelected" takes into account both primary and general election defeats. "Faced no opponent" means no major-party opponent. Figures for 2000–2008 are derived from the 2002, 2004, 2006, and 2008 elections.

Among senators, constituency size is also a crucial variable in elections. Small-state senators in many respects resemble representatives. Compared with their large-state colleagues, they are more visible, more accessible, and more able to raise the campaign money they need. But they are not electorally safe because their challengers, too, have an easier time mounting their campaigns and gaining visibility.[101]

Strategic Politicians. A very important and frequently underrated factor contributing to incumbent reelection success is simply the quality of candidates who typically run against incumbents. Jacobson surely captures the normal state of affairs when he observes that "most incumbents face obscure, politically inexperienced opponents whose resources fall far short of what is necessary to mount a formidable campaign."[102] As discussed in Chapter 3, it is often difficult to recruit strong candidates to run against incumbents. Incumbents are reelected at high rates not just because of the advantages they have over challengers in terms of funding and visibility, but simply because they are often far more skilled and more experienced politicians than their opponents.

Incumbency advantage has a self-fulfilling aspect, because good potential challengers will typically perceive the long odds of defeating an incumbent and therefore choose not to enter the race. Incumbents prevail because the system of candidate recruitment throughout the United States often fails to offer voters viable alternatives.

Issue Voting

Issue preferences and even ideological beliefs figure prominently in voters' decisions. Even if most Americans devote only modest attention to political affairs, a significant number of voters are attuned to issues and base their choices on a specific issue or cluster of issues. Not a few elections turn on those margins.

Congressional Party Platforms. Partisans care deeply about the issues with which their parties are linked. In studying the 1998 House elections, Owen G. Abbe and his colleagues found that "voters are more likely to support candidates whom they deem competent on their issues." They concluded that "party leaders and individual candidates must campaign on a well-defined agenda for party-owned issues to have an impact."[103]

At least since the mid-1970s, congressional parties have forged campaign platforms. The most notable example was the GOP's "Contract with America," the brainchild of then-representative Newt Gingrich of Georgia.[104] The contract was a set of ten proposals that candidates promised to bring to the House floor if Republicans won a majority in the 1994 midterm elections. Similarly, more than a year before the 2006 balloting, House Democrats, led by the minority leader, Nancy Pelosi of California, came up with another list of initiatives known as the "Six for '06" platform. It embraced such popular goals as national security, energy independence, and economic strength. In the lead-up to the 2010 elections, congressional Republicans embraced a platform called the "Pledge to America." It included such proposals as a $100 billion cut in federal spending, an end to tax hikes, and curbs on new federal regulations.[105]

Issues and Partisanship. Voters' responses to political issues show up in the different patterns of choice displayed by demographic groups (see Figure 4-4). Americans sort themselves out politically according to their age, sex, income, education, race or ethnicity, region, and even by frequency of attendance at religious services.

A demographic snapshot of the two parties' voters would start at the much-discussed gender gap, the difference in voting between men and women. Women lean toward Democratic candidates, men toward Republicans. The gender gap appears in virtually all recent contests. As pollster Celinda Lake remarked, "You'll get [a gender gap] in a race for dogcatcher in Montana, if it's a Republican against a Democrat."[106] The gender gap was 7 percentage points in 2008 and 2010 and 8 points in 2012. The explanation for the gender gap probably lies in differing responses to political and social issues. Men are more apt to favor military expenditures, tough anticrime laws, and restrictions on welfare recipients and immigrants. Women are more supportive of social programs such as government-sponsored health benefits, job training, child care, and assistance to needy families.[107]

A host of similar patterns is found among congressional voters. "There's a family gap, a generation gap, a gender gap," said GOP pollster Neil Newhouse of the fissures among the voting population.[108] Many of the patterns are familiar. The Republicans attract upper-income and conservative voters; the Democrats engage lower-income and liberal voters. The Republicans draw upon married people, whites, regular churchgoers, gun owners, small-business owners, and older people; the Democrats attract singles and young people, African Americans, Hispanics, Jews, the secular, and occasional churchgoers. Such loyalties are built on issues and themes adopted by parties and candidates over the years.

Issues and Campaigns. Legislators and their advisers try to anticipate voters' reactions to their stands on issues. They devote much energy to framing positions, communicating them (sometimes in deliberately vague language), and assessing their effect. Moreover, every professional politician can relate cases in which issues tipped an election one way or another. Frequently cited is the electoral influence of single-interest groups. Some citizens vote according to a single issue they regard as paramount—for example, gun control, abortion, or gay marriage. Even if few in number, such voters can decide close contests. For that reason, legislators often shrink from taking positions on hot-button issues such as these.

Public policy issues also have powerful indirect effects on election outcomes. Issues motivate "opinion leaders," voters who can influence support far beyond their single vote. Organized interests also carefully monitor lawmakers' behavior and then channel or withhold funds, publicity, and other campaign assistance accordingly. Legislators devote time and attention to promoting and explaining issues to attentive publics because it pays for them to do so.

FIGURE 4-4   Who Were the Voters in 2010?

Percentage of voters		For Democrat		For Republican
	Total vote	45		52
48	Men	41		55
52	Women	48		49
77	White	37		60
11	Black	89		9
8	Hispanic/Latino	60		38
2	Asian	58		40
12	Under 30 years	55		42
24	30–44 years	46		50
43	45–59 years	45		53
21	60 years and older	38		59
3	Not a high school graduate	57		36
17	High school graduate	46		52
28	College incomplete	43		53
51	College graduate	45		53
21	East	54		44
25	Midwest	44		53
31	South	37		61
23	West	49		48
44	White Protestant	28		69
25	White fundamentalist	19		77
23	Catholic	44		54
2	Jewish	—		—
17	Union household	61		37
—	Under $15,000	—		—
17	$15,000–29,999	57		40
19	$30,000–49,999	51		46
21	$50,000–74,999	45		51
42	Over $75,000	41		58
35	Democratic	91		7
29	Independent	37		56
35	Republican	5		94
20	Liberal	90		8
38	Moderate	55		42
42	Conservative	13		84

Source: Adapted from Harold W. Stanley and Richard G. Niemi, *Vital Statistics on American Politics, 2011–2012* (Washington, DC: CQ Press, 2011), table 3-8.

Notes: Percentages based on Democratic, Republican, and other (not shown) votes. Data based on questionnaires completed by voters leaving polling places around the nation on election day, 2010.

ELECTION OUTCOMES

The two Congresses are apparent throughout congressional elections. House and Senate contests are waged one by one on local turf, but always against a backdrop of national events, issues, and partisan alignments. The involvement of national party entities and their allied interest groups has imposed a greater degree of national coordination on congressional campaigns, especially those in marginal states and districts. The resulting fusion of local and national forces shapes the content and results of congressional elections.

Party Balance

Despite the oft-claimed independence of candidates and voters, almost all races are run under either the Democratic or Republican Party label, fought on playing fields tilted toward one party or the other, and aimed mainly at loyalists who are likely to turn out for their party's candidates.

Shifting Majorities. In some respects, the overall partisan outcome of the 2012 contests was fixed months and even years before the actual balloting. With an anemic economy and presidential approval ratings hovering around 50 percent, it was clear that the elections would be a close contest. Senate Democrats were heavily "exposed" going into 2012 in that the party had to defend more than twice as many seats as Republicans. Conventional wisdom early in the cycle held that Democrats would lose control of the Senate. Meanwhile, benefiting from both incumbency advantage and their command of the redistricting process in many states, Republicans were well positioned to maintain their House majority. In the end, the outcome of the 2012 elections largely reinforced the status quo. The incumbent president was reelected, Democrats retained their Senate majority, and Republicans retained their House majority.

Taking a longer view, the outcome was predictable in that either the Democrats or the Republicans have controlled Congress since 1855 (see Appendix A for a list of the partisan majorities in the House and Senate since 1901). Between 1896 and 1920, the two parties had approximately equal numbers of partisans in the electorate, but lower participation rates in Democratic areas favored the Republicans. The GOP's relative position improved further after 1920, when women received the vote.

The New Deal realignment of the 1930s shifted the balance to the Democrats. For many years after that, the Democrats were virtually a perennial majority and the Republicans a permanent minority on Capitol Hill. Between 1932 and 1994, the Republicans controlled both chambers simultaneously for only four years (1947–1949, 1953–1955). Democratic sweeps in 1958, 1964, and 1974 padded their majorities. Republicans found the Democratic dominance in Congress hard to overcome, even in years when voters strongly backed Republican presidential candidates. Democrats were able to maintain their majorities, as long-serving incumbents effectively exploited their positions of influence and their ability to steer government benefits back home.

In recent decades, however, no party has been able to take control of Congress for granted. Since Republicans won control of the Senate in 1980, neither party has been secure in its control of that chamber. Similarly, control of the House has been a far more open question since the Republican victory of 1994 than during the long years of Democratic dominance. Even while Republicans clung to their post-1994 majority in the House for the next decade, Democrats steadily gained seats throughout the 1990s, and Republicans' control of the chamber progressively narrowed. In 2006 Democrats returned to majority status in both the House and the Senate. They then expanded these margins of control in the 2008 elections.

In 2010, however, all the House Democratic gains of 2006 and 2008 were wiped out. Republicans retook House control (242–193), gaining their largest majority in that chamber in sixty-four years. Republicans retained their House majority in 2012, with only a loss of eight seats. Even so, no analyst believes that the era of intense two-party competition for control of Congress has yet come to an end.

Regional Patterns. Recent elections have cemented long-term shifts in the two parties' power bases. Historically, the Grand Old Party was dominant in the populous states of the Northeast and Midwest. "The Democracy," by contrast, owned the solid South from the Civil War era through the 1970s, as well as the large urban political machines. Today, many of the old patterns are precisely reversed, with the Republican Party dominant in the South and the Democratic Party ascendant in the Northeast.[109] The tectonic plates of political alliances move slowly, but they sometimes produce changes of earthquake proportions.

The 1994 earthquake signaled the Republicans' conquest of the South. For the first time in history, the GOP claimed a majority of the South's seats. The party's grip on the region continued to tighten in subsequent election cycles. In 2013, Republicans hold 75 percent of House seats and 72 percent of Senate seats belonging to the eleven states of the Confederacy. The modern-day GOP is currently the party of choice for conservative white southerners.

Regionally, the South, the Great Plains, and the Mountain West form the backbone of the congressional GOP. More than 45 percent of the Republican Conference in both chambers is now from the South, even though that region accounts for only a quarter of the Senate and a third of House districts. In its other regional bastions, the Great Plains and the Mountain West, Republicans claim 65 percent of senators and 77 percent of House districts. Taken together, these regions account for approximately half of the GOP's House majority and two-thirds of its Senate contingent. The Great Lakes states constitute a competitive region, with Republicans controlling 58 percent of its House seats but only 25 percent of its Senate seats.

Democrats are strongest on the coastal edges of the national map—the Northeast, the Mid-Atlantic, and the West Coast. The eleven states of New England and the mid-Atlantic are overwhelmingly Democratic (though some have lost population and thus House seats). In these states—all of which were in the Democratic Party's column in the last three presidential elections—the party claims 70 percent of House seats and 77 percent of Senate seats. In New England, the GOP holds no House seats and only two out of twelve Senate seats. Similarly, Democrats dominate the country's western coast. All four Pacific Rim states (excluding Alaska) were won by Democratic candidates in the last four presidential elections. Democrats control fifty of the region's seventy House seats and all eight of its Senate seats.

Looking beyond such regional patterns, the two parties tend to represent different kinds of districts. Democratic strength lies in cities, inner suburbs, and majority-minority districts, including those in the South and Midwest. Republicans dominate rural, small town, and exurban areas. Meanwhile, Democratic voters are more packed together in the districts held by Democrats than are Republican voters in the districts held by their party, which means that Democratic candidates tend to win by larger majorities than Republican winners normally do. Put another way, more Democratic votes are wasted (that is, inefficiently distributed across congressional districts), giving the GOP a structural advantage.[110]

Polarized Parties, Polarized Voters? Underlying this geographic distribution is what might be called a cultural divide between the two parties. Democrats tend to represent urban areas, where most voters favor social welfare spending and environmental and other business regulations. Urban voters also tend to take a more tolerant view of the diversity of racial, ethnic, and sexual identities. Republicans tend to be traditionalists—economic and cultural conservatives who promote businesses large and small, advocate certain religious causes, and generously support military expenditures. Such long-standing issue commitments flatly contradict anyone who claims that there is scant difference between the two parties.

How pervasive are these partisan differences within the electorate? Political elites—candidates, officeholders, activists, and strong party identifiers—have long been found at the extremes of the ideological spectrum: Democrats to the left, Republicans to the right.[111] Such activists do not represent the majority of citizens, average voters, or even average party identifiers. Most voters either identify as "moderate" or reject any ideological term to describe themselves.[112] Rank-and-file party identifiers have, however, become more ideologically polarized than in the past.[113] Many, after all, respond to the rising amount of ideological rhetoric in the contemporary political arena, including that dispensed by congressional representatives and biased cable, Internet, and other partisan communications. Moreover, these loyal voters are ardently wooed by parties and candidates, both of whom seek reliable supporters (rather than waverers) to turn out at the polls.

Party Alignment and Realignment

Historically, political upheavals have shifted party control in the House or Senate with decisive results. Political scientists and journalists often talk of "critical elections" or "critical periods" in which one party yields preeminence to another, or major voting groups alter the shape of the parties' coalitions, or both. Such watershed eras include the Civil War, the turbulent 1890s, the New Deal of the 1930s, and the Republican revolution of 1994. Each of these upheavals brought to Capitol Hill new lawmakers, new voting patterns, and new legislative priorities.[114]

Between the civil rights upheavals of the 1960s and the mid-1990s, the congressional party system went through a gradual transformation that realigned the parties on ideological lines and brought them into competitive balance. The Republican Party achieved ideological consistency by co-opting southern and rural conservatives and by shedding most of its moderate wing, especially members from the Northeastern, Mid-Atlantic, and Pacific Rim states. In losing most of the South to Republicans, the Democrats also became more ideologically coherent. Long split by divisions between conservative southerners and northern liberals, by the 1990s the Democratic Party was smaller than in the past but considerably more unified.

Realignments of the party system are only apparent in hindsight. It now seems clear that the Democratic majorities of the 110th and 111th Congresses (2007–2011) were not grounded in any long-term shifts of voter alliances. Political scientist James Campbell views the post-2010 Republican House majority as a "return to the normal party balance of recent decades," reflecting the temperament of the United States as a center-right country.[115] Indeed, Republicans may enjoy an enduring congressional majority post-2010, especially in view of the hurdles to defeating incumbents and the structural advantages they hold in congressional districts. Still, the Republican margin of control is narrow and vulnerable to a partisan wave election. Today's party system remains in the same tight competitive balance characteristic of the 1990s.

Turnover and Representation

Reelection rates should not be confused with turnover rates. Even in years when few members are turned out of office by the voters, many leave Capitol Hill voluntarily—to retire, to run for another office, or to follow other pursuits. In other words, the natural process of membership change is continuous. More than 90 percent of both House and Senate incumbents seeking reelection won in 2012. Nevertheless, when the new Congress convened in January 2013, there were fourteen new senators and seventy-five new House members. More than 30 percent of both chambers had served less than two years.[116]

For Congress to be a responsive institution, constant turnover of members is essential—whether by steady increments or by watershed elections. Even when few lawmakers are turned out of office, all of them are keenly aware of the threat of defeat. Most take steps to prevent that eventuality by continually monitoring constituents' needs and opinions through personal visits and polls. But are voters' views accurately reflected by the representatives they elect to Congress? This question is not easily answered. Popular control of policy makers is not the same thing as popular control of policies. Constituents' views are not precisely mirrored by legislators' voting behavior or by the laws passed by the legislature.

CONCLUSION

What links voters' attitudes and members' voting on issues? In the 1960s, Warren E. Miller and Donald E. Stokes found that constituency attitudes correlated differently depending on the kind of policy.[117] In foreign affairs, constituents' attitudes and legislators' votes exhibited a negative correlation; in social and economic welfare issues the correlation was moderate; in civil rights issues the correlation was very high. In other words, in at least one and possibly two major policy areas the linkage was weak enough to cast some doubt on constituency control.

Political scientists explain the absence of strong linkages by noting how difficult it is to meet all the conditions needed for popular control of policies. Voters would have to identify the candidates' positions on issues, and they would have to vote by referring to those positions. Differences among candidates would have to be transparent, and winners would have to vote in accord with their pre-election attitudes. These conditions are not routinely met. Candidates' stands are not always clear, and candidates do not invariably differentiate themselves on issues.

Nevertheless, winning candidates learn from their campaign experiences, even from issues raised by their opponents. *Issue uptake* is the term coined by political scientist Tracy Sulkin to describe this effect. From her study of the issue agendas of 473 House and Senate campaigns and the winners' subsequent legislative activity, she demonstrates that the victors embrace many of their opponents' campaign themes when they return to Capitol Hill. "Congressional campaigns have a clear legacy in the content of legislators' agendas," she writes, "influencing the areas in which they choose to be active and the intensity with which they pursue these activities."[118] Legislative responsiveness is best thought of as a process:

> It begins in campaigns as candidates learn about the salience of issues and their strengths and weaknesses on them; continues throughout winning legislators' terms in office, influencing not just how they vote but also the content of legislation they introduce, cosponsor, and speak about on the floor; goes on to inform their career decisions and future electoral prospects; and leaves a tangible trace on public policy outputs.[119]

If ideological or attitudinal links between voters and their representatives are rough and variable, actual contacts between constituents and individual legislators are numerous and palpable. Much of lawmakers' time and effort while in office is devoted to responding to the folks back home. Constituency politics are ever present in the daily lives of senators and representatives. The two Congresses are distinct but inextricably linked.

Lawmakers on the Hill and at Home Newly elected Rep. Tammy Duckworth, D-Ill., after taking her oath of office in January 2013 (left). An Asian American, she is the first disabled woman to serve in the House, having lost both her legs in the Iraq war. Sen. Max Baucus, D-Mont., chair of the Senate Finance Committee, played a key role in shaping President Obama's health-care legislation—here (bottom left) appearing with ranking Republican Sen. Chuck Grassley of Iowa. And two lawmakers elected in 2008 reach out to their constituents: Rep. Lynn Jenkins, R-Kan., talks with district voters in Valley Falls (top right), while Rep. Aaron Schock, R-Ill., greets constituents at a Peoria restaurant (bottom right).

Being There: Hill Styles and Home Styles

"After years of studies, it's time to cut through the red tape and put Montanans to work on the Keystone Pipeline," declared Sen. Max Baucus, D-Mont., to a standing ovation.[1] Baucus was addressing a joint session of the Montana state legislature, with the governor and other statewide officials in attendance. No line in his speech got a bigger round of applause. Keystone is a planned new pipeline project to transport oil from the oil sands region in Alberta, Canada, to the Gulf Coast. The project is controversial because of environmental concerns about oil spills along the pipeline, as well as the greenhouse gases emitted from oil sands extraction. In early 2012, the Obama administration rejected a permit for the pipeline. The Senate's Democratic leadership also indicated that it would not do anything to facilitate the project's approval.[2] But in Montana, virtually every elected official wants the project underway.[3] "All I care about is working right now to get the most jobs for Montanans, and Keystone is a part of that solution," said Baucus. "To me, it's a no-brainer. . . . People at home, they want this."[4]

Max Baucus is not just a faithful representative of local opinion in Montana. As chair of the Senate Finance Committee, he is also one of the most powerful lawmakers in the United States. A low-profile senator from one of the nation's least-populated states, his is no household name. Nevertheless, a considerable share of the most significant legislation of recent years bears Baucus's mark. The health care reform proposal forged under his leadership was, in most key respects, the legislation that President Barack Obama eventually signed. Years earlier, Baucus helped shepherd President George W. Bush's $1.35 trillion tax cut through the chamber in 2001.[5] In 2003 Baucus was one of only two Democrats permitted in the room during conference committee negotiations over landmark legislation creating a new federal prescription drug benefit program for seniors.[6]

Baucus's reputation as a lawmaker is matched only by his reputation for constituency service. On his desk stands a plaque that reads, "Montana comes first." He is renowned for his ability to bring federal dollars to Montana. Dubbed a "high plains grifter" by the *Washington Post*,[7] Baucus has coaxed federal help for his state, including its roads, farmers, ranchers, and doctors. The shape of national policy is indelibly influenced by the concerns of Baucus's local constituency. To win endorsement of Baucus's Finance Committee, trade legislation must take into account Montana's beef producers.[8] Health legislation must make special provision for rural providers.[9]

Baucus's political success did not always come easily. Representing a state that has voted Republican in ten of the last eleven presidential elections, Baucus faced some tough electoral challenges. To stay in close touch with constituents, he scheduled regular "work days," working a full day alongside Montanans in various jobs and professions. And before he announced his plans to retire in 2015, he consistently raised large sums for his reelection efforts long before the identity of his challengers were known.

A local champion and a national leader, Max Baucus personifies the two Congresses. All members live and work in these two worlds: one on Capitol Hill and the other back home in their states and districts.

HILL STYLES

Congress is a body of transplanted locals who naturally speak up for their constituents. However, the ability of Congress to reflect the nation's large and varied population is affected by the diversity of its membership. There is no substitute for having a member of one's own group in a position of influence, and many groups do not receive representation commensurate with their presence in the population.

Who Are the Legislators?

Elections, as Aristotle first observed, are essentially oligarchic affairs that involve few active participants. The active participants are self-starters and risk-takers willing to seek an electoral "contract" for two or six years with no guarantee of renewal. In addition, by almost any measure senators and representatives constitute an economic and social elite. They are well educated. They come from prestigious occupations. The pay of senators and representatives ($174,000 since 2009) alone puts them in the top 1 percent of the nation's wage earners, but many members also have earned or inherited considerable wealth.[10] In 2013 around half of House members were millionaires, along with about two-thirds of senators.[11]

The elite character of the congressional membership raises questions of representation. One central purpose of a representative body is to bring together diverse individuals to deliberate on public policy. When the diversity of viewpoints is systematically limited, important interests and concerns are likely to be overlooked or undervalued. As John Stuart Mill argued a century and a half ago, "In the absence of its natural defenders, the interest of the omitted is always in danger of being overlooked."[12]

To meet Mill's standards for representation, must Congress closely mirror the demographics of the populace? Hannah Pitkin distinguishes between two types of representation: *descriptive* and *substantive*.[13] "Descriptive representation" refers to whether a legislature's membership reflects the diversity of backgrounds and interests in society. "Substantive representation" occurs when legislators consciously act as agents for constituents and their interests—an activity legislators can perform regardless of their personal background or group memberships. For example, legislators can voice farmers' concerns even if they have never plowed a field. Whites can champion equal opportunities for minorities.

Although descriptive representation and substantive representation are conceptually distinct, a wide range of empirical research has found that they are intertwined in the real world. The social identity of legislators affects representation in myriad ways. Representatives' racial, ethnic, and gender identities shape their priorities, positions, and legislative styles.[14] Whether constituents and representatives share a common identity has also been shown to affect trust and patterns of contact between them.[15]

Education and Occupation. By every measure, Congress is a highly educated body.[16] When the 113th Congress convened in January 2013, 93 percent of House members and 99 percent of senators held university degrees. Nearly two-thirds had graduate degrees. Twenty-five had medical degrees.

Historically, law and politics have been closely linked in the United States. A humorist once quipped that the U.S. government "of laws and not men" is really "of lawyers and not men." And indeed at the beginning of the 113th Congress, 168 representatives and 57 senators were law school graduates.

That so many members have law degrees does not necessarily mean that they possess extensive experience in the practice of law. "They are not, by and large, successful lawyers who left thriving partnerships to run for public office," observes Alan Ehrenhalt. "Rather, they are political activists with law degrees."[17] Legal training develops skills that are useful in gaining and holding public office, such as verbalization, advocacy, and negotiation. A law degree also serves as a stepping-stone into public service at many levels. Lawyers monopolize elected law enforcement and judicial posts, two main pathways to Congress. Hill staffers are often expected to have law degrees, and many members of Congress start out on Capitol Hill as staff aides. The 113th Congress is home to at least one hundred former congressional staffers.

The historical dominance of lawyers on Capitol Hill has nevertheless declined in recent decades. Lawyers are now outnumbered by members from other careers. Today's Congress is filled with professional public servants or, in common parlance, "career politicians." The 113th Congress includes thirty-three former mayors, ten former governors, eight former lieutenant governors, seven former judges, one former cabinet secretary, and two ambassadors. Half of senators (fifty-one) are former House members.

A significant contingent of Congress members have served in the military, though the veterans' ranks have thinned over time. After World War II, returning veterans surged into Congress. Among them were Reps. John F. Kennedy, D-Mass.; Richard M. Nixon, R-Calif.; Gerald R. Ford, R-Mich.; and Bob Dole, R-Kan. By the 1970s, more than seven of ten members were veterans. As the World War II era receded and draftees were replaced by a volunteer force, fewer veterans were elected. Just 20 percent of the members of the 113th

Congress have served in the military.[18] A small group of members currently serve in the Reserves and the National Guard.

Today's media-centered campaigns have spawned a few celebrity legislators. Several astronauts, including Sen. Bill Nelson, D-Fla., have served. Name recognition from his career as a writer and performer on *Saturday Night Live* helped launch the political career of Sen. Al Franken, D-Minn.

Many occupations are, and always have been, drastically underrepresented in Congress. Low-status occupations—including farm labor, service trades, manual and skilled labor, and domestic service—are extremely rare on Capitol Hill.[19] Not a few members, however, held menial jobs at some point in their lives. For example, at a hearing on Social Security taxes for household help, Rep. Carrie P. Meek, D-Fla. (1993–2003), a granddaughter of slaves, brought her own vivid experiences to the proceedings. "I was once a domestic worker," she told her colleagues. "My mother was a domestic worker. All my sisters were domestic workers."[20] Such perspectives are valuable for congressional representation and deliberation.

Race. African Americans, who make up 13.1 percent of the nation's population, account for 9 percent of the membership of the House of Representatives. There are two African American senators, both appointed and neither currently serving a full term. In 2013, forty-three African Americans (including two delegates) served in the House; all were Democrats. One of the two African American senators (Sen. Tim Scott, S.C.) is Republican. Although African American representation in Congress still does not reflect their proportion of the nation's population, black legislators have gained seniority and congressional influence over time.[21]

Other minorities are more severely underrepresented. Latinos make up 16.7 percent of the U.S. population but only 6.7 percent of the members on Capitol Hill. Of the thirty-three Latino representatives, most are Mexican Americans. All three Latino senators, however, are Cuban Americans. Of the Latino members of the 113th Congress, twenty-seven are Democrats and nine are Republicans. Asians and Pacific Islanders claim twelve representatives and one senator—all of them Democrats. There is one Native American, a House Republican.

The growing presence of racial minorities in Congress has had beneficial effects on representational bonds with minority communities. African Americans represented by black lawmakers, for example, tend to know more about their representatives and hold them in higher esteem.[22] "Even controlling for party affiliation," Katherine Tate's survey of black constituents found, "black legislators received significantly higher ratings on average than their white counterparts."[23] Another study showed that constituents of the same race as the incumbent were 27 percent more likely than constituents of other races to recognize the name of their representative.[24]

A growing scholarly literature also suggests that descriptive representation on Capitol Hill yields substantive benefits for minority communities. Black legislators are more active on issues of importance to their constituents of color—that is, they are more likely than their white colleagues to introduce bills on subjects of special concern to black Americans.[25] Systematic studies have also found that black members were more active than white members on policy issues of importance to African Americans in attending committee meetings, voting, offering amendments, and participating in deliberations.[26]

Gender. Neither chamber accurately reflects the nation in terms of gender. Congress historically has been a male bastion. In international comparisons, it still is: the United States ranks seventy-seventh worldwide in the proportion of women serving in the national legislature.[27] Diversity has developed slowly.

Unable to vote nationally until 1920, women have always been underrepresented in Congress. Beginning in 1917 with Rep. Jeannette Rankin, R-Mont., the presence of women in Congress has grown very slowly. A record number of women serve in the 113th Congress—eighty representatives (eighteen of them in the California delegation) and twenty senators (two each from California, New Hampshire, and Washington).[28] More than three-quarters are Democrats. Among them, Nancy Pelosi, D-Calif., serves as House Democratic leader and was the first woman to serve as Speaker of the House (2007–2011).

The advent of a critical mass of women has changed Congress. Policy concerns once labeled "women's issues"—which in truth affect everyone—now receive a respectful hearing. Gender discrimination, women's health, and issues involving the balance between family and workplace are more seriously addressed. Rep. Nita M. Lowey, D-N.Y., whose mother died of breast cancer, pressed for increased funding for research on the disease. During a debate over family leave policy, Sen. Patty Murray, D-Wash., recalled having to quit a secretarial job sixteen years earlier when she was pregnant with her first child. "When a person in this body gets up and speaks from personal experience, it changes the whole nature of the debate," observed Sen. Chris Dodd, D-Conn.[29] Referring to the women serving in the Senate, Senator Murray declared, "We've made it okay for men to talk about these [women's] issues, too."[30] Political science research offers systematic confirmation that the presence of women has had notable effects on Congress. Women legislators are more likely than men to introduce, sponsor, and press for bills of special concern to women and children.[31]

Only a handful of women members are mothers of school-age children. They undoubtedly face special challenges. Asked about the hardest thing about being a mother of young children while serving in Congress, Rep. Kristi Noem, R-S.D., said: "It isn't easy being away from my kids during the weeks I spend in D.C."[32] Nevertheless, the presence of moms on the Hill undoubtedly enriches representation. "Having kids is very relevant for a member of Congress," says former representative Pat Schroeder, D-Colo. (1973–1997), whose children were young when she arrived on Capitol Hill.[33]

Women legislators today are active far beyond the so-called women's issues. For example, Sen. Susan Collins, R-Maine, steered a complex intelligence reform bill through fierce turf battles while chairing the Senate Homeland Security and Governmental Affairs Committee in 2004.[34] Another challenge that women lawmakers face is that voters tend to view them as less competent on military and security issues.[35] To counter voters' stereotypes of female politicians in the post-9/11 environment, scholar Michele Swers finds that women legislators have expanded their activity and visibility on defense issues, particularly on homeland security matters.[36]

Sexual Orientation. Gays and lesbians passed a milestone in 1998 when Tammy Baldwin, D-Wis., became the first lesbian representative whose sexual orientation was known before her initial election. (Other congressional gays and lesbians revealed their sexuality or were outed after they had served for some time; some remain in the closet.) Baldwin did not shy away from the issue. Her campaign slogan was "A different kind of candidate." In 2013 Baldwin became the nation's first openly gay senator. The 113th Congress also includes the first openly bisexual person.[37]

As with other types of social identity, electing gay and lesbian representatives matters for the group's representation. Indeed, one recent study found that the presence of lesbian and gay elected officials was the single most important factor affecting local adoption of domestic partner benefits.[38] Still, as Rep. Barney Frank, D-Mass., has pointed out, the hardest part of running as a gay man is "convincing voters that you will not disproportionately focus on that minority's issues."[39]

Religion. Ninety-eight percent of all members of Congress cite a specific religious affiliation. By comparison, about 16 percent of Americans do not identify with any particular faith; indeed, the fastest-growing category in recent surveys of American religion is "unaffiliated."[40] Protestants collectively make up a majority of the 113th Congress, but about 30 percent of House and Senate members are Roman Catholics, the largest single religious denomination. Jews account for 7 percent. The 113th Congress also includes fifteen Mormons, three Buddhists, two Muslims, and one Hindu.[41]

Age and Tenure. When the 113th Congress convened in 2013, the average age of members was among the highest in history: fifty-seven for representatives, sixty-two for senators.[42] Tenure as well as age has risen since the early days. "Few die, and none retire," it was said as the twentieth century began. Today, the average member of Congress has served for approximately a decade.[43]

Age and tenure levels fluctuate over time. Periods of relatively low turnover (the 1980s, for example) are punctuated by dramatic changings of the guard. The 2010 election was one such moment. Fully 21 percent of the House and 15 percent of the Senate were freshmen in the 112th Congress. Similar turnovers occurred in the 1970s and the 1990s, involving both senior and junior members of Congress.[44] Electoral defeats play some role, but the majority of members leave voluntarily. Of course, many departing members retire just because they anticipate electoral difficulty.[45]

A certain balance between new blood and stable membership is undoubtedly optimal for legislative bodies. Rapid turnover—the early 1990s and 2006–2012, for example—can sharpen generational conflict. Many newly elected members indulge in Congress-bashing in their campaigns and want to shake up the institution, and not a few of them shun the idea of making a career of public service. The anti-establishment attitudes of members of the Tea Party caucuses on Capitol Hill are not unusual among large classes of relative newcomers. Reflecting on these troublesome freshmen, former Senate majority leader Trent Lott, R-Miss., said, "As soon as they get here, we need to co-opt them."[46] If past is prologue, many will eventually settle into the established power structure on Capitol Hill.

Equal Representation of States. The equal voice that all states have in the Senate is a central feature of congressional representation. The Senate's divergence from a population-based representation affects the welfare of many social and economic groups. It enlarges the voice of farmers, ranchers, mining interests, and users of federal lands—all groups that have far more presence in the less populous states than in the nation as a whole. At the same time, racial and ethnic minorities—already underrepresented in Congress relative to their share of the nation's population—are further disadvantaged by the Senate's makeup.[47] The nation's populous states are more racially and ethnically diverse than its less populous ones, and so one effect of Senate representation is to boost the voting power of the predominantly white residents of lightly populated states and to confer less voting power on the more racially diverse residents of populous states.[48]

Equal state representation in the Senate has other meaningful effects as well. Bonds between senators and their constituents are closer and more personalized in less populous states than in more populous ones.[49] And when Congress makes decisions about distributing federal dollars, less populous states receive more benefits than they pay in taxes, whereas populous states provide more revenue but receive fewer returns. Small-population states are advantaged across most federal spending programs, with the effect most pronounced on the types of programs over which Congress maintains tightest control.[50]

Collective Representation. Representation does not always follow state or district boundaries. It occurs when citizens feel they are served by any member of Congress, not just their local member. Congressional representation is, as Robert Weissberg put it, "collective," not just "dyadic."[51] In other words, representation involves more than the interactions between individual members and the residents of their geographic constituencies. Citizens can feel a sense of connection to Congress when the body as a whole includes members who speak for them. When someone from an ethnic or racial minority background goes to Congress, it is often a matter of pride for an entire identity group. Such legislators speak for people like them throughout the nation.[52]

Many constituencies are represented in the same way. One member who suffers from epilepsy defends job rights for other sufferers of the condition; another whose grandson was born prematurely champions funds for medical research into birth defects; members who are openly gay speak out for the rights of homosexuals everywhere. Such causes are close to members' hearts, even though they may pay scant political dividends. Legislators' backgrounds, religious beliefs, social identities, and experiences all shape their views and priorities. Political scientist Barry C. Burden refers to such influences as "the personal roots of representation," and he argues that analysts must take them into account to understand legislators' policy activism in Congress.[53]

Congressional Roles

Members of Congress, as Richard F. Fenno Jr. explains, spend their lives "moving between two contexts, Washington and home, and between two activities, governing and campaigning."[54] The two contexts and the two activities are continuously interwoven. How members govern is deeply affected by their constituency roots and their campaign experiences. In turn, their Capitol Hill activities affect all their subsequent contacts with people back home. As members carry out their representational functions, it is possible to distinguish three roles undertaken to some degree by most members of Congress: legislator, constituency servant, and partisan.

Legislator. The rules, procedures, and traditions of the House and Senate impose many constraints on members' behavior. To be effective, new members must learn their way through the institutional maze. Legislators therefore stress the formal aspects of Capitol Hill duties and routines: legislative work, investigation, and committee specialization. Sen. Charles E. Schumer, D-N.Y., an elected official for most of his life (he was elected to the state assembly at age twenty-three and served nine terms in the U.S. House), explained his commitment as a professional legislator during his successful 1998 Senate campaign:

> I love to legislate. Taking an idea—often not original with me— shaping it, molding it. Building a coalition of people who might not completely agree with it. Passing it and making the country a little bit of a better place. I love doing that.[55]

Legislators pursue information and expertise on issues, not only because of their personal interest in public policy but also because it sways others in the chamber. To influence other members, a legislator must be perceived as credible and knowledgeable—in other words, someone worth listening to.

The legislator's role often dovetails with that of representing constituents. Most members seek committee assignments that will serve the needs of their states or districts. One House member related why he sought a seat on the committee handling flood control and water resource development. "The interests of my district dictated my field of specialization," he explained, "but the decision to specialize in some legislative field is automatic for the member who wants to exercise any influence."[56]

Members soon learn the norms, or folkways, that expedite legislative productivity. Examining the post–World War II Senate, Donald R. Matthews identified folkways that restrained and channeled members' legislative activity. Senators were encouraged to serve an apprenticeship, deferring to elders in their early years; to concentrate on Senate work instead of on gaining publicity;

to specialize in issues within their committees or affecting their home states; and to extend reciprocity to colleagues—that is, provide willing assistance with the expectation that it would be repaid in kind one day.[57]

These folkways have faded in importance in the contemporary Senate, though they have not entirely disappeared. Barbara Sinclair's major reassessment of senators' Hill styles concluded that the restrained activism of the 1950s Senate had given way to unrestrained activism in the contemporary era.[58] New senators now actively take part in most aspects of the chamber's work, ignoring the apprenticeship norm. Many senators, especially those with an eye on the White House, work tirelessly to attract national publicity and personal attention. Committee specialization, although still common, is less rigid than it once was. Senators now have many overlapping committee assignments and are expected to express views on a wide range of issues.

The House relies more on formal channels of power than on informal norms. From interviews, however, Herbert B. Asher uncovered some key House norms.[59] Among them are the beliefs that the important work of the House should be done in committees, and that members should specialize in the issues before their committees. Members should be prepared to bargain and trade votes. Members should learn the procedural rules of the chamber. They should not personally criticize a colleague on the House floor.

As in the Senate, House norms of earlier eras have weakened. New members, impatient to make their mark, assert themselves more quickly, aided by party leaders who worry about getting the freshmen reelected. Leadership comes earlier to members than it used to. Specialization remains more compelling in the House than in the Senate, but many members branch out into unrelated issues. No longer are committees the sole forums for influencing legislation. Many of today's members, more partisan and ideologically driven than their predecessors, shun norms such as reciprocity and compromise. One of the most striking violations of civility norms occurred during the highly contentious spring of 2010. While staunchly pro-life representative Bart Stupak, D-Mich., was announcing his support for health care reform legislation on the House floor, another House member interrupted him by shouting, "Baby killer!"[60]

Constituency Servant. As constituency servants, members of Congress attempt to give voice to local citizens' concerns, solve problems constituents encounter with federal programs, and ensure that their states and districts receive a fair share of federal dollars. Often the task is performed by legislators and their staffs as casework—individual cases triggered by constituent letters or visits. Even though mostly delegated to staff aides, this is a chore that weighs heavily on members. A House member expressed the philosophy of most legislators this way:

> Constituent work: that's something I feel very strongly about. The American people, with the growth of the bureaucracy, feel nobody cares. The only conduit a taxpayer has with the government is a congressional office.[61]

One recent field experiment analyzing members' response time to letters dealing with policy and letters requesting constituent services found that members prioritize service over policy.[62] Sometimes, members stress constituency service to gain breathing room for legislative stands that stray from district norms.

Research has shown that developing a reputation as working hard on behalf of constituents in these ways makes a positive difference for legislators' careers. A recent study found that "a constituent-service reputation generates the most positive notice among citizens . . . [while] policy expertise appears to be less valuable to, or less noticed by, constituents."[63]

Procuring pork-barrel projects for local constituencies tends to improve representatives' name recognition back home,[64] reduce their likelihood of facing a strong challenger,[65] and enhance vulnerable members' reelection chances.[66] Even while Congress has adopted bans against earmarking special projects for members' constituencies and creating tax breaks for ten or fewer beneficiaries, they recognize that their constituents still expect them to bring home the bacon. An Arkansas lobbyist tells the story of going to visit one of his state's Republican members known for his anti-pork speeches. "I know you're anti-pork," the lobbyist began, "but I have to tell you about our needs and how to position yourself." "What do you mean?" the representative retorted. "As far as I can tell, it's not pork if it's for Arkansas."[67] Members have especially strong incentives to perform the constituency servant role whenever Congress considers government programs with highly visible local benefits, such as highway or mass transit grants, water projects, and homeland security contracts.

Partisan. Members of Congress are elected not just as individual representatives, but as members of a political party. Nearly every member of Congress formally affiliates with one of the two major parties, and even the few members elected as independents organize with one of the two parties to receive their committee assignments. Party affiliation is more than a mere label for most members. Members work with and for their parties, and their partisan ties and activities have a pervasive effect on congressional elections, representation, and legislation.

Members have a personal stake in the collective fate of their parties. Whether their party commands a majority of seats in the House or Senate affects their power in the chamber and their ability to achieve personal legislative goals. The majority party elects leaders with agenda-setting responsibilities and controls the chairmanships of all committees and subcommittees in the two chambers. In addition, members know that voters' feelings about the parties will affect their own electoral chances. Former Republican senator Lincoln Chafee of Rhode Island (currently governor of that state) lost his seat in 2006, despite high personal approval ratings, in large part because of his party's unpopularity in Rhode Island. "I give the voters credit," he said. "They made the connection between electing even popular Republicans at the cost of leaving the Senate in the hands of a leadership they had learned to mistrust."[68]

Many members hold posts within their congressional parties. Legislative party organizations are extensive, with whips, deputy whips, regional whips, and a variety of task forces. Elections for party positions are often hotly contested. As discussed in more detail in Chapter 6, members who hold or seek party positions dedicate significant effort to party causes. They do favors for fellow partisans and exhort them to vote the party position. They seek to impress leaders and other party members with their prodigious fund-raising and campaigning on behalf of their party's candidates.[69]

Even those members who do not serve as party officers attend and participate in the party caucus. In the contemporary Congress, the House and Senate caucuses of both parties meet at least weekly. Members engage in internal party communications and party message development. They stage press conferences, reach out to sympathetic groups and opinion leaders, and coordinate floor speeches as they seek to shape media coverage to partisan advantage.[70] In short, partisan activities today place significant demands on legislators' time and energy. Not only do members seek to enact good policy as legislators and advance local concerns as constituency servants, but they also are partisans, heavily invested in the collective fortunes of their parties.

How Do Legislators Spend Their Time?

For senators and representatives, time is their most precious commodity, and lack of it is their most frequent complaint about their jobs.[71] Allocating time requires exceedingly tough personal and political choices. Members are barraged with requests for meetings with groups and constituents. They are expected to spend considerable amounts of time in their home states and districts.

Scheduling is complicated by the large number of formal work groups—mainly committees and subcommittees, but also joint, party, and ad hoc panels. The average senator sits on three full committees and seven subcommittees; representatives average two committees and four subcommittees. With so many assignments, lawmakers are hard-pressed to control their crowded schedules. Committee quorums are difficult to achieve, and members' attention is often focused elsewhere. All too often working sessions are composed of the chair, the ranking minority member, perhaps one or two interested colleagues, and staff aides.[72]

Repeated floor votes, which lawmakers fear missing, are another time-consuming duty. In a typical Congress, more than a thousand recorded votes may be taken in the House chamber and perhaps six hundred in the Senate. "We're like automatons," one senator complained. "We spend our time walking in tunnels to go to the floor to vote."[73] Rep. Debbie Wasserman-Schultz, D-Fla., shuns the House gym, explaining, "I get my exercise running around the Capitol."[74]

Members are under relentless pressure to raise campaign funds. As mentioned in Chapter 4, the Democratic Congressional Campaign Committee recommends that new members spend between 40 and 50 percent of their time in Washington on fund-raising. "Call time" takes a large bite out of members' daily schedule. In addition, members must set aside time for fund-raising events and other personal meetings.

Taken together, lawmakers' daily schedules in Washington are "long, fragmented, and unpredictable," according to a study based on time logs kept by senators' appointment secretaries.[75] "In Congress you are a total juggler," recalls former representative Pat Schroeder. "You have always got seventeen things pulling on your sleeve."[76] Often members have scant notice that their presence is required at a meeting or a hearing. Carefully developed schedules are frequently disrupted.

Political scientists may claim that Congress runs in harmony with members' needs, but the members know otherwise. In a survey of 114 House and Senate members, "inefficiency" was the thing that most surprised them about Congress (45 percent gave this response).[77] "[Congress] is a good job for someone with no family, no life of their own, no desire to do anything but get up, go to work, and live and die by their own press releases," quipped former representative Fred Grandy, an Iowa Republican who left Congress in 1995. "It is a great job for deviant human beings."[78]

The dilemma legislators face in allocating their time is far more than a matter of scheduling; it is a case of conflicting role expectations. More members want to devote extra time to legislative duties than their schedules allow. There are always pressing demands to spend more time on constituency and political chores.[79] The two Congresses pull members in different directions. As a retiring House committee chair remarked:

> One problem is that you're damned if you do and damned if you don't. If you do your work here, you're accused of neglecting your district. And if you spend too much time in your district, you're accused of neglecting your work here.[80]

The Shape of the Washington Career

Once a short-term activity, congressional service has become a career. Accompanying this careerism, or longevity, is a distinctive pattern of Washington activity: the longer members remain in office, the more they sponsor bills, deliver floor speeches, and offer amendments. Despite the democratizing trends of the reform era (1960s and 1970s), senior lawmakers continue to take the lead in legislative activities.[81]

Long tenure also tends to pull members toward legislative specialization. Settling into their committee slots, members gain expertise in a distinct policy field and spend their time managing legislation and conducting oversight in that field. Seniority tends to boost legislative achievement. Veterans usually enjoy significantly more success than do freshmen in getting their bills passed.

The link between members' service and their effectiveness reflects the indispensable role careerists play in the legislative process. As John R. Hibbing observed:

Senior members are the heart and soul of the legislative side of congressional service. Relatively junior members can be given a subcommittee chairmanship, but it is not nearly so easy to give them an active, focused legislative agenda and the political savvy to enact it. Some things take time and experience, and successful participation in the legislative process appears to be one of those things.[82]

The wisdom of this statement is repeatedly borne out. One recent study drawing on the uniquely detailed data available for the North Carolina General Assembly reports that legislators' "effectiveness rises sharply with tenure," and "there is no evidence that effectiveness eventually declines with tenure, even out to nine terms."[83] The study concludes that "the increased effectiveness [of senior legislators] is due to the acquisition of specific human capital, most likely through learning-by-doing."[84] A comprehensive study of U.S. House members' abilities to get their bills past significant stages in the legislative process reports that "as members become more senior they become more efficient at arranging deals with key office-holders."[85] Newcomers bring with them zeal, energy, and fresh approaches. And yet many of them lack patience, bargaining skills, institutional memory, and respect for the lawmaking process.

LOOKING HOMEWARD

Not all of a representative's or a senator's duties lie in Washington, D.C. Legislators not only fashion policy for the nation's welfare, but they also act as emissaries from their home states or districts.

Independent Judgment or Constituency Opinion?

Although found in virtually every political system, representation is the hallmark of democratic regimes dedicated to sharing power among citizens. In small communities, decisions can be reached by face-to-face discussions, but in populous societies such personalized consultation is impossible. Thus, according to democratic theory, citizens can exert control by choosing "fiduciary agents" who will then deliberate on legislation just as their principals, the voters, would do if they could be on hand themselves.[86] But in attempting to serve as a faithful agent for constituents, legislators are faced with a central dilemma of representation: whether to take actions that are popular with constituents or to do what the legislator believes is in their best interest. As Pitkin explains,

> The representative must act in such a way that, although he is independent, and his constituents are capable of action and judgment, no conflict arises between them. He must act in their interest, and this means he must not normally come into conflict with their wishes.[87]

Recent opinion surveys seem to echo Pitkin's formulation. As one analyst puts it, "The public seems to want elected officials to internalize the majority's values and then try to assess how those values come to bear on an issue." No less than 85 percent agreed with the following statement: "The goal of Congress should be to make the decisions that a majority of Americans would make if they had the information and time to think things over that Congress has."[88]

To represent their constituents, legislators must do more than register prevailing constituency opinion. Public opinion often changes when controversy arises and constituents become more informed about issues. Legislators must instead use their superior information about policy, their broader perspective, and their personal judgment in making decisions. Legislators have to anticipate constituents' future views if an issue becomes more salient and more broadly understood.

Some representatives reject the idea that they ought to represent public opinion and instead see themselves as Burkean trustees charged with doing what is in constituents' interests. Speaking to a group of newly elected House members, Rep. Henry J. Hyde, R-Ill. (1974–2007), voiced the Burkean ideal:

> If you are here simply as a tote board registering the current state of opinion in your district, you are not going to serve either your constituents or the Congress well. You must take, at times, a national view, even if you risk the displeasure of your neighbors and friends back home. If you don't know the principle, or the policy, for which you are willing to lose your office, then you are going to do damage here.[89]

Nearly every member can point to conscience votes cast on deeply felt issues. A few, such as Rep. Mike Synar, D-Okla. (1979–1995), compile a contrarian record, challenging voters to admire their independence if not their policies. Synar was an unabashed liberal Democrat from a state that now elects mostly conservative Republicans. "I want to be a U.S. congressman from Oklahoma, not an Oklahoman congressman," Synar declared when he arrived in the capital.[90] If turned out of office by hostile sentiment (as Synar later was), the Burkean can at least hope for history's vindication.

In practice, legislators assume different representational styles according to the occasion. They ponder factors such as the nation's welfare, their personal convictions, and constituency opinions. "The weight assigned to each factor," writes Thomas E. Cavanagh, "varies according to the nature of the issue at hand, the availability of the information necessary for a decision, and the intensity of preference of the people concerned about the issue."[91]

Members of Congress are challenged to explain their choices to constituents—no matter how many or how few people truly care about the matter.[92] The anticipated need to explain oneself shapes a member's decisions and is part of the dilemma of choice. A cynical saying among lawmakers asserts that "a vote on anything [is] a wrong vote if you cannot explain it in a 30-second TV ad."[93]

What Are Constituencies?

Senators and representatives cannot respond equally to all the people within a given state or district. A subset of their constituents elected them, and so they interact more with supporters than with opponents. The constituencies that legislators see as they campaign or vote are quite different from the boundaries found on maps. Fenno describes a "nest" of constituencies, ranging from the widest (geographic constituency) to the narrowest (personal constituency), which is made up of supporters, loyalists, and intimates.[94]

Geographic and Demographic Constituencies. The average House district today numbers more than 720,000 people. As for senators, fourteen represent states with only one House district; the rest represent multidistrict states with as many as 37 million people.[95] Such constituencies differ sharply from one another. More than half of the people in Manhattan's Upper East Side (New York's Twelfth District) have college degrees, compared with only 6 percent in California's central valley (Twenty-first District). Median family income ranges from $79,000 (New Jersey's Eleventh District, Morris County) to less than $21,000 in New York's Sixteenth District in the South Bronx, where 40 percent of the families live in poverty. Such disparities among districts shape their representatives' outlooks.

Demographically, constituencies may be homogeneous or heterogeneous.[96] Some constituencies, even a few whole states, remain uniform and one-dimensional—mostly wheat farmers or inner-city dwellers or small-town citizens. Because of rising population, economic complexity, and educational levels, however, virtually all constituencies, House as well as Senate, have become more heterogeneous than they used to be. The more diverse a constituency, the more challenging is the representative's task.

Another attribute of constituencies is electoral balance, especially as manifested in the incumbent's reelection chances. Heterogeneous districts tend to be more competitive than uniform ones. Incumbents predictably prefer safe districts—that is, those with a high proportion of groups leaning toward their party. Not only do safe districts favor reelection, but they also imply that voters will be easier to please.[97]

Truly competitive districts are not the norm, especially in the House of Representatives. The 2012 elections were reasonably competitive by recent standards. In the last month leading up to the elections, analysts at the *Cook Political Report* estimated that eighty-five House seats were either toss-ups or merely leaning toward one political party. Despite this, the majority of incumbents won handily: 61 percent of House victors won by 20 percentage points or more, and 10 percent faced no challenger at all. Less than 20 percent of House districts were decided by narrow margins.

As Table 5-1 shows, competitiveness varies over time. Senate seats are more likely to be closely contested than House races, but most incumbents still win in a walk.

Whatever the numbers might show, few incumbents regard themselves as truly safe. The threat of losing an election is very real. Even with incumbent reelection rates at above 90 percent, incumbent officeholders understandably fear even a 10 percent chance of losing a job they have worked so hard to win. Most lawmakers have a close call at some time in their congressional careers, and many of them eventually suffer defeat.[98] In addition to the incumbents who went down to defeat in 2012, a number of others—including three senators and some thirty House members—survived while receiving what might be called warning signs from the home folks. Incumbents thus worry not only about winning or losing but also about their margins of safety. Downturns in normal electoral support narrow the member's comfort zone in the job, may invite challengers in future years, and could block chances for further advancement.[99]

Political and Personal Constituencies. As candidates or incumbents analyze their electoral base, three narrower constituencies can be discerned: supporters (the reelection constituency), loyalists (the primary constituency), and intimates (the personal constituency).[100] Supporters are expected to vote for the candidate on election day, but some do not. Candidates and their advisers constantly monitor these voters, reassessing precinct-level political demography—registration figures, survey data, and recent electoral trends. The more elections incumbents have survived, the more precisely they can identify supporters. Areas and groups with the biggest payoffs are usually targeted.

Loyalists are the politician's staunchest supporters. They may be from pre-electoral ventures—civil rights, environmental, or Tea Party activists, for example. They may hail from religious or ethnic groups, or political or civic clubs. They may be friends and neighbors. Whatever their source, they are willing volunteers who can be counted on to lend a hand in reelection campaigns.

Candidates dare not ignore these loyalists. A favorite story of House Speaker Thomas P. "Tip" O'Neill Jr., D-Mass. (1953–1987), emerged from his first campaign for city council (at which he failed). A neighbor told him, "Tom, I'm going to vote for you even though you didn't ask me." "Mrs. O'Brien," replied a surprised O'Neill, "I've lived across the street from you for 18 years. I shovel your walk in the winter. I cut your grass in the summer. I didn't think I had to ask you for your vote." To this the lady replied, "Tom, I want you to know something: people like to be asked."[101] Expressions of gratitude are equally important. The elder George Bush reportedly "always carried a box of note cards with him on the campaign trail and penned a personal note immediately following each event to the volunteers and hosts."[102]

Even entrenched officeholders worry about keeping their core supporters energized. Loyalists are a politician's defenders in times of adversity. "There's a big difference between the people who are for you and the people who are excitedly for you," an Iowa politician told Fenno, "between those who will vote if they feel like it and those for whom the only election is [your] election. You need as many of that group as you can get."[103]

TABLE 5-1 **House and Senate Margins of Victory, 1974–2012**

Chamber and election year	Percentage of vote				Number of seats
	Under 55	55–59.9	60 plus	Unopposed	
House					
1974	24	16	46	14	435
1976	17	14	56	12	435
1978	17	14	53	16	435
1980	18	14	60	8	435
1982	16	16	63	6	435
1984	12	13	61	14	435
1986	9	10	64	17	435
1988	6	9	67	18	435
1990	11	16	58	15	435
1992	20	18	58	3	435
1994	22	17	52	9	435
1996	22	18	57	3	435
1998	10	17	63	10	435
2000	18	12	56	14	435
2002	10	10	70	10	435
2004	7	14	64	15	435
2006	15	14	62	9	435
2008	14	16	57	12	435
2010	24	16	54	6	435
2012	17	21	59	2	435
Senate					
1974	41	18	35	6	34
1976	30	33	30	6	33
1978	24	33	36	6	33
1980	58	18	21	3	34
1982	30	27	43	—	33
1984	18	21	58	3	33
1986	38	15	47	—	34
1988	33	15	52	—	33
1990	26	11	49	14	34
1992	34	34	32	—	35
1994	32	34	34	—	35
1996	59	18	24	—	34
1998	29	9	62	—	34
2000	29	15	55	—	34
2002	32	18	46	4	34
2004	32	15	50	3	34
2006	24	21	55	—	33
2008	26	20	51	3	35
2010	32	27	38	3	37
2012	39	27	33	0	33

Sources: CQ Weekly and authors' calculations.

Notes: Percentages may not add to 100 because of rounding. "Unopposed" includes districts or states where only one major-party candidate was on the ballot.

Intimates are close friends who supply political advice and emotional support. They may be members of the candidate's family, trusted staff members, political mentors, or individuals who shared decisive experiences early in the candidate's career. The setting and the players differ from state to state and from district to district. Tip O'Neill's inner circle was made up of the "boys" of Barry's Corner, a local clubhouse in Cambridge, Massachusetts, whose families O'Neill had known intimately over more than fifty years of political life. When Rep. David E. Price, D-N.C., first decided to run for Congress, he relied on what he called the "Wednesday night group," which he described as "an inner circle without whom the effort would never have gotten off the ground."[104] Such intimates play an indispensable role. Beyond their enthusiastic support, they provide unvarnished advice on political matters and serve as sounding boards for ideas and strategies.

Home Styles

Legislators evolve distinctive ways of presenting themselves and their records to their constituents—what Fenno calls their home styles. These styles are exhibited in members' personal appearances, mailings, newsletters, press releases, telephone conversations, radio and television spots, and websites. Little is known about how home styles coalesce, but they are linked to members' personalities, backgrounds, constituency features, and resources. The ways members interact with constituents have a powerful effect on their electoral success. As Fenno notes, "It is the style, not the issue content, that counts most in the reelection constituency."[105]

Presentation of Self. A successful home style will elicit trust—constituents' faith that legislators are who they claim to be and will do what they promise.[106] Winning voters' trust does not happen overnight; it takes time, persistence, and consistency. Members must establish their qualification for office—that is, the belief that they are capable of handling the job. Members also strive to convey identification, the impression that legislators resemble their constituents, and empathy, the sense that legislators understand constituents' problems and care about them.

Because of the variations among legislators and constituencies, the use of many different home styles can effectively build the trust relationship. The legendary Speaker "Mr. Sam" Rayburn represented his East Texas district for nearly fifty years (1913–1961) as a plain dirt farmer. Once he was back in his hometown of Bonham, his drawl thickened; his tailored suits were exchanged for khakis, an old shirt, and a slouch hat; and he traveled not in the Speaker's limousine, but in a well-dented pickup truck. His biographer relates:

> If Rayburn ever chewed tobacco in Washington, a long-time aide could not recall it, but in Bonham he always seemed to have a plug in his cheek. He made certain always to spit in the fireplace at his home when constituents were visiting, so that if nothing else, they would take away the idea that Mr. Sam was just a plain fellow.[107]

The aim of a member's home style is to become "one of us" in constituents' estimation. Accomplishing this is a "difficult feat—far more difficult than establishing a reputation as a fine constituency servant or policy expert."[108]

Today's legislators are no less inventive in fashioning home styles. Representative A's direct style features face-to-face contacts with people in his primary constituency. He rarely mentions issues because most people in his district agree on them. Representative B, a popular local athlete, uses national defense issues to symbolize his oneness with a district supportive of the military. Representative C displays himself as a verbal, issue-oriented activist, an outsider ill at ease with conventional politicians. Senator D, articulate and personable, comes across as "a mom in tennis shoes." The repertoire of home styles is virtually limitless.

Voters are likely to remember style long after they forget issue statements or voting records. Even so, legislators know full well that they must explain their decisions to others.[109]

Explaining Washington Activity. Explaining is an integral part of decision making. In home district forums, constituents expect members to be able to describe, interpret, and justify their actions. If they do not agree with the member's conclusions, they may at least respect the decision-making style.

Although few incumbents fear that a single vote can defeat them, all realize that voters' disenchantment with their record can be fatal—more so in these days of Internet communications when lobby groups publicize voting records. Although local news media coverage of Congress is often uncritical, it can promote political accountability. Local media devote more time and resources to monitoring representatives who are "out of step" with their district's presidential vote than those who are perceived to be in step. Such members face additional media scrutiny and must therefore account for their Washington decisions more frequently.[110]

Members stockpile reasons for virtually every position they take, often more than are needed. Facing especially thorny choices (for example, on aid to Wall Street firms, health care reform, or the war in Iraq), they might seek a middle-of-the-road route. More often, they huddle under the umbrella of their party's line. Whatever course they choose, they will find that inconsistency is mentally and politically costly. Contrary to the popular stereotype of politicians speaking out of both sides of their mouths, members give much the same account of themselves regardless of the group they are talking to.

Constituency Careers. Constituency bonds evolve over the course of a lawmaker's career. Constituency careers have at least two recognizable stages: expansionism and protectionism. In the first stage, the member builds a reelection constituency by solidifying the help of hard-core supporters and reaching out to attract additional blocs of support. Aggressive efforts to reach out to new voters—exploiting the perquisites of incumbency, such as fund-raising and an election-year avalanche of messages to constituents—account for the "sophomore surge," in which newcomers typically boost their margin in their first reelection bid. In the second stage, the member stops expanding the base, content with protecting support already won. Once established, a successful home style is rarely altered.

Certain developments, however, can lead to a change in a member's home style. One is demographic change in the constituency, as population movement or redistricting force a member to confront unfamiliar voters or territory. A second cause is a strategic reaction, such as when a fresh challenger or a novel issue threatens established voting patterns. Because coalitions may shift over time, members and their advisers pore over the results of the most recent election (and available survey results).

Finally, home styles may change with new personal goals and ambitions. Achieving positions of power in Washington can divert a member's attention from home state business. Family responsibilities or the need to improve one's financial situation may also lead to a shift in priorities. Faced with new aspirations or shifting constituency demands, some members decide to retire. Others struggle ineffectively and are defeated. Still others survive by rejuvenating their constituency base.

OFFICE OF THE MEMBER INC.

Home style includes the way a member answers day-to-day questions: How much attention should I devote to state or district needs? How much time should I spend in the state or district? How should I keep in touch with my constituents? How should I deploy staff aides to handle constituents' concerns?

Road Tripping

During the nineteenth century, legislators spent most of their time at home, traveling to Washington only when Congress was in session. However, after World War II (and the advent of both air travel from home and air-conditioning on Capitol Hill), congressional sessions lengthened until they spanned most of the year.

By the 1970s, both houses had adopted parallel schedules of sessions punctuated with district work periods (House) or nonlegislative periods (Senate). At the same time, members were permitted more paid trips to states or districts. Today, senators and representatives are allowed as many trips home as they want, subject to the limits of their official expense allowances. Many members (even those from the West Coast) go home every weekend. Today's home styles thus entail frequent commutes.

Seniority is also a factor. Senior members tend to make fewer trips to their districts than do junior members, perhaps reflecting junior members' greater attentiveness to their districts or senior members' greater Washington responsibilities. Finally, members' decisions to retire voluntarily are usually accompanied by large drops in trips home.

Constituency Casework

"All God's chillun got problems," exclaimed Rep. Billy Matthews, D-Fla. (1953–1967), as he pondered mail from his constituents.[111] In the early days, lawmakers lacked staff aides and wrote personally to executive agencies for help in matters such as pension or land claims and appointments to military academies. The Legislative Reorganization Act of 1946 provided de facto authority for hiring caseworkers, first in Senate offices and later in the House.

What are these cases all about? As respondents in a nationwide survey reported, the most frequent reason for contacting a member's office (16 percent of all cases) is to express views or obtain information on legislative issues. Requests for help in finding government jobs form the next largest category, followed by cases dealing with government services such as Social Security, veterans' benefits, or unemployment compensation. Military cases (for example, transfers, discharges, personal hardships) are numerous, as are tax, legal, and immigration problems. Constituents often ask for government publications. And there are requests for flags that have flown over the U.S. Capitol.

Many citizen appeals, moreover, betray a hazy understanding of the officeholder's duties. Rep. Luis V. Gutierrez, D-Ill. (1993–2009), reported being barraged with all manner of complaints and requests when he shopped in his North Side Chicago neighborhood. Examples of what he has heard are: "They haven't picked up my trash!" (the city's job). "Can you get my son a scholarship to the state university?" (a state matter). Or "I can't pay my child support" (personal). Rep. Gutierrez's personal favorite was: "I own property in Puerto Rico and someone is blocking my driveway."[112]

Cases arrive in legislators' offices by letter, phone, e-mail, fax, or in person at district or mobile offices. All representatives and senators now have e-mail addresses and websites with contact information. Occasionally, members themselves pick up cases from talking to constituents. Indeed, many hold office hours in their districts for this purpose. When a constituent's request is received, it is usually acknowledged promptly by a letter that either fills the request or promises that an answer will be forthcoming.

Keeping up with incoming communications is a priority for all congressional offices. If the constituent's request requires contacting a federal agency, the contact in the executive agency is usually a liaison officer, although some caseworkers prefer to deal directly with line officers or regional officials. Once the problem has been conveyed, it is a matter of time before a decision is reached and a reply forwarded to the congressional office. The reply is then sent along to the constituent, perhaps with a cover letter signed by the member. If the agency's reply is deemed faulty, the caseworker may challenge it and ask for reconsideration; in some cases the member may personally intervene to lend weight to the appeal.

The volume of casework varies from state to state and from district to district. Demographic variation affects casework volume because some types of citizens simply are more likely to have contact with government agencies. Senators representing the smallest states often have casework loads that exceed those of House members, because their greater institutional clout makes them even more attractive to small-state residents than their state's House members. By contrast, large-state senators are perceived as being more distant, so constituents in those states are more likely to turn to their House members for casework requests.[113]

From all accounts, casework pays off in citizen support for individual legislators. In one National Election Study (NES) survey, 17 percent of all adults reported that they or members of their families had requested help from their own representatives. Eighty-five percent said they were satisfied with the response they received.[114] "Casework is all profit," contends Morris P. Fiorina. Unlike the positions members take on issues, casework wins friends without alienating anyone. But casework benefits do not entirely supplant issue positions or party loyalties.

Some criticize constituency casework as unfair or biased in practice. Citizens may not enjoy equal access to senators' or representatives' offices. Political supporters or cronies may receive favored treatment at others' expense. But in the great bulk of cases, help is universally dispensed.

Personal Staff

Legislators head sizable office enterprises that reflect their responsibilities within the institution and toward their constituents. Staff members assist with legislative and constituency duties. Constituent representation is deemed so essential that when a member dies, resigns, or is incapacitated, the staff normally remains on the job (supervised by the secretary of the Senate or the clerk of the House, as the case may be).

Each House member is entitled to a member representational account (MRA) that ranges from $1.3 to $1.6 million annually. From this account, members pay the salaries of no more than eighteen full-time and four part-time employees. The average House member's full-time staff actually numbers about fifteen. Representatives also are entitled to an annual office allowance, which is used for travel, telecommunications, district office rental, office equipment, stationery, computer services, and mail.[115]

Senators' personal staffs range in size from thirteen to seventy-one; the average is from thirty to thirty-five full-time employees. Unlike the House, the Senate places no limits on the number of staff a senator may employ. A senator's office expense account depends on factors such as the state's population and its distance from Washington, D.C.

Members' offices always seem crowded and overburdened, but freezes on staff size have been partially offset by computerization, shifting work to state and district offices, and use of volunteers. Congressional offices depend heavily on unpaid help, mainly college-age interns. On average, each House and Senate office uses about nine interns every year (see Appendix B for information on internships).

Staff Organization. No two congressional offices are exactly alike. Each is shaped by the personality, interests, constituency, and politics of the individual legislator. State and district needs also influence staff composition. A senator from a farm state likely will employ at least one specialist in agricultural problems; an urban representative might hire a consumer affairs or housing expert. Traditions are important. If a legislator's predecessor had an enviable reputation for a certain kind of service, the new incumbent will dare not let it lapse.

The member's institutional position also affects staff organization. Committee and subcommittee chairs have committee staff at their disposal. Members without such aides rely heavily on personal staff for their committee work.

Staff Functions. Most personal aides in the House and Senate are young, well educated, and transient. Senate and House aides have served on average less than four years in their posts. Their salaries, although somewhat above the average for full-time workers in the United States, fall well below those for comparably educated workers.[116]

The mix of personal staff functions is decided by each member. Most hire chiefs of staff, legislative assistants (LAs), caseworkers, and press aides, as well as a few people from the home state or district. Chiefs of staff supervise the office and impart political and legislative advice. Often they function as the legislator's alter ego, negotiating with colleagues, constituents, and lobbyists. LAs work with members in committees, draft bills, write speeches, suggest policy initiatives, analyze legislation, and prepare position papers. They also monitor committee sessions that the member is unable to attend.

To emphasize personal contacts, many members have moved casework staff to their home districts or states. Virtually all House and Senate members have home district offices. Some members have as many as five or six such offices. Field offices have lower staff salaries, cheaper rents, and less overhead. They also are more accessible to constituents, local and state officials, and regional federal officers. Members' district staffs fill the role once performed by local party workers and simultaneously enhance members' reelection prospects.

This organizational division reflects the fundamental duality of legislative roles. Legislative functions are centered on Capitol Hill, whereas constituency functions are based in field offices. In other words, "Office of the Member, Inc." is increasingly split into headquarters and branch divisions—with the Capitol Hill office handling legislative duties and the state or district office dealing with constituents.

Because members' resources—offices, staffs, and allowances—are funded by the taxpayers, they are restricted to the conduct of official business. "Any campaign work by staff members must be done outside the congressional office, and without using any congressional office resources," states a 2006 House ethics memorandum.[117] This distinction may seem cloudy; after all, members' offices are suffused with electoral concerns, and what constitutes "campaign activity" is unclear. During the campaign season, certain aides go on leave and transfer to the campaign organization's payroll.

MEMBERS AND THE MEDIA

Office allowances in both chambers amply support lawmakers' unceasing struggle for media attention. A member's office bears some resemblance to the communications division of a medium-size business. Nearly every day, messages are released for wide distribution. In addition to turning out press releases, newsletters, and individual and mass mailings, members communicate through telephone, interviews, radio and TV programs, e-mail and text messages, official and personal websites, and through Internet social networking services. Most of the time, these publicity barrages are aimed not at the national media but at individuals and media outlets back in the home state or district.

Mail

The traditional cornerstone of congressional publicity is the franking privilege—the right of members to send out mail at no cost with their signature (the frank) instead of a stamp. This practice, which dates from the First Continental Congress in 1775, is intended to facilitate official communication between elected officials and the people they represent (a rationale accepted by federal courts in upholding the practice).

Critics point out that franked mail is largely unsolicited and often politically motivated. The fact that outgoing mail costs are much higher in election years than in nonelection years seems to bear that criticism out. Most items are mass mailings, not individual letters. Mass mailings are either general-purpose newsletters blanketing home states or districts or special messages targeted to certain categories of voters. Recipients are urged to share their views or contact local offices for help. Sometimes, the newsletter may feature an opinion poll asking for citizens' views on selected issues. Whatever the results, the underlying message is that the legislator cares what folks back home think.

Current law forbids franked mail that is "unrelated to the official business, activities, and duties of members." It also bars the frank for a "matter which specifically solicits political support for the sender or any other person or any political party." In addition, chamber rules forbid mass mailings (five hundred or more pieces) sixty days (Senate) or ninety days (House) before a primary, runoff, or general election. Congress has also placed caps on newsletters and on total outgoing mail. In the two months before the beginning of each cut-off period, streams of U.S. Postal Service trucks are seen pulling away from the loading docks of the congressional office buildings.

The advent of e-mail poses the problem of whether, or how, the much-debated franking restrictions should apply. The Senate has generally applied the franking rules to electronic mail. The House, however, has declined to adopt such strict rules.

Americans increasingly rely on the Internet for news. It is no wonder, then, that lawmakers have rapidly set up websites and even blogs.[118] Most sites feature the member's biography, committee assignments, and votes on major issues. Capitol Hill websites exhibit variety in their content, usability, and interactivity.[119] Some members' websites include streaming audio or video of members' speeches or appearances on news programs. Few of them include such potentially sensitive information as the member's financial disclosure reports, travel spending, and meetings with lobbyists.

Members are quick to embrace new communication technologies. Many members now make use of social networking services such as Facebook and Twitter. Reporting on lawmakers using their BlackBerries throughout President Obama's first address to a joint session of Congress, *Washington Post* journalist Dana Milbank joked, "It's bad enough that Americans are paralyzed by economic jitters. Now the president has to deal with lawmakers paralyzed by Twitter."[120]

Feeding the Local Press

News outlets in North America are decentralized and dispersed. These include daily and weekly newspapers, radio and TV stations, and cable systems. Virtually all these media outlets are locally based, centered on local issues, and funded by local advertising.

Most local media outlets have inadequate resources for covering their congressional delegations. In fact, very few have their own Washington reporters. Most rely on syndicated or chain services that rarely follow individual members consistently. "If they report national news it is usually because it involves local personalities, affects local outcomes, or relates directly to local concerns," stated a Senate report.[121]

Relations with the press receive close attention from members. Most legislators have at least one staffer who serves as a press aide; some have two or three. Their job is to generate coverage highlighting the member's work. Executive agencies often help by letting incumbents announce federal grants or contracts awarded in the state or district. Even if the member had nothing to do with procuring the funds, the press statement proclaims, "Senator So-and-So announced today that a federal contract has been awarded to XYZ Company in Jonesville." Many offices also prepare weekly or biweekly columns that small-town newspapers can reprint under the lawmaker's byline.

The House, the Senate, and the four Capitol Hill parties (House and Senate Republicans and Democrats) have fully equipped studios and satellite links where audio or video programs or excerpted statements (called actualities) can be produced for a fraction of the commercial cost.[122] Some incumbents produce regular programs that are picked up by local radio or television outlets. More often, these outlets insert brief audio or TV clips on current issues into regular news broadcasts—to give the impression that their reporters have gone out and obtained the story. Members also create their own news reports and beam them directly to hometown stations, often without ever talking to a reporter. With direct satellite feeds to local stations, members regularly go "live at five" before local audiences.

Like printed communications, radio and TV broadcasts pose ethical questions. House and Senate recording studios are supposed to be used only for communicating about legislation and other policy issues, but the distinction between legitimate constituent outreach and political advertising remains blurred. (The studios run by the parties have no such limits.) Some radio and television news editors have qualms about using members' programs. "It's just this side of self-serving," said one television editor of the biweekly "Alaska Delegation Report."[123] Others claim to see little difference between these electronic communications and old-fashioned press releases. Local editors and producers still have to decide whether to use the material, edit it, or toss it.

Local Press Boosterism?

With a few notable exceptions, local media convey little information about their representatives. Most stories are uncritically positive: only 6 percent of the news stories compiled by R. Douglas Arnold cited anyone who criticized the incumbent's performance.[124] As a result of this pervasive positive tilt, when members successfully cultivate local coverage, they are more likely to win reelection.[125]

In the eyes of home district media outlets, incumbents simply fare splendidly. Michael J. Robinson cited the case of "Congressman Press," a midlevel House member, untouched by scandal, who had an average press operation. Drawing on 144 press releases from his office over the course of a year, his local paper ran 120 stories featuring or mentioning him. "On average, every other week, Congressman Press was featured in a story virtually written in his own office."[126]

Even when local stories are not drawn from press releases, they tend to be respectful if not downright laudatory.[127] Broadcast media are even more benign than print media. As one legislator said, "TV people need thirty seconds of sound and video at the airport when I arrive—that's all they want."[128] Most local reporters for radio and TV are on general assignment and do little preparation for interviews. Their primary goal is to get the newsmaker on tape.

Local radio and television's weakness for congressionally initiated communications magnifies the advantages incumbents enjoy. ABC News commentator Cokie Roberts observed, "The emergence of local TV has made some members media stars in the home towns and, I would argue, done more to protect incumbency than any franking privilege or newsletter ever could, simply because television is a more pervasive medium than print."[129] A recent study reports a strong link between the expansion of local television stations across the country and the rise of incumbency advantage in the post-1960s era.[130]

Reports on Congress from the national press corps are far more critical than those from local news organizations. Following the canons of investigative journalism, many national reporters are on the lookout for scandals or evidence of wrongdoing. The national press reports primarily on the institution of Congress, whereas the local press focuses mostly on local senators and representatives. Individual members tend to be reported on far more favorably than the institution. The content and quality of press coverage in local and national media underscore the differences between the two Congresses. Congress as collective policy maker, covered mainly by the national press, appears in a different light from the politicians who make up Congress, covered mainly by local news outlets.

CONCLUSION

How members of Congress manage the two Congresses dilemma is reflected in their daily tasks on Capitol Hill and in their home states or districts. Election is a prerequisite to congressional service. Legislators allocate much of their time and energy, and even more of their staff and office resources, to the care and cultivation of voters. Their Hill styles and home styles are adopted with this end in mind.

Yet senators and representatives do not live by reelection alone. Many bemoan the need for constant campaigning. "What drives me nuts about this place is that, when I came here, it used to be that you had at least a year after you were elected where you could get the people's business done before the next election intruded," complained former representative David Obey, D-Wis. (1969–2011). "Now the way politics has been nationalized, the election intrudes every day."[131] For those who remain in office, reelection is not usually viewed as an end in itself, but as a lever for pursuing other goals—policy making or career advancement. Fenno once remarked to a member that "sometimes it must be hard to connect what you do here with what you do in Washington." "Oh no," the lawmaker replied, "I do what I do here so I can do what I want to do there."[132]

P *arty Leaders.* Former House Speaker Nancy Pelosi, D-Calif., hands the gavel to the new Speaker, John A. Boehner, R-Ohio (top left), on January 5, 2011, the first day of the 112th Congress. House Minority Whip Steny H. Hoyer, D-Md., and Minority Leader Pelosi walk with President Obama to a Democratic Party caucus on budget policy (top right). Senate Republican minority leader Mitch McConnell, R-Ky., speaks to the press after a GOP issues meeting (bottom right). The House GOP leadership team (bottom left)—Speaker Boehner, Chief Whip Kevin McCarthy, Calif., and Majority Leader Eric Cantor, Va.—leave the White House, where they discussed government spending and job creation.

Leaders and Parties in Congress

Congress began on a high note for the new Speaker of the House. On January 5, 2011, John A. Boehner, R-Ohio, smiled as he received the gavel from outgoing Speaker Nancy Pelosi, D-Calif. Jubilant Republicans thundered their applause in a House chamber filled with representatives and their children, grandchildren, and other family members. "I now pass this gavel and the sacred trust that goes with it to the new speaker," said Pelosi. "God bless you, Speaker Boehner."[1]

But leadership of the contemporary Congress has proved extremely difficult for Boehner. The first session of the 112th Congress concluded in 2011 with the Republican House leadership's "remarkable capitulation"[2] on a payroll tax cut extension. Rank-and-file House Republicans, many affiliated with the Tea Party movement, had rejected the extension, even though it had passed the Senate with eighty-nine votes. The House Republican opposition to continuing a tax cut that benefited most working Americans quickly became politically untenable. Defections within Republican ranks as well as the prospect of suffering blame for raising taxes in a weak economy made it impossible to hold out. After Senate Republican leader Mitch McConnell, R-Ky., released a statement imploring the House to agree to the Senate bill, Boehner was forced to completely reverse course and allow the extension to pass, in an ending described on all sides as a "debacle."[3]

The second session of the 112th Congress concluded in 2012 with a similar drama. Facing the imminent expiration of a set of tax cuts adopted during the George W. Bush administration, Boehner pursued a deal with the president and the Republican led Senate to preserve as many of the tax cuts as possible. To increase his bargaining leverage, Boehner asked the House to pass a measure that would extend all the Bush tax cuts except those affecting income above $1 million per year. Even though the leadership personally whipped the vote and held the members in session late in expectation of passing the measure, Boehner was forced to withdraw the plan at the last minute. Conservatives had opposed the bill because it tacitly acceded to tax increases on high-income individuals, even though the measure was only designed as a bargaining chip. Recognizing his defeat, Boehner, near tears, led his conference in the serenity prayer, "God grant me the serenity to accept the things I cannot change, the courage to change the things I can, and the wisdom to know the difference."[4]

The upshot was that the weakened Boehner moved to the sidelines as Senate leaders negotiated a deal.

Every political leader finds it more difficult to govern than to oppose, but the political environment of the 113th Congress presents special challenges. With divided government and hard questions on the political agenda—such as government retrenchment, fiscal balance, immigration, gun control, and the debt limit—Boehner must find solutions that can command the support of his party in the House and then win approval by the Senate and, in most cases, the administration. This is no simple task.

To complicate matters further, Boehner had committed to lead the chamber in a more open, participatory fashion than other recent House Speakers. On his first day as Speaker, Boehner gained approval of a set of revisions to House rules to make the body operate "with greater openness, deliberation, and efficiency."[5] The new rules require legislation to be available for review for three calendar days before a vote. They also mandate that committees quickly post information about pending legislative proposals, as well as the outcomes of votes and any amendments adopted. Such revisions addressed many of Boehner's criticisms of his predecessor. But they also reflect the reality of a large group of enthusiastic Republican newcomers who had no intention of being shut out of power. As former House Speaker Newt Gingrich remarked, "None of these folks are coming in saying, 'Mommy, may I?'"[6] Along the same lines, GOP strategist Frank Luntz observed, Boehner has "some very ornery folks to deal with."[7]

Building electoral majorities, managing internal party politics, and presiding over the House and its internal rules are among the Speaker's wide-ranging duties. These responsibilities must be carried out with careful attention to the two Congresses. Leaders must facilitate lawmaking, while at the same time attending both to party members' representational ties with their constituents and to the party's public image. Of his fellow Republicans, Boehner says, "You've got to give them room to grow. You've got to give them room to be rebellious from time to time. If you tighten down the pressure cooker too much, it's going to explode."[8] Making national policy means finding ways of persuading members who represent different constituencies, regions, ideologies, values, and interests to support legislation that addresses national concerns. "The only thing that counts is 218 votes, and nothing else is real," a House leader declared. "You have to be able [to attract a majority of the House] to pass a bill."[9] Implicit in this party leader's statement is recognition that mobilizing winning coalitions is not easy. Party leaders encounter what scholars call a "collective action" dilemma.[10] How can leaders mobilize a majority to pass legislation for the collective or public good when it is in the self-interest of lawmakers to reject the difficult trade-offs that are frequently required? Lawmakers prefer to free ride on the efforts of their colleagues. If legislation is enacted, members can claim credit and their constituents can receive benefits, but they do not want to suffer the political pain that typically accompanies successful negotiation. Instead, they want to dodge responsibility for making the compromises necessary to pass legislation, especially the difficult concessions required during conditions of divided government. Of course, when there are too many free riders, little lawmaking gets done. Congressional leaders resolve the collective action problem in two main ways: devising sufficient incentives (political, policy, or procedural) to attract majority support, and coordinating the work of the bill's champions to win desired objectives.

Taking account of the two Congresses requires party leaders to assume roles both inside and outside the institution. In their inside role, party leaders formulate policy agendas and use their procedural and organizational authority to advance them. In their outside role, party leaders articulate and publicize issue positions designed to galvanize partisan support and swing voters. They also help recruit candidates for Congress and assist in their campaigns. Leaders' inside and outside roles are inextricably intertwined. They serve as their party's link to the president, the press, the public, and the party faithful. In today's era of ideological polarization and intense electoral competition, the line between campaigning and governing has all but disappeared. Locked in a permanent campaign, leaders try to generate public momentum either to force legislative action on party priorities or to create issues to take to the voters in the next election. "The reality is, to get something done in this town you've got to deal with the policy and the politics," explained representative (now senator) Rob Portman, R-Ohio.[11]

Congress is a partisan body—that is, legislative organization is partisan organization. The majority party in the House and Senate controls not only the top leadership posts but also the chairmanships and majorities on committees and subcommittees. With these tools, the majority party is generally able to control the legislative agenda.

THE SPEAKER OF THE HOUSE

No other congressional leader possesses the visibility and authority of the Speaker. "Because the Speakership is the only leadership position in Congress whose existence and method of selection is mandated by the Constitution," writes political scientist Matthew N. Green, "the office possesses considerable prestige."[12] Although the Constitution does not require the Speaker to be a House member, all of them have been. Under the Presidential Succession Act of 1947, the Speaker is next in line behind the vice president to succeed to the presidency.

The office of Speaker combines procedural and political prerogatives with policy and partisan leadership. Speakers preside over the House, meaning that they rule on points of order, announce the results of votes, refer legislation to committees, name lawmakers to serve on conference committees and select committees, and maintain order and decorum in the House chamber. In addition to these procedural prerogatives, they exercise important political powers. They set the House's agenda of activities, control the Rules Committee, chair or influence the decisions of their party's committee assignment panel, bestow or withhold various rewards, coordinate policy making with Senate counterparts, and, in this age of television and Internet communications, expound party and House positions to the public at large. In practice, Speakers today seldom actually preside over the House because they focus so much attention on external activities, such as campaigning for party members, fund-raising, and message development.

Speakers are formally elected by the members of the House. Today's Speakers have served long careers in the House, over which they have built relationships with fellow members and risen through the ranks of their party. Speakers elected since 1899 have served, on average, more than twenty years before their election to the post. Both Boehner and Pelosi had served twenty years before becoming Speaker.

Once in office, Speakers traditionally have been reelected as long as their party has controlled the House. Members typically vote for the speakership along straight party lines. Not since 1923 has there been a floor battle over the speakership, because one party has always enjoyed a clear majority. As chief parliamentary officer and leader of the majority party (see Figure 6-1), the Speaker enjoys unique powers in scheduling floor business and in recognizing members during sessions. Occasionally, Speakers will relinquish the gavel to join in the floor debate. Recent Speakers, including Dennis Hastert and Pelosi, often voted on issues before the House.[13]

The Speaker is also in charge of administrative matters. The current administrative structure was established after Speaker Newt Gingrich took office in 1994. Gingrich's reforms abolished administrative units, streamlined and modernized management, undertook an independent audit of the accounting systems, and assigned responsibility to a new chief administrative officer—elected by the House at the start of each Congress—for running the House's administrative operations in a professional manner.[14]

The Changing Role of the Speaker

House rules permit a determined majority to achieve its policy objectives, but it was not always so. Before 1890, intense battles were fought over the majority party's right to govern and the minority party's right to have input. Throughout most of the nineteenth century, the House minority possessed a variety of stalling tactics that often frustrated House decision making.[15] In the 1890s, however, Republican Speaker Thomas "Czar" Reed of Maine finally curtailed the minority's capacity for obstruction. The House adopted procedures (the famous Reed Rules) to facilitate action on the basis of majority rule, including an 1890 House rule, still in effect: "No dilatory motion shall be entertained by the Speaker."

By 1910 Speaker Joseph G. Cannon, R-Ill., dominated the House: assigning members to committees, appointing and removing committee chairs, referring bills to committee, regulating the flow of bills to the House floor as chair of the Rules Committee, and controlling floor debate. Taken individually, Cannon's powers were little different from those of his immediate predecessors, but taken together and exercised to their limits, they bordered on dictatorial. The result was a revolt. Progressive Republicans joined with discontented minority Democrats to reduce the Speaker's authority.

FIGURE 6-1 Organization of the House of Representatives, 113th Congress, 2013–2015

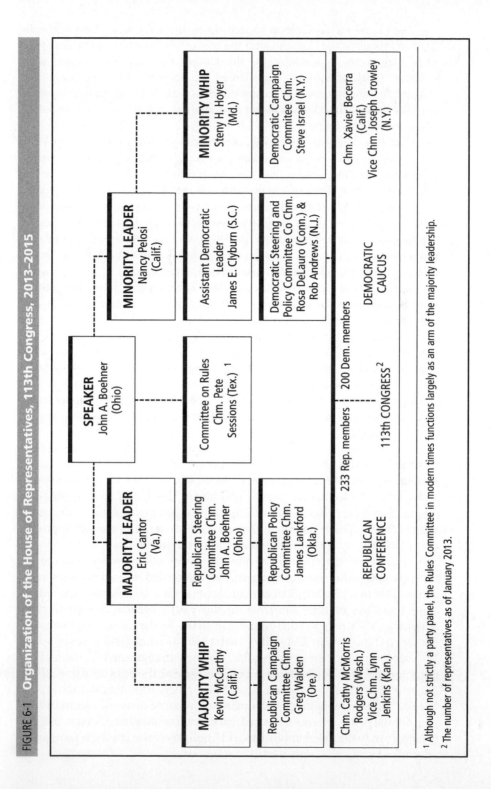

SPEAKER
John A. Boehner
(Ohio)

Committee on Rules
Chm. Pete
Sessions (Tex.) [1]

MAJORITY LEADER
Eric Cantor
(Va.)

Republican Steering
Committee Chm.
John A. Boehner
(Ohio)

Republican Policy
Committee Chm.
James Lankford
(Okla.)

MAJORITY WHIP
Kevin McCarthy
(Calif.)

Republican Campaign
Committee Chm.
Greg Walden
(Ore.)

Chm. Cathy McMorris
Rodgers (Wash.)
Vice Chm. Lynn
Jenkins (Kan.)

REPUBLICAN
CONFERENCE

MINORITY LEADER
Nancy Pelosi
(Calif.)

Assistant Democratic
Leader
James E. Clyburn (S.C.)

Democratic Steering and
Policy Committee Co Chm.
Rosa DeLauro (Conn.) &
Rob Andrews (N.J.)

MINORITY WHIP
Steny H. Hoyer
(Md.)

Democratic Campaign
Committee Chm.
Steve Israel (N.Y.)

Chm. Xavier Becerra
(Calif.)
Vice Chm. Joseph Crowley
(N.Y.)

DEMOCRATIC
CAUCUS

233 Rep. members   200 Dem. members

113th CONGRESS [2]

[1] Although not strictly a party panel, the Rules Committee in modern times functions largely as an arm of the majority leadership.

[2] The number of representatives as of January 2013.

The House forced Cannon to step down from the Rules Committee in 1910 and required the House to elect the committee's members. The next year, when Democrats took control of the House, the new Speaker, James B. "Champ" Clark of Missouri, was denied the authority to make committee assignments, and his power of recognition was curtailed. The speakership then went into long-term eclipse as power flowed briefly to party caucuses and then to the committee chairs.

Over time after the 1910 revolt, committees became more powerful relative to party leaders. Power in Congress was diffused among a relatively small number of committee chairs, who were often called the "dukes" or "barons" of Capitol Hill. These chairs rose to power by means of a nearly inviolable seniority system, in which each committee's longest-serving majority party member served as chair until death, resignation, or retirement. This system tended to elevate to top committee posts the long-serving conservative southern Democrats from safe seats, a process that eventually yielded committee chairs who were out of step with the preferences of party leaders.

Working from a more constricted office, Speakers after Cannon exhibited various leadership styles. The longest-serving Speaker in history, Democrat Sam Rayburn of Texas (1940–1947, 1949–1953, 1955–1961), functioned largely as a broker or mediator, negotiating with the powerful chairs to report out legislation supported by the Democratic majority. Rayburn used his personal prestige as well as his long political experience and immense parliamentary skills to provide coherence for a decentralized chamber. As he explained, "The old day of pounding on the desk and giving people hell is gone. A man's got to lead by persuasion and kindness and the best reason—that's the only way he can lead people."[16]

The distribution of power in the House of Representatives changed fundamentally during the 1970s. Activist, liberal lawmakers elected during the Vietnam War and the Watergate era found themselves frustrated by the conservative tilt of the committee barons. This liberal bloc joined forces with other longtime members disgruntled with the status quo to curb the power of committee chairs. These reformist Democrats took a two-pronged approach toward transforming the distribution of power in the House.

First, the reformers sought to limit the ability of committee chairs to act independently. After years of agitation, they succeeded in making chairs more accountable to their party. Rather than allowing them to hold their chairmanships regardless of their adherence to the party's agenda, new party rules adopted in 1973 required that committee chairs be elected by secret ballot of the Democratic Caucus. Committee chairs were also obligated to share power with subcommittee chairs. Second, the reformers strengthened the hand of the party leadership. The Speaker, for example, gained the right to name all the majority party members of the Rules Committee, including the chair. The Speaker was also permitted to refer measures to more than one committee.

Although the reforms enhanced party leaders' powers, Speakers did not exploit them to the fullest immediately. Instead, power was gradually centralized in the majority party leadership over many subsequent Congresses. By the late 1970s, rank-and-file Democrats were encouraging their party leaders to use their new powers to overcome institutional fragmentation and to curb the minority Republicans' ability to obstruct action on the floor. Longtime Speaker Thomas P. "Tip" O'Neill Jr. (D-Mass., 1977–1987) strengthened the office by drawing Democratic rank-and-file members into the leadership orbit, expanding the whip structure, and creating leadership task forces to allow them input on party priorities.[17] O'Neill's successor, Speaker Jim Wright (D-Texas, 1987–1989), pushed the prerogatives of the office further. His unyielding personal style and knack for making "minority status more painful," as one House GOP leader put it, embittered Republicans (and even some of his own party).[18] Wright's tenure in office ended in the wake of ethics charges successfully initiated against him by an energetic up-and-coming Republican, Newt Gingrich. Speaker Thomas S. Foley, D-Wash. (1989–1995), had a reputation for being a judicious, low-key, and consensus-oriented leader, and his initial objectives were to restore civility and bipartisan cooperation. Although Republicans found Foley easier to deal with than Wright, they soon lamented the Speaker's willingness to use procedural rules to frustrate GOP objectives. Foley began to make far more extensive use of the Rules Committee to shape the floor agenda and restrict amending opportunities. In a departure from his predecessors, Foley favored the use of restrictive rules to govern the consideration of most legislation.[19]

The Contemporary Speaker. Speaker Newt Gingrich, R-Ga., took the office of Speaker to new heights. In the lead-up to the 1994 elections, Gingrich had spearheaded a ten-point party platform called "The Contract with America." Almost all House Republican candidates pledged to act on every item in the platform within the first hundred days of the 104th Congress if their party won a majority. Gingrich was widely credited with the GOP's sweeping victory in the 1994 elections: "[Gingrich is] the one responsible for leading the Republican Party out of the wilderness of the minority to the promised land of the majority," said one GOP House member.[20]

In the immediate aftermath of the Republicans' taking control of the House, GOP lawmakers observed a parliamentary model of governance marching in lockstep with their "prime minister." Everything in the ten-point contract except term limits for lawmakers passed the House within a hundred days. Gingrich also adopted a wide array of institutional changes that centralized power in his office. He curbed the independence of committees by personally selecting committee members and chairs who would strongly support his agenda—and, when necessary, he ignored seniority in the process. In addition, he required the GOP members of the Appropriations Committee to sign a written pledge that they would heed the leadership's directives for spending reductions. During his speakership, he often bypassed committees entirely by establishing leadership task forces to process legislation. Most significant, he changed the House rules to impose a six-year term limit on all committee and subcommittee chairs, so no chair could accumulate enough influence to challenge the central party leaders. In short, party power came to dominate committee power.

But Gingrich did not remain Speaker for long. Two extended face-offs with President Bill Clinton in late 1995 and early 1996 resulted in highly unpopular shutdowns of ongoing government operations, for which the public blamed the Republicans, not President Clinton.[21] In 1996, after President Clinton was reelected, Gingrich faced ethics charges of his own. Two weeks after Gingrich's reelection as Speaker, the House voted 395–28 to reprimand and fine him for ethical misconduct related to inaccurate financial information he had given the House Ethics Committee. Weakened, Gingrich no longer dominated the House as he once had. When the 1998 midterm results came in, Republicans were shell-shocked at their poor showing, and many blamed Gingrich for the losses. He then left the speakership and resigned from the House.

Gingrich's successor as Speaker, Dennis Hastert, R-Ill. (1999–2007), played a less visible role outside the House, but inside the institution he was no less powerful than Gingrich. The longest-serving GOP Speaker, Hastert exercised "top-down" command of the House and followed a partisan governing strategy on party-preferred measures. "The job of the Speaker," he said, "is not to expedite legislation that runs counter to the wishes of the majority of his majority."[22] Hastert maintained a modest public profile, sharing his national spokesman's role with other Republicans: "I don't think I have to be [at] the head of every news release or press conference, and on every Sunday talk show," he mused.[23] At the same time, he consolidated power in the party's top leadership.

Hastert and his leadership team were not reluctant to direct rank-and-file members or committee chairs to toe the line on issues important to the party. For example, during a GOP conference meeting, Veterans' Affairs chair Christopher H. Smith of New Jersey criticized the Republicans' budget resolution and the White House's spending proposals for veterans. Speaker Hastert "got up and shut him down," said a witness to the tongue-lashing. "I've never seen anything like that. It was scathing."[24] When Smith refused to curb his advocacy of more spending for veterans, GOP leaders removed Smith as Veterans' Affairs chair and even from the committee itself.

The trend toward centralization of power in the Speaker's office was not reversed under Hastert's successor, Nancy Pelosi (D-Calif., 2007–2011). Her elevation to the speakership was historic in that she was the first woman to rise so high in American politics, but Speaker Pelosi's leadership style largely tracked the "top-down," centralized model of her two immediate predecessors, Gingrich and Hastert. Despite having criticized the Republican majority's restrictions on open debate and full committee consideration of bills, Pelosi employed similar limitations on committees and inputs from the minority party. Under Pelosi's leadership, committee chairs enjoyed a somewhat more prominent role, but this shift did not entail a more decentralized process in which committees enjoyed free rein. Instead, legislation was often worked out in an ad hoc manner behind closed doors in leadership offices.[25] A wide-ranging Brookings Institution report on congressional operations and policy making in the 110th Congress (2007–2009) concluded that "a pattern of tighter, more centralized control—which began more than two decades ago under Democratic rule and then intensified under Republican majorities, especially after the 2000 election—continues unabated."[26]

Although the current Speaker, John Boehner, indicated an intention to lead the House in a more inclusive manner than his recent predecessors, there is no indication that the balance of House power has shifted back in the direction of committee chairs. Even as minority leader, Boehner demonstrated a willingness to bring ranking members to account when they acted in ways harmful to the party. For example, when Joe L. Barton, R-Texas, ranking member of the Energy Committee, apologized to BP's CEO for President Barack Obama's "$20 billion shakedown" of the company to cover damages from the 2010 Gulf oil spill, Boehner quickly summoned Barton to demand a public retraction.[27] After becoming Speaker, Boehner signaled that he would ensure committee activities were carried out in a way that would serve the leadership's broader interests.[28] Following the 2012 elections, Boehner's Steering Committee stripped four members of their committee assignments as punishment for their intransigence and willingness to criticize fellow Republicans.[29]

Although Boehner has asserted discipline over committees, he has taken a more tolerant stance toward the Republican rank and file. "The House works best when it is allowed to work its will," says Boehner.[30] Boehner has repeatedly been unable to hold his party's ranks together on high-stakes issues. With conservatives refusing to go along with bipartisan deals, Boehner has had to rely on Democratic votes to pass important legislation, such as to raise the debt ceiling or to keep the government operating. The tension between ardently conservative rank-and-file Republicans skeptical of compromise and the need to pass legislation that can also win approval from a Democratic Senate and president presents challenges for centralized leadership in the 113th Congress.

The Speaker's Influence: Style and Context

Congressional analysts disagree about the extent to which congressional leaders can influence policy outcomes. Compared with legislative party leaders in many other democracies, party leaders in Congress unquestionably have fewer tools to induce party loyalty among lawmakers. Nevertheless, congressional leaders enjoy more institutional authority at some times than at others. In general, political scientists stress context over personal style as the main factor affecting the Speaker's institutional clout. Political scientists have developed a theory—conditional party government—to explain why congressional leaders appear to be stronger during some eras than others.[31]

Conditional party government theory posits that if partisans share common policy views and confront an opposition party with sharply different policy preferences, then these dual conditions favor strong centralized leadership. Rank-and-file partisans (the principals) will empower their party leaders (agents) to advance an agenda that nearly all of them support. According to the two leading proponents of this theory:

> These two considerations—preference homogeneity [or policy agreement within parties] and preference conflict [or policy disagreement between parties]—together form the "condition" in the theory of conditional party government. As these increase, the theory predicts that party members will be progressively more willing to create strong powers for leaders and to support the exercise of those powers in specific instances. But when diversity grows within parties, or the differences between parties are reduced, members will be reluctant to grant greater powers to leaders. This is the central prediction of [conditional party government].[32]

Conditional party government theory provides an explanation for the changing role of the Speaker. Speaker Sam Rayburn's role as cautious broker and negotiator, for example, makes sense in light of fractures within the Democratic Party during the 1950s. During Rayburn's era—and for many years afterward—congressional Democrats were deeply divided between their northern and southern wings. Southern Democrats tended to be more conservative than their northern colleagues on a number of significant political issues, particularly civil rights and labor regulations (such as minimum wage laws, union organizing, and business-labor relations). On such matters, southern Democrats often allied themselves with Republicans in a voting pattern known as the conservative coalition. Recognizing these divisions, Rayburn had to lead cautiously. Just bringing the Democratic Caucus together could be politically explosive, so Rayburn rarely convened the caucus.[33] Instead, he dealt with members on a personalized, individual basis.

According to the theory of conditional party government, Rayburn's style of leadership was not merely a personal stylistic choice, it was also a way of coping with intractable conflict within the party. Under such conditions, rank-and-file Democrats simply would not trust their Speaker with expansive procedural and political powers.

By the same token, the conditional party government perspective views the forceful leadership of recent Speakers in light of changes in the political context. Since the 1960s, regional realignments have created far more ideological consensus *within* each of the two congressional parties, and considerably less ideological agreement *between* the two parties than existed during the 1950s and 1960s. After the enfranchisement of southern African Americans in the 1960s, the Democratic Party in the South began to elect Democrats (such as John Lewis of Georgia) who were more responsive to African American constituents and more ideologically compatible with their party colleagues from the rest of the country. Meanwhile, conservative southern whites gradually moved into the Republican Party. Because the South is now largely in the GOP camp, today's Democratic Party mostly lacks the deep regional divisions that characterized the earlier era. Constituency change in the North reinforced this ideological homogenization of the parties. Moderate "Rockefeller

Republicans" have largely disappeared in the Northeast, and the conservative coalition is no longer an important voting bloc in Congress. As a result of these constituency changes, the two parties are more internally coherent in their policy preferences.

This new context helps explain the assertive styles of contemporary Speakers. The rank-and-file members of both parties are more willing to trust their leaders with institutional authority. For example, contemporary Speakers of both parties have been given more influence over committee assignments, allowing them to appoint like-minded members to coveted committees. By stacking important committees with loyal partisans, a Speaker raises the likelihood that they will report legislation that the Speaker favors. Individual members also recognize that they owe their committee assignments in part to the Speaker. Given the greater willingness of members to tolerate hierarchical leadership, recent Speakers have been able to dictate to committee chairs, advance party agendas, and take procedural actions to hamstring the minority party. Their personal talents have been augmented by formal and informal procedural changes that have raised the likelihood that their objectives would be realized.

Not all scholars accept the conditional party government account. An alternative theory—the pivotal voter theory—eschews intense focus on parties and leaders as a way to understand Congress. This perspective points to the many limits on the ability of party leaders to shift policy outcomes away from what a majority of the chamber prefers toward the policy preferences of the majority party.[34] Proponents of this theory argue that policy outcomes on the floor rarely diverge from what is acceptable to the pivotal voter—in the House, the member who casts the 218th vote. Furthermore, they argue that majority members who disagree with the leadership's position are unlikely to change their policy views to back the party. Why would they vote to support a policy with which they disagree? Instead, they will join with members of the other party to form a winning coalition, just as conservative southern Democrats once did with conservative Republicans—the so-called conservative coalition that shaped legislative policy making for a good part of the twentieth century. When a majority party is internally unified, there will be no difference between what it prefers and what the chamber majority will agree to, but when the majority party is divided, it is unable to enforce its agenda unless it can command a majority. Simply observing party leaders engaged in frenetic activity—often seeking pivotal votes—does not mean that they can skew legislative outcomes in the majority's favor. From this vantage point, the important question for understanding Congress is simply the distribution of policy preferences in the chamber as a whole, not the activities and powers of party leaders and party organizations.

Other critics of conditional party government emphasize that leadership is by no means entirely determined by the political context. "Leadership in Congress occurs within an institutional context that imposes limits," writes Randall Strahan, "but some leaders take advantage of those opportunities and others do not. Leadership involves not only the conditions that make leadership possible but also the choice of the leader to act."[35] Adroit and forceful Speakers can lead by molding circumstances and seizing opportunities favoring their own objectives.[36] In short, Speakers' personal capacities allow them to exercise that elusive quality called leadership—that is, an ability to persuade others to follow even when they disagree with their leaders' views.

House Floor Leaders

The Speaker's principal deputy—the majority leader—is the party's floor leader. As former majority leader Tom DeLay (R-Texas, 1997–2003) said of his relationship with Speaker Hastert, "I see it that Hastert is the chairman of the board and I am the chief executive officer."[37] Elected every two years by secret ballot of the party caucus, the floor leader is not to be confused with a floor manager. Floor managers—usually two for each bill and frequently the chair and ranking minority member of the committee that reported the bill—are appointed to steer particular bills to a final vote.

The House majority leader is usually an experienced legislator. The current majority leader, Eric Cantor, R-Va., rose to the post fairly quickly; he was elected to Congress in 2000, only ten years before taking on that position. His elevation to top leadership reflected his skill as party whip in bridging divergent elements in the Republican Conference, as well as his energetic, forward-looking approach to getting House Republicans to embrace new communications technologies to reach supportive groups beyond Capitol Hill.[38]

House and party rules are largely silent about the majority's leader's duties. By tradition, the primary duties are to serve as principal strategist and spokesperson for the party and to monitor the House floor. By modern custom, neither the Speaker nor the Democratic or Republican leaders chair committees,[39] but they may serve on formal or informal task forces or panels. For example, the Speaker and minority leader are ex officio members of the Permanent Select Intelligence Committee.

To plan the daily, weekly, and annual legislative agendas, Cantor must consult widely. He meets regularly with committee chairs to discuss their schedule of activities, review pertinent legislative issues, and coordinate chamber action with the party's floor managers. He also gauges sentiment on legislation among rank-and-file members and urges them to support or reject measures. As one majority leader said, "The Majority Leader has prime responsibility for the day-to-day working of the House, the schedule, working with the committees to keep an eye out for what bills are coming, getting them scheduled, getting the work of the House done, making the place function correctly." He added that the majority leader must also "articulate to the outside world" what his or her party stands for and is trying to do.[40]

The minority leader is the floor leader of the loyal opposition. Like the majority leader, the minority leader promotes unity among party colleagues, monitors the progress of bills through committees and subcommittees, and forges coalitions in support of proposals. However, the minority leader is more often in a reactive position, criticizing the majority party's initiatives and developing alternatives to them. Bertrand Snell, R-N.Y., minority leader from 1931 to 1939, described the duties:

> He is spokesman for his party and enunciates its policies. He is required to be alert and vigilant in defense of the minority's rights. It is his function and duty to criticize constructively the policies and program of the majority, and to this end employ parliamentary tactics and give close attention to all proposed legislation.[41]

Former Speaker Nancy Pelosi is minority leader in the 113th Congress, "the first sitting speaker to move across the hall to the minority leader's office since 1955."[42] Most members of the Democratic Caucus decided to keep Pelosi, a seasoned leader, rather than go with a newcomer. While a sizable contingent questioned the wisdom of retaining Pelosi—with her low approval ratings—as the public face of the party after Democrats lost their majority in 2010, she held onto the office on a 129–68 vote. Her prodigious fund-raising—more than $328 million for Democratic candidates since joining the elected party leadership as whip in 2002—established a track record that many members were reluctant to question.[43] There was also no question about her effectiveness in holding the party together to achieve remarkable legislative victories.[44] In 2012 she was reelected to the minority leadership unanimously.

The minority leader must forge party unity by managing internal conflicts and resolving intraparty disagreements. Perhaps the most important job of the minority leader is to craft a strategy to win back majority control of the House. In this respect, the minority leader must decide whether to cooperate with or to confront the majority party. By working with the majority, the minority party can often influence legislation more to its followers' liking. However, cooperation entails supporting the majority party's legislation on the floor— an often unpleasant task.

A minority party can instead pursue a strategy of confrontation. By consistently offering an alternative vision on issues of the day, the minority party can build the case for its return to power. In the 111th Congress, then–minority leader Boehner signaled that House Republicans would focus more on confrontation than on cooperation. "I have been trying to get my Republican colleagues to understand that we are not in the legislative business," Boehner remarked at a lunch with reporters.[45] There is no set formula for how to win back majority control of the House, because many of the electoral and political forces and events that influence majority status are beyond party leaders' control.[46]

House Whips

Another top elective party post is that of chief whip. As the term implies, the whip and the whip's team of deputies and regional whips encourage party discipline, count votes, and, in general, mobilize winning coalitions on behalf of partisan priorities. To do so, the chief whip serves as liaison between the party's rank-and-file membership and its leaders. The whip assembles and communicates political and policy intelligence, assigns deputy whips to take the "temperature" of the various factional groups within the party, and provides the party's members with scheduling information.

Accurate vote counting is a whip's most important skill. When Kevin McCarthy, R-Calif., the new House Republican majority whip, asked veteran former whips for advice, they told him, "You need to know your count, and you don't share your count."[47] Members' voting predilections on important procedural and substantive issues are typically classified as "yea," "leaning yea," "undecided," "leaning no," and "no." Former majority whip James Clyburn, D-S.C., used a fishing metaphor to explain his procedure for forging winning coalitions:

> When it comes to working with the Democratic Caucus I have to fish in a lot of ponds. I go fishing with the Blue Dogs [fiscally conservative Democrats]. I go fishing with the New Dems [moderate Democrats]. I go fishing with the Hispanics and I go fishing with the Asian Pacific Islanders, trying to cobble together the 218 votes I need.[48]

First elected to the House in 2006, McCarthy's rise to top leadership as majority whip in 2011 was quick. Despite the short time frame, he had distinguished himself as lead author of the House Republican "Pledge to America," a party platform document for the 2010 elections. In addition, he is one of the coauthors (along with Paul Ryan from Wisconsin and Eric Cantor) of *Young Guns,* a small-government manifesto designed to raise the authors' profiles as young, reform-minded Republican leaders.[49] McCarthy's effectiveness as whip is enhanced by his ability to avoid being too closely associated with any one faction in his party. "Moderates think he's a moderate. Conservatives think he's a conservative," says Tony Strickland, a former Republican colleague of McCarthy's in the California Assembly.[50]

In recent years, both parties have expanded their whip teams. The whip team meets regularly to discuss issues and strategy. The larger the whip team, the larger the number of members involved in leadership decision making and the more incentives they have to back their top leaders. As a former GOP majority whip stated, with a sixty-person GOP whip organization, it is feasible "to reach everybody in the [Republican] Conference and deliver their votes when it counts."[51] A larger whip team also ensures leadership representation for important party groups and broadens the party's appeal to outside constituencies. In a conference with 234 members, an extended whip team allows a division of labor as well. "Grunt work is subcontracted out to whip team members," such as Rep. Jeff Denham, R-Calif., and Rep. Devin Nunes, R-Calif. "Each is typically assigned two or three House colleagues.... [W]hip team members take cards from the GOP cloakroom, approach their assigned colleagues and check the appropriate box on the card reflecting the lawmaker's intentions."[52]

LEADERS OF THE SENATE

Unlike the House, today's Senate is an institution that tolerates and even promotes individualism. Candidate-centered elections, the proliferation of policy and ideological interest groups, the large role of money in campaigns, the staff resources available to every senator, and senators' needs to seek news media coverage are among the factors that have led to today's individualistic Senate. Senators cherish and assert their independence, which intensifies the challenges faced by those elected to lead them. Unlike their House counterparts, Senate leaders lack institutional prerogatives and procedures designed to facilitate majority rule, and therefore must rely heavily on personal skills and negotiation with colleagues of both parties.

Presiding Officers

The House majority's highest elected leader, the Speaker, has the authority to preside over the House. By contrast, the Senate's majority leader, the majority party's highest leader, almost never presides in the Senate chamber.

The Senate has three kinds of presiding officers. First, the constitutional president of the Senate is the vice president of the United States (see Figure 6-2). Except for ceremonial occasions, the vice president seldom presides over Senate sessions and can vote only to break—not make—a tie. When votes on major issues are expected to be close, party leaders make sure that the vice president is presiding so he can break the tie.

Second, the Constitution provides for a president pro tempore to preside in the vice president's absence. In modern practice, this is the majority party senator with the longest continuous service. Sen. Patrick Leahy, D-Vt., is president pro tempore of the Democratic-controlled Senate of the 113th Congress (2013–2015). By passing a simple resolution, the Senate sometimes appoints a deputy president pro tempore. This majority party official presides over the Senate in the absence of the vice president and president pro tempore.

Third, a dozen or so senators of the majority party, typically junior members, serve approximately one-hour stints each day as the presiding officer. The opportunity to preside helps newcomers become familiar with Senate rules and procedures.

Floor Leaders

The majority leader is the head of the majority party in the Senate, its leader on the floor, and the leader of the Senate. Similarly, the minority leader heads the Senate's minority party (today, minority leaders prefer to be called "Republican leader" or "Democratic leader," as the case may be). The majority and minority leaders are elected biennially by secret ballot of their party colleagues. Neither position is mentioned in the Constitution; they are relatively recent creations that date from the early 1900s.

Emergence of the Floor Leader. Historically, the Senate has always had leaders, but no single senator exercised central management of the legislative process in the fashion of today's floor leader. During the Senate's first century or so—especially in the 1790s and early 1800s, when there was no system of permanent standing committees or organized senatorial parties—leadership flowed from the personal talents and abilities of individual legislators.

FIGURE 6-2 Organization of the Senate, 113th Congress, 2013–2015

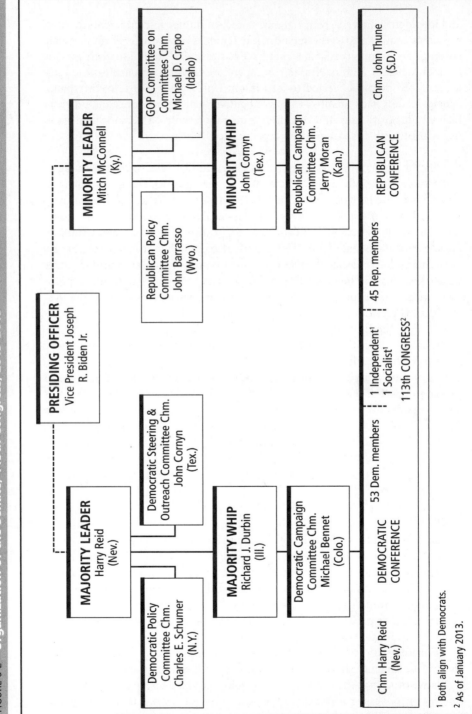

[1] Both align with Democrats.

[2] As of January 2013.

The small size of the early Senate promoted an informal and personal style of leadership. Throughout the nineteenth century, scores of prominent senators were called "leaders" by scholars and other observers. Some were sectional or factional leaders; others headed important committees (by the mid- to late 1840s committees and their chairs were centers of power); and still others (such as Henry Clay, John C. Calhoun, and Daniel Webster) exercised wide influence because of their special political, oratorical, or intellectual gifts. Even as late as 1885, however, Woodrow Wilson could write: "No one is *the Senator*. No one exercises the special trust of acknowledged leadership."[53]

By the turn of the twentieth century, the political landscape had changed. Party structures and leaders emerged as clearly identifiable forces for organizing and managing the Senate's proceedings. This important development occurred, according to a historian of the Senate, because of the influx of a "new breed" of senators who valued party unity and "the machinery of [party] organization," especially the party caucus.[54] Soon, those senators who chaired their respective party caucuses acquired levers of authority over senatorial affairs. They chaired important party panels, shaped the Senate's agenda of business, and mobilized party majorities behind important issues. By 1913 the position of majority leader had informally emerged out of the caucus chairmanship.[55]

Not until Lyndon B. Johnson (LBJ) became majority leader in 1955 was the post transformed into one of great authority and prestige.[56] Considered by many analysts to be the most influential majority leader ever, the Texas Democrat had an extensive network of trusted aides and colleagues who gave him better information about more issues than any other senator. Opposition party control of the White House under President Dwight D. Eisenhower gave the aggressive Johnson the luxury of choosing which policies to support and which strategies to employ to get them enacted. Armed with a pragmatic outlook, domineering style, and legendary arm-twisting abilities, Johnson became the premier vote-gatherer in the Senate. The majority leader's display of face-to-face persuasion was called the "Johnson Treatment":

> The Treatment could last ten minutes or four hours. It came, enveloping its target, at the LBJ Ranch swimming pool, in one of LBJ's offices, in the Senate cloakroom, on the floor of the Senate itself. Its tone could be supplication, accusation, cajolery, exuberance, scorn, tears, complaint, the hint of threat. It was all of these together. It ran the gamut of human emotions. Its velocity was breathtaking, and it was all in one direction. Interjections from the target were rare. Johnson anticipated them before they could be spoken. He moved in close, his face a scant millimeter from his target, his eyes widening and narrowing, and his eyebrows rising and falling. From his pockets poured clippings, memos, statistics. Mimicry, humor, and the genius of analogy made The Treatment an almost hypnotic experience and rendered the target stunned and helpless.[57]

Buttressing Johnson was an inner club, a bipartisan group of senior senators. A particularly important ally within this inner club was Richard B. Russell of Georgia. The leader of southern Democrats and a lawmaker of immense influence, Russell endorsed Johnson as Democratic leader. (The Russell Senate Office Building on Capitol Hill is named for the Georgia senator.) The club, observers said, wielded the real power in the Senate through its dominance of most of the Senate's key committees and leadership positions.[58] Furthermore, unwritten rules of behavior (for example, junior members should be seen and not heard) encouraged new senators to defer to the establishment.

Today's majority leaders encounter a Senate that is much different from the one led by Johnson. Gone is the seniority-ruled, club-like, relatively closed Senate of old. It was ended largely by three key developments: the influx of independent-minded and activist senators who wanted and expected to be major policy participants; internal senatorial changes that promoted egalitarianism, such as the provision of staff resources to all members; and external developments in the broader political environment (such as the twenty-four-hour news cycle).

Together, these developments led to an individualistic Senate where leaders were expected to serve members' personal needs and advance their individual agendas. As former majority leader Robert C. Byrd, D-W.Va. (1977–1981, 1987–1989), once remarked about the egalitarian, individualistic, and C-SPAN–covered Senate: "Circumstances don't permit the Lyndon Johnson style. What I am saying is that times and things have changed. Younger Senators come into the Senate. They are more independent. The 'establishment' is a bad word. Each wants to do his 'own thing.'"[59] Similarly, the current majority leader, Harry Reid, D-Nev., said:

> I don't dictate how people vote. If it's an important vote, I try to tell them how important it is to the Senate, the country, the president. . . . But I'm not very good at twisting arms. I try to be more verbal and non-threatening. So there are going to be . . . a number of opportunities for people who have different opinions not to vote the way that I think they should. But that's the way it is. I hold no grudges.[60]

Limits on Today's Leadership: Individualism and Partisanship. If individualism characterizes the post-Johnson Senate, another development has added to leaders' difficulties in managing and processing the Senate's business: escalating partisanship. Unlike in the House, having a strong and cohesive party does not necessarily enable a Senate majority leader to govern. As discussed in more detail in Chapter 8, the Senate's rules do not permit the majority party leadership to set the agenda without input from the minority party. The majority leader must negotiate with the minority leader in scheduling legislation for floor consideration. To lead the Senate successfully, then, Senate leaders must achieve considerably more cross-party consensus than is necessary in the House.

As in the House, the two Senate parties have become, in the words of journalist David S. Broder, "more cohesive internally and further apart from each other philosophically."[61] Or, as Sen. Orrin G. Hatch, R-Utah, put it, "Today, most Democrats are far left; most Republicans are to the right; and there are very few in between."[62] The wide differences between the parties are grounded not only in members' personal policy preferences but also in the two parties' electoral interests, as each party seeks to establish clear reasons for voters to prefer it to the opposition.[63] Groups allied with the parties contribute to the widening divide. The two Congresses are very much in evidence as Democratic senators champion policies favored by their core national constituencies (such as environmentalists, gays, minorities, and union members), and Republican lawmakers do the same for their constituency base (such as the religious right, the Tea Party, business owners, gun owners, and antiabortion advocates).

What all this means for the majority leader is extraordinary difficulty in achieving the consensus needed to enact legislation and approve nominations. Any senator, regardless of party, has significant parliamentary powers to stymie action, which puts a premium on the leader's skill in negotiating and deal making. Lacking formidable leadership tools to exert tight control over chamber proceedings, Senate leaders rely heavily on patience, perseverance, personal ties, and, on occasion, procedural hardball to move legislation. If one or more senators engage in a filibuster (extended debate) on a matter, the majority leader faces an even higher hurdle: acquiring the sixty votes needed to end debate (that is, invoking a procedure called cloture) so the Senate can vote on the measure or matter. As a former majority leader reminisced:

> It's a tough job [being majority leader], and it has gotten tougher and tougher. Part of it is that now you don't need 50 votes—you've got to have 60 votes. The filibuster and cloture used to be used occasionally for big issues. [In more recent years], it has become an instrument used on almost every bill. You can have 51 votes, you can have 55 votes, but if you don't get 60 votes, [the bill] can die. And it is very hard to dredge up 60 votes.[64]

Majority leader Harry Reid frequently finds it impossible to push legislation past the procedural hurdles erected by the Senate minority. A former Golden Gloves boxer, he is, by all accounts, a blunt, tough, and savvy leader. "He's very shrewd and effective," points out former senator John Ensign, R-Nev. "Behind the scenes he is tenacious."[65] Despite his leadership skills and extensive legislative experience, Reid says: "The biggest challenge I have is results. If you have more than half [in the Senate], that doesn't mean you are going to win. You need to have multiple instances where you can create different coalitions to get to 60."[66] Part of Reid's game plan for achieving results is "a highly centralized leadership operation" with floor strategy and message operations managed from his office.[67] He promotes partisan cohesion by keeping note cards in a breast pocket of his jacket, "on which he records favors asked and promises made."[68] Nevertheless, many measures that cleared the Democratic-majority House in the 111th Congress (2009–2011) failed to pass the Democratic-majority Senate.

Minority Leader. The Senate minority leader consults continually with the majority leader because the Senate usually operates by consensus. Republican leader Mitch McConnell from Kentucky has said that he's "very fond" of Majority Leader Reid. "I think he wants to get solutions to problems, and so do I."[69] Getting things done in the Senate almost always requires cooperation across party lines.

The minority leader acts as his party's representative in any dealings with the president. When the minority leader is a member of the president's party, he or she has the traditional duties of pushing the administration's program and responding to partisan criticisms of the president. When in opposition, the minority leader has to calculate when to cooperate with and when to confront the president. Several times in recent years McConnell has taken on the role of deal-maker in negotiations with Vice President Joe Biden. For example, during the 2012 lame-duck session, the duo crafted a compromise that became law, averting a major tax increase on Americans scheduled to take effect at the start of 2013.

McConnell meets regularly with Senate Republicans to build party consensus, craft policy alternatives, and devise tactics to block or modify Democratic initiatives. He also works with his House counterpart to coordinate strategy and to develop and communicate a party agenda. Sen. Lamar Alexander, Tenn., said of his leader: "Mitch McConnell's strength is he knows the Senate and understands it is almost entirely based on personal relationships. Most successful leaders' strategy is silent, but he has a very good understanding of where each of us is, and he works with us privately."[70]

McConnell has also made it clear that the only way the Senate can function is on a bipartisan basis, with legislation containing provisions that appeal to Republicans. During the closely divided 110th Congress, he remarked that there is nothing Democrats "can do without some degree of cooperation from a very robust forty-nine-vote minority."[71]

At the same time, the minority leader is also always striving to win back control of the Senate. In pursuit of that goal, it is often useful for a minority leader to shun compromise. Bipartisan deals tend to blur the differences between the parties, and a minority party seeking to win more seats often wants to present clear alternatives to voters. McConnell made much use of this approach during the unified Democratic government of the 111th Congress (2009–2011). Reflecting on the party's strategy on health care reform, the budget, and economic stimulus, McConnell observed, "It was absolutely critical that everybody be together because if the proponents of the bill were able to say it was bipartisan, it tended to convey to the public that this is O.K., they must have figured it out. It's either bipartisan or it isn't."[72] The approach achieved many of its desired effects: it excited the Republican base, intensified media controversy, defined party lines, and weakened public confidence in President Obama and the Democratic congressional leadership. It did not, however, win back the Senate for the GOP, as the party remained in the minority following both the 2010 and 2012 elections.

Party Whips. The Senate's whip system carries out functions similar to those of the House, such as counting noses before crucial votes, monitoring floor activity, and fostering party consensus. Sen. Richard J. Durbin of Illinois is the majority whip of the 113th Congress, the Democrats' second in command in the senate. He heads a whip structure that includes a chief deputy whip and four deputy whips. Durbin and Reid complement each other. Reid excels at knowing the procedural "nuts and bolts" of the Senate. Durbin, also quite knowledgeable about procedure, is "very good at taking issues and making them resonate with the public, and he is good on the [Senate] floor and at message" development.[73] As Sen. Patty Murray, D-Wash., has noted, "He puts issues we're dealing with in real American language. I think he's really a good face for our party."[74]

The Senate's minority whip in the 113th Congress is Sen. John Cornyn of Texas. Cornyn was chair of the National Republican Senatorial Committee from 2009 to 2012, and he might have been seen as partly responsible for the party's disappointing failure to pick up seats in the 2012 election. His elevation to the whip position in November 2012 nevertheless reflects the esteem in which he is held by his party colleagues. In 2011 Cornyn tied seven other senators as "the most conservative senator," according to *National Journal*.[75] Cornyn's selection likely signals that the Senate Republicans will continue their strategy of shunning compromise with the Obama administration and Senate Democrats in the 113th Congress.

SELECTION OF LEADERS

Before the opening of each new Congress, senators and representatives elect their top leaders by secret ballot in their party caucuses. Although the whole House votes for the Speaker, the election is pro forma. With straight-party voting—the modern unspoken rule on this and other organizational matters— the majority party elects the Speaker.

Candidates for party leadership positions usually wage elaborate campaigns to win support from their partisan colleagues, with some launching websites to support their candidacy. Jack Kingston, R-Ga., launched a "video blog outlining his credentials" in his unsuccessful attempt to be the House GOP conference chair.[76] Occasionally, last-minute entrants successfully bid for leadership positions. But whether brief or lengthy, campaigns for party leadership positions are intense. Members understand that a party leadership post can be a "career launching pad either within the [Congress] or outside it."[77]

Both House and Senate leaders are generally chosen from the mainstream of their respective parties. As political scientist David Truman observed as long ago as 1959, party leaders tend to be "middlemen" in their parties—in ideological terms, from neither the far left nor the right fringes.[78] A recent study examining all open leadership contests over the past hundred years determined that leaders tend to be closer to their party's ideological median than would happen by chance, but also that Democratic leaders tend to come from the left of the party median and Republican leaders from the right of the party median.[79] It also appears that these patterns are evident early in the selection process, suggesting that candidates with these profiles are more likely to seek leadership positions in the first place.

Seniority in Congress is one of many criteria that influence the election of party leaders. Other considerations are geographical balance within the leadership; parliamentary expertise; competency in organizational matters; skill in forging winning coalitions; fund-raising prowess; communication skills; sensitivity to the mood of the membership; and personal attributes such as intelligence, fairness, persuasiveness, political shrewdness, and media savvy. Gender balance may be becoming a more important consideration, as the number of women lawmakers rises. For example, female representation was a prominent consideration in the most hotly contested leadership battle of 2012, as Republicans selected Rep. Cathy McMorris Rodgers, R-Wash., for the number four leadership slot over Rep. Tom Price, R-Ga.[80]

Although serving as a party leader in the House is typically a full-time position, every party leader in the Senate sits on one or more committee. The smaller size of the Senate allows leaders to participate in committee work while discharging their leadership duties. In the Senate of the 113th Congress, for example, Reid, McConnell, Durbin, and Cornyn each serve on standing committees.

LEADERSHIP ACTIVITIES

Leadership duties can be broadly described as institutional maintenance (ensuring that Congress and its members perform their lawmaking and oversight duties and preserving Congress's reputation and integrity) and party maintenance (crafting winning coalitions among partisan colleagues and providing assistance to their members).[81] These two tasks are often blended, as leaders perform their institutional tasks in ways that simultaneously serve their party. Nevertheless, congressional leaders have responsibilities for the basic functioning of Congress that transcend party politics.

Institutional Tasks

From an institutional perspective, party leaders have various obligations. To help them carry out these diverse responsibilities, their chamber gives them extra staff resources.

Organizing the Chamber. Party leaders select the top administrative officers of both houses of Congress, such as the clerk of the House and the secretary of the Senate. These officers are important for the day-to-day functioning of the chambers even if they are invisible to the public. Party leaders also oversee committee jurisdictional revisions and revise congressional rules. Speaker Gingrich backed the abolition of three standing committees in 1995, and Speaker Hastert supported a major recodification of House rules in 1999, the first since 1880.

Scheduling Floor Business. "The power of the Speaker of the House is the power of scheduling," Speaker O'Neill once declared.[82] Or, as Newt

Gingrich put it, "When you are Speaker you get to set the agenda. . . . [Y]ou get to decide what legislation is up."[83] After consulting with committee leaders, interested members, the president, and others, House and Senate party leaders decide what, when, how, and in which order measures should come up for debate. Setting the chamber's agenda and schedule—determining what each chamber will debate—is perhaps the single most important prerogative of the Speaker and Senate majority leader. Scheduling legislation is a basic task that must be managed for the institution to function at all, but leaders also act strategically in their party's interests as they make these decisions.

Once a bill is scheduled for action, the job of the leaders is to see that members vote—a task more difficult than merely herding bodies into the chamber. Party leaders may seek out certain members to speak on an issue because their endorsement can persuade other legislators to support it. Or they may delay action until the bill's sponsors are present. "The leadership must have the right members at the right place at the right time," said Robert Byrd (D-W.Va.)when he was the Senate majority whip.[84] Although leaders generally seek to influence members of their own party and chamber, they also try to win cooperation from the other chamber and from the opposition party.

Leaders' scheduling prerogatives mold policy outcomes; the point at which bills reach the floor can seal their fate. A week's delay in scheduling a controversial White House initiative, for example, may give the president, lobbying groups, and others additional time to muster votes for the proposal. Depending on the circumstances, delay may also afford the opposition an opportunity to mobilize its forces.

Legislative business is also scheduled with forthcoming elections in mind. Measures are postponed to avoid an electorally embarrassing defeat, or they may be brought to the floor to satisfy groups allied with the party. What better time to take up legislation revamping the Internal Revenue Service than on or around April 15, the filing deadline for federal income taxes? Reflecting the two Congresses, both parties use the floor as an election platform to raise issues that appeal to external audiences. After passing measures advocated by its electoral base, a party can say, "Look what we did for you." Conversely, a party that fails to pass a measure can say to its bedrock supporters, "Look what we tried to do."

Consulting the President. A traditional duty of party leaders is to meet with the president to discuss the administration's goals and to convey legislative sentiment about what the executive branch is doing or not doing. Although presidents spend more time dealing with leaders of their own party in Congress, they also consult with opposition leaders.

Party Tasks

From a party perspective, congressional party leaders have a number of formal and informal responsibilities. Each party's rules formally specify certain functions and responsibilities for their leaders. Parliamentary precedents and chamber rules assign additional duties to party leaders. Party leaders have also assumed a wide range of duties on an informal basis.

Organizing the Party. Congressional leaders help to organize their party by selecting partisan colleagues for standing committees, revising party rules, choosing other party leaders, and appointing party committees. A couple of examples illustrate the point. Senate Republicans' rules authorize their leader, Senator McConnell, to appoint party colleagues to certain committees. In the House, Speaker Boehner ensured that many freshmen elected in 2010 received plum committee assignments.[85] To reward Sen. Charles Schumer, D-N.Y., for his success in helping Democrats win back majority control of the Senate, Senator Reid "installed him in a newly created leadership post—vice chairman of the Democratic Conference."[86] Later, when the position opened up, Schumer was also selected chair of the Democratic Policy Committee.

Promoting Party Unity. Another leadership responsibility is to encourage party unity in Congress on priority legislation. Sen. Everett Dirksen, R-Ill. (minority leader, 1959–1969), used social gatherings to accomplish this goal:

> Dirksen brought party members together in a series of social affairs. He held cocktail parties at a Washington country club, inviting all Republican senators and sometimes their wives too. These were calculated by Dirksen to improve party harmony and to build a friendly feeling for himself with the Republican senators.[87]

Party leaders' efforts to foster party cohesion go far beyond extending social invitations. Leaders perform many services for their party rank and file that build goodwill and a sense of common purpose. They schedule members' bills, provide them with timely political information, advise them on electoral issues, visit with their constituents, help them obtain good committee assignments, and work with them to forge policy agendas. "You really have to make people feel part of the process," remarked a Senate Democratic leader.[88] Periodically, leaders organize partisan retreats where members discuss party and policy goals, consider specific legislative initiatives, air differences, and resolve disputes.

Party leaders do not have to rely solely on their powers of persuasion. Informal political networks and access to strategic information give them an edge in influencing colleagues:

> Because members will respond more candidly to leadership polls than to lobbyist or White House polls, [leaders] have perhaps the most important information in a legislative struggle—information on where the votes are and (sometimes) what it will take to win certain people over.[89]

Top leaders also can bestow or withhold a variety of tangible and intangible rewards, such as naming legislators to special or select committees, influencing assignments to standing committees, aiding reelection campaigns, and smoothing access to the White House or executive agencies.

Publicizing Party Views. Leaders are expected to publicize their party's policies and achievements. They give speeches in various forums, appear on radio and television talk shows, write newspaper and journal articles, hold press conferences, organize town meetings around the country, and establish websites that highlight party issues and images. Leaders are also expected to develop public relations strategies to neutralize the opposition's arguments and proposals.[90] The advocacy role has increased in importance in recent years, in part because of the twenty-four-hour news cycle. "We've created a situation," noted a scholar, "where the real way you drive the legislative process is by influencing public opinion, rather than by trading for votes."[91]

Party leaders also provide members with talking points for meetings with journalists or constituents. Parties often create communications teams that meet regularly to discuss message development and delivery and to recommend their more telegenic members to present party positions. "We're focused on making sure we deliver the [party] message both here in Washington and out in the hinterlands," said a chair of the Senate Republican Conference.[92]

Providing Campaign Assistance. Leaders must be energetic campaigners and fund-raisers on behalf of their partisan colleagues. They help party candidates raise campaign funds. They establish their own leadership political action committees (PACs) to solicit contributions and donate to candidates of their party. They direct campaign dollars to groups running issue ads in the months leading up to the November elections. They travel widely to campaign for incumbents and challengers from their party. They encourage outside groups to contribute to the party's electoral efforts. They also help vulnerable colleagues gain a higher profile by giving them a lead role on a major issue or by creating working groups to provide members running for reelection with greater public exposure.[93]

In both the House and the Senate, the ability to raise funds for colleagues is an increasingly important criterion for judging prospective party leaders.[94] Members anticipating a run for a leadership post distribute campaign funds as standard operating practice. According to one account, "It seems that the job of fundraiser is becoming more important to senators' expectations of what a majority leader should do. . . . [They] are not trying to buy votes so much as to demonstrate how well they can fulfill that role."[95] Leaders stand at the intersection of the two Congresses—the representative assembly, where money is needed to win elections, and the lawmaking body, where power calls the shots.

PARTY CAUCUSES, COMMITTEES, AND INFORMAL GROUPS

House and Senate leaders operate in diverse institutional settings. In the larger, more impersonal House, majority party leaders sometimes ignore the wishes of the minority party. But this seldom happens in the Senate, where leaders must cope with the extensive rights of individual senators and the minority party. Despite these differences between the House and the Senate, parties in the two chambers are organized into the same three components: caucuses, committees, and informal party groups.

Party Caucuses

The organization of all partisans in a chamber is called the caucus or (in the case of Republicans) the conference. Party caucuses or conferences elect leaders, approve committee assignments, provide members with services, debate party and legislative rules and policies, appoint task forces or issue teams, develop themes to keep members on message, enable members to vent their frustrations, and discuss outreach programs that appeal to voters. In an explanation which applies equally well to both parties and chambers, a senior House Democrat said:

> The caucus is the place where a great deal of freewheeling debate over an issue takes place and where sometimes a consensus develops. Most of the discussions, although they have taken place at leadership meetings and at chairmen's meetings and in whips' meetings, have ended up in the broader forum of the caucus where every member of the Democratic party participates. You don't take a vote, but you try to develop a consensus and make concessions where they're necessary and develop the strongest possible position that can be supported by the maximum number of Democrats.[96]

In brief, party caucuses are useful forums where party members and leaders can assess sentiment on substantive or procedural issues and forge party unity. On rare occasions, party caucuses consider whether to strip particular members of their committee seniority or to oust committee leaders. Sometimes presidents attend their party's House or Senate caucus to rally the troops, as President Obama did just before the House of Representatives voted on health care reform in 2010.[97]

Party Committees

Each of the four congressional party groups—Senate and House Democrats, Senate and House Republicans—establishes committees to serve partisan needs and objectives (see Table 6-1). Three of the four party groups on Capitol Hill have policy committees, for example.[98]

Party committees do not make policy, but they do provide advice on scheduling, study substantive and political issues, distribute policy papers, track votes on issues, and discuss and implement party policy. Their influence has varied over the years, assuming greater importance when the party does not control the White House and thus needs policy and oversight assistance. The Senate Democratic Policy Committee, for example, conducted extensive oversight during President George W. Bush's tenure, including investigations of government contracting in Iraq and Afghanistan.[99] The policy committees also maintain websites that party members and staff can access for information. Other important party panels are the campaign committees (discussed in Chapter 3) and the committee assignment committees (discussed in Chapter 7).

TABLE 6-1	**Party Committees in the Senate and House**

Committee	Function
Senate Democratic	
Policy and Communications Policy	Considers party positions on specific measures and assists the party leader in scheduling bills; facilitates communication between Senate Democrats and to external audiences
Steering and Outreach	Assigns Democrats to committees and coordinates policy, legislative, and message issues for the Democratic Conference
Campaign	Works to elect Democrats to the Senate
Senate Republican	
Policy	Provides summaries of GOP positions on specific issues; researches procedural and substantive issues; drafts policy alternatives
Committee on Committees	Assigns Republicans to committees
Campaign	Works to elect Republicans to the Senate
House Democratic	
Steering and policy	Assists the leadership and Democratic Caucus in establishing, implementing, researching, and communicating party priorities; assigns Democrats to committees
Campaign	Works to elect Democrats to the House
House Republican	
Policy	Considers majority party proposals and works for consensus among Republican members
Steering	Assigns Republicans to standing committees
Campaign	Works to elect Republicans to the House

Note: The official names of the parties' campaign committees are as follows: Democratic Senatorial Campaign Committee, National Republican Senatorial Committee, Democratic Congressional Campaign Committee, and National Republican Congressional Committee.

Informal Party Groups

In addition to party committees, a variety of informal partisan groups operate on Capitol Hill. Among party groups in the House are the conservative Republican Study Committee, the Tea Party Caucus, the centrist New Democrat Coalition, and the fiscally conservative Blue Dog Democrats. The conservative Republican Study Committee and the 30-Something Caucus (moderate to liberal Democrats) regularly reserve time at the end of the legislative day to spotlight their party's priorities and successes and to criticize the other party. Most of the hundreds of informal groups on Capitol Hill are not explicitly partisan. Instead, they typically have a policy focus—such as boating, steel, mining, soybeans, rural health, electricity, automobiles, children, bicycles, or the Internet—and promote public awareness of related issues, sometimes favoring specific policies.

PARTY CONTINUITY AND CHANGE

Several features of the contemporary party system on Capitol Hill stand out: the intensity of party conflict, the persistence of the two-party system, and the advent of new coalition-building practices.

Intense Party Conflict

By any test one can use, the four Capitol Hill party groups are flourishing. The organizational elements are healthy and active, their leaders are increasingly prominent, and party voting is at very high levels. The congressional parties are well assisted by professional staff.

The strength of today's parties has definite virtues. For one, it enables voters to better comprehend the divergent views, values, and principles of the two parties, and it may even encourage voter turnout. "Confrontation fits our strategy," said Richard B. "Dick" Cheney when he was in the House (1979–1989). "Polarization often has very beneficial results. If everything is handled through compromise and conciliation, if there are no real issues dividing us from Democrats, why should the country change and make us the majority?"[100]

Nevertheless, compromise is a traditional hallmark of legislative decision making. The intensity and extent of partisan conflict in the contemporary Congress raises questions about the body's ability to engage in meaningful bipartisan deliberation and mutual accommodation. Partisan polarization is decried by observers and members alike. In today's House, the two parties are not "just opponents or rivals now. [They] are enemies, with every fight being zero-sum," exclaimed a senior GOP lawmaker. "Compromise is seen as weakness by many of your constituents, and by all your potential opponents in the next primary."[101]

The goal of bipartisanship is an oft-heard refrain on Capitol Hill—but it is an elusive one. President Obama campaigned in 2008 on a promise to "turn the page" on the bitter party politics that had characterized the Geroge W. Bush presidency. But his first major initiative, an economic stimulus package, elicited an almost purely partisan response in Congress. No House Republican and only three Senate Republicans supported the president's package.[102] Similarly, just before the opening of the 110th Congress, Senate Majority Leader Reid convened a closed-door meeting of all senators.[103] Its purpose was to infuse a spirit of bipartisanship in the working relationships between the two parties. A few weeks later, the Senate was in gridlock as the two parties bitterly clashed over how to debate a measure disapproving of President Geroge W. Bush's deployment of more troops to Iraq.[104] As former senator Olympia J. Snowe,

R-Maine, observed, "The whole Congress has become far more polarized and partisan so it makes it difficult to reach bipartisan agreements. The more significant the issue, the more partisan it becomes."[105]

The Two-Party System

The Democratic and Republican Parties have dominated American politics and Congress since the mid–nineteenth century. Scholars have advanced various theories for the dualistic party politics of a country as diverse as the United States. Plurality elections in single-member congressional districts encouraged the creation and maintenance of two major parties. Under the winner-takes-all principle, the person who wins the most votes in a state or district is elected to the Senate or House. This principle discourages the formation of third parties, but other countries using this system of representation, such as Canada and the United Kingdom, have nonetheless had a tradition of successful third parties. Some scholars also trace the origins of the national two-party system to early conflicts between Federalists (advocates of a strong national government) and Antifederalists (advocates of limited national government).[106] In addition, many states have laws that make it difficult to create new parties. Constitutional, political, and legal arrangements all contribute to the existence and maintenance of the two-party system.

Whatever mix of causes produced the two-party system, one thing is clear: few third-party or independent legislators have been elected to Congress during the last century. The high-water mark was the Sixty-third Congress (1913–1915), which had one Progressive senator and nineteen representatives elected as Progressives, Progressive-Republicans, or independents. Since World War II, only a handful of lawmakers have been elected from minor parties or as independents.[107] Most of these legislators have converted to one of the major parties or have voted with them on procedural and substantive matters. The 113th Congress has only two independent lawmakers, each of whom affiliates with the Democratic Party: socialist senator Bernie Sanders of Vermont and freshman senator Angus King of Maine. Third-party or independent members participate in Democratic or Republican affairs by invitation only.

Advances in Coalition Building

In Capitol Hill's highly competitive environment, party leaders are constantly searching for new ways to get the legislative results they want. Fierce competition has prompted continual innovation in media, public relations, and legislative strategies.

Media and Public Relations. Party leaders understand that media strategies—that is, the use of the press, television, radio, polls, the Internet, speeches, and so on—are essential to advance or block legislation. They form issue teams, message groups, "war rooms," or theme teams to orchestrate, organize, and coordinate political events and communications strategies that promote the party's message to the general public. No longer is the inside game—working behind the scenes to line up votes—sufficient to pass major legislation.

Also necessary is the outside game—influencing public opinion, coordinating with advocacy groups, and creating grassroots support for policy initiatives. Today, both parties use the media to complement their parliamentary strategies in order to raise issues, define and frame priorities, and respond to partisan criticisms. Both congressional parties understand the importance of words as political weapons. GOP consultants found, for example, that characterizing the tax on inheritances as the "death tax"—and having GOP officeholders repeat it again and again over several years—aroused public ire against the tax. This sentiment was instrumental in the dramatic reductions of the estate tax as part of President Geroge W. Bush's successful 2001 tax cut plan.

President Obama can use his bully pulpit to advance Democratic initiatives, but congressional Republicans have no messenger who can focus the nation's attention as effectively as a president. As a result, Republicans have embraced a wide array of communications techniques to shape national debate. Meanwhile, they have augmented the number of leadership staff handling new media, communications, and grassroots outreach. "Our effort will work to help build dynamic, multilayered, outside-the-Beltway coalitions that will help the Republican Conference explain the value of our policies and the impact they will have on the American people," predicted a House Republican coalitions director.[108] Republican leaders hold press conferences, appear on diverse media outlets, organize town meetings, prepare talking points for the press (and their own members), develop party themes, participate in Web forums and blogs, write newspaper editorials, circulate data and statistics, organize policy forums, and engage in a variety of other activities to promote their legislative agenda to the public and to criticize Democratic proposals.

Omnibus Bills. A phenomenon of modern lawmaking is the rise of megabills—legislation that is hundreds or thousands of pages in length, encompassing disparate policy topics. Many of Congress's most significant recent policy departures have been enacted through omnibus bills.

Joining several bills in a single package can help leaders garner support. In such megabills, sweeteners can be added to woo supporters, and provisions that could not win majority support in stand-alone bills can be tucked out of sight. Bundling popular programs with painful spending cuts limits the number of difficult votes lawmakers must cast and provides them with political cover. Members can explain to angry constituents or groups that they had to support the indivisible whole because its discrete parts were not open to separate votes. Leaders, however, must be wary of the reverse concern that a megabill can attract a coalition of opponents with the votes needed to reject the measure.

Megabills can also strengthen Congress's leverage with the executive branch. Measures that a president might veto if presented separately can be folded into megabills and signed in that fashion.

Party leaders command the resources and authority to influence the packaging process. "Omnibus bills place a huge amount of power in the hands of a few key leaders and their staffs," pointed out one House member.[109] Rank-and-file members look to party leaders to formulate a package acceptable to a majority, if not all, its members. Nevertheless, these megabills often arouse lawmakers' suspicions and complaints. "These omnibus bills . . . are abominations," one member complained. "No one member of Congress has a chance to read much of them, let alone understand them, before they are voted on."[110]

CONCLUSION

Congressional parties have elaborate organizations, and their leaders fulfill a multiplicity of roles and duties. As Sen. Robert Byrd explained when he held that post, the Senate majority leader performs many duties: "He facilitates, he constructs, he programs, he schedules, he takes an active part in the development of legislation, he steps in at crucial moments on the floor, offers amendments, speaks on behalf of legislation and helps to shape the outcome of the legislation."[111] And yet typically party leaders cannot command their colleagues. Their leadership rests chiefly on their skill in giving others reasons to follow them.

The party system organizes Congress. The committee system shapes the measures on which Congress acts. These two systems are often in conflict. The first emphasizes aggregation; the second, fragmentation. Party leaders have historically struggled to manage an institution that distributes policy-making authority to a large number of working groups. In short, leaders provide the centripetal force to offset committees' centrifugal influence.

Committee Hearings and Mark-Ups. Rep. Fred Upton, R-Mich., House Energy and Commerce Committee chair (top left), testifies before the Rules Committee in favor of his panel's bill to repeal the Patient Protection and Affordable Care Act. He is flanked by GOP colleagues Steve King, Iowa, and John Kline, Minn. (Top right) Sen. Chuck Grassley and Sen. Mazie Hirono, D-Haw., at a 2013 Senate Judiciary Committee hearing on immigration reform. Sen. John Cornyn, R-Tex., (center) consults staff aides during the Judiciary Committee mark-up of the ill-fated bill to ban assault weapons. (Bottom) Committee aides sort through amendments during a break in the House Energy and Commerce Committee's mark-up of a 2009 bill designed to reduce greenhouse gasses.

Committees:
Workshops of Congress

C ongress's committees serve two broad purposes: individual and institutional. Individually, lawmakers are able to use their committee assignments to benefit their constituents. "As far as I can see, there is really only one basic reason to be on a public works committee," admitted a House member. "Intellectual stimulation" is not it. "Most of all, I want to be able to bring home projects to my district."[1] At the start of the 112th Congress (2011–2013), no less than twenty House GOP freshman lawmakers won assignment to the Transportation and Infrastructure Committee, in part because the panel's agenda (highways, mass transit, and water projects) addresses investments that can bring jobs and economic growth to their districts. Nine more GOP "frosh" were added to the panel in the 113th Congress. Legislators know that their letters and telephone calls to the pertinent agency officials can influence the funding of member-proposed federal projects. They also fully understand the connection between their committee assignments and their reelection potential.

Committees also enable legislators to utilize or develop expertise in areas that interest them. A former teacher, for example, may seek assignment to the committee overseeing education policy. And some panels, such as the tax and appropriations committees, enable members to wield personal influence among their colleagues. For much of congressional history, members sought out the House Appropriations Committee, explained a GOP leader, because "instantaneously . . . they have a host of new friends, and we all know why": that panel controls the distribution of discretionary federal money (over $1 trillion in 2013).[2]

Institutionally, committees are the centers of policy making, oversight of federal agencies, and public education (largely through the hearings they hold). By dividing their membership into a number of "little legislatures," the House and Senate are able to consider dozens of proposed laws simultaneously.[3] Without committees, a legislative body of 100 senators and 441 House members[4] could not handle biennially the roughly 10,000 bills and nearly 100,000 nominations, a national budget of nearly $4 trillion, and a limitless array of controversial issues. Although floor actions often refine legislation, committees are the means by which Congress sifts through an otherwise impossible jumble of bills, proposals, and issues.

Congressional committees serve another important institutional function in the political system: they act as safety valves—that is, they are outlets for national debates and controversies. Military and economic challenges, demographic shifts, trade agreements, global environmental concerns, the drug war, social dislocations caused by technological advances, and the cost of health care place enormous strains on the political system. As forums for public debates, congressional committees help to vent, absorb, and perhaps resolve these strains. The safety valve function also gives citizens a greater sense of participation in national decision making and helps educate members about public problems.

At times, the individual and institutional purposes of the committee system come into conflict. Because members tend to gravitate to committees for constituency or career reasons, they are not the most impartial judges of the policies they authorize. "It's one of the weaknesses of the system that those attracted to a committee like Agriculture are those whose constituents benefit from farm programs," acknowledged Sen. Charles E. Schumer, D-N.Y. "And so they're going to support those programs and they're not going to want to cut them, even the ones that are wasteful."[5]

THE PURPOSES OF COMMITTEES

Senator Schumer's comment highlights an ongoing debate about the development and fundamental purposes of the committee system. To explain the organizational logic of legislatures and the behavior of their committees, scholars have advanced the distributional, informational, and party hypotheses.

The *distributional* hypothesis suggests that legislatures create committees to give lawmakers policy influence in areas critical to their reelection. Members seek committee assignments to "bring home the bacon" (public goods and services) to their constituents. Because lawmakers self-select these kinds of committees, the committees become filled with what scholars call preference outliers—members whose homogeneous preferences for benefits to their constituents put them out of step with the heterogeneous views of the membership as a whole. Chamber majorities, in brief, may need to restrain overreaching committees by rejecting or amending their recommended actions.[6]

The *informational* hypothesis proposes that legislative bodies establish committees to provide lawmakers with the specialized expertise required to make informed judgments in a complex world. Furthermore, the division of labor under the committee system augments Congress's role in relation to the executive branch. Instead of being composed primarily of preference outliers, committees under this model have a diverse membership with wide-ranging perspectives. The basic goal of committees, then, is to formulate policies that resolve national problems.[7]

The *party* hypothesis views committees as agents of their party caucuses. According to this perspective, committee members are expected to support their party's programs or, at minimum, not advance policies opposed by a majority of their own party.

Each of these hypotheses captures an aspect of the committee system. Lawmakers are concerned with local issues of immediate concern to constituents, but every district and state are also affected by broad national concerns—the condition of the economy and the environment, for example. Certain issues may lend themselves on occasion more to the distributional than to the informational or party theory of policy making.

Because good public policy may be impeded by the parochial orientations of individual members, Congress has a small number of control, or centralizing, committees that promote institutional and policy integration over committee and programmatic particularism. For example, each house has a Budget Committee, which proposes limits on how much Congress can spend on designated functional areas.[8] However committees are characterized, they concentrate on the policy and oversight activities of individual lawmakers.

EVOLUTION OF THE COMMITTEE SYSTEM

Committees in the early Congresses were generally temporary panels created for specific tasks. Proposals were considered on the House or Senate floor and then were referred to specially created panels that worked out the details—the reverse order of today's system. The Senate, for example, would "debate a subject at length on the floor and, after the majority's desires had been crystallized, might appoint a committee to put those desires into bill form."[9] About 350 ad hoc committees were formed during the Third Congress (1793–1795) alone.[10] The parent chamber closely controlled these temporary committees. It assigned them clear-cut tasks, required them to report back favorably or unfavorably, and dissolved them when they had completed their work.

By about 1816, the Senate—and the House a bit later—had developed a system of permanent, or standing, committees, some of which are still in existence. Standing committees, as historian DeAlva Stanwood Alexander explained, were better suited than ad hoc groups to cope with the larger membership and wider scope of congressional business. Another scholar, George H. Haynes, pointed out that the "needless inconvenience of the frequent choice of select committees" taxed congressional patience. Lawmakers recognized that debating bills one at a time before the whole chamber was an inefficient way of processing Congress's legislative business. Perhaps, too, legislators turned to standing committees as counterweights to presidential influence in setting the legislative agenda.[11] Permanent committees changed the way Congress made policy and allocated authority. The House and Senate now reviewed and voted on recommendations made by specialized, experienced committees. Permanent committees also encouraged oversight of the executive branch. Members have called them "the eye, the ear, the hand, and very often the brain" of Congress.[12]

As committees acquired expertise and authority, they became increasingly self-reliant and resistant to chamber and party control. After the House revolt against domineering Speaker Joseph G. Cannon, R-Ill., in 1910, power flowed to the committee chairs. Along with a few strong party leaders, committee chairs held sway over House and Senate policy making during much of the twentieth century. In rare instances, committee members rebelled and diminished the chair's authority. But most members heeded the advice that Speaker John W. McCormack, D-Mass. (1962–1971), gave freshmen: "Whenever you pass a committee chairman in the House, you bow from the waist. I do."[13]

The chairs' authority was buttressed by the custom of seniority that flourished with the rise of congressional careerism. The majority party member with the most years of continuous service on a committee virtually always became its chair. As a result, committee chairs owed little or nothing to party leaders, much less to presidents. This automatic selection process produced experienced, independent chairs but concentrated authority in a few hands. The have-nots wanted a piece of the action and objected that seniority promoted the competent and incompetent alike. They objected, too, that the system promoted members from safe one-party areas—especially conservative southern Democrats and midwestern Republicans—who could ignore party policies or national sentiments.

The late 1960s and 1970s saw a rapid influx of new members, many from the cities and suburbs, who opposed the conservative status quo. (In the House, this surge was abetted by U.S. Supreme Court–mandated reapportionments, as discussed in Chapter 3.) Allying themselves with more senior members seeking a stronger voice in Congress, these reformers sponsored changes that diffused power and shattered seniority as an absolute criterion for leadership posts. Today, House and Senate committee chairs (and ranking minority members) are elected by their party colleagues. No longer free to wield arbitrary authority, they must abide by committee and party rules and be sensitive to majority sentiment within their party's caucus or conference.

In fact, there has been a dramatic shift in the post-1970s power of committee chairs, especially since the mid-1990s. Committee chairs are far less independent today than they were in the late 1970s, after the party, House, and Senate reforms of that decade. Once the dominant central players in the House and Senate, contemporary chairs are often hand-picked by party leaders, expected to raise money for the party, toe the line on top party issues, and use the media to advance party goals. Committee chairs are still important actors, but they are a shadow of what they once were.

TYPES OF COMMITTEES

Today, Congress boasts a shopper's bazaar of committees—standing, select, joint, and conference—and within each of these general types are variations. Standing committees, for example, can be classed as either authorizing or appropriating panels. Authorizing committees (such as Agriculture, Armed

Services, and Judiciary) are the policy-making centers on Capitol Hill. As substantive committees, they propose solutions to public problems and advocate what they believe to be the necessary levels of spending for the programs under their jurisdictions. The House and Senate Appropriations Committees recommend how much money agencies and programs will receive. Not surprisingly, the two types of panels, authorizing and appropriations, tend to come into conflict. Typically, authorizers press for full funding of their recommendations, whereas appropriators usually recommend lower spending levels, especially in an era of spending austerity.

Standing Committees

A standing committee is a permanent entity created by public law or House or Senate rules. Standing committees continue from Congress to Congress, except in rare instances when they are eliminated or new ones are created. Table 7-1 identifies the standing committees in the 113th Congress.

Standing committees process the bulk of Congress's daily and annual agenda. Typically, measures are considered on the House or Senate floor after first being referred to, and approved by, the appropriate committees. At the same time, committees are the burial ground for most legislation—that is, committees select from the thousands of measures introduced in each Congress those that merit floor debate. Of the hundreds of bills that clear committees, fewer still are enacted into law.

Sizes and Ratios. The biennial congressional election results frame the party negotiations over setting committee sizes and ratios (the number of majority and minority members on a panel). At the beginning of each new Congress, each chamber adopts separate resolutions, offered by Democrats and Republicans, electing party members to the committees and thus setting their sizes and ratios. In practice, committee sizes and ratios are established in the House by the majority leadership. Because the majority party has the votes, it is the final arbiter if the minority protests its allotment of seats.

At the opening of the 113th Congress, the ratio of Republicans to Democrats in the 433-member House (there were two vacancies) was 54 percent (233 Republicans) to 46 percent (200 Democrats). In the main, this was the approximate ratio on most House committees. As a result, there was no public protest from minority members about being underrepresented on most committees, a common complaint in years past. To be sure, some committees, such as Rules (69 percent to 31 percent in the 113th) and Ways and Means (59 percent to 41 percent in the 113th), traditionally have disproportionate ratios to ensure firm majority party control. The Ethics Committee has an equal number of majority and minority members, and the Speaker names the committee chair.

In the Senate, sizes and ratios are negotiated by the majority and minority leaders. (Senate rules, unlike those of the House, establish the sizes of the standing committees, but these can be adjusted up or down with the agreement of the majority and minority leaders.) Once it became clear after the 2012 elections by what margin the Democrats had retained Senate control (55D,

TABLE 7-1 **Standing Committees of the House and Senate, 113th Congress, 2013–2015**

House	Senate
Agriculture	Agriculture, Nutrition, and Forestry
Appropriations	Appropriations
Armed Services	Armed Services
Budget	Banking, Housing, and Urban Affairs
Education and the Workforce	Budget
Energy and Commerce	Commerce, Science, and Transportation
Ethics	Energy and Natural Resources
Financial Services	Environment and Public Works
Foreign Affairs	Finance
Homeland Security	Foreign Relations
House Administration	Health, Education, Labor, and Pensions
Judiciary	Homeland Security and Governmental Affairs
Natural Resources	Indian Affairs
Oversight and Government Reform	Judiciary
Rules	Rules and Administration
Science, Space, and Technology	Small Business and Entrepreneurship
Small Business	Veterans' Affairs
Transportation and Infrastructure	
Veterans' Affairs	
Ways and Means	

Sources: House and Senate committee web pages.

45R), the two party leaders—Democrat Harry Reid, Nev., and Republican Mitch McConnell, Ky.—were responsible for negotiating committee sizes and ratios. "We'll be negotiating committee ratios, the two of us, like we always do," remarked Senator McConnell.[14] Given the Democratic gain of two seats in the 113th Senate, Senator Reid proposed that the eight committees—Aging, Agriculture, Budget, Commerce, Foreign Relations, Homeland Security, Small Business, and Veterans—from the previous Congress that only had a single-seat advantage be increased to a two-seat advantage for all committees. This change was agreed to, underscoring the adage that elections have consequences. In general, Senate leaders usually change party ratios on committees "by shifting seats between the parties, rather than by adding seats to panels."[15] The Senate's Select Committee on Ethics—which is chaired by a majority party member—always has an equal number of majority and minority members.

Party leaders sometimes enlarge panels to accommodate lawmakers competing for membership on the same committees. They recognize that intraparty harmony can be maintained by boosting the number of committee seats. In 2011, however, Speaker John Boehner, R-Ohio, downsized most House committees to boost productivity and to cut costs. For example, the Appropriations Committee went from sixty seats to fifty, Energy and Commerce from fifty-nine seats to fifty-four, Transportation and Infrastructure from seventy-five seats to fifty-nine, and Ways and Means from forty-one seats to thirty-seven. The Armed Services Committee maintained its size (sixty-two), becoming the largest House panel. Minority Leader Nancy Pelosi, D-Calif., faced some discontent from her Democratic flock once the size reductions became known. Many Democrats lost their seats on major committees with the GOP's reset of sizes and ratios. After bipartisan discussions, some committee sizes were adjusted. For example, Democrats were granted one more seat on the Energy and Commerce Committee to accommodate a returning Democrat who had taken a leave of absence. "Republicans also gave themselves an additional seat" on Energy and Commerce.[16]

Subcommittees. Subcommittees perform much of the day-to-day law-making and oversight work of Congress. Like standing committees, they vary widely in rules and procedures, staff arrangements, modes of operation, and relationships with the full committee as well as its other subcommittees. They are created for various reasons, such as lawmakers' need to subdivide a committee's wide-ranging policy domain into manageable pieces, their wish to chair these panels and to have a platform to shape the legislative agenda, and their desire to respond to the policy claims of specialized constituencies.

Under House rules, most standing committees are limited to no more than five subcommittees. Committees bound by the limit of five may create a sixth subcommittee if it is devoted to oversight. There are some exceptions to the limit of five, such as Appropriations (which has twelve subcommittees), Armed Services (seven), Foreign Affairs (seven), and Transportation and Infrastructure (six). Various reasons account for these deviations: long-standing custom, acquisition of additional jurisdiction, accommodations of lawmakers, and bicameral concerns. A committee authorized to establish additional subcommittees may choose not to do so. For example, a committee chair decided to reduce the number of subcommittees from seven to five. His new subcommittee structure was created "so that the jurisdiction of each subcommittee will have broad appeal and will engage the attention of the subcommittee members."[17]

Another House rule limits members to serving on no more than four subcommittees. Such limits—on the number of subcommittees for each standing committee and subcommittee assignment restrictions for each member—are designed to make Congress "more deliberative, participatory, and manageable by reducing scheduling conflicts and jurisdictional overlap."[18] Republicans are in control of the House of the 113th Congress, and their party conference rules state that the "method for the selection of Chairmen of the

Committee's Subcommittees [and GOP subcommittee assignments] shall be at the discretion of the full Committee Chairman, unless a majority of the Republican Members of the full Committee disapprove the action of the Chairman." Furthermore, the chair "shall formalize in writing for the other Republican Members of the Committee the procedures to be followed in selecting Subcommittee Chairmen and individual subcommittee assignments and shall do so in advance of the Committee's organization." In the case of the Appropriations Committee, the chair submits nominees for subcommittee chairs to the Republican Steering Committee for approval.

The two Congresses are also evident in the composition of subcommittees. A good example occurred in the 112th House when Lamar Smith, R-Texas, chaired the Judiciary Committee. He passed over Steve King, R-Iowa, for chairmanship of the Immigration Subcommittee. King had been the ranking GOP member on the panel in the previous Congress. But, worried that King's inflammatory statements about immigrants would alienate Latino voters in the 2012 elections, Smith selected Elton Gallegly of California, "who has a lower profile and a less strident tone than King," to head the subcommittee.[19]

In dealing with House subcommittees, the minority Democrats in the 113th Congress followed the detailed procedures outlined in their party rules. Simply put, once the subcommittee structure and jurisdictions are established, committee Democrats bid for a subcommittee ranking slot (or assignment) in order of their seniority on the full committee (or seniority on the Appropriations subcommittee), with the most senior Democrat choosing first. The choices are then subject to approval by secret ballot of the Democratic committee members. The ranking positions on four of the most powerful committees— Appropriations, Energy and Commerce, Financial Services, and Ways and Means—require approval by the Democratic Steering and Policy Committee. If the Steering and Policy Committee rejects a member to serve as the ranking committee minority leader, the relevant committee is obliged to submit a new nominee to the party panel.

Assignment to the most important committees is generally "exclusive." Democrats who serve on exclusive committees may serve on no other standing committees unless they are granted an exemption, or waiver, from this requirement. (Waivers of the rule are quite common.) Waivers are granted to permit members to sit on an extra major committee that they deem important to their reelection prospects. This is another example of the two Congresses— the institution bending to suit the preferences and constituency needs of individual members. House Republicans refer to their generally exclusive panels as the "A" committees (Appropriations, Energy and Commerce, Rules, and Ways and Means).

Although silent on the number of subcommittees that standing committees may establish, Senate and party rules set subcommittee assignment limits for senators and prohibit them from chairing more than one subcommittee on any given committee. The number of subcommittees, not surprisingly, often equals the number of majority party members on a committee eligible to chair a subcommittee. Subcommittee chairs and assignments are determined in one of two ways: by the committee chair in consultation with the ranking member or by senators' order of seniority on the full committee. It is traditional in both chambers for committee members to defer to the chair on organizational matters, such as the number of subcommittees and their respective jurisdictions. For example, at the beginning of the 113th Congress, House Oversight and Government Reform Committee chair Darrell Issa, R-Calif., decided to consider legislation involving the District of Columbia at the full committee rather than in a subcommittee, where it was handled in the previous Congress. Chairman Issa is "one of the city's staunchest allies on Capitol Hill."[20] These matters, however, are subject to majority approval of the panel.

Unlike in the House, where every standing committee except Budget and Ethics has subcommittees, in the Senate four standing committees customarily function without subcommittees—Budget, Rules and Administration, Small Business, and Veterans' Affairs—as do four other permanent panels—Indian Affairs, Ethics, Intelligence, and Aging. These panels are able to process their legislative business without subcommittees because of their relatively small workloads compared with those of other Senate committees.

Select, or Special, Committees

Select, or special, committees are temporary panels that typically go out of business after the two-year life of the Congress in which they are created. But some select committees take on the attributes of permanent committees. The House, for example, has a Permanent Select Intelligence Committee. Select committees usually do not have legislative authority (the right to receive and report out measures) unless it is granted by their authorizing measure; they can only study, investigate, and make recommendations.

Select panels are created for several reasons. First, they can accommodate the concerns of individual members. Indeed, the chairs of these panels may attract publicity that enhances their political careers. For example, Democrat Harry S. Truman of Missouri came to the public's (and President Franklin D. Roosevelt's) attention as head of a special Senate committee investigating World War II military procurement practices. Second, special panels can be an access point for interest groups such as the elderly. Third, select committees supplement the standing committee system by overseeing and investigating issues that the permanent panels on may lack adequate time for or prefer to ignore. A recent example of an issue-based select committee was the House's creation in the 110th and 111th Congresses of a select panel on global warming. When Republicans took charge of the House in the 112th Congress, they discontinued the global warming panel, contending that its demise would save money and that the panel duplicated the work of other standing committees. Republicans also wanted to "deny Democrats a key bully pulpit for advancing their environmental agenda."[21]

Finally, select committees can be set up to coordinate consideration of issues that overlap the jurisdictions of several standing committees. A good example occurred following the establishment in 2003 of the Department of Homeland Security (DHS). It was formed by merging twenty-two federal agencies with a workforce at the time of 180,000 employees. Because numerous House committees exercised jurisdiction over parts of DHS, Speaker Dennis Hastert, R-Ill., created a select homeland security panel to determine whether a new, single-focused standing committee should be created to oversee DHS. As a result of the select panel's review, the House created a standing Committee on Homeland Security in the following Congress. (The formation of this panel is discussed in more detail later in this chapter.)

Joint Committees

Joint committees, which include members from both chambers, have been used since the First Congress for study, investigation, oversight, and routine activities. Unless the composition of a joint committee is prescribed in statute, House members of these committees are appointed by the Speaker; senators are appointed by that chamber's presiding officer. The chairmanship of joint committees rotates each Congress between House and Senate members. There are now four joint committees: Economic, Library, Printing, and Taxation. The Joint Library Committee and the Joint Printing Committee oversee, respectively, the Library of Congress and the Government Printing Office. The Joint Taxation Committee is essentially a holding company for staff who work closely with the tax-writing committees of each house. The Joint Economic Committee conducts studies and hearings on a wide range of domestic and international economic issues.

Conference Committees

Before legislation can be sent to the president to be signed, it must pass both the House and the Senate in identical form. One way this result is obtained is to create a conference committee (see Chapter 8 for more on conferences). Sometimes called the third house of Congress, these bicameral panels reconcile differences between similar measures passed by both chambers. They are composed of members from each house.

Conference bargaining can be classified roughly in four ways: traditional, offer-counteroffer, subconference, and pro forma. Traditional conferences are those in which the participants meet face to face, haggle among themselves about the items in bicameral disagreement, and then reach an accord. The bulk of conferences are of this type. In offer-counteroffer conferences, often used by the tax-writing committees, one side suggests a compromise proposal; the other side recesses to discuss it in private and then returns to present a counteroffer. Conferences with numerous participants (on omnibus bills, for example) usually break into small units, or subconferences, to reconcile particular matters or to address special topics. Pro forma conferences are those in which issues are resolved informally—by preconference negotiations between conferee leaders or their staffs. The conference itself then ratifies the earlier decisions.[22]

Some scholars argue that congressional conference committees are powerful because they have unilateral authority to veto or negotiate alterations in legislation at a late stage in the process. Others dispute this contention and claim that the "ex post veto is not a significant institutional foundation of congressional committee power."[23] Another model suggests that conferees serve as agents of their respective chamber majorities, advocating their policy positions instead of conference committee viewpoints.[24] Whatever the claims, increasingly the top party leaders in each chamber are taking a direct and active role in determining those who should (or should not) be conferees. On occasion, the top leaders, such as the Senate majority leader or House majority leader, serve as conferees on priority measures to increase their leverage in the bicameral bargaining process.

Several recent Congresses have witnessed a decline in the convening of conference committees (see Chapter 8). The Senate, compared to the House, has difficulty at times in convening conferences for interconnected political and procedural reasons. Politically, the majority party has sometimes excluded minority party conferees from the negotiating sessions. Procedurally, it is more difficult to get to conference if senators want to filibuster motions to do so. As a form of payback, minority party senators who are conferees in name only can stymie the creation of conference committees by extended debate.

THE ASSIGNMENT PROCESS

Every congressional election sets off a scramble for committee seats. Legislators understand the linkage between winning desirable assignments and winning elections. Newly elected representatives and senators quickly make their preferences known to party leaders, to members of the panels that make committee assignments, and to others—such as friendly lobbyists or generous contributors. They may be able to help the newcomers obtain their preferred committee seats. At the same time, incumbents may try to move to more prestigious panels.

The Pecking Order

The most powerful, and thus most desirable, standing committees are House Ways and Means and Senate Finance, which pass on tax, trade, Social Security, and Medicare measures. The House and Senate Appropriations Committees, which hold the federal purse strings, are also influential panels and usually much sought after. However, their attractiveness has waned somewhat given "the recent political focus on cutting spending, the now-routine inability of lawmakers to fund the government by the statutory deadline of Oct. 1 each year and the moratorium on earmarks that Republicans have successfully imposed on Congress."[25] Moreover, in today's contentious partisan environment, party leaders have taken a much larger role in shaping appropriations measures.

The consequence of these developments is to make some lawmakers wary of either chairing or serving on the appropriating panels. When Republicans took control of the 112th House, several GOP lawmakers declined to serve on the Appropriations Committee. "We sent a sheet around, people gave us their preferences, and there weren't that many members that chose to serve on the Appropriations Committee," said Speaker John Boehner, R-Ohio.[26] These lawmakers recognized the potential perils of the two Congresses: they could be challenged electorally either by conservative and Tea Party supporters for not cutting enough, or by constituents angry at spending cuts to favorite programs. As a result, budget-cutting fiscal hawks have been recruited to the panel. Their mission is to practice the "politics of subtraction," by cutting or terminating agencies and programs. The Appropriations Committee has been "a favor factory for years; now it is going to be [an antispending] slaughterhouse," declared a House critic of the favor factory.[27]

The Senate has also seen evidence of the panels' diminished allure. When the longtime chair of the Appropriations Committee, Democrat Daniel Inouye of Hawaii, died, the two most senior Senate Democrats on that panel—Patrick Leahy, Vt., and Tom Harkin, Iowa—each chose not to head it. Although Appropriations was considered for decades to be the most powerful Senate committee, Senators Leahy and Harkin decided to remain as chairs of their respective committees, Judiciary and Health, Education, Labor, and Pensions. Their decisions would have confounded many senatorial colleagues from a different era. The Leahy-Harkin result: the third-ranking Democrat on the panel, Barbara Mikulski, Md., became in the 113th Congress the first woman to chair the Appropriations Committee.

The Budget Committees, established in 1974, are sought-after assignments because of their important role in economic and fiscal matters and their guardianship of the congressional budgeting process. The House and Senate Commerce Committees, along with each chamber's banking and financial services committees, are also coveted panels: not only do they command broad jurisdictional mandates, but the many interest groups they affect can supply cash donations for the committee members' future election campaigns. To boost the reelection chances of a number of House Republican freshmen, the GOP leadership named twelve newcomers to Financial Services, five to Energy and Commerce, three to Appropriations, and two to Ways and Means. "The amount of money you can raise is almost entirely determined by committee membership," a GOP insider confided.[28]

Among those panels that seldom have waiting lists are the House and Senate Ethics Committees. These committees are not popular because legislators are reluctant to sit in judgment of their colleagues. "Members have never competed for the privilege of serving on the ethics committee, and I am no exception," remarked a House Democrat after his party's leader prevailed on him to join the ethics panel. Or as one GOP member grumbled after serving as ethics chair, "I've paid my debt to society. It's time for me to be paroled."[29]

The attractiveness of committees can change over time, as noted with respect to the appropriating panels. Another example is the Senate Foreign Relations Committee, a panel that long elicited great interest among members, especially during the Vietnam War era. Once the Cold War ended, however, the panel often had trouble filling its vacancies. Throughout the 1990s, senators viewed it largely as a debating society without much influence either inside or outside the Senate. Later, because of heightened public concern about the global war on terrorism, an ongoing war in Afghanistan, instability in the Middle East, and a large array of other pressing global issues, the committee played a larger role in shaping the nation's policies in an uncertain world. "Yeah, they've got clout," one foreign policy expert explained. "You control money, you control nominations, you control treaties, and you control the microphone," in discussions on an array of global issues. "That's a lot of power in Washington."[30] On the other hand, some commentators question its current influence in the international realm. The panel seldom approves treaties, in part because they require a two-thirds vote of the Senate; it has not passed a foreign aid authorization bill since 1985; and members avoid seeking assignment to the panel because it lacks jurisdiction over issues that generate campaign contributions. Still, as Sen. Marco Rubio, R-Fla., a committee member, stated: "I still think the committee is an important place to be."[31]

Preferences and Politicking

In his analysis of six House committees, Richard F. Fenno Jr. found that three basic goals of lawmakers—reelection, influence within the House, and good public policy—affected the committee assignments that members sought. Reelection-oriented members were attracted to committees such as Natural Resources (then called the Interior Committee). Appropriations and Ways and Means attracted influence-oriented members. Policy-oriented members sought membership on the Education and Labor Committee (now Education and the Workforce) and the Foreign Affairs Committee. Members with similar goals found themselves on the same committees, Fenno concluded. Such homogeneity of perspectives may result in harmonious but biased committees (see Table 7-2).[32]

Since Fenno's study, scholars have elaborated on the link between members' goals and committee assignments. They have divided House committees into reelection (or constituency), policy, and power panels, and they concur that some mix of the three goals motivates most of the committees' activities. They agree, too, that members' goals "are less easily characterized in the Senate than in the House."[33] After all, most every senator has the opportunity to serve on one of the top committees, such as Appropriations, Armed Services, Commerce, and Finance. Thus the power associated with a particular committee assignment is less important for senators than for representatives.

Members campaign vigorously for the committees they prefer. In *Hit the Ground Running,* his guidebook for GOP newcomers to Congress, House

TABLE 7-2 House and Senate Committee Comparison

Category	House	Senate
Number of standing committees	20	16
Committee/subcommittee assignments per member	About 6	About 11
Power or prestige committees	Appropriations, Budget, Commerce, Financial Services, Rules, Ways and Means	Appropriations, Armed Services, Commerce, Finance, Foreign Relations[1]
Treaties and nominations submitted by the president	No authority	Committees review
Floor debate	Representatives' activity is somewhat confined to the bills reported from the panels on which they serve	Senators can choose to influence any policy area regardless of their committee assignments
Committee consideration of legislation	More difficult to bypass	Easier to bypass[2]
Committee chairs	Subject to party and speakership influence that can limit the chair's discretionary authority over committee operations	Freer rein to manage committees
Committee staff	Often assertive in advocating ideas and proposals	More influential in shaping the legislative agenda
Subcommittee chairmanships	Representatives of the majority party usually must wait at least one term	Majority party senators, regardless of their seniority, usually chair subcommittees

[1] Almost every senator is assigned to one of these committees.

[2] For example, by allowing riders—unrelated policy proposals—to measures pending on the floor.

majority leader Eric Cantor, R-Va., outlined the key steps for securing committee assignments (see Box 7-1).

Although both parties try to accommodate assignment preferences, some members still receive unwelcome assignments. A classic case was that of Democratic representative Shirley Chisholm of Brooklyn (1969–1983), the first African American woman elected to Congress. Initially, she was assigned to the House Agriculture Committee. "I think it would be hard to imagine an assignment that is less relevant to my background or to the needs of the predominantly black and Puerto Rican people who elected me," she said. Chisholm's protests won her a seat on the Veterans' Affairs Committee. "There

BOX 7-1   **How to Get the Committee Assignment You Want**

The first step is to decide which committee assignments are right for you and your district. Soon after the organizational conference, you will receive a Dear Colleague letter from your leadership requesting that you submit your committee preferences. Expect this form by early December at the latest. Your personal policy interests, the needs of your district and state, and your future goals are important factors in deciding which committees to request.

Obtaining a seat on your preferred committee may be a multi-year process depending on vacancies and which committees you select. This applies especially to the "A" committees.

Second, be prepared to make your case as to why you should be selected to your committee of choice. The competition for committees such as Financial Services, Transportation and Infrastructure, and Armed Services can be intense.

Successful arguments may include highlighting your professional experience or policy expertise within the committee's jurisdiction, the critical needs of your district or state, the fact that your region of the country may be under-represented on the committee, or the fact that you may be a vulnerable freshman. Bottom Line: This is about marketing yourself, your experience, your abilities, and your district.

Finally, you should engage the Steering Committee (the GOP's committee assignment panel). First, reach out to your class representative. They will be your primary voice on the Steering Committee and it is important that they be an advocate for your request. Keep in mind that your class representative must prioritize and balance the needs of your entire class.

You should also discuss your committee choices with the elected leaders. They hold a substantial bloc of votes on the Steering Committee. In addition, you may want to reach out to other members of the Steering Committee. Ideally, you want to have someone other than your class and regional representative speak in support of your request when the Steering Committee convenes.

are a lot more veterans in my district than there are trees," she later observed.[34] Yet some urban lawmakers welcome service on the Agriculture Committee, where they can fuse metropolitan issues with rural issues through food stamp, consumer, and other legislation.

How Assignments Are Made

Each party in each house has its own panel to review members' committee requests and dispense assignments to standing committees: the House Republican and Democratic Steering Committees, the Senate Republican Committee on Committees, and the Senate Democratic Steering and Outreach Committee. The decisions of these panels are the first and most important step in a three-step procedure. The second step involves approval of the assignment lists by each party's caucus. Finally, there is a pro forma election by the full House or Senate.

Formal Criteria. Both formal and informal criteria guide the assignment panels in choosing committee members. One formal rule is that each member be treated equitably. However, some lawmakers enjoy "grandfather" rights, meaning that newly adopted party rules governing committee service do not apply to them. For example, Senate GOP conference rules state that two Republicans from the same state should not serve on the same committee. House Democratic rules state that any member who served on either the Appropriations or Ways and Means Committees in the preceding Congress must be reported to the caucus for appropriate action.

Since 1953, when Senate Democratic leader Lyndon B. Johnson of Texas announced his "Johnson rule," all Senate Democrats have been assigned one major committee before any party member receives a second major assignment. In 1965 Senate Republicans followed suit. Senate rules also classify committees into different categories, popularly called "A," "B," and "C." There is even a separate category of prestigious "Super A" committees. Senators may sit on only one of the four Super A panels: Appropriations, Armed Services, Finance, and Foreign Relations (unless they are granted a waiver of the rule). Senate Rule XXV states that members must serve on no more than two committees in the A category, which includes the four Super A panels; one in the B grouping (such as Budget, Rules and Administration, and Small Business); and any number of C committees (Ethics, Indian Affairs, Joint Library, Joint Printing, and Joint Taxation).

Informal Criteria. Many informal criteria affect committee assignments—including party loyalty, geography, substantive expertise, gender, and electoral vulnerability. In their party rules, House Democrats instruct the Steering Committee to consider "merit, length of service, degree of commitment to the Democratic agenda, and Caucus diversity" in granting committee assignments. When House Republicans completed their selection of committee chairs for the 113th Congress, there were no women committee leaders. As a result, female party members made it known to Speaker Boehner that he must rectify this situation by naming women to head the two committees (Ethics and House Administration) with leadership vacancies for which he had appointment authority. The Speaker complied with this request.

Members' own wishes are another criterion. Lawmakers who represent districts or states with large military installations may seek assignment to the Armed Services Committee. Or lawmakers with a specific policy interest (education, health, and so on) may strive to win appointment to panels that deal with those topics. Finally, the committee assignment panels of each congressional party typically respect what is referred to as a "property norm." Returning lawmakers of each party are generally permitted to retain their committee seats (unless they are bumped because of committee ratio changes) before new members bid for vacant committee positions. Lawmakers who do lose their committee positions because of ratio changes may be returned to those panels in the next or subsequent Congresses.

The two Congresses are always intertwined in committee assignment decisions. Each party seeks to boost the electoral resources of its members. House Democratic and GOP leaders, for example, sometimes grant electorally vulnerable freshmen an extra committee assignment or two to broaden their appeal as they head toward their reelection contests. "All of these committees have constituents," said Democratic leader Steny Hoyer of Maryland. "And all of these [freshmen Democratic appointees] have people in their districts who are members of these constituencies."[35] More seasoned members who could face tough electoral competition may seek plum assignments as well, in order to boost their influence and capacity for fund-raising.

Party leaders also promise committee assignments to candidates to help them win election. In the 2010 elections, when Senate GOP leader Mitch McConnell, R-Ky., was campaigning in Arkansas for John Boozman—who successfully challenged incumbent senator Blanche Lincoln, D-Ark.—McConnell vowed he would appoint Boozman to the Agriculture Committee. "John will be on the Agriculture Committee on Day One when we make the committee assignments," declared Senator McConnell. "I have the ability to put him on the Agriculture Committee, and I'm going to do that."[36] Senator Lincoln was the chair of the Agriculture Committee, and McConnell's promise helped to blunt Lincoln's claim that as the chair she could deliver for the farmers and consumers of Arkansas.

After the November 2012 elections, Senate Democratic leader Reid rewarded certain party members with plum committee assignments if they had survived arduous contests or had agreed to take on a difficult party assignment. For example, Sen. Michael Bennet of Colorado accepted the chairmanship of the Democratic Senatorial Campaign Committee for the November 2014 election cycle, likely to be an uphill challenge for the party to defend several vulnerable seats. Bennet was assigned to the Finance Committee. Elizabeth Warren won a tough election in Massachusetts against incumbent GOP senator Scott Brown. She was assigned to the Banking Committee because of her large role in creating the Consumer Financial Protection Bureau and championing financial regulatory reform.[37]

Seniority. Normally, the assignment panels observe seniority when preparing committee membership lists. The member of the majority party with the longest continuous committee service is usually listed first. Senate Republicans—unlike House Republicans and House and Senate Democrats—apply seniority rigidly when two or more GOP senators compete for either a committee vacancy or chairmanship. As a senator noted, "When I first came to the Senate, I was skeptical [of the seniority tradition]. But as I've become more senior, I've grown more fond of it."[38] (The Senate GOP leader fills half of all vacancies on the A committees; seniority determines the other half.)

By contrast, the two House party groups do not observe seniority as strictly as Senate Republicans typically do. House Democratic Caucus rules even state that the party's Steering and Policy Committee "need not necessarily follow seniority" in nominating members for committee posts (see Box 7-2 on party assignment committees). The following overview of how the four most recent Speakers—Newt Gingrich, Hastert, Pelosi, and Boehner—handled the selection of chairs reveals the changing character of the process.

BOX 7-2   **Party Assignment Committees**

House Republicans. Before the 104th Congress began in 1995, incoming Speaker Newt Gingrich, R-Ga., revamped his party's Committee on Committees, which he would chair. Gingrich renamed it the Steering Committee, transformed it into a leadership-dominated panel, eliminated a weighted voting system wherein a GOP member of the assignment panel cast as many votes as there were Republicans in his state delegation, and granted the GOP leader the right to cast the most votes (five). These reforms continued in the subsequent Congresses. The Republican leader also appoints all GOP members of the Rules, House Administration, and Ethics Committees.

House Democrats. Democrats on the House Ways and Means Committee functioned as their party's committee on committees from 1911 until 1974, when the Democratic Caucus voted to transfer this duty to the Steering and Policy Committee. The Steering Committee, co-chaired by Rosa DeLauro of Connecticut and Robert Andrews of New Jersey in the 113th Congress, recommends Democratic assignments to the caucus, one committee at a time.

Senate Republicans. The chair of the Republican Conference appoints the assignment panel of about three to five members. The floor leader is an ex officio member. Idaho senator Michael D. Crapo chairs the panel during the 113th Congress.

Senate Democrats. The Steering and Outreach Committee makes assignments for Democrats. Its size (about twenty-five members) is set by the party conference and may fluctuate from Congress to Congress. The party's floor leader appoints the members of this panel and its chair (Sen. Mark Begich of Alaska, for the 113th Congress).

Gingrich (1995–1999). Speaker Gingrich simply bypassed the seniority custom on several occasions to give chairmanships to lower-seniority colleagues whom he judged could move the party's agenda more vigorously than senior members. Gingrich also was instrumental in having the House adopt a rule imposing a six-year limit on committee and subcommittee chairs. This rule both promotes party direction of committees and triggers "musical chairs" whenever the chairs' six years have expired. (The Rules chair, appointed by the Speaker, is not subject by House rule to the six-year limit.) Republicans also adopted term limits as a House rule.

Hastert (1999–2007). When Dennis Hastert assumed the speakership, he decided to use an interview procedure to determine replacements for full committee chairs who had completed their six years. In a letter to GOP members, Speaker Hastert explained several features of the interview process: "The candidates [for each open chairmanship] will be given an opportunity to discuss their legislative agenda, oversight agenda, how they intend to organize the committees, and their communication strategy."[39] Party loyalty and fundraising prowess were also factors. "You can't tell me a Member who raises $1 million for the party and visits 50 districts is not going to have an advantage over someone who sits back and thinks he's entitled to a chairmanship. Those days are gone," said a top GOP leadership aide.[40] Even with term limits, there is no guarantee that chairs will be permitted to serve their full six years if they rouse the ire of party leaders. In an unprecedented event, GOP leaders ousted a colleague in 2004 (Christopher Smith of New Jersey) as chair of the Veterans' Affairs Committee, removed him from the panel, and named another member as chair. Smith's offense: his outspoken advocacy of more spending on veterans' benefits, which angered Speaker Hastert. The message of Smith's removal was plain to every Republican: toe the party line and be a team player or you will be benched.

Pelosi (2007–2011). Democratic Speaker Nancy Pelosi, unlike her GOP predecessors, chose to follow seniority in designating committee chairs. As a result, many of the Democratic chairs were liberal "old bulls" who either headed or were senior members of several of the most influential committees prior to the GOP takeover in 1995. The so-called old bulls included David Obey, Wis., of Appropriations; George Miller, Calif., of Education and Labor; Barney Frank, Mass., of Financial Services; John Conyers, Mich., of Judiciary; and Charles Rangel, N.Y., of Ways and Means. Few doubt that Pelosi exercised firm control of the Steering Committee's assignment process, however. The panel was chaired by two handpicked allies of the Speaker: California's Miller and Rosa DeLauro of Connecticut. Although Pelosi largely kept the chairs on a short leash, she did allow trusted allies, such as chairs Miller and Obey, greater independence. (Pelosi retained term limits for committee chairs in the 110th Congress but dropped them from the House rulebook in the 111th.)

In the minority after the 2010 elections, a group of disgruntled Democrats wanted to reduce Pelosi's power by taking away her authority to name the Steering Committee co-chairs and transferring it to the Democratic Caucus. Pelosi, now minority leader, sidestepped that effort by offering an amendment to permit the members of the Steering Committee—stacked with Pelosi supporters—to select the co-chairs. Not surprisingly, committee members chose Miller and DeLauro. They also co-chaired the party panel in the 113th Congress.

Boehner (2011–). As chair of the GOP's Steering Committee, with the right to cast more votes (five) than any other panel member, Speaker Boehner had to make several early chairmanship decisions because of the term limits on committee and subcommittee chairs. He wanted the term-limit rule honored for chairs who had reached their six-year limit, and his position was upheld by the Steering Committee. Two examples make the point.

First, at the start of the 112th Congress (2011–2013), Joe Barton of Texas had reached his six-year limit as the top Republican on the Energy and Commerce Committee. He sought a waiver to continue in that role. However, Speaker Boehner was not pleased that as the panel's ranking member, he had publicly apologized to the head of British Petroleum (BP) for the federal government's heavy pressure on the company over the massive oil spill in the Gulf of Mexico in 2010. Speaker Boehner rejected the waiver request, and the Steering Committee named Fred Upton of Michigan to lead the panel despite the opposition of many conservative and Tea Party critics. Upton's conservative critics argued that he had cooperated too much with Democrats and lacked sufficient zeal in cutting federal spending. (Upton, like every candidate for a committee chairmanship, touted conservative credentials and promised to conduct vigorous oversight of the Obama administration.) He remains Energy chair in the 113th House.

Second, there were term-limited chairs, such as Transportation Committee head John Mica, Fla., at the start of the 113th Congress who wanted waivers to continue as panel leaders. Speaker Boehner rejected all such requests except in the special case of Paul Ryan, Wis., who was term-limited as head of the Budget Committee. Representative Ryan's case was special for several reasons. He had been selected as Mitt Romney's vice presidential candidate; he was the GOP's most prominent and authoritative spokesperson on fiscal and budgetary matters; and he was a rising star in the national Republican Party. Moreover, there was broad consensus among party leaders and rank-and-file Republicans that Ryan should be granted a waiver to continue as Budget Committee chair, especially during a period of continuing fiscal challenges among the two parties, chambers, and branches of government.

In addition to upholding the term-limit rule with only rare exceptions, Speaker Boehner took decisive action against four conservative lawmakers who opposed the party on numerous issues. The four were removed from influential panels: Justin Amash, Mich., and Tim Huelskamp, Kan., from the Budget Committee; David Schweikert, Ariz., from Financial Services; and Walter Jones, N.C., from Foreign Affairs. In the view of a House GOP aide, Speaker Boehner's purpose in stripping these members of their committee assignments was to send a message to his GOP colleagues: "You want good things in Congress and to have a good career? Better play nicely."[41] A related explanation was provided by Lynn Westmoreland, Ga., a member of the GOP's assignment panel. He refuted the public contention of the purged members that they had been removed from their panels because of lack of party loyalty as determined by a "secret leadership scorecard." No, declared Representative Westmoreland. "It had to do with their inability to work with other members, which some people might refer to as the [a—hole] factor."[42]

On the Senate side, Republicans adopted in 1997 a party rule restricting committee chairs (or ranking members) to six years of service. "The whole thrust behind this," said the Senate author of the term-limit change, "is to try to get greater participation, so new members of the Senate don't have to wait until they've been here 18 years to play a role."[43] This goal is not easy to achieve because long-serving Republicans are often senior on more than one committee. Thus when they hit the six-year limit, party rules permit them to seek the chairmanship (or ranking minority position) of another committee and leapfrog over a party member with less committee seniority. For example, after serving six years as either chair or ranking member of the Finance Committee, Sen. Charles Grassley, R-Iowa, in the 112th Congress became the ranking member on the Judiciary Committee. Grassley's predecessor on Judiciary was Sen. Orrin Hatch of Utah, who claimed the ranking post on Finance.

Senate Democrats have no term-limit rule for their committee leaders. Their long-standing tradition is to allow seniority on a panel to determine who will be either the chair or ranking minority member of a standing committee. But Senate rules also limit members to one chairmanship. Recall the reference earlier in this chapter to Senator Mikulski and how she became chair of the Appropriations Committee. As another example, in 2011 Democratic senator Barbara Boxer, Calif., returned as head of the Environment and Public Works Committee, even though she was outranked by two of her colleagues—Max Baucus, Mont., who opted to continue as Finance chair, and the now-retired Joseph Lieberman, I-Conn., who continued to chair the Homeland Security and Governmental Affairs Committee.

Biases. The decisions made by the assignment panels inevitably determine the geographical and ideological composition of the standing committees. Committees can easily become biased toward one position or another. Farm areas are overrepresented on the Agriculture Committees and small-business interests on the Small Business Committees. It is no wonder, then, that committees are policy advocates. They propose laws that serve the interests of their members and the outside groups and agencies that gravitate toward them.

Both who gets on a panel and who does not affect committee policy making. Committees that are carefully balanced between liberal and conservative interests can be tilted one way or the other by new members. Meanwhile, the number of women on a committee can sometimes change committee dynamics and outcomes. And new committee leaders can shift a panel's policy agenda and outlook. Senator Boxer's views on environmental policy diverged sharply from those of the previous chair, Sen. James Inhofe, R-Okla.: "Inhofe calls global warming a hoax; Boxer ranks curbing global warming as one of her two top priorities."[44] When Sen. Robert Menendez of New Jersey replaced Sen. John Kerry of Massachusetts (now secretary of state) as chair of the Foreign Relations Committee, there was a shift in attitude toward Cuba. Unlike his predecessor and President Obama, Chairman Menendez is not in favor of relaxing economic sanctions against the island nation. "The time for U.S. engagement" with Cuba, he argued, "will be when we see verifiable market and democratic reforms on the island."[45] A committee's political philosophy influences its success on the House or Senate floor. Committees ideologically out of step with the House or Senate majority are more likely than others to have legislation defeated or significantly revised by floor amendments.

Approval by Party Caucuses and the Chamber

For most of the last century, each chamber's party caucuses either simply ratified the assignment decisions of their committees on committees or took no action on them at all. Beginning in the 1970s, however, party caucuses became major participants in the assignment process. Chairs and ranking minority members were subjected to election by secret ballot of their party colleagues. Clearly, committee leadership is no longer an automatic right.

Although seniority still encourages continuity on committees, the seniority system has now become more flexible and is under party control. House

Democratic rules for the 113th Congress state that upon "a demand supported by 10 or more Members, a separate vote, by secret ballot, shall be had on any member of a committee. . . . If the noes prevail on any such vote, the committee list . . . in question shall be returned to the [Steering Committee] for the sole purpose of implementing the direction of the Caucus." The term-limit rule for House Republicans prevents their members from becoming independent committee barons, as occurred in earlier eras. In the Senate, the parties can exercise control over committees but nearly always defer to the seniority rankings of lawmakers in determining who becomes ranking member on or heads a committee or subcommittee.

Each chamber's rules require that all members of standing committees, including chairs, be elected by the entire House or Senate. The practice is for each party's leaders to offer the caucus-approved assignment lists to the full chamber. Normally, these are approved quickly by voice vote.

COMMITTEE LEADERSHIP

Committee chairs call meetings and establish agendas, hire and fire committee staff, arrange hearings, recommend conferees, act as floor managers, allocate committee funds and rooms, develop legislative strategies, chair hearings and markups, and regulate the internal affairs and organization of their committees. For example, as Senate Judiciary chair Patrick Leahy D-Vt., told a journalist, "I've always set the agenda in Judiciary."[46]

A chair's procedural advantages are hard for even the most forceful minority members to overcome. The chair may be able to kill a bill simply by refusing to schedule it for a hearing. Or a chair may convene meetings when proponents or opponents of the legislation are unavoidably absent. The chair's authority derives from the support of a committee majority and a variety of formal and informal resources, such as substantive and parliamentary experience and control over the agenda, communications, and financial resources of the committee. When told by a committee colleague that he lacked the votes on an issue, House Energy and Commerce chair John Dingell, Mich., reminded him, "Yeah, but I've got the gavel."[47] Dingell banged his gavel, adjourned the meeting, and the majority had no chance to work its will before the legislative session ended.

The Dingell example highlights the formidable ability of chairs to stymie action on legislation they oppose. However, committee chairs also are among the most substantively and strategically knowledgeable members of their panel and of the chamber. They are advantageously positioned to form ideas into law. When Bill Thomas, R-Calif., headed the Ways and Means Committee (2001–2007), he was acknowledged as hard-working, assertive, and shrewd. On many controversial issues (tax, trade, and health), he skillfully mobilized winning coalitions in committee, in the chamber, and in conference with the Senate. Thomas even sought out senatorial advice on how to move legislation in the House in a way that would maximize its chances in the Senate. "He will venture to the Senate floor to run options by key senators of both parties, or to stop in Senate leadership offices, before returning to the House to brief appropriate leaders on the latest state of play."[48]

The ranking minority party members on committees are also influential figures. Among their powers on various committees are nominating minority conferees, hiring and firing minority staff, sitting ex officio on all subcommittees, assisting in setting the committee's agenda, managing legislation on the floor, and acting as committee spokespersons for their party. Ranking members, as appropriate, present minority alternatives to majority proposals, challenge the chair on procedural and policy matters, develop tactics and strategies to foil the majority's plans, and highlight party goals and views to the attentive public. For example, Elijah Cummings, D-Md., won the ranking position on the Oversight and Government Reform Committee over other competitors because he was viewed as more able than the others to counterattack the aggressive and media-savvy chair of the panel, Darrel Issa of California.[49]

POLICY MAKING IN COMMITTEE

Committees foster deliberate and collegial but often fragmented decisions. They encourage bargaining and accommodation among members. To move bills through Congress's multiple decision points from subcommittee to committee, authors of bills and resolutions typically make compromises in response to important committee members, among others. These gatekeepers may exact numerous alterations in a bill's substance. The proliferation of committees also multiplies the points of access for outside interests.

Overlapping Jurisdictions

The formal responsibilities of standing committees are defined by the rules of each house, various public laws, and precedents. Committees do not have watertight jurisdictional compartments. Any broad subject overlaps numerous committees. The Senate has an Environment and Public Works Committee, but other panels also consider environmental legislation. The same is true in the House. These House bodies, along with a brief sketch of some of their environmental responsibilities, are as follows:

Agriculture: pesticides; soil conservation; some water programs

Appropriations: funding for environmental programs and agencies

Energy and Commerce: health effects of the environment; environmental regulations; solid waste disposal; clean air; safe drinking water

Financial Services: open space acquisition in urban areas

Foreign Affairs: international environmental cooperation

Natural Resources: water resources; power resources; land management; wildlife conservation; national parks; nuclear waste; fisheries; endang-ered species

Oversight and Government Reform: federal executive branch agencies for the environment

Science, Space, and Technology: environmental research and development

Small Business: effects of environmental regulations on business

Transportation and Infrastructure: water pollution; sludge management

Ways and Means: environmental tax expenditures

Jurisdictional overlaps can have positive results. They enable members to develop expertise in several policy fields, prevent any one group from dominating a topic, and promote healthy competition among committees. Committees with overlapping jurisdictions sometimes formulate a written memorandum of understanding that informally outlines how policy topics are to be referred among them.[50] But healthy competition can quickly turn into intercommittee warfare. Various House and Senate committees periodically clash over issues that do not fit neatly into any single panel's area of responsibility (energy and environmental issues, for example). Committees' formal jurisdictional mandates have not kept pace with change—nor can they, given the constant emergence of new issues (such as global warming). Another trigger of turf battles is forum shopping by outside interests, who want their carefully drafted bills referred to sympathetic committees.

The expansionist tendency of some committees also can create intercommittee tussles. The "bold jurisdictional power grab" by the House Energy and Commerce Committee for an intellectual copyright bill will not stand, declared the bipartisan leaders of the Judiciary Committee. "Rest assured, we will wholeheartedly oppose this move in a bipartisan fashion, as we would expect Energy and Commerce leaders to do if we attempted to write energy legislation."[51] At the start of the 112th Congress, the incoming chair of the Natural Resources Committee, Doc Hastings, R-Wash., urged GOP leaders to transfer energy jurisdiction from the Energy and Commerce Committee to his panel. "In terms of legislative power, it is a Goliath," Hastings declared. "[Energy and Commerce] is the committee that spawned Obamacare and the Democrats' cap-and-trade national energy tax."[52] Energy and Commerce chair Fred Upton, R-Mich., quickly defended his panel's jurisdiction. "To diminish the authority of the Energy and Commerce Committee," he wrote, "is to weaken the power of the House—the people's body—and give an upper hand to the Democrat[ic] White House and Senate."[53] Another GOP Energy and Commerce panel member bluntly stated that Hastings's move "will not be successful. You don't spend four years getting back into the majority and immediately go into cannibal mode."[54] In the end, the GOP Steering

Committee rejected Hastings's effort to capture part of the Energy and Commerce panel's jurisdiction.[55]

Multiple Referrals

When a bill is introduced in the House, it usually is referred to a single committee. House rules traditionally made no provision for multiple referrals, although informally at times more than one panel reviewed the same bill. In 1975, however, the rules were changed to permit several types of multiple referrals. This change augmented the Speaker's authority and granted him additional flexibility in referring measures to various committees.

When Republicans assumed control of the House in 1995, they streamlined multiple referrals and placed them firmly under the Speaker's control. The Speaker must "designate a committee of primary jurisdiction upon the initial referral of a measure to a committee." The primary committee concept increases accountability for legislation while retaining for the Speaker flexibility in determining whether, when, and for how long other panels can receive the measure.

At the time of initial referral, the Speaker identifies the primary committee. It has predominant responsibility for shepherding the legislation to final passage. The Speaker may also send the measure to secondary panels. The House parliamentarian calls this practice an additional initial referral. In the following example of referral language, the Energy and Commerce Committee is the primary committee and Judiciary is the additional initial panel:

> H.R. 650. A bill to establish reasonable legal reforms that will facilitate the manufacture of vital, life-saving vaccines, and for other purposes; to the Committee on Energy and Commerce, and in addition to the Committee on the Judiciary, for a period to be subsequently determined by the Speaker, in each case for consideration of such provisions as fall within the jurisdiction of the committee concerned.

Multiple referrals may promote integrated policy making, broader public discussion of issues, wider access to the legislative process, and consideration of alternative approaches. They also enhance the Speaker's scheduling prerogatives. The Speaker can use the referral power to intervene more directly in committee activities and even to set deadlines for committees to report multiply referred legislation. The reverse is also possible: the Speaker can delay action on measures by referring them to other committees. Thus multiple referrals can be employed to slow down legislative decision making. (About 20 percent of measures introduced in the House are multireferred.)

The Senate usually sends measures to a single committee—the committee with jurisdiction over the subject matter that predominates in the legislation. Although multiple referrals have long been permitted by unanimous consent, they are used infrequently, mainly because senators have many opportunities to influence policy making on the floor. Senate procedures provide lawmakers with relatively easy ways either to bypass the referral of legislation to committees or to raise issues for chamber consideration (see Chapter 8).

Where Bills Go

Many bills referred to committee are sent by the chair to a subcommittee. Others are retained for review by the full committee. In the end, committees and subcommittees select the measures they want to consider and ignore the rest. Committee consideration usually consists of three standard steps: public hearings, markups, and reports.

Hearings. When committees or subcommittees conduct hearings on a bill, they listen to a wide variety of witnesses. These include the bill's sponsors, federal officials, pressure group representatives, business leaders, public officials, and private citizens—sometimes even celebrities. Celebrity witnesses can help give a bill national visibility. As a senator put it, "Quite candidly, when Hollywood speaks, the world listens. Sometimes when Washington speaks, the world snoozes."[56]

Equally important are witnesses who add drama to hearings because of their first-hand experience with an issue or problem. The Senate Finance Committee, for example, attracted national headlines with its hearings on alleged wrongdoings by the Internal Revenue Service (IRS). Taxpayers recounted their horrendous experiences, and IRS agents donned black hoods to tell about the organization's mistreatment of taxpayers.[57] Testimony by employees who lost their jobs and retirement savings because of corporate scandals and mismanagement helped to galvanize congressional enactment of corporate accounting and accountability laws, such as the Dodd-Frank Wall Street Reform and Consumer Protection Act (P.L. 111–203).[58] Dueling hearings in the House and Senate during the 112th Congress featured as witnesses citizens who had experienced first-hand the effect of the health care overhaul. Witnesses in the GOP House hearings castigated and criticized what they called Obamacare. In response, Senate Democratic committee hearings in defense of the health care law heard "testimony from people who live outside the Beltway."[59] Hearings, then, are often orchestrated as political theater in which witnesses put a human face on a public problem and tell stories that may generate public momentum for or against legislation.[60]

Hearings also provide opportunities for committee members to be heard on issues. Frequently, lawmakers present their views on legislation in their opening statements and in the guise of questioning witnesses. By revealing the patterns and intensity of support or opposition and by airing substantive problems, hearings indicate to members whether a bill is worth taking to the full chamber. Most hearings follow a traditional format. Each witness reads a prepared statement. Then each committee member has a limited time (often five minutes) to ask questions before the next witness is called. To save time and promote give and take, committees occasionally use a panel format in which witnesses sit together and briefly summarize their statements.

Committees will sometimes convene joint hearings with other relevant House or Senate panels. They also may organize field hearings in cities around the country to generate and solicit public support for an issue, or, in a two Congresses theme, schedule hearings in the chair's state or district to win him or her favorable publicity and visibility prior to the November elections. Party committees, ad hoc legislative groups, or individual lawmakers also may conduct informal hearings of their own. Committees may even hold pre-hearings so committee members can be better informed about the issues likely to be raised during a scheduled hearing.

Committees are harnessing contemporary technology to conduct Capitol Hill hearings. Recent Speakers urged all committees to utilize technology to provide live broadcasts of their hearings online ("Webcasts") in order to make the legislative process "fully accessible and transparent" to the public.[61] House and Senate panels have used interactive video, teleconferencing, e-hearings, and other technology to collect testimony from witnesses who may be located in other parts of the nation or world. The Internet has been used to transmit testimony, and cable television viewers have e-mailed or faxed questions to witnesses.[62] And, in a first, an astronaut became the only person ever to deliver testimony from space to a committee hearing on Capitol Hill.[63]

Some of the overlapping purposes served by hearings are the following:

- To explore the need for legislation
- To build a public record in support of legislation
- To publicize the role of committee chairs
- To stake out committee jurisdictions
- To review executive implementation of public laws
- To provide a forum for citizens' grievances and frustrations
- To educate lawmakers and the attentive public on complex issues
- To raise the visibility of an issue

Hearings are shaped mainly by the chairs and their top staff, with varying degrees of input from party leaders, the ranking minority member, and others. Chairs who favor bills can expedite the hearings process; conversely, they can kill with kindness legislation they oppose by holding endless hearings. When a bill is not sent to the full chamber, the printed hearings are the end product of the committee's work. Committee chairs, mindful of the two Congresses, can also use hearings to try and win reelection by addressing issues that appeal to various voting groups in their state or district.

Markups. After hearings are held, committee members decide the bill's actual language—that is, they mark up or amend the bill (see Box 7-3 on committee decision making). Chairs may circulate their "mark" (the measure open for amendment) to committee colleagues and solicit their comments and suggestions.

To promote greater transparency and accountability, House Republicans adopted chamber rules that require committees to make their markup vehicle available online to the public at least twenty-four hours prior to markup meetings. In addition, committees are obligated to make amendments adopted during markup publicly available online within twenty-four hours, and record votes during markups are to be publicly available in electronic form within forty-eight hours.

Some panels adhere closely to parliamentary rules during the committee amending phase; others operate by consensus with few or no votes taken on the issues; and still others have "conceptual markups." A senator explained that Finance Committee markups "are not about legislative language. They are concept documents that are then put into legislative language and brought to the floor."[64] Concepts may include, for example, whether going to school counts as work for welfare recipients or what kind of tax plan best fosters economic growth. Proponents try to craft a bill that will muster the backing of their colleagues, the other chamber, lobbyists, and the White House.

The markup process can be arduous because members often face the two Congresses dilemma: whether to support a bill that might be good for the nation or oppose it because of the opposition of their constituents. Not surprisingly, the bill that emerges from markup is usually the one that can attract the support of the most members. As a former chair of the House Ways and Means Committee stated, "We have not written perfect law; perhaps a faculty of scholars could do a better job. A group of ideologues could have produced greater consistency. But politics is an imperfect process."[65] Or as Sen. Pat Roberts, R-Kan., said about a bill revamping the intelligence community: "While this is not the best possible bill, it is the best bill possible."[66]

Outside pressures often intensify during markup deliberations. Under House and Senate sunshine rules, markups must be conducted in public, except on national security or related issues. Compromises can be difficult to achieve in markup rooms filled with lobbyists watching how each member will vote. Thus committees sometimes conduct pre-markups in private to work out their positions on various issues.

After conducting hearings and markups, a subcommittee sends its recommendations to the full committee. The full committee may conduct hearings and markups on its own, ratify the subcommittee's decision, take no action, or return the matter to the subcommittee for further study.

Reports. If the full committee votes to send the bill to the House or Senate, the staff prepares a report, subject to committee approval, describing the purposes and provisions of the legislation. Reports emphasize arguments favorable to the bill, summarizing selectively the results of staff research and hearings. Reports are noteworthy documents. The bill itself may be long, highly technical, and confusing to most readers. "A good report, therefore, does more than explain—it also persuades," commented a congressional staff aide.[67] Furthermore, reports may guide executive agencies and federal courts in interpreting ambiguous or complex legislative language.

The Policy Environment

Executive agencies, pressure groups, party leaders and caucuses, and the entire House or Senate form the backdrop against which a committee makes policy. (To be sure, outside groups, the 24/7 media, and the broad issue context of a particular period all influence committees' policy environment.) These environments may be consensual or conflictual. Some policy questions are settled fairly easily; others are bitterly controversial. Environments also may be monolithic or pluralistic. Some committees have a single dominant source of outside influence; others face numerous competing groups or agencies.

Environmental factors influence committees in at least four ways. First, they shape the content of public policies and thus the likelihood that these policies will be accepted by the full House or Senate. The Judiciary Committees are buffeted by diverse and competing pressure groups who feel passionately about volatile issues such as abortion, immigration, and gun control. The committees' chances for achieving agreement among their members or on the floor depend to a large extent on their abilities to deflect such issues altogether—or to accommodate diverse groups through artful legislative drafting and political accommodation.

Second, policy environments foster mutual alliances among committees, federal departments, and pressure groups—the "iron triangles." The House and Senate Veterans' Affairs Committees, for example, regularly advocate legislation to benefit veterans' groups, the second point in the triangle. This effort is backed by the Department of Veterans' Affairs, the third point in the triangle. At the very least, issue networks emerge. These are fluid and amorphous groups of policy experts who try to influence any committee that deals with their subject area.[68]

Third, policy environments establish decision-making objectives and guidelines for committees. Clientele-oriented committees, such as the House and Senate Small Business Committees, try to promote the policy views of their clientele groups, small-business enterprises. Alliances between committees and federal departments also shape decisions, such as the traditional support given the military by the House and Senate Armed Services Committees.

Finally, environmental factors influence the level of partisanship on committees. Some committees are relatively free of party infighting, but other committees consider contentious social issues that often divide the two parties. The House Judiciary Committee is filled with conservative Republican and liberal Democratic firebrands. Their sharp ideological clashes sometimes receive wide publicity, such as the panel's nationally televised impeachment of President Bill Clinton along party lines. To try to reduce the intense partisanship on various committees, their chairs have organized informal gatherings or bipartisan retreats as a way for committee members "to find common ground despite the strong feelings on a lot of issues."[69]

BOX 7-3   **Committee Decision Making: A Formal Model**

Political scientists use a variety of sophisticated techniques to understand legislative decision making. Employing concepts from economics such as rational choice—the notion that individuals (or lawmakers) have preferences or desires and that they will act in their self-interest to achieve their goals—these scholars utilize a number of analytical tools to consider how lawmakers devise strategies to accomplish their policy objectives. One such analytical approach is called spatial theory. The term *spatial* refers to a mathematical idea that theorists rely on called a policy space. An easy-to-understand example is that certain policy preferences can all be arrayed along a straight line, or unidimensional continuum. For example, one end of the line might be labeled "more spending" and the other "less spending." Different spending preferences could be placed at different points, or spaces, along the line.

In employing spatial theory to model legislative decision making, scholars make a number of assumptions. Two are especially important: (1) lawmakers hold consistent preferences, and (2) members have an ideal policy outcome that they prefer. Put differently, lawmakers will vote for policy alternatives that bring them closer to their policy ideal and oppose those that do the reverse. The work of these scholars highlights the importance of institutional rules and procedures in determining which of several policy alternatives will prevail. Analysts have also found that the median voter—the midpoint lawmaker with an equal number of other members to his or her left or right—is the ultimate determiner of outcomes in unidimensional cases. Another way to view the median voter is the 218th vote in the House, the Supreme Court justice who casts the fifth vote in a 5–4 decision, or the member who casts the sixth vote in a committee of eleven members.

To depict this graphically, assume that a House Appropriations subcommittee has sent to the floor a spending bill that reflects its committee median (CM). The subcommittee also must take into account a floor median (FM) if it wants its majority position to carry the day on the floor. The current policy status quo (Q) means that, if the bill does not pass, last year's funding level remains in force. If the subcommittee's bill is brought to the floor under a no-amendment rule, then the House membership can either accept or reject the panel's position. If the House rejects the subcommittee's policy recommendation, it has agreed to retain the status quo. Whether the subcommittee's position prevails on the floor can be depicted using these two examples.

If the subcommittee's position is to win on the House floor, it must devise a strategy that takes account of the majority preferences of the membership. Furthermore, the subcommittee

COMMITTEE STAFF

Staff aides play a big role in the three principal stages of committee policy making—hearings, markup, and report. Representatives and senators (the latter to a greater degree because there are fewer of them) cannot handle their large workloads on their own, so they must rely heavily on their unelected employees. Indeed, Congress needs qualified professional staff to counter the expertise lodged in the executive branch and in the lobbying community. In the House, committee resources are roughly divided between the majority and minority parties on a two-thirds to one-third basis; in the Senate, it is a 60 to 40 percent ratio. Informally, both parties rely on a network of outside experts to help them evaluate proposals from the executive branch, forge policy must have some way to acquire information about the policy options likely to be accepted by at least a majority of the House. These types of considerations are commonplace in the real world of Capitol Hill policy making.

Example 1

More spending			Less spending
FM	CM		Q

In Example 1, the preferences of a majority of the House clearly are closer to the committee's position than the status quo. Thus, the committee's position prevails.

Example 2

More spending			Less spending
FM		Q	CM

In Example 2, a majority of the House clearly favors the policy status quo instead of the committee's position, which loses in an up-or-down floor vote.

Most bills concern not a single dimension, such as more or less spending, but a multitude of dimensions. For example, a bill might be close to a member's ideal point on the spending dimension but be far away on another dimension, such as which governmental level (federal or state) should handle the issue. The introduction of additional dimensions (multidimensionality) produces greater difficulty in analyzing legislative decision making. By employing spatial theory and other analytical approaches, political scientists strive to better understand and explain congressional politics and decision making.[1]

[1] See, for example, Kenneth Shepsle and Mark Boncheck, *Analyzing Politics* (New York: Norton, 1977); Charles Stewart, *Analyzing Congress* (New York: Norton, 2001); and Gerald Strom, *The Logic of Lawmaking: A Spatial Theory Approach* (Baltimore: Johns Hopkins University Press, 1990).

---

proposals, or provide strategic advice. For example, think tanks provide lawmakers and their staff with numerous domestic, defense, and foreign policy options and proposals.

The discretionary agenda of Congress and its committees is powerfully shaped by the congressional staff. Their influence can be direct or indirect, substantive or procedural, visible or invisible. In the judgment of one former senator, "Most of the work and most of the ideas come from the staffers. They are predominantly young men and women, fresh out of college and professional schools. They are ambitious, idealistic, and abounding with ideas."[70] However, staff tenure is relatively short. According to a 2010 survey conducted by the House's Chief Administrative Office, the tenure of personal staff ranges from

6.7 years for chiefs of staff to 1.8 years for staff assistants. The average tenure for Senate aides is about 5.3 years. Many committee, personal, and leadership aides use their experience as a stepping-stone to other jobs, such as lobbying.

Policy proposals emanate from many sources—the White House, administrative agencies, interest groups, state and local officials, scholars, and citizens—but staff aides are strategically positioned to advance or hinder these proposals. As one Senate committee staff director recounted, "Usually, you draw up proposals for the year's agenda, lay out the alternatives. You can put in some stuff you like and leave out some you don't. I recommend ideas that the [chair is] interested in and also that I'm interested in."[71] Many committee staff members are active in outside communications and issue networks (health or the environment, for example) that enhance lawmakers' abilities to make informed decisions.[72]

Staff aides negotiate with legislators, lobbyists, and executive officials on issues, legislative language, and political strategy. Staff members do the essential spadework that can lead to changes in policy or new laws. For example, a "team totaling 20 [Senate Governmental Affairs] aides, including detailees from the FBI and CIA" drafted the 2004 bill that reorganized the nation's intelligence community.[73] Staff aides sometimes make policy decisions. Consider their crucial role on a defense appropriations bill:

> The dollar figures in the huge piece of legislation [were] so immense that House-Senate conferees, negotiating their differences. . . , relegated almost every item less than $100 million to staff aides on grounds that the members themselves did not have time to deal with such items, which [a senator] called "small potatoes."[74]

During hearings, aides recruit witnesses, on their own or at the specific direction of the chair, and plan when and in what order they appear. In addition, staff aides commonly accompany committee members to the floor to give advice, draft amendments, and negotiate compromises. The number of aides who can be present on the floor is limited, however, by House and Senate regulations.

For information, analyses, policy options, and research projects, committee staff can turn to the three legislative support agencies: the Congressional Research Service, established in 1914; the Government Accountability Office, established in 1921 (as the General Accounting Office and renamed in 2004); and the Congressional Budget Office, established in 1974. Unlike committee or personal aides, the Congressional Research Service, the Government Accountability Office, and the Congressional Budget Office operate under strict rules of nonpartisanship and objectivity. Staffed with experts, they provide Congress with analytical talent matching that in executive agencies, universities, and specialized groups.

Staffing reflects members' dual roles in the two Congresses: national policy maker and constituency representative. It can sometimes be a controversial process. A New Jersey senator, for example, was criticized by African American clergy in his state for "failing to appoint blacks to important positions on his personal staff" as he had promised he would when he was running for office. The senator responded that he had hired professional black staffers and "defended his efforts to hire members of racial minorities."[75] During the electoral season, staffers frequently take unpaid leave to work as campaign volunteers for their boss or "to boost their party's prospects in pivotal races."[76]

COMMITTEE REFORM AND CHANGE

Since passage of the Legislative Reorganization Act of 1946, Congress has made numerous attempts to reform the committee system but has only rarely succeeded. Because of strong opposition from members who stood to surrender subcommittee chairmanships or favored jurisdictions, Congress has had only mixed success in reorganization efforts. Two changes to the committee system illustrate some of the difficulties associated with changing the committee structure. One revision created a homeland security panel in each chamber; another concerned the formation and then the demise of a select intelligence panel within the House Appropriations Committee.

Homeland Security Committees

The National Commission on Terrorist Attacks upon the United States (also called the 9/11 Commission) urged the House and Senate to each create a single authorizing committee for homeland security. Its report stated that at least eighty-eight committees and subcommittees in Congress had some jurisdiction over the Department of Homeland Security. Arguably, the formation of House and Senate homeland security panels would minimize turf conflicts, reduce the number of panels before which top DHS officials would have to appear as witnesses, and strengthen congressional oversight of the new department. Eventually, both chambers responded to the commission's suggestion, but in different ways.

In the Senate, the GOP and Democratic leaders created in August 2004 a twenty-two-person working group (headed by Sens. Mitch McConnell and Harry Reid) to review the commission's recommendations for improving oversight of intelligence and homeland security. Two months later, the Senate debated the McConnell-Reid plan (S. Res. 445), which called for renaming the Governmental Affairs Committee the Homeland Security and Governmental Affairs Committee and assigning it broad authority for overseeing domestic security and DHS. Achieving that objective, however, would require ten standing committees to give up some of their jurisdiction to the renamed Governmental Affairs panel.

During floor action on S. Res. 445, several amendments were successfully offered by committee chairs and ranking members reclaiming the jurisdiction that would have been lost to the renamed Governmental Affairs Committee if the resolution was adopted unchanged. "We're creating a shell," lamented Joseph I. Lieberman of Connecticut, the ranking Democrat on the Governmental Affairs Committee. "We're calling a committee a homeland security committee. But if you pick up the shell, there's not much homeland security under it."[77] The chair of the Governmental Affairs Committee, Susan Collins, R-Maine, said the changes made to S. Res. 445 left her newly renamed panel with "less than 38 percent of the Department of Homeland Security's budget and 8 percent of its personnel."[78] Dismayed by these events, both Collins and Lieberman voted against S. Res. 445, which was approved on October 9, 2004, by a 79–6 vote. S. Res. 445 also called for the creation of a Senate Appropriations Subcommittee on Intelligence, but that proposal was not acted upon.

At the opening of the 109th Congress, the House replaced its temporary select panel on homeland security with a standing committee. The permanent panel was given, among other responsibilities, jurisdiction over general homeland security policy and the organization and administration of the Department of Homeland Security. The new committee also was assigned broad oversight authority over all government "activities relating to homeland security, including the interaction of all departments and agencies with the Department of Homeland Security." Even with the creation of the new panel, however, oversight of homeland security is still spread among nine other authorizing committees.

The turf-conscious committee chairs negotiated with their party leaders to preserve some portion of their panels' jurisdiction that had been given to the new standing committee. A detailed analysis of how homeland security legislation was to be referred among all the committees with homeland security jurisdiction was included in the *Congressional Record*.[79] To illustrate, the Homeland Security Committee was to receive bills dealing with "transportation security," and the Transportation and Infrastructure Committee retained its jurisdiction over measures dealing with "transportation safety." Plainly, this jurisdictional distinction is somewhat akin to the adage "two sides of the same coin."

At the start of the 112th Congress, House GOP leaders considered—and rejected—giving the Homeland Security Committee the predominance of jurisdiction over the Department of Homeland Security. Peter King, R-N.Y., the chair of the Homeland Security panel, urged party leaders to consolidate significant policy and oversight responsibility in his committee rather than maintain the status quo of having DHS subject to the marching orders of numerous committees and subcommittees. But John Mica, R-Fla., the head of the Transportation Committee, along with other committee chairs, argued that "their committees should get more homeland security turf, not less."[80] Plainly, GOP leaders did not want to open the new Congress with a bitter and divisive jurisdictional battle over committee turf and quietly quashed the matter. Similarly, when three House Republicans urged their party colleagues to create a new standing Committee on Health Care in the 113th Congress, their idea faded quickly. Most Republicans did not want to provoke an acrimonious fight over jurisdictional turf.[81]

Select Intelligence Oversight Panel

The 9/11 Commission declared congressional oversight of intelligence "dysfunctional." It recommended that the House and Senate create a single panel with the authority to both authorize and appropriate funds for the intelligence community. On the November 2006 campaign trail, the Pelosi-led Democrats vowed to implement all the outstanding recommendations of the commission, including the merger of the authorizing and appropriating processes for intelligence. In partial fulfillment of that promise, Speaker Pelosi successfully advocated a plan that achieved the goal of strengthening intelligence oversight without implementing the commission's exact recommendation.

Her proposal, which the House adopted on January 9, 2007, established a Select Intelligence Oversight Panel on Appropriations as a component of the Appropriations Committee. The panel was composed of thirteen members (eight majority members, five minority)—ten from the Appropriations Committee and three from the Permanent Select Intelligence Committee. The job of the select panel was to submit its recommendation for the intelligence community budget to the Appropriations Subcommittee on Defense for the determinative spending level for intelligence. House Republicans opposed the select panel's formation, in part because it did not implement the 9/11 Commission's proposal to merge the authorizing and appropriating functions in one committee.

When Republicans reclaimed control of the House after the November 2010 elections, they abolished the Select Intelligence Oversight Panel. They argued that the panel was a redundant layer of committee bureaucracy. Other committees—Armed Services, Homeland Security, and Permanent Select Intelligence—could achieve the goal of intercommittee coordination between authorizers and appropriators that led to the select panel's formation in the first place. House Democrats urged Republicans to reestablish the panel, but they were not successful. Rush Holt, D-N.J., the outgoing chair of the select panel, said Republicans supported its elimination because the idea for it originated with their nemesis, Speaker Pelosi.[82] A House GOP leadership aide contended that the "sub-panel created by Democrats" did not establish one committee with both authorizing and appropriating authority over the intelligence community. Instead, the Democratic plan "diffused rather than consolidated oversight."[83]

However, during the GOP-controlled 112th House, the chair of the Permanent Select Intelligence Committee devised a new arrangement between his panel and the Appropriations Committee. Three appropriators would participate in Intelligence Committee hearings and meetings. Under the panel's rules for the 113th Congress, members and staff may share pertinent intelligence information with the House and Senate Committees on Appropriations. For its part, the relevant Senate committees (Appropriations and Select Intelligence) signed a memorandum of agreement "pledging greater cooperation."[84]

Committees are remarkably durable, resilient, and stable institutions, despite the periodic forces for change that buffet them (such as public criticism of Congress and reformist sentiment among institutionally minded lawmakers). Major committee restructuring plans, as the several committee reform efforts in the post–World War II period attest, almost always fail or produce only marginal adjustments in committees' jurisdictional mandates, policy-making influence, or method of operation. Scholars and lawmakers posit various theories to explain why it is difficult to accomplish major jurisdictional realignment. For example, because the control of jurisdictional turf is viewed as power, Speaker Thomas P. "Tip" O'Neill Jr., D-Mass., explained the House's rejection of a major 1973–1974 committee realignment plan in this succinct manner: "The name of the game is power, and the boys don't want to give it up."[85] A political scientist offered an electoral explanation for the demise of committee reshuffling plans that embodies the two Congresses concept:

> [A] primary and constant force hindering committee restructuring movements has been the electoral objectives of members of Congress. Under pressure to bolster their reelection prospects in order to achieve long-term legislative and personal goals, rational politicians with the ability to shape legislative structures utilize the arrangement of rules and procedures to secure targeted government benefits for needy constituents and voting blocs. Any widespread change in the established order of policy deliberation—particularly its centerpiece—the committee system—would create far too much uncertainty in members' electoral strategies and therefore would be broadly opposed from the start.[86]

Whatever other factors (such as interest group, party leadership, or committee member and staff opposition) impede major committee overhaul, these workshops of Congress evolve in response to new events and circumstances. Several recent developments highlight the dynamic quality of the committee system. These include ebbs and flows in the authority of committee chairs, the use of task forces, and the circumvention of the committee process.

Constricting the Authority of Committee Chairs

When Republicans took control of both houses of Congress in the mid-1990s, many GOP committee chairs had to take more direction from their top leaders, especially in the House. Committee chairs "have been at the mercy of top House and Senate Republican leaders," wrote two congressional analysts, "who—given the high level of partisanship and the small size of their majorities—have resorted to dictating legislation from the top down in order to maintain some semblance of control."[87] Centralized control over committees was plainly evident during the speakership of Newt Gingrich (1995–1999), who sometimes circumvented committee consideration of legislation, dictated legislative changes to committees, used the Rules Committee to redraft committee-reported measures, and engaged in other actions that undermined the committee system, such as creating partisan task forces.

Speaker Hastert, too, was not reluctant to rein in committee chairs. The removal of the Veterans' chair, noted earlier, underscores that point. The Speaker also exercised tight control over the Appropriations Committee. After

Hastert won adoption in 2003 of a party rules change requiring the Appropriations subcommittee chairs to be approved by the Steering Committee, one of the subcommittee leaders said, "Now the leadership gets to have the [subcommittee chairs] come in and grovel before them."[88] Two years later, the Steering Committee warned a subcommittee chair that he could lose the chairmanship of his Appropriations subcommittee if he "does not raise or donate more money to Republicans."[89]

Speaker Pelosi worked to keep the committee chairs under control and to shape the party message and agenda at the top leadership level. After all, a major focus of Pelosi was to retain Democratic control of the House in the November 2008 and 2010 elections. She could not permit independent-minded committee chairs to do their own thing and jeopardize this fundamental party goal. At the same time, Speaker Pelosi recognized the need to have a productive relationship with her chairs, because much of the House's work is carried out by these "little legislatures." Achieving the right balance between "top-down" command and committee autonomy is no easy task. Henry Waxman, D-Calif., a committee chair and a Pelosi ally, put it this way: "I think there has to be a lot more direction from the leadership to the committees of jurisdiction. We don't want to return to the days of committee chairs that felt they didn't have to be accountable. There has to be a balance."[90] When asked, Waxman declined to say whether the correct balance had been achieved.

As a former committee chair, Speaker Boehner wanted to follow the "regular order" and allow committees to produce legislative products by observing the usual deliberative process of hearings, markups, and reports. He promised that in the 112th House "no more bills [would be] written behind closed doors in the speaker's office. Bills should be written by legislators in committee in plain public view."[91] The reality was somewhat different, however. The regular order was followed in the House on many measures, but the Democratic Senate often viewed them as "message" bills and took no action. (The reverse pattern also occurred: Senate-passed bills languished in the Republican House.) On nearly every major bill considered in the contentious 112th Congress, political reality trumped the regular order. The most significant measures were the product of private negotiations among the top House party leaders, particularly the Speaker, Senate leaders (with Senate GOP leader Mitch McConnell often playing a key role), Vice President Joe Biden, and President Obama. Key staff aides to these party and executive branch leaders were also instrumental negotiators on the critical bills highlighted in various chapters of this book, such as the summer 2011 battle to raise the borrowing authority of the federal government and the December 2012 effort to avert the so-called "fiscal cliff."

Committees were bypassed by the top-down legislating. "The declawing of committees and their chiefs," wrote several congressional journalists, "is a direct result of the deadline-busting approach to lawmaking that has dominated" the 112th Congress. Democrats and Republicans "wait until the last possible moment to reach agreement on major bills, a habit that short-circuits the committee process in favor of direct negotiations between House and Senate leaders," the president, and other executive officials.[92] In short, policy making by brinksmanship has strengthened party leaders and weakened committee leaders. Tellingly, Speaker Boehner stated that he wants the 113th House to rely on committees to process legislation through the regular order. Sometimes the Speaker's goal cannot be achieved as aspiration meets legislative reality.

Senate committee chairs also are subject to direction from their party leadership, as these several examples illustrate. Senate majority leader Harry Reid told Finance chair Max Baucus "to stop chasing Republican votes on [President Obama's] massive health care reform bill."[93] Earlier, when political momentum began to build for a patients' bill of rights measure, another majority leader took the issue away from the chair of the Health, Education, Labor, and Pensions Committee and "created a [party] task force . . . to write the . . . bill."[94] That majority leader also gave the Finance Committee a deadline to report a priority bill or else he would call up the proposal he favored.[95] As for the brinksmanship practiced by the 112th Congress, Sen. Bob Corker, R-Tenn., exclaimed that the Senate is "not working and it's not working because nothing [major] passes through committees anymore. It's airdropped from the top."[96] The point is that on measures of utmost party importance, congressional leaders will often override the prerogatives of committee chairs to take control of crucial agenda items. Senate majority leader Reid stated that during the 113th Congress, he is relying on the committee system to deal with such major issues as immigration reform and gun control.[97]

The ability of today's party leaders, particularly in the House, to exercise significant control over committee leaders represents a major change in how today's Congress works. The chairs are subject to centralized leadership direction on the party's top priorities and might face sanctions if their performance does not comport with party expectations. On the one hand, this development ensures that the chairs (and ranking minority members) are ultimately accountable for their actions to the Democratic Caucus or Republican Conference. On the other hand, tight leadership control, combined with term limits for House and Senate Republicans, could gradually diminish the traditional role of committees as the policy specialization system for the legislative branch. Why bother to devote years of effort to becoming substantive experts, some committee members might ask, if policy on major issues is decided at the top and committee leaders are forced to relinquish their posts after six years (if not sooner)?

Party Task Forces

Speaker Gingrich was noted for creating numerous party task forces, in part because he could determine their mandate and timetable, appoint the chair and members, and assign a deadline for drafting a product. Many of these task forces did little, but some wrote legislation. Indeed, task forces can forge consensus, draft legislation, coordinate strategy, promote intraparty communication, and involve noncommittee members and junior members in issue areas.

Gingrich's use of task forces provides a practical look at the three theories of legislative organization: the distributional hypothesis, the informational hypothesis, and the party hypothesis. The Speaker's Task Force on California was established in large measure to ensure that the politically important state of California received its fair share of federal funds from the GOP-controlled House. This panel's formation buttressed the committee autonomy or distributive politics view of congressional organization: committees are designed to accommodate important constituencies. The Task Force on Immigration underscored the chamber-dominated, or informational, perspective. Its work enhanced the expertise of all members by providing them with specialized information on the complexities of immigration policy. Finally, the Task Force on the Environment was formed in part to promote the GOP's deregulatory agenda. A partisan perspective shaped much of its work.

Speaker Hastert de-emphasized the use of party task forces, but he still occasionally employed them to address issues of importance to the party. For example, Hastert created task forces to deal with health and terrorism issues. Speaker Pelosi established a bipartisan task force to consider whether the House should create an outside body to investigate ethical misconduct by lawmakers.[98] Her initiative led the House in March 2008 to create an independent Office of Congressional Ethics (OCE) with authority to initiate investigations of alleged misconduct by lawmakers.[99] Speaker Boehner, who retained the OCE, relies on a GOP high-tech working group "to propose measures that would spur growth in the high-tech industry."[100] He also named William "Mac" Thornberry, R-Texas, to coordinate the work of at least a half-dozen committees and produce cybersecurity legislation that might be enacted into law.

Senate leaders also form party task forces, sometimes to showcase senators up for reelection and to promote party priorities. For example, a senator up for reelection was named by GOP leader McConnell to head the GOP's high-tech task force. The aims of the task force are "to advise the Republican Conference on technology issues and act as an advocate for the industry."[101] Party task forces are also created to develop legislative plans or ameliorate internal party conflict. For example, Senate GOP leader Bob Dole, Kan., established a task force to cool the passions of junior Republicans who wanted to oust the Appropriations chair (Mark Hatfield of Oregon) because he did not vote for a top GOP priority, a constitutional balanced budget amendment. The task force came up with term limits for committee chairs, which, as noted earlier, is still observed by Senate Republicans.

Bypassing Committees

It has not been unusual in recent years, as noted above, for House and Senate party leaders to bypass some or all of the stages of committee consideration of legislation. In general, the circumvention of committees reflects the dominance of party power over committee power. It also represents Congress's focus on short-term lawmaking and emphasis on partisan gain over cooperative policy making. Specific reasons for bypassing committees are noteworthy. For example, heightened partisanship in certain committees encourages party leaders to take charge of priority measures to avoid negative media coverage of committee markups. Or factional disputes within committees may prevent them from reaching agreement on measures deemed important to party leaders. Time is a factor as well. Party leaders may believe there is not enough time for committees to hold hearings and markups on major bills they want to consider within a certain time period. Along these lines, Sen. Barbara Mikulski, D-Md., lamented that "legislative malpractice" occurred during the Senate debate on a medical liability bill: "First of all, the procedure for considering this bill is seriously flawed. The bill was brought to the full Senate without hearings, without consideration by the Judiciary Committee."[102] Senate GOP leader McConnell claimed that Democrats in the 111th Congress regularly bypassed Senate committees. Democrats set a record, declared McConnell, "bypassing committees 43 times or double the previous average."[103] The Democratic leader blamed dilatory procedural abuses by Republicans for the high number. Some analysts contend that "there are few consequences if [committees are bypassed] because nobody outside Congress cares whether a bill went through committee or not."[104] Today, committee review of major legislation can be problematic. This development has frustrated committee chairs and rank-and-file lawmakers in both chambers. As Senate Finance chair Max Baucus, D-Mont., put it: "We're all frustrated. We all wish there was more legislating and less messaging."[105] Only time will tell whether committees' policy-making role on consequential measures will increase in the 113th Congress.

CONCLUSION

Several generalizations can be made about congressional committees today. First, they shape the House and Senate agendas. Not only do they have negative power—pigeonholing legislation referred to them—but they have positive power as well. The bills they report largely determine what each chamber will debate and in what form. As one House chair stated in his testimony before the Joint Committee on the Organization of Congress, committees

> provide Congress with the expertise, skill, and organizational structure necessary to cope with the increasingly complex and technical questions in both the domestic and international arenas. They also ensure a forum for the broadest possible participation of diverse interests and constituencies in the formative stages of the legislative process. They are, in short, the window through which much of the democratic participation in lawmaking is made possible.[106]

Second, committees differ in their policy-making environments, mix of members, decision-making objectives, and ability to fulfill individual members' goals. Recruitment methods reinforce committees' autonomy; they frequently are imbalanced ideologically or geographically. And they are likely to advocate policies espoused by agencies and outside groups interested in their work.

Third, some committees often develop an *esprit de corps* that flows across party lines, in part because these panels have developed a culture of bipartisanship. The military panels are a good example. Despite intermittent partisan clashes, for the past straight fifty-one years the House and Senate Armed Services Committees have never failed to win enactment into law of the annual National Defense Authorization Act. Committee members usually will defend their panels against criticisms or jurisdictional trespassing and criticize attempts to bypass them.

Fourth, committees typically operate independently of one another. This longtime custom fosters an attitude of mutual noninterference in the work of other committees. However, multiple referrals of bills spawn broader interrelationships among committees.

Fifth, the committee system contributes fundamentally to policy fragmentation, although a few committees—such as the House's Rules and Budget Committees—act as policy coordinators for Congress. "This is one of the anomalies here," remarked a House member. "In order to attain legislative efficiency, we say that we have to break down into committees with specialized jurisdictions. When you do that, you lose your ability to grapple with the big problems."[107] As a result, party leaders are more involved than ever in coordinating policy making and forging winning coalitions in committees and on the floor.

Finally, committee autonomy is far weaker today than it was before the 1970s, as assertive party leaders strive to move the party's agenda forward and enforce party discipline—with or without the committee leaders' cooperation. Gone are the days when committee chairs were known as the "dukes" and "barons" of Capitol Hill. Moreover, the House and particularly the Senate have even witnessed a surge in the formation of "gangs"—informal bipartisan groups of lawmakers—that draft legislation for chamber consideration. This development has occurred in part because committees are sometimes unable to report important measures because they are riven by partisan divisions. In brief, the balance of power in Congress has shifted to party leaders. In theoretical terms, the pressure on autonomy may be seen as a shift in committee roles from distributional purposes to partisan-programmatic goals.

AMENDMENTS ONLY
FOR PREPRINTING IN THE
CONGRESSIONAL RECORD

***H**ouse and Senate chambers.* Senators sit at assigned desks in the elegant Senate chamber (top). The House Speaker's chair is in front of the flag and to the left of the Mace—a symbol of national unity that on rare occasions may be hoisted and displayed to quell disturbances in the chamber. The seats below are for clerks, and the box in the foreground is the "hopper," where members may place amendments for House consideration (center). The House chamber, seen from the rear, shows the Speaker's rostrum but also the galleries and lawmakers' seats. Members do not have assigned seats, but the majority and minority committee leaders' tables are seen to the right (bottom).

Congressional Rules and Procedures

Congress needs written rules to do its work. Compiling the Senate's first parliamentary manual, Thomas Jefferson stressed the importance of a known system of rules:

> It is much more material that there should be a rule to go by, than what the rule is; that there may be uniformity of proceeding in business not subject to the caprice of the Speaker or captiousness of the members. It is very material that order, decency, and regularity be preserved in a dignified public body.[1]

Jefferson understood that how Congress operates affects what it does. Thus Congress's rules protect majority and minority rights, divide the workload, help contain conflict, ensure fair play, and distribute power among members. Because formal rules cannot cover every contingency, precedents—accumulated decisions of House Speakers and Senate presiding officers—fill in the gaps. These precedents are codified by House and Senate parliamentarians, printed, and distributed. There are also informal, unwritten codes of conduct, such as courtesy to other members. These folkways are commonly transmitted from incumbent members to newcomers.[2]

Before bills become laws, they typically pass successfully through several stages in each house (see Figure 8-1 for a simplified view of lawmaking). Bills that fail to attract majority (sometimes supermajority) support at any critical juncture may never be passed. Congress, in short, is a procedural obstacle course that favors opponents of legislation and hinders proponents. This defensive advantage promotes bargaining and compromise at each decision point.

Congressional rules are not independent of the policy and power struggles that lie behind them. There is very little the House and Senate cannot do under the rules so long as the action is backed by votes and inclination. And yet votes and inclination are not easily obtained, and the rules persistently challenge the proponents of legislation to demonstrate that they have both resources at their command. Little prevents obstruction at every turn except the tacit understanding that the business of the House and Senate must go on. Members recognize that the rules can be redefined and prerogatives taken away or modified. Rules also can be employed against those who use them abusively. In short, rules can be employed to block or advance actions in either chamber, and proponents or opponents of measures or matters do not look on them as neutral devices.

INTRODUCTION OF BILLS

Only members of Congress can introduce legislation. Often embedded in these measures are a number of assumptions—for example, that a problem exists; that it can best be resolved through enactment of a federal law instead of allowing administrative agencies or state and local governments to handle it; and that the proposed solution contained in the bill ameliorates rather than exacerbates the problem. The GOP-controlled House of the 112th and 113th Congresses adopted a rule requiring all lawmakers to provide with the bills (H.R.) and joint resolutions (H. J. Res.) they introduce a constitutional authority statement specifying the power or powers granted to Congress in the Constitution to enact the bill or joint resolution. Often these statements are quite brief—"Article I, section 8," for example.[3]

Lawmakers introduce legislation for many reasons, such as constituency, electoral, policy, political, and so on. When gasoline prices start to go up significantly, members respond in two Congresses fashion by introducing numerous energy-related bills. But there is also a motivator that is rarely discussed and can be just as potent: a personal brush with adversity. Congress is an intensely human place where personal experience sometimes has powerful repercussions.[4] As a senator stated, "Each of us, as United States senators, comes to . . . this public place with the sum of our beliefs, our personal experience and our values, and none of us checks them at the door."[5] For example, former senator Pete V. Domenici, R-N.M., whose daughter suffers from mental illness, was Congress's acknowledged champion for the mentally ill. "In the field of mental health," said a Democratic House member, "I think it's possible that nothing at all would have been done by Congress if it weren't for legislators like Domenici who were galvanized by personal experience."[6] Rep. Carolyn McCarthy, D-N.Y., has long been a forceful advocate for gun control. Why? A deranged gunman on a commuter train killed her husband and seriously wounded her adult son. Personal experience, however, is not the only source of legislative proposals. Often members get ideas for bills from the executive branch, interest groups, scholars, state and local officials, constituents, the media, and their own staff.

A member who introduces a bill becomes its sponsor. He or she may seek cosponsors to demonstrate wide support for the legislation. Outside groups also may urge members to cosponsor measures. "We were not assured of a hearing," said a lobbyist of a bill that his group was pushing. "There was more hostility to the idea, so it was very important to line up a lot of cosponsors to show the over-all concern."[7] A two Congresses dimension is also evident in signing on (or not) to legislation. For example, a lawmaker may cosponsor a labor bill to win the support of union workers back home. Conversely, the

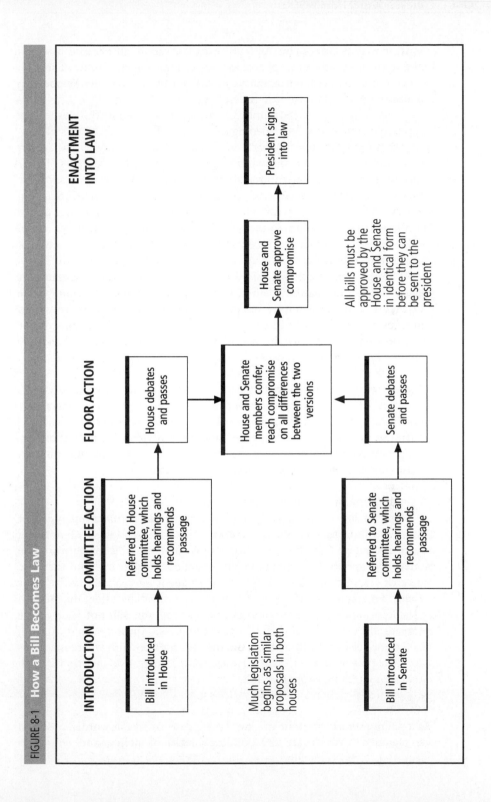

FIGURE 8-1 How a Bill Becomes Law

INTRODUCTION   COMMITTEE ACTION   FLOOR ACTION   ENACTMENT INTO LAW

Bill introduced in House

Referred to House committee, which holds hearings and recommends passage

House debates and passes

House and Senate members confer, reach compromise on all differences between the two versions

House and Senate approve compromise

President signs into law

Bill introduced in Senate

Referred to Senate committee, which holds hearings and recommends passage

Senate debates and passes

Much legislation begins as similar proposals in both houses

All bills must be approved by the House and Senate in identical form before they can be sent to the president lawmaker may decide against cosponsoring the labor bill because it would mobilize business groups to oppose his reelection. Vulnerable lawmakers up for reelection may cosponsor measures offered by opposition members to broaden their appeal to voters in both major parties.

Equally important as the number of cosponsors is their identity, especially their leadership status and ideological stance. Members often seek out cosponsors from the opposing party to signal that the bill transcends partisan politics. In an unusual cosponsorship pairing, the former House chairs of their respective party campaign committees, Chris Van Hollen, D-Md., and Pete Sessions, R-Texas, joined to introduce bipartisan legislation.[8] When Sen. Ted Kennedy, D-Mass., an outspoken liberal, served in the Senate with Sen. Strom Thurmond, R-S.C., a southern conservative, he exclaimed, "Whenever Strom and I introduce a bill together, it is either an idea whose time has come, or one of us has not read the bill."[9]

Although identifying a bill's sponsors is easy, pinpointing its real initiators may be difficult. Legislation is "an aggregate, not a simple production," wrote Woodrow Wilson. "It is impossible to tell how many persons, opinions, and influences have entered into its composition."[10] President John F. Kennedy, for example, usually is given credit for initiating the Peace Corps. But Theodore Sorensen, Kennedy's special counsel, recalled that the Peace Corps was

> based on the Mormon and other voluntary religious service efforts, on an editorial Kennedy had read years earlier, on a speech by General [James] Gavin, on a luncheon I had with Philadelphia businessmen, on the suggestions of [Kennedy's] academic advisers, on legislation previously introduced and on the written response to a spontaneous late-night challenge he issued to Michigan students.[11]

In short, many bills have complex origins.

Required legislation, particularly funding measures, make up much of Congress's annual agenda. Bills that authorize programs and specify how much money can be spent on them (authorization bills) and bills that provide the money (appropriation bills) appear on Congress's schedule at about the same time each year. Other matters recur at less frequent intervals, every five years perhaps. Emergency issues require Congress's immediate attention. Activist legislators also push proposals onto Congress's program. Bills not acted on die automatically at the end of each two-year Congress. "Anybody can drop a bill into the hopper [a mahogany box near the Speaker's podium where members place their proposed bills]," said a House GOP leader. "The question is, Can you make something happen with it?"[12]

Drafting

"As a sculptor works in stone or clay, the legislator works in words," observed one member.[13] Words are the building blocks of policy, and legislators frequently battle over adding, deleting, or modifying terms and phrases. Members increasingly give their bills eye-catching titles to attract media attention and for partisan message purposes. For example, GOP lawmakers have introduced bills with titles such as "The Reducing Barack Obama's Unsustainable Deficit Act." As an analyst pointed out, "If Republicans can take a silly name like Repealing the Job-Killing Health Care Act Law and make it stick, they've helped communicate its meaning and importance to audiences they're trying to reach."[14]

Acronyms are increasingly popular on Capitol Hill because they attract public attention. Consider the USA PATRIOT Act (Uniting and Strengthening America by Providing Appropriate Tools Required to Intercept and Obstruct Terrorism) or the JOBS (Jumpstart Our Business Startups) bill. Members also affix popular phrases to legislation, such as "bill of rights." As a Senate GOP leader pointed out, "If you ask [voters], 'Are you for the Bill of Rights?' Yeah, they're for the Bill of Rights. 'Bill of Rights' is a great term. It's the new term. It may even be supplanting reform."[15] And then there is the time that, instead of proposing to reduce or terminate estate taxes, Republicans called for an end to "the death tax."

Conversely, opponents of measures try to attach unattractive labels to them. Defenders of the estate tax refer to its abolition as the "Paris Hilton Benefit Act." Critics of an energy bill dubbed it the "Hooters and Polluters Bill" because the legislation contained a provision benefiting a Hooters restaurant in Louisiana. Opponents of the JOBS bill referred to it as "just old bills." And "Obamacare" is how Republicans pejoratively characterized the president's landmark overhaul of the health care system. (Recognizing that Republicans had won the branding war on the health law, the president also refers to it as Obamacare.) The health overhaul was also referred to as "socialized medicine," a "government takeover," and a measure that contained "death panels." How measures are framed influences how the public will view them. "Whoever controls the language controls the debate," asserted one commentator.[16] And this is why, in the current 24/7 media environment, an effective "messaging" or public relations strategy is critical both to the fate of major legislation and to a party's electoral success.

Although bills are introduced only by members, anyone can draft them.[17] Expert drafters in the House and Senate offices of the legislative counsel assist members and committees in writing legislation. Executive agencies and lobbying groups also often prepare measures for introduction by friendly legislators. Many home-state industries, for example, draft narrowly tailored tariff or regulatory measures that enhance their business prospects. These proposals are then introduced by local lawmakers—another instance of the two Congresses linkage. As a senatorial aide explained, the senator sometimes "just introduces [bills] as a courtesy to his constituents."[18] (See Box 8-1 outlining the four basic types of legislation: bills, joint resolutions, concurrent resolutions, and simple resolutions.)

BOX 8-1 Types of Legislation

Bill

◄ Most legislative proposals before Congress are in a bill form.

◄ Bills are designated H.R. (House of Representatives) or S. (Senate) according to where they originate, followed by a number assigned in the order in which they were introduced, from the beginning of each two-year congressional term.

◄ Public bills deal with general questions and become public laws if approved by Congress and signed by the president.

◄ Private bills deal with individual matters, such as claims against the government, immigration and naturalization cases, and land titles. They become private laws if approved and signed by the president.

Joint Resolution

◄ A joint resolution, designated H. J. Res. or S. J. Res., requires the approval of both houses and the president's signature, just as a bill does, and has the force of law.

◄ No significant difference exists between a bill and a joint resolution. The latter generally deals with limited matters, such as a single appropriation for a specific purpose.

◄ Joint resolutions are used to propose constitutional amendments, which do not require presidential signatures but become a part of the Constitution when three-fourths of the states have ratified them.

Concurrent Resolution

◄ A concurrent resolution, designated H. Con. Res. or S. Con. Res., must be passed by both houses but does not require the president's signature and does not have the force of law.

◄ Concurrent resolutions generally are used to make or amend rules applicable to both houses or to express their joint sentiment. A concurrent resolution, for example, is used to fix the time for adjournment of a Congress and to express Congress's annual budgeting plan. It might also be used to convey the congratulations of Congress to another country on the anniversary of its independence.

Resolution

◄ A simple resolution, designated H. Res. or S. Res., deals with matters entirely within the prerogatives of one house.

◄ It requires neither passage by the other chamber nor approval by the president and does not have the force of law.

◄ Most resolutions deal with the rules of one house. They also are used to express the sentiments of a single house, to extend condolences to the family of a deceased member, or to give advice on foreign policy or other executive business.

Nowadays, Congress frequently acts on comprehensive (omnibus) bills or resolutions (sometimes called packages or megabills by the press). Packages contain an array of issues that were once handled as separate pieces of legislation. Their increasing use stems in part from members' reluctance to make hard political decisions without a package arrangement. A House Budget Committee chair once explained their attractiveness. As he stated:

> Large bills can be used to hide legislation that otherwise might be more controversial. By packaging difficult issues in measures that command broad support, they enable members to avoid hard votes that they would have to account for at election time and allow members to avoid angering special-interest groups that use votes [to decide] contributions to campaigns. Leaders can also use them to slam-dunk issues that otherwise might be torn apart or to pressure the President to accept provisions that he objects to.[19]

Sometimes, Congress has little choice but to use the omnibus approach. Difficulties in enacting the twelve annual appropriations bills often mean that all or many ("omnibus") or two, three, or so ("minibus") are rolled into one comprehensive package. In this way, procedural action on the outstanding measures is expedited by majority party leaders, who, in doing so, minimize the opportunities for further delay. A goal of Speaker John Boehner, R-Ohio, was to "put an end to so-called comprehensive bills with thousands of pages of legislative text that make it easy to hide spending projects and [detrimental] policies."[20] House Republicans employed the two Congresses theme when they highlighted the size of the president's health overhaul measure—over 2,700 pages—as a symbol of big-government intervention in health care, a potent GOP electoral theme in the November 2010 elections. ("I think we paid a terrible [electoral] price for health care," exclaimed Rep. Barney Frank, D-Mass.[21]) Some Democrats disagree with Speaker Boehner's view of big bills. "I don't think the issue's the length of the bills," said Rep. Diana DeGette, D-Colo. "I think the issue is the clarity of the explanation."[22]

Timing

"Everything in politics is timing," Speaker Thomas P. "Tip" O'Neill Jr., D-Mass., used to say. A bill's success or failure often hinges on when it is introduced or brought to the floor. A bill that might have succeeded early in a session could fail as adjournment nears. However, controversial legislation can sometimes be rushed through during the last hectic days of a Congress. "You do learn that everything has its time," noted Sen. Bob Corker, R-Tenn. You "just wait for the moment which is going to be the best environment to introduce something."[23]

Elections greatly influence the timing of legislation. Policy issues can be taken off or kept on Congress's agenda because of electoral circumstances—a good illustration of how the two Congresses are inextricably connected. For example, coming off major electoral successes both House parties in recent years moved to capitalize on their momentum with quick action early in the new Congress. Examples are the House's action in 1995 on the ten-point, hundred-day Contract with America agenda heralded by Speaker Newt

Gingrich, R-Ga., and the hundred-hour legislative agenda pushed in 2007 by Speaker Nancy Pelosi, D-Calif. And, as one of its first orders of business under Speaker Boehner, the House on January 26, 2011, passed a bill to repeal Obamacare. (President Obama's second-term victory and his veto prerogative effectively end any chance that the Affordable Care Act will be rescinded.)

REFERRAL OF BILLS

After bills are introduced, they are referred formally to the appropriate standing committees by the Senate presiding officer or the House Speaker. (In practice, however, measures are referred by the Senate or House parliamentarian, who is the official procedural adviser to each chamber's presiding officer.) A bill's phraseology can affect its referral and therefore its chances of passage. This political fact of life means that members use words artfully when drafting legislation. The objective is to encourage the referral of their measures to sympathetic, not hostile, committees. If a bill mentions taxes, for example, it invariably is referred to the tax panels. In a classic case of circumventing the Finance Committee, Senator Domenici avoided the word *tax* in a bill proposing a charge on waterborne freight:

> If the waterway fee were considered a tax—which it was, basically, because it would raise revenues for the federal treasury—the rules would place it under the dominion of the Senate's tax-writing arm, the Finance Committee. But Finance was chaired by Russell B. Long, of Louisiana, whose state included two of the world's biggest barge ports and who was, accordingly, an implacable foe of waterway charges in any form. Domenici knew that Long could find several years' worth of bills to consider before he would voluntarily schedule a hearing on S. 790 [the Domenici bill]. For this reason, [Domenici staff aides] had been careful to avoid the word *tax* in writing the bill, employing such terms as *charge* and *fee* instead.[24]

Domenici's drafting strategy worked. His bill was jointly referred to the Commerce Committee and the Environment Committee, on which he served. Because committees' jurisdictional mandates are ambiguous and overlap, it is not unusual for legislation to be referred to two or more committees—the concept of "one bill, many committees." Indeed, multiple referrals are common in the House, less so in the Senate. In the Senate, they require unanimous consent to implement. Furthermore, all senators have many opportunities to influence committee-reported measures or matters, regardless of whether they serve on the panel of jurisdiction (see Box 8-2, which describes how parliamentary convention affects the reference of legislation).

Of the thousands of bills introduced each year, Congress takes up relatively few. During the 112th Congress (2011–2013), 10,569 public bills and joint resolutions were introduced, but only 238 (2.3 percent) became public

BOX 8-2   **Rules and Referral Strategy**

Sometimes, the Senate's rules can be so arcane that it takes major strategy sessions to get even the most routine bills through the legislature.

That was the case when Sen. Bob Graham, D-Fla. (1987–2005), drafted a bill (targeted only at Florida) to permit the Forest Service to sell eighteen tracts of land and use the proceeds to buy up patches of private lands within the Apalachicola National Forest. To ensure that such a low-profile bill moved, Graham wanted it to go through the Energy and Natural Resources Committee, on which he sat.

Instead, Parliamentarian Alan S. Frumin told Graham's aides that the bill, which was soon to be introduced, would be referred to the Agriculture, Nutrition, and Forestry Committee. Because Graham was not a member, such a move could have guaranteed the bill a quiet death.

Why the Agriculture Committee? For at least four decades, the jurisdiction over land bills has been split between the two committees. Bills affecting land east of the 100th Meridian—which runs through North Dakota and South Dakota and the middle of Texas—are assigned to Agriculture, while bills that affect lands west of it go to Energy.

Graham's bill dealt with the wrong side of the country. To change Frumin's mind, Graham's aides needed to turn the rules to their advantage.

They found their opportunity by uncovering the roots behind the 100th Meridian rule. The idea was to divide jurisdiction between public lands and privately owned lands. Because most land on the East Coast is privately owned, that side of the country went to Agriculture, which had jurisdiction over private lands. Everything in the West fell to Energy, which had jurisdiction over public lands.

Graham's aides, however, found out that a majority of tracts in Florida were always public lands. That persuaded Frumin that the bill belonged to the Energy panel.

Source: Adapted from David Nather, "Graham Turns Rules to His Advantage," *CQ Weekly,* June 8, 2002, 1494.

laws. More public laws were enacted in earlier Congresses: for example, 640 in the 90th (1967–1969) and 590 in the 99th (1985–1987). Part of the general decline in the number of laws enacted can be explained by the use of omnibus or megabills. The decline may also stem from the widespread congressional sentiment that more laws may not be the answer to the nation's problems. But the decline also reflects political stalemates resulting from the complexity of issues, the intensity of partisanship, legislative-executive and bicameral conflicts, and the narrow party divisions in Congress. It is worth emphasizing that lawmakers understand that most of the bills they introduce are unlikely, as stand-alone measures, to become law. However, the ideas encapsulated in their legislation can be "added as amendments to a larger bill or negotiated into a markup or conference report."[25]

Lawmaking is an arduous and intricate process. As a Senate GOP leader noted, "That's the way Congress works. You work for two years and finally you get to the end and either it all collapses in a puddle or you get a breakthrough."[26] Or as John Dingell, D-Mich., the longest-serving lawmaker in U.S. history in either chamber, phrased it: "Legislation is hard, pick-and-shovel work," and it often "takes a long time to do it."[27] Recall the decades-long efforts by numerous lawmakers and presidents—from Teddy Roosevelt to, finally, Barack Obama—to comprehensively overhaul the nation's health care system.

Once committees complete action on the bills referred to them, the House and Senate rules require a majority of the full committee to be physically present to report (vote) out any measure. If this rule is violated and neither waived nor ignored, a point of order can be made against the proposal on the floor. (A point of order is a parliamentary objection that halts the proceedings until the chamber's presiding officer decides whether the contention is valid.)

Bills reported from committee have passed a critical stage in the lawmaking process. The next major step is to reach the House or Senate floor for debate and amendment. The discussion that follows begins with the House because tax and appropriation bills originate there—the former under the Constitution, the latter by custom.

SCHEDULING IN THE HOUSE

All bills reported from committee in the House are listed in chronological order on one of several calendars—that is, the lists that enable the House to put measures into convenient categories. Bills that raise or spend money are assigned to the Union Calendar. The House Calendar contains all other major public measures, such as proposed constitutional amendments. Private bills, such as immigration requests or claims against the government, are assigned to the Private Calendar. There is no guarantee that the House will debate legislation placed on any of these calendars. The Speaker, in consultation with party and committee leaders, the president, and others, largely determines whether, when, how, and in what order bills come up. Outside events and influencers also shape agenda-setting, including input from citizens and bloggers around the country.[28] The power to set the House's agenda constitutes the essence of the Speaker's institutional authority. The Speaker's agenda-setting authority is bolstered by rules and precedents upholding the principle of majority rule. This means that in the House a united and determined voting majority—whether partisan or bipartisan—will prevail over resolute opposition.

Shortcuts for Minor Bills

Whether a bill is major or minor, controversial or noncontroversial, influences the procedure employed to bring it before the House. Most bills are relatively minor and are taken up and passed through various shortcut procedures.

One shortcut is the designation of special days for considering minor or relatively noncontroversial measures. An especially important routine and time-saving procedure is suspension of the rules. It is in order Monday, Tuesday, and Wednesday of each week. The procedure is controlled by the Speaker through the power of recognizing who may speak ("Mr. Speaker, I move to suspend the rules and pass H.R. 1234"). The vote simultaneously suspends House rules and enacts (or rejects) the measure. Most public laws enacted by the House are accomplished through this procedure. A study by Donald R. Wolfensberger, former staff director of the House Rules Committee, determined that since the early 2000s from 75 to over 80 percent of bills enacted into public law came to the House floor via this procedure, compared with about 33 percent two decades ago.

In 2011, the first year of GOP control of the 112th Congress, there was a decline in the use of suspension procedure. As House majority leader Eric Cantor, R-Va., noted, the "percentage of bills that have come to the floor under suspension of the rules has dramatically declined from [over] 80 percent [in 2010] to 55 percent this year."[29] One reason for this decline in suspension procedure was the GOP leadership's goal of focusing the House's attention on reducing the fiscal deficit, repealing the health care law, and shrinking the size and scope of the federal government. Suspensions increased the following year to bolster the chamber's productivity and thus avoid or minimize the political "do nothing" charge on the campaign trail, and to castigate the Democratic Senate for refusing to act on House-passed legislation. Press reports had indicated that the 112th Congress, compared to its predecessors, was at historic lows in the enactment of laws.[30]

Legislation considered under suspension of the rules does not have to be reported from committee before the full House takes it up. Importantly, the suspension procedure permits only forty minutes of debate, allows no amendments, and requires a two-thirds vote for passage. The procedure is often favored by bill managers who want to avoid unfriendly amendments and points of order against their legislation. Bills that fail under suspension can return again to the floor by a rule issued by the Rules Committee (discussed later in this chapter). The heightened partisanship in the closely divided House raises the question of why the suspension procedure, which requires bipartisanship to attract the two-thirds vote, is being employed more and more in such a polarized institution. The answer seems to involve a trade-off. "As members are increasingly being denied opportunities in special rules to offer amendments to more substantive bills on the floor," explained Wolfensberger, "the leadership is providing alternative mechanisms to satisfy members' policy influence and reelection needs through the relatively non-controversial and bipartisan suspension process."[31] Thus, greater use of suspensions serves two prime purposes: it provides an outlet for members to achieve their policy and political goals and keeps the lid on members' frustration with limited or closed amendment procedures.

The current rules of the House Republican Conference establish specific guidelines for using the suspension procedure. Under Conference Rule 28, bills and resolutions are not to be scheduled using the suspension procedure if, for example, they are opposed by more than one-third of the committee members reporting the bill; if they fail to include a cost estimate; or if they create new programs, unless they also eliminate or reduce a program of equal or greater size. The majority leadership "does not ordinarily schedule bills for suspension unless confident of a two-thirds vote."[32] Lawmakers often refer to measures on the "suspension calendar" even though there is no formal calendar for this purpose.

To accommodate lawmakers' constituency and legislative activities (the two Congresses concept), the House instituted a cluster voting rule. The Speaker announces that record votes on a group of bills debated under the suspension procedure will be postponed until later that day or within the next two days. The bills are then brought up in sequence and disposed of without further debate. Cluster voting accommodates lawmakers returning from weekends in their district. It also minimizes interruptions of committee or constituency meetings when the House is in session throughout the week. Absent cluster voting, members would be required to run back and forth to the chamber scores of times throughout the day to vote on issues.

At times, the minority party gets upset with the majority leadership for not scheduling enough of their bills via the suspension procedure. To protest, minority party members may vote against suspension bills until more of their routine measures are taken up on the floor. They also may castigate the majority leadership for using the suspension of the rules procedure on bills that in their estimation merit more debate than forty minutes and require the offering of amendments.

Another expedited procedure is unanimous consent. The Speaker, however, will recognize a lawmaker to call up bills or resolutions by unanimous consent "only when assured that the majority and minority floor leadership and the relevant committee chairs and ranking minority members have no objection."[33] Without these clearances, unanimous consent is not a viable avenue to the floor.

Major measures reach the floor by different procedures. Budget, appropriation, and a limited number of other measures are considered "privileged"—meaning that the House rulebook grants them a "ticket," or privileged access, to the floor. Privileged measures may be called up from the appropriate calendar for debate at almost any time. (Remember, the Speaker sets the agenda, even for privileged business.) Most major bills, however, do not have an automatic green light to the floor. Before they reach the floor they are assigned a rule (a procedural resolution) by the Rules Committee.

The Strategic Role of the Rules Committee

The House Rules Committee has existed since the First Congress. During its early years, the committee prepared or ratified a biennial set of House rules and then dissolved. As House procedures became more complex because of the growing membership and workload, the committee became more important. In 1858 the Speaker became a member of the committee and the next year its chair. In 1880 Rules became a permanent standing committee. Three years later, the committee launched a procedural revolution. It began to issue rules (sometimes called special rules), which are privileged resolutions that grant priority for floor consideration to virtually all major bills.

Arm of the Majority Leadership. In 1910 the House rebelled against the arbitrary decisions of Speaker Joseph G. Cannon, R-Ill., and removed him from the Rules Committee. During the decades that followed, as the committee became an independent power, it extracted substantive concessions in bills in exchange for rules, blocked measures it opposed, and advanced those it favored, often reflecting the wishes of the House's conservative coalition of Republicans and southern Democrats.

The chair of the Rules Committee from 1955 to 1967 was Howard W. "Judge" Smith, D-Va., a diehard conservative and a master at devising delaying tactics. He might abruptly adjourn meetings for lack of a quorum, allow requests for rules to languish, or refuse to schedule meetings. House consideration of the 1957 civil rights bill was temporarily delayed because Smith absented himself from the Capitol, and his committee could not meet without him. Smith claimed he was seeing about a barn that had burned on his Virginia farm. Retorted Speaker Sam Rayburn, D-Texas, "I knew Howard Smith would do most anything to block a civil rights bill, but I never knew he would resort to arson."[34]

Liberals' frustration with the bipartisan coalition of conservatives who dominated the committee finally boiled over. After John F. Kennedy was elected president in 1960, Speaker Rayburn recognized that he needed greater control over the Rules Committee if the House was to advance the president's activist New Frontier program. Rayburn proposed enlarging the committee from twelve members to fifteen. This proposal led to a titanic struggle between Rayburn and the archconservative Rules chair:

> Superficially, the Representatives seemed to be quarreling about next to nothing: the membership of the committee. In reality, however, the question raised had grave import for the House and for the United States. The House's answer to it affected the tenuous balance of power between the great conservative and liberal blocs within the House. And, doing so, the House's answer seriously affected the response of Congress to the sweeping legislative proposals of the newly elected President, John Kennedy.[35]

In a dramatic vote, the House agreed to expand the Rules Committee. Two new Democrats and one Republican were added, loosening the conservative coalition's grip on the panel.

During the 1970s, the Rules Committee came under even greater majority party control. In 1975 the Democratic Caucus authorized the Speaker to appoint, subject to party ratification, all Democratic members of the committee, including the chair. (Thirteen years later, Republicans authorized their leader to name the GOP leader and members of the Rules Committee.) The majority party maintains a disproportionate ratio on the panel (currently nine Republicans and four Democrats in the 113th Congress). The Rules Committee, in short, has once again become the Speaker's committee. As a GOP Rules member said about the panel's relationship with the Speaker, "How much is the Rules Committee the handmaiden of the Speaker? The answer is, totally."[36] GOP representative Pete Sessions of Texas heads the panel in the 113th Congress.

The Speaker's influence over the Rules Committee ensures that the Speaker can both bring measures to the floor and shape their procedural consideration. Because House rules require bills to be taken up in the chronological order listed on the calendars, many substantial bills would never reach the floor before Congress adjourned. The Rules Committee can put major bills first in line. Equally important, a rule from the committee sets the conditions for debate and amendment.

A request for a rule is usually made by the chair of the committee reporting the bill. The Rules Committee conducts hearings on the request in the same way that other committees consider legislation, except that only members testify. The House parliamentarian usually drafts the rule after consulting with majority committee leaders and staff. The rule is considered on the House floor and is voted on in the same manner as regular bills (see Box 8-3 for an example of a generally open rule from the Rules Committee).

Types of Rules. Traditionally, the Rules Committee has granted open, closed, modified, or structured rules as well as waivers. An open rule means that any lawmaker may propose germane amendments. A closed rule prohibits the offering of amendments by rank-and-file members. A modified rule comes in two forms: modified open and modified closed (also called a "structured" rule by some lawmakers). The distinction hinges in part on the number of amendments made in order by the Rules Committee—few or only one under modified closed, more under modified open. In addition, modified open rules may also require the pre-printing of amendments and impose a time limit on the amendment process, or both. Modified closed rules often grant only one amendment to the minority party: a complete substitute alternative to the pending bill. Structured rules restrict the number of amendments to those specified in the rule itself or in the Rules Committee's report on the procedural resolution. It is common today for the Rules Committee to announce in advance that it will provide a structured (i.e., "restricted") rule and require lawmakers to submit their proposed amendments to the committee. The committee will then review the amendments and determine which to make in order for chamber consideration. The requirement that all amendments be either pre-printed in the *Congressional Record* or submitted in advance to Rules aids the majority party in preparing its floor strategy. Waivers of points of order set aside technical violations of House rules to allow bills or other matters to reach the floor. Waivers are commonly included in the different types of rules.

Whether Democrats or Republicans control the House, their majority on the Rules Committee displays procedural creativity and imagination:

Instead of choosing from among a few patterns the Rules Committee has demonstrated a willingness to create unique designs by

BOX 8-3   **Example of a Rule from the Rules Committee**

*T*his is a modified open rule (H. Res. 92) that sets the terms for debating and amending the Full-Year Continuing Appropriations Act, 2011 (H.R. 1). It allows any member to offer a germane amendment as long as it is pre-printed in the Congressional Record. The House adopted the rule on February 15, 2011, by a 242–174 vote.

Resolved, That at any time after the adoption of this resolution the Speaker may, pursuant to clause 2(b) of rule XVIII, declare the House resolved into the Committee of the Whole House on the state of the Union for consideration of the bill (H.R. 1) making appropriations for the Department of Defense and the other departments and agencies of the Government for the fiscal year ending September 30, 2011, and for other purposes. The first reading of the bill shall be dispensed with. All points of order against consideration of the bill are waived. General debate shall be confined to the bill and shall not exceed one hour equally divided and controlled by the chair and ranking minority member of the Committee on Appropriations. After general debate the bill shall be considered for amendment under the five-minute rule. No amendment to the bill shall be in order except: (1) those received for printing in the portion of the Congressional Record designated for that purpose in clause 8 of rule XVIII dated at least one day before the day of consideration of the amendment (but no later than February 15, 2011); and (2) pro forma amendments for the purpose of debate. Each amendment so received may be offered only by the Member who submitted it for printing or a designee and shall be considered as read if printed. When the committee rises and reports the bill back to the House with a recommendation that the bill do pass, the previous question shall be considered as ordered on the bill and amendments thereto to final passage, without intervening motion except one motion to recommit with or without instructions.

Source: Congressional Record, 112th Cong., 1st sess., February 15, 2011, H815–H816.

recombining an increasingly wide array of elements, or by creating new ones as the need arises, to help leaders, committees, and members manage the heightened uncertainties of decision making on the House floor.[37]

The trend toward creative use of complex rules reflects several developments. Among the most important are the wider use of multiple referrals, which requires Rules to play a larger coordinative role in arranging floor action on legislation; the rise of megabills hundreds of pages in length that contain priorities the Speaker does not want picked apart on the floor; the desire of majority party leaders to exert greater control over floor procedures; members' impatience with dilatory floor challenges to committee-reported bills; members' demand for greater certainty and predictability in floor decision making; and efforts by committee leaders either to limit the number of amendments or to keep unfriendly amendments off the floor. The sharp rise in partisanship has also triggered an increase in creative rules (see Box 8-4 on examples of creative rules).

BOX 8-4 Examples of Creative Rules

Queen-of-the-Hill Rule

◄ Under this special rule, a number of major alternative amendments—each the functional equivalent of a bill—are made to the underlying legislation, with the proviso that the substitute that receives the most votes is the winner.

◄ If two or more alternatives receive an identical number of votes, the last one voted upon is considered as finally adopted by the membership.

Self-Executing Rule

◄ This special rule provides that when the House adopts a rule it has also agreed simultaneously to include another measure or matter in the bill made in order by the special rule.

◄ Adoption of a self-executing rule means that the House has passed one or more other proposals at the same time it agrees to the rule.

◄ Whether this rule is controversial or not usually depends on the nature of the policy being agreed to in the two-for-one vote.

Structured Rule

◄ The essential feature of the structured rule is that it limits the freedom of members to offer germane amendments to the bills made in order by those rules.

◄ The number of structured rules has increased since the 1980s. The majority party uses these rules to minimize debate, prevent unwanted amendments, and maximize its ability to mobilize winning majorities.

◄ Rank-and-file members often rail against these rules because they restrict their opportunities to amend committee-reported measures or majority party initiatives.

Multiple-Step Rule

◄ This type of rule facilitates an orderly amendment process.

◄ One variation is for the Rules Committee to report a rule that regulates the debating and amending process for specific portions of a bill and then report another follow-on rule to govern the remainder of the measure and amendments to it.

◄ Another variation is for the Rules Committee to state publicly that if a measure encounters difficulties on the floor, the panel will report a subsequent rule that limits time for further debate or further amendments.

Anticipatory Rule

◄ To expedite decision making on the floor, the Rules Committee may grant a rule even before the measure or matter to which it would apply has been reported by a House committee or conference committee.

When Republicans took control of the House in 1995 after four consecutive decades in the minority, they remembered their bitter experience with rules that restricted their right to offer amendments. Speaker Gingrich promised more openness and greater opportunities for all lawmakers to offer floor amendments to pending legislation. Republicans did work to provide more open amendment procedures when they first took control of the House. However, as Republican majorities declined in subsequent Congresses, the number of open rules dropped markedly (see Table 8-1), the result of heightened partisan acrimony and the GOP's preference to enact its agenda priorities with few or no changes.

Like the Republicans in 1995 when Democrats reclaimed the House majority in the 110th Congress (2007–2009), Speaker Pelosi pledged to manage the chamber in an open, fair, and deliberative manner. But it was not long before the Democrats brought their legislative priorities to the floor under closed or structured rules. Meanwhile, regularly the Republicans took the floor to criticize the Democratic majority for reneging on its promises. The majority is "failing to live up to its commitment to run the House in an open and fair manner," exclaimed a Rules Republican.[38] In the next Congress, still under Democratic control, there were no open rules at all—even on the twelve appropriations measures, which traditionally are open to amendment—unless one counts as open a rule with a pre-printing requirement for amendments. Overall, as one analyst wrote, the two Houses under Democratic control were "worse than Republicans were at their worst, producing restrictive amendment rules for 86 percent and 99 percent of legislation, respectively, versus 81 percent under Republicans in the 109th Congress."[39] In response to the GOP

TABLE 8-1 **Open and Structured Rules, 103d–112th Congresses**

Congress and years		Total rules granted	Open/modified Open rules		Restrictive rules	
			Number	Percent	Number	Percent
103d	(1993–1995)	104	31	30	73	70
104th	(1995–1997)	151	86	57	65	43
105th	(1997–1999)	142	72	51	70	49
106th	(1999–2001)	184	93	51	91	49
107th	(2001–2003)	112	41	37	71	63
108th	(2003–2005)	128	33	26	95	74
109th	(2005–2007)	138	24	17	114	83
110th	(2007–2009)	159	23	15	136	85
111th	(2009–2011)	95	0	0	95	100
112th	(2011–2013)	140	25	18	115	82

Source: Don Wolfensberger, resident scholar, Bipartisan Policy Center, Washington, D.C. Wolfensberger is a former decades-long professional staff aide and staff director of the House Rules Committee.

complaints, Democrats said the GOP's floor strategy was to offer "gotcha" amendments designed for campaign attack ads or to undermine the majority's policy priorities. Steny Hoyer of Maryland, then the majority leader, added, "I said we were going to be fair, not stupid."[40]

Speaker Boehner has also promised to run an open, fair, and deliberative lawmaking process with ample opportunities for the minority Democrats to offer amendments. Let legislators legislate is his stated objective. "To my friends in the minority," he said, "I offer a commitment: Openness . . . will be the new standard. There were no open rules in the House in the last Congress. In this one, there will be many."[41] Note that Speaker Boehner did not say all rules would be open or that he would tolerate minority party disruption of floor proceedings. To be sure, Democrats regularly criticize GOP-crafted rules. As the ranking Rules Democrat, Louise Slaughter, N.Y., said on one occasion: while "this rule may have the word 'open' in the title, I assure [my colleagues] that this is not an open process. [T]he Republican majority has provided an extremely convoluted and restrictive process."[42]

Open rules generally clash with a fundamental objective of any majority party: enactment of priority legislation. As Table 8-1 reveals, only 18 percent of rules in the 112th Congress were either open or modified open, a better percentage than under Speaker Pelosi but not compared to Boehner's two GOP predecessors (Gingrich and Hastert). However, unlike previous Speakers, Boehner has consistently brought appropriations bills to the floor under open rules, returning to the traditional practice of the House.

In summary, rules establish the conditions under which most major bills are debated and amended. They determine the length of general debate, permit or prohibit amendments, and often waive points of order. Writing the rules is the majority party's way of ensuring that measures reach the floor under terms favorable to the party's preferred outcomes. Put differently, the majority party limits and structures the votes to get the legislative and political results it intends, keeping the two Congresses in mind. In this era of message politics and partisan polarization, innovative rules can both protect majority party members from casting electorally perilous votes or, alternatively, make amendments in order that appeal to diverse party constituencies. Rarely are rules rejected by the House. As Speaker Thomas "Tip" O'Neill, D-Mass. (1977–1987), once said: "Defeat of the rule on the House floor is considered an affront both to the [Rules] Committee and to the Speaker."[43]

For their part, minority lawmakers object strongly to the wider use of restrictive rules that block them from offering and getting votes on their policy alternatives. "We don't expect to win," said a minority member, "but we do expect to be able to at least offer amendments so the two parties can define their differences."[44] Special rules are as or more important to a bill's fate as a favorable committee vote.

Dislodging a Bill from Committee

Committees do not necessarily reflect the point of view of the full chamber. What happens when a standing committee refuses to report a bill or when the

Rules Committee does not grant a rule? To circumvent committees, members have three options: the discharge petition, the Calendar Wednesday rule, and the ability of the Rules Committee to extract a bill from committee. However, these tactics are rarely employed and seldom successful.

The discharge petition permits the House to relieve a committee of jurisdiction over a stalled measure. This procedure also provides a way for the rank and file to force a bill to the floor, even if the majority leadership, the committee chair, and the Rules Committee oppose it. If a committee does not report a bill within thirty legislative days after the bill was referred to it, any member may file a discharge motion (petition) requiring the signature of 218 members, a majority of the House. Once the signatures are obtained, the discharge motion is placed on the Discharge Calendar for seven days. It can then be called up on the second and fourth Mondays of the month by any member who signed the petition. If the discharge motion is agreed to, the bill is taken up right away. Since 1910, when the discharge rule was adopted, only three discharged measures have ever become law. Its threatened or actual use, particularly as the number of signatures closes in on 218, may stimulate a committee to act on a bill and the majority leadership to schedule it for floor action.

The discharge procedure is rarely successful as a lawmaking device largely because members are reluctant to second-guess committees; to write legislation on the floor without the guidance of committee hearings and reports; and to use a procedure that may one day be used against committees on which they serve. Moreover, 218 signatures are not easy to obtain. The Speaker, too, is not reluctant to pressure majority party members who sign discharge petitions to remove their names, because their actions could jeopardize the majority's control of the floor schedule. If majority lawmakers add or refuse to remove their names, the message being sent, according to Tom Cole, Okla., former House GOP campaign chair, is that "you're thumbing your nose at your own leadership."[45] Unwanted consequences, as noted below, might result to majority members who refuse to heed their leader's advice.

The minority party may employ discharge petitions to spotlight the two Congresses. For example, minority members may promote and publicize their high-priority issues and then circulate discharge petitions "in an attempt to force House votes—and provide a contrast with [the majority party] in an election year."[46] When Republicans were in the minority in the 111th Congress (2009–2011), they filed discharge petitions to try to force floor votes on repealing the health care law. Their objective was "to capitalize on the public's divided feelings on the health care law as the [2010] midterm elections approach[ed]."[47] In brief, vulnerable House members can be subject to attack ads for failing to sign a discharge petition supported by many voters in their respective districts.

The discharge rule also applies to the Rules Committee. A motion to discharge a rule is in order after seven legislative days, instead of thirty days, as long as the bill made in order by the rule has been in committee for thirty days. Any member may enter a discharge motion, but majority members rarely break ranks with their party leaders to sign the petition. When Rep. Christopher Shays, R-Conn., signed a successful discharge petition to force House action on a landmark campaign finance reform bill (the Bipartisan Campaign Reform Act of 2002) opposed by the GOP leadership, there were charges of treason against Shays and rumblings that he might face a GOP challenger in the Republican primary. Signing discharge petitions, "along with other kinds of procedural betrayals, are being considered and discussed by members" of the GOP's committee on committees, remarked the Republican Conference chair.[48] Shays was subsequently passed over as chair of the Oversight and Government Reform Committee, even though he had more seniority than the two other Republicans in contention.

Adopted in 1909, the Calendar Wednesday rule provides that on Wednesdays committees may bring up from the House Calendar or Union Calendar their measures that have not received a rule from the Rules Committee. However, the clerk will not call committees on Wednesdays unless the committee chair gives notice on Tuesday that he or she will seek recognition to call up a measure under the rule. Calendar Wednesday is cumbersome to employ, seldom used, and generally dispensed with by unanimous consent. Since 1943, fewer than fifteen measures have been enacted into law under this procedure.[49]

Finally, the Rules Committee has the power of extraction. The committee can propose rules that make bills in order for House debate even if the bills have been neither introduced nor reported by standing committees. Based on an 1895 precedent, this procedure is akin to discharging committees without the required 218 signatures. It stirs bitter controversy among members who think it usurps the rights of the other committees, and therefore it is seldom used.

HOUSE FLOOR PROCEDURES

The House meets Monday through Friday, often convening at noon. In practice, it conducts the bulk of its committee and floor business during the middle of the week (the so-called Tuesday to Thursday Club). To infuse greater predictability in the schedule, and to provide more time for members to spend in their districts, the GOP leaders of the 112th Congress crafted a legislative schedule somewhat different from previous House patterns. "Under the new calendar, House members will have a cycle of being in session for two weeks in Washington [with five-day workweeks] and then spending the following week in their home districts."[50] Majority Leader Eric Cantor, R-Va., also promised that there would be no votes each legislative day earlier than 1 p.m. (to permit committees to meet without interruption), no votes after 7 p.m., and on Fridays voting would conclude by 3 p.m.[51] However, this scheduling pattern was modified in 2012 to accommodate the congressional and presidential election season. Lawmakers wanted to spend more time at home to campaign.

At the beginning of each day's session, bells ring throughout the Capitol and the House office buildings, summoning representatives to the floor. The bells also notify members of votes, quorum calls, recesses, and adjournments. Typically, the opening activities include a daily prayer; approval of the *Journal* (a constitutionally required record of the previous day's proceedings); recitation of the Pledge of Allegiance; receipt of messages from the president (such as a veto message) or the Senate; announcements, if any, by the Speaker; and one-minute speeches by members on any topic. On Mondays and Tuesdays, a period of morning-hour debate takes place after the opening preliminaries but before the start of formal legislative business.

After these preliminaries, the House generally begins considering legislation. For a major bill, a set pattern is observed: adopting the rule, convening in Committee of the Whole, allotting time for general debate, amending, voting, and moving the bill to final passage.

Adoption of the Rule

The Speaker, after consulting other majority party leaders and affected committee chairs, generally decides when the House will debate a bill and under what kind of rule. Speakers rely on their majority leader to help draft and manage the floor agenda. When the scheduled day arrives, the Speaker recognizes a majority member of the Rules Committee for one hour to explain the rule's contents. By custom, the majority member yields half the time for debate to a minority member of the Rules Committee. At the end of the debate, which may take less than the allotted hour, the House votes on the previous question motion. Its approval brings the House to an immediate vote on the rule. Rejection of the previous question (a rare occurrence) allows the minority party an opportunity to amend the rule.

Opponents of a bill can try to defeat the rule and avert House action on the bill itself. But rules are rarely defeated because majority party members generally vote with their leaders on procedural votes and the Rules Committee is sensitive to the wishes of the House. During the speakership of Dennis Hastert, R-Ill. (1999–2007), the House rejected only two rules offered by the Rules Committee. Splits within the majority party account for the defeats. Nancy Pelosi never lost a rule during her four years as Speaker (2007–2011), nor has Speaker Boehner (2011–) had any rules turned down by the House. Procedural votes are usually party-line votes. Once the rule is adopted, the House is governed by its provisions. Most rules state that "at any time after the adoption of [the rule] the Speaker may declare the House resolved into the Committee of the Whole."

Committee of the Whole

The Committee of the Whole House on the state of the Union is a parliamentary artifice that the House borrowed long ago from the British House of Commons. Its function in the contemporary House is to expedite consideration of legislation and to promote member involvement in general debate and the amendment process, if amendments are permitted by the special rule. It is simply the House in another form with different rules. For example, a quorum in the Committee of the Whole is only 100 members, compared with 218 for the full House. Debate on amendments is governed by the five-minute rule rather than the one-hour rule that applies in the House. By custom, Speakers never preside over the Committee; they always appoint a majority party colleague to act as chair of the committee, which then begins general debate of a bill.

General Debate

A rule from the Rules Committee specifies the amount of time, usually one to two hours, for a general discussion of the bill under consideration. Controversial bills require more time, perhaps four or more hours. Control of the time is divided equally between the majority and minority floor managers—usually the chair and ranking minority member of the committee that reported the legislation. (When bills are referred to more than one committee, a more complex division of debate time is allotted among the committees that had jurisdiction over the legislation.) The majority floor manager's job is to guide the bill to final passage; the minority floor manager may seek to amend or kill the bill.

After the floor managers have made their opening statements, they parcel out several minutes to colleagues on their side of the aisle who wish to speak. General debate rarely lives up to its name. Most legislators read prepared speeches. Give-and-take exchange occurs infrequently at this stage of the proceedings.

The Amending Phase

The amending process is the heart of decision making on the floor of the House. Amendments determine the final shape of bills and often dominate public discussion. Former representative Henry J. Hyde, R-Ill., for example, repeatedly and successfully proposed amendments barring the use of federal funds for abortions. Hyde's 1977 anti-abortion amendment remains today a regular provision of many public laws.

An amendment in the Committee of the Whole is considered under the five-minute rule, which gives the sponsor five minutes to defend it and an opponent five minutes to speak against it. The amendment then may be brought to a vote. Amendments are routinely debated for more than ten minutes, however. Legislators gain the floor by saying, "I move to strike the last word" or "I move to strike the requisite number of words." These pro forma amendments, which make no alteration in the pending matter, simply serve to give members five minutes of debate time.

If there is an open rule, opponents may try to load a bill with so many objectionable amendments that it will sink under its own weight. The reverse strategy is to propose sweetener amendments that attract support from other members. Offering many amendments is an effective dilatory tactic because each amendment must be read in full, debated for at least five to ten minutes, and then voted on.

In this amending phase, the interconnection of the two Congresses is evident: amendments can have electoral as well as legislative consequences.

Floor amendments enable lawmakers to take positions that enhance their reputations with the folks back home, put opponents on record, and shape national policy. For example, "put-them-on-the-spot amendments," as one representative dubbed them, can be artfully fashioned by minority lawmakers to force the majority to vote on issues such as gun control or stem cell research that can be used against them in the next campaign.[52] The majority party's control of the Rules Committee minimizes the use of this tactic because the panel may "script" the amendment process. For example, only the amendments made in order by Rules can be offered, often in a set order, and only by a specific member. Structured rules of this sort block spontaneous amendments and debates on issues that might stymie passage of the majority party's priorities.

The minority guards the floor to demand explanations or votes on amendments brought up by the majority. As a minority floor guardian wrote, "So long as a floor watchdog exists all members of the House are afforded some additional protection from precipitous actions."[53] In the 113th Congress, various minority members assume this role for Democrats in the House.

Voting

Before passage of the 1970 Legislative Reorganization Act, the Committee of the Whole adopted or rejected amendments by voice votes or other votes with no public record of who voted and how. Today, any legislator supported by twenty-five colleagues can obtain a recorded vote. (The member who requested a recorded vote is counted as one of the twenty-five who rise to be counted by the chair.)

Since the installation of an electronic voting system in 1973, members can insert their personalized cards (about the size of a credit card) into one of more than forty voting stations on the floor and press the "Yea," "Nay," or "Present" button. A large electronic display board behind the press gallery provides a running tally of the total votes for or against a motion. The voting tally, said a representative, is watched carefully by many members:

> I find that a lot of times, people walk in, and the first thing they do is look at the board, and they have key people they check out, and if those people have voted "aye," they go to the machine and vote "aye" and walk off the floor.
>
> But I will look at the board and see how [members of the state delegation] vote, because they are in districts right next to me, and they have constituencies just like mine. I will vote the way I am going to vote except that if they are both different, I will go up and say "Why did you vote that way? Let me know if there is something I am missing."[54]

After all pending amendments have been voted on, the Committee of the Whole rises. The chair hands the gavel back to the Speaker, and a quorum once again becomes 218 members.

Final Passage

As specified in the rule, the full House must review the actions of its agent, the Committee of the Whole. The Speaker announces that under the rule the previous question has been ordered, which means in this context that no further debate is permitted on the bill or its amendments. The Speaker then asks whether any representative wants a separate vote on any amendment. If not, all the amendments agreed to in the committee will be approved.

The next important step is the motion to recommit, which provides a way for the House to return, or recommit, the bill to the committee that reported it. The motion to recommit has two forms: (1) the rarely used "straight" motion to return the measure to committee (which effectively kills it), and (2) a motion to recommit with instructions that the committee report "forthwith," which means the bill never really leaves the House. If this form of the motion is adopted, the bill, as modified by the instructions, is automatically before the House again. By precedent, either form of the motion is always made by a minority party member who opposes the legislation. Each form of the motion is also subject to ten minutes of debate, five per side. Recommittal motions are usually not successful because they are so heavily identified as an opposition party prerogative, but they do serve to protect the rights of the minority. When Republicans won majority control in 1995, they amended the House rules to guarantee the minority leader or his or her designee the right to offer a recommittal motion with instructions (the instructions embody the minority's policy alternative and must be germane to the bill). This rule still remains in place.

Recent Congresses have seen a change in the major purposes of the motion to recommit. Although still employed by the minority party to force the House to vote on its alternative policy proposal (the "instructions" in this motion), the motion to recommit is now frequently employed to achieve two political purposes: to defeat, delay, or eviscerate majority party policies and to force vulnerable majority lawmakers to vote on "gotcha amendments" certain to cause them electoral grief if they do not vote for the minority proposal. As Democratic leader Hoyer exclaimed, "The unfortunate fact is that the motion to recommit with instructions has for more than a decade become a hollow vehicle and farce."[55] For example, whether a Democratic or Republican minority, the instructions in motions to recommit are artfully drafted to require members to vote on "hot button" issues—preventing child molestation, for example—while also undermining the majority party's policy objectives. Clearly, many lawmakers would be reluctant to vote against a motion to recommit with this kind of instruction because they would likely face a barrage of campaign attack ads suggesting that they support child molestation.

If the motion to recommit with instructions is adopted, the minority proposal is incorporated into the bill. If it is rejected, as commonly occurs, the Speaker will declare, "The question is on passage of the bill." Passage of the measure, by the House in this case, marks about the halfway point in the lawmaking process. The Senate must also approve the bill, and its procedures are strikingly different from those of the House. It is an institution noted for protecting the rights of the minority, hence its reliance on the unanimous consent of all senators to accomplish much of the chamber's business.

SCHEDULING IN THE SENATE

Compared with the larger and more clamorous House, which needs and follows well-defined rules and precedents, the Senate operates more informally. And, unlike the House, where the rules permit a determined majority to make decisions, the Senate's rules emphasize individual prerogatives (freedom to debate and to offer amendments, including nonrelevant amendments) and minority rights (those of the minority party, a faction, or even a single senator). "The Senate," said one member, "is run for the convenience of one Senator to the inconvenience of 99."[56] No wonder some commentators say the Senate has only two rules (unanimous consent and exhaustion) and three speeds (slow, slower, and slowest). As former senator Byron Dorgan, D-N.D., said, "The only thing it's easy to do in the Senate is slow things down. The Senate is 100 human brake pads."[57]

The scheduling system for the Senate appears relatively simple. There is a Calendar of Business on which are listed public and private bills reported by the committees and a separate Executive Calendar for treaties and nominations. The Senate has nothing comparable to the scheduling duties of the House Rules Committee, and the majority and minority leadership actively consult about scheduling. The Senate majority leader is responsible for setting the agenda and is aided in controlling the scheduling by the priority given him when he seeks recognition on the floor. What this means is that if several senators are seeking recognition from the presiding officer and the majority leader is among them, the chair will always give preference to the majority leader.

Despite the Senate's smaller size, establishing a firm agenda of business is harder in the Senate than in the House. As a majority leader once said:

> The ability of any Senator to speak without limitations makes it impossible to establish total certainty with respect to scheduling. When there is added to that the difficulty and very demanding schedules of 100 Senators, it is very hard to organize business in a way that meets the convenience of everybody.[58]

Legislation typically reaches the Senate floor in two ways: by unanimous consent or by motion. But senators, too, can also force Senate consideration of their proposals by offering them as nonrelevant amendments to pending business. Unanimous consent agreements are of utmost importance to the smooth functioning of the Senate.

Unanimous Consent Agreements

The Senate frequently dispenses with its formal rules and instead follows negotiated agreements submitted to the Senate for its unanimous approval (see Box 8-5 on unanimous consent agreements). The objectives are to expedite work in an institution known for extended debate, to impose some measure of predictability on floor action, and to minimize dilatory activities. As a party floor leader observed:

> We aren't bringing [measures] to the floor unless we have [a unanimous consent] agreement. We could bring child-care legislation to the floor right now, but that would mean two months of fighting. We want to maximize productive time by trying to work out as much as we can in advance [of floor action].[59]

It is not uncommon for party leaders to negotiate piecemeal unanimous consent agreements—limiting debate on a specific amendment, for example—and to hammer them out in public on the Senate floor.

Unanimous consent agreements (also called time-limitation agreements) limit debate on the bill, any amendments, and various motions. Occasionally, they specify the time for the vote on final passage and typically impose constraints on the amendment process. For example, to facilitate enactment of an omnibus crime package that contained provisions with widespread Senate support, senators agreed to a unanimous consent request barring floor amendments on controversial issues such as gun control or the death penalty.[60]

The Senate's unanimous consent agreements are functional equivalents of special rules from the House Rules Committee. Both waive the rules of their respective chambers and must be approved by the members—in one case by majority vote and in the other by unanimous consent. These accords are binding contracts and can be terminated or modified only by another unanimous consent agreement. Senators and aides often negotiate and draft and circulate unanimous consent agreements privately, whereas the Rules Committee hears requests for procedural rules in public sessions.

Ways to Extract Bills from Committee

If a bill is blocked in committee, the Senate has several ways to obtain floor action. It can add the bill as a nonrelevant floor amendment to another bill, bypass the committee stage by placing the bill directly on the calendar, suspend the rules, or discharge the bill from committee. Only the first two procedures are effective; the other two are somewhat difficult to employ and seldom succeed.[61]

In recent years, however, various senators have employed motions to suspend the rules to force votes on amendments that would normally be out of order under Senate rules and precedents. The suspension rule requires one day's written notice (published in the *Congressional Record*) of the terms of the

BOX 8-5   **Example of a Unanimous Consent Agreement**

*O*rdered, That notwithstanding cloture having been invoked on H.R. 1, and following any Leader remarks on Friday, December 28, 2012, the Senate resume consideration of H.R 5949, an act to extend the FISA Amendments Act of 2008 for five years; provided, that the only first degree amendment in order to the bill be the Wyden amendment, the text of which is at the desk; provided further, that there be 30 minutes of debate equally divided on the amendment prior to the vote; further, that there be no amendments in order to the amendment prior to the vote, and that upon disposition of the amendment, the bill be read a third time and the Senate vote on passage of the bill, as amended, if amended; further that there be a 60 affirmative vote threshold for the amendment and for passage of the bill.

Ordered, That upon disposition on Friday, December 28, 2012, the Senate resume consideration of H.R. 1, an act making appropriations for the Department of Defense and other departments and agencies of the Government for the fiscal year ending September 30, 2011, and for other purposes; provided, that notwithstanding Rule XXII, the following [21] amendments be in order:

-Cardin #3393 (surety bonds),

-Grassley #3348 (DOJ—vehicles)

Ordered further, That all after the first vote be 10 minute votes; provided further, that upon disposition of the pending amendments listed, the Senate vote in relation to Amdt. No. 3395, offered by the Senator from Nevada (Mr. Reid), as amended, if amended; provided further that upon disposition of Amdt. No. 3395, the cloture motion on H.R. 1 be withdrawn, the bill be read a third time and the Senate vote on passage of H.R. 1, as amended, if amended.

Source: U.S. Senate, Calendar of Business, 112th Cong., 2d sess., December 28, 2012, 2.

Note: The unanimous consent agreement for H.R. 1 is a selected version of the provisions contained therein, while still highlighting its main features. For example, only two of the twenty-one amendments are listed.

debatable suspension motion and a high voting threshold (two-thirds) to succeed. (See the discussion below on how Sen. Harry Reid, D-Nev., foiled the minority party's use of suspension motions for message purposes.)

Because the Senate has no general germaneness (or relevancy) rule, senators can take an agriculture bill that is stuck in committee and add it as a nonrelevant floor amendment to a pending health bill. "Amendments may be made," Thomas Jefferson noted long ago, "so as to totally alter the nature of the proposition." However, unanimous consent agreements can limit or prohibit nonrelevant amendments.

Senators can also bypass the referral of measures to committee by invoking one of the chamber's formal rules (Rule XIV). Typically, when senators introduce bills or joint resolutions (or when bills or joint resolutions are passed by the House and sent to the Senate), they are referred to the appropriate committee of jurisdiction. Rule XIV specifies that those measures are to be read twice by title on different legislative days before they are referred. If a senator interposes an objection after the first reading and again the next day after the second reading, the bill or joint resolution is automatically placed on the Senate's Calendar of Business (see Box 8-6 for how Rule XIV works). Although not used for the vast majority of measures, Rule XIV is increasingly invoked on party issues of high priority. The majority leader, for example, may employ it to circumvent committees because no time is available for a lengthy committee review, or because he wants an issue ready to be called up at his discretion. As Sen. Lamar Alexander, R-Tenn., noted, "From the 103rd to the 109th Congress, Rule XIV to bypass [committees] was used on average 24 times per Congress. This was shattered in the 110th Congress when it was used 57 times."[62]

SENATE FLOOR PROCEDURES

The Senate, like the House, often convenes at noon, sometimes earlier, to keep pace with the workload. Typically, it opens with a prayer, followed by the

---

BOX 8-6 Senate Rule XIV: Bypassing Committee Referral

MEASURE READ THE FIRST TIME—S. 192

Mr. BEGICH. Madam President, I understand that S. 192, introduced earlier today by Senator DEMINT, is at the desk and I ask for its first reading.

The PRESIDING OFFICER. The clerk will read the bill by title.

The bill clerk read as follows:

A bill (S. 192) to repeal the job-killing health care law and health care-related provisions in the Health Care and Education Reconciliation Act of 2010.

Mr. BEGICH. Madam President, I now ask for its second reading and object to my own request.

The PRESIDING OFFICER. Objection is heard.

The bill will be read the second time on the next legislative day.

Source: Congressional Record, January 26, 2011, S263.

MEASURE PLACED ON THE CALENDAR—S. 192

Mr. REID. Mr. President, I understand S. 192 is at the desk and is due for a second reading.

The ACTING PRESIDENT pro tempore. The clerk will read the title of the bill for the second time.

The legislative clerk read as follows:

A bill (S. 192) to repeal the job-killing health care law and health care-related provisions in the Health Care and Education Reconciliation Act of 2010.

Mr. REID. Mr. President, I object to further proceedings with respect to this legislation.

The ACTING PRESIDENT pro tempore. Objection having been heard, the bill will be placed on the calendar under rule XIV.

Source: Congressional Record, January 27, 2011, S295.

Pledge of Allegiance and then leaders' time (usually ten minutes each to the majority leader and the minority leader to discuss various issues). If neither leader wants any time, the Senate typically either permits members who have requested time to make their statements, or it resumes consideration of old or new business under terms of a unanimous consent agreement. The Senate, too, must keep and approve the *Journal* of the previous day's activities. Commonly, the *Journal* is "deemed approved to date" by unanimous consent when the Senate adjourns or recesses at the end of each day.

Normal Routine

For most bills, the Senate follows four steps:

1. The majority leader secures the unanimous consent of the Senate to an arrangement that specifies when a bill will be brought to the floor and the conditions for debating it.
2. The presiding officer recognizes the majority and minority floor managers for opening statements.
3. Amendments are then in order, with debate on each amendment regulated by the terms of the unanimous consent agreement.
4. A roll call vote takes place on final passage.

As in the House, amendments in the Senate serve various purposes. For example, floor managers might accept "as many amendments as they can without undermining the purposes of the bill, in order to build the broadest possible consensus behind it."[63] Some amendments are designed with the two Congresses in mind. Such amendments may bestow benefits to the electorate or embarrass members who must vote against them. "My amendment can be characterized as a 'November amendment,'" remarked a Republican senator, "because the vote . . . will provide an opportunity for Senators to go home and say, 'I voted to reduce Federal taxes' and 'I voted to cut Federal spending.'"[64] Senate Democrats make "vigorous use of amendments to strike a contrast with Republican policies."[65] Unless constrained by some previous unanimous consent agreement, senators generally have the right to offer an unlimited number of floor amendments.

Significantly, recent majority leaders have increasingly used their right of first recognition on the floor to "fill the amendment tree": a chart that imposes a limitation on the number of amendments to a measure that may be offered and pending at the same time. The right of first recognition brings up two points. First, the presiding officer always recognizes the majority leader first if other senators are trying to catch the eye of the chair. Second, despite Senate precedents stating that members lose the floor when they offer amendments, the first recognition principle trumps that determination, enabling the majority leader to offer amendment after amendment until the so-called amendment tree (a chart that depicts the number of permissible amendments to a measure) is filled. Majority Leader Reid has employed tree-filling far more than his Democratic or Republican predecessors. During the 111th Congress (2009–2011), Reid used the procedural device forty-four times compared to a combined forty by the majority leaders in office from 1985 to 2008. In the 112th Congress, Reid filled the tree sixty-three times. The surge in tree-filling largely reflects two general and overlapping developments: heightened partisan conflict in the chamber and wider use of amendments by the minority party for political message-sending.

Once the amendment tree is filled, no other senator may offer amendments—that is, the amending process is frozen "until action is taken to dispose of one or more of those already pending."[66] This practice is controversial and angers many lawmakers, especially those in the minority. Regularly, GOP leader Mitch McConnell, Ky., blasts Reid for undermining the unique deliberative character of the Senate by preventing Republicans from offering their nonrelevant amendments. From Senator Reid's perspective, tree-filling is done for several specific reasons, such as blocking unwanted, nonrelevant amendments; protecting vulnerable colleagues from voting on amendments crafted to cause them electoral grief; or promoting negotiations with the opposition so an accord might be reached on the number of amendments each side is willing to vote on. If an accord is reached, the majority leader will drop some of his amendments so others may offer theirs.

A bill is brought to a final vote whenever senators stop talking. (The Senate has no motion to end debate and vote on a measure or matter.) This can be a long process, particularly in the absence of a unanimous consent agreement. On some bills, unanimous consent agreements are foreclosed because of deliberate obstructive tactics, particularly the threat or use of the filibuster (extended debate). In these instances, bills cannot be voted upon until the filibuster has ended. Every measure might face at least two primary filibusters: the first on the motion to take up the legislation and the second on the consideration of the bill. "Double filibusters" underscore the expansive scope of minority rights that characterizes Senate procedure. (A number of laws, such as trade or budget reconciliation measures, restrict a senator's right to prolong debate. As a former Senate parliamentarian noted, "We have on the books probably a couple hundred laws that set up specific legislative vehicles that cannot be filibustered or only amended in a very restricted way.")[67]

Holds, Filibusters, and Cloture

The old-style filibuster has long been associated with the 1939 movie *Mr. Smith Goes to Washington*, which featured a haggard Jimmy Stewart conducting a dramatic solo talkathon on the floor of the Senate to inform the public about political wrongdoing. In its new incarnation, the filibuster is usually threatened more than invoked to gain bargaining power and negotiating leverage. Today, the threat to filibuster is sufficient to block action on many bills or nominations, in large measure because it is so hard to mobilize sixty votes to invoke cloture (closure of debate). Moreover, cloture is a time-consuming procedure (at least two days) that impedes the Senate's ability to process its extensive workload.

Filibusters involve many blocking tactics besides extended debate in which senators might hold the floor for hours of endless speeches. In today's polarized Senate, contemporary filibusters are commonly waged by those who skillfully exploit Senate rules. For example, senators might offer scores of amendments, raise many points of order, or demand numerous and consecutive roll call votes. Holds also function as a form of silent filibuster.

Holds. Long an informal custom, a hold permits one or more senators to block floor action on measures or matters by asking their party leaders not to schedule them. A hold, explained Sen. Charles E. Grassley, R-Iowa, is "a notice by a Senator to his or her party leader of an intention to object to bringing a bill or nomination to the floor for consideration."[68] The majority leader decides whether, or for how long, to honor a colleague's hold. The power of holds is grounded in the implicit threat of senators to conduct filibusters or to object to unanimous consent agreements.

Holds have come under criticism because they often lead to delays or even the death (choke holds) of measures or nominations. Originally intended as a way for senators to get information about when the majority leader planned action on a measure, holds have become devices to kill measures by delaying them indefinitely or to gain bargaining leverage by, for example, stalling action on presidential nominees. On one occasion, so many holds on nominations were pending before the Senate that a Democratic leader felt left out. As he explained, "I'm going to have to pick out a nominee to get to know him or her a lot better because it works that way. I mean, it's 'Hello, I'm your holder . . . come dance with me.'"[69]

For years, Sens. Grassley and Ron Wyden, D-Ore., joined by Sen. Claire McCaskill, D-Mo., have tried to reform—not eliminate—the holds process. Specifically, they want to end secret holds where one anonymous senator can block bills or nominations. Some success for the trio came in 2007 when the Senate established a procedure for ending secret holds (formally called a "notice of intent to object"). However, there was no enforcement mechanism. When the 112th Congress opened, the Senate adopted a "standing order"—the functional equivalent of a formal rule—that requires every senator to make his or her hold public. If a senator does not come forward to be the claimant, then whoever objected on his or her behalf, including the two party leaders, would be identified in the *Congressional Record* as the "holder." Still, anonymous pre-floor objections to calling up measures or matters have not disappeared in the Senate. In the view of Majority Leader Reid, "We tried to do something on secret holds, but that hasn't helped [the nominations process] much at all."[70] In short, there are still secret holds in the Senate.

Filibusters and Cloture. The right of extended debate is unique to the Senate. Any senator or group of senators can talk continuously in the hope of delaying, modifying, or defeating legislation. In 1957 South Carolina senator Strom Thurmond, then a Democrat, set the record for the Senate's longest solo performance—twenty-four hours and eighteen minutes; he was trying to kill a civil rights bill.

The success of a filibuster depends not only on how long it takes but also on when it is waged. A filibuster can be most effective late in a session because there is insufficient time to break it.[71] Even the threat of a filibuster can encourage accommodations or compromises between proponents and opponents of legislation.

Defenders of the filibuster say it protects minority rights, permits thorough consideration of bills, and dramatizes issues. "In many ways," noted Sen. Robert C. Byrd, D-W.Va., "the filibuster is the single most important device ever employed to ensure that the Senate remains truly the unique protector of the rights of our people."[72] Critics contend that talkathons enable minorities to extort unwanted concessions. During most of its history, the Senate had no way to terminate debate except by unanimous consent, exhaustion, or compromise. In 1917 the Senate adopted Rule XXII, its first cloture (debate-ending) rule. After several revisions, Rule XXII now permits three-fifths of the Senate (sixty members) to shut off debate on substantive issues or procedural motions. (A two-thirds vote is required to invoke cloture on a proposal to change the rules of the Senate.)

Once cloture is invoked, thirty hours of debate time remain before the final vote occurs on the matter identified in the cloture motion. There might also be multiple cloture votes on a measure: on the motion to proceed, on the bill itself, and to amendments. If the Senate is in a procedural "hard ball" situation, opponents of the legislation will consume the entire thirty hours of post-cloture debate on each clotured item. These actions "can grind legislative business to a halt and leave the Senate in an interminable purgatory."[73]

Senators complain about the frequent use of filibusters, filibuster threats, and cloture attempts. In the past, filibusters generally occurred on issues of great national importance. Today, they occur on a wide range of less momentous topics. As one majority leader pointed out,

> Not long ago the filibuster or threat of a filibuster was rarely undertaken in the Senate, being reserved for matters of grave national importance. That is no longer the case. . . . The threat of a filibuster is now a regular event in the Senate, weekly at least, sometimes daily. It is invoked by minorities of as few as one or two Senators and for reasons as trivial as a Senator's travel schedule.[74]

Unsurprisingly, many commentators call it the "sixty-vote Senate." Or as a senator observed, "It isn't good enough to have the majority. You've got to have 60 votes."[75] Today, it is not uncommon for unanimous consent agreements to require bills or amendments to attract sixty votes for passage rather than a simple majority. The interests of both sides are served by this development. Majority advocates get a vote, and the supermajority threshold protects minority opponents. Moreover, this accord saves the Senate's time by avoiding use of the cloture procedure.

Attempts to invoke cloture also have increased, particularly in recent Congresses. For example, in the decade from 1961 to 1971 there were 5.2 cloture votes per Congress, but during the 109th Congress (2005–2007) there were fifty-two cloture votes.[76] The 110th Senate seemingly broke all records when the chamber voted on 112 cloture motions, "twice the number in the previous Congress and more than double the average number over the previous twenty years."[77] But then another new record was set in the 111th Congress—132 cloture votes.[78] If the cloture votes of the 112th Congress are counted with the totals from the 110th and 111th Congresses, there have been more than 385 cloture votes in the Senate.

Tellingly, when Majority Leader Reid forces cloture votes, he wins a majority of them by attracting sufficient GOP votes to attain the sixty required to invoke cloture.[79] Why would Republican senators force Reid to resort to the cloture process even when they plan to vote for cloture? To consume the most precious commodity in the Senate: time. As a top floor aide to Senator Reid wrote: "By requiring the cloture vote and then voting for it, the minority has been able to waste considerable time and thus reduce the amount of time available to act on other items of [President Obama's] agendas."[80] Filibustering actions frustrate the majority party's ability to govern, which might make the minority the majority party after the next election. Remember, with forty-one votes, the minority's threat of extended debate (the "silent filibuster") is often enough to prevent legislation from even reaching the floor.

Moreover, the norm of one cloture vote per measure has changed. The modern Senate reached a record of eight cloture votes (all unsuccessful) on a controversial campaign financing measure during the 100th Congress (1987–1989). Cloture is also sometimes employed for purposes unrelated to ending a filibuster. For example, if the sixty votes are obtained under Senate Rule XXII, there is the requirement that all amendments be germane to the clotured measure. Or the majority leader may schedule repeated cloture votes, knowing that they will fail, in order to tar the other party as "obstructionists" in the next election.

There is little question that contemporary senators wield their procedural prerogatives for partisan advantage. The new normal today in the Senate is that nearly everything requires sixty votes to pass. It is not surprising, then, that the two parties provide different interpretations of the circumstances that provoke their dismay and frustration with Senate proceedings. A co-chair of the Senate Democratic Policy Committee declared that there was "less cooperation and more determination to block almost anything than at any time I have seen in the 30 years I have served here." He added:

> We have a noncontroversial issue, a motion to proceed [to the consideration of] something on which there is no controversy, and it is subject to a filibuster, and then a cloture motion has to be filed. Then 2 days have to pass before it ripens. We have a cloture vote, and

then following the cloture vote, the minority says: Well, we insist that the 30 hours postcloture be used. So 30 hours has to be burned off. Only then can you get a vote on a noncontroversial issue. Then you have a vote, and it is 98 to 1. That has happened throughout this [Congress]—continual efforts to block everything; deciding that the best strategy politically, apparently, for the minority here in the U.S. Senate is to block everything.[81]

Sen. Lamar Alexander insists that the "real obstructionists have been the Democratic majority which, for an unprecedented number of times, have used their majority advantage to limit debate, not allow amendments and bypass the normal committee consideration of legislation." He continued:

So the real "party of no" is the majority party that has been saying "no" to debate and "no" to voting on amendments that minority members believe improve legislation and express the voices of the people they represent. In fact, the reason the majority leader can claim there have been so many filibusters is because he actually is counting as filibusters the number of times he filed cloture—or moved to cut off debate.[82]

This clash of viewpoints on which party provoked the intense parliamentary warfare led a number of mainly junior senators to try—at the start of the 112th Congress—to change the Senate rules. One reform group favored use of the so-called constitutional or nuclear option.[83] Its advocates argue that a newly elected Senate should not be bound by preexisting rules. Instead, they argued, the Senate has the constitutional right "to determine the rules of its proceedings" by majority vote at the start of a new Congress, notwithstanding any inherited (or continuing) rules from the previous Congress. Under inherited Senate rules, however, ending a talkathon on any rules change requires a supermajority vote of two-thirds, a very high hurdle for reform proposals.

In the end, the Senate adopted a series of modest changes, leaving Rule XXII (cloture/filibuster) untouched. The revisions included another attempt to end secret holds (noted earlier); elimination of the reading requirement for amendments—employed as a dilatory tactic—if they have been available to lawmakers for at least seventy-two hours; and, as mentioned in Chapter 11, agreement that the number of federal positions subject to the advice and consent of the Senate should be reduced by one-third. In addition, the two party leaders announced a nonbinding "gentlemen's agreement." GOP leader Mitch McConnell said that Republicans would restrict filibusters on the motion to proceed to consider legislation. For his part, Democratic leader Reid stated that he would exercise restraint in filling the tree to block Republican amendments. The gentlemen's agreement did not last long.[84] There was an increase in the use of tree-filling and no shortage of filibuster threats on the motion to proceed to a measure or matter.

The 112th Congress also saw the majority Democrats use a reinterpretation of the rules to mobilize a simple floor majority to crack down on Republican obstruction. In 2010 and 2011, minority Republicans began to use suspension motions as a way to circumvent germaneness requirements for amendments when cloture (closure of debate under Senate Rule XXII) was invoked by the required sixty-vote supermajority. None of the GOP's suspension motions attracted the required two-thirds vote to suspend Senate rules, but they afforded Republicans an opportunity to discuss their "message" proposals and to foil Majority Leader Reid's scheduling plans.

Upset at the GOP's delaying tactic of arranging multiple suspension motions, Senator Reid took steps on October 6, 2011, to establish a new Senate precedent to end the practice. First, he emphasized that cloture is a process to bring Senate rules to a close. Unless the Senate changes its precedents, he explained, "we will be faced with an endless series of motions to suspend the rules after the Senate has voted overwhelmingly to bring consideration to a close, and that is a result a functioning democracy cannot tolerate."[85] Second, Reid called up one of the GOP's suspension motions and raised a point of order (a parliamentary objection) against it. Although the presiding officer, following the advice of the Senate parliamentarian, overruled the point of order, Senator Reid appealed the ruling. The Senate then voted to overturn the chair's ruling and uphold Reid's point of order, creating a new Senate precedent. Under this precedent, "it will now be against the rules to seek the 67 votes needed to suspend the cloture rules and bring up an amendment that is non-germane, or unrelated, to the bill in question after a successful cloture vote."[86] Some Republicans accused Reid of "going nuclear," though establishment of new precedents by majority vote is not uncommon. Reid's maneuver, however, may have foreshadowed the more significant reform actions of the 113th Congress (2013–2015).

In January 2013, the Senate adopted bipartisan packages of new filibuster changes negotiated by the two party leaders (Reid and McConnell). Among the fundamental objectives of the revisions were to expedite Senate action on legislation by minimizing the threat of a filibuster on the motion to proceed by allowing a simple majority to take up a bill, if amendment opportunities are guaranteed to the majority and minority parties, thus inhibiting "filling the tree"; collapsing into a single debatable motion, rather than three, the process for taking a bill to conference with the House (although that single motion is still subject to a filibuster); and shortening post-cloture debate time on certain nominations.

A number of senators and outside groups criticized the changes for not going far enough. For example, some wanted majority cloture rather than the current sixty-vote requirement to shut down extended debate. However, the incremental approach to change avoided a potential parliamentary meltdown if the "nuclear option"—changing Senate rules with majority support—had been used by Senator Reid. Moreover, Senator Reid understood that Democrats would one day be in the minority and need the filibuster when the GOP controlled the Senate. Furthermore, use of the nuclear option was viewed as a "slippery slope" that any majority could use at any time to change Senate rules. The Senate might then become more like the majoritarian House.

The recent initiatives to revise Senate rules reflect an erosion of the Senate's customary norms of collegiality, civility, and accommodation. The various explanations for this development include the election to the Senate of House members who bring with them the aggressive partisanship common to the House, heightened demands placed on senators by constituents and lobbyists, intense electoral competition, and the escalating costs of campaigns. "Daily priorities [are] shaped more by personal agendas—campaign needs, interest-group demands, personal staff, obligations to meet constituents, and off-the-Hill speeches—and less by the expectations of colleagues and the needs of Senate colleagues," wrote congressional scholar Steven S. Smith. "Pressed by constituencies and lobbyists and more strongly motivated to grab a headline, senators now more routinely and more fully exploit their procedural prerogatives than at any other time in the Senate's history."[87] The upshot of these developments is a more individualistic and partisan Senate, which means that compromises and accommodations are harder to achieve on significant substantive and procedural issues.

RESOLVING HOUSE-SENATE DIFFERENCES

Before bills can be sent to the president, they must be passed by the House and the Senate in identical form. Conference committees are the best known method used to resolve bicameral differences when the two chambers pass dissimilar versions of the same bill. Another approach is to ping-pong House and Senate amendments between the chambers until each chamber is satisfied with the product.[88] Recent Congresses have seen greater use of the ping-pong method because of the Senate's difficulty in getting to conference, largely because the procedural steps to convene a conference are subject to extended debate. If neither chamber will accept the other's changes via the exchange of amendment process, a House-Senate conference committee may be appointed to reconcile the differences. There are occasions, too, when ping-ponging is used in combination with conference committees. For example, the chambers may start out using the exchange of amendments and then convene a conference to resolve the outstanding matters in bicameral disagreement.

Worth re-emphasizing is that the ping-pong procedure has increased in importance and prominence in recent Congresses. Instead of convening a conference, there is greater use of the exchange of amendment procedure on controversial and consequential legislation. A major reason was the Senate's difficulty in convening a conference with the other chamber because of its own internal partisan disagreements. To get to conference, the Senate's majority leader makes a routine, three-part request to convene a conference with the House. He would say: "Mr. President, I move that the Senate insist on its amendments [to the House-passed bill], request a conference with the House on the disagreeing votes thereon, and that the Chair be authorized to appoint conferees." Traditionally, the leader's motion would be quickly agreed to by unanimous consent. As explained by Robert Dove, the former parliamentarian of the Senate, "The three steps are usually bundled into a unanimous consent [request] and done within seconds. But if some senators do not want a conference to occur and they are determined, they can force three separate cloture votes to close depart [on each of the discrete parts], and that takes a lot of time. It basically stops the whole process of going to conference."[89] As noted earlier, the 113th Senate combined the three-part request into a single debatable motion to facilitate the Senate's ability to convene a conference with the House.

Most public laws are approved without conferences. Either they pass each chamber without any changes (roughly 70 percent of the time), or the House and Senate amend a bill in turn until both chambers agree on the wording (about 20 percent of laws follow this shuttle route). Only about 10 percent of the measures passed by Congress—usually the most important and controversial—are subject to bicameral reconciliation by conference committees.

Under each chamber's rules and precedents, conference committees meet to resolve the matters in bicameral dispute; they are not to reconsider provisions already agreed to, and they are not to write new law by inserting matter that neither house may have considered. However, parliamentary rules are not self-enforcing, and either chamber can waive or ignore them. It is not unusual for conference reports to contain new matter that neither chamber debated nor amended in committee or on the floor. No wonder conference committees are called the third house of Congress.

Selection of Conferees

Conferees usually are named from the committee or committees that reported the legislation. Congressional rules state that the Speaker and the Senate presiding officer select conferees. In fact, that decision typically is made by the relevant committee chairs and the ranking minority members. House and Senate party leaders commonly get involved in naming conferees on major legislation to ensure that the conferees will back leadership positions on the legislation.

House and Senate party leaders are sometimes named as conferees—a sign that they want to direct conference negotiations on high-stakes issues important to their party. The House majority leader, for example, often serves on important tax conferences. When the top majority party leaders of either chamber are named as conferees, this signals, as one senator declared, a "majority-party driven" conference.[90]

Each chamber may name as many conferees as it wants, and some conference delegations have become very large. The 1981 omnibus reconciliation conference set the record, with more than 250 House and Senate conferees working in fifty-eight subconferences to resolve more than three hundred matters in bicameral disagreement. The ratio of Republicans to Democrats on a conference committee generally reflects the proportion of the two parties in the House and Senate.

Today's conference committees represent a sharp departure in size and composition from the pre-1980 era, when conference delegations generally ranged from five to twelve conferees from each house. And before the mid-1970s, conferees nearly always were the most senior lawmakers from the committees that reported the legislation. Although seniority frequently determines who the conferees will be, it is not unusual for junior and even first-term members to be conferees. Furthermore, conferees today commonly are chosen from several standing committees and reflect intricate selection arrangements. For example, House conferees may be named to negotiate only certain items in disagreement instead of the entire bill. Multiple referrals and megabills are the driving forces behind these two developments.

In conference each chamber has a single vote determined by a majority of its conferees, who are generally expected to support the legislation as it passes their body. But, a senator confessed, as conference committees drag on, the "individual attitudes of the various members begin to show."[91] A standard objective of conferees is to fashion a compromise product—the conference report—that will be acceptable to a majority of the membership of both chambers and that the president will sign into law.

Openness and Bargaining

Secret conference meetings were the norm for most of Congress's history. In 1975 both houses adopted rules requiring open meetings unless the conferees from each chamber voted in public to close the sessions. Two years later, the House went further, requiring open conference meetings unless the full House agreed to secret sessions. Sometimes, the Cable-Satellite Public Affairs Network (C-SPAN) televises conference proceedings.

The open conference is yet another instance of individual–institutional cleavage. Under the watchful eye of lobbyists, conferees fight harder for provisions they might have dropped quietly in the interest of bicameral agreement. And yet private bargaining sessions still permeate conference negotiations.

Senators and representatives expect certain bills to go to conference and plan their bargaining strategy accordingly. For example, whether to have a recorded vote on amendments can influence conference bargaining. In the absence of a recorded vote, amendments may be easier to drop in conference. Bargaining techniques in conference cover a range of techniques: from logrolling ("you accept my chamber's position on this provision and I'll accept yours on another provision") to threats to walk out of the negotiations unless the other side compromises. One side may fight hard for a position on which it plans to yield, so the conferees can tell their parent chamber that they put up a good battle but the other side would not relent. Conference committees are where the final version of the law is often written, sometimes making changes or additions to legislation that neither chamber ever reviewed or considered in committee or on the floor.

The Conference Report

A conference ends when its report (the compromise bill) is signed by a majority of the conferees from each chamber. House and Senate staff then prepare the conference report and the accompanying joint explanatory statement, which summarizes the conferees' recommendations. The House and Senate then vote on the conference report without further amendment. If either chamber rejects the conference report—an infrequent occurrence—a new conference may be called or another bill introduced. Once passed, the compromise bill is sent to the president for approval or disapproval.

CONCLUSION

The philosophical bias of House and Senate rules reflects the character of each institution. Individual rights are stressed in the Senate, majority rule in the House. In both chambers, however, members who know the rules and precedents have an advantage over procedural novices in affecting policy outcomes. The late senator Byrd—the longest-serving Senate member in history—was the acknowledged procedural expert in the Senate. Byrd understood that passing measures often involved unorthodox processes and procedures (for example, forgoing committee hearings or markups or even floor debate).[92]

In addition to congressional rules, persistence, strategy, timing, compromise, and pure chance are important elements in the lawmaking process. To make public policy requires building winning coalitions at successive stages where pressure groups and other parties can advance their claims. Political, procedural, personal, and policy considerations shape the final outcome. Passing laws, as one former representative said, is like the "weaving of a web, bringing a lot of strands together in a pattern of support which won't have the kind of weak spots which could cause the whole fabric to fall apart."[93]

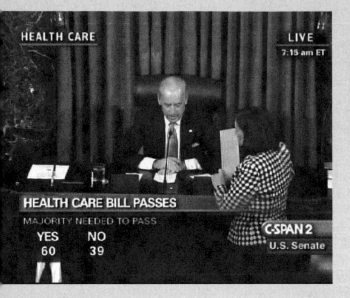

HEALTH CARE — LIVE 7:15 am ET

HEALTH CARE BILL PASSES
MAJORITY NEEDED TO PASS

YES	NO
60	39

C-SPAN 2
U.S. Senate

Congressional Decision Making
Covered by C-SPAN, Vice President Joseph R. Biden Jr. (top left) announces the final Senate vote on President Obama's health-care measure. The House then votes along party lines to accept the Senate version of the bill (bottom left). The House's electronic voting system records members' floor votes (top right). Members insert plastic cards into voting boxes throughout the chamber to vote "yea," "nay," or "present." Members' votes are scrutinized and rated by hundreds of interest groups, including the Humane Society (bottom right).

U.S. HOUSE - HEALTH CARE — LIVE 10:47 pm ET

HOUSE PASSES SENATE BILL
AHEAD - Vote on Reconciliation Bill

H R 3590

	YEA	NAY	PRES	NV
DEMOCRATIC	219	34		
REPUBLICAN		176		2
INDEPENDENT				
TOTALS	219	210		2

TIME REMAINING 0:00

C-SPAN

HUMANE SCORECARD
The 112th Congress in Review

HUMANE SOCIETY

Decision Making in Congress

"I know that everyone is anxiously awaiting the 8:15 time," joked Senate majority leader Harry Reid to a group of unhappy senators waiting on the Senate floor at 8:40 p.m. on a Thursday evening. Only a few could even muster a smile in response.[1] Earlier that day, Reid had announced that senators could tentatively expect a roll call vote to take place at 8:15 p.m. Nearly half an hour after the vote was expected, it had become clear that Democrats lacked the support needed to advance a critical $410 billion omnibus spending measure. "It appears at this time that we are going to have to continue work on this bill," said Reid. "We would probably be a vote short."[2]

Democratic leaders were thrown off guard by dissent in their party's ranks. They had expected to pass the measure easily.[3] But passing the bill turned out to be a "tough slog."[4] Republicans denounced as wasteful the bill's increased spending—an average boost of 8 percent for domestic programs.[5] In the wake of the controversy, a few centrist Democrats signaled their concern and criticized the bill as "bloated" and "business as usual."[6] Even with these defections, however, Reid thought that he had won the needed support. Instead, he was blindsided by the opposition of Sen. Robert Menendez, D-N.J., who was "deeply offended" by a few provisions in the 1,132-page measure that would relax some travel and trade restrictions on Cuba.[7] Menendez's opposition was especially unexpected because senators serving in the party leadership— Menendez at the time was chair of the Democratic Senate Campaign—rarely opposed their party on priority issues. "It's been surprising," Reid said of the failure to move the bill.[8]

Reid postponed the vote to buy time for building support. In the meantime, he was forced to allow Republicans to offer a series of amendments requiring Democrats to cast politically painful votes. Sen. David Vitter, R-La., for example, successfully demanded a vote on an amendment to eliminate automatic cost-of-living increases in congressional salaries.[9] Senators of both parties knew these votes would figure in future ads against Democratic candidates. "This is all about developing campaign commercials," said Sen. Mark Begich, D-Alaska.[10] "Democrats effectively used the pay raise issue against several Republican candidates in past cycles," noted a National Republican Senatorial Committee spokesperson, "so I don't think they should be at all surprised if this emerges as an issue in some of their own campaigns."[11]

While the debate on amendments went forward, leaders began to round up new support for the bill. "We're working on it," said Majority Whip Richard J. Durbin, D-Ill. "I hope at the end of the day we don't lose [as many as four or five Democrats]."[12] Of the whip team's efforts, Sen. Claire McCaskill, D-Mo., commented, "I think it's fair to say that there's an extraordinary amount of pressure on this particular bill."[13] Treasury Department officials were dispatched to discuss the Cuba trade provisions with Menendez. Having received assurances about the way the administration would interpret the legislative language, Menendez finally announced his support of the bill at a Democratic Caucus meeting to a round of applause.[14] In the end, the Senate passed the legislation after an additional week of work, and President Barack Obama signed the measure into law.

This large-scale spending measure (and hundreds more that have a lower profile) required lawmakers to make tough policy choices collectively—after discussion, debate, bargaining, and problem-solving. "The Senate requires consensus," remarked a top Senate leadership staffer. "Senator Reid is not a king. If he had the ability to snap his fingers and make things fall into place, he would."[15] The end product is almost always an imperfect compromise. Indeed, "imperfect" was precisely how President Obama described the omnibus spending bill when he signed it.[16] Legislative assemblies are deliberative bodies, and in the United States this deliberation takes place in the context of the two Congresses. Individual members confront thousands of choices: how and when to participate, how to decide, how to find allies, and how to explain their actions to constituents back home.

THE POWER TO CHOOSE

All members of Congress have the ability to shape public policy, although some members are far more influential than others. At a minimum, every legislator has the right, indeed the obligation, to vote. Legislators must cast their own votes; no colleague or staff aide may do it for them. To exchange their votes or other official acts for money or for any other thing of value is a federal crime. But aside from bribery or corruption there are no legal grounds for challenging legislators' deliberations or decisions. As discussed in Chapter 2, the U.S. Constitution specifies that "for any Speech or Debate in either House, [members of Congress] shall not be questioned in any other place."

Policy making in Congress involves far more than casting roll call votes. Matters that come before Congress for a vote have already been shaped by the participation of members at many prior stages. Some of this work, like members' votes, is a matter of public record: formal meetings, markups, debates, and amending activities. Of equal importance are the less-visible informal negotiations that surround nearly every enactment—away from the eyes of reporters and lobbyists. Separating formal and informal modes of participation in a study of members' committee activity, Richard L. Hall found that members' formal and informal activities do not always coincide.[17]

Sometimes, members use formal actions to signal concern to constituents and other groups, but then do not follow through with the hard informal work needed to shape the legislation.

A full accounting of lawmakers' performance, then, would embrace not only how members participate in floor and committee deliberations but also how much effort they expend overall. How much attention do they pay to issues? How do they gain expertise? Whom do they consult for information on legislative decisions? How influential are party leaders? How do they hire, deploy, and supervise their staffs? Countless such decisions define what it means to be a member of Congress.

TYPES OF DECISIONS

One basic decision facing legislators is how to spend their time and energy while in the nation's capital. Some try to digest the mountains of studies and reports that cross their desks. They "do their homework," in Capitol Hill parlance. Others seem to know or care little about legislative matters. They pursue other duties—communication, outreach, visits with constituents or lobby groups, partisan politics, and fund-raising. Such members may rarely contribute to committee or floor deliberations. Their votes usually follow cues from party colleagues, staff aides, the White House, or interest groups. Some are found in the ranks of the "Obscure Caucus," a list of unnoticed members compiled periodically by *Roll Call*, a Capitol Hill newspaper. "These Members pay strict attention to parochial issues and would much rather attend a hog-calling contest back home than appear on a cable news show. They deliver for their districts and shun any entreaties to become part of the Washington, D.C., culture."[18]

Specializing

Within the legislative realm, members may dig deeply in a particular area or range widely across issues and policies. Senators are more apt to be generalists, while representatives tend to cultivate a few specialties. Former senator Jim DeMint, R-S.C., once explained why members should specialize:

> If you've got twenty things you want to do, see where everything is. You'll find that maybe ten of those are already being worked on by people, and that while you may be supportive in that role, you don't need to carry the ball. But you can find those two or three things that are important to you that no one seems to be taking the lead on. But if you try to play the lead on everything, you'll be wasting your time.[19]

In both houses, key policy-making roles are played by those whom Rep. David E. Price, D-N.C., a political scientist, calls *policy entrepreneurs*—that is, those recognized for "stimulating more than . . . responding" to outside political forces on a given issue.[20] Often nearly invisible to the mass of citizens, these legislators are known to specialized publics for their contributions to specific policies—for example, Sen. Jeff Flake, R-Ariz., on immigration; Rep. Earl Blumenauer, D-Ore., on bike trails; Rep. Mac Thornberry, R-Texas, on cybersecurity; and Sen. Tom Harkin, D-Iowa, on policies for the disabled.

Members' policy reaches can go beyond their committee assignments—through speeches, floor amendments, caucuses, and task forces, to name a few. When only in his second term, Rep. Dick Armey, R-Texas (1985–2003), who was not a member of the Armed Services Committee, devised an ingenious scheme to employ an outside commission—the Base Realignment and Closure Commission (BRAC)—to decide which unneeded military bases should be closed. His proposal smoothed political sensitivities regarding base closures in members' constituencies and won bipartisan support for its enactment into law (P.L. 100–526). Such feats are not everyday occurrences, but the fluidity of today's procedures makes even the most junior member a potential policy entrepreneur.

A member's knowledge and perceived expertise on issues is a vital source of legislative influence. As Sen. Edmund S. Muskie, D-Maine (1959–1980), put it:

> People have all sorts of conspiratorial theories on what constitutes power in the Senate. It has little to do with the size of the state you come from. Or the source of your money. Or committee chairmanships, although that certainly gives you a kind of power. But real power up there comes from doing your work and knowing what you're talking about. Power is the ability to change someone's mind. . . . The most important thing in the Senate is credibility. Credibility! That is power.[21]

Timing of Decisions

Lawmakers do more than specialize in a particular policy field. They are constantly forced to make decisions on issues, many far from their areas of specialization. Timing is key. *When* members make decisions has important consequences for the deliberative process, a point that Richard F. Fenno Jr. discussed in his work on the "politics of timing."[22]

From a study of a vote on selling AWACS (airborne warning and control system) reconnaissance planes to Saudi Arabia, Fenno identified three types of decision makers: early deciders, active players, and late deciders.

Early deciders are fervent supporters who want to get out front in the debate. "I'd rather come out early and be part of the fight," said Rep. Peter T. King, R-N.Y., of his ready support for fast-track trade authority.[23] These members are buoyed by friendly lobbyists but ignored by others because their commitments are known at the outset from declarations, bill sponsorship, or prior voting records.

Active players, by contrast, delay their commitments, inviting bids from various sides of the issue at hand and often gaining leverage over the final language of legislation.

Late deciders delay their decision (or reconsider an earlier commitment) until the very last moment. They forfeit influence over the basic framework of the measure. But late deciders are eagerly courted by all sides and may gain specific concessions. With every vote critical to Senate passage of President Obama's health care overhaul plan and pressure mounting to conclude action, Sen. Byron Dorgan, D-N.D., informed Majority Leader Reid that he would not vote for the Patient Protection and Affordable Care Act unless it included Native American health care. "That's not a threat, just a statement of fact," he said.[24] (Dorgan, now retired, was chair of the Committee on Indian Affairs.) Native American health care was included as part of the larger bill.

Taking the Lead

Senators and representatives differ widely in the rate at which they introduce and sponsor bills. Some lawmakers are inveterate initiators of bills and resolutions. Others shy away from sponsoring measures. Still others commonly take the lead in sponsoring legislation because of the position they occupy, such as the chair of the relevant committee of jurisdiction. A study by Wendy Schiller found that bills in the Senate are most likely to be introduced by senior senators, those who are chairs or ranking members of high-volume committees (such as Commerce), and those who represent large, diverse states.[25]

Senate and House rules do not limit the number of members who can cosponsor bills or resolutions. Thus cosponsorship has become common. Most bills are cosponsored; according to one study, the average Senate bill had 7.2 cosponsors and the average House bill had 22.2 cosponsors.[26] Authors of measures often circulate a "Dear Colleague" letter detailing the virtues of the bill and soliciting cosponsors to demonstrate broad support and urge committee action. A researcher found that more than twelve thousand such letters were sent electronically by House members in 2007, an average of more than twenty-five letters per member.[27]

Occasionally, however, some members shun cosponsors. Introducing his waterway users' fee bill, Sen. Pete V. Domenici, R-N.M. (1973–2009), decided against seeking cosponsors for several reasons.[28] First, as ranking Republican on the subcommittee, he could arrange for hearings without the support of cosponsors. In addition, single sponsorship is easier. ("If you've got cosponsors you have to clear every little change with them.") And, finally, if the bill became law, he would get more credit on his own.

Do legislators favor the bills and resolutions they introduce? Normally they do, but as Sportin' Life, the *Porgy and Bess* character, said, "It ain't necessarily so." Members may introduce a measure to stake out jurisdiction for their committee or to pave the way for hearings and deliberations that will air a public problem. Or they may introduce measures they do not personally favor to oblige an executive agency or to placate an important interest group.

Taking Part

As members in any organization, some lawmakers take a passionate interest in what goes on; others pay selective attention to issues; a few seem just to be going through the motions. In a detailed study of three House committees, Richard L. Hall uncovered great variation in members' levels of participation. Although members' attendance at committee and subcommittee sessions was respectable (about three-quarters of the members showed up for at least part of each session), active participation—taking part in markup debate, offering amendments, and the like—was far less common. Perhaps half a subcommittee's members could be considered players, by a generous counting. The rest were nonplayers. As a subcommittee staffer remarked, "On a good day half of [the members] know what's going on. Most of the time it's only five or six who actually mark a bill up."[29]

Constituency interests strongly propel members to participate in committee business. This is true even when the negotiations are informal and out of the public's sight. In formal subcommittee markup sessions, "the public forum has the benefit of allowing members at once to promote—through their votes, arguments, amendments, obstructionism—constituency interests and be seen doing so."[30]

Constituency-driven activity was especially common in the House Agriculture Committee, a panel historically buffeted by regional and commodity pressures. Because of the committee's composition, its membership is more favorable to agriculture programs than the House as a whole. Furthermore, only a subset of the committee's members participates in most matters, and those who choose to take part tend to be more biased in favor of the programs under consideration than even the rest of the Agriculture Committee. Hall found in his late 1990s study, in a pattern that is not known to be true across the board, that members representing constituencies with large numbers of dairy farmers and peanut growers, for example, were the most active in influencing policy affecting dairy and peanut interests. Neither the full committee nor floor deliberations counterbalanced the enthusiastic advocacy of the dozen or so lawmakers from districts that produced those commodities. Whether this pattern of activity continues into the 2000s and 2010s requires additional analysis. Participation on Agriculture was the most biased toward members with a constituency stake in the legislation being considered; in debates over job training legislation in another committee, participating members tended to represent areas with higher unemployment rates than those of nonparticipants. No participatory biases were found when concentrated district benefits were not at stake.

Members in formal leadership positions are also more likely to take an active part in committee deliberations. Members often forgo participation because there are so many demands on their time that they must prioritize issues which are important to their constituents. Committee and subcommittee leaders, however, face fewer obstacles to participation because their seniority and authority "[place] them at the epicenter of the communications network in which most important legislative interactions take place."[31] In other words, holding leadership posts puts members "in the know" and enables them to be major players on legislation even when they do not personally have a significant constituency stake in the outcome.

Participation in House or Senate floor debates is equally varied: members who do not serve on the relevant committees, or who have only peripheral interests in the matter, are tempted to speak simply "for the record." A study of three major congressional debates determined that it is "typically no better than moderately informed." Gary Mucchiaroni and Paul J. Quirk concluded: "Legislators frequently assert claims that are inaccurate or misleading, and reassert them after they have been effectively refuted."[32] The good news about floor debates is that opposing members often—though not always—counter erroneous or distorted arguments.

Offering Amendments

Another important way of participating is to offer amendments to bills or resolutions. Amendments propose specific changes in legislative language: they delete or add words or substitute one provision for another. They are a chief means of shaping legislation during committee and floor deliberation. However, amendments are not always intended to enact policy changes. They can instead be used as a tool of obstruction or to derail legislation. They also can serve political purposes by putting members on the record on specific issues. For example, Sen. Claire McCaskill, who won reelection in a tight 2012 contest, exclaimed that in the leadup to the election, Senate GOP leader Mitch McConnell, R-Ky., had been "trying to figure out what amendments he could put on the floor to make my life miserable." McConnell's goal, she said, was "to figure out some way to put something on the floor that would get me to vote against my own mother."[33]

House majority leaders, who control the floor agenda, regularly employ special rules to limit the amendments that members can offer to particular bills. By so doing, the leaders often can engineer favored policy outcomes, expedite floor action, and prevent politically difficult issues from being raised on the floor. During the 112th Congress, for example, the House considered in 2012 a GOP tax reform bill under a structured rule that granted a specific minority Democrat the opportunity to offer one free-standing amendment to the bill (H.R. 6169) that the majority Republicans knew they could defeat. The measure was entitled "Pathway to Job Creation through a Simpler, Fairer Tax Code Act." A senior minority member of the Rules Committee blasted the rule, stating that other than one minority amendment, "every single amendment the Democrats had to try to influence this bill was defeated [in the Rules Committee] on a strictly partisan vote—every single one of them." This bill, he added, is "a press release masquerading as a meaningful piece of legislation."[34] The measure passed the House on a party-line vote just before the members began their traditional August recess.

Compared to the House, in the Senate—because of individual senators' prerogatives—germane and nonrelevant amendments are more freely offered and form a central part of floor debate. Sometimes, amendments are offered simply to test the strength of support for a proposal rather than to immediately alter policy outcomes. During a debate on reauthorizing the National Aeronautics and Space Administration, a House member introduced an amendment to cancel the costly space station program. Instead of losing by a wide margin (as in previous years), the amendment failed by only a single vote. That narrow margin signaled plunging support for the space station and other "big science" projects.[35]

Some amendments are designed to force members to declare themselves on issues that command public attention. Sen. David Vitter's, R-La., amendment to an omnibus appropriations bill to end automatic cost-of-living increases in congressional salaries is an example. Lawmakers who vote for salary increases, especially during hard economic times, risk having the voters turn them out of office.

Other amendments are poison pills. So-called killer amendments are intended to make a bill so unpalatable that if adopted, they will kill the underlying measure. Although killer amendments upset the sponsors and managers of bills, they rarely alter a measure's ultimate fate. Examining seventy-six killer amendments considered in the mid-1990s, a scholar concluded that they "rarely, if ever, cause bills to fail. . . . Most were easily defeated."[36]

Casting Votes

Lawmakers' most visible choices are embodied in the votes they cast. Voting is a central ritual of any legislative body. Members know that their voting records communicate a great deal of information about their policy and political commitments to their constituents. Reflecting on his vote on a financial institutions bailout package, a House member said, "This is a legacy vote; these are the votes you have to live with for the rest of your life."[37] Several months after the 112th Congress convened, many Tea Party–supported congressional Republicans found themselves facing a legacy vote. These lawmakers, having promised in the 2010 elections to cut and curb government spending, now faced an unavoidable vote: the electorally painful decision to raise the national debt ceiling, allowing the government to spend hundreds of billions of dollars more. Raising the "must-pass" debt ceiling is "beautiful politics—the brutal kind," declared former senator Alan Simpson, R-Wyo. (1979–1997), co-chair of President Obama's deficit reduction commission.[38]

Members anticipate that constituents will review their votes at reelection time. Outside groups closely follow members' votes on specific measures and publicize them during election campaigns. Special interests want to know whether members' promises on the campaign trail tracked their voting decisions in Congress. Groups may grade lawmakers as "heroes" or "zeros" based on their votes for environmental or business measures. Nevertheless, members' own personal judgments sometimes outweigh political expedience. Members may be willing to risk their reelection chances by casting a vote contrary to the strong preferences of many of their constituents (for example, voting for gun control in a state or district with a pro-gun culture), especially if they have explained to voters in advance the reasons for their decision.

Senators and representatives strive to be recorded on as many floor and committee votes as possible. On 945 roll call votes on the House floor in 2011, members voted a record-setting 96.6.percent of the time. In 2012, an election year, the voting participation of House members on 657 roll call votes declined to 95.3 percent. In 2011 senators recorded a participation rate on 235 votes of 97 percent; their participation rate in 2012 dropped slightly to 96.6 percent.[39] Members seek to compile a record of diligence to forestall charges of absenteeism by potential opponents. They also want to compile a good voting record to demonstrate their commitment to the voters back home. Just before casting her 5,000th consecutive vote, Sen. Susan Collins, R-Maine., said, "While I recognize that not every vote is a critical vote, at this time when the public's confidence is so low, casting every single vote sends a strong signal to one's constituents of dedication to the job and to respect for the high privilege that we have been given."[40]

House and Senate leaders make it easier for members to fulfill high expectations by trying to schedule votes at predictable times; stacking votes back to back in midweek; or holding fewer votes on Mondays, when lawmakers are returning to Capitol Hill from their states or districts, and Fridays, when many members are anxious to depart for their constituencies. Majority party leaders of the House and Senate sometimes avoid controversial votes on priority bills by promising colleagues that their proposals will be voted on separately later in the session. Or they might schedule votes to attract public attention to their party message. "We're not going to do that at midnight tonight," stated Senate majority leader Harry Reid. "We're going to have the votes when you [reporters] can write about it during a decent news cycle."[41]

If members cannot vote in person, they can still be recorded on an issue by announcing their views in floor statements or in press releases. Pairing is a voluntary arrangement that allows members to go on the record without voting or affecting the final tabulation. A member who wishes to be recorded on an issue but cannot be present for the roll call vote may also ask another member who plans to vote on the other side for a "pair" arrangement in which both announce their positions in the *Congressional Record* but neither casts a vote (they cancel each other out). Members often grant such requests as a courtesy to their colleagues. Members might also vote "present" for various reasons. For example, Sen. Charles Schumer, D-N.Y., cast a rare "present" vote on a judicial nominee because the nominee was married to his sister.[42]

What Do Votes Mean?

Like other elements of the legislative process, votes are open to multiple interpretations. House and Senate floor votes do not perfectly register members' views. Members sometimes vote against a bill that they prefer to the status quo because they hope that a better bill on the matter might emerge later. Members know that a weak reform can deplete political will for bolder action. Politicians will also refuse to accept a compromise when they can force a confrontation that will sharpen the differences between the parties. At times, members prefer to keep the issue alive rather than to pass a bill. As a scholar wrote, "Advocates often anticipate that having the party differences clearly displayed will help them win in the next election, after which they will be able to enact an unadulterated form of the bill."[43] Killing a modest measure may lead to action on a more wide-ranging proposal later.

Members also may vote for a bill that they do not favor because they fear that if they fail to support it the end result will be something even worse. For example, some conservative Republicans voted for a federal program providing prescription drug coverage for elderly Americans because they believed it was the best bill they could get. "I don't think we'll write a better bill if we defeat this," explained a conservative senator.[44] Members will often go along with legislation because on the whole they deem the bill a step forward, even though they dislike specific provisions.

In some cases, recorded votes are wholly misleading. Given the multiplicity of votes—procedural as well as substantive—on many measures, lawmakers can come out on more than one side of an issue, or at least appear to do so. For example, members may vote to authorize a program and later vote against funding it. Or they may vote against final passage of a bill but for a substitute version. This tactic, which may open a lawmaker to the charge of being a "flip-flopper," assures the bill's backers that the lawmaker favors the concept, while pleasing voters who oppose the bill. Such voting patterns may reflect either a deliberate attempt to obscure one's position or a thoughtful response to complex questions. As in so many aspects of human behavior, lawmakers' motivations are often difficult to evaluate fully, and only in light of specific cases.

Members can also take advantage of "free votes" when their own individual vote will not affect the final outcome. Some members delay voting until the outcome of the vote is already assured. For example, during the debate on a constitutional amendment to prohibit flag burning, there was "strategic waiting" on the part of members.[45] Democratic members were cross-pressured on the issue—Democratic leaders opposed the anti–flag burning amendment, but it was very popular with constituents. Before it was clear that the amendment was going to fail, only 28 percent of the voting Democrats supported the amendment. Once enough votes had been cast to defeat the amendment, 73 percent of the remaining Democrats voted in favor of it. After the amendment had failed, members could take the popular position without any legislative consequences. Opportunities for insincere votes proliferate in the U.S. system of the separation of powers. Members can deliberately vote for measures that they believe will fail in the other chamber of Congress or be vetoed by the president. And they can support popular measures that they expect the courts will strike down as unconstitutional.

Lawmakers' voting rationales are sometimes hard to explain to outsiders. In some cases, members face a dilemma: either vote their convictions and deal with the consequences, or swallow their misgivings and vote for appearance's sake. A GOP House member chose the former course when he joined fourteen other Republicans in voting against a popular bill authorizing U.S. sanctions against nations that persecute religious minorities—an appealing idea but fraught with problems. "This was an awfully awkward vote, and I know I'll hear from the folks back home," he explained. "But the devil was in the details."[46]

More often, lawmakers decide to go with the crowd. Regarding a highly appealing constitutional amendment requiring a balanced budget, a senator admitted that he planned to vote for it because he got "tired of explaining" its deficiencies. It was easier "just to say put it in."[47]

Scholars and journalists often mistakenly treat votes as if they were unambiguous indicators of legislators' views. Lobbyists, too, are prone to assess lawmakers on the basis of floor votes. Many groups construct voting indexes that label legislators as "friendly" or "unfriendly." Citizens should be cautioned to examine such indexes closely. How many votes does the index include? Are they a fair sample of the group's concerns? Does the index embody a partisan or ideological agenda, hidden or otherwise? The bottom line is: beware of an interest group's voting scorecards, even if you agree with its policy leanings.

DETERMINANTS OF VOTING

Votes, particularly on single issues, should be examined, interpreted, and categorized with care. Among several factors that shape congressional voting are party affiliation, ideological leanings, constituents' views, and presidential leadership.

Party and Voting

Party affiliation is the strongest single correlate of members' voting decisions. In a typical year, from half to two-thirds of all floor votes could be called party unity votes, defined as votes in which a majority of voting Republicans oppose a majority of voting Democrats. Figure 9-1 depicts House and Senate party unity votes from 1953 to 2012. Party voting is far more prevalent today than in the 1970s or early 1980s. Indeed, contemporary levels of party voting recall the militant parties of the late nineteenth century.

In the GOP-controlled 112th House, party unity was at record-setting levels.[48] In 2012, 72.8 percent of 657 House roll call votes divided the parties, "the highest incidence of such party unity votes ever in a presidential election year." The previous year was a record-setter: 75.8 percent of all House votes (716 of 945) were party unity. House party unity scores were high in large measure because, with eighty-seven freshmen Republicans—many Tea Party–endorsed and committed to slashing spending and reducing or eliminating federal programs—"GOP leaders tacked to the right. They brought divisive bills to the floor, measures meant to show what government would look like if their party ran the whole show."[49] In 2012 in the Senate, "59.8 percent of 251 votes split along party lines, the most in a presidential election year since 1996."[50]

Figure 9-2 depicts unity votes for the two parties in each chamber from 1956 to 2012. House and Senate Democrats voted on average with their party 92 percent of the time in 2011 and 2012. House Republicans voted on average almost as consistently as the Democrats in those years. Similarly, Senate Democrats were as united in their votes as members of the two parties in the House. "Only Senate Republicans showed a noteworthy departure from the partisan norm; their average party unity score fell from 86 percent" in 2011 to 80 percent.[51] This change occurred because six vulnerable Republican senators "departed from their party's majority on at least a third" of the party unity votes.[52]

Party cohesion stems from a number of roots. Members of a political party vote similarly because they are elected by many of the same sorts of constituencies and organized interests throughout the country. As one study noted, on a wide range of unrelated issues—"gun control, the economy, war, same-sex marriage, abortion, the environment, the financial bailout—the views of Republicans and Democrats have become increasingly monolithic."[53]

Party members also vote together because of their shared ideological commitments. Changes in the ideological composition and the constituency base of the two congressional parties have contributed to the increased levels of partisanship in the contemporary Congress. Each of these sources of party unity—constituency and ideology—is discussed here. However, it is important

FIGURE 9-1 **Party Unity Votes in House, Senate, and Congress, 1953–2012**

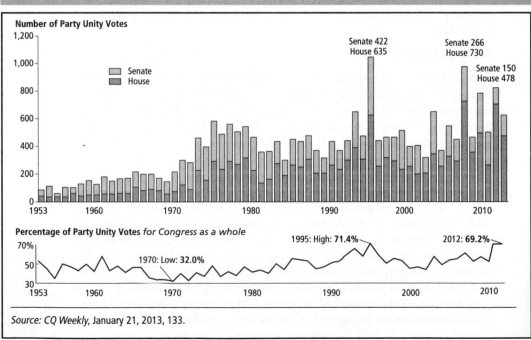

Source: *CQ Weekly*, January 21, 2013, 133.

FIGURE 9-2   **Average Party Unity Votes in the House and Senate, 1956–2012**

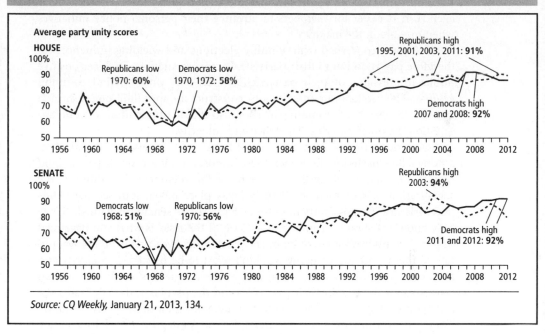

Source: *CQ Weekly,* January 21, 2013, 134.

to note that congressional party unity also has a source in explicitly *partisan* motives, meaning party members' shared political interests in helping their party win elections and control Congress.[54] These interests bring fellow partisans together despite the diversity of their policy preferences. Indeed, even when interparty conflict in Congress was at a low ebb in the late 1960s and early 1970s, the parties still successfully organized the committees and leadership of Congress, and party affiliation remained the strongest single predictor of members' voting behavior.

Members of Congress cooperate with their fellow partisans in part because their personal fate as politicians is bound up with their party's public image and collective reputation. Members know that they do not win or lose elections solely as individual legislators. Voters' attitudes about the national parties affect their choices in particular congressional elections.[55] (Three "wave" elections in a row—'06, '08, and '10—demonstrate that voters will turn out the majority party when they believe it has messed up.) As a result, members take into account how their individual actions will affect public perceptions of their party as a whole. There are exceptions, however. Numerous Republicans unsuccessfully urged GOP representative Todd Akin, Mo. (of "legitimate rape" fame), to drop out as the Senate challenger to Democratic incumbent Claire McCaskill. As former Missouri GOP senator John Danforth stated, Akin "damages the Republican brand."[56]

Members also care about the collective image of their party because they want their party to command a congressional majority. Members gain power personally when their party is in the majority. Members of the majority party chair all committees and subcommittees, and majority leaders set the floor agenda. It is easier for members to advance their personal policy initiatives when they are in the majority.

Members concerned with winning elections and wielding influence will therefore pay attention to their party's collective reputation. To foster positive public impressions of their party, fellow partisans work to find common ground. They collaborate in efforts to construct an appealing policy agenda and then cooperate in promoting it. They also exploit opportunities to call into question the other party's competence and integrity.

Common political interests nurture bonds of trust and communication among fellow partisans. To deepen these bonds, the congressional parties hold regular lunches, conferences, and retreats for members. In addition, the socialization of new members largely takes place in partisan settings. Thus fewer friendships cross party lines these days. As one senator explained, "If the only knowledge you have of 'the other side of the aisle' is what you have read in an attack press release written by the party operatives, you wouldn't want to talk to them, and you certainly wouldn't want to be friends."[57] Majority and minority party leaders regularly appeal to their members' common partisan interests in order to rally their troops behind the party agenda. The leaders of both parties strive to give the electorate a favorable view of the party's "brand." They hire consultants to devise messages and strategies crafted to generate broad public support for their policy goals and objectives. Contrasting his party's image with the clearer Republican brand, a Democratic senator said, "I can tell you what the Republicans stand for in eight words: family values, strong defense, lower taxes and less government."[58] Reflecting on these partisan motives, political scientists Gary Cox and Mathew McCubbins wrote, "Modern political parties facing mass electorates, similar to corporations facing mass markets, have a strong incentive to fashion and maintain a brand name."[59]

The common political interests of Democrats and Republicans mean they are predisposed to support their party. Political scientists who have studied members' voting decisions have found that members decide mainly by consulting the views of their partisan colleagues.[60] The typical member of Congress feels "duty bound to ascertain the views of the party leaders and [to] go along in the absence of contrary inclinations."[61] In other words, members cooperate with their parties unless they have a reason to defect. Wavering members who have reservations about the party's position may be subject to heavy pressure from party leaders. A classic example involved House Speaker Newt Gingrich, R-Ga. (1995–1999), and his lieutenants. During the GOP's first year in power after forty consecutive years of Democratic control, a junior Republican described the leadership's approach at persuasion:

> They pull us into a room before almost every vote and yell at us. . . .
> They say, "This is a test of our ability to govern," or "This is a gut
> check," or "I got you here and you hired me as your coach to get you
> through, but if you want to change coaches, go ahead."[62]

Party leaders in both chambers can usually rely on a high level of reflexive support from fellow partisans, especially on procedural matters. Political scientists have repeatedly shown that members are more likely to vote with their parties on procedural motions than directly on the substance of legislation.[63] Indeed, members often support their party leaders on procedural matters related to a bill, even when they do not intend to support the bill on final passage. Procedural votes, in brief, are usually partisan votes. As a senator once observed, "This is a procedural vote, and in the Senate we traditionally stick with the leadership on such votes."[64]

House leaders have broad authority to exploit procedures to strengthen party unity. Through their control of key committees, scheduling powers, and use of special rules, majority party leaders arrange for votes they are likely to win and avoid those they are apt to lose. For example, the majority leadership can use their agenda-setting prerogative in positive and negative ways. They can bring legislation to the floor under procedures that advantage the majority party, or the leaders can block unwanted measures (or amendments) from even being brought up for chamber consideration.

Senate leaders have fewer procedural tools than do House leaders, but majority leaders can use their right to be recognized first on the floor to regulate the timing, order, and content of debates to partisan advantage. For example, Senate majority leader Reid deliberately scheduled a series of votes he knew he would lose. Why? He wanted to portray Republicans as "obstructionists," to indicate to the bill's supporters that he tried, to demonstrate that Senate rules need revision (the measures were blocked by filibuster threats), and to direct the public's attention to these issues. Minority Leader McConnell viewed the entire exercise as political theater: "Are we here to perform, or are we here to legislate?"[65] At the same time, minority party members also have strong incentives to stick together on procedural and other matters, forcing vulnerable majority party members to cast difficult votes and making it increasingly difficult for the majority party to pursue its program.

Ideology and Voting

Most lawmakers today are committed partisans who hold strong ideological views on such topics as the proper role and purpose of government.[66] Indeed, many members of Congress entered politics through various ideological causes. Opposition to the Iraq war and the huge income disparity between the rich 1 percent and the other 99 percent spurred political activism for members on the left of the political spectrum. Many members on the right entered politics because of their small-government views or traditionalist social values. Long before they take their first oath of office, members bring ideological loyalties that inspire voting decisions throughout their political careers.

Both political parties encompass ideological diversity, which reflects their demographic and behavioral differences. The Republican Party, for example, embraces both economically conservative voters—educated, higher-income cohorts who are often associated with business—along with less-educated, lower- or middle-income people who are drawn to the party's traditional social values and its emphasis on limited government, national and border security, and a hard line on crime. How to balance the party's ideological wings is not an easy assignment for GOP congressional leaders. They work to accommodate both the party's social and religious conservatives, as well as their economically conservative business wing, not to mention the Tea Partiers.

Thus the journey to an acceptable compromise among House Republicans in the 112th Congress was difficult to muster. Many junior Republicans were in no mood to contain their zeal to cut spending, repeal health care, and overturn unwanted federal regulations. During a House GOP Conference meeting, freshman representative Steve Southerland, Fla., said he understood the party leadership's plea for party unity. "I want you to know there is a limit to how far I will follow. I may lose in 2012 [he won reelection] but I will not lose me."[67] The 113th Republican House is also likely to confront continued disunity within party ranks. For example, several junior GOP lawmakers, such as Matt Salmon of Arizona, have stated that they will vote to defeat procedural resolutions ("rules") from the Rules Committee if they make in order legislation that deviates from their principles (no tax increases, for example).

The Democratic Party also embraces ideological variety. It includes, according to one analysis, several types, such as "urban liberals" or "god and government" Democrats (largely nonwhite individuals who attend weekly religious services). In brief, Democrats include across-the-board liberals who are committed to a vigorous government redressing economic grievances, to tolerant stances on social and lifestyle issues, and to international treaties and institutions guiding foreign policy. But the party also includes factions advocating for a more conservative position on economic issues or on social issues, such as abortion. For example, a group of centrist House Democrats who belong to the informal New Democratic Coalition tacks left on social issues but veers "toward the center on business- and economic-oriented policies that could appeal to independent and moderate voters."[68] The party's diversity reflects its voters, who range from union members—who are concerned with economic issues but unsupportive of liberalism on social causes—to the "creative class" of professionals in university towns and urban enclaves who are far more libertarian on social issues.[69] Free trade pacts also tend to split these groups: union members fear losing jobs to low-wage foreign labor, while educated professionals tend to be more open toward globalization. Democratic leaders have to navigate these ideological divisions, often by avoiding issues that fracture the party.

When political scientists began seriously to analyze congressional roll call voting in the 1950s, ideological diversity within each of the two parties was far greater than it is today. Conservatives and liberals had a meaningful presence in both legislative parties. Although members often voted along party lines, at other times they would unite across parties in recognizable ideological coalitions. Frequently, Republicans and southern Democrats would cooperate in a voting pattern known as the conservative coalition.[70] Historically, this coalition was stronger in the Senate than in the House. Its success rate was impressive in both chambers during the 1939–1965 period—no matter which party controlled the White House or Capitol Hill.

Since the 1960s, the two legislative parties have sorted themselves out along ideological lines, with conservatives largely in the Republican Party and liberals exclusively in the Democratic Party. Scholars have found that "the most conservative Democrat is more liberal than is the most liberal Republican," with Republicans moving further to the right than Democrats to the left (called "asymmetric polarization").[71] As a consequence, the cross-party conservative coalition surfaces so rarely these days that the respected *CQ Weekly* has stopped scoring it.[72] Bipartisan conservatism fell victim to the increasing ideological consistency of both political parties. In short, "Democrats are perched on the left, Republicans on the right, in both the House and the Senate as the ideological centers of the two parties have moved markedly apart."[73]

The polarization of the contemporary Congress—in which partisanship and ideology are closely intertwined—can be shown spatially on a left–right (liberal–conservative) continuum. Using the congressional roll call voting record, political scientists Keith T. Poole and Howard Rosenthal have devised a scaling methodology to generate ideological scores for all members of Congress.[74] Their data show marked divergence between the parties in recent years.

Figure 9-3 displays the distribution of ideological preferences for Republicans and Democrats among activists and the general public and within Congress. When voters are asked to locate themselves on the ideological spectrum, the result roughly follows a normal bell-shaped curve. As shown in panel A, citizens are bunched together around the middle of the ideological spectrum, with relatively few respondents identifying themselves as very liberal or very conservative.[75] The same centrist pattern appears when voters are asked to position themselves on specific policy issues, even on hot-button topics such as taxes and abortion. By contrast, political activists are more likely to identify as either liberal or conservative. The surveys of delegates to the national presidential nominating conventions displayed in panel A of Figure 9-3 reveal Republican and Democratic activists clustering to the left or right of the median, with far less overlap between the two parties at the elite level than exists in the mass public.

In 1968 the ideological divisions in the House of Representatives (displayed in panel B in Figure 9-3) looked similar to those of the party elites. Democrats appeared in almost every ideological niche, from far left to far right. Although Republicans were more tightly clustered on the right, a number spilled over to the liberal side of the scale.[76] Political moderates—members at or near the midpoint between the parties—constituted a substantial bloc.

The contemporary Congress (represented by panel C) is almost completely polarized along party lines. Only a handful of members fall at the midpoint— not a single Republican falls on the liberal side of the scale, and only a few Democrats stray into the conservative category. (Panels B and C were compiled from the Poole-Rosenthal data by scholar Sean M. Theriault.)

FIGURE 9-3   **Ideological Divisions in Congress and the Public**

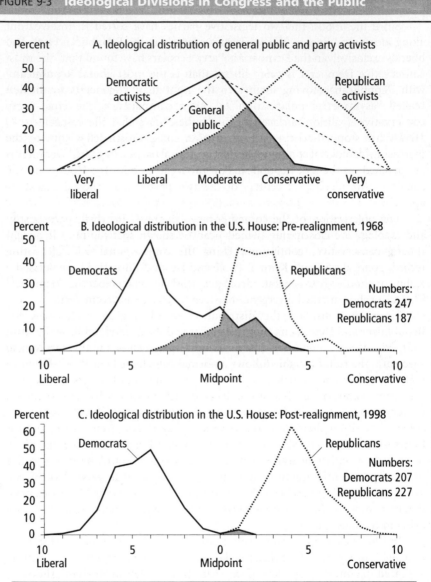

Percent   A. Ideological distribution of general public and party activists

Percent   B. Ideological distribution in the U.S. House: Pre-realignment, 1968

Numbers:
Democrats 247
Republicans 187

Percent   C. Ideological distribution in the U.S. House: Post-realignment, 1998

Numbers:
Democrats 207
Republicans 227

Sources: Panel A: *Washington Post*/ABC News survey, *Washington Post*, August 11, 1996, M8, and August 25, 1996, M4. Panels B and C: Adapted from Sean M. Theriault, "The Case of the Vanishing Moderates: Party Polarization in the Modern Congress" (paper presented at the Western Political Science Association, Denver, Colorado), March 2003, fig. 1. These data are derived from Keith T. Poole and Howard Rosenthal's DW-NOMINATE ideology scores. See Keith T. Poole and Howard Rosenthal, *Congress: A Political-Economic History of Roll-Call Voting* (New York: Oxford University Press, 1997). Scores for adjacent years (1969–1970 and 1999–2000) yield virtually identical results. See Morris P. Fiorina et al., *Culture War? The Myth of a Polarized America*, 2d ed. (New York: Pearson Longman, 2006), fig. 2.2.

In today's Congress, members' party affiliation and ideological views overlap almost perfectly. (These figures are for the House; patterns in the Senate are similar though somewhat less dramatic.) This polarization and the resulting collapse of the middle (the "shrinking center") have produced clear ideological battle lines between the parties. Although partisan rigidity gets a bad rap from commentators, one must consider how closely political convictions are linked to partisanship in the minds of lawmakers and their activist supporters. "If you can't find common ground, that doesn't mean you're partisan," explained Nancy Pelosi when she was Speaker (2007–2011). "It just means you believe different things." Of her Republican foes—often blamed for obstructing her party's proposals—she noted, "They vote the way they believe. . . . I think that they vote with more integrity than they get credit for."[77]

The proportion of political moderates—conservative Democrats or liberal Republicans—hovered at about 30 percent in the 1960s and 1970s. Today, however, fewer than one in ten lawmakers fall into this centrist category.[78] Conservative Democrats, the larger of the two centrist groupings, once represented a third of their party's members; today they could caucus in a small room. The fiscally conservative "Blue Dog" Democrats, as they called themselves, saw their ranks cut in half (from a little over fifty to twenty-six) in the November 2010 elections. Their membership was reduced to about a dozen or so in the 2012 elections. Even rarer are moderate Republicans, who account for no more than 2 percent of all House GOP members and no more than 3 to 6 percent of senators.[79]

Constituency and Voting

Constituency context is another powerful influence on members' vote choices. Constituencies control lawmakers' choices in two ways. First, people usually elect representatives whose views mirror their own. In this sense, representatives vote their constituency because they are transplanted locals. Second, members listen to constituents because it is politically imperative to do so. Representatives feel great electoral pressure to respond to the dominant political interests and opinions in their constituencies. For example, pleas for stronger gun control laws are unlikely to resonate with members from Idaho, where the culture embraces the right of men and women to purchase guns.

Constituency concerns can either reinforce or undermine party unity in Congress. For much of the twentieth century, it was not unusual for conservative-leaning states to elect Democrats and for liberal-leaning states to elect Republicans. During that period, constituency influence often led members to buck their party. But since the 1960s, constituencies have gradually sorted themselves out according to ideological and policy preferences. In the current era, constituency pressure tends to bolster party unity.

Relatively few Democrats in the 113th Congress represent conservative districts or states. In 1960 all senators from the South were Democrats, and they constituted a large conservative bloc who often resisted Democratic Party leaders and cooperated across party lines with Republicans. But in the 113th Congress (2013–2015), only six southern Democrats are in the Senate.[80] By the same token, many areas once represented by GOP liberals have been captured by Democrats. New England, an area of the country that was once a moderate Republican stronghold, now elects Democrats almost exclusively. The decline of conservative Democrats and moderate Republicans underlies much of the ideological cohesion within, and the chasm between, today's Capitol Hill parties.[81]

Partisans in the contemporary Congress vote together in great part because they reflect the same kinds of states and districts. Republicans tend to represent rural areas and outer suburbs. Democrats tend to represent urban areas, inner-ring suburbs, and majority-minority districts.[82] Two interrelated demographic trends are worth noting briefly. Today, the GOP is largely a white, male-dominated party. By contrast, minority groups and women tend to vote for Democrats. There is no certainty that this pattern will continue into the future, however.

Second, diversity characterizes House Democrats more than any of the other three party groups on Capitol Hill. When the 113th Congress convened, "white males [are] for the first time in American history . . . a minority" in the party's caucus.[83] The consequences of having a white-male-dominated, largely "southernized" House Republican Party and a minority and female-dominated House Democratic Party are not self-evident. However, it is reasonable to suggest that compromises on significant issues may be harder to obtain, disagreements over the role of government are likely to be more contentious, and conflicts over social issues could increase. In the judgment of a political scientist, "When you have parties so divergent in views, regions, and genders, the culture wars could escalate from conventional to nuclear weapons."[84]

The few remaining party mavericks in today's Congress tend to come from parts of the country where their party generally does not do well electorally. Democratic mavericks tend to be from nonminority southern or midwestern areas, such as Sen. Ben Nelson, D-Neb., who chose not to run for reelection to the 113th Congress. Similarly, the most independent Republicans are those representing northeastern and mid-Atlantic states. In 2011–2012, for example, Maine's two Republican senators, Susan Collins and Olympia Snowe, were not reluctant to side with Democrats rather than their own party on a number of votes. Snowe was so dismayed by the partisan polarization in Congress that she decided not to run for reelection in 2012.

Constituency affects congressional decision making as politicians take both attentive and inattentive publics into account. Political scientist R. Douglas Arnold has tracked how both groups can influence members' electoral calculations.[85] Attentive publics are those citizens who are aware of issues facing Congress and hold decided opinions about what Congress should do. It is thus relatively easy for politicians to consider their views. A politician's natural instinct is to yield to the strongly voiced preferences of an attentive public, unless the issue in question mobilizes two equally vociferous but opposing interests. Especially feared are single-interest groups that threaten to withhold electoral support if their preferences—for example, on abortion or gun control—are ignored.

Inattentive publics are those who lack extensive knowledge or firm preferences about a specific issue. Frankly, this definition describes most people most of the time. People pay attention to only a small fraction of the issues before Congress, yet a reelection-minded legislator dare not ignore those who seem indifferent to an issue. "Latent or unfocused opinions," Arnold cautions, "can quickly be transformed into intense and very real opinions with enormous political repercussions. Inattentiveness and lack of information today should not be confused with indifference tomorrow."[86] Legislators are well advised to approach even the most minor choices with this question in mind: Will my decision be defensible if it were to appear on the front pages of major newspapers in my state or district?

Calculating the electoral consequences of a lawmaker's multitude of daily decisions is no easy task. Arnold summarizes the components of such calculations:

> To reach a decision, then, a legislator needs to (1) identify all the attentive and inattentive publics who might care about a policy issue, (2) estimate the direction and intensity of their preferences and potential preferences, (3) estimate the probability that the potential preferences will be transformed into real preferences, (4) weigh all these preferences according to the size of the various attentive and inattentive publics, and (5) give special weight to the preferences of the legislator's consistent supporters.[87]

Fortunately, lawmakers need not repeat these calculations every time they face a choice. Most issues have been around for some time. The preferences of attentive and even inattentive publics are fairly well known. Moreover, Congress is well structured to amass information about individual and group preferences. And prominent officials—party leaders and acknowledged policy experts, for example—can often legitimize members' choices and give them cover in explaining those choices to voters.

The Presidency and Voting

Although Congress often pursues an independent course and members differ in their feelings toward the occupant of the White House, presidents can persuade members to support their agendas. Figure 9-4 depicts the percentage of the time presidents—from Dwight D. Eisenhower to Barack Obama—have prevailed in congressional roll call votes on which they announced a position. Presidents take positions on a wide range of issues, from the momentous (health care and financial reforms, in Obama's case) to large numbers of routine and noncontroversial matters (most Senate confirmations of executive nominations, for example).[88]

During President Obama's first two years in office, he enjoyed large success in winning congressional support on those issues where he took a clearly stated position. In fact, in 2009 he had a 96.7 percent success rate. A year later, his success rate dropped to 85.8 percent, "the tenth highest on record and the fourth highest for a president in his second year." Moreover, his 2010 score "does not capture the sheer size of the legislation enacted during his second year: the tax deal [extending President George W. Bush's 2001 and 2003 tax cuts to 2012], in addition to overhauls of [the] health care system and financial regulations, not to mention student loans, food safety, a strategic weapons treaty with Russia and a repeal of the ban on gays serving openly in the military."[89]

President Obama's legislative success rate declined significantly in the aftermath of the November 2010 elections. Republicans reclaimed control of the House and gained seats in the Senate. One result: Obama won on "just 54 percent of the votes where he made his preference known, the lowest success score of his presidency."[90] House Republicans opposed the president at almost every turn, while their partisan colleagues in the Senate blocked much of the president's legislation through dilatory tactics, such as the filibuster. The battles between the president and congressional Republicans meant that "Obama signed fewer new laws than any president this century, or in the half-century before that."[91]

Figure 9-4 reveals a common pattern: presidents in their fourth year witness a decline in their success rate with Congress. Only President George H. W. Bush had a lower success rate (43 percent) than Obama's (53.6 percent) at the same point in his presidency. Despite the president's relatively low legislative success rate, Obama won reelection to a second term, in part by campaigning against an unpopular and dysfunctional 112th Congress.

Party control of Congress dramatically affects presidential success rates. As long as their party controls Congress, presidents win at least three of every four votes on which they take a position; when the government is divided, presidents fall well below that level. Another important pattern evident in Figure 9-4 is that presidents tend to lose congressional support as their administrations age. Presidents' best years in dealing with Congress are usually their first.

LEGISLATIVE BARGAINING

Whatever their sources of influence, in the end individual legislators have only a single vote on any given bill or, more typically, on an amendment. At that moment, the vote is reduced to a "yea" or "nay" question, with no hedging or nuance allowed. Legislators have to decide how to cast these binary votes on a bewildering array of issues. They rarely have adequate—or even much—information on any particular bill or amendment. Legislators must weigh their goals—which often may conflict—and process their limited information in a relatively short period of time to arrive at a decision.[92]

Such a state of affairs—disparate goals and widely scattered influence—is hazardous. Stalemate is a constant threat. The "collective action problem" is the

FIGURE 9-4   **Presidential Success History, 1953–2012**

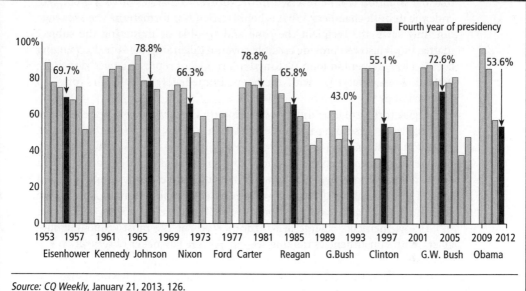

Source: *CQ Weekly*, January 21, 2013, 126.

Note: Presidential success is defined as the percentage of the time the president won his way on roll call votes on which he had taken a clear position.

way political scientists refer to the challenge of merging individual goals into group achievements. To overcome this predicament, members have to resort to politicking—that is, they must trade off goals and resources to get results. It is no wonder, then, that Congress is "an influence system in which bargain and exchange predominate."[93]

Implicit and Explicit Bargaining

Bargaining is a general term that refers to several related types of behavior. It describes in an overall sense, the process by which two or more parties arrive at a mutually beneficial exchange. Such processes may be implicit or explicit.

   Implicit Bargaining. Implicit bargaining occurs when legislators take actions designed to elicit certain reactions from others, even though no negotiation has taken place. For example, legislators often introduce bills or sponsor hearings not because they expect the measure to pass but to prod someone else—an executive branch official, or a committee chair with broader jurisdiction on the question—to take action. Or a bill's managers may accept a controversial amendment knowing full well that the objectionable provision will be dropped in the other chamber or in conference. These are examples of the so-called law of anticipated reactions.[94]

Another type of implicit bargaining occurs when legislators seek out or accept the judgments of colleagues with expertise on a given matter, expecting that the situation will be reversed in the future. Exchanges of voting cues are endemic in both chambers. What is being traded is information. The exchange not only saves the recipient the time and trouble of mastering the subject matter, but it also can provide credible cover in defending the vote. Exchanging cues is a key element in John W. Kingdon's model of representatives' decisions, derived from interviews with members immediately after their votes on specific issues.[95]

Legislators have little difficulty making up their minds when they receive no conflicting cues from party leaders, respected fellow members, constituents, or key interest groups. If all the cue-givers in their field of vision concur, members operate in a consensus mode of decision making. If the actors are in conflict, the lawmaker will have to weigh the alternatives. For example, a liberal senator who finds himself alone in voting on the same side as most conservative senators may reevaluate his position.

Fellow members emerge in Kingdon's study as the most influential cue-givers, with constituencies ranking second. As one lawmaker observed:

> I think that the other members are very influential, and we recognize it. And why are they influential? I think because they have exercised good judgment, have expertise in the area, and know what they are talking about.[96]

When members deviate from a consensus stance among their cue-givers, it is usually to follow their own conscience or their constituencies. Adding up these short-term forces, Kingdon's model successfully predicted about 90 percent of the decisions.

Explicit Bargaining. Explicit bargains also take several forms. In making compromises, legislators may agree to split their differences. Compromises are straightforward on issues dealing with quantitative elements that can easily be adjusted upward or downward—for example, funding levels or eligibility criteria. Compromise on substance is also possible. For example, members who favor a major new program and members who oppose any program at all may agree to a two-year pilot project to test the idea.

"You cannot legislate without the ability to compromise," declared former senator Alan Simpson, R-Wyo., who often found fault with militant junior members of his own party. He recounted the following tale:

> On a recent bill, I went to [conservative House members] and said: "Here's what I'm doing. I've got six senators who will vote this far, and then the next time if you go any further, they will not be there." So [my GOP colleague] and I delivered on this singular bill, and they said, "We want you to get more." And we said, "There is no more to get." Next vote on this bill, we lost six votes. Then they came in and said, "We are going to probably kill the whole thing. . . ." [A]nd they got nothing.[97]

The lesson is that compromise is inevitable in crafting laws; those who are unwilling to give ground are bound to be disappointed. On occasion, both parties avoid compromise and engage in brinksmanship, with each expecting the other to "blink" first before the interparty deadlock produces bad political and policy repercussions. Winning concessions from the opposing side is a key aim of this form of strategic bargaining.[98]

The classic compromise—a "win win" for the contending sides—has been hard to achieve in recent Congresses because a significant number of lawmakers have preferred a "no compromise" strategy. There was simply an unwillingness on their part to engage in the traditional "give and take" negotiating process: members give up legislative provisions or positions but take others they find acceptable enough to move legislation forward. A view expressed by a House Republican reflected one shared by many others on Capitol Hill: "When it comes to compromise, half of a bad deal is still a bad deal."[99] Effective governance is challenged when issues provoke high-stakes brinksmanship and compromise implies political weakness, a sellout, or a betrayal of principle.

Logrolling

Logrolling is bargaining in which members exchange support so that all parties to the deal can attain their individual goals. The term originated in the nineteenth century when neighbors helped each other roll logs into a pile for burning. Its most visible form is a something-for-everyone enactment, sometimes called a "Christmas tree" bill. Such bills are prevalent in legislative areas such as public works, omnibus taxation, or tariffs and trade. Describing a classic logroll, former representative Edward J. Derwinski, R-Ill. (1959–1983), explained how the country's two million farmers put together a majority coalition every five years to pass the omnibus farm bill's basket of price supports, acreage allowances, and marketing agreements:

> What [the farmers] do is very interesting. The agriculture people from North Carolina, where agriculture means tobacco, discuss their problems with the man representing the rice growers in Arkansas or California. The sugar beet growers in Minnesota and sugar cane interests in Louisiana and Hawaii and the wheat and corn and soybean and other producers just gather together in one great big happy family to be sure there is a subsidy for every commodity. They put those numbers together again so that they have at least 218 supporters in the House and 51 in the Senate. A supporter of the tobacco subsidy automatically becomes a supporter of the wheat subsidy, or the sugar quota, or the soybean subsidy, or whatever else follows.[100]

Logrolling draws lawmakers into the finished legislative product by embracing their special interests, proposals, or amendments. Henry M.

"Scoop" Jackson, D-Wash. (House, 1941–1953; Senate, 1953–1983), when asked how he had assembled a majority for a new proposal, responded this way: "Maggie [Sen. Warren Magnuson of Washington] talked to Russell, and Tom promised this if I would back him on Ed's amendment, and Mike owes me one for last year's help on Pete's bill."[101] Such reciprocity especially pervades the Senate, dominated as it is by individuals. Sponsors of a Senate bill often must placate most or all interested legislators to gain clearance to bring a bill to the floor.

Lawmakers who enter into, and stand to profit from, a logroll are expected to support the final package, regardless of what that package looks like. A broad-based logroll is thus hard to stop. "It's not a system of punishment. It's a system of rewards," explained a House member.[102]

In an austere fiscal environment, logrolling is often aimed at equalizing sacrifices instead of distributing rewards. Broad-spectrum bills—authorizations, omnibus tax measures, continuing resolutions, and budget resolutions—may include numerous less than optimal provisions, many of which would fail if voted on separately. Such a negative logroll enables lawmakers to support the measure as "the best deal we can get."

Logrolling can turn narrowly targeted programs into broad-scale ones, as many lawmakers want a piece of the policy pie. This development can dilute a program's impact by spreading funds throughout the nation rather than in targeted areas. Similarly, if resources are spread too thinly among too many sites, the program may not make a noticeable difference in any single area.

In a time logroll, members agree to support one measure in exchange for later support for another measure. A time logroll was crucial to the initial House passage in 2003 of a major new prescription drug benefit for seniors. Rep. Jo Ann Emerson, R-Mo., had been fighting for years to allow U.S. consumers to purchase generic drugs from Canada and other countries where prices were lower, but she could not convince her Republican leadership to permit a vote. "I felt like a darned broken record," Emerson said.[103] When Emerson realized that Republican leaders would need her vote to pass the new prescription drug benefit, she took advantage of the opportunity. She demanded that they promise to bring her reimportation bill up for a vote, and eventually she was able to get a good-faith pledge from the leadership to greenlight her bill. "I'm extremely pleased with the outcome," she said.[104] Republican leaders fulfilled their promise to Emerson the following month by permitting the House to take a vote on the matter.[105]

Sometimes, logrolls can be constructed on the basis of side payments to members. A lawmaker's support is exchanged for benefits on an unrelated issue—for example, a federal project for the state or district, a better committee assignment, inclusion in an important conference, help with fund-raising, or access to the White House. Although such side payoffs may seem trivial or parochial, they can enable members to achieve valued goals.

Bargaining Strategy

For bargaining to take place, participants in the House and Senate must be able to rely on one another's future actions. Rep. John P. Murtha, D-Pa. (1974–2010), a master dealmaker, cited two elements of power on Capitol Hill: "Develop expertise on an issue that makes you vital to colleagues, and keep your word."[106] Relying on his expertise and contacts within the defense community, he often cut deals quietly in the back corner of the Democratic side of the House. On the Senate side of the Capitol, the same kind of deal-making occurs. Majority Leader Reid, for example, was not reluctant to provide Sens. Ben Nelson, D-Neb., and Mary Landrieu, D-La., with what each wanted in order to win their votes for the president's controversial health overhaul plan. The press soon called the special health benefits each received for their states, respectively, the "Cornhusker Kickback" and the "Louisiana Purchase."[107]

For bargaining to succeed, the participants must agree on the need for a legislative product—that is, the benefits of reaching a decision must exceed the costs of failing to do so. In many cases, politicians may prefer a course of strategic disagreement, the "efforts of politicians to avoid reaching an agreement when compromise might alienate supporters, damage their prospects in an upcoming election, or preclude getting a better deal in the future."[108]

According to bargaining theory, a measure's sponsors will yield only what they absolutely must to gain a majority of supporters. "Parties wish to use their votes efficiently, winning victories at the cheapest possible price."[109] By this logic, if bargainers act rationally and have perfect information about one another, minimum winning coalitions should predominate.[110] Recounting Senate majority leader Lyndon B. Johnson's meticulous vote counting before a floor fight, a top Senate aide concluded: "And once a sufficient majority had been counted, Johnson would seldom attempt to enlarge it: Why expend limited bargaining resources which might be needed to win future battles?"[111]

Most legislative strategists, however, lack Johnson's extraordinary skills. Uncertainty about outcomes leads them to line up more than a simple majority of supporters. Moreover, at many points in the legislative process supermajorities are required—for example, in voting under suspension of the rules, in overriding vetoes, or in ending Senate filibusters. Not surprisingly, therefore, minimum winning coalitions are not typical of Congress, even in the majoritarian House of Representatives.[112]

Yet coalition size is the crux of legislative strategy. Bargainers repeatedly face the dilemma of how broadly or how narrowly to frame their issues and how many concessions to yield in an effort to secure passage.

CONCLUSION

Congressional deliberation is at risk today. With both parties unified and seemingly uninterested in debate or compromise, life on Capitol Hill has become, in Hobbes's words, "nasty" and "brutish" (though hardly "short"). Take-no-prisoners strategies are encouraged by today's highly competitive, polarized party system. As a senator observed,

> The pressure on congressional leaders both from interests in the party and from outside groups is severe. Many would rather fight and lose, rather than reach out and find common ground. Congress should not be like the Super Bowl, in which one team always has to win and the other team inevitably loses. There's nothing wrong with reaching legitimate compromise and getting something done for the American people.[113]

Political scientist Sarah Binder's findings echo this sentiment. "The decline of the political center," she writes, "has produced a political environment that more often than not gives legislators every incentive not to reach agreement."[114] The result is often legislative inaction, which may be criticized as stalemate or gridlock.

Yet the enterprise of lawmaking rests on the premise that at least where urgent matters are concerned, bargainers will normally prefer some sort of agreement to none at all. As Everett M. Dirksen, R-Ill., the legendary Senate Republican leader (1959–1969), once remarked, "I am a man of fixed and unbending principle, and one of my principles is flexibility."[115] Flexibility is especially crucial with "must-pass" legislation which, if not approved, can imperil government functions. When dealing with some reauthorizations and appropriations, the alternative to lapses in the timely enactment of appropriations bills—called "funding gaps"—can be the total or partial shutdown of federal activities and programs and the furlough of governmental employees.[116] Indeed, budget impasses have resulted in seventeen funding gaps since 1977. The two most controversial funding gaps occurred when the GOP-controlled 104th Congress (1995–1997) and President Bill Clinton clashed over spending policy. Two partial government shutdowns occurred (November 15–16, 1995, and December 16–January 6, 1996) that led to the furlough of about 800,000 federal employees (Thousands of federal furloughs also occurred in 2013 due to the fiscal sequester: across-the-board spending cuts in domestic and defense programs.)

Bargaining is a necessary part of legislative life. It shapes the character of bills, resolutions, and other forms of congressional policy making. It also underlies many attributes of the legislative process—delay, obfuscation, compromise, and norms such as specialization and reciprocity.

Deliberation is the hallmark of legislative decision making. Coalitions are constructed as diverse views are voiced and a variety of members, executive officials, and interest groups participate. It is yet another point of contact and conflict between within Congress—the Congress of individual wills and the Congress of collective decisions.

Multiple Presidential Roles. President Barack Obama meets with bipartisan Senate leaders to discuss his Supreme Court nomination of Sonia Sotomayor (top). From left to right, Sen. Jeff Sessions, R-Ala., ranking minority member of the Judiciary Committee; Minority Leader Mitch McConnell, R-Ky; Vice President Joseph R. Biden Jr.; President Obama; Senate Majority Leader Harry Reid, D-Nev.; and Judiciary Committee chair Patrick Leahy, D-Vt. (Center): The president signs the Affordable Care Act in the East Room in March 2010, surrounded by Democratic champions of the measure. He is flanked by 11-year-old Marcelas Owens of Seattle, whose mother died without health insurance, and long-serving Rep. John Dingle, D-Mich. The president is mobbed by lawmakers seeking a handshake before delivering the annual State of the Union (SOTU) address (bottom).

Congress and the President

"We want you to lead, Mr. President!" declared Speaker John Boehner, R-Ohio, in a carefully delivered speech read from a teleprompter (a rarity for the Speaker) a few days after Barack Obama's reelection victory in 2012. The Speaker's remarks were particularly targeted at finding a bipartisan, interbranch solution to avoid going over the so-called "fiscal cliff." The fiscal cliff was a combination of congressionally imposed fiscal deadlines: "a year-end fiscal apocalypse of expiring Bush-era tax cuts and across-the-board spending reductions [dubbed sequestration, see Chapter 14 for details] meant to be so perilous that Congress would be forced to find a more rational solution."[1] Many economists stressed that without a deal between Congress and the White House to prevent large tax increases and spending reductions divided equally between defense and domestic programs, the country would be pushed into another recession.

When the bipartisan and bicameral party leaders met with the president shortly after the November 2012 elections, all expressed optimism that a framework agreement could be developed during the postelection "lame-duck" session. The agreement would "replace the year-end fiscal cliff [to be automatically triggered after January 1, 2013] with a less abrupt and economically damaging debt-reduction plan."[2] Optimism for such an agreement soon faded given resistance by both President Obama and Speaker Boehner, the lead fiscal negotiators, to accept the tax and spending proposals of the other.

During his successful bid for a second term, Obama campaigned on the idea that the wealthiest 2 percent of Americans would pay higher taxes if he won reelection. He urged Speaker Boehner to accept higher income tax rates for those earning more than $250,000 per year. Boehner counteroffered with $800 billion in revenue through tax reform, rather than higher income tax rates.[3] With negotiations at a standstill, Speaker Boehner in mid-December 2012 developed his own fiscal cliff plan, dubbed "Plan B" by the media. Boehner's plan involved House action on two bills. The first, which narrowly passed the House on a strict party-line vote (215 to 209), delayed sequestration for a year. The second measure (the heart of Plan B) would extend the 2001 Bush-era tax cuts for everyone with income under $1 million. Despite predictions by top House GOP leaders that they had the votes to pass the bill, antitax

Republicans refused to support any tax hike for anyone. Boehner's plan never reached the floor for lack of votes—a significant setback.

Uncertainty reigned on Capitol Hill, as lawmakers left town for the Christmas holiday and President Obama departed Washington for his family's annual Hawaii vacation. When the Senate reconvened on December 27, negotiations resumed in earnest among the president (who returned from his abbreviated vacation) and the top House and Senate party leaders and their aides. The House reconvened three days later, a Sunday, to consider whatever legislation the Senate could pass that day or the next to avert the fiscal cliff. (Technically, the 112th Congress could work to midnight, January 2, 2012, when it would officially end and the new 113th Congress would begin.) With the failure of Plan B, the Speaker wanted the Democratic-controlled Senate to take the lead in crafting a bill; this would make it more likely that a compromise bill arriving in the House would have enough Democratic support to ensure passage—even if Republicans remained divided. Speaker Boehner realized that if he lost the support of about half of his party, his influence as party leader would be weakened, his hold on the speakership might be jeopardized, and he would have to accommodate Democratic demands to win their support. Having the Senate go first also gave the House the option to amend the Senate's bill. The amended measure could then be returned to the Senate for further review.

In the end, although Congress technically went over the cliff by a few hours, Senate GOP leader Mitch McConnell and Vice President Joe Biden devised a compromise that the Senate adopted (89 to 8) on New Year's Day at 2 a.m. After some contretemps in the House, that chamber enacted the legislation (257 to 167) around 11 p.m. of the same day. Most Republicans voted against the McConnell-Biden compromise, but it passed with considerable Democratic support. The compromise prevented tax increases for most Americans, but raised income tax rates for high earners (individuals earning more than $400,000 and families earning over $450,000). The McConnell-Biden plan, among other things, also postponed sequestration for two months (until March 1, 2013).

Compared to the interchamber and interbranch battles that characterized the 112th Congress, there was considerable legislative-executive cooperation during President Obama's first two years in office, when Democrats controlled both legislative chambers. Although the president inherited huge problems (two wars, a financial meltdown, and high unemployment, among others) from the previous administration, Obama in his first two years won passage of truly consequential legislation. Some analysts called the achievements transformative, comparable to President Lyndon B. Johnson's "Great Society" accomplishments such as Medicare in 1965. With a Democratic-controlled 111th Congress, the president won enactment of a massive overhaul of the health care system, something many of his predecessors from Theodore Roosevelt on had wanted but had failed to do. He revamped the financial regulatory system; championed a $787 billion stimulus package to revive the economy and prevent another

Great Depression; and, during one of the most productive "lame-duck" sessions in decades, succeeded in winning Senate approval of a major nuclear arms treaty with Russia and terminated the "don't ask, don't tell" law that prevented gay and lesbian people from serving openly in the military.

However, the president failed to win GOP votes for his major legislative accomplishments, despite his 2008 pledge to be a postpartisan president and to change the way Washington works. Almost from the start of the 111th Congress, congressional Republicans organized to try to frustrate the ambitious agenda of the president and congressional Democrats. Senate GOP leader McConnell gathered his party colleagues together and told them, "Republicans need to stick together as a team." Or, as GOP senator George Voinovich of Ohio said of McConnell's strategy, "If Obama was for it, we had to be against it."[4] A statement on the president's health overhaul plan by GOP senator Jim DeMint, S.C. (now the head of the conservative Heritage Foundation), reflected the Republican strategy: "If we're able to stop Obama on [health care reform], this will be his Waterloo. It will break him."[5]

The president sought to negotiate with Republicans on policy but had little success in forging personal relationships with GOP lawmakers. President Obama, by many accounts, is not someone who enjoys socializing or schmoozing with lawmakers. During his first term, for instance, in his "104 rounds of golf as president, Obama has played with only two members of Congress" (Speaker Boehner and Rep. James Clyburn, D-S.C.).[6] In the judgment of a sophisticated Washington insider, President Obama largely ignored the Republicans during his first two years in office.[7] As Senate Minority Leader McConnell noted about much of the president's first two years, "They had the numbers, they had the agenda, and they didn't need us."[8]

Major legislative successes were much harder to come by in the 112th Congress (2011–2013). Republicans controlled the House—many Tea Party–supported—and there were more Republicans in the Democratic Senate. Much of the work of the 111th Congress became the agenda of the 112th Congress, except in reverse—cut entitlement spending, eliminate government programs, overturn unwanted federal regulations, and so on. For example, House and Senate Republicans acted quickly but unsuccessfully to fulfill their 2010 campaign pledge to "repeal and replace" the Obama-championed Patient Protection and Affordable Care Act (which they derisively called Obamacare). In doing so, they proposed legislation to eviscerate the law, holding numerous hearings and offering floor amendments, and enlisted outside groups and media outlets to continue their drumbeat of criticism against the act. (The president later adopted the term Obamacare and used it periodically in his speeches, especially after the U.S. Supreme Court upheld most provisions of the health law as constitutional.)

The GOP-controlled House also launched scores of hearings to review critically the administration's issuance of rules and regulations viewed as economically harmful to business. The House even passed a resolution directing its standing committees to highlight regulatory overreach by federal agencies. Spencer Bachus, R-Ala., chair of the House Financial Services Committee, exclaimed that the "more than 300 new rules and regulations being written per the new [Dodd-Frank Wall Street Reform and Consumer Protection Act, P.L. 111–203] are proving detrimental to businesses and the economy."[9] Over in the Senate, GOP leader McConnell candidly proclaimed that for the 112th Congress, "the single most important thing we want to achieve is for President Obama to be a one-term president."[10]

Instead, despite the struggling national economy, President Obama won a second term handily, with Republicans losing eight seats in the House (but still in control) and Democrats unexpectedly picking up two Senate seats. Republicans were devastated by their losses. Many had been convinced that they would win the White House, retain the House, and take control of the Senate. Tellingly, President Obama approached Congress differently than he did in his first term. He was more willing to challenge congressional Republicans and less willing to accommodate their demands. For example, the president stated that he would neither negotiate with Speaker Boehner as he did in 2011 over raising the statutory borrowing limit nor follow the informal Boehner rule (every dollar of debt increase must be matched by a dollar of spending cuts). The Speaker's rule fell by the wayside in January 2013, when Congress passed a three-month debt-ceiling increase. The president's response to the Speaker was that proposals to cut spending must be accompanied by more revenue. Obama's tougher line with Congress, administration officials said, reflected a new reality: the president "will never have to seek reelection again."[11]

Tensions between the executive and legislative branches are inevitable. The two policy-making branches have divergent responsibilities and different constituencies and terms of office, and typically they are jealous of each other's prerogatives. Executive officials see the decentralized Congress as inefficient and meddlesome. Legislators perceive the hierarchical and highly centralized executive branch as arrogant and arbitrary. At times, these differences lead to conflicts that the news media dramatize as the "battles on the Potomac." Several times during the 112th Congress, the elective branches engaged in the "politics of brinksmanship" before legislation was enacted to resolve bitter interbranch clashes. A dramatic instance occurred during summer 2011 over legislation to raise the debt ceiling (see Chapter 14). This legislative-executive struggle even led to a book about the controversy (*The Price of Power*, 2012) by noted journalist and author Bob Woodward.

Yet day in and day out Congress and the president work together. Even when their relationship is guarded or hostile, bills are passed and signed into law. Presidential appointments win Senate approval. Appropriation measures are eventually enacted and the government is kept afloat. This cooperation continues even when control of the White House and the Congress is divided between the two major parties.

Divided government often complicates relationships between Congress and the executive branch, as was evident in the highly polarized 112th Congress

(2011–2013). Gridlock was often the order of the day on major legislation. The GOP House passed many measures on largely party-line votes that simply died in the Democratic Senate, with the reverse the case as well. This Congress enacted "fewer bills into law than any Congress in decades." In response, GOP representative Jason Chaffetz of Utah exclaimed, "Numbers of bills passed should not be a litmus test for a Congress."[12] But unified partisan control of both branches is no guarantee of harmony, as Presidents Jimmy Carter and Bill Clinton (in his first two years in office) learned. Political scientist Ross K. Baker has summarized President Clinton's rocky start with Congress. For example, the collapse of the administration's national health insurance initiative, captained by Hillary Rodham Clinton, contributed to the Republican capture of both houses of Congress in the 1994 elections.[13]

President Obama also experienced pushback from various congressional Democrats to his major initiatives. During the 111th Congress, some Democrats complained that the president was overloading the legislative circuits by proposing so many major initiatives all at once—a massive stimulus package and major proposals to reform health care, energy, and education. "There's only so much that we can absorb and do at one time," explained Sen. Daniel Inouye, D-Hawaii, chair of the Senate Appropriations Committee.[14] The president responded that Congress is capable of dealing with more than one major problem at a time. Still, a handful of moderate Senate Democrats pushed to pare down Obama's health care initiative; only after months of bargaining was the bill enacted.

THE PRESIDENT AS LEGISLATOR

The president is sometimes called the chief legislator because of his close involvement in congressional decision making. Article II, section 3, of the Constitution directs the president from time to time to "give to the Congress Information of the State of the Union and recommend to their Consideration such Measures as he shall judge necessary and expedient." (Today, this means annually and during television's prime time.) Soon after delivering the annual State of the Union address, the president sends to Congress draft administration bills for introduction on his behalf. By enlarging the list of messages required from the president—the annual budget and economic reports, for example— Congress has further involved the chief executive in designing legislation. Indeed, Congress often delegates authority to the president because it appreciates the strengths of the White House—such as its capacity for coordination—and recognizes its own shortcomings, such as its decentralized committee structure, which inhibit swift and comprehensive policy making. Crises, partisan considerations, and public expectations all make the president an important participant in congressional decision making. And the president's constitutional veto power ensures that White House views will be listened to, if not always heeded, on Capitol Hill.

The legislative presidency emerged after World War II. By then, it was conceded that this new presidential role was institutionalized, performed not because of some unique combination of personality and circumstance but because everyone expected it—including Congress, the press, and the public.[15] This deeply entrenched expectation will not change anytime soon.

Understanding the chief executive's relations with Congress is no easy task. The founders did not clearly define the legislative-executive relationship, and so it has always been a work in progress. Presidents bring their own style to the relationship, which political scientist Charles O. Jones characterizes as either the "partnership model" or the "independent model." The partnership model means that presidents consult regularly with lawmakers and involve them directly in the policy and political affairs of the White House. The independent model holds that presidents should minimize their involvement with Congress and strive on their own to accomplish their top priorities.[16]

Scholars and others have long analyzed America's complex system of separate institutions sharing, and competing for, power. Different theories, such as Jones's, have been formulated to define effective presidential leadership. Some studies focus on the person in the White House; others examine the bureaucracy and the institutional functions and structures of the presidency; and still others analyze discrete aspects of the relationship between Congress and the president, such as presidential spending power versus the legislative branch's power of the purse.[17] Here we discuss four prominent presidential theories—persuasion, rhetoric, administrative, and the "two presidencies"—as a way to illuminate important aspects of the chief executive's relations with Congress. To varying degrees, these analytical perspectives overlap and capture the activities of all presidents.

The Power to Persuade

"Presidential power is the power to persuade," wrote Richard E. Neustadt, a former staff aide in the Truman White House and adviser to President-elect John F. Kennedy.[18] Power, Neustadt asserted, meant more than the executive's ability to persuade Congress to enact a bill. "Strategically, the question is not how he masters Congress in a peculiar instance, but what he does to boost his chances for mastery in any instance."[19] Presidents striving to be successful are urged to employ all their powers—constitutional, political, bureaucratic, personal, and more—to persuade Congress and others to follow their lead. Setting Congress's agenda—that is, determining the policies that the legislature heeds by taking them up in committee and on the floor—epitomizes the president's power to persuade.

Presidents have shaped Congress's agenda since the earliest days of the Republic. The First Congress of "its own volition immediately turned to the executive branch for guidance and discovered in [Treasury Secretary Alexander] Hamilton a personality to whom such leadership was congenial."[20] Two decades later (by 1825), the "initiative in public affairs remained with [Speaker Henry] Clay and his associates in the House of Representatives" and not with the president.[21] Thus dominance in national policy making may pass from one branch to the other. Strong presidents sometimes provoked efforts by Congress to reassert its own authority and to restrict that of the executive. Periods of presidential ascendancy are often followed by eras of congressional assertiveness. Still, Congress has usually expected the White House to outline its legislative program in the annual State of the Union message and in other formal and informal presidential messages.

Presidents follow different patterns in setting agendas. They also study the decisions of their predecessors to learn from their mistakes and successes. For example, President Ronald Reagan (1981–1989) and his staff studied the clumsiness of his predecessor, Jimmy Carter (1977–1981), in dealing with his two Congresses (with large Democratic majorities). Reagan found that Carter quickly overloaded Congress's agenda and never made clear what his priorities were. There were three major consequences:

> First . . . there was little clarity in the communication of priorities to the American public. Instead of galvanizing support for two or three major national needs, the Carter administration proceeded on a number of fronts. . . . Second, and perhaps more important, the lack of priorities meant unnecessary waste of the President's own time and energy. . . . Third, the lack of priorities needlessly compounded Carter's congressional problems. . . . Carter's limited political capital was squandered on a variety of agenda requests when it might have been concentrated on the top of the list.[22]

By contrast, agenda control was the hallmark of Reagan's leadership during his first year in office. By limiting his legislative priorities, Reagan focused Congress's and the public's attention on one priority issue at a time. Most were encapsulated as "Reaganomics"—tax and spending cuts. He exploited the usual honeymoon period for new presidents by moving his agenda quickly, during a moment of widespread anticipation of a new era of GOP national political dominance.

Reagan also dealt skillfully with Congress, meeting, negotiating, and socializing with lawmakers, including a private dinner with Democratic Speaker Thomas P. "Tip" O'Neill Jr. of Massachusetts and his wife. Enjoying a Republican majority in the Senate, the Reagan White House focused primarily on lobbying the Democratic House to pass the president's economic program—the "greatest selling job I've ever seen," said Speaker O'Neill. Reagan personally called or telegraphed all of the "Boll Weevils," the forty-seven southern Democrats in the Conservative Democratic Forum.[23] And he persuaded several governors to meet with members from their states who were opposing the program. Top executive officials were dispatched to targeted Democratic districts to drum up public support. On the key House vote, all 191 GOP members and 63 Democrats backed the president's budget plan.

Overall, after only eight months in office Reagan scored some of the biggest victories of his eight years in office. Later, when his control over the agenda slackened, Congress was still confined to a playing field he had largely set out. Lawmakers were forced to respond to, though not always accept, the positions the president had staked out on taxes, spending, defense, and social issues.

President Obama—the first sitting senator since John Kennedy (1960) to move directly to the White House—promised the voters "change" if elected. During his first two years in office, the president enjoyed major successes in advancing a consequential agenda. Facing the worst economic recession since the 1930s and having a Congress heavily controlled by Democrats, Obama won enactment of landmark comprehensive laws. Many Americans failed to give the president much credit for his initiatives because, according to the Pew Research Center, his "achievements were seen through the prism of, 'He hasn't fixed the economy.'" President Obama concurred in that assessment: "It's perfectly sensible that they are holding out an overall assessment [of my presidency] until they see changes in their lives."[24]

Several other factors also account for the first-term disconnect between major policy success and public discontent, even giving rise to the conservative Tea Party movement. Four merit some mention.

First, some analysts hold that Obama misinterpreted the meaning of his historic 2008 victory. His resounding 53-percent victory margin reflected many things—public disapproval of George W. Bush and the Iraq war, the woeful state of the economy, and so on—but it is doubtful that the electorate endorsed a "new New Deal" that would dramatically expand the role, reach, and cost of government. At least a plurality of the public viewed the health law (the Affordable Care Act) as an unwanted and intrusive "government takeover" of health care, which provoked numerous efforts in Congress to repeal or weaken the law. One result was a public backlash against Democrats in the 2010 midterm elections. Democrats suffered a "shellacking," according to President Obama. As Rep. Barney Frank, D-Mass., stated: "I think we paid a terrible price for health care."[25]

Obama campaigned on "change you can believe in," but to many people it was change they did not want or support, especially when confidence in government was low and federal expenditures were a Niagara Falls of red ink. A Gallup pollster remarked that it was paradoxical that in 2008, when trust in government was at an historic low of about 25 percent, Obama was offering "government as the primary solution to most of the nation's woes."[26] What people wanted most from the government and the private sector were three things: jobs, jobs, jobs. As a Democratic House member recounted, "Everybody [in Washington] talked about health care, and I went home [to Kansas City, Missouri] and everyone there talked about jobs."[27]

Second, the president's governing agenda was summed up by many as too much spending—four years of annual deficits (over $1 trillion), too much debt (over $16 trillion in 2012 and rising), too much government (scores of new federal programs, entities, and regulations), and too little success in creating economic growth. "Where's my bailout?" was the refrain heard on Main Street. By contrast, on Wall Street many business executives awarded themselves large bonuses from the bailout funds provided by taxpayers. The president could claim that his policies prevented another 1930s depression, but it is hard to gain much public credit for preventing something that did not happen.

Third, public expectations for the president were simply too high, as they often are for presidents. He and his supporters wanted many things to happen fairly quickly (recall White House chief of staff Rahm Emanuel's comment that great crises should not be wasted because they beget great opportunities): revival of the economy, enactment of climate change legislation, closure of the Guantánamo Bay detention camp, labor law reform, an overhaul of the health care system (including a public option), immigration reform, and more. The founders, however, had devised a complex three-way bargaining process among the House, Senate, and White House that is inherently slow-moving. As Speaker Dennis Hastert, R-Ill. (1999–2007), once said: "The art of what is possible is what you can get passed in the House, what you can get passed in the Senate and signed by the president. We're playing a three-sided game here."[28] Added to that reality were the difficulties of moving legislation through the Senate, where sixty votes had become the new normal to advance legislation.

Senate Republicans employed a confrontational "party of no" strategy in both the 111th and 112th Congresses, blocking numerous measures and nominations. As Senate GOP leader McConnell said of Obama's 111th Congress (2009–2011) program, "I wish I could have blocked more"; it was anathema to many Republicans. Absent GOP votes on many administration priorities, the public watched a messy sausage-making process as Democratic leaders attracted ("bought" from the public's perspective) votes by including in the legislation special-interest provisions sought by their party colleagues. It was of little surprise, then, that Obama's goal of being a postpartisan president who could change the way Washington works was never reached.

Fourth, as scholar William Galston put it, there was a clash between the president's "agenda of choice" for the 111th Congress—his campaign promises—and his "agenda of necessity"—the economic crisis.[29] His agenda of choice prevented a laser-like focus on what seemed to interest the public most: restoration of a healthy economy that would put many unemployed people back to work. Health care, climate change, education reform, and other important issues absorbed the president's time and energy, reinforcing the view among many people that Obama was a "big government" liberal who was taking the country in a direction they did not want to go.

In short, President Obama's record of accomplishment during his first two years in office is something that most chief executives would not be able to achieve over their full four-year terms. Much of the president's time during the 112th Congress was spent defending and protecting from GOP assaults the policy successes of his first two years.[30] Similarly, the 113th Congress faced holdover issues from the previous Congress that required relatively early action in 2013. Three are especially noteworthy. First, the president and congressional leaders spent considerable time trying unsuccessfully to reach an agreement to avert the March 1 sequestration: automatic and indiscriminate across-the-board spending cuts equally divided between defense and nondefense programs. (Most mandatory programs, such as Social Security, were exempt from spending cuts.) Sequester's effects occurred in fairly short order, such as unpaid furloughs for federal employees, delays at airports, services cut at national parks, and the cancellation of maintenance on military ships and planes. Second, Congress enacted a new continuing resolution (CR) before a March 27 deadline—the expiration date of the CR passed in the previous Congress that prevented a government shutdown. The new CR funded the government until the end of the fiscal year (September 30, 2013). Third, another hike in the debt ceiling was projected to be required around mid-May. However, the combination of more revenue flowing into the federal treasury and less spending meant more time—perhaps until autumn 2013—for "President Obama and Congress to come up with an agreement to raise the $16.4 trillion debt ceiling" and avoid breaching the statutory borrowing limit.[31] In brief, a major challenge for President Obama in his second term has been whether he can persuade some "Republicans that their self-interest lies in helping him govern, after years of obstruction."[32]

For the most part, presidents recognize the importance of maintaining informal contacts with Congress because they understand it is not easy to persuade Congress to act in a certain way. As Lyndon Johnson—who had served as Senate minority leader (1953–1955) and majority leader (1955–1960)—once declared, "Merely placing a program before Congress is not enough. Without constant attention from the administration, most legislation moves through the congressional process at the speed of a glacier."[33] Johnson regularly (and sometimes crudely) admonished his aides and departmental officers to work closely with Congress. "[Get off] your ass and see how fast you can respond to a congressional request," he told his staff. "Challenge yourself to see how quickly you can get back to him or her with an answer, any kind of an answer, but goddamn it, an answer."[34]

To persuade members to support their programs, presidents often grant or withhold their patronage resources. Broadly conceived, patronage involves not only federal and judicial positions but also federal construction projects, location of government installations, campaign support, access to strategic information, plane rides on *Air Force One*, White House entree for important constituents, and countless other favors, large and small. Some presidents even keep records of the political favors they grant to lawmakers, IOUs that they can cash in later for needed support in Congress. There are limits, however, to the persuasive power of patronage. As one White House congressional relations chief said, "The problem with congressional relations is that with every good intention, at the end of the day you can't accommodate all the requests that you get."[35] More important, many factors influence how members vote on issues important to the White House. Although a president's persuasive skills can sometimes tip the balance, other considerations—lawmakers' constituency interests, policy preferences, and ideological dispositions, as well as public opinion and the number of partisan seats in each chamber—usually are more important in shaping congressional outcomes.

Going Public: The Rhetorical President

"With public sentiment, nothing can fail; without it nothing can succeed," Abraham Lincoln once observed.[36] Lincoln's idea is the essence of the rhetorical presidency: how and when a chief executive strategically employs contemporary campaign techniques and the technology of the mass media to promote "himself and his policies in Washington by appealing to the American public."[37] The rhetorical president's ultimate objective is to produce an outpouring of public support that encourages lawmakers to push his ideas through the congressional obstacle course. However, "if he had the votes he would pass the measure first and go to the public only for the bill-signing ceremonies."[38]

Going public on an issue is not without its risks. The strategy may alienate legislators who feel that the president is going over their heads, cutting them out of the process, and disregarding their constitutional role. The president can also raise expectations that cannot be met, make inept appeals, or stiffen the opposition. Furthermore, many legislators are more popular than the president in their districts or states. Political scientists, such as George Edwards, argue that presidents rarely succeed in moving public opinion.[39] Presidents do better when they champion issues that the public already favors. Contextual factors, such as the mood of the country, the state of the economy, the president's popularity, and the president's partisan strength in Congress, largely account for their legislative success.

President Reagan was an acknowledged master at using the electronic media to orchestrate public support. The Hollywood actor-turned-president was at home in front of cameras and microphones, and he had a keen sense of public ritual and symbolism as means of rallying support. After the March 30, 1981, assassination attempt, Reagan returned a month later and made a dramatic appeal for his economic program. "The White House shrewdly tied Reagan's return to action to the budget and tax debate, scheduling an April 28 comeback speech before a joint meeting of Congress. It was a triumph, and people began to call him the 'Great Communicator.' "[40] Reagan's adroitness with the media, primarily during his first year in office, is a legacy that looms large for subsequent presidents and Congresses. He showed that "one man using the White House's immense powers of communication can lift the mood of the nation and alter the way it does business."[41]

President Clinton used various media technologies to reach voters and employed campaign-style practices to generate public support for his programs. His empathetic response to the April 1995 bombing of a federal office building in Oklahoma City reminded people of the human face of the federal government, the very entity House Republican "revolutionaries" were warring against. When Republicans added provisions that Clinton opposed to a flood relief bill, the president used the bully pulpit to paint the GOP position as "extreme" and generated a flurry of favorable publicity for his position. One reporter noted:

> News accounts portrayed Republicans as, well, crazy extremists bent on playing games with flood victims. Rank-and-file Republicans writhed in political agony. Michigan Republican Fred Upton's mother watched the news accounts with alarm and warned her son, "You're getting killed." "When your mom tells you that, you know you're in trouble," said Upton.[42]

The White House also used "nightly tracking polls and weekly focus groups to help determine its daily message and the approach President Clinton should take to important national issues."[43]

George W. Bush was initially dubbed "the reticent president" by some analysts on several grounds: his preference for not seizing the public spotlight and addressing every major event or issue that might arise; his determination to stay "on message" by sticking to prepared talking points; his predilection for carefully staged and scripted appearances; and his propensity for committing verbal gaffes. Nevertheless, Bush worked diligently to win public and political support for his policy and political objectives.[44] Bush also became the first president to deliver his weekly radio address in Spanish—political recognition of the electoral potential of the growing Hispanic population.

Bush came into his own as both communicator in chief and commander in chief in the aftermath of the terrorist attacks on the World Trade Center in New York City and the Pentagon. He gave powerful and eloquent speeches in a variety of forums, such as before Congress and at the United Nations (UN), on the need to go after terrorists who threatened the United States and to disarm Saddam Hussein's regime in Iraq. His direct and confident manner resonated with most Americans and boosted domestic and congressional support for his antiterrorism and war plans.

In addition, the Bush White House went to great lengths to use television to promote the president, employing former network television aides with expertise in lighting, camera angles, and backdrops. The most elaborately staged event was Bush's flight to and speech on the aircraft carrier *Abraham Lincoln,* during which he prematurely announced the end of major military combat in Iraq. White House aides "choreographed every aspect of the event, even down to the members of the *Lincoln* crew arrayed in coordinated shirt colors over Mr. Bush's right shoulder and the 'Mission Accomplished' banner placed to perfectly capture the president and the celebratory two words in a single shot."[45] As the war continued for years without producing stability and security in Iraq, those same images were used to ironic effect by war critics, Democratic candidates, and late-night comedians.

President Obama, like Reagan, is an exceptionally skilled and eloquent speaker who enjoys addressing citizens in a variety of locales and settings. Winston Churchill once said that of "all the gifts bestowed upon [modern leaders], none is so precious as the gift of oratory."[46] Obama has that gift.[47] In a modern version of Franklin Roosevelt's "fireside" chats, Obama became the first president to appear on *The Tonight Show,* a late-night television program that draws about five million viewers. The president's purpose was "to broaden his audience beyond cable news junkies and political elites, appealing to those who don't already know the intricacies" of his policy proposals.[48]

President Obama recognized that "in a fragmented media universe, presidents must communicate nearly constantly across an array of platforms, both traditional and new."[49] One of those new platforms was a live Internet "town hall" meeting in which Obama fielded questions in the White House from citizens across the nation as well as from a live audience in the East Room. That video chat was the first of its kind for any modern presidency.[50] Another first for the president was to hold a Twitter town hall meeting with people who tweet, as well as participating in town hall events conducted on YouTube and Facebook.[51] The president also created a Web page called "We the People" where citizens were "able to create and sign petitions seeking the government's action on a range of issues."[52] In the Internet age with its 24/7 media cycle, "presidents must exploit an array of traditional and nontraditional communication methods if they are to influence and shape the public conversation. The pace at which news travels" in the social media age also means that it is difficult at times for presidents to stay on message, because issues or stories can quickly go viral and require a response from the administration.[53]

Despite his communication innovations and gifts as a speaker, which helped him twice win the presidency, Obama—by many accounts, including his own—has not employed the "bully pulpit" in an effective manner as chief executive. He has delivered many important, thoughtful speeches, but they appear to have done little in moving public opinion toward supporting his ambitious first-term agenda. As a Democratic governor put it, "Ironically, the best communicator I ever saw in a campaign has turned out to be not so good at getting out the message as president."[54] Or, as a Democratic senator explained, "[W]e spent too much time legislating and way too little messaging. Essentially, when we passed a bill, we moved on to the next one. . . . [We] didn't spend time letting [the public] know what we were doing."[55] The president agreed with some of this criticism. As Obama said during an interview: "What I have not done as well as I would have liked to is to consistently communicate to the general public why we're making some of these decisions."[56] President Obama held fewer press conferences (79) during his first term than Presidents George H. W. Bush (143), Bill Clinton (133), and George W. Bush (89). And, according to political scientist Martha Kumar, President Obama engaged in far fewer informal question-and-answer sessions with reporters (107) than any of his recent predecessors during their first four years in the White House— Reagan (158), the elder Bush (313), Clinton (612), and G. W. Bush (354).[57]

Obama's defenders might note that political science research suggests presidential speeches seldom move public opinion. Nonetheless, many political observers believe that a more comprehensive messaging strategy would have helped his program during his first term. In today's hyperpartisan environment, the president has "powerful incentives to skip negotiations with members across the aisle in order to avoid ceding [message] control of the public arena to [his] opponents."[58]

By not employing the huge megaphone of the White House, the president enabled congressional Republicans, hostile media outlets, and others who opposed his agenda to dominate the public relations battle. Health care is a prime example. Republicans constantly and successfully framed the national debate on health care reform as a "government takeover," "socialized medicine," or a bill with "death panels." President Richard Nixon made a keen observation on how administrations can win favorable congressional action on their policies: "In the final analysis, [legislative successes] are not won or lost by programs. They are won or lost on how these programs are presented to the country, and how all the political and public relations considerations are handled."[59] His comment underscores the importance of presidential communication strategies, especially in this fast-paced, 24/7 competitive media environment. Thus, advancing administration priorities requires skill at both the inside game of mobilizing winning coalitions on Capitol Hill and the outside game of stirring popular support for the president's agenda.

The Administrative President

Presidents understand that getting Congress to pass legislation is an arduous process, and that even when laws are enacted bureaucratic indifference may hamper implementation of presidential initiatives. Thus a president's core administrative strategy is to win policy goals by statute whenever feasible but, when such an effort falls short, to accomplish those aims through organizational or managerial techniques. Administrative presidents employ a variety of methods, such as naming loyal political appointees to supervise and monitor agency activities, reorganizing executive departments to advance presidential goals, using the budget process to reduce unwanted programs or increase favorite activities, and employing executive orders and rule-making authority to achieve outcomes blocked by Congress.[60] In short, presidents have an array of methods to bypass Congress and act unilaterally to advance their objectives.

Using executive orders and reorganization plans, presidents can act on their own to create entirely new administrative entities. In doing so, presidents are able to institutionalize policies that Congress would never have created. Based on a study of all the administrative agencies established between the end of World War II and 1995, William G. Howell and David E. Lewis report that "presidents have unilaterally created over half of all administrative agencies in the United States."[61] Among them are such important agencies as the Peace Corps. Facing significant opposition in Congress to the Peace Corps idea, President Kennedy opted to create the agency by executive order. By the time

Congress got around to reviewing the president's actions, the Peace Corps already had 362 employees and 600 volunteers at work in eight countries.[62] By establishing this "fact on the ground," the president pressured Congress into accepting the new organization. Another example stems from the September 11, 2001, terrorist attacks. In the immediate aftermath of the attacks, President George W. Bush unilaterally created an Office for Homeland Security in the White House, constructed a prison for suspected terrorist noncitizens at Guantánamo Bay, Cuba, and established a new court system for handling cases involving "unlawful enemy combatants."[63] Despite candidate Obama's 2008 campaign promise to close the Guantánamo Bay military prison, the facility to date remains open.

For his part, President Obama created by executive order several executive entities. Examples are the Export Coordination Enforcement Center, the President's Council on Jobs and Competitiveness, the Interagency Trade Enforcement Center, and the National Commission on Fiscal Responsibility and Reform, co-chaired by Erskine Bowles, former White House chief of staff to President Clinton, and former senator Alan Simpson, R-Wyo. After a gunman in December 2012 killed twenty elementary school students and six adults at the Sandy Hook Elementary School in Newtown, Connecticut, President Obama created a working group of top administration officials, headed by Vice President Biden, to propose ways to curb gun violence in the United States. In mid-January 2013, Obama issued twenty-three presidential memoranda and instructions to federal officials on actions to take to reduce gun violence.[64] Biden explained that "the administration might use 'executive orders' to curb gun violence," in addition to recommending legislative and further administrative action.[65]

Presidents have long employed executive orders—a form of administrative lawmaking using (or expanding) authority that the legislative branch has delegated—to achieve objectives not explicitly authorized by Congress.[66] President Harry S. Truman, for example, issued an executive order racially integrating the armed services. Stymied by the GOP-controlled Congress on issues such as antismoking legislation, a patients' bill of rights, and subsidies for school construction, President Clinton made extensive use of executive orders. "His formula include[d] pressing the limits of his regulatory authority, signing executive orders and using other unilateral means to obtain his policy priorities when Congress fail[ed] to embrace them."[67] Congressional Republicans railed against Clinton's "go-it-alone" governing.

George W. Bush similarly exploited administrative tools to advance his policy goals. For example, Bush quickly exercised executive authority to roll back, suspend, or challenge many Clinton-era regulations. He also was not reluctant to implement by executive fiat administration programs stalled in Congress. When the Senate blocked action on Bush's faith-based initiative (assisting religious groups in winning government grants for charitable and social service work), the president ordered his administration to implement the program through executive orders and changes in agency regulations.[68]

Moreover, like presidents before him, Bush encouraged his departments and agencies to move rapidly to enact a wide array of so-called "midnight regulations." Rushing them through in the administration's waning months, executive officials could burnish the president's legacy and—as a senior think tank analyst observed—"extend its influence into the future."[69]

Upon entering office in 2009, the Obama administration moved quickly to block or reverse many of Bush's rules and regulations. Even before Obama was sworn into office, his transition team "compiled a list of about 200 Bush administration actions and executive orders that could be swiftly undone to reverse White House policies on climate change, stem cell research, reproductive rights and other issues."[70] True to form, in his first seven days in office President Obama blocked action on Bush's last-minute rules. And like many other presidents, Obama has not shied away from using executive power to overcome legislative gridlock and advance his goals. "If Congress refuses to act [on my priorities]," declared the president, "I've said that I'll continue to do everything in my power to act without them."[71]

After legislation addressing global warming stalled in Congress, for example, President Obama used executive power to promulgate greenhouse gas emission regulations issued by the Environmental Protection Agency. When Congress failed to reauthorize the No Child Left Behind law, the president waived many of its requirements for more than half the states—so long as they followed guidelines issued by the administration, such as promoting charter schools.[72] With Congress unable to enact comprehensive immigration legislation, he issued a directive granting a reprieve from deportation to 800,000 or more young people under the age of thirty "brought to the country illegally as children who are enrolled in high school or college or who join the military."[73]

The "Two Presidencies"

"The United States has one president, but it has two presidencies; one presidency is for domestic affairs, and the other is concerned with defense and foreign policy."[74] According to this formulation by political scientist Aaron Wildavsky, presidential proposals are likely to achieve more success in the international arena than in the domestic arena, in part because Congress asserts itself more in domestic policy making than in foreign policy. Since its emergence, Wildavsky's thesis has sparked considerable controversy on, for example, how to measure success rates in the two arenas and whether the concept is relevant today in a world in which the international and domestic constantly overlap.[75] Whatever the strengths or weaknesses of the two-presidencies idea as Wildavsky laid it out, the concept seems especially relevant to the presidency of George W. Bush before and after the September 11, 2001, terrorist attacks. The pre-9/11 period constituted George W. Bush's first presidency, with its focus on domestic issues; then the post-9/11 era constituted his second presidency, with its strong focus on defense and national security issues.

The Pre-9/11 Phase. Despite Vice President Al Gore's plurality in the 2000 popular vote tally, the absence of any mandate from the voters, and the lack of any presidential coattails (the GOP lost seats in both chambers, though it held onto the majority in each), President Bush quickly advanced an ambitious agenda as though he had won a huge victory. This approach surprised the many pundits who had predicted that Bush would move slowly to implement his "compassionate conservative" campaign promises. "This is the farthest thing from a caretaker administration you could get," declared a Brookings Institution analyst. "It's the farthest thing from a president saying I lost the popular vote, I'm here because of a 5 to 4 vote on the Supreme Court [*Bush v. Gore*]. I'd better [advance] some centrist positions."[76]

Bush scored major policy successes early in his first term, largely by staking out an assertive policy-making approach that combined bipartisan and partisan governing strategies. Three days after being sworn into office, for example, Bush proposed the No Child Left Behind Act. A bipartisan and bicameral group of lawmakers worked cooperatively with the administration to win passage of the legislation. Bush took a more partisan approach in pushing Congress to enact the largest across-the-board tax cut ($1.35 trillion) since Ronald Reagan's presidency. Although there were partisan complaints that the tax cut was too large, lawmakers on both sides of the aisle were reluctant to vote against tax reductions for their constituents.

A different legislative dynamic emerged after May 2001, when Vermont GOP senator Jim Jeffords switched parties and Senate Democrats suddenly found themselves the majority party (Jeffords became an independent but caucused with the Democrats). Democratic control of the Senate produced significant problems for the Bush administration. Now the Democrats could initiate and force votes on their priorities, hold hearings to spotlight their agenda and critique Bush's, modify or block administration bills coming from the GOP House, reject the president's nominations, and require the White House to develop "a defensive strategy for responding to Democratic ideas."[77] Bush responded by renouncing bipartisanship and adopting a partisan model of governance.

But the president soon encountered vocal opposition to many of his ideas in Congress and the country. Polls indicated public concern about the country's direction and revealed that the public preferred the Democrats' positions over GOP ones. By June 2001, Bush's public standing had fallen "to a tepid 50 percent approval rating, the lowest presidential approval rating in more than five years."[78] As a result, congressional Democrats became increasingly optimistic that they could reclaim control of Congress in the midterm elections of November 2002. It was not to be, however.

The Post-9/11 Phase. The George W. Bush presidency was transformed by the terrorist attacks. After an uncertain response during the first days, Bush became a confident, resolute, decisive, and strong commander in chief. Images of the president consoling firefighters and others at the site of the World Trade Center, his calm and confident demeanor, and his eloquent statements to the public—including the September 20, 2001, national address before a joint meeting of Congress—rallied the nation to fight a global war against terrorists and the states that provided them safe haven. He called this global struggle "the first war of the twenty-first century," an open-ended fight that continues to this day.

Meanwhile, Bush's public approval ratings soared to a record-level 91 percent, breaking his father's record of 89 percent during the 1991 Persian Gulf War.[79] The levels of bipartisanship on Capitol Hill were also remarkable in the first weeks after the terrorist attacks. Congress moved quickly to enact some significant measures, including passage of legislation authorizing the president to employ "all necessary and appropriate force" against those groups or nations involved in the terrorist attacks. Subsequently, as directed by the president, the military ousted the Taliban regime in Afghanistan, which had provided safe haven for Osama bin Laden, the al Qaeda leader behind the September 11 attacks. (On May 2, 2011, bin Laden was killed at his compound in Pakistan in a daring U.S. Navy commando operation authorized by President Obama.)

President Bush's focus then turned to Iraq, a nation he declared to be part of the "axis of evil" that threatened the world. In October 2002, the administration persuaded Congress to enact a joint resolution granting the president unilateral authority to launch a preemptive military strike against Iraq. On March 19, 2003, President Bush went on national television and informed the nation of the start of the war in Iraq. Three weeks later, on April 9, U.S. forces entered Baghdad, ending the regime of longtime dictator Saddam Hussein.

President Bush justified the invasion of Iraq on several grounds: al Qaeda operated in Iraq, and Saddam Hussein was somehow involved in the 9/11 attacks; Saddam had weapons of mass destruction (chemical and biological), and he posed a threat to American and world safety; and, as the president stated in his 2003 State of the Union address, Saddam was obtaining uranium from Niger for his nuclear weapons program. However, the rationales for invading Iraq proved to be false. A few weeks before he left office, in a valedictory interview with ABC News, Bush came close to admitting that the Iraq war had been a mistake. "The biggest regret of all the presidency has to have been the intelligence failure in Iraq," he said.[80]

President Obama confronted an array of overlapping issues that involve the two presidencies because so many of today's problems are transnational in character. They range from global warming, to international criminal organizations, to global economic crises, to the ongoing struggle against terrorism. No single nation is capable of effectively addressing these global issues alone; nor is any nation insulated from their effects. The international position of the United States is inextricably linked to the well-being of the domestic economy. "Our whole foreign policy has to be anchored in economic strength here at home," President Obama observed. "And if we are not strong, stable, [and] growing" economically, "then our foreign [and defense] policy leadership will diminish as well."

THE VETO POWER

Article I, section 7, of the Constitution requires the president to approve or disapprove bills passed by Congress. When the president disapproves (vetoes) a measure, it dies unless it "shall be repassed by two thirds of the Senate and House of Representatives." Because vetoes are so difficult to override, the veto power transforms the president into, in Woodrow Wilson's words, a "third branch of the legislature."[81] Presidents can usually attract enough of their supporters in Congress to sustain a veto, who may also publicly pledge to sustain vetoes of certain bills to show solidarity with the chief executive. From 1789 through the end of Barack Obama's first term, thirty-six of forty-four presidents exercised their veto authority on 2,564 occasions. Congress overrode these vetoes on 110 occasions (4.3 percent).[82] During his first two years in office, President Obama vetoed just two bills—the average (one veto per year) during periods of unified government[83] (see the section "Pocket Vetoes" for more discussion of Obama's two vetoes during his entire first term).

When contemplating a veto, presidents seek advice from numerous administration sources, such as agency officials, the Office of Management and Budget, and White House aides. Presidents commonly give various reasons for vetoing a bill: the bill is unconstitutional, it encroaches on the president's independence, it is unwise public policy, it cannot be administered, or it costs too much. Political calculations may underlie any or all of these reasons. The veto is more than a negative power, however. Presidents use the threat of a veto to advance their policy objectives by, for example, inducing legislators to accommodate executive preferences and objections. "We try to use the veto threat wisely, to change votes or to change the language of the underlying document," explained a top White House legislative aide. "And we succeed."[84]

Presidents also practice the politics of differentiation through the veto: a veto fight with Congress may suit presidents who want to underscore how their views differ from the other party's. For its part, Congress can discourage vetoes by adding items to must-pass legislation or to measures the president strongly favors. Congress may also deliberately send the president of the opposite party a measure that lawmakers want him to veto, so they can use the issue on the campaign trail—a "winning by losing" strategy. Bills may also be signed in a public ceremony closer to the November elections as a way to energize the electoral base of the president's party—another example of the two Congresses.

Veto Options

Once the president receives a bill from Congress, he has ten days (excluding Sundays) in which to exercise one of four options:

1. He can sign the bill. Most public and private bills presented to the president are signed into law. The president also may issue a signing statement that expresses his interpretation of the provisions of the new law.

2. He can return the bill with his veto message to the originating house of Congress.

3. He can take no action, and the bill will become law without his signature. This option, which is seldom employed, is reserved for bills the president dislikes but not enough to veto.

4. He can pocket veto the bill. Under the Constitution, if a congressional adjournment prevents the return of a bill, the bill cannot become law without the president's signature.

Veto Strategies

George H. W. Bush (1989–1993) was among the most successful chief executives in employing the veto against an opposition Congress. He used it to block unwanted legislation and as a potent bargaining weapon to wring concessions from the Democratic-controlled Congress. Not until his term was nearly over, and after thirty-five consecutive veto victories, did Congress manage to override a Bush veto—on a 1992 measure to reregulate the cable television industry. Part of the explanation for Bush's veto successes was that he announced his intentions early and stuck by them unless the compromises he wanted were agreed to. Furthermore, he convinced congressional Republicans that their strength depended on sustaining his vetoes. (Of his forty-four vetoes, only the cable bill veto was overridden by Congress.)

By contrast, President Clinton did not veto a single measure during his first two years in office—something that had not happened since the days of Millard Fillmore in the 1850s. Part of the explanation is that Clinton was dealing with a Democratic Congress. Not until 1995 did Clinton use his veto pen, rejecting an appropriations bill sent to him by the Republican Congress. Subsequently, the president either exercised or threatened to exercise the veto against numerous GOP-sponsored bills. (Presidents often use Statements of Administration Policy to express their concerns about measures moving through Congress, even threatening to veto them.)

President George W. Bush claimed that he would not hesitate to use his veto power to enforce his budgetary goals if Congress passed legislation he considered excessive or objectionable. But he did not veto a single bill, spending or otherwise, during his entire first term, although he did issue 145 veto threats during that time. One has to reach back all the way to James Garfield (1881) to find a veto-less president, and Garfield did not even serve a full year before being assassinated. Partial-term presidents William Henry Harrison, Zachary Taylor, and Millard Fillmore never issued a veto, nor did one-termers John Adams and John Quincy Adams. Only Jefferson survived two terms without one.[85]

Several factors account for Bush's no-veto first term: unified Republican control of the House and Senate during much of the period and the resulting consensus on many issues; the refusal of top party leaders, such as Speaker Dennis J. Hastert, R-Ill., to send to the White House bills that Bush might veto;

the desire of Republicans to demonstrate their capacity to govern with narrow majorities; the ability of the White House and GOP congressional leaders to work out their disagreements; and the president's pragmatism in redefining his positions "to accommodate the direction in which lawmakers were leaning."[86]

Like other presidents, Barack Obama has threatened several times to veto measures because of objections to provisions in the legislation. During President Obama's 2011 State of the Union address, he declared, "If a bill comes to my desk with earmarks in it, I will veto it" (as discussed in Chapter 14, earmarks are special-interest provisions in measures that benefit members' districts or states). The president's threat had a direct effect on the lawmakers. As Senate majority whip Richard Durbin, D-Ill., exclaimed, "We're out of the earmark business."[87] President Obama has seldom followed through on veto threats: "only twice in his first term, on relatively inconsequential bills," in large measure because the Democratic Senate could block anti-administration bills coming out of the GOP House.[88]

Once Congress has enacted a bill and the president has signed it, the measure is printed on special paper called parchment and delivered by hand to the White House. A copy is also sent to the Government Printing Office for online public distribution. (Obama is the first president to use an autopen [a mechanical device] to affix his signature to legislation. He did this three times during his first term. For example, while the president was vacationing in Hawaii, he "directed the ['fiscal cliff'] bill be signed by autopen."[89] Several House Republicans objected to the president's use of the autopen.)

Post-Veto Action

Just as the president may feel strong pressure to veto or to sign a bill, Congress may feel intense political heat after it receives a veto message. A week after President Nixon's televised veto of a 1970 bill funding welfare programs, House members received more than 55,000 telegrams, most of them urging support for the veto. And Congress did uphold the veto, in part because of Nixon's televised appeal. However, despite a massive telephone campaign to congressional offices (as many as 80,000 calls an hour) urging members to sustain President Reagan's veto of a 1988 civil rights bill, the House and Senate easily overrode the veto.[90]

Actually, Congress need not act at all on a vetoed bill. If party leaders lack the votes to override, the chamber that receives a vetoed measure may refer it to committee or table it. Even if one house musters the votes to override, the other body may do nothing. A vetoed bill cannot be amended—it is all or nothing at this stage—and the Constitution requires that votes on overriding a veto be recorded.

Signing Statements

At times, presidents issue proclamations called "signing statements" to accompany bills they have signed into law. Even though they are not mentioned in the Constitution, signing statements have been used since James Monroe's presidency (1817–1825). George W. Bush, however, employed them more often than any other president to reassert and strengthen the so-called unitary theory of executive power.[91] As interpreted by Bush, this theory allowed the president to override laws that he claimed would impinge upon his constitutional prerogatives as commander in chief. When Congress banned torture of war prisoners, for example, the president held that the law trespassed on his powers as commander in chief. Ronald Reagan was the first president to use signing statements as a way to challenge congressional enactments on constitutional grounds. Of his 276 signing statements, 71 (or 26 percent) raised constitutional objections. By comparison, 127 (or 85 percent) of President Bush's 149 signing statements contained "multiple constitutional and statutory objections . . . to over 700 distinct provisions of law."[92] (See Box 10-1 for three examples of Bush's signing statements.)

BOX 10-1 Examples of Signing Statements

	Congressional directive	Signing statement
Intelligence Reform and Terrorism Prevention Act of 2004 (P.L. 108-458) Signed December 17, 2004	Created a position for a national intelligence director, in response to past intelligence failures, and required the president to consult with Congress on the person's responsibilities.	"To the extent that provisions of the Act . . . purport to require consultation with the Congress as a condition to execution of the law, the executive branch shall construe such provisions as calling for, but not mandating, such consultation."
Fiscal 2006 Defense Appropriations (P.L. 109-148) Signed December 30, 2005	Outlawed "cruel, inhumane or degrading treatment" of suspected terrorists in U.S. custody.	"The executive branch shall construe Title X in Division A of the Act, relating to detainees, in a manner consistent with the constitutional authority of the President to supervise the unitary executive branch and as Commander in Chief."
Department of Defense Appropriations Act, 2007 (P.L. 109-289) Signed September 29, 2006	Blocked money from being spent to process foreign intelligence if it was gathered unlawfully. Stipulated that information gathered on U.S. citizens must comply with constitutional limits on searches and seizures.	"The executive branch shall construe [the provision] in a manner consistent with the President's constitutional authority as Commander in Chief, including for the conduct of intelligence operations, and to supervise the unitary executive branch."

Source: Adapted from Chris Wilson, "Memo to Congress: Bush Asserts Final Say," *CQ Weekly*, October 30, 2006, 2863.

Even though the Constitution requires the president to "take care that the laws be faithfully executed," Bush's signing statements asserted that he had "the power to set aside the laws when they conflict with his legal interpretation."[93] Signing statements have raised concerns in Congress because they seem to provide the president with an unofficial line-item veto, allowing him to decide which parts of bills to implement or ignore. However, some observers believe that signing statements have little effect on the administration of laws. Studies have shown that "federal agencies seem to have generally complied with thousands of legislative provisions that [Bush] had questioned."[94]

Running for president in 2008, Obama criticized President Bush's use of signing statements. As president, Obama vowed he would use such statements with restraint and "only when it is appropriate to do so as a means of discharging my constitutional responsibilities."[95] On March 11, 2009, President Obama issued his first signing statement, "reserving a right to bypass dozens of provisions in a $410 billion government spending bill even as he signed it into law."[96] Sen. Charles E. Grassley, R-Iowa, attacked the signing statement for setting back "whistleblower protections and [violating] two promises with one stroke of the pen."[97] The two promises, according to Grassley, were protecting whistleblowers and avoiding Bush's sentiment that some parts of laws are optional. In a White House memorandum to all departments and agencies, President Obama made clear that signing statements are appropriate in limited circumstances, and that "they promote a healthy dialogue between the executive branch and Congress."[98]

Healthy dialogue or not, Obama's signing statements roused the ire of lawmakers and influential outside organizations. The American Bar Association, for example, sent a letter to President Obama in 2011 "urging him instead to veto bills if he thinks sections [of a measure] are unconstitutional."[99] Nonetheless, President Obama continues to use signing statements, albeit sparingly compared to President George W. Bush. During their first three years in office, Obama issued ten signing statements, Bush sixty-three. Moreover, the objections that each raised in their respective signing statements were often similar: that the legislation contained provisions that infringed on the constitutional prerogatives of the president.[100]

Pocket Vetoes

The pocket veto has been a source of some controversy and confusion over the years. Article I, section 7, of the Constitution states:

> If any bill shall not be returned by the President within ten days (Sundays excepted) after it shall have been presented to him, the same shall be a law, in like manner as if he had signed it, unless Congress by the adjournment prevents its return, in which case it shall not be a law.

The framers wanted to ensure that presidents would not be forced into signing last-minute legislation and that Congress would have time to consider, and perhaps override, the president's objections. The issue, however, is exactly when a congressional adjournment prevents the return of the president's veto. Several court decisions, such as *Kennedy v. Sampson* (1974), established the principle that pocket vetoes are not to be used during congressional sessions but only after Congress's final adjournment at the end of its second session.

The Ford and Carter administrations adhered to this understanding, but not other administrations. For example, President Reagan twice used intersession (between the first and second sessions) pocket vetoes, and President Clinton employed intrasession (in the middle of a session) pocket vetoes. In December 2007, President Bush invoked the pocket veto and returned it to the House (which originated the measure) "to leave no doubt the bill is being vetoed." The House majority voiced strong objection, with Speaker Pelosi declaring, "Your successful return of H.R. 1585 establishes that you were not prevented from returning it."[101]

President Obama's two vetoes were what some refer to as "hybrid vetoes" or "protective return" pocket vetoes (see Box 10-2). Obama returned the two unsigned bills to the originating chamber as if he were exercising a regular (or traditional) veto. In both cases, Congress objected to his pocket veto approach, treated it as a regular veto, and sustained the veto.

Thus it appears that neither an intra- nor an intersession pocket veto prevents its return to Congress. Until the Supreme Court makes a definitive ruling involving the use of the pocket veto both during and between legislative sessions, it is likely that legislative-executive conflicts over the pocket veto will occur periodically. In summary, the scope of the pocket veto power, as public law scholar Louis Fisher has written, "has been left largely to practice and to political understandings developed by the executive and legislative branches."[102]

The Line-Item Veto

Congress's habit of combining numerous items into a single measure obliges the president to accept or reject the entire package. Presidents and supporters of executive power have long advocated allowing the president to veto items selectively. They argue that it would give the president an effective way to eliminate wasteful spending and reduce the federal deficit. Opponents counter that the item veto is about interbranch power and not fiscal restraint. Granting the item veto to the president, they argue, would undermine Congress's power of the purse and give chief executives added bargaining leverage over lawmakers. "The president could say, 'I'm going to zap your dam, but I've got another piece of legislation coming around, and I won't be so inclined to do that [if you support me],'" said Rep. Jack Kingston, R-Ga.[103] Critics also say that presidents already have the only tool they need to control spending: the veto.

After much debate, Congress in 1996 expanded the president's rescission (cancellation of spending) authority. It eventually passed the line-item veto, as part of the "Contract with America," despite concern among congressional Republicans that President Clinton would use it against GOP-passed riders (extraneous policy provisos) in appropriations bills. The Line-Item Veto Act

BOX 10-2   Deep Presidential Pockets

When he quietly vetoed his first piece of legislation last week—a stopgap military appropriation that turned out not to have been needed—Barack Obama renewed a rather obscure constitutional debate about the way recent administrations have employed the "pocket veto," in which a president fails to either sign or veto a bill after Congress has already adjourned.

In his Dec. 30 "memorandum of disapproval," the term usually applied when announcing a pocket veto, Obama indicated that he was withholding his signature from the short-term continuing resolution that Congress sent him to ensure military spending until the fiscal 2010 Defense spending bill could be signed into law—which Obama had done Dec. 19. But the president also returned the short-term bill to the House.

There is no question that, as Obama asserts in his memorandum, his signing the Defense bill made the short-term continuing resolution unnecessary. But constitutional law experts question whether Obama and other recent presidents who have done the same thing actually have the authority to issue hybrid veto messages that combine both a traditional and pocket veto.

"This never made any sense," says Louis Fisher, a specialist on constitutional law at the Library of Congress. "It seems you have either a returned veto or a pocket veto, but not both."

President Gerald R. Ford was the first to use one of these "protective return" vetoes, though he agreed to limit its use after a court challenge by Democratic Sen. Edward M. Kennedy of Massachusetts, who prevailed in federal District Court, according to Robert Spitzer, a political science professor at the State University of New York at Cortland, who wrote a 2005 book on the presidency and the Constitution.

Nevertheless, presidents of both parties subsequently issued several hybrid vetoes. The most recent example was George W. Bush's rejection of the fiscal 2008 defense authorization bill in Dec. 2007. Bush objected to a provision that could have allowed lawsuits against Iraq in U.S. courts for acts committed under Saddam Hussein's regime.

Although it may seem like just "constitutional trivia," Spitzer says he views it as a way that presidents of both parties have quietly tried to expand executive power.

Presidents view the pocket veto, originally envisioned as protection against Congress passing laws and then skipping town before a president had a chance to veto them, as particularly attractive because there's no way legislators can override them.

"This whole protective return pocket veto is a back-door way to expand the pocket veto so that the president can use it any time Congress is literally not in session," Spitzer says.

Source: Reprinted from Seth Stern, "Deep Presidential Pockets," *CQ Weekly,* January 4, 2010, 10.

gave the president a fifth veto option. After a president signed a bill into law, he could exercise the line-item veto prerogative to cancel dollar amounts specified in any appropriations law, or even in the accompanying House or Senate committee reports; strike new entitlement programs or expansions of existing programs; and delete tax breaks limited to one hundred or fewer beneficiaries. The measure required the president, after using the line-item veto, to send a special message to Congress identifying what he had rescinded. To overturn his decisions, Congress would have to pass another bill that the president could then veto, requiring Congress to override it by a two-thirds vote of each chamber. Under the law, then, the president could block something if he had the support of only one-third plus one of the members of each chamber. The act became effective on January 1, 1997, and was originally set to expire at the end of 2004.

Contrary to the expectations of pundits, President Clinton exercised caution in his use of the line-item veto. The president apparently chose not to anger lawmakers whose support he might need later to enact administration priorities. As one account noted, the president "has deferred to Congress on the overwhelming majority of projects that members added to budget bills, even when the Administration could find no compelling public interest to justify them."[104]

On June 25, 1998, in the case *Clinton v. New York City*, the Supreme Court by a 6–3 vote held the Line-Item Veto Act to be unconstitutional because it gave the president "unilateral authority to change the text of duly enacted statutes," as Justice John Paul Stevens wrote for the majority.[105] The Clinton administration soon announced that it would release funds for the projects that had been subjected to line-item vetoes.

Since the Court's decision, and in view of today's record expenditures during the economic crisis and heightened concern about wasteful spending, there has been renewed interest among some lawmakers in enacting a constitutionally valid line-item veto. President Obama also supports enactment of enhanced rescission legislation that would guarantee within a specified number of days an up or down vote on a package of spending cuts. Many lawmakers oppose rescission bills, because they believe it would cede too much power to the president.

SOURCES OF LEGISLATIVE-EXECUTIVE COOPERATION

Unlike the legislative assemblies of many nations where executive authority is lodged in the leader of parliament—called the prime minister or premier—Congress truly is separate from the executive branch. And yet the executive and legislative branches are mutually dependent in policy making. The 124 volumes (as of 2011) of the *United States Statutes at Large* underscore the cooperative impulses of the two branches. Each volume contains the joint product of Congresses and presidents over the years, from the 108 public laws enacted by the First Congress (1789–1791) to the 283 enacted by the 112th Congress (2011–2013). These accomplishments are the result of party loyalties and public expectations, bargaining and compromise, and informal links between the president and lawmakers.

Party Loyalties and Public Expectations

Presidents and congressional leaders have met informally to discuss issues ever since the First Congress, when George Washington frequently sought the advice of Virginia representative James Madison. But meetings between the chief executive and House and Senate leaders were not common until

Theodore Roosevelt's administration (1901–1909). Today, congressional party leaders are two-way conduits who communicate legislative views to the president and inform other members of executive preferences and intentions.

A president and the members of his party are linked psychologically and ideologically. This means that "bargaining 'within the family' has a rather different quality than bargaining with members of the rival clan."[106] Congressional Democrats want President Obama to succeed in moving his agenda, even though they do not always share his priorities. As Rep. Chris Van Hollen, D-Md., said, "Our political fortunes are tied to Barack Obama's" and that the 2010 midterm elections would be "a report card not only on Congress but the White House, too."[107] The voters did in fact send a "report card" to lawmakers: congressional Democrats suffered, in President Obama's words, a "shellacking." Two years later, voters rewarded congressional Democrats with higher electoral grades as they won additional seats in the Senate and House, but not enough to take control of the latter.

Bargaining and Compromise

The interdependence of the two branches provides each with the incentive to bargain. Legislators and presidents have in common at least three interests: shaping public policy, winning elections, and attaining influence within the legislature. In achieving these goals, members of Congress may be helped or hindered by executive officials. Agency personnel, for example, can heed legislators' advice in formulating policies, help them gain favorable publicity back home, and give them advance notice of executive actions. Meanwhile, executive officials rely on legislators for help in pushing administrative proposals through the legislative process.

Bargains and compromises are essential to public policy making in a diverse nation of over 300 million people. Most recently, compromise-making has proven to be exceptionally difficult among the parties, chambers, and branches. Many factors account for this development, such as the ideological divide between the two political parties. Bipartisan compromises may be good or bad, but they cannot be achieved if the two parties emulate parliamentary systems: one party governs (or tries to) and the other is united in opposition. The polarized 112th Congress managed after several deadline crises and arduous legislative-executive negotiations to avoid a government default or shutdown. One result of the apparent government dysfunction was that Standard and Poor's, a national credit-rating agency, for the first time ever downgraded the creditworthiness of the United States from AAA to AA+.

Deal-making between the branches is hard because, as a GOP House member said after the November 2012 elections, "Compromise has a very small constituency—very small."[108] This view, combined with the country's political and ideological polarization, has created what might be called a new normal on Capitol Hill: policy making by brinksmanship. Each side waits until the final hours before accepting a compromise in the belief that it heightens their bargaining leverage. A scholar summed up the pitfalls of the high-risk, "no compromise" brinksmanship tactic: it "aims at claiming a large portion of the pie: 'Give me everything or I walk.' That's a very aggressive approach, and doesn't foster creative deal-making at all." He added that President Obama and House Speaker Boehner both "need a face-saving way to reach a compromise. Each needs to get something to sell to its constituency."[109] In brief, these leaders face the challenge of how they can come together to address the nation's problems when many in both parties disdain the idea of compromise.

Informal Links

Some presidents deal with Congress more adeptly than others. Lyndon Johnson assiduously courted members. He summoned legislators to the White House for private meetings, danced with their wives at parties, telephoned greetings on their birthdays, and hosted them at his Texas ranch. He also knew how to twist arms to win support for his programs. Johnson's understanding of what moved members and energized Congress was awe-inspiring. "There is only one way for a President to deal with the Congress," he said, "and that is continuously, incessantly, and without interruption."[110]

President Obama meets periodically with the bicameral leadership—the Speaker, House minority leader, Senate majority leader, and Senate minority leader—to discuss issues of common concern. His top legislative aides are often present at every key stage of a major bill's development, suggesting ways to resolve contentious issues. As a former senator, the president also has informal and friendly relationships with several lawmakers, such as Sen. Tom Coburn, R-Okla. To a large extent, Obama has outsourced the congressional liaison role to Vice President Joe Biden—given his more than three decades of Senate service. Biden's close ties to many House and Senate members, especially Senate GOP leader McConnell, have enabled him to craft bipartisan compromises on major measures that have passed both chambers. When Senator McConnell found he could not reach a compromise resolution to the 2012 "fiscal cliff" with Senate Democrats, he opened negotiations with Vice President Biden to produce a successful result in what many commentators called a dysfunctional Congress. "The vice president and I have worked together on solutions before," remarked Senator McConnell, because of the trust they developed after decades of serving together in the Senate.[111]

Informal and personal relationships between the president and the top House and Senate party leaders, as well as rank-and-file members, can promote, but not guarantee, productive problem-solving. "These kinds of relationships just don't pop up out of the air or out of necessity," observed a former aide to Speaker Boehner. "They require trust, and they take time. You just don't grow that necessary trust and relationship overnight."[112]

SOURCES OF LEGISLATIVE-EXECUTIVE CONFLICT

Legislative-executive conflicts were evident in 1789, they are present today, and they can be expected in the future for at least three reasons. First, the Constitution specifies neither the precise policy-making roles of Congress and the president nor the manner in which they are to deal with one another. Second, presidents and Congresses serve different constituencies. Third, important variations exist in the timetables under which the two branches operate.

Constitutional Ambiguities

Article I invests Congress with "all legislative powers," but it also authorizes the president to recommend and to veto legislation. In several specific areas, the Constitution splits authority between the president and Congress. The Senate, for example, is the president's partner in treaty making and nominations under the "advice and consent" clauses. And before treaties can take effect, they require the concurrence of two-thirds of the Senate. The Constitution is silent, however, on how or when the Senate is to render its advice to the president.[113]

In 1919 and 1920, a historic confrontation occurred when the Senate vehemently opposed the Treaty of Versailles negotiated by President Woodrow Wilson. The treaty contained an agreement binding the United States to the proposed League of Nations. Many senators had warned the president against including the League provision in the treaty, and during floor deliberations the Senate added several reservations that the president strongly opposed. Spurning compromise, Wilson launched a nationwide speaking tour to mobilize popular support for the treaty. Not to be outdone, senators opposed to the pact organized a "truth squad" that trailed the president and rebutted his arguments. During his tour, Wilson suffered a stroke from which he never fully recovered. And in the end, the treaty was rejected. This example illustrates that under the Constitution's separation of powers, presidents' abilities to achieve even their most urgent foreign policy goals are limited by Congress's institutional prerogatives.

Different Constituencies

Presidents and their vice presidents are the only public officials elected nationally. To win, they must create vastly broader electoral coalitions than are necessary for legislators, who represent either states or districts. Only presidents, then, can claim to speak for the nation at large. It is important to note, however, that

> there is no structural or institutional or theoretical reason why the representation of a "single" broader constituency by the President is necessarily better or worse than the representation of many "separate" constituencies by several hundred legislators. Some distortion is inevitable in either arrangement, and the question of the good or evil of either form of distortion simply leads one back to varying value judgments.[114]

Presidents and legislators tend to view policies and problems from different perspectives. Members of Congress often subscribe to the view that "what's good for Portland is good for the nation." Presidents are apt to say that "what's good for the nation is good for Portland."

In other words, public officials may view common issues differently when they represent diverging interests. For example, a president might wish to reduce international trade barriers. A representative from a district where a manufacturer is threatened by imported products is likely to oppose the president's policy, whereas retailers of imported products are likely to support the president. The challenge to national policy making is to forge consensus within an electorate that simultaneously holds membership in two or more competing constituencies.

Disparities in constituencies are underscored by differences in the ways voters judge presidents and members of Congress. Studies of presidential popularity ratings suggest that presidents are judged on the basis of general factors—economic boom or bust, the presence or absence of wars or other crises, the impact of policies on given groups.[115] The news media, too, can affect the assessment of presidents. Legislators, by contrast, tend to be assessed on the basis of their personalities, their communication with constituents, and their service in material ways to the state or district. Not only do presidents and legislators serve different constituencies, but they also labor under divergent incentives.

Different Time Perspectives

Finally, Congress and the president operate on different timetables. Presidents have four years, at most eight, to win adoption of their programs. They are usually in a hurry to achieve all they can before they leave office. In practice, they have even less time because of the typical falloff in presidential support after the initial "honeymoon." Indeed, presidents and their advisers actually often have a year, perhaps less, to sell their basic programs to Congress and the public. "A president's most effective year is his first," explained Sen. Richard Durbin, D-Ill., President Obama's close friend and confidant. "He is brand new to the office, has a national mandate of varying degrees, and Congress is usually more open to working with him. After the first year, an election year is under way and people look at him differently."[116] Presidents think in terms of four years; most lawmakers think in terms of two.

On major, long-standing issues, however, Congress typically moves slowly. Seldom does it pass presidential initiatives quickly unless an emergency or crisis of some sort is looming. Moreover, many legislators are careerists. Once elected, House members are likely to be reelected, and senators serve six-year terms. Most members hold office a good deal longer than the presidents they deal with. Skeptical legislators, reluctant to follow the president, realize that if they resist long enough someone else will occupy the White House.

THE BALANCE OF POWER

"The relationship between the Congress and the presidency," wrote Arthur M. Schlesinger Jr., "has been one of the abiding mysteries of the American system of government."[117] Part of the mystery inheres in the Constitution, which enumerates many powers for Congress as well as those "necessary and proper" to carry them out, while leaving the president's powers largely unstated. Where does the balance of power lie? There is no easy answer, but at certain times the scale has tipped toward Congress and at other times toward the president. Scholars have even identified periods of "congressional government" or "presidential government."[118]

Four points need to be remembered about the ups and downs of Congress and the presidency. First, even during periods in which one branch appears to dominate, the actual balance of power in specific policy areas is complex. The stature of either branch is influenced by issues, events, partisan circumstances, personalities, or public opinion.

The mid-1960s and early 1970s, for example, are cited as a time of "imperial presidents" and compliant Congresses.[119] Although Congress enacted much of President Johnson's Great Society program, it also initiated scores of laws, including consumer, environmental, health, and civil rights legislation. Nor did executive actions go unchallenged. Nationally televised hearings conducted in 1966 by the Senate Foreign Relations Committee helped to mobilize congressional and public opposition to the Vietnam War. The refrain "imperial presidents" and compliant Congresses was heard again when Republicans were in charge of Congress from 2001 to 2007 and George W. Bush was in the White House. More recently, House majority leader Eric Cantor, R-Va., has called President Obama an "imperial president" for using his regulatory and executive authority to govern without Congress.[120]

Second, power also shifts within each branch. In Congress, aggressive leaders may be followed by less assertive leaders. In the executive branch, the forces for White House leadership regularly battle the forces for agency decentralization. These internal power fluctuations clearly affect policy making. During the Eisenhower presidency in the 1950s, powerful committee and party leaders could normally deliver blocs of votes to pass legislation. Today, even with the resurgence of partisanship on Capitol Hill, the president can never be sure which of the 535 members will form a winning coalition.

Third, legislative-executive relationships are not zero-sum games. If one branch gains power, the other does not necessarily lose it. If one branch is up, the other need not be down. The expansion of the federal government since World War II has augmented the authority of both branches. Their growth rates were different, but each expanded its ability to address complex issues, initiate legislation, and frustrate the proposals of the other. According to the conventional wisdom, wars, crises, nuclear weapons, military expansion, and public demands fostered the imperial presidency. Such factors certainly enlarge the likelihood of executive dominance, but in the wars of 1812 and 1898, for example, military action was encouraged in part by aggressive Congresses. Economic panics and depressions under Presidents James Monroe, James Buchanan, and Ulysses S. Grant did not lead to losses of congressional power.

Political scientist David Mayhew has asserted that with respect to productivity of laws and investigations, it "does not seem to make all that much difference whether party control of the American government happens to be unified or divided."[121] Mayhew examined the period from 1946 to 1990, when the mobilization of cross-party majorities on Capitol Hill was commonplace. President Ronald Reagan, for example, enjoyed large successes on his policy priorities (tax cuts, defense hikes, and program reductions) in 1981 when he won the support of conservative "Reagan Democrats" in the Democratic-controlled House. Today, in an era of strong, largely cohesive, and ideologically distinct congressional parties—reflecting the conditional party government model discussed in Chapter 6—presidents confront a heightened potential for partisan impasses, especially in the Senate, regardless of whether the government is unified or divided.

Conflict between Congress and the president is embedded in the system of separation of powers and checks and balances. But the founders also expected their governmental arrangement to promote accommodation between the branches. Historical patterns have veered between these two extremes. The two branches worked together in the early days of Woodrow Wilson's progressive New Freedom (1913–1916); during the New Deal (1933–1937) and World War II (1941–1945); during the brief Great Society years (1964–1966) following John F. Kennedy's assassination in 1963; for the even briefer "Reaganomics" juggernaut during Ronald Reagan's first year in office (1981); during most of George W. Bush's first six years in office (2001–2007); and during Barack Obama's first two years (2009–2011). At other times, the two branches fought fiercely—during Wilson's second term (1919–1921); after 1937 during the Franklin Roosevelt administration; after 1966 during the Lyndon Johnson administration; and for much of the Nixon, Reagan, George H. W. Bush, and Clinton administrations, the final two years of George W. Bush's presidency, and Obama's last two years of his first term.

Finally, a wide gap often separates what presidents want from what they can achieve. Congress can influence what, when, how, or even whether executive recommendations are sent to Capitol Hill. Expectations of what will pass Congress frequently shape White House agendas. This indirect priority-setting power of the House and Senate can affect whether the president even transmits certain proposals to Congress. It also works in the other direction. Recommendations may be forwarded or endorsed because the White House knows they have broad legislative support. "The president proposes, Congress disposes" is an oversimplified adage.

Congress and the president are institutions shaped by diverging imperatives. Executive officials want flexibility, discretion, and long-range commitments from Congress. They prefer few controls and consultations with a limited number of legislators. The executive tends to be hierarchical, or vertical, in decision making, whereas Congress tends to be collegial and horizontal— with power spread among 535 independent-minded lawmakers. One of the legislative branch's strengths is that it is able to give voice and visibility to diverse viewpoints that the executive branch may have overlooked or ignored. The dispersion of power can slow down decision making, but it also can promote public acceptance of the nation's policies. Thus what are often viewed as Congress's vices are also genuine virtues.

CONCLUSION

Conflict would seem to be the inevitable result of a system that intentionally divides lawmaking and other powers between the executive and legislative branches. Much of the relationship between Congress and the executive, however, is better characterized as accommodation than as conflict. Neither branch is monolithic. Presidents find supporters in both chambers even when presidents are opposed by congressional majorities. Both branches seek support for their policy preferences from each other and from outside allies. Congress and the president must find ways to work together to achieve common goals.

Nevertheless, confrontation is a recurring element in dealings between Capitol Hill and the White House. The framers of the Constitution consciously distributed and mixed power among the three branches. They left it unclear how Congress or the president would assert control over the bureaucracy and over policy making. Even when both houses of Congress are controlled by the same party as the White House, the two branches have different constituencies and often become adversaries.

Finally, legislative-executive relations are constantly evolving. Either branch may be active on an issue at one time and passive at another time. So many circumstances affect how, when, what, or why shifts occur in the relationship that it is impossible to predict the outcome.

The General Services Agency—the federal government's procurement arm—ran into trouble over an expensive 2010 meeting held at a Las Vegas resort. GSA's Inspector General Brian Miller and Deputy Administrator Susan Brita (top left) prepare to be grilled by a House subcommittee. The House GOP's chief watchdog over the Obama administration is Rep. Darrell Issa, R-Calif. (top right), who chairs the House Oversight and Government Reform Committee; ranking Democrat is Elijah Cummings, D-Md. A Transportation Safety Administration (TSA) agent (bottom left) shows a passenger how to pass through a full-body scanner at Washington's Dulles International Airport. Another passenger (center right) finds a unique way to protest TSA's invasion of privacy at Phoenix Sky Harbor Airport. President Obama (bottom right) makes his fourth trip to examine the Gulf oil spill damage in southern Alabama with local officials and Coast Guard Admiral Thad Allen, his on-the-scene coordinator.

Congress and the Bureaucracy

In his 2013 State of the Union address, President Barack Obama emphasized an activist role for the national government and recommended that Congress address such issues as climate change, energy, and infrastructure. "Progress does not compel us to settle centuries-long debates about the role of government for all time," he said, "but it does require us to act in our time." Opponents of big government castigated the president for suggesting a larger federal role in policy making, particularly during a time of huge deficits and debt and when the public's lack of trust and confidence in the government was at an all-time low.[1]

Public confidence and trust in government exhibit an ebb and flow over time. In 1964 nearly 80 percent of Americans said they trusted the government "to do the right thing most of the time."[2] Different eras, in brief, can provoke different views of government. Confidence was high during World War II, low during the Vietnam War and the Watergate scandal. In short, the proper role of government has been a constant and continuous source of debate since the nation's founding. Suffice it to say, as a noted scholar put it, "The role of government in a free society must be a matter of continuous negotiation among members of its public."[3]

The national government has grown under presidents of both parties throughout the modern era despite pronouncements such as that of President Bill Clinton in 1996, "The era of big government is over." The administration of Republican president George W. Bush (2001–2009) oversaw substantial governmental growth, only in part triggered by domestic security, law enforcement, and military requirements after the terrorist attacks of September 11, 2001. As respected journalist David S. Broder wrote, President Bush presided over one of the largest expansions of government in history: "He has created a mammoth Cabinet department [Department of Homeland Security], increased federal spending, imposed new federal rules on local and state governments, and injected federal requirements into every public school in America."[4]

When Democratic president Obama began his first term, the country was in the midst of the most serious national economic crisis since the Great Depression. The government intervened dramatically in the marketplace, spending trillions of taxpayer dollars to try and revive the ailing economy. The effort undoubtedly helped halt the recession's downward spiral, perhaps preventing another depression. "Not since Lyndon B. Johnson and Franklin D. Roosevelt," wrote a congressional journalist, has a president "moved to expand the role of government so much on so many fronts—and with such a demanding sense of urgency."[5] Many in the public reacted negatively to the "governmentalizing of the economy" by the Obama administration and the huge sums spent to jumpstart the ailing economy.[6] With the public deeply split over Obama's agenda, the elections of November 2010 and 2012 produced four years (2011–2015) of divided government. The two elections also reignited a national conversation between those who view government as a constructive force for collective action and those who emphasize individual, private sector, and nongovernmental problem-solving. A Washington insider summarized the clash of views over the government's role:

> Should we have a smaller federal government with lower taxes and fewer federal regulations that would leave people to largely take care of themselves, as Republicans generally favor? Or should the federal government help prop up the elderly, the poor, and low-income workers, as most Democrats believe?[7]

Today's philosophic disconnect between the two branches, legislative chambers, and parties over the government's role hit home on March 1, 2013, when an agreement could not be reached to stop a process called sequestration: indiscriminate, across-the-board spending cuts of about $1 trillion over a decade divided between domestic and defense agencies and programs. Many Republicans backed sequestration as a guaranteed way to shrink the government and reduce the fiscal deficit and debt. Many Democrats opposed spending reductions on scores of domestic and defense programs regardless of merit, and lamented the impact of the cuts on the less-well-off, the economy, and federal services.

President Obama provided his own perspective on the government's size and scope. "It's not an issue of big government versus small government. It's an issue of smart government," where "we can probably do more and do it smarter with less money, if we are actually making some tough choices."[8] A key challenge for the president's concept of smart government is an unsettled political and policy reality: today's big government is supported with revenue for a small government. In the judgment of a former representative, Democrat Lee Hamilton of Indiana: "The nation's current fiscal difficulties will surely force government to do less than many people want, and the public sector will have to become smarter, more effective, and more efficient. This is not a bad thing."[9]

Yet history demonstrates that it is often difficult for presidents or Congress to shrink the size, role, or reach of the federal government. Setting aside war and other national crises, one basic reason is the ambivalence of the public. Although they profess to wanting to get the government off their backs, Americans of virtually all ideological persuasions often turn to the government to help fulfill their goals and to provide assistance during times of need. As William S. Cohen, former GOP senator from Maine (1979–1997) and defense secretary during the Clinton administration, put it: "The government is the enemy until one needs a friend."[10]

The paradox, then, is that citizens and various groups oppose the general idea of big government, but they support many of the government's specific roles—and may even welcome selective expansion of those roles—in ensuring clean air and water, a strong national defense, access to quality health care, the safety of prescription drugs, and protection from terrorist attacks. Understandably, lawmakers typically defend government programs supported by their constituents. As a senior citizen told a lawmaker: "Tell the government to keep its hands off my Social Security!" To implement any government program, an organized bureaucracy is required—often federal *and* state bureaucracies.

The recent expansion of the federal government under both Democratic and Republican presidents has spawned a wave of interest in "states' rights." Governors, state legislatures, and attorneys general have shown no reluctance to challenge federal authority. Legislative leaders in twelve states, for example, back a "repeal amendment" to the U.S. Constitution that would permit any federal law or regulation to be overturned "if the legislatures of two-thirds of the states voted to do so."[11] Many states, too, have adopted "sovereignty resolutions," which allow state legislatures, referendums, or special conventions to declare federal laws, such as the recent health care reforms, "null and void within their state borders."[12]

Tension is common in the U.S. system of federalism, in part because of conflicts over which level of government can best perform what types of functions. The federal government can preempt state laws or impose federal mandates on the states. When the national government fails to address important issues (such as immigration, energy conservation, or climate change), states step in to deal with them. Meanwhile, the national government looks to the states for ideas and innovations. For example, President Obama's landmark health care overhaul law was patterned after various state initiatives. The reality is that today's federal-state relationship is usually more symbiotic than confrontational. Each level of government needs the other. Washington relies on the states to administer various national programs, and states rely on federal resources to fund many of their health care, transportation, and education priorities.

The two Congresses contribute to an expanding bureaucracy. In today's complex and interdependent world, constituents typically look to the national government rather than the private sector to secure collective goods such as security, justice, and protection. Members of Congress respond to their constituents' demands. Regardless of which party is in control, the national government is not reluctant to supersede state authority to regulate electricity, define what constitutes drunk driving, or combat child abductions. Similarly, nationwide corporations often lobby for federal regulation so they do not have to contend with the different rules of the fifty states. Indeed, businesses often prefer federal regulations because these are sometimes "considerably weaker than those being imposed these days by many of the tougher states."[13] As former senator Ernest F. Hollings, D-S.C. (1966–2005), said, "We have armies who protect us from enemies from without and the [Federal Bureau of Investigation] protects us from enemies within. We have Social Security to protect us from the ravages of old age. We have Medicare to protect us from ill health. We have clean air and clean water [laws] to protect our environment. We have [laws that mandate] safe working places and safe machinery. Our fundamental duties here are to protect."[14]

CONGRESS ORGANIZES THE EXECUTIVE BRANCH

Just as the president and Congress share influence over lawmaking, they share responsibility for the executive branch of government—the bureaucracy. The Constitution requires the president to implement the laws, and by implication it empowers him to manage the executive branch. But Congress "has at least as much to do with executive administration as does an incumbent of the White House."[15] Congress is constitutionally authorized to organize and fund the executive branch. The framers, of course, did not foresee the huge federal bureaucracy that has arisen from their sparse references to "executive departments." George Washington supervised only three departments (State, War, and Treasury); Barack Obama heads fifteen. Beyond the cabinet departments, the federal bureaucracy also includes independent agencies (such as the Central Intelligence Agency), independent regulatory commissions, and government corporations (see Figure 11-1).

Congress has extensive influence over the structure and composition of the federal bureaucracy.[16] Among other things, it can enact statutes that establish or abolish executive agencies and departments (see Table 11-1). The newest cabinet creation is the Department of Homeland Security (DHS). Congress can also instruct departments and agencies to reorganize themselves or establish an outside commission to recommend how departments or agencies might be merged or abolished. Or it can authorize the president to reorganize on his own initiative or to propose reorganization plans that will then be subject to some form of congressional review. In addition to establishing federal entities such as DHS, Congress extends its long arm into the bureaucracy in many different ways. The Senate confirms (or not, as the case may be) presidential appointments of high-level officials. Congress authorizes the basic personnel systems of federal entities. It also grants rule-making authority to administrative agencies.

Senate Confirmation of Presidential Appointees

High-level federal appointments—executive, diplomatic, and judicial—are subject to the Senate's "advice and consent" under Article II, section 2, of the Constitution. After the president has decided whom to nominate, the Senate decides whether to confirm (see Figure 11-2).

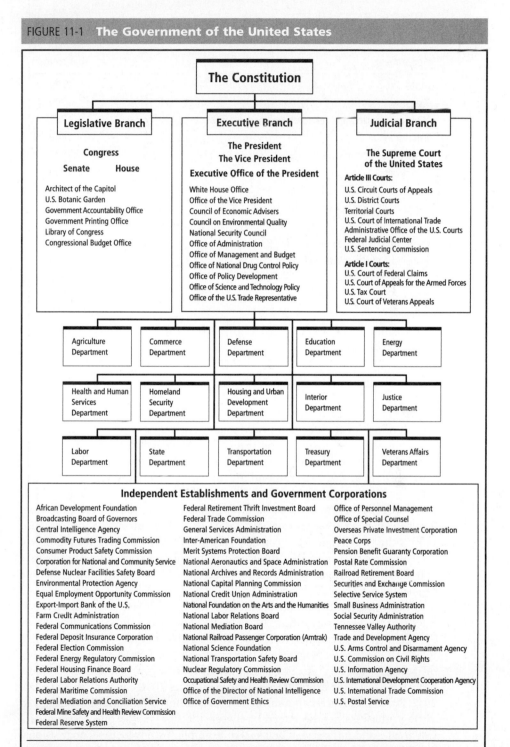

FIGURE 11-1   **The Government of the United States**

The Constitution

Legislative Branch

Congress

Senate   House

Architect of the Capitol
U.S. Botanic Garden
Government Accountability Office
Government Printing Office
Library of Congress
Congressional Budget Office

Executive Branch

The President
The Vice President
Executive Office of the President

White House Office
Office of the Vice President
Council of Economic Advisers
Council on Environmental Quality
National Security Council
Office of Administration
Office of Management and Budget
Office of National Drug Control Policy
Office of Policy Development
Office of Science and Technology Policy
Office of the U.S. Trade Representative

Judicial Branch

The Supreme Court
of the United States

Article III Courts:

U.S. Circuit Courts of Appeals
U.S. District Courts
Territorial Courts
U.S. Court of International Trade
Administrative Office of the U.S. Courts
Federal Judicial Center
U.S. Sentencing Commission

Article I Courts:

U.S. Court of Federal Claims
U.S. Court of Appeals for the Armed Forces
U.S. Tax Court
U.S. Court of Veterans Appeals

Agriculture Department	Commerce Department	Defense Department	Education Department	Energy Department
Health and Human Services Department	Homeland Security Department	Housing and Urban Development Department	Interior Department	Justice Department
Labor Department	State Department	Transportation Department	Treasury Department	Veterans Affairs Department

Independent Establishments and Government Corporations

African Development Foundation
Broadcasting Board of Governors
Central Intelligence Agency
Commodity Futures Trading Commission
Consumer Product Safety Commission
Corporation for National and Community Service
Defense Nuclear Facilities Safety Board
Environmental Protection Agency
Equal Employment Opportunity Commission
Export-Import Bank of the U.S.
Farm Credit Administration
Federal Communications Commission
Federal Deposit Insurance Corporation
Federal Election Commission
Federal Energy Regulatory Commission
Federal Housing Finance Board
Federal Labor Relations Authority
Federal Maritime Commission
Federal Mediation and Conciliation Service
Federal Mine Safety and Health Review Commission
Federal Reserve System

Federal Retirement Thrift Investment Board
Federal Trade Commission
General Services Administration
Inter-American Foundation
Merit Systems Protection Board
National Aeronautics and Space Administration
National Archives and Records Administration
National Capital Planning Commission
National Credit Union Administration
National Foundation on the Arts and the Humanities
National Labor Relations Board
National Mediation Board
National Railroad Passenger Corporation (Amtrak)
National Science Foundation
National Transportation Safety Board
Nuclear Regulatory Commission
Occupational Safety and Health Review Commission
Office of the Director of National Intelligence
Office of Government Ethics

Office of Personnel Management
Office of Special Counsel
Overseas Private Investment Corporation
Peace Corps
Pension Benefit Guaranty Corporation
Postal Rate Commission
Railroad Retirement Board
Securities and Exchange Commission
Selective Service System
Small Business Administration
Social Security Administration
Tennessee Valley Authority
Trade and Development Agency
U.S. Arms Control and Disarmament Agency
U.S. Commission on Civil Rights
U.S. Information Agency
U.S. International Development Cooperation Agency
U.S. International Trade Commission
U.S. Postal Service

Source: The United States Government Manual, 2012 (Washington, DC: Office of the Federal Register, Government Printing Office), 22.

TABLE 11-1 **Growth of the Cabinet**

Department	Year created
State	1789
Treasury	1789
War (reorganized and renamed Defense in 1947)	1789
Interior	1849
Justice (position of attorney general created in 1789)	1870
Agriculture	1889
Commerce (created as Commerce and Labor)	1903
Labor (split from Commerce and Labor)	1913
Health, Education, and Welfare (reorganized and renamed Health and Human Services in 1979)	1953
Housing and Urban Development	1965
Transportation	1966
Energy	1977
Education	1980
Veterans Affairs	1989
Homeland Security	2002

Source: CQ Daily Monitor, January 10, 2003, 3.

Senators use their confirmation power to wield influence over executive branch priorities. Senate committees usually elicit the following promise from departmental and agency nominees they have confirmed: "The above nomination [a cabinet secretary, for example] was approved subject to the nominee's commitment to respond to requests to appear and testify before any duly constituted committee of the Senate."[17] Or, as Sen. Charles Grassley, R-Iowa, declared, "I'm going to hit every [Obama] nominee with the question, 'Are you open to congressional oversight?'"[18] The confirmation process also reflects the two Congresses principle. As a top Senate official once remarked, "It looks very, very good in California or some place to put out a press release that says, 'Today, I questioned the new Secretary of Transportation about the problems of our area.'"[19]

Presidents can bypass the Senate's advice and consent role in three broad ways. First, the Constitution (Article II, section 2) provides that "[t]he President shall have Power to fill up all Vacancies that may happen during a Recess of the Senate, by granting Commissions which shall expire at the End of their next Session." Recess appointees then serve until the end of the next Senate session—for example, a person named in 2011 could serve until late 2012. Presidential recess appointments are not unusual, and they have occurred during intersession—the interval between the first and second sessions of a Congress—and intrasession breaks. For example, a study by the Congressional

FIGURE 11-2   **The Appointments Process**

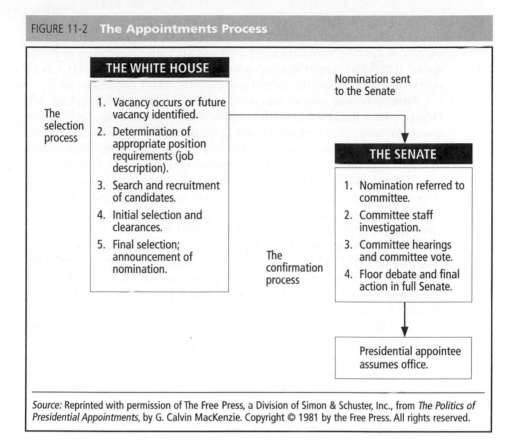

THE WHITE HOUSE

The selection process

1. Vacancy occurs or future vacancy identified.
2. Determination of appropriate position requirements (job description).
3. Search and recruitment of candidates.
4. Initial selection and clearances.
5. Final selection; announcement of nomination.

Nomination sent to the Senate

THE SENATE

1. Nomination referred to committee.
2. Committee staff investigation.
3. Committee hearings and committee vote.
4. Floor debate and final action in full Senate.

The confirmation process

Presidential appointee assumes office.

Research Service found that since the inauguration of President Ronald Reagan in 1981, "presidents have made 329 intrasession recess appointments and 323 intersession appointments."[20]

On January 25, 2013, the president's constitutional recess authority was called into question by a decision of the U.S. Court of Appeals for the District of Columbia Circuit. The three-judge panel ruled that presidents can only make recess appointments to fill vacancies during the break between the first and second sessions (intersession) of a Congress and not during the short or long breaks (the August recess, for example) that take place intrasession. As the chief judge of the circuit court wrote, the president's interpretation of the recess clause gives him "free rein to appoint his desired nominees at any time he pleases, whether that time is a weekend, lunch, or even when the Senate is in session and he is merely displaced with its action."[21]

Unless this decision (*Noel Canning v. National Labor Relations Board* [NLRB]) is reversed by the Supreme Court, it will limit the president's recess authority to intersession periods. Moreover, it calls into question the decisions made by hundreds of current and past recess appointees and opens those rulings to legal challenge. Three weeks after the court case, President Obama renominated the two Democratic members of the NLRB whose appointments were invalidated by the circuit court. In April 2013, the Department of Justice appealed to the Supreme Court to review the January ruling of the D.C circuit court. (In May 2013, another circuit court supported the decision of the first.)

Another consequence of the circuit court's decision was highlighted by a Department of Justice attorney who handled recess appointments for President George W. Bush: "If this opinion stands, I think it will fundamentally alter the balance between the Senate and the president by limiting the president's ability to keep offices filled."[22] Two key reasons bolster this judgment. First, there are many intrasession recesses but only one intersession break, which can be short or exceedingly brief. Second, presidents have come to rely more on recess appointments in response to the wider use of Senate filibusters and holds to block the confirmation of presidential appointments. (Recall that sixty votes are required to bring an end to a filibuster.) As a congressional expert noted, partisan filibusters "can stop a president's appointees in their tracks and in the process can kill agencies and stymie programs."[23] Indeed, without his appointees in place, the president's constitutional authority to "take Care That the Laws be faithfully executed" is weakened.

In addition, senators have long resented presidential use of the recess appointment option, especially if the chief executive is not of their party, because it undermines their constitutional advice and consent role. Mindful that the Constitution (Article I, section 5) states neither chamber can adjourn for more than three days without the consent of the other house, the Senate would sometimes adopt a simple formula to block recess appointments: no Senate recesses, no presidential recess appointments. The Senate would meet in *pro forma* session every third day, convening for only a few seconds and seldom conducting any official business. Technically, because the Senate is meeting in a *pro forma* session, it would be able to act on nominations received from the White House.[24] Use of these sessions prevented President Obama from employing recess appointments for people opposed by Senate Republicans. By precedent, presidents respected the fiction that the Senate was in session during *pro forma* meetings and did not make recess appointments.

However, in 2012 President Obama broke precedent, ignored the Senate's *pro forma* sessions, and recess-appointed Richard Cordray as chair of the new Consumer Financial Protection Bureau. His approval was blocked by Senate Republicans for months because they wanted a law enacted to have a commission-led agency rather than one person in overall charge of the bureau. In addition, because the National Labor Relations Board (NLRB) lacked a quorum to function, the president recess-appointed three individuals during the Senate's *pro forma* meetings. The president contended that the Senate was not actually in session because nearly every senator, except for a few Republicans, had departed for the winter holidays. Senate Republicans countered that official business was conducted during the *pro forma* sessions, and that the president had no business determining what constitutes sessions of the Senate. Obama's action set off a storm of protest in the Senate, provoked legal challenges, and prompted the president, as noted, to renominate for Senate consideration both Cordray and the NLRB recess appointments. (The impact of the *Canning* decision on the Senate's use of *pro forma* sessions to block executive appointments remains to be seen.)

The other two ways that the chief executive can bypass the Senate's advice and consent role have not aroused as much controversy in recent years as the recess appointment process. The president can name individuals, on a temporary acting basis, to fill vacant positions that require confirmation by the Senate. Senate dissatisfaction with this procedure led to enactment of the Federal Vacancies Reform Act of 1998 (P.L. 105-277), which imposed time restrictions on how long officials can serve in an acting capacity, typically 210 days. In some cases, Congress has enacted laws that permit the president, an agency head, or an automatic mechanism to fill temporary vacancies. For example, if the director of the Office and Management and Budget (OMB) is absent or unable to serve, the deputy director then acts as the OMB director.[25]

Third, many prominent officials, such as White House advisers, are not subject to the advice and consent of the Senate. President Obama may be a record-breaker in naming so many individuals, informally called "czars," to head up important policy initiatives—the "environmental czar," the "economic czar," the "information czar."[26] Czars oversee and coordinate the forming of policies that cut across the jurisdictions of several departments and agencies. For example, Harvard professor (now U.S. senator) Elizabeth Warren was asked to set up the new Bureau of Consumer Financial Protection in the Treasury Department. The bureau was created as part of the landmark financial regulatory reform bill (P.L. 111-203), and she was largely the intellectual force behind its creation. Because of significant Senate opposition to Warren, President Obama bypassed the nominations process and named Warren an assistant to the president and special adviser to the Treasury secretary. GOP senator Bob Corker of Tennessee dubbed Warren "the czar of all czars."[27] (Of note: Senator Warren, newly elected in 2012, asked Senator Corker to mentor her in the ways of the Senate. Corker agreed.)

The appointment of numerous czars reflects the amassing of further power in the White House. Many presidents have appointed "czars," but President Obama "has made the most appointments of such officials in U.S. history—nearly 50," and they "exercise substantial regulatory and policy authority without any system of normal democratic controls in place."[28] Yale law professor Bruce Ackerman contends, "We need to seriously consider requiring Senate approval of senior White House staff positions."[29] And yet the slow pace of confirmations no doubt provides incentives for presidents to name policy czars as a way to avoid lengthy Senate approval.

Indeed, today nominations to high-level executive posts are subject to standards of judgment and evaluation that go far beyond reasonable questions of competence or conflict of interest; nominees' personal lives and backgrounds are scrutinized as well. As one commentator explained:

These days, if you want to run for office or accept a position of public trust, everything is relevant. Your moral, medical, legal and financial background, even your college records, become the subject of public scrutiny. In the old days, the scrutiny was done in private, and certain transgressions could be considered irrelevant.[30]

This shift in standards stems in part from a change in attitudes by the press, the public, the White House, and the Senate. The press, for example, now more aggressively reports on the private activities of public officials.[31] In the 1980s, use of marijuana could derail nominees. In the 1990s, it was hiring an illegal immigrant as a nanny or domestic helper. In 2009, tax issues caused problems for several of Obama's top nominees, such as Thomas Daschle, the former Senate Democratic leader. He was forced to withdraw as the president's choice to head the Department of Health and Human Services because of his failure to pay $146,000 in taxes.[32] This trend is also driven in large measure by a hyperpartisan environment in which the president's opponents seek to embarrass or obstruct the administration at every turn.

These developments have produced a rigorous vetting process for nominees. Each nominee must fill out several lengthy questionnaires and undergo security checks. According to Norman Ornstein, "Each security check is a massive operation, involving up to 40 face-to-face interviews, and is basically the same for the assistant secretary of Education for public affairs as it is for the secretary of State."[33] The Senate Finance Committee "borrowed" staff from the Internal Revenue Service (IRS) to examine the tax returns of Obama's nominees. Investigators from the White House, Federal Bureau of Investigation (FBI), IRS, and Senate ask nominees difficult and uncomfortable questions about their personal and professional lives. "I have never been subjected to such personally insulting and expensive scrutiny in my life," said one Obama nominee, who was asked for receipts for furniture he donated to charity more than a decade ago. Another nominee was questioned about "his wife's sexual activity when she was at university."[34] The importance of a thorough vetting process was emphasized by an Obama adviser: "The real purpose of vetting is to understand the person's ability to perform the job and be confirmed for the position. We also want to avoid surprises."[35] "Avoiding surprises" is a goal not always achieved. For example, Treasury Secretary Timothy Geithner encountered unexpected tax problems that delayed his eventual confirmation.

A study by the Brookings Institution, a Washington, D.C.–based think tank, found that one result of the rigorous vetting process is a drop-off in "the number of talented Americans willing to accept the call to presidential [service]. Presidential recruiters report that it takes more calls to find candidates willing to subject themselves to the process and more work to keep the candidates from bolting once the process begins."[36]

Today, there is substantial frustration with the confirmation process. "The nomination system is a national disgrace," wrote a scholar of the presidential appointment process.[37] The problems are many, afflicting the administrations of both parties—even when the same party controls the White House and the Senate. Although the Senate eventually confirms most nominees, three concerns with the process merit mention.

First, it takes longer and longer to fill the full-time cabinet and agency positions requiring Senate confirmation. Public administration expert Paul C. Light studied five hundred of Obama's nominees for full-time jobs in his administration "and found they've waited an average of more than nine months to be confirmed, longer than at any time since the 1960s."[38] As an Obama White House press secretary noted, "There is certainly an advise and consent, a very important [constitutional] provision. It is not advise, delay and consent. It should not be that way."[39] To be sure, delays are also caused by the administration's slowness in nominating people to serve in high federal positions.[40]

To try and resolve the problem as well as related issues, the bipartisan Senate leadership created on the opening day of the 112th Congress a "working group," headed by Sens. Charles Schumer, D-N.Y., and Lamar Alexander, R-Tenn., to suggest reforms to the confirmation process. Two measures emerged from the working group, and both were agreed to by the Senate. First, the president signed into law (P.L. 112-166) the Presidential Appointment Efficiency and Streamlining Act. This law reduced by 163 the number of non-policy-making executive positions subject to the advice and consent of the Senate, such as nominations to various federal boards and commissions. The law grants the president unilateral authority to make the 163 appointments and implies that the Senate would devote more time to reviewing the roughly 1,000 or so executive nominations that still require confirmation. The law also established a working group of government officials to develop recommendations for improving the selection and vetting processes.

In June 2011, the Senate adopted a resolution (S. Res. 116) that expedited chamber consideration of 272 nominations—different from the 163 noted above—to various federal entities (departmental posts, independent agencies, federal advisory boards, etc.). These noncontroversial nominations are expected to bypass committee referral and receive faster chamber action. When the Senate receives presidential nominations for the 272 positions, they are placed on the Senate's Executive Calendar in a special section entitled "Privileged Nominations; Information Requested." The committee of jurisdiction then gathers background and financial information from the individual nominated for one of the 272 positions. Once the committee chair certifies that the information has been received, the nominee is listed for ten days in another section of the Executive Calendar entitled "Privileged Nominations; Information Received" and then assigned to the "Nominations" section. During any stage of this process, any senator can request any nominee in the 272 group to be referred to the appropriate committee for the regular confirmation review.[41] Otherwise, these nominations can be called up and passed by unanimous consent.

Second, the expanding bureaucracy raises concerns beyond the general slowness of the confirmation process, particularly the issue of public accountability. In the 1970s, writes Paul C. Light, "Congress discovered executive structure . . . and began to mine it."[42] Since then, Congress and the president have made many changes in the top four layers of officials in cabinet departments (secretary, deputy secretary, undersecretary, and assistant secretary), all while creating more new job titles in the top echelons of government than ever before. The result is additional layers of bureaucracy—in some federal agencies there are as many as fifty layers between the president and frontline executive employees—"a bureaucratic fog in which Congress and the president are hopelessly isolated from the people they most need to guide."[43] Among the numerous new titles are deputy associate deputy secretary, principal assistant deputy undersecretary, principal senior deputy assistant secretary, deputy associate assistant secretary, and deputy executive associate administrator.[44]

As a result of "title creep," Light explains that it is difficult to know whom to hold accountable for what goes wrong in the executive branch, and "impossible for the bottom to hear the top when messages go through dozens of interpretations on their journey down."[45] The Pentagon is a glaring example of the burgeoning bureaucracy. In 1960 there were 78 deputy assistant secretaries of defense, and today there are 530.[46] Light brands title creep as the "thickening of government" and attributes much of it to "an indelible belief that more leaders equals more leadership."[47] Several other reasons accounting for the invention of new titles include the "use of promotions rather than pay raises to reward senior employees [and] the creation of new positions by Congress and attempts by presidents to tighten their hold on the bureaucracy with a greater number of political appointees."[48]

Third, the Senate's confirmation process can be mean and nasty, especially in this period of polarized politics. "With law so hard to make and so hard to change, influencing the choice of the implementers and adjudicators of the law becomes an essential strategic option."[49] Many nominees are, therefore, subjected to rough treatment. For example, former GOP senator Chuck Hagel, Neb., Obama's defense secretary and a decorated Vietnam War combat officer, confronted harsh criticism and interrogation from many Republicans on the Senate Armed Services Committee, some of whom were his former colleagues. In the end, the Senate confirmed Hagel as defense secretary despite an outside media campaign funded by secret donors "unmatched in the annals of modern presidential cabinet appointments."[50]

Ideological groups, as in Hagel's case, may organize attack campaigns to defeat nominees who appear unsupportive of their agendas. Sometimes, the purpose of Senate confirmation hearings "seems less to ensure that nominees are fit than to cripple the chief executive's political leadership. A defeated nomination can embarrass a president, demoralize his supporters, and reduce public confidence in his judgment."[51] Others argue that although the confirmation process may be tough, so are the positions for which nominees seek assignment. "If you can't fight your way through the process," says a former head of the Central Intelligence Agency (CIA), "you might not just do a hot job as director."[52]

Individual senators, too, are not reluctant to threaten filibusters or to place holds on nominations—that is, senators notify party leaders that they oppose floor consideration of certain nominees (see Box 11-1). The Senate may also refuse to consider a nominee if members invoke senatorial courtesy. This tradition, dating from the nation's earliest years, means that the Senate will usually delay or not act on nominees for offices in a state if opposed by a senator of the president's party from that state.

The Personnel System

Congress wields constitutional, legal, and informal authority over the federal personnel system. The civil service itself was created after a disgruntled job seeker assassinated President James A. Garfield in 1881. That event prompted Congress to curb the abuses of the spoils system, the practice of handing out federal jobs to supporters of the party that had won the presidency. In 1883 Congress passed the first civil service law that substituted merit for patronage. But those patronage practices have a modern equivalent: the political appointee system. The latest figures show that the fifteen cabinet departments are home to more than 2,500 political appointees (see Table 11-2).[53] The number of political appointees, however, is small compared with the number of federal employees: 2.8 million civil servants and 1.4 million uniformed personnel.

Not all political appointees have the requisite experience to meet the challenges of their office. A classic example involved Hurricane Katrina, which devastated the Gulf Coast in late August 2005. At the time, the chief of the Federal Emergency Management Agency (FEMA) was Michael Brown. A former commissioner of the International Arabian Horse Association, Brown had little experience in emergency management. Despite President George W. Bush's praise—"Brownie, you're doing a heck of a job!"—FEMA's response to this crisis was widely viewed as inept and inadequate. One response by Congress was to pass the Post-Katrina Emergency Management Reform Act of 2006 (P.L. 109-295), which requires that any nominee named to head FEMA must meet certain qualifications.[54]

Periodically, various lawmakers recommend a reduction in the number of political appointees. They contend that there are simply far more appointees than the president can manage effectively. Far from enhancing responsiveness, said one senator, the large number of political appointees undermines "presidential control of the executive branch."[55] Not everyone agrees. Amid rising partisanship, one scholar argued, "presidents need to stock departments with people who understand politics and the importance of interaction with Congress, lobbyists and the media."[56]

Pay and Other Legal Standards. By law, Congress has wide control over federal employees. It can establish retirement programs; special requirements for holding office; personnel ceilings; employee performance standards; wages,

BOX 11-1 **Lifting of Objection**

*M*r. GRASSLEY. Madam President, on June 27, I provided notice of my intent to object to proceeding to the nominations of Mark J. Mazur, to be an Assistant Secretary of the Treasury, and Matthew J. Rutherford, to be an Assistant Secretary to the Treasury. My support for the final confirmation of these nominees depended on receiving information from both the Treasury Department and the Internal Revenue Service regarding their implementation of the tax whistle-blower program. Since I have received the responses, I no longer object to proceeding to these nominations. [...]

I began asking questions about the program's implementation in 2010. I wrote again in 2011 and then again on April 30 of this year. Unfortunately, I did not get complete answers until I objected to proceeding to the nominations of Mr. Mazur and Mr. Rutherford. [...]

It is unfortunate that objecting to these nominees, both of whom were approved by the Finance Committee by unanimous, bipartisan votes, was the only way I could get information about the whistleblower program. At least there is now more information than ever before about the IRS whistleblower program.

Source: An excerpt from the *Congressional Record*, July 30, 2012, S5655–S5656.

benefits, and cost-of-living adjustments (COLAs); and protections from reprisals for whistleblowers (employees who expose waste and corruption). The 1939 Hatch Act, named for Sen. Carl Hatch, D-N.M. (1933–1949), restricts federal employees' partisan activity. The act was passed during the New Deal after reports that civil servants were being coerced to back President Franklin D. Roosevelt in his reelection efforts. Today, civil servants can engage in political activity in accord with regulations prescribed by the U.S. Office of Special Counsel. For example, most career civil servants can run for nonpartisan office, contribute to political organizations, or distribute campaign literature. They may not run for partisan office, use their authority to exert influence over an election, or wear political buttons while on duty.[57] As a sign of the times, the special counsel's office has also issued guidelines for federal employees on the use of social media such as Facebook and Twitter in election campaigns.[58]

Other limits are placed on bureaucrats as well. After leaving public office, many executive officers, top legislative staffers, and legislators themselves pass through the "revolving door" to jobs with private firms that deal with the government. However, various laws impose a "cooling-off" period before these officials and employees may lobby their former agencies, departments, or branches of government. For example, under the Honest Leadership and Open Government Act, which President George W. Bush signed into law on September 14, 2007, high government officials and senators are subject to a two-year cooling-off period after leaving office; House members must comply with a one-year cooling-off period.[59] Nevertheless, government officials regularly move to the private sector and vice versa. Enactment of the landmark Dodd-Frank Wall Street Reform and Consumer Protection Act (P.L. 111-203)

TABLE 11-2   **Political Appointees by Department and Appointment Type, 2012**

Department	Presidential appointment requiring Senate approval	Presidential appointment not requiring Senate approval	Noncareer Senior Executive Service	Schedule C	**Total**
Agriculture	14	2	43	168	**227**
Commerce	22	3	33	103	**161**
Defense	51	0	94	134	**279**
Education	15	3	14	112	**144**
Energy	22	0	30	66	**118**
Health and Human Services	19	2	48	66	**135**
Homeland Security	16	5	61	102	**184**
Housing and Urban Development	14	1	18	49	**82**
Interior	17	0	30	36	**83**
Justice	218	5	45	68	**336**
Labor	16	3	29	105	**153**
State	220	5	36	125	**386**
Transportation	20	3	31	41	**95**
Treasury	29	4	23	45	**101**
Veterans Affairs	11	4	8	9	**32**
Total	704	40	543	1,229	**2,516**

Sources: Henry B. Hogue, Maureen Bearden, and Betsy Palmer, "Filling Advice and Consent Positions at the Outset of a New Administration," Congressional Research Service Report RLWP19, April 1, 2010, 2; and Maeve P. Carey, "Presidential Appointments, the Senate's Confirmation Process, and Changes Made in the 112th Congress," Congressional Research Service Report R41872, October 9, 2012, Appendix A.

in 2010 saw many government regulators walk through the revolving door to join various Wall Street firms.[60] Similarly, top White House officials have also left the administration to take high-paying jobs in business, law, and public relations firms, despite signing Obama-required pledges barring them for two years from trying to influence executive officials on behalf of their clients. However, the pledge does not prevent "outgoing Obama aides from lobbying Congress or from helping employers or clients influence the administration by charting strategy or even supervising lobbyists."[61]

Size of Government. Americans have debated the size and reach of the federal government since the nation's founding. At least since the twentieth century—from the Progressive Era to World War I, from the New Deal to the Great Society, to today's governmental interventions in the private sector—the national government has expanded dramatically. Growth has been driven by overlapping factors. Wars and crises, of course, expand federal obligations. The intelligence community mushroomed during the Cold War as the United States faced a major threat from the other nuclear-armed superpower, the Soviet Union, and expanded dramatically after the September 11, 2001, terrorist attacks. As a result, some 854,000 people with supersecret clearances are now in place at ten thousand sites across the United States.[62]

Complexity is another factor triggering governmental growth. New problems and issues repeatedly demand national action. Today, the federal government must address issues with global dimensions, from trade to currency exchange rates, to climate change. As the nation's population grew to over 300 million and government expanded its responsibilities and capacities, it was only natural that individuals and groups would look to their national officeholders to solve problems in health care, transportation, law enforcement, energy, and so on.

People often complain about the overly large federal establishment, but what does "too big" really mean? Much of the disagreement centers on how government size should be measured: the share of the gross domestic product (GDP) devoted to federal expenditures, the magnitude of the federal budget, or the number of federal employees. As to the first standard, federal spending relative to the size of the U.S. economy is a mixed picture, from 21.8 percent of GDP in 1990 to 18.4 percent in 2000, 19.8 percent in 2004, 20.2 percent in 2008, 23.8 percent in 2010, and 22.8 percent in 2012. Moreover, since 2011 and despite Congress's penchant for legislating by crisis, the federal deficit is projected to shrink by nearly $4 trillion over a decade because of large cuts in discretionary spending, some tax increases, and savings on interest payments. However, this is a short-term outlook. In this decade, explained the Congressional Budget Office, "total government spending is falling compared with the size of the economy but will rise again in the next decade" because of more baby boomer retirements and rising medical costs.[63] Another measure of the government's size is the federal budget, which keeps growing ($3.8 trillion in 2013), but so, too, have the nation's population and obligations. Recall that discretionary spending has been cut back significantly but entitlement spending keeps growing.

Contrary to what many people believe, the federal workforce has remained relatively constant in size. How can the government continue to perform services while generally keeping its size down? One answer is that much of what the federal government does is to transfer money to eligible recipients, such as the elderly who receive Social Security. This function does not require large numbers of federal workers. Another answer is that federal work has been outsourced to contract firms, or privatized. The Pentagon, for example, reached a milestone in 2001 when the number of its private sector employees (734,000) exceeded its civilian workforce (700,000). Nine years later, the Defense Department said it employed 766,000 contractors compared with 745,000 civilian employees; however, another study calculated that Pentagon-employed contractors numbered 1.2 million.[64] These contract employees "perform service jobs from mowing lawns to testing weapons systems."[65] As one analyst explained, "Everybody wants the federal government to look smaller than it really is. By contracting out jobs rather than having civilian workers in those jobs, you can say, 'Look, the government's smaller.'"[66] Another scholar has put the true personnel size of the government at about 15 million employees: the 4.1 million civilian, military, and postal workers plus the 10.5 million "shadow" employees who work "under federal contracts and grants or mandates imposed on state and local governments."[67] Unless undone, the sequestration triggered on March 1, 2013, will lead to fewer federal and "shadow" employees, furloughs of current government employees, and limits on new governmental hires.

Whatever the outcome of this debate about government size, privatizing (or outsourcing) the federal government's work has certain benefits and costs. Outsourcing has distinct advantages in many instances: contractors can be faster, more flexible, and cheaper than the career bureaucracy. They can provide security services, technological skills, intelligence capabilities, and other benefits that government agencies are unable to fulfill. However, many analysts believe that certain functions are inherently governmental, which means they are "so intimately related to the public interest as to require performance by a federal government employee."[68] Moreover, because contractors are not directly responsible to Congress, the so-called third-party (or shadow) government raises serious questions of accountability, resulting in fraud, waste, and cost overruns.

The Rulemaking Process

Congress creates and funds executive agencies and defines their legal mandates, but rarely can it specify the details needed to implement policies and programs. By statute, Congress delegates to federal entities its inherent legislative authority to craft the implementing rules and regulations (the terms are interchangeable) for carrying out the mandates contained in laws. As Senator Grassley explained, "All regulations are based ultimately on the authority granted by this Congress. When an agency promulgates a rule, it is engaging in a legislative task—in effect, filling in the gaps on the implementation that we in Congress have established through statute."[69] Executive agencies through their rule-writing authority (their final regulations have the full force and effect of statutes) enact more "laws" annually than the legislative branch. In other words, executive branch officials who write regulations are lawmakers operating in a bureaucratic context.

Lawmakers can employ the expedited procedures (restrictions on the length of debate, for example) specified in the Congressional Review Act (CRA) to try to nullify, one at a time, unwanted regulations promulgated by executive agencies. The CRA is a section of the 1996 small-business regulatory fairness law requiring regulators to submit all proposed major rules and regulations—those with an economic impact over $100 million in any one year—to the House and Senate. Lawmakers then have sixty legislative days from the time a regulation is published in the *Federal Register*—the government's daily publication of regulatory activities—to reject it under expedited procedures by enacting a joint resolution of disapproval (see Box 11-2).[70]

Important to note is that the president can veto joint resolutions of disapproval, and mustering the two-thirds vote needed to override the chief executive is a high hurdle. Nevertheless, as an aide to a former Senate GOP

BOX 11-2 **Resolution of Disapproval**

Republicans may be in the minority in the Senate, but they have a number of tools that will allow them to bring up votes on the health care law that Democrats may want to avoid. One little-discussed method allows opponents of the law to bring up a resolution that could kill health policy regulations that the administration issues. Such a resolution would not have to overcome amendments, filibusters or motions to move to other business.

The technique, authorized in the 1996 Congressional Review Act (CRA), gives Congress 60 days to overturn a major regulation after an agency publishes a rule or informs Congress of its release (whichever is later).

If Congress succeeds in shepherding through a disapproval resolution that the president will sign, federal regulators cannot publish a new rule that is "substantially" similar to the one that was rejected.

Earlier this year [2010], Sen. Michael B. Enzi was the first to target a regulation resulting from the health care overhaul. The Wyoming Republican sought to overturn a rule setting guidelines for grandfathering health plans that were in existence when the health care law passed in March.

Enzi's proposal (SJ Res 39) was rejected, 40–59, on a party-line vote. Even if Congress had passed the measure, President Obama probably would have vetoed it.

Opponents of rules have succeeded only once in overturning a policy. In March 2001, the House and Senate Republicans who controlled Congress, joined by moderate Democrats, overturned an Occupational Safety and Health Administration ergonomics rule that was issued during the waning days of the Clinton administration. President George W. Bush signed the resolution into law.

Even though the prospects for killing a regulation are slim under the CRA, Republicans still see it as a valuable tool that can keep the issue in the public's sights and force Democrats to defend the law.

Source: Rebecca Adams, "The Anti-Regulation Route," *CQ Weekly*, November 29, 2010, 2757.

majority leader noted, the CRA "provides an important public relations tool to highlight real concerns and perhaps force the administration to make some changes [to the challenged regulation] that they would otherwise not be willing to make."[71] Disapproval resolutions also signal regulatory agencies that Congress is keeping a close eye on their work. According to a Texas House Republican, the CRA will be a major weapon, able "to block the implementation of these bad laws, and to educate the public with laser clarity on the specifics of what these regulations will do to our freedoms."[72]

Statutory Standards for Rulemaking. In the Administrative Procedure Act (APA) of 1946 and later amendments to it, Congress established standards for rulemaking by government agencies. Under the APA, regulatory agencies are required to publish a notice in the *Federal Register* of their proposed rule-making. The notice includes such information as where and when "interested parties" can comment on the proposed rule. Typically, the public comment period runs for at least thirty days. Interested parties can take part in the process by testifying in public about the merits or demerits of proposed regulations. Citizens can comment on federal rulemaking through the government's official websites—www.federalregister.gov or www.reginfo.gov—as well as through comparable sites. The Obama administration has been considering a change in how rulemaking would work: agencies would first draft a rule, then solicit public comments, make revisions based on the comments, and then publish the final rule. The new approach would use blogs, electronic town hall meetings, and social media sites to involve the citizenry in determining whether a rule is needed, and if so, what should be in it. As the White House's deputy chief technology officer said, "Instead of starting with a finished product, we're co-creating from the get-go and asking people what should be in such a rule before we write it."[73]

The federal courts also ensure that executive officials do not repeal rules by fiat. A federal appeals court has held that once a rule is published in the *Federal Register*, "it cannot be reversed without a lengthy administrative process, even if [the rule] has not yet taken effect."[74] Although presidents can overturn executive orders with the stroke of a pen, they cannot treat regulations the same way. "It is not easy for a president to stop a final rule that has been published in the *Federal Register* short of putting the whole process [as prescribed in the Administrative Procedures Act of 1946] in reverse and beginning the process of rulemaking anew—with public notices, comment periods and agency reviews that could take years."[75]

Legislative-Executive Clashes. Congress and the White House frequently skirmish over rulemaking. GOP administrations tend to have a pro-business regulatory perspective, favoring voluntary compliance and giving key regulatory jobs to corporate and industry officials who are keen on easing or reducing regulation. Democratic presidents appoint individuals to head agencies who support worker safety and consumer and environmental protections. Inevitably, these disparate party views of federal regulation produce sharp disagreements. Congressional Republicans blame President Obama for creating job-killing regulations that stifle economic growth by imposing expensive costs and red tape on businesses. For his part, President Obama contends that Republicans want the end of regulations "that protect Americans from risky financial deals and other reckless behavior that crashed our economy."[76] Nonetheless, the Obama administration has directed federal agencies to be "sensitive to the costs and cumulative effects of regulations on businesses." The president also issued an executive order (13563) requiring "executive agencies to reduce regulations that place unnecessary burdens on U.S. businesses and the public." House majority leader Eric Cantor, R-Va., called Obama's regulatory initiatives "underwhelming."[77]

A recent ongoing controversy between Congress and the executive agencies has centered on the authority of the Environmental Protection Agency (EPA) to regulate carbon emissions. When the Democratic-controlled 111th Congress (2009–2011) failed to enact legislation to curb greenhouse gas emissions found to promote climate change and to endanger public health and welfare, the EPA used its authority under the Clean Air Act (P.L. 101-549) to require power plants, electric utilities, and oil refineries to employ the best available technologies to reduce their carbon emissions. (On April 2, 2007, the U.S. Supreme Court, in *Massachusetts v. EPA,* agreed that greenhouse gases were air pollutants and subject to regulations imposed by the EPA.) In response to the EPA's actions, House and Senate members from energy-producing states immediately went on the offensive to limit or strip the EPA's climate change authority. "We are not going to let this administration regulate what they've been unable to legislate," declared House Energy and Commerce chair Fred Upton, R-Mich.[78] Upton also promised that the EPA administrator would be testifying so frequently before his committee "that he'll guarantee her a permanent parking space on Capitol Hill."[79]

However, after two years of committee hearings and passing bills in their chamber repealing EPA regulations, House Republicans started to recognize that their chances of curbing environmental regulations are not good. As Joe Barton, R-Texas, chair *emeritus* of the House Energy and Commerce Committee, explained: "Congress can do something [about EPA regulations], but you need a majority in the House and 60 percent in the Senate, plus the president to avoid a veto. In this environment, we don't have that." Instead, mindful of the two Congresses, Barton said Republicans should push messaging bills. "Message bills are different. I'm open to that," he said.[80]

Hundreds of rules and regulations issued each year by executive agencies must be reviewed by the White House regulatory "czar." This czar is the chief of the Office of Information and Regulatory Affairs (OIRA) within the Office of Management and Budget. OIRA devotes considerable time to analyzing economically significant regulations, those that would impose more than $100 million in costs on affected industries. OIRA can reject these major rules, require their revision, or approve them in line with the president's priorities. A study by a former chief of OIRA found that with Republicans in control of the

House, there had been a slowdown in the growth of new regulations. The Obama administration "averaged 63 economically significant final rules annually in 2009 and 2010—and then 44 annually since then."[81] (For a list of the number of all final federal rules published for selected years, see Table 11-3.)

Proposed rules and regulations are typically subject to cost-benefit review. Measuring costs and benefits is at best a tricky undertaking. Risk analysis experts hold that this traditional tool should be used "to sort through a complex world of threats to human and environmental health so we can identify the choices that will do the most people the most good at the least cost."[82] Critics of this approach, however, point out that measuring costs is usually easier than estimating benefits; costs are more easily quantified, whereas benefits are often intangible and long-term. How valuable are regulations? Lawmakers, like their constituents, are of two minds. Some, such as Sen. Barbara Boxer, D-Calif., emphasize their positive aspects:

TABLE 11-3 **Total Number of Final Rules Published in the *Federal Register*, 2000–2012**	
Year	Number of final rules
2000	4,079
2001	3,423
2002	3,559
2003	3,744
2004	3,661
2005	3,301
2006	3,065
2007	2,947
2008	3,085
2009	3,471
2010	3,261
2011	3,835
2012	2,482

Source: Maeve Carey, regulatory expert, the Congressional Research Service.

Note: The data are provided by the Government Accountability Office (GAO) in its Federal Rules Database, available on GAO's website.

> The purpose of the Federal regulatory process is to improve and protect the high quality of life that we enjoy in our country. Every day, the people of our Nation enjoy the benefits of almost a century of progress in Federal laws and regulations that reduce the threat of illness, injury, and death from consumer products, workplace hazards, and environmental toxins.[83]

Others call for regulators to issue "smarter, more cost-effective regulations."[84] A difficult challenge is to distinguish between inflexible, pointless, or overly burdensome and costly regulations and the beneficial regulations that are necessary to promote and protect the public's health and safety.

Whatever their view of the regulatory process, legislators must act as intermediaries between their constituents and federal agencies. Constituents' problems are handled within members' offices by personal staff aides called caseworkers. In addition to courting the electoral payoff of effective casework—evidence of the two Congresses once again—some members appreciate its value as oversight. "The very knowledge by executive officials that some Congressman is sure to look into a matter affecting his constituents acts as a healthy check against bureaucratic indifference or arrogance," wrote a former senator.[85]

CONGRESSIONAL CONTROL OF THE BUREAUCRACY

"Congressional power, like chastity," explained a scholar, "is never lost, rarely taken by force, and almost always given away."[86] Because no law can be sufficiently detailed to cover every conceivable circumstance, Congress allows executive officials wide discretion in implementing the laws it passes. This delegation of authority occurs because legislators lack the time, knowledge, or expertise to address the complexities of contemporary administration.

Congress is often sharply criticized for drafting vague or sloppy legislation that gives executive officials and judges too much leeway in interpretation and administration. "Administration of a statute is, properly speaking, an extension of the legislative process," pointed out political scientist David B. Truman, and, therefore, Congress must watch over its programs lest they undergo unintended change.[87] Because of the size and reach of the executive establishment, Congress's oversight role is even more important today than when Woodrow Wilson wrote in 1885, "Quite as important as lawmaking is vigilant oversight of administration."[88]

The Constitution does not refer explicitly to the oversight role, but it does implicitly flow from Congress's right, among other things, to make laws, raise and appropriate money, give advice and consent to executive nominations, and impeach federal officials. Congress has, however, formalized its oversight duties. The Legislative Reorganization Act of 1946 directed all House and Senate committees to exercise "continuous watchfulness" over the programs and agencies under their jurisdiction. Subsequent statutes and House and Senate rules have extended Congress's authority and resources for oversight. The Government Accountability Office (GAO), the chief investigative arm of the legislative branch, provides the House and Senate at the start of each new Congress with "high risk" reports on the management and accounting practices of federal agencies and departments. The high risk reports also identify "areas in need of broad-based transformation."[89] Overall, GAO issues annually more than a thousand audits and reports on administrative management.

Members understand their review responsibilities. "Congress's duty didn't end in passing this law," remarked a senator. "We have to make sure the law works." Another senator said, "I have always felt that one-third of the role of Congress should be in oversight."[90] The purposes of oversight are many, but three are especially important: (1) to check the power of the executive branch; (2) to determine how laws are being implemented and whether they need adjustments and refinements; and (3) to shine the spotlight of public attention on significant executive actions and activities. As Woodrow Wilson wrote in

1885, "The informing function of Congress should be preferred even to its legislative [lawmaking] function." He went on to say:

> Unless Congress [has] and use[s] every means of acquainting itself with the acts and dispositions of the administrative agencies of government, the country must be helpless to learn how it is being served; and unless Congress both scrutinize[s] these things and sift[s] them by every form of discussion, the country must remain in embarrassing, crippling ignorance of the very affairs which it is most important it should understand and direct.[91]

Political purposes are served by oversight as well, such as generating favorable publicity for programs; urging the elimination or reduction of agencies; responding to requests from special interests to influence agency decisions; or winning electoral support from constituents or groups. Oversight thus occurs in a political context, within which Congress's relationship with administrative agencies can range from cooperation to conflict.

To ensure that laws are working, Congress relies on a varied array of formal and informal processes and techniques. Each has its strengths and weaknesses, and it is often necessary to use several in combination if the House and Senate are to challenge or assess executive branch performance. Many oversight activities are indirect, ad hoc, and not subject to easy measurement or even recognition. "Oversight isn't necessarily a hearing," said John D. Dingell, D-Mich., a noted House overseer when he chaired the Energy and Commerce Committee. "Sometimes it's a letter. We find our letters have a special effect on a lot of people."[92]

Hearings and Investigations

Many of Congress's most dramatic historical moments have occurred during legislative probes into administrative or business misconduct or manmade or natural disasters. Examples are the Teapot Dome inquiry (1923); the Senate's Watergate hearings (1973–1974); the Iran-contra investigation (1987); the joint hearings into the disintegration of the space shuttle *Columbia* (2003); the hearings on the Iraq war (2007); the hearings into taxpayer-funded bonuses for Wall Street executives (2009); or, more generally, the scores of 2011–2012 hearings by the GOP-controlled House committees searching for ways to slash federal spending. The mere threat of a congressional hearing is often enough to keep agencies in line. But Congress's investigative authority is not without limits. Earl Warren, when he was chief justice of the U.S. Supreme Court, wrote in *Watkins v. United States* (1957):

> There is no general authority to expose private affairs of individuals without justification in terms of the functions of Congress. . . . Nor is the Congress a law enforcement or trial agency. These are functions of

the executive and judicial departments of government. No inquiry is an end in itself; it must be related to, and in furtherance of, a legitimate task of the Congress.[93]

By collecting and analyzing information, House and Senate inquiries can clarify whether new laws are needed to address public problems. They also sharpen Congress's ability to scrutinize executive branch activities, such as the expenditure of funds, the implementation of laws, and the discharge of duties by administrative officials. Investigations also inform the public by disseminating and revealing information. "Congress provides a forum for disclosing the hidden aspects of governmental conduct," wrote two Senate members of the Iran-contra investigating committee. It allows a "free people to drag realities out into the sunlight and demand a full accounting from those who are permitted to hold and exercise power."[94] Hearings and investigations are, in short, valuable devices for making government accountable to the people. They can spawn new laws or their functional equivalent: change in bureaucratic operations.

Congressional Vetoes

Congress has little choice but to delegate sweeping authority to administrative agencies. The question, then, is how Congress can control those agencies. One answer historically has been the legislative veto (or congressional veto), a statutory enactment that permits presidents or agencies to take certain actions subject to later approval or disapproval by one or both houses of Congress (or in some cases by committees of one or both houses). Legislative vetoes are arrangements of convenience for both branches. Executives gain decision-making authority they might not have otherwise, and Congress retains a second chance to examine decisions.

In 1983 many forms of the legislative veto were declared unconstitutional by the Supreme Court (*Immigration and Naturalization Service v. Chadha*). The Court's majority held that the device violated the separation of powers, the principle of bicameralism, and the presentation clause of the Constitution (legislation passed by both chambers must be presented to the president for his signature or veto). The decision, wrote Justice Byron R. White in a vigorous dissent, "strikes down in one fell swoop provisions in more laws enacted by Congress than the court has cumulatively invalidated in its entire history."[95]

Congress has repealed some veto provisions since *Chadha* and amended others, while continuing to employ a wide range of oversight techniques to monitor executive actions. Yet despite the *Chadha* ruling, legislative vetoes of the committee variety continue to be enacted into law. Public law scholar Louis Fisher has summed up the status of legislative vetoes:

Are they constitutional? Not by the Court's definition. Will that fact change the behavior between committees and agencies? Probably not. An agency might advise the committee: "As you know, the requirement in this statute for committee prior-approval is unconstitutional under the Court's test." Perhaps agency and committee staff will nod their heads in agreement. After which the agency will seek prior approval of the committee.[96]

Self-interest impels agencies to pay close attention to the wishes of members of Congress, especially those who sit on their authorizing or appropriating panels.

Mandatory Reports

Congress can require the president, federal agencies, or departments to assess programs and report their findings.[97] Reports can act "as a mechanism to check that laws are having the intended effect." Moreover, they can "drive a reluctant bureaucracy to comply with laws it would otherwise ignore."[98] Each year, executive agencies prepare several thousand reports for submission to Congress. Because of the massive size and important role of the Defense Department, it is not surprising that the Pentagon is tasked with preparing numerous reports for Congress. During an August 2010 departmental briefing, Defense Secretary Robert Gates noted, "In 1970, the Pentagon produced a total of 37 reports for the Congress, a number that topped off at more than 700 reports in last year's cycle."[99] Trying to reduce the number of outdated or duplicative reports—which Congress does periodically—often comes with the requirement that agencies be more responsive to committees' requests for information. A spokesperson for Howard "Buck" McKeon, R-Calif., the former chair of the House Armed Services Committee, said his boss would be happy to work with the secretary of defense to eliminate various reporting requirements if the Pentagon would do "a better job of providing specific programmatic and policy information in a timely manner" to the committee.[100]

Nonstatutory Controls

Congressional committees also use informal means to review and influence administrative decisions. These range from telephone calls, letters, personal contacts, and informal understandings to statements in conference reports, hearings, and floor debates.[101] Committee reports frequently contain phrases such as "the committee clearly intends that the matter be reconsidered" or "the committee clearly intends for the Secretary to promote" or "the committee clearly expects."

On occasion, OMB directors tell federal agencies to ignore report language because it is not legally binding. Lawmakers of both parties and chambers (and even executive officials), however, may seek to thwart such directives. Sometimes, members threaten to make all report language legally binding on agencies, thereby limiting the agencies' flexibility and discretion in resolving issues.[102] Although their usage is not measured, nonstatutory controls may be the most common form of congressional oversight.

Inspectors General

In 1978 Congress created a dozen independent offices for inspectors general (IGs). Since then, Congress has established inspectors general offices in nearly every federal department and agency. IGs conduct audits and investigations of agency programs and operations; prevent and detect fraud and abuse in such programs and operations; and keep Congress and agency heads fully informed on a timely basis about problems and the need for corrective actions. Granted wide latitude and independence, IGs are "the government's first line of defense against fraud."[103]

Inspectors general testify frequently before congressional committees and submit directly to Congress reports on their efforts to root out waste, fraud, and abuse. For example, the Labor Department IG determined that a departmental initiative to improve worker safety in hazardous industries "rarely fulfilled its promise" because of uneven inspections and enforcement. The result was fifty-eight fatalities that might have been prevented.[104] The Pentagon's IG detailed billions of dollars in waste and fraud by military contractors.[105]

The Appropriations Process

Congress probably exercises its most potent oversight of agencies and programs through the appropriations process. By cutting off or reducing funds (or threatening to do so), Congress can abolish agencies, curtail programs, or obtain requested information. Upset that the secretary of the Department of Housing and Urban Development (HUD) was flying off to various conferences rather than dealing with the housing foreclosure crisis, appropriators eliminated the secretary's travel budget. "Frankly, I want to cause [HUD] officials a little personal pain," declared one legislator. He said he wanted them to "just plant their butts at their desks and do the job that they were appointed to do."[106] In another case, a House Appropriations subcommittee chair, angry because the Homeland Security Department had not provided reports on its spending priorities, declared, "They've just been ignoring us. They'll pay for that."[107] By the same token, Congress can build up program areas by increasing their appropriations—sometimes beyond the levels that the administration has requested.

The appropriations power is exercised mainly through the House and Senate Appropriations Committees, especially through each panel's twelve standing subcommittees. These panels annually recommend funding levels for federal agencies and departments so that they have the funds to carry out their program responsibilities. The budgetary recommendations of the Appropriations subcommittees are generally accepted by their parent committee and by the House or Senate.

The Appropriations Committees and their subcommittees, or members from the House or Senate floor, may offer amendments that limit the purposes for which money may be spent ("limitation riders") or that impose other spending limits on federal agencies. Funding bills also may contain various policy directives to federal agencies—for example, prohibiting agencies from using funds to promulgate or issue certain regulations. Such directives are often in the form of floor amendments. "These amendments," wrote two GOP senators, "are an important way for Congress to save taxpayers from wasteful agency spending, and they enjoy a long-standing precedent because of their use by Republican and Democratic Congresses alike to rein in the excesses of Republican and Democratic administrations."[108] Political scientist Jason A. McDonald has also underscored the legislative importance of limitation amendments in influencing agency actions. They provide "Congress with much more influence than scholars have appreciated over not only everyday policy decisions within agencies (which in and of itself would be significant), but also over the substance of regulations about which members of Congress, and their constituencies, care for political and policy reasons."[109]

Impeachment

Article II, section 4, of the Constitution states: "The President, Vice President, and all Civil Officers of the United States, shall be removed from office on Impeachment for, and Conviction of, Treason, Bribery, or other high Crimes and misdemeanors." This removal power is the ultimate governmental check vested in Congress.[110] The House has the authority to impeach an official by majority vote. It then tries the case before the Senate, where a two-thirds vote is required for conviction.

Only impeached federal judges have been convicted by the Senate. The most recent case occurred on December 8, 2010, when the Senate voted for only the eighth time to convict and remove from office a federal district judge in Louisiana.[111] As for presidents, the House impeached President Andrew Johnson in 1868, after Radical Republicans in the House charged that he had violated the Tenure of Office Act by dismissing the secretary of war. The Senate acquitted Johnson by a single vote. Facing probable impeachment and conviction, President Richard M. Nixon resigned in 1974 after the House Judiciary Committee voted articles of impeachment. In December 1998, President Clinton became the first elected president to be impeached by the House. (Johnson was not elected; he became president when Abraham Lincoln was assassinated.) The charges against Clinton were perjury and obstruction of justice. Two months later, the Senate voted acquittal on both articles of impeachment.[112]

Oversight: An Evaluation

Congress's willingness to conduct regular and meaningful oversight stems from several factors: public dissatisfaction with government; revelations of executive agency abuses; the influx of new legislators skeptical of government's ability to perform effectively; concern about the growth of a regulatory state; the availability of seasoned congressional staff; and recognition by Congress that it must make every dollar count.[113] Of these several factors, two stand out as especially important motivators of oversight since Republicans' capture of the House in November 2010 and again in November 2012. First, top GOP leaders have made cutting agencies and programs a major priority, and second, many in the populace want to rein in the reach of the federal government.

The perspective of the two Congresses highlights the electoral, political, and policy incentives that encourage members to oversee the bureaucracy. One of these incentives is the opportunity to claim credit for assisting constituents and to receive favorable publicity back home. Another is the prodding by interest groups and the media. Committee and subcommittee chairs "seek a high pay off—in attention from both the press and other agencies—when selecting federal programs to be their oversight targets."[114] Members on the relevant committees of jurisdiction are also motivated to induce favorable agency and departmental action on pet policies or programs.

Divided government—the president of one party, Congress (or one chamber) controlled by the other—encourages vigorous congressional oversight. Oversight simultaneously enables opposition lawmakers to supervise agency activities and look for ways to undermine the administration's policy goals or public reputation. Simply responding to scores of subpoenas issued by committees controlled by the opposition party can sap the time and energy of the White House and agency officials. By comparison, under unified government, the majority party in Congress tends to engage in less oversight. As one senior GOP lawmaker said of the unified period (2003–2007) when Republicans were in charge, "Our party controls the levers of government. We're not about to go out and look beneath a bunch of rocks to cause heartburn."[115] Party loyalty, in short, overcame institutional responsibility.

Whether there is unified or divided government, congressional oversight may not probe as deeply as some might wish. "We have not done our job in terms of oversight," declared Sen. Tom Coburn, R-Okla.[116] Friendly alliances can develop among the committees that authorize programs, the agencies that administer them, and the interest groups that benefit from governmental services. Many committees are biased toward the programs or agencies they oversee. They want to protect and nurture their progeny and make program administration look good. Without concrete allegations of fraud or mismanagement, committees may lack the incentive to scrutinize and reevaluate their programs. This kind of cooperative oversight can dissuade committees from conducting meaningful inquiries that require agencies to justify their existence and contribution to the public's well-being

A standard rationale for oversight is that it ensures that laws are carried out according to congressional intent. But because many laws are vague and replete with multiple objectives, they are difficult to assess. Moreover, proof that programs are working as intended may not emerge for years. Congressional patience may wane as critics conclude that there are no demonstrable payoffs for the taxpayer. Alternatively, oversight may identify program flaws but not reveal what would work or even whether there is any ready solution.

In the 112th Congress, the need to establish oversight priorities was underscored by Darrell Issa, R-Calif., the House's leading investigator as chair of the Oversight and Government Reform Committee. "I don't need to be looking at every failure of government," he said. "I need to be looking at where failure of government needs reform. You bring it back to Congress and we fix it."[117] Chairman Issa solicited the input of 150 companies, trade associations, think tanks, and scholars, "asking them to come up with a list of the most onerous existing and proposed regulations that are hurting job creation and economic growth."[118] Democrats complained that this initiative catered too much to moneyed interests rather than the broad middle class.

Each oversight technique has limitations. Hearings may provide dramatic episodes, but they often result in minimal follow-up. The appropriations process is usually hemmed in by programmatic needs for financial stability. And statutes are often blunt instruments of control. Other obstacles to effective oversight include inadequate coordination among committees sharing jurisdiction over a program; sporadic review by committees of departmental activities; and frequent turnover among committee staff aides, a situation that limits their understanding of the programs created by Congress.

Critics who fault Congress's oversight may be erecting unattainable standards. Many analysts are looking for what scholars have come to call "police-patrol" oversight—active, direct, systematic, planned surveillance of executive activities. Instead, Congress often waits until the "fire alarms" sound—set off by interest groups, the press, staff aides, and others concerned about administrative violations—before it begins to review in detail agencies' activities.[119]

Congress may be benefitting from some extra police-patrol assistance offered by a combination of civic-minded individuals and technology. A current trend is the "public as watchdog." A good example is the enactment in 2006 of the Federal Funding Accountability and Transparency Act, informally called the "Google your government" law because it required OMB "to provide a user-friendly, searchable database" of nearly $1 trillion in federal grants and contracts.[120] Websites such as recovery.gov or stimuluswatch.org allow citizens to monitor the projects that receive taxpayer dollars. The GAO has a website and hotline to enable citizens to report allegations of waste, fraud, or mismanagement of federal funds. And Chairman Issa has established a whistleblower website where agency employees can alert committee staff of fraud and abuse in their agency. Majority Leader Cantor's website contains a feature dubbed YouCut that permits the public to vote on "which government programs should be cut."[121]

There are even informal "citizen regulators" who test children's toys and clothing to protect them from harmful chemicals. "I'm not going to rely on an agency that changes personnel based on administrations and takes years to make any kind of change," remarked the mother of a three-year-old.[122] The promise of these actions is that they enable any interested person or watchdog group to monitor federal spending or products available in stores across the nation and make their evaluations known to congressional lawmakers. The blogosphere, in short, adds millions of extra eyes to congressional oversight.

Micromanagement

Because oversight often means legislative intrusion into administrative details, executive branch officials sometimes complain about congressional micromanagement. Even though the executive bureaucracy may react with dismay, Congress's focus on administrative details is as old as the institution itself. The structural fragmentation of the House and Senate encourages examination of manageable chunks of executive actions. Members realize that power inheres in details, such as prescribing personnel ceilings for agencies. Presidents who oppose certain programs can starve them to death by shifting employees to favored activities. Thus Congress may specify personnel ceilings for some agencies. "It is one of the anomalies of constitutional law and separated powers," writes Louis Fisher, "that executive involvement in legislative affairs is considered acceptable (indeed highly desirable) while legislative involvement in executive affairs screams of encroachment and usurpation."[123]

CONCLUSION

Because of continual shifts in the balance of legislative and executive prerogatives, the age-old issue of executive independence versus congressional scrutiny will not be settled. Yet the recent interest in oversight has had almost no discernible effect on the size and scale of the executive branch or on the main roles and responsibilities of the legislative branch. After all, committees are not disinterested overseers but rather guardians of the agencies and programs under their purview. Together with their satellite interest groups, committees and agencies form subgovernments or issue networks that dominate many policy-making areas.

Court Politics. Solicitor General Elena Kagan (top) begins the third day of Senate Judiciary Committee hearings on her nomination to the Supreme Court. President Obama hugs Justice Ruth Bader Ginsburg as he arrives for his 2011 State of the Union message (center); Justices Anthony Kennedy and Stephen Breyer look on. In March 2013 gay rights organizations (bottom) protested two days of Supreme Court consideration of LGBT issues, including the 1996 "Defense of Marriage Act" (DOMA), which among other things prevents legally married same-sex couples from collecting earned federal benefits.

Congress and the Courts

"Scarcely any political question arises in the United States that is not resolved, sooner or later, into a judicial one," wrote Alexis de Tocqueville in *Democracy in America*, his classic 1835 study of early American life.[1] Perhaps no controversy has illustrated Tocqueville's truism as well as the events following passage of the Patient Protection and Affordable Care Act of 2010 ("Obamacare"). Obamacare was quickly challenged as unconstitutional in courts across the country. The lower courts split, some upholding it, others agreeing with the opponents of the law. But no one thought that the lower courts would have the last word on such an important "political question" as the constitutionality of a landmark piece of legislation.

The Supreme Court heard extended arguments on multiple challenges to Obamacare. Following the oral arguments in the case, commentators wrote innumerable analyses of the justices' questioning of the attorneys and the attorneys' performance and speculated intensely on how the Court would decide the fate of the law. On the fateful day (June 28, 2012) when the justices handed down their decision, hundreds of demonstrators gathered outside the Supreme Court building in a circus-like atmosphere that included Tea Party activists, dueling chants and signs, and even a trio of belly dancers gyrating in Obamacare's favor. In the end, the Court, in a rather convoluted fashion, upheld the most controversial aspect of Obamacare, the individual mandate to purchase health insurance. But the complexity of the Court's ruling caused CNN initially to report that Obamacare had been struck down, leading its opponents gathered outside to cheer. Those cheers quickly turned to groans and angry words as the actual nature of the Court's 5–4 decision to uphold the individual mandate became clear.

As in the Obamacare decision, the Supreme Court is typically viewed as having the final, authoritative interpretation of the Constitution—a power referred to as "judicial review." The U.S. Supreme Court first asserted the prerogative of judicial review in the landmark case of *Marbury v. Madison* (1803).[2] At the same time, Congress and the president also interpret the Constitution. As the Supreme Court stated in *United States v. Nixon* (1974), "In the performance of assigned constitutional duties each branch of the Government must initially interpret the Constitution, and the interpretation of its powers by any branch is due great respect from the others."[3]

Conflicts between Congress and the federal courts are inevitable. The most famous episode occurred during the New Deal when the Supreme Court invalidated thirteen acts of Congress in one term (1935–1936). Frustrated, President Franklin D. Roosevelt proposed legislation to increase the number of justices, and thus to provide him the opportunity to nominate judges more sympathetic to his program. Widespread legislative and public opposition, however, defeated Roosevelt's Court-packing scheme. Nevertheless, the Court, perhaps sensitive to the changes under way in the country, became more accommodating in interpreting key constitutional provisions. In 1937 the Court handed down a decision that upheld a state minimum wage law similar to one that it had previously ruled unconstitutional.[4] In that same year, the Court also upheld a federal law governing management-labor relations, recognizing a far greater congressional power to regulate commerce than the Court's precedents had permitted. This abrupt turnaround by the Court was, as a wit of the period put it, "the switch in time that saved nine."

THE FEDERAL COURTS

Although the framers detailed the structure and authority of Congress in Article I of the Constitution, Article III leaves the creation of the federal courts other than the Supreme Court wholly to the discretion of Congress. Thus the judicial branch owes less to constitutional mandates and more to the legislation establishing its structure and the rulings of the early justices, such as Chief Justice John Marshall (1801–1835). As a noted legal scholar explained:

> Congress was created nearly full blown by the Constitution itself. The vast possibilities of the presidency were relatively easy to perceive and soon, inevitably materialized. But the institution of the judiciary needed to be summoned up out of the constitutional vapors, shaped and maintained. And the Great Chief Justice, John Marshall—not single-handed, but first and foremost—was there to do it and did.[5]

The most important constitutional provision related to the courts is the guarantee of lifetime tenure for Article III judges. The framers of the Constitution wanted an independent judiciary—that is, a judiciary insulated from political pressure. This independence is an important part of the American system of separation of powers and a source of friction between Congress and the courts. Although Congress is not without influence, the federal courts, including the Supreme Court, have the institutional ability to frustrate congressional policy.

The federal court system today is comprised of district courts, courts of appeals, and the Supreme Court. The district courts are the federal trial courts, which deal with a range of civil matters and federal criminal cases. In addition to Article III district judges, the district courts are staffed by magistrate judges, who serve a fixed term and assist the district judges in handling the civil and criminal caseloads. The district courts also house the federal bankruptcy courts, which are staffed by specialized judges serving a fixed term.

District courts are analogous to congressional committees in the sense that most of the work of the federal courts is done at that level. District courts are organized by state, in a manner similar to congressional districts. Each state, and the District of Columbia, has at least one, with larger states (such as Texas and California) having as many as four. The primary function of the district courts is "norm enforcement"—that is, applying relatively settled law to disputes.

Above the district courts are the courts of appeals, which are organized in eleven regional circuits. There is also a circuit for the District of Columbia, and one additional circuit, the Federal Circuit, with a nationwide but specialized jurisdiction centering mainly on appeals of administrative agency rulings. Parties unhappy with the outcome of a case at the district court level typically have an automatic right of appeal to the appellate level. These courts are staffed by judges typically called circuit judges. The courts of appeals hear oral arguments and decide cases in three-judge panels. In rare circumstances, a three-judge panel's decision will be reviewed by a larger number of circuit judges, sitting "en banc." The primary function of the courts of appeals is "error correction"—that is, reviewing the work of lower courts, and some executive branch agencies, for mistakes of law or fact.

Parties unhappy with the outcome of an appeal can seek Supreme Court review of their cases, but unlike at the court of appeals level, Supreme Court review is almost never automatic. Instead, the Court decides which cases from the courts of appeals and the state courts of last resort it will hear. Typically, the Supreme Court will hear and decide about 1 percent of the cases in which one or both parties have requested review. As a result, the Court's docket is dominated by cases raising important questions of constitutional and statutory interpretation. Unlike the lower federal courts, the Supreme Court does not engage in norm enforcement, and it rarely takes a case for the sole purpose of correcting an error committed by a lower court. Instead, its policy-making role is paramount.

The Supreme Court's policy making is carried out in three main ways. First, its interpretive decisions can uphold or broaden the legislative powers of Congress. The ruling upholding Obamacare, for example, was a significant victory for President Barack Obama and his congressional allies. In deciding that Congress's powers extended far enough to mandate that all Americans purchase health insurance, the Court established what is arguably a new "outer limit" for Congress's power over interstate commerce. Five justices agreed that Congress could not impose the individual mandate using its "commerce clause" power because those being regulated were not, in a practical sense, engaged in economic activity when not buying health insurance. However, five justices (with only Chief Justice John Roberts in both majorities) agreed that Congress could achieve the same result using its taxation power—indeed, the penalty for failing to purchase health insurance is to be administered by the Internal Revenue Service.[6]

Second, it can check overreaching by Congress through its implied power of judicial review. Checking Congress was, naturally, the role that opponents of Obamacare argued the Court should play. Third, and equally significant, the Supreme Court can act as a policy-making catalyst, especially when the House or Senate is stymied in making decisions. The landmark civil rights case of *Brown v. Board of Education* (1954) is a classic example. The decision struck down the separate-but-equal doctrine that had upheld state laws mandating racially segregated public schools. Before this decision, filibusters by southern senators had thwarted enactment of meaningful civil rights bills. The *Brown* ruling galvanized Congress to enact the Civil Rights Act of 1957, the first civil rights law enacted by Congress since 1875. "The genius of a system of divided powers," wrote one law professor, "is that when one branch is closed to the desires of the populace or the demands of justice, another may open up."[7] Even so, the *Brown* decision alone had little impact on the actual desegregation of public schools until Congress began to pass landmark legislation such as the Civil Rights Act of 1964 and the Elementary and Secondary Education Act of 1965.

THE COURT AS REFEREE AND UMPIRE

The Supreme Court serves as both referee between the two nationally elective branches and umpire in federal-state relations. Ever since the Court claimed the power of judicial review in 1803, it has considered a large number of separation-of-powers and federalism issues. Whether acting as referee or umpire, the Supreme Court is often attacked for usurping the prerogatives of the other national branches, or of the state and local governments. Members of Congress "often reserve their most vituperative criticism of federal courts for decisions that, in their view, unduly limit the prerogatives of state and local governments to regulate such matters as abortion, school prayer, prison overcrowding, school busing, local elections, and so on."[8]

A common refrain in criticism of the courts is that judges are acting as a "super legislature" in their rulings—that is, they are legislating from the bench. The charge of "judicial activism" is premised on the view that at least in some cases, judges are making decisions based on their personal values and not the dictates of law, or that they are making decisions that their critics believe should be settled by the elective branches of government.

Judicial activism, however, is frequently in the eye of the beholder. When, for example, the Supreme Court ruled 5–4 in *District of Columbia v. Heller*[9] that the Second Amendment protects an individual's right to own firearms— thereby overturning long-standing law in the District and, by implication, elsewhere—relatively few conservative commentators charged the Court with judicial activism. Many liberals, by contrast, saw the *Heller* case as a clear example of conservative judicial activism.[10] On the other hand, when the Supreme Court ruled, also 5–4, in *Kelo v. City of New London* that the power of eminent domain could be used to condemn a private residence to promote local economic development, liberals praised the Court's judicial restraint in permitting democratically accountable local governments to make such decisions free from judicial second-guessing.[11] Meanwhile, conservatives denounced the case as "liberal activism."[12]

The charge of judicial activism often serves as a way of denouncing judicial decisions that politicians and opinion leaders oppose on other grounds. In the broader context of partisan and ideological polarization, the judiciary has come in for harsh attacks from many quarters. Retired Supreme Court justice Sandra Day O'Connor commented that "the breadth and intensity of rage currently being leveled at the judiciary may be unmatched in American history. The ubiquitous 'activist judges' who 'legislate from the bench' have become central villains on today's domestic political landscape."[13]

The Referee

Like the federal courts, Congress interprets the Constitution. When it makes national policy through its lawmaking processes, it is also asserting that it has the constitutional power to do so. As a result, it is not uncommon for the two branches to view issues differently. To be sure, the Supreme Court often exercises restraint when it addresses the powers of Congress or the president for two key reasons: to avoid charges of judicial overreaching and to acknowledge that only the elective institutions can implement judicial judgments. But the Court sometimes frustrates congressional or executive policy, which can, in some cases, trigger a reaction.

The Lily Ledbetter case (2007) illustrates how congressional majorities may react to Supreme Court decisions with which they strongly disagree. Ledbetter received less pay than her male counterparts at Goodyear. After twenty years on the job, she learned of Goodyear's discriminatory treatment and sued on the grounds of gender-based pay and employment discrimination. The Supreme Court determined, however, that the statute of limitations in Title VII of the Civil Rights Act had expired and precluded Ledbetter's suit. The Court ruled, in a 5–4 decision, that Ledbetter's lawsuit was not timely because she did not file the suit within 180 days of the date on which the lower pay had been agreed to by the parties. The Court rejected the argument that the statute of limitations restarted with every discriminatory paycheck. A vigorous dissent by Justice Ruth Bader Ginsburg chided the Court's majority for their ignorance of workplace realities and noted that Congress could clarify the law.

Many lawmakers rejected the Court's interpretation of legislative intent in the *Ledbetter* decision. As one of its first actions, the 111th Congress (2009–2011) passed legislation, which President Obama signed into law, overturning *Ledbetter* and resetting the statute of limitations with every discriminatory paycheck, thereby making it easier for workers to challenge gender-based employment discrimination.[14]

Mindful of the courts' referee role, lawmakers have sought to employ it for their own goals. On a number of occasions, members of Congress have tried to enlist the courts to defend congressional prerogatives against usurpation by the president. War making is the principal example. Recent presidents of both parties have committed American troops to combat on their own initiative. In response, some members have gone to court to seek limits on the president's powers. As for war power suits brought by lawmakers, scholar Louis Fisher takes a cautionary view:

> In most of these cases, the courts held that the lawmakers lacked standing to bring the case. Even when legislators were granted standing, the courts refused relief on numerous grounds. Judges pointed out that the legislators represented only a fraction of the congressional membership and that often another group of legislators had filed a brief defending the president's action. Courts regularly note that Congress as a whole has failed to invoke its institutional powers to confront the president.[15]

Usually courts dismiss these suits and offer two rationales: first, the lawsuits raise political questions best left to the elective branches to resolve; and second, they represent conflicts between groups of lawmakers, not constitutional clashes between Congress and the president.

The fundamental question is how much deference the Court should show to the elected branches. Lawmakers and presidents are accountable to their constituents every time they face reelection. Although judges are not immune to the tides of public opinion, they do not face accountability through elections. On the other hand, a key virtue of an independent judiciary is that it can, in theory, protect unpopular or politically weak minority groups against unconstitutional deprivations of liberty. The tension between policy making by elected officials versus judge-made decisions is perennial.

The Umpire

As the federalism umpire, the Supreme Court is the arbiter of federal and state powers. This role was also front and center in the Supreme Court battle over Obamacare. One controversial aspect of the law was its expansion of the state mandates under the federal Medicaid program. Medicaid is a health insurance program for low-income Americans. Under a cooperative federalism model, the federal government provides funding to states to establish their own Medicaid programs, provided that the states comply with federal rules that create minimum standards for who and what is covered by the (state) program. States thus have a choice to participate in the Medicaid program or not, in keeping with their residual sovereignty. Medicaid funding has become an important part of many state budgets, and by the 1980s, all fifty states participated in the program. From time to time, however, state governors complain that the regulations imposed as a condition of receiving Medicaid funding are onerous on the states.

The Obamacare legislation imposed new Medicaid guidelines on the states to expand health insurance coverage to the uninsured poor not previously covered by existing Medicaid guidelines. To encourage all states to adopt these new guidelines, the legislation included a provision that states rejecting the new Medicaid coverage requirements would lose not only the expansion of Medicaid dollars, but also the support they currently received for their Medicaid programs. Several states argued this was federal coercion—that is, because Medicaid has become such an important part of state budgets, a threat to deprive states of all Medicaid revenue would leave the states with no choice at all but to accept the new expansion of the program.

As with the individual mandate, the Court decided this issue in a rather convoluted manner. Indeed, seven justices agreed that the conditions attached to the Medicaid expansion were unconstitutional, but they split in terms of the remedy. The two justices who would have upheld the conditions in their entirety joined with three justices who rejected the new mandate to hold that states declining to expand Medicaid under Obamacare could maintain their existing Medicaid funding as long as they complied with the applicable federal guidelines for that funding. In the end, the ruling permitted states to choose whether or not to expand their Medicaid rolls to cover those newly qualified under Obamacare without losing all federal support for their existing Medicaid program.[16] In this case, as in many others, the Court regulates the balance between federal and state power.

Statutory Interpretation

The distinction between statutory and constitutional interpretation is very important. In statutory interpretation, federal judges construe the meaning, or intent, of the often vague language embedded in laws. Constitutional interpretation occurs when federal or state laws are challenged as violating the U.S. Constitution.

Carr v. United States provides a recent example of the Court engaging in statutory interpretation. In 2006 Congress enacted the Sex Offender Registration and Notification Act (SORNA), which, among other things, made it a federal crime for sex offenders who travel "in interstate or foreign commerce" to fail to register in a new jurisdiction. The defendant in the case had moved from Alabama, where he was a registered sex offender, to Indiana prior to SORNA's enactment. The lower court, however, held that SORNA's registration requirement was retroactive. The Court, in an opinion by Justice Sonia Sotomayor, disagreed, holding that the text of the statute showed that Congress did not intend the "travels in" provision to have retroactive effect. That the provision "sets forth the travel requirement in the present tense ('travels') rather than in the past or present perfect ('traveled' or 'has traveled') reinforces the conclusion that preenactment travel falls outside the statute's compass," she wrote.[17] In short, statutory interpretation in this case and in others requires the Court to construe what is and is not covered by laws passed by Congress.

In determining whether national or state actions violate the Constitution, federal judges examine the text of the Constitution, the intentions of the drafters, and judicial precedents relevant to the controversy. In the death penalty area, the Court also considers society's evolving standards regarding such punishment because the Eighth Amendment forbids "cruel *and unusual* punishments" (emphasis added).

The major difference between statutory and constitutional interpretation is the ease with which Congress can reassert its understanding of the law against the Supreme Court. When the Court misinterprets a statute, Congress can simply amend or clarify the law, as it did in the *Ledbetter* case. By contrast, a constitutional decision of the Court is binding on Congress and can be undone only by a subsequent constitutional amendment—which is very rare—or by the Court itself when it overrules one of its precedents.

Judicial interpretation of federal statutes is fraught with difficulty because communications between Congress and the federal courts are highly imperfect. Neither branch understands the workings of the other very well.[18] Ambiguity, imprecision, or inconsistency can often be the price of winning enactment of legislative measures. The more legislators try to define precisely the language of a bill, the more they may divide or dissipate congressional support for it. Abner J. Mikva, a four-term House Democrat from Chicago who went on to become a federal judge and later counsel to President Bill Clinton, recounted an example from his Capitol Hill days. The issue involved a controversial strip-mining bill being managed by Arizona Democrat Morris K. Udall, then chair of the House Interior (now called Natural Resources) Committee:

> They'd put together a very delicate coalition of support. One problem was whether the states or the feds would run the program. One member got up and asked, "Isn't it a fact that under this bill the states would continue to exercise sovereignty over strip mining?" And Mo replied, "You're absolutely right." A little later someone else got up and asked, "Now is it clear that the Federal Government will have the final say on strip mining?" And Mo replied, "You're absolutely right." Later, in the cloakroom, I said, "Mo, they can't both be right." And Mo said, "You're absolutely right."[19]

Called upon to interpret statutes, judges may not appreciate the efforts required to get legislation passed on Capitol Hill or understand how to examine legislative history, as manifested in hearings, reports, and floor debate. Within the courts and among legal scholars, there is a lively debate over the proper way to approach statutory interpretation. Should judges focus only on the plain meaning of the statutory language, or should they delve into legislative history to ascertain what Congress intended when it employed certain statutory phrases? A group of federal judges, led by Supreme Court justice Antonin Scalia, argues that legislative history is unreliable as an indicator of legislative intent because it is open to manipulation by lawmakers, executive officials, and congressional staffers.

One remarkable example of the manipulation of legislative history occurred in the context of the Senate passage of the Detainee Treatment Act (DTA) in late 2005. An important issue before the federal courts at the time was whether the DTA would retroactively nullify all the pending legal challenges of the Guantánamo detainees. Two sponsors of the legislation, Sen. Lindsey O. Graham, R-S.C., and Sen. Jon Kyl, R-Ariz., sought to quash all such challenges, while another sponsor, Sen. Carl Levin, D-Mich., wanted to allow cases filed before the passage of the DTA to go forward.[20] But just before passage of the legislation, Graham and Kyl inserted into the *Congressional Record* a colloquy designed to show that the Senate intended to invalidate all pending legal challenges brought by Guantánamo detainees. Written in informal style, the colloquy contained banter suggesting that the exchange occurred live on the Senate floor. Such a colloquy would have alerted all senators that Graham and Kyl believed the legislation would foreclose all pending cases, and the absence of subsequent objections would imply that senators agreed with this interpretation. However, a C-SPAN recording showed that the discussion never actually occurred on the Senate floor. Justice Department lawyers nevertheless cited the colloquy in their legal brief arguing that Congress intended to remove all the pending cases from federal jurisdiction.[21] In response, a lawyer for one of the detainees objected: "This colloquy is critical to the government's legislative history argument, and it's entirely manufactured and misrepresented to the court as having occurred live on the Senate floor before a crucial vote."[22]

Rather than relying on legislative history, Scalia contends that justices should follow a textualist approach, examining the wording of laws or constitutional clauses and interpreting them according to what they meant at the time of enactment.[23]

Justice John Paul Stevens expressed a contrary opinion, saying that a "stubborn insistence on 'clear statements' [in the law] burdens the Congress with unnecessary reenactment of provisions that were already plain enough." Former representative Barney Frank, D-Mass., once remarked that if Scalia's view on legislative history became dominant, Congress would be required to develop a new category of legislation: "the 'No, we really meant it' statute."[24] The chief counsel of the Senate Judiciary Committee observed that difficulty in textual interpretation "encourages us to write clearer legislation. But unclear bills are still written. If they were not, we would not have this fight over [the confirmation of] judges."[25]

Legislative Checks on the Judiciary

Many factors are likely to generate conflict between Congress and the courts. With federal judges serving life tenure, turnover on the courts is often far slower than in Congress. Meanwhile, the ideological and partisan composition of Congress can diverge widely from that of the federal courts. In addition, some Supreme Court rulings have direct and profound effects on Congress and its members. Cases involving the redistricting of House seats and campaign finance are recent examples. Scores of interest groups also monitor court decisions, and, when they disagree with them, these groups are not reluctant to lobby Congress to seek their statutory reversal.

Congress has a variety of tools by which it can influence the Supreme Court and lower federal courts. In addition to the Senate's constitutional advice and consent role regarding judicial nominations, four legislative powers merit some mention: (1) to withdraw jurisdiction; (2) to impeach judges; (3) to influence the size, procedures, and pay scales of the courts; and (4) to pass constitutional amendments.

Withdrawal of Jurisdiction. The jurisdiction of the federal courts, including the Supreme Court, is delimited by both Article III and statute. Congress can thus alter the jurisdiction of the federal courts to achieve policy goals.

In some circumstances, Congress may seek to expand federal court jurisdiction—usually at the expense of state courts—to achieve particular policy goals. In the post–Civil War period, for example, Congress expanded federal court jurisdiction in an effort to protect the civil rights of African Americans.[26] Republican Congresses in the latter half of the nineteenth century also expanded federal court jurisdiction in order to protect commercial interests against state controls.[27] Similarly, the Class Action Fairness Act of 2005 expanded federal jurisdiction over many large class-action lawsuits, a key goal of business groups that had been frustrated by plaintiff lawyers' "forum shopping" to find the most friendly state courts.

But Congress's power over the jurisdiction of the federal courts, including the Supreme Court, serves as a potential check on judicial overreach. Under its constitutional authority to determine the Supreme Court's appellate jurisdiction, for example, Congress may threaten to withdraw the Court's authority to review certain categories of cases. Recent years offer several examples of such threats. One issue concerned a Ninth Circuit Court of Appeals decision that a 1954 federal law adding the phrase "one Nation under God" to the Pledge of Allegiance was unconstitutional on First Amendment grounds. In response, House majority leader Tom DeLay, R-Texas, remarked, "I think that [legislation limiting the court's jurisdiction] would be a very good idea to send a message to the judiciary [that] they ought to keep their hands off the Pledge of Allegiance."[28] Other topics—such as same-sex marriage and the public display of the Ten Commandments—evoked similar responses. Some scholars have argued that such threats of court-curbing legislation affect judicial decision making. One recent study found that the Supreme Court responds to the introduction of court-curbing legislation by striking down fewer laws in subsequent years.[29]

Despite the ongoing conflicts between Congress and the courts, on only one occasion in U.S. history did Congress prevent the Supreme Court from deciding a case by removing its appellate jurisdiction:

> This extraordinary action was taken by a Congress dominated by Radical Republicans who wanted to prohibit the Supreme Court from reviewing the constitutionality of the Reconstruction Acts of 1867. The acts substituted military rule for civilian government in the ten

southern states that initially refused to rejoin the Union and established procedures for those states to follow to gain readmittance and representation in the federal government.[30]

Congress simply passed legislation repealing the Supreme Court's right to hear appeals involving these matters, thereby preventing "a possibly hostile Court from using the power of judicial review to invalidate a piece of legislation."[31] Various scholars have identified a variety of reasons why court-curbing legislation is so rarely adopted: "the historically broad consensus in Congress to protect, or at least tolerate, an independent judiciary; judicial opponents' reluctance to emasculate an institution that they may someday need as an ally; ... and resistance by the organized bar."[32]

Impeachment of Judges. Federal judges, like other national civil officers, are subject to impeachment under Article II of the Constitution. They are appointed "during good behavior," effectively for life. Only one Supreme Court justice, Samuel Chase, has ever been impeached by the House. It occurred in 1804, during bitter partisan battles between Federalists and Jeffersonian Republicans. The judiciary was the last bastion of Federalist influence after Thomas Jefferson won the presidency in the 1800 election. Chase's intemperate and arrogant behavior—he even campaigned for John Adams's reelection in 1800—raised the ire of Jefferson and his allies in Congress. On March 12, 1804, the House voted 73–32 along party lines to impeach Chase. The Senate, however, failed to convict (and thus remove) him. The importance of Chase's acquittal by the Senate was underscored in a book by Chief Justice William Rehnquist:

> The acquittal of Samuel Chase by the Senate had a profound effect on the American judiciary. First, it assured the independence of federal judges from congressional oversight of the decisions they made in the cases that come before them. Second, by assuring that impeachment would not be used in the future as a method to remove members of the Supreme Court for their judicial opinions, it helped to safeguard the independence of that body.[33]

Other Supreme Court justices have been either threatened with impeachment or subjected to impeachment investigations. One example is William O. Douglas in 1953 and in 1970.

Fifteen federal judges have been impeached, and eight have been removed by a two-thirds vote in the Senate.[34] The 111th Congress (2009–2011) saw active impeachment proceedings against two district judges. In May 2009, Judge Samuel B. Kent of the Southern District of Texas was convicted of obstruction of justice, resulting from an investigation of claims that he had sexually abused two female court staffers. He was sentenced to thirty-three months in prison. He did not, however, resign from the bench, meaning that he continued to collect his judicial salary. His refusal to step down drew protests from Capitol Hill, which prompted Kent to announce that he would resign in one year. Press reports suggested that Kent believed that it would take at least that long for the House and Senate to act. This frankness led to immediate initiation of impeachment proceedings in the House, and the House soon voted unanimously to impeach Kent. He then resigned, before the Senate could try him.

On December 8, 2010, the Senate voted unanimously to remove Judge Thomas Porteous Jr. of the Eastern District of Louisiana from the bench. Porteous was impeached on four articles, based on corruption and making false statements on his financial disclosure reports.

These recent examples of judicial impeachments are representative of such cases throughout U.S. history. Judges have been impeached for unethical and illegal acts, but not because of the legal and policy judgments rendered during the course of their judicial duties. The "Impeach Earl Warren" billboards and bumper stickers that appeared all across the South in the 1960s in the wake of *Brown v. Board of Education* do not represent how impeachment has been used. It is outside congressional norms to employ impeachment as a mechanism to exert political influence over the judiciary.

Size, Procedure, and Pay. Historically, the size of the Supreme Court has varied anywhere from six to ten members. "Generally, laws decreasing the number of justices have been motivated by a desire to punish the president; increases have been aimed at influencing the philosophical balance of the Court itself" (such as Roosevelt's Court-packing plan).[35] But since 1869 Congress has not changed the Court's size from its current nine justices, so this power is unlikely to be invoked in the foreseeable future.

Procedurally, lawmakers have occasionally proposed that Supreme Court decisions overturning federal laws be accomplished by a supermajority vote of the justices. Some of the "more extreme proposals have urged that such decisions be unanimous."[36] None of these proposals has been adopted. Instead, they serve as signals to the judiciary that lawmakers disapprove of certain court decisions. Lawmakers have also communicated complaints to the judicial branch by calling for stronger ethical guidelines for judges to ensure their impartiality, though the judicial branch claims that such oversight would violate judicial independence.[37]

Another legislative proposal that has generated interbranch controversy is opening federal courtrooms to television cameras. Several justices have opposed televising Supreme Court proceedings, in part because the cameras might alter decision making, intrude on the privacy of the justices by making them public celebrities, and threaten their personal security. During an appearance before the Senate Judiciary Committee, Justice Anthony Kennedy implored senators not to pass legislation mandating the televising of their open proceedings.[38] His concern was that televised Court sessions would eventually undermine the collegial character of the Court and encourage the justices to speak in sound bites. Attitudes toward cameras in the courtroom may be changing, however. In her confirmation hearings, the Court's newest member,

Elena Kagan, said that she thought "it would be a great thing for the institution and for the American people" to be able to watch Supreme Court arguments on television.[39] Justice Sotomayor has expressed similar views.

A current concern is that fewer aspirants are seeking federal judgeships. Part of the reason is pay. "Salaries are far lower [for federal judges] than what fresh-faced law-school grads can make at big corporate firms."[40] Chief Justice John Roberts devoted much of his 2008 annual year-end report on the federal judiciary to the inadequacy of judicial salaries. The judicial branch as a whole made a major push in the 110th Congress for a judicial pay increase. The effort won the support of House and Senate leaders and President George W. Bush, but a few powerful members of Congress axed the bill.

Congressional opposition to increased judicial pay stems from so-called linkage. Under current law, the salaries of federal judges and members of Congress are linked.[41] Lawmakers' reluctance to raise their own salaries—for obvious political reasons—is a large part of the reason why federal judges' salaries have not kept pace with inflation. To raise judicial salaries substantially, members of Congress would have to agree to "de-link" their salaries from those of judges, thereby depriving members of political cover on the occasions when they decide to raise their own salaries. The chief justice currently receives an annual salary of $223,500, associate justices $213,900, appeals court judges $184,500, and federal district judges $174,000.[42] By comparison, law school deans can earn over $400,000 a year and top law firm partners $1 million or more a year.[43] Some analysts, however, question whether there are benefits to paying judges more.[44] The present state of the federal budget makes any substantial increase in judges' salaries unlikely in the near future.

Constitutional Amendments. On four occasions, Congress successfully used the arduous process of amending the Constitution to overturn decisions of the Supreme Court. In *Chisholm v. Georgia* (1793), the Court held that citizens of one state could sue another state in federal court.[45] To prevent a rash of citizen suits against the states, Congress oversaw passage of the Eleventh Amendment to reverse this decision and protect states' sovereign immunity from lawsuits brought by citizens of other states and foreign countries. The *Dred Scott v. Sandford* (1857) decision[46]—denying African Americans citizenship under the Constitution—was nullified by the Thirteenth Amendment (abolishing slavery) and Fourteenth Amendment (granting African Americans citizenship). The Sixteenth Amendment overturned *Pollock v. Farmer's Loan and Trust Co.* (1895), which struck down a federal income tax. The Twenty-sixth Amendment invalidated *Oregon v. Mitchell* (1970), which held that Congress had exceeded its authority by lowering the minimum voting age to eighteen for state elections.[47]

Generally, lawmakers are reluctant to amend the Constitution. The view of Rep. Melvin Watt, D-N.C., reflects that of many members: "I just think the Constitution has served us very well over a long, long period of time, and one needs to make a compelling case before we start amending the Constitution to do anything."[48] However, certain constitutional amendments have appeared regularly on the legislative agenda. One would ban desecration of the American flag. The proposal is a response to a 1989 Supreme Court ruling in *Texas v. Johnson* that state laws banning flag burning violate the First Amendment right of free speech. The House has passed an anti–flag desecration amendment several times, but the Senate has never approved the measure.

Eliminating life tenure for federal judges is another proposal that some-times surfaces on Capitol Hill. Bitter judicial nomination battles have prompted some observers to suggest term limits (such as fifteen years) for federal judges. "If the Senate can't figure out how to reach a [partisan] truce in its battles over these all-important jobs," wrote one analyst, "maybe the best solution is to make the jobs not quite so important."[49] Others simply contend that Supreme Court justices serve too long. Aging justices, it is argued, may become arrogant, out of touch with contemporary values, or too impaired to serve. To avoid the difficulties of winning approval of a constitutional amend-ment, they propose a legislative approach that would move "justices into senior status after roughly eighteen years on the high court."[50]

ADVICE AND CONSENT FOR JUDICIAL NOMINEES

Article II, section 2, of the Constitution states that the president "shall nomi-nate, and by and with the Advice and Consent of the Senate, shall appoint . . . Judges of the Supreme Court." The founders rejected giving the power to appoint judges solely to the executive, to Congress as a whole, or to the Senate. In the end, they compromised and required joint action by the president and the Senate. The president has the sole prerogative to nominate, but the power to confirm (or not) belongs to the Senate. Alexander Hamilton, in *Federalist* No. 66, viewed this division of responsibility in stark terms: "There will, of course, be no exertion of CHOICE on the part of the Senate. They may defeat one choice of the Executive and oblige him to make another; but they cannot them-selves CHOOSE—they can only ratify or reject the choice he may have made."

Hamilton's perspective, however, requires some refinement. Giving two elective institutions a voice in the appointments process necessarily means that the Senate is able to influence the president's choice of nominees. Indeed, indi-vidual senators, House members, interest groups, the American Bar Association (which since 1952 has rated judicial candidates), the Federalist Society, the press and media, and even sitting judges can all sometimes influence both the choice of judicial nominees and Senate action, if any, on those nominees. The fact that federal district and appellate court jurisdictions are geographically based means that senators from those states (especially if they are of the presi-dent's party) commonly have a big say in recommending judicial candidates to the White House (see Table 12-1 for judgeship appointments by presidents).

Any discussion of the various norms, practices, and controversies associ-ated with the confirmation process for federal judges must be prefaced by a description of the half-dozen principal stages in filling a vacancy on the Supreme Court.

TABLE 12-1	**Judgeship Appointments by President, 1933–2013**

President	Supreme Court	Regional Court of Appeals	USCAFC[1]	District Courts	Total
F. Roosevelt (1933–1945)	9	52	—	136	197
Truman (1945–1953)	4	27	—	102	133
Eisenhower (1953–1961)	5	45	—	127	177
Kennedy (1961–1963)	2	20	—	102	124
L. Johnson (1963–1969)	2	41	—	125	168
Nixon (1969–1975)	4	48	—	182	231
Ford (1974–1977)	1	12	—	52	65
Carter (1977–1981)	0	56	—	206	262
Reagan (1981–1989)	3	78	5	292	378
G. H. W. Bush (1989–1993)	2	37	5	149	193
Clinton (1993–2001)	2	62	4	306	374
G. W. Bush (2001–2009)	2	61	2	261	326
Obama[2] (2009–2013)	2	32	4	157	195

Sources: Adapted from "Judgeship Appointments by President," *The Third Branch,* newsletter of the federal courts, February 2009. Data for the Obama administration are from the Federal Judicial Center, www.fjc.gov/history/home.nsf/page/research_categories.html. The work of CRS experts Steven Rutkus and Barry McMillion is gratefully acknowledged.

[1] The U.S. Court of Appeals for the Federal Circuit (USCAFC) was established in 1982.

[2] Data are through June 17, 2013.

First, the president puts together a short list of nominees. Considerable thought and research go into the list. Presidents want to nominate individuals who reflect their political and policy views and are generally perceived as highly competent and knowledgeable. Many political considerations also enter the selection process. The gender, race, geographic, and religious makeup of the Court may be relevant to the choice. Presidents consider the nominee's age, seeking a qualified candidate who will be able to serve a lengthy tenure on the Court. They look to the composition of the Senate and assess the prospects of an easy or difficult confirmation battle.

The contemporary selection process also includes careful vetting of potential nominees' personal and professional lives. Typical of recent presidents, the research process conducted for the nominees on Obama's short list when Justice David Souter announced his retirement was intensive. Researchers scoured "the real estate transactions, taxes, ethics, the backgrounds of spouses and adult children, as well as a particularly close look at the early jobs held right after law school—often at the Justice Department—when early views could have been formed and when a paper trail of thousands of documents was probably created."[51]

Second, once the president has made his choice, he sends a written nomination to the Senate, which is then referred to the Judiciary Committee. The nominee is escorted to various Hill offices to meet and talk with key senators. Meanwhile, the nominee begins extensive preparation for the hearings before the Judiciary Committee. Part of the preparation commonly involves participation in mock confirmation hearings called "murder boards."

Third, the Judiciary Committee launches its own investigation of the nominee's background and qualifications. After that stage is completed, the Judiciary chair schedules public hearings on the nomination. The members of the committee have the opportunity to ask the nominee questions and also to receive testimony from other witnesses. Although it is unthinkable today that the committee would not proceed in this way, it is notable that confirmation hearings were unheard of for most of the nation's history. In 1925 Attorney General Harlan Fiske Stone was the first Supreme Court nominee to testify in public before the Judiciary Committee. Stone had made political enemies cleaning up the Justice Department in the aftermath of the Teapot Dome scandal—and by vigorously enforcing the nation's antitrust laws. Certain senators signaled that they might block Stone's appointment in light of the Justice Department's handling of a related indictment against Sen. Burton K. Wheeler, D-Mont. To answer questions about his handling of the Wheeler case, Stone apparently offered to appear before the committee in a public hearing.[52] Still, confirmation hearings did not become customary until the mid-1950s.

Fourth, after the hearings are concluded, the Judiciary Committee meets in open session to report the nomination to the Senate either with a favorable or negative recommendation, or with no recommendation at all. Dating back to at least the 1880s, the "Judiciary Committee's traditional practice has been to report even those Supreme Court nominations that were opposed by a committee majority, thus allowing the full Senate to make the final decision on whether the nominee should be confirmed."[53] (This practice does not apply to nominees for district or appellate court judgeships.) Once reported by the committee, the nomination is assigned to the Senate's executive calendar.

Fifth, the Senate majority leader decides when to call up the nomination for chamber consideration after consultation with various lawmakers, including the minority leader. Once the nomination reaches the floor, all senators have an opportunity to discuss the nominee's credentials, philosophy, or anything else they believe is relevant for the public record. Extended debate, or a filibuster, is unusual on Supreme Court nominations. Cloture is available to curb talkathons but has been moved only four times: in 1968, on Abe Fortas's nomination to be chief justice; in 1971, on William Rehnquist's nomination to be an associate justice; in 1986, on Rehnquist's nomination to be chief justice;[54] and in 2006, on Samuel A. Alito's nomination to replace Justice Sandra Day O'Connor. After debate ends, in a practice begun in 1967, the Senate decides whether to confirm the Supreme Court nominee by a roll call vote.[55]

Sixth, if a majority of the Senate votes to confirm, the secretary of the Senate transmits the resolution of confirmation to the president. The president then signs a document called a commission that officially appoints the nominee to the Supreme Court. The attorney general signs the engraved commission and delivers it to the nominee, who then takes the constitutional oath of office making him or her a justice of the U.S. Supreme Court.

Norms and Practices

Extraconstitutional norms and practices shape the confirmation process. President George Washington, for example, quickly learned the importance of the newly emerging norm of senatorial courtesy—an informal practice in which presidents consult home-state senators before submitting nominees for federal positions in their state. When he "failed to seek the advice from the Georgia senate delegation regarding a nomination for a federal position in Savannah, Washington was forced to withdraw the nomination in favor of the person recommended by the senators."[56]

Related to senatorial courtesy is the blue slip policy of the Judiciary Committee, which applies only to district and court of appeals nominees. In recent years, the practice has been for both home-state senators to be consulted through this procedure, regardless of party. Interestingly, the Obama administration worked diligently to secure the blue slip approval of GOP home-state senators and had a great deal of early success in doing so.[57] That success was undercut, however, by what one observer described as "systematic leadership-led refusal to consent" to moving ahead with nominations.[58] It seems that as in many other aspects of Senate procedures, the individual prerogatives of senators are losing ground to the leadership's partisan strategies.

An array of other Senate practices also influence whether any action occurs on judicial nominations, such as the hold, the committee chair's prerogative of determining whether hearings will be held, and the majority leader's willingness to schedule floor consideration of the nominations. As for holds, the 112th Congress adopted Res. 28, the Wyden/Grassley/McCaskill Secret Holds Resolution, with the intention of eliminating the practice of secret holds.[59] Sen. Ron Wyden, D-Ore., said of the resolution, "If you want to exercise that extraordinary power, you ought to do it in the sunlight."[60] Whether eliminating secret holds—which can be used to block judicial nominees—will actually reduce delays in confirming judges remains to be seen.

An unresolved issue is the balance between advice and consent. Presidents usually favor consent over advice. The Senate tilts in the other direction. "It's advice and consent, not nominate and rubber stamp," declared Sen. Patrick Leahy, D-Vt.[61] The qualifications appropriate for service as a federal jurist are not self-evident. The Constitution makes no reference to what presidents or senators should consider when exercising their respective roles (being a lawyer is not even a prerequisite). Setting aside the standard qualifications that everyone expects in prospective judges—legal experience, ethical behavior, recognized competence, and so on—an age-old question is whether people should be subject to litmus tests to be either nominated or confirmed for a judicial position. Should judicial nominees disclose their views on hot-button issues likely to come before the Court? Most recent nominees have studiously refused to reveal much about their views on such issues when questioned by senators.

Nomination Battles

Over the last two centuries, the Senate has "rejected about 20 percent of all Supreme Court nominees."[62] Most of the rejections occurred in the nineteenth century, with President John Tyler holding the record: five of his six nominees were rejected by the Senate (see Table 12-2).

The bitter confirmation battles of the present originate with President Ronald Reagan's nomination of conservative Robert H. Bork to the Supreme Court in 1987. A Democratic-controlled Senate rejected Bork, who was perceived as too conservative, by a 58–42 margin. The political campaign mobilized against the nomination gave rise to a new verb, to bork. Conservative groups were outraged by the ways in which Bork was treated by the Democratic-controlled Senate.

Since the failed Bork nomination, senators have become increasingly unwilling to support Supreme Court nominees selected by presidents of the opposing party.[63] In 1986 Antonin Scalia was confirmed by the Senate 98–0, even though it was clear that he was a staunch judicial conservative. President Clinton's two nominees in the early 1990s—Ruth Bader Ginsburg in 1993 and Stephen Breyer in 1994—each garnered opposition from a handful of conservative senators. President George W. Bush's nominees—John Roberts and Samuel Alito—were met with even more widespread Democratic opposition, with only half of Senate Democrats voting in favor of Roberts and only four Democrats in favor of Alito. Senate votes on President Obama's Supreme Court nominations— Sonia Sotomayor and Elena Kagan—broke down along party lines, with only nine Republicans voting for Sotomayor and only five Republicans voting for Kagan. "We have shifted from a basic expectation that absent a reason to vote against a nominee members of the opposing party will support a president's nominee," said Benjamin Wittes, senior fellow at the Brookings Institution. "In a very short period of time, that has reversed to a presumption that members of the opposition party will oppose the president's nominee, absent a reason to support him or her. That is a very profound change."[64]

The Kagan nomination in many ways illustrates the underlying partisan logic of opposition to Supreme Court nominees in the contemporary era. One criticism raised of Kagan's nomination was her lack of judicial experience. Other than Kagan, every current justice is a former federal appeals court judge. It is, of course, an open question whether membership on the highest court should reflect a broader diversity of backgrounds. From Chief Justice John Marshall's day through Earl Warren's, for example, the Court typically included members steeped in legislative or executive experience. In the Court's recent history, only Supreme Court justice Sandra Day O'Connor ever held an elective office; she was an Arizona state senator. Some legal scholars suggest that a wider range of occupational experiences on the Court would serve an important representational function and enhance decision making "with a variety of issues in the electoral and legislative spheres."[65] Opponents of her nomination, nevertheless, cast Kagan's lack of judicial experience as a "qualifications" issue.

Rather than oppose a nominee based on ideology, there is every reason to think that a president's partisan opponents prefer to fight Supreme Court nominations on the qualifications issue. Sen. Charles E. Schumer, D-N.Y., has argued that senators should forthrightly take ideology into account in voting on Supreme Court nominations rather than look for other pretexts for opposing judges with whom they disagree. "For one reason or another, examining the ideologies of judicial nominees has become something of a Senate taboo," writes Schumer. "Unfortunately, the taboo has led senators who oppose a nominee for ideological reasons to justify their opposition by finding non-ideological factors, like small financial improprieties from long ago. This 'gotcha' politics has warped the confirmation process."[66]

Recent research suggests that the relationship between qualifications and the ideology of nominees has shifted since the Bork nomination fight. Political scientist Lee Epstein and her coauthors found that before Bork, senators were willing to vote for moderately qualified nominees, even if there was some ideological distance between them and the nominee. Post-Bork, however, they found that senators were less willing to vote for ideologically distant nominees, regardless of qualifications. Epstein and her coauthors summed up the situation: "the president's discretion over whom to nominate to the Supreme Court has grown far more circumscribed over the last two decades."[67] Perhaps this observation helps to explain recent presidents' preferences for nominees with court of appeals experience rather than controversial political records.

Consent and Dissent

Until recently, little controversy was associated with scrutinizing judges named to serve on the lower federal courts. Today, fierce conflict between the parties and branches overlays the confirmation process for many judicial nominees, especially for the appellate courts. "The politicization of the judiciary has recently been the most focused, and most virulent, at the appellate, or circuit level," said federal judge James Robertson.[68]

The George W. Bush presidency saw intense clashes over federal appeals court nominees, with minority party Democrats using numerous obstructionist techniques to delay Senate consideration of the president's nominees.[69] In the spring of 2005, Republican frustration over judicial filibusters became so

TABLE 12-2 **Supreme Court Nominations Not Confirmed by the Senate**

Nominee	President	Date of nomination	Senate action	Date of Senate action
William Paterson	George Washington	February 27, 1793	Withdrawn[1]	
John Rutledge[2]	Washington	July 1, 1795	Rejected (10–14)	December 15, 1795
Alexander Wolcott	James Madison	February 4, 1811	Rejected (9–24)	February 13, 1811
John J. Crittenden	John Quincy Adams	December 17, 1828	Postponed	February 12, 1829
Roger Brooke Taney	Andrew Jackson	January 15, 1835	Postponed (24–21)[3]	March 3, 1835
John C. Spencer	John Tyler	January 9, 1844	Rejected (21–26)	January 31, 1844
Reuben H. Walworth	Tyler	March 13, 1844	Withdrawn	
Edward King	Tyler	June 5, 1844	Postponed	June 15, 1844
Edward King	Tyler	December 4, 1844	Withdrawn	
John M. Read	Tyler	February 7, 1845	Not acted upon	
George W. Woodward	James K. Polk	December 23, 1845	Rejected (20–29)	January 22, 1846
Edward A. Bradford	Millard Fillmore	August 16, 1852	Not acted upon	
George E. Badger	Fillmore	January 10, 1853	Postponed	February 11, 1853
William C. Micou	Fillmore	February 24, 1853	Not acted upon	
Jeremiah S. Black	James Buchanan	February 5, 1861	Rejected (25–26)	February 21, 1861
Henry Stanbery	Andrew Johnson	April 16, 1866	Not acted upon	
Ebenezer R. Hoar	Ulysses S. Grant	December 15, 1869	Rejected (24–33)	February 3, 1870
George H. Williams[2]	Grant	December 1, 1873	Withdrawn	

Nominee	President	Date	Action	Date of final action
Caleb Cushing[2]	Grant	January 9, 1874	Withdrawn	
Stanley Matthews	Rutherford B. Hayes	January 26, 1881	Not acted upon[1]	
William B. Hornblower	Grover Cleveland	September 19, 1893	Rejected (24–30)	January 15, 1894
Wheeler H. Peckham	Cleveland	January 22, 1894	Rejected (32–41)	February 16, 1894
John J. Parker	Herbert Hoover	March 21, 1930	Rejected (39–41)	May 7, 1930
Abe Fortas[2]	Lyndon B. Johnson	June 26, 1968	Withdrawn	
Homer Thornberry	Johnson	June 26, 1968	Not acted upon	
Clement F. Haynsworth Jr.	Richard M. Nixon	August 18, 1969	Rejected (45–55)	November 21, 1969
G. Harrold Carswell	Nixon	January 19, 1970	Rejected (45–51)	April 8, 1970
Robert H. Bork	Ronald Reagan	July 1, 1987	Rejected (42–58)	October 23, 1987
Douglas H. Ginsburg	Ronald Reagan	October 29, 1987	Withdrawn	
Harriet Miers	George W. Bush	October 3, 2005	Withdrawn	

Source: Joan Biskupic and Elder Witt, Guide to the U.S. Supreme Court, 3d ed., vol. 2 (Washington, DC: Congressional Quarterly, 1997), 707: authors' notes.

[1] Later nominated and confirmed.

[2] Nominated for chief justice.

[3] Later nominated for chief justice and confirmed.

great that Senate majority leader Bill Frist, R-Tenn., threatened to use a parliamentary maneuver called the "nuclear option" to end the talkathons. Under the maneuver, the majority leader would raise a point of order that further debate on a controversial nominee was dilatory. The Republican presiding officer would rule in his favor, and if the Democrats appealed the ruling, Frist would move to table (or kill) the appeal. The result: judicial nominations would be subject to an up-or-down majority vote rather than the Senate's cloture process (which requires sixty votes). The maneuver was never executed, however, because a bipartisan group of fourteen senators opposed Frist's plan while also simultaneously providing sufficient votes to secure Senate approval of some of the disputed nominees.

The level of conflict over judicial nominations has not abated under President Obama. In fact, during the Obama administration even district court nominations became more controversial. Several factors explain these developments.

First, interest groups are aware that federal judges make critical decisions across a broad spectrum of policy issues. Both parties understand that although the Supreme Court is viewed as the court of last resort, it decides only about 70 to 80 cases each year (a decade ago the number was 107).[70] By contrast, the twelve regional appeals courts and the federal circuit courts decide more than 63,000 cases annually.[71] The courts of appeals are "playing a more important role in setting law for vast areas of the country. A decision by the Ninth Circuit, for example, is binding on nine states, where 19 percent of the nation's population lives."[72] According to one law professor, the courts of appeals are "the Supreme Courts for their region."[73] Interest groups may also be growing more sensitive to the discretion of district judges, especially in complex commercial litigation and employment discrimination cases. Many of the procedural rulings of district judges in such cases are not generally reviewed by appellate courts, but can seriously affect cases involving corporate defendants.

Second, some confirmation fights are clearly warm-ups for potential Supreme Court vacancies down the line. Because of the preferences of recent presidents for court of appeals judges, blocking a (potentially) controversial nominee from the appellate bench likely eliminates that person from future consideration for the high court.

Third, in presidential election years there is often a drop-off in the number of judges confirmed by the Senate. Senate majority leader Harry Reid, D-Nev., has even called this informal slowing down the "Thurmond rule," after former senator Strom Thurmond, R-S.C. In the 112th Congress, press reports indicated that Senate minority leader Mitch McConnell, R-Ky., implemented the Thurmond rule for court of appeals judges in June, but that district court confirmations would end sometime in September.[74] Although some dispute that there is a so-called Thurmond rule, and in order to share the blame with Democrats others prefer to call it the "Leahy-Thurmond rule,"[75] the political reality is indeed a marked decline in the number of appellate judges confirmed during presidential election years. One study concluded that for "all judicial nominations submitted between 1947 and 2008, appointees for the Courts of Appeals pending in the Senate in a presidential election year were nearly 40 percent less likely to be confirmed than nominees pending in other years."[76] A law professor explained why this pattern occurs: "The priority for the party not in control of the White House is not so much in stopping candidates based on their ideology, but keeping as many vacancies open as possible on the theory that the next president may be someone of your party and will be able to fill those slots."[77]

Finally, it is simply far more difficult for the Senate to provide advice and consent for lifetime judicial appointments in an environment where the ideological chasm between the two parties is so wide. Unlike legislation, once the Senate confirms a judicial nominee there is no opportunity for a subsequent Senate to reverse the decision except through the impeachment process. After all, confirmation battles represent a clash between the president and the opposition party in the Senate over who will control the ideological balance of power on the courts. President George W. Bush, for example, was "more consistent and insistent than, say, [Gerald R.] Ford or Reagan" in nominating conservatives to the bench.[78] "If Democrats just rolled over on Bush's nominations," said one political analyst, "they would be guilty of oppositional malpractice."[79] There is no doubt that President Bush was successful in recasting federal courts in a more conservative direction.

President Obama has not been equally aggressive. On the ideological front, the Obama administration has gravitated toward relatively centrist jurists, perhaps in an effort to avoid "culture war" issues in the confirmation process. That effort has been largely unsuccessful, as Senate Republicans have, in the words of one prominent journalist, "ratchet[ed] up partisan warfare over judges . . . by delaying even uncontroversial picks who would have been quickly approved in the past."[80]

Many supporters of the Obama administration have also been disappointed by the administration's slow pace in making nominations.[81] The slow nominations pace in the 111th Congress may have been caused, at least in part, by staffing issues at both the Office of White House Counsel and the Office of Legal Policy (OLP) at the Department of Justice—the two executive branch entities with responsibility for vetting judicial nominees. Senate Republicans held up the nomination for the assistant attorney general to head up the OLP for over a year.[82] Obama's first White House counsel, Gregory Craig, was focused on national security issues, including the decision whether to close the prison at Guantánamo Bay, Cuba.[83] As one administration critic commented, "I don't see anything that they . . . did to make it a priority. They didn't staff it sufficiently at the White House."[84]

As of the end of June 2013, there were eighty-one vacancies on the lower federal courts but only twenty-nine nominees awaiting Senate consideration.[85] In other words, the Obama administration had not yet put forward names for more than half the existing vacancies. To some extent this may reflect the consultative approach the Obama administration has taken to making nominations. But this is also consistent with longer-term trends. Political scientists Sarah Binder and Forrest Maltzman found that presidents in the postwar period have been taking progressively longer in making lower-court nominations, even after taking into account other factors.[86] The Obama administration's slow rate of nominations is consistent with these broader historical trends.

It is likely that much of the growing delay in making nominations results from enhanced vetting of potential nominees. Binder and Maltzman suggest that because of the increased incentives of the opposition party to obstruct lower-court nominations, presidents may react by scouring nominees' backgrounds in search of possible grounds for Senate opposition. In other words, to avoid a stalled nomination, presidents may be stalling before making the nominations. Whatever the reason, the sixty lower-court judges confirmed during Obama's first two years in office is the lowest number in thirty-five years.[87]

CONCLUSION

Federal courts, like Congress and the president, are central forums for resolving the political, social, and economic conflicts that characterize American society. All three branches of government interact constantly to shape the laws under which Americans live. Sometimes, as presidents say, "the buck stops here." In Congress, the buck may stop nowhere, and either elective branch may pass the buck to the courts when it is unable to resolve certain issues. "Through this process of interaction among the branches," writes scholar Louis Fisher, "all three institutions are able to expose weaknesses, hold excesses in check, and gradually forge a consensus on constitutional values."[88]

Interest Group Influence. A staff member for AARP (American Association of Retired Persons, the nation's largest membership lobby) weighs members' responses to the controversial Medicare drug bill—a boon to drug and insurance companies that the organization backed (top). Lobbying partners— former Sens. Trent Lott, R-Miss. (1989–2002), and John Breaux, D-La. (1987–2005)—represent Shell Oil Co. to promote ratification of the Law of the Sea Treaty (center left). "Tea Party" activists rally on Capitol Hill to "hold the line" on federal spending (bottom left). Mass demonstrations seek to impress lawmakers through sheer numbers: hundreds march on the Capitol grounds to protest the Obama administration's health-care bill (bottom right).

13

Congress and Organized Interests

Comprehensive and controversial legislation inevitably provokes large lobbying efforts by proponents and opponents of the measures. Popular protests for and against such legislation are part of the nation's democratic fabric, as individuals and special interests mobilize to influence policy outcomes. Consider a brief example of the lobbying forces activated during consideration of President Barack Obama's massive and successful overhaul of the nation's health care system.

Three weeks before the landmark health care overhaul plan—the Patient Protection and Affordable Care Act—was signed into law by President Obama on March 23, 2010, five thousand protestors picketed the Ritz Carlton Hotel in Washington, D.C. Inside, America's Health Insurance Plans (AHIP), the trade association of the health insurance industry, was holding its annual lobbying conference. Among the goals of the conference was to lay out a strategy to oppose passage of health reform unless it protected the interests of the industry. The protestors outside the conference, members of a broad coalition of over a thousand organizations (such as labor, consumer, and civil rights), were seeking to confront the insurance industry and win media attention, gain public support for health care reform, and secure legislative backing for President Obama's health care plan. "The message we have is simple," exclaimed the director of Health Care for Americans Now (HCAN), the group that organized the protest at the Ritz Carlton. "Congress should listen to us, not the insurance industry."[1]

Meanwhile, lawmakers could not help but hear the cacophony of messages and voices advocating for and against health care reform. Record numbers of pressure group lobbyists and citizen activists were swarming Washington, seeking influence over virtually every facet of the health plan. Health companies and trade associations hired "more than 4,500 lobbyists to influence health reform—amounting to about eight lobbyists for each member of Congress."[2] MoveOn.org sponsored a "virtual march" on Capitol Hill, sending more than one million pro-reform e-mails to lawmakers' offices. Conservative groups such as the National Right to Life Committee purchased television ads and organized grassroots campaigns to pressure wavering congressional Democrats to vote against "Obamacare." Marches, rallies, demonstrations, conferences, radio and television advertising, the print media, YouTube, blogs, and more were used to influence congressional decision makers. The U.S. Chamber of Commerce even commissioned an economic study to portray the health bill as a job killer and harmful to the nation's economy, budgeting $50,000 to hire a prominent economist to do the study. The next step called for the economist to circulate "a sign-on letter to hundreds of other economists saying that the bill will kill jobs and hurt the economy." The open letter would be used "to produce advertisements, and as a powerful lobbying and grass-roots document."[3]

Groups on all sides of the health care issue spent huge sums to mold the final product. The medical interests alone (doctors, hospitals, drug companies, and various health businesses), which were not monolithic in their preferences, spent a record $876 million (for a business sector) over fifteen months (January 2009 to March 2010) to influence the debate and shape the measure to their liking. Unlike the Clinton administration's 1993–1994 health reform plan, when the health industry was united in its opposition, much of the $876 million was spent in support of President Obama's plan. Even after the plan was enacted into law, lobbying expenditures on health care continued. According to Tony Podesta—whose firm, the Podesta Group, ranked second in fees received during the debate on Obama's plan—his clients were keen on influencing "how the measure is implemented and in any corrections Congress might make."[4]

AMERICAN PLURALISM

The fifteen-month battle to enact comprehensive health care reform—an idea advocated at least since the administration of President Teddy Roosevelt— illustrates the dual nature of American pluralism. On the one hand, a vast array of organized interests, most of them headquartered in the nation's capital, seek to influence government policy. This is the "Washington system" of lobbyists and insider access that inspires so much populist rhetoric and public distaste.[5] Narrow profit motives were hardly absent from the health reform debate, as lobbyists sought legislative concessions to line their clients' pockets.

On the other hand, also weighing in on the issue were membership organizations, some of them huge. By means of such organizations, Americans assemble "to petition the government for redress of grievances," in the words of the Constitution's First Amendment. Groups of Americans legitimately concerned about how health care reform might affect the quality, affordability, and accessibility of medical treatments made their concerns known.

The controversy surrounding health care reform illustrates the ambivalence that characterizes both scholarly and journalistic considerations of American pluralism. The world of interest groups prompts fears of a government corrupted by narrow special interests. And yet organized interests are not only constitutionally protected, but also a foundation of civil society and a natural by-product of democratic freedom. President Harry S. Truman, in a wry response to a reporter's question—"Mr. President, would you be against lobbyists who are working for your program?"—remarked: "Well, that's a different matter. We probably wouldn't call these people lobbyists. We would call them citizens appearing in the public interest."[6]

A Capital of Interests

Capitol Hill lobbyists regularly fill committee hearings and markups, jam into conference committee rooms, and pack House and Senate galleries. These emissaries of organized interests do more than observe congressional events. They wield their vast resources—money, connections, personnel, information, and organization—to win passage of legislation they favor and reward the politicians who help them. Practically every major corporation, trade association, and professional group has Washington lobbyists. Lobbyists even have their own association: the American League of Lobbyists. Mindful that lobbyists have long been criticized and demonized by scores of public officials, pundits, and others, the league's president organized a public relations offensive to "help people understand that the 'L' word is not a bad word." He added:

> We're going to be demonstrating that everybody has a lobbyist out there. The second you get up in the morning and you have your toast and eggs, the wheat and poultry lobbyists are involved. Then you get into your car, and you have the Toyota lobbyists. When you log on to your computer and surf the Web, don't forget about the Google lobbyists. Most people have no idea that they have so many lobbyists in their day.[7]

A look inside the Washington telephone directory under "associations" reveals as much as the Constitution about what moves Congress. Washington is home to more national associations (and the 260,000 people they employ) than any other city.[8] Numerous law, financial, technology, and public relations firms have opened offices in the District of Columbia, and the growing cadres of consultants and lawyers represent diverse clients, including foreign governments. As the head of a financial trade group noted, "A financial institution—whether it's a bank or a nonbank of any size—needs to have a Washington office. It puts you at a competitive advantage to have a Washington presence [because you] can have input into the [lawmaking] process."[9]

The lobbying community probably constitutes the third-largest industry employer in the nation's capital, behind government and tourism. Indeed, President Obama's successful initiative to overhaul the financial regulatory system prompted banks, securities firms, and Wall Street firms to hire "more than 3,000 lobbyists to shape the bill," or roughly five lobbyists per Capitol Hill lawmaker.[10] "The more the government gets involved in an industry's affairs," declaimed an experienced lobbyist, "the more industry hires people to figure that out."[11] When control of one or both houses of Congress moves from one party to another, the changeover often sparks a boost in lobbying hiring and expenditures as organized interests seek out better access to new congressional leaders. "It's standard operating procedure in Washington that whenever there is a shift in power, there is a scramble by companies to make sure they have adequate representation with the new power brokers," explained the head of the Center for Responsive Politics, a D.C.-based think tank.[12]

Spending on lobbying usually grows despite broader economic downturns. Lobbying expenditures by companies, associations, and their clients totaled $3.5 billion in 2010—over twice as much as in 2000.[13] However, in 2011 and 2012 lobbying expenditures declined somewhat, in part because of the sluggish job-producing economy, the low legislative productivity, partisan gridlock in Congress, the ban on earmarks, and other factors. For example, just "six of the top 25 lobbying practices posted revenue growth last year over 2011." One result is that the "big K Street practices are trying to replace lost lobbying dollars with messaging, grass-roots organizing or social media advocacy," as well as doing more work for state and foreign governments.[14] "Lobbyists are also beating a path to the agencies more than the House and Senate," noted a lobbyist, because of the extensive regulatory activity associated with the statutory enactment of financial reform legislation and the Affordable Care Act.[15]

An experienced lobbyist emphasized that the recent dip in revenue for many lobbying groups must be assessed in the context of the past several years: "The fact that I'm down 10 percent [in 2011], I'm still up from where I was a few years ago" when revenue growth was nearly 50 percent.[16] To be sure, a number of lobbying organizations witnessed revenue increases of over 10 percent in 2012, in part because they attracted new clients. (In 2011, total lobbying expenditures amounted to $3.4 billion.)

A Nation of Joiners

Americans' zest for joining groups was noted long ago by Alexis de Tocqueville. Americans of all "conditions, minds, and ages daily acquire a general taste for association and grow accustomed to the use of it," he wrote in 1835.[17] Throughout American history, groups speaking for different subsets of "the people" have swayed public policies and politics. The nineteenth-century abolitionists fought to end slavery. The Anti-Saloon League crusaded for the prohibition of alcohol in the 1900s. Liberal movements in the 1960s and 1970s protested the Vietnam War, racial discrimination, and abuse of the environment. In the 1970s and 1980s, interest groups galvanized support for or against equal rights for women. In the 1990s, conservative groups pushed term limits for lawmakers, a balanced budget amendment, and tax cuts. More recently, antiabortion groups, immigration-reform and gun-control advocates, and both liberal and conservative membership organizations, from Moveon.org to the Tea Party to Occupy Wall Street, have played a prominent role in the political debate and process.

A free society nurtures politically active groups. "Liberty is to faction what air is to fire," wrote James Madison in *Federalist* No. 10. In recent years, interest groups have grown in number and diversity. For example, the American

Medical Association dominated health lobbying for decades, but today hundreds of health advocacy groups woo lawmakers and orchestrate grassroots activity, up from about 90 in 1975 to at least 750 today. "You name a disease, there's probably a Washington lobby for it," said an official of the American Heart Association.[18] Overall, there are more narrowly based groups that focus on a single issue such as abortion or gun control. Many factors account for the proliferation of interest groups: social and economic complexity; scientific and technological developments; the government's regulatory role; the competition for federal dollars; and the diffusion of power in Congress and throughout the government, which enhances access for outside interests (see Box 13-1 on theories of interest group formation).

Some scholars have contended that Americans' civic engagement has declined. Harvard University professor Robert Putnam has argued that citizen participation in associations is on the wane, drawing his most famous example from the nation's bowling alleys. Putnam's data show that more people are bowling but are doing so outside of traditional bowling leagues, resulting in a drop in the number of bowling leagues.[19] They are, in short, "bowling alone." As for people generally, they "would rather be alone in front of a television set than out with a group," Putnam wrote.[20] Several years later, Putnam presented a more optimistic assessment of America's civic life, spotlighting citizens' engagement in a dozen community-building activities around the country.[21] Other scholars note that although membership in older groups such as Lions Clubs or Elks or Moose Lodges is down, membership is rising in newer organizations such as environmental groups and youth soccer leagues.[22] Social media (such as blogs, Facebook, and Twitter) also enable the formation of new social and political communities. Other important indicators of civic engagement—especially volunteering—have registered increases in participation.[23] Meanwhile, scholars have generally found that during times of economic crisis there is a falloff in civic participation (the Tea Party is certainly an exception). The unemployed feel depressed and pessimistic and tend to withdraw from community organizations. According to a study conducted by UCLA professor Jennie Brand, "People who lose their jobs, even once, were roughly 30% less likely to participate in community activities, and that lasted through their lives."[24]

Biases of Interest Representation

Not all societal interests are organized and represented in the pressure group system. Organizations do not necessarily emerge just because people share a common policy goal or political interest. Economist Mancur Olson Jr. famously analyzed the difficulties of organizing to bring about policy change.[25] Organizing requires time, energy, and money, and individuals know that the small contributions they can make usually will not be decisive or even important. If a group exists and successfully presses for policy changes, the benefits will spread beyond those who worked to bring about the results. If, for example, an environmental group successfully calls for clean air regulations,

BOX 13-1 **Some Theories on Interest Group Formation**

Scholars have suggested a number of theories to explain the development of interest groups. Special interests have long been a source of fascination, in part because of their ability to influence policy making even though they may not reflect majority sentiment within the country. The case of vocal minorities prevailing over apathetic or disengaged majorities often rivets scholarly attention. Among the various theories of group formation are the following.

▶ *The proliferation hypothesis* suggests that as society becomes more complex and interdependent, groups naturally form to reflect the country's intricate array of issues and entities. As new conditions, issues, or forces emerge, new groups are formed to reflect or respond to these developments. "The reasoning behind the proliferation hypothesis is straightforward: groups need a clientele from which to draw members."[1]

▶ *The disturbance hypothesis* posits that there is an unstable equilibrium among groups. If something disturbs the equilibrium, such as war, technological innovations, the emergence of new concerns (acquired immune deficiency syndrome [AIDS], homeland security, and so on), then new groups emerge. As two scholars wrote, "Groups organize politically when the existing order is disturbed and certain interests are, in turn, helped or hurt." As an example, they note: "Mobilization of business interests since the 1960s often has resulted from threats posed by consumer advocates and environmentalists, as well as requirements imposed by the steadily growing role of the federal government."[2]

▶ *The exchange hypothesis* states that groups form because of the efforts of "entrepreneurs." The argument asserts that "group organizers invest in a set of benefits which they offer to potential members at a price—joining the group. Benefits may be material [private gains], solidarity [camaraderie], or expressive [the reward of belonging to a group with shared values and causes]."[3] The implication is that organized interests are "deemed more powerful than unorganized interests."[4]

[1] Scott H. Ainsworth, *Analyzing Interest Groups* (New York: W. W. Norton and Co., 2002), 40.
[2] Alan J. Cigler and Burdett A. Loomis, eds., *Interest Group Politics*, 6th ed. (Washington, DC: CQ Press, 2002), 8. See also David B. Truman, *The Governmental Process*, 2d ed. (New York: Knopf, 1971).
[3] Robert Salisbury, "An Exchange Theory of Interest Groups," *Midwest Journal of Political Science* (February 1969): 1. Mancur Olson, in *The Logic of Collective Action* (Cambridge: Harvard University Press, 1965), suggests that many individuals are unlikely to join organizations that may benefit them personally because they will still receive the gains without the costs (fees, attending meetings, and so on) of participating in the group. This is called the free-rider problem. "For Olson, a key to group formation—and especially group survival—was 'selective' benefits. These rewards—for example, travel discounts, informative publications, and cheap insurance—go only to members." See Cigler and Loomis, *Interest Group Politics*, 9.
[4] Ainsworth, *Analyzing Interest Groups*, 39.

urban residents will benefit from the reduced smog, regardless of whether they personally made any contribution to the group's efforts. As a consequence, individuals will prefer to free ride on the work of others.

The issue of the free rider is especially problematic for large groups, where failure to help with the collective effort is totally anonymous. According to Olson's analysis, organizing is easier for small groups with a strong material stake in policy outcomes. In small groups, social pressure can be effectively applied to discourage free riding. In some cases, a single individual or firm will bankroll the cost of organizing because it can benefit even after bearing the costs alone. Under this logic, the pressure group system should be tilted toward narrow economic interests that are easier to organize, and it should underrepresent broad public interests.

According to Olson's theory of collective action, Congress will receive more input from narrow groups with a financial stake in policy issues than from groups representing broader societal interests. Consistent with this theory, there are indeed biases in the composition of the interest group universe. One survey found that business interests make up 72 percent of all interests having Washington representation.[26]

The composition of the interest group world also reflects economic inequality. Put simply, it takes money to create and sustain organized interests, so groups representing the well off are more likely to emerge and survive. As political scientist E. E. Schattschneider famously put it, "the flaw in the pluralist heaven is that the heavenly chorus sings with a strong upper-class accent."[27] Frank Baumgartner, a political scientist who was part of a group that studied the lobbying community over a ten-year period, underscored how the poor and less well off are disadvantaged in having their issues advocated on Capitol Hill. "The biggest indictment of the lobbying community is that it amplifies the voice of those who already have the most resources in society and leaves the people with the greatest needs completely voiceless."[28]

The well off and the well educated in U.S. society participate more in politics than the less fortunate, and lawmakers hear disproportionately from them. In her analysis of legislator-constituent interactions in health care policy, Kristina C. Miler discovered that legislators' perceptions of their constituencies were systematically distorted by the fact that they and their offices interacted so much more frequently with resource-rich groups.[29] The rich and poor are interested in different things. The advantaged talk about taxes, government spending, and social issues, whereas the disadvantaged are primarily concerned about "basic human needs . . . [food], jobs, housing, and health."[30] Elected officials are inundated with messages from groups that represent the politically active (such as the elderly, veterans, and small-business owners). But lawmakers receive comparatively little information about the policy preferences of the needy, who are often only marginally engaged in civic life.

An example of this political reality occurred following the March 1, 2013, sequester (across-the-board spending cuts in federal agencies and programs). A consequence of the indiscriminate fiscal reductions was nationwide flight delays because numerous air-traffic controllers were furloughed from their jobs. Powerful interests—the airlines, businesses, and an angry traveling public—lobbied Congress to get the furloughed controllers back to work. The result: a month after the sequester took effect, a law was enacted that ended the furloughs of the air-traffic personnel. As a House member noted, "When you [vote for sequester exceptions], what happens is the most politically strong groups with the most lobbyists get relief, at the expense of everybody else. Meals on Wheels, or kids on Head Start, or grants on biomedical research—all of those get left behind."[31]

PRESSURE GROUP METHODS

Since the birth of the Republic, groups have influenced Congress's decisions. During the nation's early technological and industrial expansion, railroad interests lobbied for federal funds and land grants to build their routes. Some of these early lobbyists' methods—such as offering bribes—fueled public suspicion of pressure tactics. In 1874 Sen. Simon Cameron, R-Pa., described an honest politician as one who "when he is bought, stays bought."[32] Samuel Ward, the "king of the lobby" for fifteen years after the Civil War, wrote to his friend Henry Wadsworth Longfellow:

> When I see you again I will tell you how a client, eager to prevent the arrival at a committee of a certain member before it should adjourn, offered me $5,000 to accomplish this purpose, which I did, by having [the member's] boots mislaid while I smoked a cigar and condoled with him until they could be found at 11:45. I had the satisfaction of a good laugh [and] a good fee in my pocket.[33]

Lobbying methods have evolved in variety, sophistication, and subtlety. As government has expanded in size and scope, the mutual dependence of legislators and lobbyists has deepened. The legislator-lobbyist connection is a two-way street:

> Groups turn to Congress as an institution where they can be heard, establish their positions, and achieve their policy goals. Members of Congress in turn rely on groups to provide valuable constituency, technical, or political information, to give reelection support, and to assist strategically in passing or blocking legislation that the members support or oppose. Groups need Congress, and Congress needs groups.[34]

Modern-day methods vary according to the nature and visibility of the issue and groups' resources. Among the most important practices are direct and social lobbying, group alliances, grassroots support, and electronic advocacy.

These diverse techniques are typically employed in tandem. For example, House and Senate Democratic leaders and aides meet regularly with their lobbying allies, such as labor unions.[35] The chair of the Senate Democratic Steering and Outreach Committee works "hand in hand with outside advocacy groups to raise public support for bills on the Democratic agenda."[36] Similarly, business lobbyists regularly consult with congressional GOP leaders and their top aides to formulate strategy on the party's issues and goals. House Republican leader John Boehner of Ohio even streamed live on the Internet a Capitol Hill meeting with twenty GOP lobbyists. The session was directed at gathering "suggestions for a new [GOP] policy agenda" for the November 2010 elections and the 112th Congress (2011–2013).[37] The lobbyists then mobilized grassroots support for these initiatives through petition drives, rallies, radio and television advertising blitzes, national door-to-door campaigns, and other techniques.[38] Their efforts were successful, as Boehner became Speaker of the House. Senate Republican leaders also meet regularly with business groups and key GOP-leaning grassroots organizations to discuss ways to move the party's policy initiatives.[39]

Direct Lobbying

In the traditional method of direct lobbying, lobbyists present their clients' cases directly to members and congressional staff. When a group hires a prominent lawyer or lobbyist, such as Ken Duberstein, Heather Podesta, or Gerald Cassidy, the direct approach involves personal contact with senators or representatives. An aide to Speaker Thomas P. "Tip" O'Neill Jr., D-Mass. (1977–1987), explained the importance of the personal touch:

> [Lobbyists] know members of Congress are here three nights a week, alone, without their families. So they . . . [s]chmooze with them. Make friends. And they don't lean on it all the time. Every once in a while, they call up—maybe once or twice a year [to] ask a few questions. . . . Anne Wexler [a former official in the Carter White House, and later a lobbyist] will call up and spend half an hour talking about . . . politics, and suddenly she'll pop a question, pick up something. They want that little bit of access. That's what does it. You can hear it. It clicks home. They'll call their chief executive officer, and they've delivered. That's how it works. It's not illegal. They work on a personal basis.[40]

A variation on direct lobbying is when private citizens who have the resources hire lobbyists to present their issue or case to lawmakers. The private citizens range from victims of financial fraud to individuals who "want presidential pardons or congressional help with immigration troubles."[41] Advantaged in direct lobbying are Hollywood movie stars, famous sports figures, prominent business executives (such as Microsoft's Bill Gates), and the children, spouses, and other relatives of powerful members.[42]

Former members of Congress are particularly effective at direct lobbying. Recognizing their value, lobbying firms and clients eagerly enlist the services of former lawmakers. "Each member is part of a network of reciprocity," observed scholar James A. Thurber. "You help me, and I'll help you. That's what a lobbying client is buying."[43] As a matter of courtesy and electoral reality, most incumbent lawmakers meet with former colleagues because they might soon be an ex-member. A retired twenty-year House member wrote to prospective clients that he could "unravel red tape, open doors, make appointments, work with the Administration or government agencies, influence legislation, and assist in any other service required."[44] Drawing on recent disclosure filings, the nonpartisan Center for Responsive Politics reported that "188 different corporations, organizations, and other special interest groups employed at least two former lawmakers" to lobby Congress and other federal entities.[45] (A website—www.opensecrets.org—allows citizens to track public officials who move between the government and the private sector, the so-called revolving door.) Former top Capitol Hill staff aides are similarly sought after because of their personal knowledge and understanding of key members and congressional processes.[46] Many former lobbyists also take high-ranking staff jobs on Capitol Hill.[47]

Member-to-member lobbying can be uniquely effective. No outsider has the same access to lawmakers (and certain precincts of Capitol Hill) that former colleagues have. For example, GOP senators who may be lobbyists can attend the regularly scheduled Tuesday Republican Policy Committee lunch, "where legislative tactics are plotted on issues ranging from tax cuts to foreign policy—information that gives them a decided edge over other lobbyists."[48] Some are offended by the access that lobbyists who are former legislators have to the floor and to other Capitol Hill locations that are generally not open to the public. Ethics rules do impose restrictions on the former lawmakers (for example, they may not lobby their colleagues while in the chamber), but former members still retain privileges denied to others. As former Speaker J. Dennis Hastert, R-Ill., explained, "It's hard to take away benefits from former members. We're all going to be former members one day."[49] (Hastert is now a lobbyist with a D.C.-based firm.) Turnover in Congress hampers direct lobbying by former members. The longer former members have been out of Congress, the fewer personal contacts they have with current lawmakers.

A new type of lobbyist is also much sought after these days: the experienced fund-raiser. Campaign money-raisers spend as much or more time with the lawmakers they are assisting as lobbyists. In brief, fund-raisers have significant access to members and their staff aides. The talents that some fund-raisers bring to lobbying were summarized as follows:

> The hiring equation for lobby firms is simple: Campaign fund-raisers spend time with lawmakers—often more than policy staffers. They also have the kinds of connections with CEOs and in-house government relations heads that could mean more business for the lobby shop. And they are comfortable making "the ask," not only to sign clients but also to try to get members of Congress and staff to take action on behalf of clients.[50]

Direct lobbying takes many forms. For one thing, lobbyists may organize focus groups of Hill staff aides to determine which arguments will most appeal to lawmakers.[51] The president of a telephone trade association underscored the importance of keeping congressional staffers informed. He even organized a retreat for congressional aides, in part to glean political intelligence about how best to frame his association's issues on Capitol Hill.[52] Lobbyists monitor committees; testify (or have their clients appear as witnesses) at hearings; interpret Hill decisions for clients; articulate clients' interests to legislators; draft legislation, speeches, and "Dear Colleague" letters for members; and give campaign assistance. The House offers more occasions for contacting members directly than does the Senate, where lobbyists are more likely to target staff aides.

Taken together, lobbyists are major players in congressional policy making. "Lobbyists contribute a lot to democracy," observed Rep. James P. Moran, D-Va. "They provide continuity and institutional memory. Most of them have been around longer than members."[53] Or as a GOP senator put it, "I would have to say the best information I get in the legislative process comes from people directly involved in the industry that is going to be affected—and from people who represent them: the 'nefarious' lobbyists."[54] A financial services lobbyist skilled in policy development bluntly emphasized the important role that he and his colleagues play in the lawmaking process. "Most members may know one or two issues well, if that. Then you have a 26-year-old kid, maybe he's even 30 and went to a good law school, who's on the staff working 10 hours a day and is supposed to tell his boss how to do derivatives regulation or credit-card reform. Are you kidding?"[55]

Social Lobbying

Lobbying also occurs in social settings outside the legislative context, such as at dinner parties, receptions, sporting and entertainment events, or on the golf course or tennis court. Successful direct lobbying is grounded in trust.[56] Legislators must believe that lobbyists are credible and knowledgeable before they will accept advice from or even devote time listening to them. Social interactions are extremely useful for fostering and developing the personal relationships that lobbyists need to be effective. Lobbyists thus seek out opportunities to interact casually with lawmakers, even when no client business will be discussed. On some occasions, of course, a conversation in a social setting can produce results for a lobbyist's client. As one experienced power dealer explained, "When you want to make an end run, meet someone at a party."[57]

Travel with members of Congress has long afforded many opportunities for lobbyists to engage in social lobbying, but recent ethics laws have placed restrictions on the practice. Until the 2007 ethics rules were in place, it was not unusual, for example, for legislators to accept flights on corporate jets, reimbursing their sponsors only for the cost of commercial airfare. Such settings afforded many possibilities for relationship-building and casual interaction among lobbyists, legislators, and lobbyists' clients. The 2007 ethics reforms, however, "effectively ban travel with registered lobbyists."[58] Lobbyists "may not accompany lawmakers or aides 'on any segment' of a trip."[59] And lawmakers must receive prior approval for all such travel from the Committee on Ethics of their chamber. There are exceptions built into the travel rules for nonprofit organizations, colleges, and universities. In 2012, for example, these types of groups spent more than $3.6 million "to send members of Congress and staffers on trips to far-flung locations such as Indonesia, Israel, Ghana and Turkey."[60] (Also see the section below on foreign lobbying.)

Lobbyists are not permitted to pay for meals for legislators, banning the lobbyist-funded lavish dinners that were the source of so much public distaste. There is, however, the "reception exception" or the "toothpick rule," which permits "members and aides to [eat] food [on toothpicks] at receptions, but bans them from attending sit-down meals with lobbyists."[61] As one lobbyist hosting a reception for legislators ruefully put it, "I'm sitting here as vice president of corporate affairs for the National Association of Manufacturers, and I'm making sure that there's nothing you need a fork for."[62] Members and aides may also attend lobbyist-paid events when carrying out "official duties," and when more than twenty-five people not connected with Congress are in attendance.

A large loophole in all these ethics rules involves political fund-raising. Social and direct lobbying is unrestricted at campaign events. Many fund-raising events such as golf outings, fishing trips, and sit-down dinners offer wide-open opportunities for casual interactions with lawmakers. For example, Heather Podesta hosted a dinner at her home for five Democratic female senators. The fee for attendees, who in return were given a chance to discuss issues with the senators in a private setting, was $30,400 for a "co-chair" of the event, $10,000 for a "vice chair," $5,000 for a "co-host," and $1,000 for an "individual sponsor." Checks, said Podesta, were to be made payable to the Democratic Senatorial Campaign Committee (DSCC).[63] Lawmakers can continue to invite lobbyists to attend "lavish birthday parties in a lawmaker's honor ($1,000 a lobbyist), weekend golf tournaments ($2,500 and up), a Presidents Day weekend at Disney World ($5,000), or parties in South Beach in Miami ($5,000)."[64] Lobbyists end up paying for such events because "they pay a political fund-raising committee set up by the lawmaker. In turn, the committee pays the legislator's way."[65] In short, what is illegal if done directly—such as paying for legislators' meals, travel, or gifts—is legal if done indirectly through campaign contributions.

A variation on social lobbying is worth noting. Although members are banned by law from receiving honoraria, they can ask corporations or groups to make a donation on the lawmakers' behalf to charities or other tax-exempt groups. Critics suggest that this arrangement enables members to "obtain political benefits by directing contributions to favored organizations, and some tax-exempt groups are affiliated with politicians."[66] An analysis by the *New York Times* found "at least two dozen charities that lawmakers or their families helped create or run that routinely accept donations from businesses seeking to influence them."[67] There are no financial limits on these donations, and they "typically far exceed what companies are permitted to give to candidates in campaign contributions."[68]

Still, ethics experts remain concerned that companies, banks, and other groups with business before Congress are providing thousands and even millions of dollars to fund endowed university chairs or institutes named after influential lawmakers. "The simple fact is these things should not be named after people when they are in office," declared a congressional analyst. "We all know what is going on here: the donors are trying to influence the lawmakers."[69] The donors contend that their contributions are for good causes, and various lawmakers state that they have received prior approval of congressional ethics officials to agree to these donations, or they "avoid requesting the donations themselves, instead leaving such pleas up to staff from the universities or charities involved."[70]

Coalition Lobbying

To enhance their chances of success, lobbyists often construct coalitions in support of their legislative initiatives. Coalitions bring more resources, contacts, and money to lobbying efforts. With the diffusion of power on Capitol Hill, coalitions are better able than single groups to touch all the legislative bases. When individuals and organizations "band together and support one another," noted former senator John B. Breaux, D-La. (1987–2005), now a Washington lobbyist, it makes for "a smoother and more effective [legislative] operation than if fifty or more voices [are] all arguing for the same principle without any coordination."[71]

Examples of such coalitions abound. In 2013, to fend off automatic spending cuts (called sequestration) in domestic and defense programs, "a broad coalition that includes university, military, public health and science groups" joined together to try "to put a stop to the severe budget cuts currently set to go into effect on March 1."[72] Two years earlier, environmental and public health groups came together to work against legislative efforts to strip the Environmental Protection Agency of its authority to regulate greenhouse gas emissions. The Pharmaceutical Research and Manufacturers of America (PhRMA) worked with a variety of technology and financial interests to push for more favorable tax treatment of corporate income earned overseas, and a provision was inserted in the American Jobs Creation Act of 2004. A study by researchers at the University of Kansas determined that this single tax break earned companies $220 for every dollar they spent lobbying on the issue, "a 22,000 percent rate of return on their investment."[73]

"We have no permanent friends or permanent enemies—only permanent interests." That oft-repeated line helps to explain why "coalitions, like politics, make strange bed fellows."[74] Rival lobbying interests sometimes forge temporary coalitions to promote or defend shared goals. For example, a group of trade unions and liberal-leaning consumer groups joined with PhRMA and the health insurers' main trade association, America's Health Insurance Plans, in a coalition known as the "Healthcare Reform Dialogue" to seek points of agreement when the Obama administration began its successful effort to revamp the national health care system.[75] Upset that customary farm bills mainly subsidize rich farmers while hurting poor farmers in developing countries and in rural areas of the United States, sixteen faith-based groups formed the Religious Working Group on the Farm Bill. They were joined in the effort by the liberal Environmental Defense Fund and Oxfam and the conservative Club for Growth and Citizens Against Government Waste.[76] In opposition were the large commodity trade associations, such as the American Farm Bureau Federation, American Soybean Association, and National Corn Growers Association.

A drawback of coalitions is that they are marriages of convenience—the coalition between the American Petroleum Institute and the Environmental Working Group is but one example. As the head of the environmental group observed, "This is not a sign of any great, broad alliance with the oil industry."[77] Multiple organizations are unlikely to cooperate on more than one issue, or for extended time periods. Lawmakers may also be wary of a coalition whose organizers, membership, or funding sources are murky. An attractive name (such as the Coalition for Asbestos Reform or the Climate Policy Group) may simply be a way for a single interest to bankroll an initiative while masking its identity. To combat such efforts, Congress adopted reforms in 2007 that require more disclosure of the groups that fund and lead coalition efforts.

Grassroots Lobbying

From the abolitionist crusade, to women's suffrage, to the civil rights struggle, to today's Tea Party and Occupy Wall Street movements, grassroots lobbying is perhaps the most effective pressure technique. Instead of contacting members directly, many organizations mobilize citizens in districts and states across the country to pressure their senators and representatives. For example, when eBay, the online auction website, wanted to influence federal telecommunications policy so that phone and cable companies could not favor certain types of Web traffic at the expense of others, it sent an e-mail to more than a million eBay users urging them to contact their members of Congress in support of "network neutrality."[78] The Service Employees International Union (SEIU) announced a plan to enlist its members to make ten million telephone calls to pressure members of Congress to support universal health insurance coverage.[79]

Interest groups often send mass mailings to targeted congressional districts with letters or postcards enclosed for constituents to sign and mail to their legislators. Although lawmakers recognize that lobbying groups orchestrate such mail campaigns, they also realize they may serve as a rough measure of sentiment and organizational strength behind an issue:

> Members have to care about this mail, even if it's mail that is almost identically worded. Labor unions do this sort of thing a lot. The congressman has to care that somebody out there in his district has enough power to get hundreds of people to sit down and write a postcard or a letter—because if the guy can get them to do that, he

might be able to influence them in other ways. So, a member has no choice but to pay attention. It's suicide if he doesn't.[80]

Washington lobbying and public relations firms market grassroots lobbying services to clients. Masters of grassroots lobbying know how to guide citizens in their communications with members of Congress. For example, here is what one lobbyist said when he called a sportsman about a proposal that would have made hunting no longer tax-deductible as a business expense: "Hello, Johnny Bob? This is J. D. in Washington. Got a pencil handy? Now, this is who your congressman is. This is how you write him."[81] Although the lack of disclosure requirements makes it difficult to track expenditures on grassroots lobbying, it has become a vital part of the Washington influence industry. "We are talking about lobbying firms that are providing paid advertising to influence specific legislation," observed campaign finance expert Thomas E. Mann. "These are massively funded lobbying campaigns using paid media."[82]

Lawmakers seek to distinguish between genuine grassroots and fake grassroots (often called "Astroturf"). Many so-called grassroots groups function as front organizations for their financial backers. One group with an environmentally friendly name, the Save Our Species Alliance, was actually pushing "a rewrite of the Endangered Species Act to ease paper and logging business's access to federal lands where those species live."[83] And when the House debated a major telecommunications bill, lawmakers were flooded with bogus mail from children, dead people, and constituents who said they had not sent any mailgrams. The uproar from members led to an investigation of the affair by the Capitol Police.[84]

Proponents contend that groups or individuals who can hire lobbying firms to concoct sham grassroots activity should be required to disclose publicly who they are and how much they are spending. "The point is to identify the messengers behind these communications," said a public interest advocate, "because that helps [people] evaluate the information."[85] Opponents argue that disclosure requirements run counter to the Constitution's guarantee of free speech and the right to petition the government. As noted in one federal court decision, "In a representative government such as this, these branches of government act on behalf of the people and, to a very large extent, the whole concept of representation depends upon the ability of the people to make their wishes known to their representatives."[86]

Mass mobilizations have become so common that some firms now specialize in "grass tops" lobbying. Whereas the goal of grassroots lobbying is to mobilize the masses, the goal of grass tops lobbying "is to figure out to whom a member of Congress cannot say no: his chief donor, his campaign manager, a political mentor. The lobbyist then tries to persuade that person to take his client's side" during talks with the lawmaker.[87] Big corporations may also hire "stealth" lobbyists—public relations specialists who work quietly to "influence the news media, sponsor grassroots activities and generate favorable scientific reports."[88]

Electronic Lobbying

As in most other areas of life, advances in communication technology have transformed lobbyists' work. (For example, one study found that younger staffers prefer to connect with lobbyists via e-mail; many lobbyists and the clients they represent prefer face-to-face meetings.[89]) Smartphones, tablets, and many other digital tools allow lobbyists sitting in a congressional markup to send out alerts on legislative developments to clients, coalition partners, and their home offices. Text messaging, e-mail, and the array of social networking sites available such as Twitter, YouTube, and Facebook have all greatly increased the speed with which lobbyists can influence the legislative process and galvanize their supporters. Much grassroots lobbying now occurs over the Internet. During the Senate Judiciary Committee's confirmation hearings on Supreme Court nominee Elena Kagan, a prominent advocate for Kagan sent "live Twitter updates from the confirmation deliberations" to her followers.[90] The conservative Family Research Council, which opposed Kagan, hosted webcasts with legal experts who explained why Kagan should not serve on the Supreme Court. The council also provided people visiting their website with a letter they could send to their senators objecting to Kagan's confirmation. Individuals only had to put in their ZIP code and hit "Enter."[91] Messages can now be conveyed immediately to sympathizers anywhere in the country to bring pressure to bear when and where it is most needed. A Twitter message sent to AARP members concerning President Obama's 2013 State of the Union message said: "Keep your word, Mr. President. Protect seniors. No Social Security Cuts!"[92] In short, the potent combination of technology and politics makes "it easier to organize and send a political message across the country at warp speed."[93]

Groups use computer databases to identify supporters, target specific constituencies, recruit people, and generate personalized mass mailings.[94] With the emergence of interactive websites, lobbyists can communicate directly with prospective supporters, assign tasks, and get immediate feedback on any issue. "[Lobbying] groups get to more of my voters, more often, and with more information than any elected official can do," complained one House member. "I'm competing to represent my district against the lobbyists and the special interests."[95]

Bloggers can activate an electronic network of political activists and organizations to lobby Congress on behalf of policies or issues they support or oppose. Talk radio hosts such as Rush Limbaugh (who is heard weekly on more than six hundred stations by perhaps fourteen million listeners a week) can incite an outpouring of letters, telegrams, e-mails, YouTube videos, and tweets to lawmakers. A clash between the media and technology industries over how to deal with online piracy triggered, according to one account, the "biggest online protest in history," resulting in ten million petition signatures, three million e-mails, and 100,000 telephone calls to lawmakers.[96] (The clash involved the media's ire at the illegal sharing of files by digital pirates versus the technology industry's concern about online censorship.) A month after the online piracy battle, the lobbying potency of Facebook and Twitter was demonstrated again. A decision by the Susan G. Komen for the [Cancer] Cure foundation to cut off funding for Planned Parenthood was quickly reversed by a massive outpouring of opposition (1.3 million tweets in a few days) through these social media tools. The political power of social media, according to one commentator, "really has given a voice to huge numbers of people who were previously voiceless."[97] Online lobbying campaigns are now staples in influencing public debate and legislative decision making.

A subtle form of electronic lobbying occurs when advocacy groups purchase or establish websites or newspapers and buy radio and television stations to disseminate their views, blurring the "distinction between legitimate media and propaganda to promote their causes."[98] The National Rifle Association (NRA), for example, believes that more advocacy groups will employ traditional media formats or buy radio stations to present their views to the general public without identifying them as group-owned. "We have as much right to be at the table delivering news and information to the American public as anyone else does," the NRA's executive director explained.[99] Perhaps with that in mind, heeding federal court decisions upholding the Second Amendment right to bear arms, the NRA has expanded its portfolio beyond guns to areas such as campaign finance reform.

One of the most influential of all lobbying groups, the NRA has been able to increase its leverage on Capitol Hill because congressional battles are "so closely fought now that powerful interest groups hold more sway even if they can deliver a handful of votes."[100] Fundamentally, the political clout of the NRA rests on the intensity of its commitment to gun rights and its ability, according to Sen. Charles Schumer, D-N.Y., to mobilize "2, 3, 4 million people who care passionately about this issue . . . at the drop of a hat," without a similar intense and sustained grassroots activism that backs additional gun-control legislation.[101] (In 2011 the NRA spent $2.9 million on lobbying; gun-control advocates spent $240,000.[102])

GROUPS AND THE ELECTORAL CONNECTION

Today it is often hard to differentiate the roles of interest groups and political parties in electoral politics. "The standard distinction between interest groups and parties used to be that parties were committed to winning elections and that pressure groups let elections happen and then tried to influence the people who got elected," remarked a political scientist. "Now interest groups through their PACs [political action committees] and a variety of other methods are very much involved in the pre-policy arena."[103] As one example, the grassroots operation of the U.S. Chamber of Commerce "has begun to rival those of the major political parties."[104] Box 13-2 provides an interesting example of a group that is blending issue advocacy and electoral politics. Union workers are being trained as lobbyists in order to make them more effective advocates, organizers, and potential candidates for elective office.

Some groups are so extensively involved in partisan electoral politics that they are effectively "party allies," a vital part of their party's "enduring multilayered coalition," in the words of Paul S. Herrnson.[105] Increasingly, the electoral coalitions of the two parties exhibit greater ideological homogeneity. For Democrats, group allies include labor unions, environmental and women's rights organizations, and liberal membership groups such as People for the American Way and Moveon.org. For Republicans, allied groups include the U.S. Chamber of Commerce, pro-life and pro-gun organizations, and conservative ideological groups such as the Club for Growth and Freedom Works. Between elections, congressional party leaders and their allied interest groups cooperate to promote their party's message, enhance its public image, and advance its agenda.

Interest groups help elect members to Congress in three principal ways: they raise funds and make financial contributions through political action committees; they conduct their own, independent campaigns for or against issues and candidates; and they rate the voting records of legislators.

BOX 13-2 Union Workers Trained as Lobbyists

The United Steel Workers brings a group of legislative interns to the capital several times a year. It pays them what they make in their normal jobs plus expense allowances, lodges them in hotels, and gives them desks in the Steel Workers' offices near Dupont Circle. The visitors are technically on sabbaticals authorized by the union's collective bargaining agreements.

The program combines schooling and work. Interns often are sent to Capitol Hill to track down lawmakers or congressional aides to make the union's case on legislative issues. During a typical week, they also study congressional procedures and history, attend hearings, and observe union policy meetings. The purpose is to give rank-and-file workers a deeper knowledge of Congress and to inspire activism at the local level. The union hopes its interns will go home more politically savvy and better prepared to rally coworkers on union issues and at election time.

The steel union's program is unusual in intensity, length, and agenda. The union wants to bolster its grassroots efforts and deepen its pool of potential candidates for elected offices. A spokesman for the Steel Workers said the union hopes the six-year-old program will "get more plumbers and steamfitters and electricians into public office."

Source: Adapted from Matthew Tully, "Union Program Fields Blue-Collar Washington Lobbyists," CQ Daily Monitor, March 29, 1999, 7.

Groups and Campaign Fund Raising

Legislators who dislike raising money—seemingly a majority of them—turn to lobbyists or professional fund-raisers to arrange parties, luncheons, dinners, or other social events to which admission is charged. Lobbyists buy tickets or supply lists of people who should be invited. They even serve as treasurers of members' reelection campaigns or political action committees.[106]

Fund-raising events consume more and more of legislators' limited time (recall Chapter 4) and create new scheduling conflicts—further evidence of the imperatives of the two Congresses, the representative assembly versus the lawmaking institution. Members cannot chase money and do legislative work at the same time. To minimize these conflicts, "windows" are opened in the Senate's schedule:

> A window is a period of time in which it is understood that there will be no roll-call votes. Senators are assured that they won't be embarrassed by being absent for a recorded vote. Windows usually occur between six and eight in the evening, which is the normal time for holding fund-raising cocktail parties.[107]

Sen. Robert C. Byrd, D-W.Va., the longest-serving lawmaker ever in that chamber, complained that members must spend more time raising money than legislating.[108] A former senator said he "had to become an expert [at fund-raising] to survive in California politics." He described three principles of raising money based on his experiences. First, "people who give once are likely to give again." If you stop asking, they will stop giving or give to someone else. Second, "it's a compliment . . . to ask someone for a large sum." Third, "people who have given to other causes may give to yours." For this reason, "keep track of all who give what to whom."[109] Congressional critics, and even legislators and lobbyists themselves, question the propriety of fund-raising practices. Members are concerned about implied obligations when they accept help or money from groups. For their part, lobbyists resent pressure from members to give repeatedly.

"Bundling" is a widely used fund-raising technique that allows lobbyists and fund-raising entities to raise more money for candidates than they can contribute individually under campaign finance laws. Political action committees (PACs), for example, are limited to giving a candidate $5,000 for use in the primary and general election. There are no limits, however, on "how much a PAC can forward to candidates from other donors."[110] To bundle, a lobbyist or another type of fund-raiser will solicit checks from various sources and then give them all at once to a candidate's campaign committee or to the House and Senate party campaign committees. The candidate knows the bundler's identity because the checks are submitted to the campaign together or, in some cases, because the checks contain identifying information. Lobbyists are not "bundling this cash for altruistic reasons," said the president of a nonpartisan election watchdog group. "They want to get the [lawmakers'] attention and interest."[111] Until the 2007 ethics reforms, the public was entirely in the dark about the identities of bundlers and the amounts they raised. Under the current rules, limited disclosure requirements are imposed. Campaign committees must identify persons "reasonably known" to be registered lobbyists if they have provided two or more "bundled" contributions totaling more than $16,000 during any semiannual reporting period.[112]

Groups and Advocacy Campaigns

Elections are contested today on interest group turf, with incumbents fighting opposing interests as well as other candidates. Interest groups develop and fund advertising campaigns that are designed to influence electoral outcomes, so the candidates and party they back will support the group's legislative agenda. Labor unions, for example, spent $1.1 billion from 2005 through 2011 supporting federal candidates and lobbying Washington. But they also spent considerably more ($3.3 billion) during this period on getting out the vote, persuading union members to support certain candidates, and so on. Such political mobilization efforts are not required to be reported to the Federal Election Commission.[113] Numerous other groups also spend considerable amounts targeting voters in selected states or districts, urging them to vote for or against certain candidates.

Reverse lobbying also occurs. Lawmakers lobby the lobbyists to achieve their policy priorities. They aggressively solicit legislative input, as well as campaign funds, from their interest group allies. For example, members will try to persuade key groups that are on the fence to back their proposals or not publicly oppose them. The passage in 2003 of a major prescription drug benefit for Medicare enrollees was facilitated by Speaker Hastert's wooing of the AARP—the multimillion-member seniors' lobby. Seven years later, congressional Democrats and President Obama lobbied the AARP and won its backing for enactment of the most significant health care overhaul in two generations. Top GOP aides to the House majority leadership have met with outside conservative groups (e.g., Club for Growth and Freedom Works) to solicit their input on upcoming fiscal battles in the 113th Congress, to listen to their agenda priorities, and to encourage unified support among outside conservative groups for the House Republican policy blueprint.[114]

Rating Legislators

About a hundred groups keep pressure on members of Congress by issuing "report cards" on their voting records. Groups select a number of major issues and then publicize members' scores (on a scale of zero to one hundred) based on their "right" or "wrong" votes on them. Members are often warned by colleagues that certain votes will be scored. "You'll hear this as you walk into the chamber: 'This is going to be a scored vote. The environmentalists are going to score this vote, or the AFL-CIO is going to score this vote,'" explained a House member.[115] Congressional aides sometimes check with lobbying groups to determine whether certain votes will be scored.

To be sure, advocacy groups are not reluctant to announce that they will be grading lawmakers on certain votes. The votes of lawmakers who sign pledges, such as the Taxpayer Protection Pledge or the Social Security Protectors' Pledge, are certain to have their votes monitored closely by outside organizations for any deviations from their promises. If pledges are violated, such as voting for tax hikes, members might face a primary challenge in the next election.[116]

Interest groups use scorecards to influence members' decisions on selected issues. The liberal Americans for Democratic Action and the conservative American Conservative Union issue score-based ratings that are well known and widely used. The ratings game, however, is suspect; it is always simplistic. The selected votes are often inadequate to judge a member's full record because they are selected with an agenda in mind. Group strategists defend ratings as "a shorthand way for voters to tell something about their congressman."[117] In targeting members in upcoming elections, many interest groups assign attention-getting names based on their scorecards, such as "heroes and zeroes" (from consumer advocates) or the "dirty dozen" (environmental polluters).

Groups use legislative scorecards to determine which candidates will win endorsement and receive campaign contributions. Vulnerable incumbents who hold closely contested seats and are mindful of the two Congresses are usually careful when casting their votes to avoid antagonizing powerful interest groups back home. As a lawmaker who represents a marginal district once said, "If I cast a vote, I might have to answer for it. It may be an issue in the next campaign. Over and over I have to have a response to the question: Why did you do that?"[118] Members may also use bad scores in their campaigns. A liberal lawmaker, for example, might "wear bad scores from conservative groups like a badge of honor."[119] Some of the groups that rate lawmakers maintain websites that allow visitors to compare how they personally would vote on issues with the actual voting record of their senators or representatives.[120] Interest groups may also canvass door to door in certain areas, "to talk to voters about the results" of their scorecards.[121]

GROUPS, LOBBYING, AND LEGISLATIVE POLITICS

How much influence do organized interests wield over congressional legislation? The American public is convinced that their sway is excessive. Overwhelming majorities of survey respondents agree with the statement "Congress is too heavily influenced by interest groups."[122] Political science research, by contrast, offers no such clarity on this question. According to a thorough review of the literature, the subject of interest group influence has "generated more smoke than fire, more debate than progress, more confusion than advance."[123] Moreover, the results of empirical research do not support sweeping populist characterizations of Congress as bought and paid for by moneyed interests. A ten-year study by a group of political scientists who examined ninety-eight issues found that the side with the most PAC donations, lobbyists, money, and members won only half of the time. They concluded, "A better predictor than money in winning or killing legislation was the support of government agency heads, congressmen-turned-lobbyists, high-level congressional and government officials—and best of all—party leaders and the president."[124] The study also pointed out that it is difficult for lobbyists to change the policy status quo because there are "people benefiting from the status quo" and entrenched interests on both sides of the issue.[125]

The Role of Money

Journalists and campaign reform groups often posit a direct linear correlation between members' votes and the amounts they have received from various groups. Scholarly researchers reject such simple cause-and-effect inferences. Simply correlating the campaign contributions legislators receive with their voting behavior ignores the possibility that members might just as well have voted as they did without any group influence or campaign contributions. Instead, it is necessary to determine whether lawmakers change their behavior after having received campaign assistance. The more careful research designs used by scholars frequently fail to find any causal connection between PAC contributions and members' votes.[126] As the manager of a corporate PAC pointed out, money is "only one tool. We use it to defeat people who do not agree with us and elect those who do. I wish we could just 'buy' votes, but we can't. That's not the way it works in the real world."[127]

Rather than altering members' behavior, the principal finding of empirical research on interest group behavior is that lobbyists tend to donate to members who are already friendly to their objectives. Labor unions, for example, donate the bulk of their funds to Democrats.[128] Similarly, oil and gas interests contribute primarily to Republicans.[129] Generally speaking, groups do not regard donating to legislative opponents a good investment of their campaign money. Citing E. E. Schattschneider, who said, "moneyed interests sing with an upper-class accent," political scientists Richard L. Hall and Frank W. Wayman write, "they also spend a good deal of effort singing to the choir."[130] Furthermore, as discussed in Chapter 4, the amount that interest groups can contribute to legislators' campaigns is limited. With the proliferation of interest groups and PACs, candidates have many different groups to which they can turn for fund-raising help. No single group is likely to exert overwhelming financial leverage over any given member of Congress.

In short, the patterns in campaign contributing simply do not conform to crude vote-buying theories. The relationship between lobbyists and legislators rarely resembles a simple economic exchange of money for support. Contributions signal and reinforce a relationship more often than they create one. The influence of money must be weighed along with other considerations influencing members' votes, including constituency pressures, party ties, friendships with fellow legislators or lobbyists, and personal conscience, idiosyncrasies, and prejudices. As Rep. Barney Frank, D-Mass., put it: "Votes will beat money any day. Any politician forced to choose between his campaign contributions and strong public sentiment is going to vote public sentiment. Campaign contributions are fungible, you can get new ones. You can't get new voters."[131]

This is hardly to claim that the enormous sums that interest groups spend on political campaigns have no effect on legislative politics and policy making. Contributions almost certainly buy access to legislators. "There is no question—if you give a lot of money, you will get a lot of access. All you have to do is send in the check," explained one corporate executive.[132] Nevertheless, the linkages between money and policy making are not simple or easy to trace. Under the right circumstances, organized interests can reframe issues, sway members, mobilize support, or demobilize opposition, but there is very little evidence that organized interests are able to convert outright opponents.[133]

Lobbying and Legislation

An open, decentralized institution, Congress presents lobbyists with multiple opportunities to shape the fate of legislation. Groups play a direct or indirect part throughout the congressional environment in individual members' work, committee activities, legislative agenda-setting, and floor decision making. Nevertheless, tracing the nature and extent of lobbyists' influence on legislation is no less difficult than untangling the relationship between campaign contributions and lawmaking.

Just as organized interests contribute primarily to their legislative allies, lobbyists also spend most of their time with friendly legislators. Lobbyists rarely target their opponents in Congress, nor do they generally devote significant effort to trying to influence fence-sitters.[134] Instead, they work with lawmakers who share their policy views—providing them with appropriate information, data, and political intelligence that they can perhaps use to persuade wavering colleagues.

Along these lines, many organized interests have ties to sympathetic informal congressional groups. For example, the steel industry maintains links with the Steel Caucus and textile manufacturers with the Textile Caucus. Interest groups can be instrumental in forming these informal legislative entities. The idea for the Mushroom Caucus (to protect mushroom producers from foreign imports) originated at a May 1977 luncheon for House members sponsored by the American Mushroom Institute.[135] The Institute of Scrap Recycling Industries lobbied for two years (successfully) to encourage formation of the Senate Recycling Caucus and the House Recycling Caucus. These two recycling groups focus "on ways Congress can help improve recycling and develop new markets for recycled products."[136] Several of the informal legislative caucuses are closely affiliated with nonprofit entities such as the Congressional Black Caucus Foundation, which can collect unlimited donations from corporations, unions, and others. The nonprofits often sponsor policy forums, meetings, conventions, and other events where lobbyists can mingle with lawmakers and discuss the issues of the day.[137]

The relationship between lobbyists and legislators is better understood as a "legislative subsidy" than as a simple exchange in which legislators trade policy for political support.[138] Legislators benefit from the help of lobbyists because successful legislating requires so much work and expertise. Lobbyists' primary role is to assist and underwrite the efforts of their legislative allies. Lobbyists provide their congressional supporters with information, legislative language, policy analysis, useful arguments, and political advice. Working with friendly legislators, lobbyists steer policy toward their clients' goals, exerting influence that in practice is hard to distinguish from legislators' own policy preferences.

The value of lobbyists to legislators thus extends far beyond campaign contributions. "Essentially, we operate as an extension of congressmen's staff," explained one lobbyist. "Occasionally we come up with the legislation, or speeches—and questions [for lawmakers to ask at hearings] all the time. We look at it as providing staff work for allies."[139] Or, as one of Washington's premier lobbyists, Thomas Hale Boggs Jr. (son of former House majority leader Thomas Hale Boggs Sr., D-La. [1941–1943, 1947–1973], and former representative Lindy Boggs, D-La. [1973–1991]), explained, "Congressional staffs are overworked and underpaid. Lobbyists help fill the information vacuum."[140]

Lobbyists' information and expertise are thus one of their most valuable assets. An annual survey conducted by the American League of Lobbyists revealed that lobbyists rated "good information/analysis" given directly to the member as the most effective way to influence a lawmaker.[141] Reflecting on the changing styles of modern lobbying, a lawyer-lobbyist said, "Because of the increasing sophistication of staff, you have to be armed with facts, precedents and legal points. Sure it's a political environment, but it's much more substantive. The old-style, pat-'em-on-the-back lobbyist is gone, or at least going."[142] Lobbying is substantive because Washington is a town filled with experts and saturated with data, analyses, and reports on all sides of an issue. The result: "Facts compete in Washington, just like Democrats and Republicans."[143]

Subgovernments

Many congressional committees deal with policies of concern to specific groups such as farmers, teachers, or veterans. Lawmakers whose constituencies contain many members of these groups tend to seek seats on the relevant committees. Members from farming areas seek assignment to the agriculture committees; members from states with many users of federal lands (such as ranchers and miners) seek assignment to the natural resources committees. Such committees often form alliances with the bureaucrats and lobbyists who regularly testify before them and with whom members and staff aides frequently meet. At hearings before the House or Senate veterans' affairs committees, for example, the triple alliance is on public view. In attendance are the committee members, along with witnesses from various veterans' organizations (such as the American Legion) and executive officials from the

Department of Veterans Affairs. Scholars and journalists use the term *subgovernment* for the three-way policy-making alliances of committees, executive agencies, and interest groups.

These triangular relationships dominate policy making less today than in the past. Other contending forces (citizens' groups, aggressive journalists, assertive presidents) have ended their policy monopoly. Fluid issue networks, in which diverse participants and groups influence decision making, better characterize current relationships within and among policy domains. Still, there is evidence that the triangular relationships remain influential in various policy domains. On January 17, 1961, President Dwight Eisenhower in his farewell address urged citizens to guard against a "military-industrial" complex to which political evolution has added Congress to the mix. This phenomenon, stated Sen. John McCain, R-Ariz., "should now rightly be called the military-industrial-congressional complex."[144] A description of the triple alliance was provided by former defense secretary Robert Gates in a 2009 speech:

> First, there is Congress, which is understandably concerned . . . about protecting jobs in certain states and congressional districts. There is the defense and aerospace industry, which has an obvious financial stake in the survival and growth of these programs. And there is the institutional military itself—within the Pentagon, and as expressed through an influential network of retired generals and admirals.[145]

Even this subgovernment is not immune to outside developments over which it has little control, as evidenced by the 2013 reality of sequestration that requires the Pentagon to make significant spending cuts in defense programs, projects, and accounts.

REGULATION OF LOBBYING

For more than a hundred years, Congress intermittently considered ways to regulate lobbying—a right protected by the First Amendment's free speech principle and "the right of the people . . . to petition the Government for a redress of grievances." Not until 1946 did Congress enact its first comprehensive lobbying law, the Federal Regulation of Lobbying Act (Title III of the Legislative Reorganization Act). The ineffectiveness of this law finally led to passage of the Lobby Disclosure Act of 1995.[146] In 2007 Congress enacted another major lobbying reform measure, the Honest Leadership and Open Government Act (P.L. 110-181). In general, there have been three main statutory approaches to the regulation of lobbying: defining and prohibiting abusive lobbying practices, requiring registration for lobbyists, and providing for disclosure of lobbyists' activities.[147]

The 1946 Lobbying Law

The main objective of the 1946 act was public disclosure of lobbying activities. Persons trying to influence Congress were required to register with the clerk of the House or the secretary of the Senate and to report quarterly the amounts of money they received and spent for lobbying. The law's drafters, although reluctant to propose direct control of lobbying, believed that "professionally inspired efforts to put pressure upon Congress cannot be conducive to well-considered legislation." Thus the law stressed registration and reporting:

> The availability of information regarding organized groups and full knowledge of their expenditures for influencing legislation, their membership and the source of contributions to them of large amounts of money, would prove helpful to Congress in evaluating their representations without impairing the rights of any individual or group freely to express its opinion to the Congress.[148]

The lobby law soon proved ineffective. In 1954 the Supreme Court upheld its constitutionality, but the decision (*United States v. Harriss*) significantly weakened the law.[149] First, the Court said that only lobbyists paid to represent someone else must register—exempting lobbyists who spent their own money. Second, the Court held that registration applied only to persons whose "principal purpose" was to influence legislation. As a result, many trade associations, labor unions, professional organizations, consumer groups, and law firms avoided registering because lobbying was not their principal activity. Some lobbyists claimed immunity from the law on the pretext that their job was to inform, not influence, legislators. Finally, the Court held that the act applied only to lobbyists who contacted members directly. This interpretation excluded indirect lobbying activities that, for example, generated grassroots pressure on Congress.

Lawmakers tried repeatedly to plug the 1946 law's loopholes. The attempts foundered largely because it was difficult to regulate lobbying without trespassing on citizens' rights to contact their elected representatives. After repeated efforts to "change the way Washington does business"—a campaign theme that many members advocated—the two parties finally came together to enact the first major overhaul of the 1946 act.

The Lobby Disclosure Act of 1995

The Lobby Disclosure Act of 1995 applied new rules to individuals and firms that lobby Congress and senior executive branch officials. The law broadened the definition of those who must register as lobbyists to include all those who spend at least one-fifth of their time trying to influence lawmakers, congressional aides, or high-level executive officials, and who are paid $5,000 or more over a six-month period. Registrations of lobbyists quickly soared. A study by the Government Accountability Office determined that when the law took effect "only 6,078 individuals and organizations had registered" under the outdated 1946 act. "After the new law took effect, a total of 14,912 lobbyists registered," 10,612 of them first-time registrants.[150] In 2009 there were about 15,000 registered lobbyists, although many more people who lobby do not register, in part because the statutory requirements do not apply to them. The law is administered by the public records offices of the House and Senate.

Lobbyists are required to "provide semi-annual disclosures showing who their clients are, what policies they are trying to influence, and roughly how much money they are spending for lobbying."[151] Civil fines of up to $50,000 can be imposed on those who fail to comply. Grassroots lobbying is exempt from the law, as are lobbyists paid $5,000 or less semiannually and organizations that use their own employees to lobby.

Although the 1995 lobby law was an improvement over the old one, it was minimally enforced. A 2005 report by the Center for Public Integrity said that the disclosure system was in disarray.[152] Lee H. Hamilton, former Indiana representative, vice chair of the 9/11 Commission, and cochair of the 2006 Iraq Study Group, described the situation:

> Roughly one in five of the companies registered to lobby failed to file the required forms, and overall, 14,000 documents that should have been filed are missing, while another fifth of the required lobbying forms were filed late. The Center [for Public Integrity] found that "countless forms are filed with portions that are blank or improperly filled out. An unknown number of lobbyists neglect or refuse to file any disclosure forms whatsoever." In essence, we have a lobby disclosure system in name only.[153]

Some firms and organizations also underreport their lobbying expenditures. "Companies, trade associations, and lobby firms often misreport—intentionally or inadvertently—how much money they shell out or take in."[154]

The Honest Leadership and Open Government Act of 2007

A confluence of events beyond the perception that the 1995 law was weakly enforced compelled the 110th Congress (2007–2009) to take up another major lobbying reform bill. Those events included, among other examples of transgressions by lawmakers, the Jack Abramoff bribery scandal (2005–2006), which led to the imprisonment of Abramoff and several lawmakers. Lobbyist Abramoff had developed close ties to influential lawmakers and staff aides, in part by providing them with lavish travel, meals, and gifts. As one staff aide said, "I was given tickets to sporting events, concerts, free food, free meals. In return, I gave preferential treatment to my lobbying buddies."[155] Democrats made the "culture of corruption" on Capitol Hill a major theme of the November 2006 elections, which won them majority control of both chambers. Highlighting the two Congresses theme, Democratic leaders realized that they had to make ethics and lobbying reform a top priority, as they did successfully in 2007. (Turning the tables, Republicans won back control of the House in the November 2010 elections, in part by using the corruption issue against Democrats.[156])

Some of the most notable provisions of the 2007 ethics reforms are highlighted in Box 13-3. Allegations of ethical violations are handled by each chamber's ethics committee; lobbying violations are under the purview of the Department of Justice. In March 2008, the House created an Office of Congressional Ethics (OCE) composed of eight private citizens. The OCE may investigate any alleged rules violations by members and report their findings to the House Ethics Committee for further review. OCE reports are eventually made public even if the ethics panel chooses to dismiss the cases submitted to them.[157] Whether statutory or rule-based, enforcement of the requirements is essential to gain public trust.

Public trust and enforcement remain significant issues. To promote public trust, President Obama took office promising to change the way Washington did business. He targeted "the outsized influence of lobbyists" on both ends of Pennsylvania Avenue.[158] During his administration, guidelines, memoranda, and executive orders have been issued restricting and limiting communications between federally registered lobbyists and executive branch officials and banning lobbyists from political appointments. On occasion, however, executive nominees have received waivers from the president's ethics rules so they could serve in his administration.[159] Moreover, the president has met in private with lobbyists, as have White House officials; Obama relies on them, so long as they are not registered lobbyists, for policy suggestions. He also depended on them to raise money for his 2012 reelection campaign.[160] In his January 27, 2010, State of the Union message, President Obama urged Congress to pass new lobbying restrictions: "It's time to require lobbyists to disclose each contact they make on behalf of a client with my administration or with Congress." This change did not occur, however.

Enforcement of the registration and disclosure requirements under the 1995 and 2007 laws remains problematic. A 2010 report by the Government Accountability Office stated that the "Justice Department has now received referrals regarding 2,680 lobbyists or organizations that have not filed required reports on their campaign contributions or their political spending," but the Department of Justice has taken "little or no follow-up action."[161] The U.S. Attorney's Office for the District of Columbia has the responsibility to take action against lobbyists who do not comply with the law, but enforcement appears to be minimal. From 1998 to 2008, only three cases of noncompliance were considered by the office, with $47,000 in fines collected from these actions.[162] In 2011 another enforcement case produced $45,000 in fines, and the next year witnessed fines assessed to two firms ($50,000 in one case and $30,000 in another).[163] Moreover, there appears to be a trend of registered lobbyists "de-registering," perhaps because of Obama's restrictions, the paperwork burdens, or their assertion that they do not engage in lobbying.[164]

Some Washington insiders say, "I don't lobby," because they do not meet with lawmakers directly or spend more than 20 percent of their time over three months lobbying for a client. (These individuals might be called "unlobbyists."[165]) For example, a former Senate party leader does not register as a lobbyist even

BOX 13-3   The Honest Leadership and Open Government Act of 2007

LOBBY REGISTRATION

The clerk of the House and the secretary of the Senate are required to make registration and disclosure forms available, in a searchable and suitable format, on the Internet for public inspection.

LOBBYING DISCLOSURE

Lobbyists must file quarterly reports for an electronic database, with a maximum fine of $200,000 for not complying.

GIFTS, MEALS, AND TRAVEL

Lobbyists may not give lawmakers or staff gifts, even those less than $50 in value, and they cannot pay for lawmakers' or staffers' meals or travel expenses.

Members and staff must receive advance approval from the appropriate ethics committee before accepting any travel with any private organization.

REVOLVING DOOR

Senators and very senior executive officials are prohibited from lobbying for two years after they leave government; House members, for one.

Senior staff members who left Capitol Hill would be prohibited from lobbying for one year.

All Senate staff members are prohibited from lobbying the member or committee for whom they worked for one year after leaving.

CAMPAIGN CONTRIBUTIONS

Registered lobbyists would have to reveal all their political contributions, including bundling of contributions from friends and colleagues.

LOBBYING THE EXECUTIVE BRANCH

Lobbyists who contact executive branch officials, called "covered officials," must register with the clerk of the House and secretary of the Senate and disclose their contacts and activities. (The 1946 act did not address lobbying the executive branch.)

Source: Adapted from Jack Maskell, legislative attorney, "Lobbying Law and Ethics Rules Changes in the 110th Congress," Congressional Research Service Report RL34377, September 17, 2007.

though he provides clients with lawmaking and other relevant advice. "I provide my clients with analysis, not access," he said. "I offer them strategic advice on public policy matters, including analysis of the substance, procedure and politics associated with different policy initiatives, whether they be legislative, regulatory or otherwise."[166] According to the president of the American League of Lobbyists—a professional association for lobbyists—there are "about 3,000 'nonregistered lobbyists' [or unlobbyists] who ought to be registered, in addition to more than 12,000 who are actually registered."[167]

Foreign Lobbying

The 1995 Lobby Disclosure Act also amended the Foreign Agents Registration Act of 1938, which required those who lobby on behalf of foreign governments or political parties to register with the Justice Department and file twice-yearly reports with the department on their contacts with lawmakers and federal agencies. The 1995 law broadened the definition of foreign lobbyists to include individuals who lobby on behalf of foreign-owned commercial enterprises. About five hundred lobbyists have registered with the Justice Department as agents representing foreign governments or parties (see www.usdoj.gov/criminal/fara). Although foreigners who are lobbyists cannot make campaign contributions, one "in every $8 spent lobbying Congress and federal agencies comes from foreign governments."[168]

Numerous foreign governments sponsor cultural exchange programs for lawmakers and legislative staff, which are organized by Washington-based lobbyists who work for those governments. From 2006 to 2011, there were more than 800 of these cultural exchange trips paid for by foreign countries located in most parts of the world (Asia, the Middle East, and Europe, for example). Despite the detailed rules (pre-approval, the itinerary, etc.) for congressional travel funded by corporations and other organizations that hire lobbyists, some of those rules do not apply to trips paid for by foreign governments. For example, registered foreign lobbyists may organize these trips and, importantly, accompany lawmakers and staff on the cultural trips. The benefits to these lobbyists can be significant. As one account noted, "Lobbyists for foreign countries use the trips to build relationships with staffers and often contact them about legislative business [involving the host countries] after the trips are over."[169]

Because of the role of the United States in the global economy and in military security, many foreign governments and lobbyists who work for foreign clients spend considerable amounts of time and money promoting their interests on Capitol Hill and with the broader citizenry. For example, to hasten passage of a trade agreement with the United States, the South Korean embassy "signed four different lobbying and public relations firms to advocate for the trade deal."[170] Several Washington firms lobby for the Libyan rebels who led the successful revolt against dictator Muammar Gaddafi. One firm signed a $15,000-per-month contract with the Libyan embassy. The firm will provide various services, such as a public outreach program, the promotion of investments in Libya, and the development of a website and social media.[171] Many other nations also hire lobbyists to forge closer ties with Congress, the executive branch, and various U.S. industries, such as oil.[172]

Local lobbyists also operate globally. Many U.S.-based corporations hire lobbyists who can protect their interests in Europe or other parts of the world when disputes arise about trade, agriculture, antitrust laws, the environment, and other issues.[173] The National Rifle Association formed a transnational organization of gun groups and firearms manufacturers from eleven other countries (the World Forum) to fight international restrictions and regulations that might adversely affect the gun trade.[174] The NRA also informed the United Nations that "the effort to craft international rules for weapons sales will go nowhere in Congress if it includes civilian arms."[175]

Globalization of the world's economy also influences congressional lobbying. Toyota is the world's largest auto manufacturer, with plants located in eleven states. By locating plants around the country, the company enhances its political clout on Capitol Hill, gaining supporters in the House, Senate, and state houses. Toyota can now "call on 151 House members, 22 senators, and 11 governors from the states where it operates."[176]

CONCLUSION

Since the nation's beginning, lobbying and lawmaking have been closely intertwined. Lobbying "has been so deeply woven into the American political fabric that one could, with considerable justice, assert that the history of lobbying comes close to being the history of American legislation."[177]

Recent years have witnessed an explosion in the number and types of groups organized to pursue their ends on Capitol Hill. Compared with decades past, many more industry associations, public affairs lobbies (such as Common Cause), single-issue groups, political action committees, and foreign agents are engaging in the influence trade. Some of these groups employ new grassroots and technological lobbying techniques. Many victories today are won in Washington because of sophisticated lobbying campaigns waged in home states or districts.

No one questions that groups and lobbyists have a rightful public role, but some aspects of lobbying warrant concern. Groups often push Congress to pass laws that benefit the few and not the many. They inflate disagreements and hinder compromise. They often misrepresent the voting records of legislators in their rating schemes and pour money into the campaigns of their allies (mainly incumbents). Lawmakers who defy single-issue groups find at election time that those organizations are bent on defeating them.

Built-in checks constrain group pressures, however. The immense number of organized interests enables legislators to play one competing group off against another. Knowledgeable staff aides also provide members with information to counter lobbyists' arguments. Lawmakers' own expertise is another informal check on lobbyists. Finally, there are self-imposed constraints. Lobbyists who misrepresent issues or mislead members soon find their access permanently closed off. As Rep. Barney Frank explained: "I feel better about a position when I can hear from both sides. . . . You can use [lobbyists] to inform you, as long as they know that if they lie, they lose. They will never be allowed to come back to this office."[178]

B*udgets, Taxes, and Domestic Policies.* Two citizens (top) fill out last-minute tax returns at a post office in northwest Washington, D.C. House Budget Committee chair Rep. Paul Ryan, R-Wis., challenges President Obama's budget for the fiscal year 2014 (center). Domestic tragedies like Hurricane Sandy (October 2012) compel local officials to appeal for federal aid: President Obama meets with New York Governor Andrew Cuomo, with (from left to right) Housing Secretary Shaun Donovan, Homeland Security Secretary Janet Napolitano, and New York City Mayor Michael Bloomberg. Local senators and representatives led the call for federal aid.

Congress, Budgets, and Domestic Policy Making

Whaen Republicans won control of the House of Representatives in the 2010 elections, cutting domestic spending was high on their priority list. But the new majority party had to contend with a Democratic president and Democratic Senate, all resisting the sweeping cuts that Republicans favored. How could Republicans transform America's fiscal policy while controlling just a single chamber of Congress? Their answer was to capitalize on the looming need to raise the country's debt ceiling. This decision set up a confrontation that dominated American politics for several months in 2011 and that illuminates important features of Congress as a policy-making institution.

When the government raises less in revenue than it spends, it must borrow money—by issuing bonds—to cover the difference. The debt limit is a statutory cap on the total amount of borrowing that the federal government can undertake. Treasury Secretary Timothy Geithner notified Congress in early January 2011 that the debt ceiling of $14.294 trillion would soon be breached unless Congress passed legislation raising the limit.[1]

Leaders of the new GOP majority in the House responded that they would only agree to raise the debt limit if the president and Senate accepted major budget cuts.[2] Absent an increase in the debt limit, the Treasury Department would be unable to pay the money that it owed to government program beneficiaries—such as Social Security checks—and the government would eventually default on the interest payments that it owed to existing bondholders. Austan Goolsbee, the chair of President Barack Obama's Council of Economic Advisers, bluntly warned, "If we get to the point where we damage the full faith and credit of the United States, that would be the first default in history caused by pure insanity."[3] Outside experts generally agreed that the result would be catastrophic for the U.S. economy.

Several months of arduous negotiations ensued. While the Obama administration disagreed with the idea of linking a debt ceiling increase to spending cuts, the president and his team nonetheless met with House Republican leaders to seek an agreement on a major deficit reduction package that would include a debt ceiling increase. There were moments when it appeared that a "grand bargain"—in which Obama agreed to substantial cuts in both discretionary domestic spending and in entitlement programs such as Medicare and Medicaid, and Speaker John Boehner agreed to new revenues—was within reach. But in the end, Obama insisted on increased tax revenues that Boehner could not sell to conservative members of his party, while Boehner sought greater spending cuts than Obama was willing to accept, absent major new revenues.[4]

As talks dragged into July 2011, two major credit ratings agencies threatened to lower the United States' credit rating unless action was taken to raise the debt ceiling before August 2, when the Treasury Department would no longer be able to meet all obligations for payments under existing law. President Obama took to the airwaves to warn that Social Security checks might be delayed if Congress failed to act; Republicans accused the president of trying to scare the country and of failing to negotiate in good faith.[5]

Meanwhile, as market jitters mounted, Senate minority leader Mitch McConnell, R-Ky., proposed a compromise that would shift responsibility for increasing the debt limit onto the president. McConnell's plan would authorize Obama to increase the debt ceiling in three installments over the next two years; Congress could then vote to disapprove the increases, but the disapproval resolutions would be subject to a presidential veto. This would allow Republicans to vote against the specific debt ceiling increases, while nonetheless avoiding default. House Republicans, however, rejected the plan.[6]

With time running out, President Obama announced a deal to increase the debt ceiling on July 31, 2011. The agreement consisted of two stages. The first stage included $917 billion in spending cuts that the White House and congressional leaders had agreed to, along with a corresponding $900 billion increase in the debt limit. The second stage provided for an additional $1.2 trillion increase in the debt limit but tied that increase to further deficit reduction. Under the agreement, Congress would create a special joint committee charged with identifying the additional $1.2 trillion in deficit reduction. If this so-called "supercommittee" failed to reach an agreement, across-the-board spending cuts—split evenly between domestic and defense programs—would take effect in January 2013. Supporters of the compromise argued that this "trigger" would impose such devastating cuts—hitting programs valued by both parties—that it would force both sides to negotiate in good faith and ultimately lead to a major budget deal.[7]

The House passed the agreement on August 1 and the Senate followed suit the next day, essentially at the last possible moment before the Treasury Department would have run out of room to maneuver.

When the supercommittee was appointed, however, it became apparent that there was little likelihood it would reach the sort of agreement that had eluded Obama and Boehner. House Republicans appointed stalwart conservatives—such as Jeb Hensarling of Texas—who were loath to agree to new taxes, while Democrats appointed committed liberals—such as Xavier Becerra of California—who were deeply resistant to the spending cuts sought by Republicans. The result was another stalemate. As the 112th Congress wound down, Congress voted to delay the automatic spending cuts for two more months in the hope of reaching another deal, but they began to take effect when no deal was reached by March 2013.

The two Congresses were clearly in evidence during the debt limit fight. As a lawmaking assembly, members of both parties faced the urgent need to act decisively to forestall an economic disaster. But passing legislation on the debt limit required addressing members' electoral calculations. For Republicans who believed they had been elected to cut spending and deficits, a vote to raise the debt limit was seen as a liability that could threaten their reelection. McConnell's proposal to delegate responsibility for the debt ceiling to the president reflected Congress's widespread desire to avoid tough votes.

More generally, the deep ideological split over whether dramatic spending cuts or new taxes were needed to deal with the deficit reflected the diversity of views in the country at large. For Republicans, their very public promise to constituents that they would never agree to increased taxes greatly limited their maneuvering room in discussions of a "Grand Bargain." Democrats, for their part, were mindful of the political payoff of defending popular programs such as Medicare and Social Security from Republican cuts. Constituent concerns were never far from the surface as members fought over the debt ceiling.

The debt ceiling battle also illustrates other aspects of the contemporary policy-making process in Congress. In the context of deep party divisions and frequent divided government, legislators and the president find it extremely difficult to agree unless there is a deadline that makes the consequences of stalemate disastrous. This, in turn, may create incentives for both sides to *create* deadlines as a spur to action. The result, however, tends to be a drawn-out, messy negotiating process that veers close to disaster before generating a resolution that neither side is particularly happy about and that may well once again postpone some of the difficult decisions for yet another, new deadline.

Congress's approval rating took a hit following the debt ceiling negotiations—falling to yet another low.[8] The public clearly does not like the politics of brinksmanship that has become increasingly common on Capitol Hill, but as long as the parties remain deeply divided from one another—and as long as voters do not provide a clear signal about how to resolve pressing policy challenges—more of the same may be expected.

Plainly, conflicts about policies and the money to pay for them lie at the vortex of today's lawmaking process. This chapter will first provide a general overview of the policy-making process. It will then turn to a more detailed discussion of budgeting, which has increasingly come to dominate politics and policy making in Congress.

STAGES OF POLICY MAKING

Public policy is what the government says and does about perceived problems.[9] Policy making normally has four distinct stages: (1) setting the agenda, (2) formulating policy, (3) adopting policy, and (4) implementing policy.

Setting the Agenda

At the initial stage, public problems are spotted and moved onto the national agenda, which can be defined as "the list of subjects to which government officials and those around them are paying serious attention."[10] In a large, pluralistic country such as the United States, the national agenda at any given moment is extensive and vigorously debated.

How do problems move onto the agenda? Some emerge as a result of a crisis or an attention-grabbing event—an economic depression, a terrorist attack, a devastating hurricane or earthquake, or a high-visibility corruption scandal. For example, in December 2012 a devastating shooting in an elementary school in Newtown, Connecticut, led to renewed attention to gun control on the national political agenda. Other agenda items are occasioned by the gradual accumulation of knowledge—for example, rising awareness of an environmental hazard such as global warming. Still other agenda items represent the accumulation of past problems that no longer can be avoided or ignored, such as the safety of the nation's food supply and the crumbling infrastructure.

Agendas are also set in motion by political processes—election results (1964, 1994, 2006, and 2010 are good examples), turnover in Congress, or shifts in public opinion.[11] For example, the election of 2006 resulted in the first Democratic Congress in over a decade, and with it came a new set of priorities, including opposition to President George W. Bush's handling of the Iraq war and aggressive congressional oversight of the executive branch. In the 2010 elections, Democrats took a "shellacking." The eighty-seven House GOP freshmen, backed by an assertive Tea Party movement, made cost-cutting and downsizing government their top priorities. Scores of members in both parties and both chambers shared their concerns and mobilized to address the nation's mounting deficit and debt.

Agenda items are pushed by policy entrepreneurs—that is, people who are willing to invest their time and energy in promoting a particular issue. Especially at the beginning of a new president's term, many of Washington's think tanks and interest groups issue reports that seek to influence the economic, social, or foreign policy agenda of the nation. Elected officials and their staffs or appointees are more likely to shape agendas than are career bureaucrats.[12]

Lawmakers are frequently policy entrepreneurs. Party and committee leaders are especially influential. Generally speaking, politicians gravitate toward issues that are visible, salient, and solvable. Tough, arcane, or controversial problems such as entitlements may be shunned or postponed because they arouse significant public controversy.

The nation's recent experience with record gasoline prices placed pressure on lawmakers to address difficult questions of energy policy. Energy independence has been a decades-long goal of the United States, particularly since the 1970s, when the Organization of Petroleum Exporting Countries (OPEC)—a cartel—deliberately slowed down oil production, resulting in long gas lines in cities across America. The reality is that there are no quick fixes to the demand for energy. As one analyst suggested,

> We need an energy policy that understands that the world is going to require much more energy in the future. The math is pretty simple. Today, there are about 6.7 billion people on earth. By 2050 there will be 9 billion. To sustain these extra 2.3 billion people while still raising standards of living everywhere, we will need to consume about twice as much energy as we do today. So the debate about oil vs. natural gas vs. biofuels vs. alternative energy is wholly unrealistic. If we are going to sustain and support this kind of population and economic growth, we'll need everything.[13]

Forecasters continue to predict more short- and long-term energy woes unless steps are taken to develop clean alternative fuels, change consumption habits, encourage conservation, and reduce the spiraling demand for oil, especially oil from the volatile Middle East.[14]

This kind of creeping crisis is often difficult for members of Congress to grapple with, in part because of the two-Congresses dilemma. As conscientious lawmakers, members might want to forge long-term solutions. But as representatives of their constituents, they must respond to more immediate constituent concerns about, as Obama's energy secretary phrased it, being "at the mercy of [energy] price spikes" because of the country's oil dependency.[15]

Formulating Policy

In the second stage of policy making, lawmakers and others discuss items on the political agenda and explore potential solutions. Members of Congress and their staffs play crucial roles by conducting hearings and writing committee reports. They are aided by the policy experts in executive agencies, interest groups, legislative support agencies, think tanks, universities, and private sector organizations. Another term for this stage is *policy incubation,* which entails "keeping a proposal alive while it picks up support, or waits for a better climate, or while a consensus begins to form."[16] Sometimes, this process takes only a few months; more often it requires years. During Dwight D. Eisenhower's administration (1953–1961), for example, congressional Democrats explored and refined domestic policy options that while not immediately accepted, were ripe for adoption by the time their party's nominee, John F. Kennedy, was elected president in 1960.[17]

The incubation process refines the solutions to problems and brings policies to maturity. The process may break down, however, if workable solutions are not available. The seeming intractability of many modern issues complicates problem solving. Thomas S. Foley, D-Wash. (Speaker, 1989–1995), held that in the years after he entered Congress in 1965 issues became far more perplexing. At that time "the civil rights issue facing the legislators was whether the right to vote should be federally guaranteed for blacks and Hispanics. Now members are called on to deal with more ambiguous policies like affirmative action and racial quotas."[18] Complex topics such as stem cell research, genetic discrimination, unconventional warfare, and global climate change are contemporary examples of the difficult issues facing lawmakers. Solutions to problems normally involve "some fairly simple routines emphasizing the tried and true (or at least not discredited)."[19] A repertoire of proposals—for example, blue-ribbon commissions, trust funds, or pilot projects—can be applied to a variety of unsolved problems. Problem solvers also must guard against recommending solutions that will be viewed as worse than the problem.

Adopting Policy

Laws often embody ideas whose time has come. The right time for a policy is what scholar John W. Kingdon calls the "policy window": the opportunity presented by circumstances and attitudes to enact a policy into law. Policy entrepreneurs must seize the opportunity before the policy window closes and the idea's time has passed.

Once policies are ripe for adoption, they must gain popular acceptance. This is the function of legitimation, the process through which policies come to be viewed by the public as right or proper. Inasmuch as citizens are expected to comply with laws or regulations—pay taxes, observe rules, and make sacrifices of one sort or another—the policies themselves must appear to have been properly considered and enacted. One of the lingering liabilities of the landmark Patient Protection and Affordable Care Act of 2010 is the impression among some Americans that it was rammed through without bipartisan support.

Symbolic acts, such as members voting on the House or Senate floor or the president signing a bill, signal to everyone that a policy was adopted within the traditional practices. Hearings and debates serve to fine-tune policies as well as to cultivate support from affected interests. As for the pace of the overall process, responding to critics of Congress's glacial progress in adopting energy legislation, a senator posed these questions:

> Would you want an energy bill to flow through the Senate and not have anyone consider the impacts on housing or on the automotive industry or on the energy industries that provide our light and power? Should we ignore the problems of the miner or the producer or the distributor? Our legislative process must reflect all of the problems if the public is to have confidence in the government.[20]

Legitimating policies, in other words, often requires a measured pace and attention to procedural details. But a measured pace and painstaking attention to procedural niceties often provide opponents of change with an opportunity to mobilize. In many circumstances, policy makers may be forced to enact bold changes quickly in response to public outcry or demand, knowing that the details will have to be refined and adjusted later. The legislative passage in three weeks of President Obama's economic stimulus package is an example.

Implementing Policy

In the final stage, policies shaped by the legislature and at the highest executive levels are put into effect, often by a federal agency. Most policies are not self-executing; they must be promulgated and enforced. A law or executive order rarely spells out exactly how a particular policy should be implemented. Congress and the president usually delegate most decisions about implementation to the responsible agencies under broadly worded guidelines. Implementation determines the ultimate effect of policies. Officials of the executive branch can thwart a policy by foot-dragging or sheer inefficiency. By the same token, overzealous administrators can push a policy far beyond its creators' intent.

Congress, therefore, must exercise its oversight role. It may require executive agencies to report to or consult with congressional committees or to follow other formal procedures. Members of Congress receive feedback on the operation of federal programs through a variety of channels: media coverage, interest group protests, and even casework for constituents. With such information Congress can adjust funding, introduce amendments, or recast the legislation on which the policy is based.

TYPES OF DOMESTIC POLICIES

One way to understand public policies is to analyze the nature of the policies themselves. Scholars have classified policies in many different ways.[21] Our typology identifies three types of domestic policies: distributive, regulatory, and redistributive.

Distributive Policies

Distributive policies or programs are government actions that convey tangible benefits—subsidies, tax breaks, or advantageous regulatory provisions—to private individuals, groups, or firms. These benefits are often called "pork," a derogatory term for program benefits or spending specifically designated for members' states or districts. But pork is often difficult to define objectively. After all, "one person's pork is another person's steak." The projects come in several varieties, including "old-fashioned pork" (bridges and roads), "green pork" (wind, solar, and other alternative energy projects), "academic pork" (research grants to colleges and universities), or "high-tech pork" (cybersecurity).

Distributive policy making, which makes many interests better off and few, if any, visibly worse off—comes easily to Congress, a collegial and nonhierarchical institution that must build coalitions to function. A textbook example was the $1 billion-plus National Parks and Recreation Act of 1978. Dubbed the "Park Barrel Bill," it created so many parks, historic sites, seashores, wilderness areas, wild and scenic rivers, and national trails that it sailed through the Interior (now Resources) Committee and passed the House 341–61. "Notice how quiet we are. We all got something in there," said one House member after the Rules Committee cleared the bill in five minutes flat. Another member quipped, "If it had a blade of grass and a squirrel, it got in the bill."[22]

Distributive politics of this kind throws the two Congresses into sharp relief: national policy as a mosaic of local interests.

The politics of distribution works best when tax revenues are expanding, fueled by high productivity and economic growth. When productivity declines or tax cuts squeeze revenues, it can become difficult to add new benefits or expand old ones. Yet distributive impulses remain strong even in these circumstances, as lawmakers in both parties work to ensure that money is spent for specific purposes in their districts or states. This type of particularistic spending is known by a variety of different names—"pork," "spending with a Zip code," "member projects," "congressional directed spending," or, more commonly today, "earmarks." By whatever name, the fundamental purpose of this spending is to "bring home the bacon." Recently, earmarks have fallen into disfavor, in part because of their cost, political use ("greasing" the legislative wheels), and the circumvention of competitive procedures for funding such constituency-based projects.

The Controversy over Earmarks. During the 1990s and early 2000s, the number of earmarks in spending bills increased in number and dollar value. In 1993 there were 892 earmarks worth $2.6 billion; in 1998 there were nearly 2,000 earmarks worth $10.6 billion; and by 2005 there were "nearly 14,000 earmarks, costing $27.3 billion."[23] The cost of over 9,000 earmarks peaked at $29 billion in 2006, with a falloff to $15.9 billion (9,500 earmarks) in 2010.[24] (The 2010 expenditures for earmarks represented less than half of 1 percent of the $3.7 trillion federal budget.)

Various factors accounted for the explosion in earmarks and then their rapid drop-off. As for the increase, with narrow partisan divisions in the House and Senate, party and committee leaders used earmarks to attract the votes they needed to pass priority legislation and, in a two-Congresses tactic, helped electorally vulnerable lawmakers facing tough challenges at home. A longtime GOP appropriator also stated that in 1995, when Republicans took control of the House, they "democratized the earmark process" by making earmarks "available to everyone, Republican or Democrat, leader and rank-and-file alike."[25]

The decline in earmarks occurred for three principal reasons. First, there was significant criticism of wasteful and unnecessary earmarks, especially in an era of rising fiscal deficits. The classic example highlighted by opponents of earmarks was "the bridge to nowhere"—a $230 million bridge connecting a small Alaskan town of eight thousand to an island with fifty residents.[26]

Second, there was an unseemly and sometimes corrupt connection between earmarks and campaign contributions. One lawmaker (who ended up in jail) took $2.4 million in bribes from lobbyists to insert earmarks for defense contractors, who would then contribute to his reelection campaign. Third, aggressive watchdog groups, bloggers, and several lawmakers, such as Rep. (now Sen.) Jeff Flake, R-Ariz., and Sen. John McCain, R-Ariz., exposed and challenged on the floor what they viewed as bad earmarks.

Earmark Reform. The 110th and 111th Congresses, as well as President Obama, instituted reforms intended to bring transparency and accountability to the earmark process. For example, the procedures required public disclosure of the lawmaker requesting an earmark; the name and location of the intended recipient; the purpose of the earmark; and certification that neither the requesting lawmaker nor his or her spouse had a financial interest in the earmark.

The 112th Congress went even further. The GOP-controlled House imposed a complete ban on earmarks for all House members. Their party regulation stated that "no Member shall request a congressional earmark, limited tax benefit, or limited tariff benefit, as such terms have been described in the Rules of the House." Some House committees also established their own guidelines for excluding earmarks from their measures.[27]

The Senate resisted for a time but then moved to ban earmarks. After President Obama declared in his 2011 State of the Union message that he would veto any legislation containing earmarks and the House indicated that it would not pass any bills that contained them, Senate Appropriations chair Daniel Inouye, D-Hawaii, said in a statement: "Given the reality before us, it makes no sense to accept earmark requests that have no chance of being enacted into law."[28] But key senators have promised to revisit the issue and to explore ways "to improve the earmarking process."[29] Other senators, such as Claire McCaskill, D-Mo., and Patrick Toomey, R-Pa., want to write into law the prohibition against earmarks now in party rules.[30]

The debate over earmarks did not end in either chamber for a fundamental two-Congresses reason. As one lawmaker explained, earmarking is "part of the genetic makeup of a legislator," who must try to find a way to help his or her community.[31] Earmark advocates in both chambers argued that a blanket ban impeded the lawmaking process, granted too much authority to unelected bureaucrats to make spending decisions that reside constitutionally with House and Senate members, and urged a rethinking of how to define an earmark. Writing to their Appropriations Committee's leaders, several senators stressed the need "to operationalize a clear definition" of earmarks. Authorized earmarks that benefit the entire nation, they argued, "are quite different from congressionally directed spending items, which only benefit a separate state, congressional district or region, and change year-to-year."[32]

Members also employed other, less transparent means to finance projects back home: earmarks by another name. They include "lettermarking"—lawmakers writing to administrators to urge that home-based projects be funded; "phonemarking"—calling executive officials to request money for projects in their states or districts; and "soft earmarks"—simply "suggesting" to agency officials that money should be spent on the lawmaker's project. Members also might hike the dollar amounts in certain budgetary accounts and "then forcefully request that the agency spend the money on the member's pet project."[33] Some lawmakers continue to solicit funding for earmarked local projects. They ask constituents to send in letters identifying community projects in need of federal money. As Rep. Mike Thompson, D-Calif., wrote in a letter to constituents:

> I disagree with this decision [banning earmarks] because it prevents full and open congressional consideration of many worthwhile project proposals critical to the health, safety and economic well-being of

the people of our district. As your representative in Congress, I am committed to working with you to pursue alternative strategies to support critical infrastructure improvements in our communities.[34]

To sum up, many lawmakers and analysts contend that eliminating earmarks saves a trivial amount of money, and that the lengthy debates over earmarks only detract from the big-budget items that dominate spending such as entitlements and defense, which need members' attention. Moreover, many earmarks are not wasteful and serve worthwhile national purposes, such as repairing decrepit bridges, establishing the Human Genome Project, and requiring the Pentagon "to procure Predator drone aircraft as well as to buy more body armor for troops and provide more armor protection for vehicles used in Iraq."[35]

Regulatory Policies

Regulatory policies are designed to protect the public from the harm or abuse that might result from unbridled private activity. For example, the Food and Drug Administration monitors standards for foodstuffs and tests drugs for purity, safety, and effectiveness, and the Federal Trade Commission guards against illegal business practices such as deceptive advertising.

Federal regulation against certain abuses dates from the late nineteenth century, when the Interstate Commerce Act and the Sherman Antitrust Act were enacted to protect against abuses in transportation and monopolistic practices. As the twentieth century dawned, scandalous conditions in slaughterhouses and food-processing plants led to meatpacking, food, and drug regulations. The stock market collapse in 1929 and the Great Depression of the 1930s paved the way for the New Deal's regulation of the banking and securities industries and of labor-management relations. Consumer rights and environmental protection policies came of age in the 1960s and 1970s. The reversal of some of the protections of the 1930 enactments, plus lax oversight by federal agencies, contributed to the banking crisis of 2008–2009, which in turn fueled the Great Recession. Predictably, the fresh wave of Wall Street scandals led to a new round of regulatory fervor. Among its legacies is the Consumer Financial Protection Bureau (P.L. 111-203). Its job is to act as a watchdog for consumers in their purchase of various financial products, such as credit cards or mortgages.

Regulation inevitably arouses controversy. Much of the clean air debate, for example, involves the basic issue of costs versus benefits: Do the public health benefits of cleaner air outweigh the financial costs of obtaining it?[36] Environmentalists and health advocates argue that tougher standards for regulating air pollution prevent suffering and save the lives of thousands who are afflicted with asthma and other lung diseases. Industries and conservative groups attack these claims, contending that the regulations are unnecessary, too expensive, and produce little health benefit.[37] A by-product of new regulations—such as the sweeping health care and financial reform laws enacted by the 111th Congress—has been the skyrocketing revenues for "Washington lobbyists positioned to help companies influence and comply with the new regulations."[38]

Reviewing federal agencies' regulation-writing process is a priority of today's Congress and of President Obama. Like presidents before him, Obama took steps to further centralize overall control over regulation writing in the Office of Management and Budget (OMB), specifically OMB's Office of Information and Regulatory Affairs (OIRA). For example, the president issued an executive order on January 18, 2011 (E.O. 13563), requiring agencies to produce affordable and less intrusive regulations: "We're looking at the [regulatory] system as a whole to make sure we avoid excessive, inconsistent and redundant regulation."[39] To achieve these regulatory goals, the president relies on OMB, which uses cost-benefit analysis to curb excessive and burdensome regulations. Rep. Darrell Issa, R-Calif., the chair of the House Oversight and Government Reform Committee, also cites regulatory reform as a top priority.

Redistributive Policies

The most difficult of all political feats is redistributive policy—that is, one in which the government purposefully shifts resources from one group to another. Typically controversial, redistributive policies engage a broad spectrum of political actors, not only in the House and Senate but also in the executive branch and among interest groups and the public at large. Redistributive issues tend to be ideological, dividing liberals and conservatives on fundamental questions of equality, opportunity, and property rights. Tax cuts for the wealthy at a time of rising income inequality is an example of a redistributive controversy. Redistribution can even be future-oriented: excessive amounts of deficit spending today mean larger financial burdens for the next generation.

Most of the divisive socioeconomic issues of the past generation—civil rights, affirmative action, school busing, welfare, immigration, tax reform—were redistributive problems. A redistributive issue for the twenty-first century is the growing share of the federal budget that goes to the elderly compared with everyone else in society. Spending on entitlement programs, principally Social Security and Medicare, absorbs an ever-increasing proportion of federal dollars, which then are unavailable for other important social, domestic, or security needs.

When redistributive issues are at stake, federal budgeting is almost always marked by conflict. In recent years, the conflicts have tended to be over the progressivity of the income tax code and how to cut entitlements. Various techniques have been employed to disguise cuts and to make them more palatable. Omnibus budget packages permit legislators to approve cuts en bloc instead of one by one, and across-the-board formulas (such as freezes) give the appearance of spreading the misery equally to affected groups. In all such vehicles, provisions are added to placate the more vocal opponents of change.

CHARACTERISTICS OF CONGRESSIONAL POLICY MAKING

As a policy-making body, Congress displays the traits and biases of its membership and structure, as well as those of the larger political system. As for the first, the two houses of Congress have divergent electoral and procedural traditions. As for the second, Congress is representative, especially where geographic interests are concerned, and it is decentralized, having few mechanisms for integrating or coordinating its policy decisions. As for policy itself, Congress is often inclined toward enacting symbolic measures instead of substantive ones. Finally, Congress is rarely ahead of the curve—or the public—tending to reflect conventional perceptions of problems.

Bicameralism

Differences between the House and Senate—their relative sizes, members' terms of office, the character of their constituencies—shape the policies they make. Six-year terms, it is argued, allow senators to act as statesmen for at least part of each term before the approaching elections force them to concentrate on fence-mending. Although this distinction may be more apparent than real, empirical studies of senators' behavior lend some support to the claim.[40]

Various constituencies tend to pull in divergent directions. Homogeneous House districts often promote clear, unambiguous positions on a narrower range of questions than those embraced by an entire state. A senator, then, as a representative of an entire state, must weigh the claims of many competing interests on a broad range of matters.

The sizes of the two chambers dictate procedural biases. House rules are designed to allow majorities to have their way. By contrast, Senate rules give individual senators great latitude to influence action. As a GOP senator once said, "The Senate has the strongest minority of any minority on earth, and the weakest majority of any on earth."[41]

In short, the two chambers differ in outlook, constituency, and strategy. This can make forging agreement across the two chambers more challenging and therefore adds to the more general difficulty of changing or terminating existing policies, not to mention passing new legislation.

Localism

Congressional policies respond to constituents' needs, particularly those that can be mapped geographically. Sometimes, these needs are pinpointed with startling directness. For example, an aviation noise control bill required construction of a control tower "at latitude 40 degrees, 43 minutes, 45 seconds north and at longitude 73 degrees, 24 minutes, 50 seconds west"—the very location of a Farmingdale, New York, airport in the district of the Democratic representative who requested the provision.[42]

Usually, however, programs are directed toward states, municipalities, counties, or geographic regions. Funds are often transferred directly to local government agencies, which in turn deliver the aid or services to citizens. But sometimes Congress will require states and localities to fund some national priorities without federal assistance. These "unfunded mandates" strain state budgets and rouse the ire of state and local officials. In 1995 President Bill Clinton signed into law the Unfunded Mandates Reform Act, which requires

Congress either to make provision to pay for any mandate that the Congressional Budget Office (CBO) estimates will cost state and local governments $50 million or more, or to "take a separate recorded vote to waive the requirement, thus holding members of Congress accountable for their decision."[43]

Lawmakers are therefore supposed to consider the costs of any federal requirements they impose on state and local governments. For example, the No Child Left Behind (NCLB) education law (P.L. 107-110), which President Obama is urging the 113th Congress to revise and reauthorize before 2014 (the statute's expiration date), prescribes mandatory standardized testing in all public schools in today's cash-strapped states. School systems in many states complain that the federal government has failed to provide enough money to cover the expense of meeting the law's requirement. The law's fundamental goal is to ensure that by 2014 every student in Grades 3–8 is proficient in reading and math. If not, schools might close and teachers could be fired.

National and local policies are necessarily intertwined. National policies can be advanced by state and local governments; in turn, states or localities can develop innovations that spur national action. The threat of terrorist attacks in the United States demands that any such calamity be confronted by first responders—police officers, firefighters, public health officials, and others—at the state and local levels. On other issues as well, the states are the testing grounds, or laboratories, for social, economic, and political experiments.

Many policy debates revolve around not only which government level can most effectively carry out a responsibility, but also which level best promotes particular values. Liberals tend to prefer that the national government lead in enforcing civil rights and environmental protection. Conservatives support an activist national government on defense and security matters. When it suits their purposes, both liberals and conservatives are capable of advocating either national mandates or local autonomy, depending on which level of government would best serve their objectives.

Piecemeal Policy Making

Policies all too often mirror Congress's scattered and decentralized structure. Typically, they are considered piecemeal, reflecting the patchwork of committee and subcommittee jurisdictions. The structure of a policy frequently depends on which committees have reported it. Working from varying jurisdictions, committees can take different approaches to the same problem. The taxing committees gravitate toward tax provisions to address problems; the appropriations committees will prefer a fiscal approach to issues; the commerce panels typically adopt a regulatory perspective; and so forth. Each approach may be well or ill suited to the policy objective. The approach adopted will depend on which committee is best positioned to promote the bill.

Symbolic Policy Making

Congressional policy making can be more about appearance than substance. Bills are often passed to give the impression that action is being taken, even when the measure adopted is unlikely to have any real impact on the problem. The general public and interest groups continually demand, "Don't just stand there, do something." Doing something is often the only politically feasible choice, even when no one knows exactly what to do or whether inaction might be just as effective.[44] For example, when rising gas prices provoked a national outcry in May 2008, Congress responded by passing a law cutting off the flow of oil to the nation's Strategic Petroleum Reserve. Though the move was touted as a way to boost supply and thus reduce gas prices, most analysts argued it would have no effect on energy prices.[45]

Still, symbolic actions are important to all politicians. This is not the same thing as saying that politicians are merely cynical manipulators of symbols. Words and concepts—*equal opportunity, income inequality, cost of living, affirmative action*—are contested earnestly in committee rooms and on the House and Senate floor. The result, however, is that federal goals are often stated in vague, optimistic language and not spelled out in terms of specific measures of success or failure.

Reactive Policy Making

It would be naive to expect a deliberative body to routinely adopt bold or radical solutions to problems. Elected officials are seldom far ahead of or far behind the collective views of their constituencies. Members know that out-of-the-mainstream views are unlikely to attract widespread public support. Indeed, Congress is essentially a reactive institution. As one House member explained,

> When decision rests on the consent of the governed, it comes slowly, only after consensus has built or crisis has focused public opinion in some unusual way, the representatives in the meantime hanging back until the signs are unmistakable. Government decision, then, is not generally the cutting edge of change but a belated reaction to change.[46]

Ending the statutory "don't ask, don't tell" policy toward gays in the military, for example, came late in 2010—only after public attitudes on the matter had shifted and the Joint Chiefs of Staff had assured lawmakers that the change would not adversely affect military performance.

The reactive character of Congress's policy making is evident in its budget process. Under pressures to reform in recent decades, Congress has embraced formal and informal changes in the way it makes budget decisions. The current budget process, dating from the mid-1970s, was intended to bring coherence to the way standing committees handle the president's budget. It has decisively shaped both Congress's internal decision making and its relations with the executive.

CONGRESSIONAL BUDGETING

Congressional budgeting is a complex process that involves two types of federal spending: discretionary and mandatory (entitlements). Discretionary spending is under the jurisdiction of the House and Senate Appropriations Committees; mandatory or entitlement spending embedded in statutes is the purview of the authorizing (or policy-recommending) committees of each chamber. Virtually all House and Senate members and committees, the president and executive branch officials, and scores of other participants actively seek to influence Congress's power of the purse. That congressional budgeting is usually contentious should come as no surprise considering the high political and policy stakes associated with fiscal decision making (see Box 14-1 for some of the terminology used in budgeting).

Authorizations and Appropriations

Congress's budget procedures are shaped by two customary and longtime processes: authorizations and appropriations. Generally, legislative rules stipulate that before agencies or programs receive any money, Congress should first pass authorization laws that do three fundamental things: (1) establish or continue (reauthorize) federal agencies and programs; (2) define the purposes, functions, and operations of programs or agencies; and (3) recommend (that is, authorize) the appropriation of funds for programs and agencies. As Senate Democratic leader Harry Reid explained, "Authorizations allow programs to be created and funded. When we pass an authorizing bill, we hope the authorized level will be looked at in [the] appropriations committee—as I did as a longtime member. But we realize there are competing priorities, and full funding doesn't come very often."[47]

As an example, the defense authorization bill might authorize the construction of three new submarines and recommend $15 billion for this purpose. Does that mean the Pentagon has the money to build the submarines? No. Congress must enact the defense appropriations bill that would grant the Pentagon legal authority to spend a specific amount of money for the submarines. In short, an authorization can be viewed as a "hunting license" for an appropriation, a law that actually supplies programs and agencies with public funds (budget authority).

By custom, the House initiates appropriations bills. The House Appropriations Committee (usually one of its twelve subcommittees) would recommend how much money the Pentagon should receive for the submarines. The amount is called "budget authority" (BA), and it is equivalent to depositing money in a checking account. The budget outlay (BO) is the check written by the Pentagon to the contractors hired to construct the submarines. The House Appropriations Committee can provide up to the authorized $15 billion (but not more), propose less funding, or refuse to fund the submarine purchases at all. Assume that the House votes to approve $10 billion. The Senate Appropriations Committee, acting somewhat like a court of appeals, then hears navy officials asking the Senate to approve the full $15 billion. If the Senate accedes, a House-Senate compromise is worked out, either in a conference committee or by the bicameral exchange of amendments.

The authorization-appropriation sequence, which is often observed in the breach, is not required by the U.S. Constitution. The dual procedure dates from

BOX 14-1 **A Budget Glossary**

Appropriations. The process by which Congress provides budget authority, usually through the enactment of twelve separate appropriations bills.

Budget authority. The authority for federal agencies to spend or otherwise obligate money, accomplished through enactment into law of appropriations bills.

Budget outlays. Money that is spent in a given fiscal year, as opposed to money that is appropriated for that year. One year's budget authority can result in outlays over several years, and the outlays in any given year result from a mix of budget authority from that year and prior years. Budget authority is similar to putting money into a checking account. Outlays occur when checks are written and cashed.

Cut-as-you-go (CUTGO) rule. This House rule requires new mandatory spending to be offset with cuts to existing entitlement programs. Tax increases cannot be used to offset new spending.

Discretionary spending. Programs that Congress can finance as it chooses through appropriations. With the exception of paying entitlement benefits to individuals (see mandatory spending below), almost everything the government does is financed by discretionary spending. Examples include all federal agencies, Congress, the White House, the courts, the military, and programs such as space exploration and child nutrition. About a third of all federal spending falls into this category.

Fiscal year. The federal government's budget year. For example, fiscal year 2014 runs from October 1, 2013, through September 30, 2014.

Mandatory spending. Made up mostly of entitlements, which are programs whose eligibility requirements are written into law. Anyone who meets those requirements is entitled to the money until Congress changes the law. Examples are Social Security, Medicare, Medicaid, unemployment benefits, food stamps, and federal pensions. Another major category of mandatory spending is the interest paid to holders of federal government bonds. Social Security and interest payments are permanently appropriated. And although budget authority for some entitlements is provided through the appropriations process, appropriators have little or no control over the money. Mandatory spending accounts for about two-thirds of all federal spending.

Pay-as-you-go (PAYGO) rule. This Senate rule requires that all tax cuts, new entitlement programs, and expansions of existing entitlement programs be budget-neutral—that is, offset either by additional taxes or by cuts in existing entitlement programs.

Reconciliation. The process by which tax laws and spending programs are changed, or reconciled, to reach outlay and revenue targets set in the congressional budget resolution. Established by the 1974 Congressional Budget Act (P.L. 93-344), it was first used in 1980.

Rescission. The cancellation of previously appropriated budget authority. This is a common way to save money that already has been appropriated. A rescissions bill must be passed by Congress and signed by the president (or enacted over his veto), just as an appropriations bill is.

Revenues. Taxes, customs duties, some user fees, and most other receipts paid to the federal government.

Sequester. The cancellation of spending authority as a disciplinary measure to cut off spending above preset limits. Appropriations that exceed annual spending caps can trigger a sequester that will cut all appropriations by the amount of the excess. Similarly, tax cuts and new or expanded entitlement spending programs that are not offset under the pay-as-you-go law could trigger a sequester of nonexempt entitlement programs.

Source: Adapted from Andrew Taylor, "Clinton's Strength Portends a Tough Season for GOP," *CQ Weekly,* February 6, 1999, 293.

the nineteenth century and stems from inordinate delays caused by adding riders—extraneous policy amendments—to appropriations bills. "By 1835," wrote a legislator, "delays caused by injecting legislation [policy] into these [appropriations] bills had become serious and [Massachusetts representative] John Quincy Adams suggested that they be stripped of everything save appropriations."[48] Two years later, the House required authorizations to precede appropriations. The Senate followed suit. Both chambers have rules and precedents designed "to segregate decisions about what the government should do [authorizations] from those about how much it can afford [appropriations]."[49] However, as discussed shortly, policy riders are often added to appropriations bills despite the dual procedure.

The Constitution provides that "No Money shall be drawn from the Treasury, but in Consequence of Appropriations made by Law" (Article I, section 9). As a result, appropriations have priority over authorizations. An appropriations measure may be approved even if the authorization bill has not been enacted. Some programs have not been authorized for years, but they still continue to operate. Why? If money is sprinkled on programs or agencies, they continue to exist and function even if their authorization has lapsed. As one House Appropriations subcommittee chair said about the "must-pass" appropriations bills, "It's not the end of the world if we postpone the Clean Air Act or a tax measure. But the entire government will shut down if . . . appropriations [are not enacted annually]."[50]

Authorizations can be annual, multiyear, or permanent. Through the end of World War II, most federal agencies and programs were permanently authorized. They were reviewed annually by the House and Senate Appropriations Committees, but not by the authorizing committees (such as Agriculture or Commerce). Since the 1970s, the trend has been toward short-term authorizations, giving the authorizing committees more chances to control agency operations.[51] Generally, authorizing committees are eager to enact their bills on a timely basis, because otherwise they cede their lawmaking power to the appropriating panels. As Sen. Dianne Feinstein, D-Calif., the chair of the Intelligence Committee, exclaimed, "If this committee can't pass authorization bills . . . which give scope and force of law to what we do, we are in fact a paper tiger."[52] But authorizers also try from time to time to hitch a ride on an appropriations bill heading to the White House. "Ideally, it's not great to use [appropriations] bills," remarked Rep. Barney Frank, D-Mass. "But they may be the only vehicles we can use [for] some [authorization measures] where we're facing a veto or we have problems in the Senate."[53]

In practice, it is hard to keep the two stages distinct. Authorization bills sometimes carry appropriations, and appropriations bills sometimes contain legislation (or policy provisions). Chamber rules that forbid these maneuvers can be waived. In the House, so-called limitation riders make policy under the guise of restricting agency use of funds. Phrased negatively ("None of the funds may be used for a specified purpose . . ."), limitations on the use of federal funds bolster congressional control of the bureaucracy. A well-known limitation amendment—barring the use of federal funds for abortions except under limited circumstances—was first adopted in 1976 and has been readopted ever since in appropriations bills. The Senate, too, is not reluctant to add extraneous policy proposals to appropriations bills. Angered that a major immigration proposal was added to a supplemental appropriations bill, Democratic leader Harry Reid exclaimed, "This is the mother of all authorizing legislation on an appropriations bill."[54] Policy riders can provoke, as noted by Representative Frank, bicameral, party, and legislative-executive disputes.

Committee Roles and Continuing Resolutions. Among the authorizing committees, House Ways and Means and Senate Finance have especially powerful roles in the budget process. These tax panels have access to the staff experts of the Joint Taxation Committee. Because the House under the Constitution initiates revenue measures, it usually determines whether Congress will act on legislation to raise, lower, or redistribute the tax burden. Occasionally, however, the Senate takes the lead. The Senate technically complies with the Constitution by appending a major tax measure to a minor House-passed revenue bill. In 1981 the Republican-controlled Senate used this tactic to act on President Ronald Reagan's sweeping tax cut plan. It used the same ploy the next year on the president's tax increase package. The House jealously guards its constitutional authority to originate tax measures and typically will return to the Senate any bill that violates the origination clause.[55]

Whenever Congress cannot complete action on one or more of the twelve regular appropriations bills (generally one for each subcommittee) by the beginning of the fiscal year (October 1), it provides temporary, stopgap funding for the affected federal agencies through a joint resolution known as a continuing resolution. In the past, continuing resolutions were usually employed to keep a few government agencies in operation for short periods (usually one to three months). In some years, Congress has packaged all the regular appropriations bills into one massive continuing resolution. Each year, Congress also passes one or more supplemental appropriations bills to meet unforeseen contingencies. To sum up, there are three basic types of appropriations: *regular* (made annually), *supplemental* (furnishing funds for unexpected contingencies), or *continuing* (providing funds when one or more annual appropriations bills have not been enacted by the start of the fiscal year).

A Shift in Thinking. Congress has witnessed shifts in the role and culture of the two Appropriations Committees over time. Once known as guardians of the federal Treasury, the two panels gradually developed an affinity for spending as they evaluated and compared the budgetary requests of federal agencies and departments. Some lobbyists even referred to the committees as "favor factories" where taxpayer dollars could be won for their clients. Several committee members won the appellation the "King of Pork" or the "Prince of Pork" for the hundreds of millions of dollars they earmarked for projects in their states or districts.

Recently, a House appropriator called the panel "the Dis-Appropriations Committee."[56] Subtraction, not addition, now characterizes budgeting by the two panels. As Harold Rogers, R-Ky., the chair of House Appropriations, said, "The atmosphere in the country is that government has to get serious about cutting spending. We've finally come to the realization, and now we understand how deep the [deficit] problem is. And the place where the spending is controlled is the Appropriations Committee."[57]

To what extent and for how long the "atmosphere in the country" will support program funding reductions is unclear. Government programs have constituencies—which is often why they were created in the first place—likely to oppose severe funding cuts or outright program terminations. As scholars and others have long known, people favor spending cuts in the abstract but not for programs they support and benefit from. For example, senior citizens often tell lawmakers, "Keep your hands off my Social Security!" A key question, then, is, are Americans ready and willing to shrink the size and scope of government and roll back federal spending?[58]

Backdoor Spending Techniques

To sidestep appropriators' abilities to slash their recommended funding levels, authorizing committees evolved backdoor funding provisions to bypass the front door of the two-step authorization-appropriation sequence. Backdoors are authorization laws that mandate, rather than simply recommend, the expenditure of federal funds. This type of spending legislation, which is reported solely by the authorizing committees, is called direct (or mandatory) spending, as opposed to the discretionary spending under the House and Senate Appropriations Committees. There are three types of backdoor or direct spending provisions: (1) contract authority permits agencies to enter into contracts that subsequently must be covered by appropriations; (2) borrowing authority allows agencies to spend money they have borrowed from the public or the Treasury; and (3) entitlement programs grant eligible individuals and governments the right to receive payments from the national government.

The fastest-growing of the three types is entitlements, which establish legally enforceable rights for eligible beneficiaries. Spending for entitlement programs (such as Medicare and Social Security) is determined by the number of citizens who qualify and the benefit levels established by law. No fixed dollar amount is established for these programs. Budget wonks sometimes call entitlements "uncontrollable under existing law." Statutory changes are difficult to make because entitlements benefit millions of people. Tellingly, the GOP controlled House of the 112th Congress sought to defund President Obama's health care law by changing the mandatory spending features embedded in the health law into discretionary spending. If such a law were enacted, it would be easier for House appropriators to defund the statute's implementation.[59]

The Challenge of Entitlements

Entitlements are the real force behind the escalation of federal spending (see Figure 14-1). Approximately two-thirds of federal spending consists of entitlements that avoid the annual appropriations review process. This ratio of

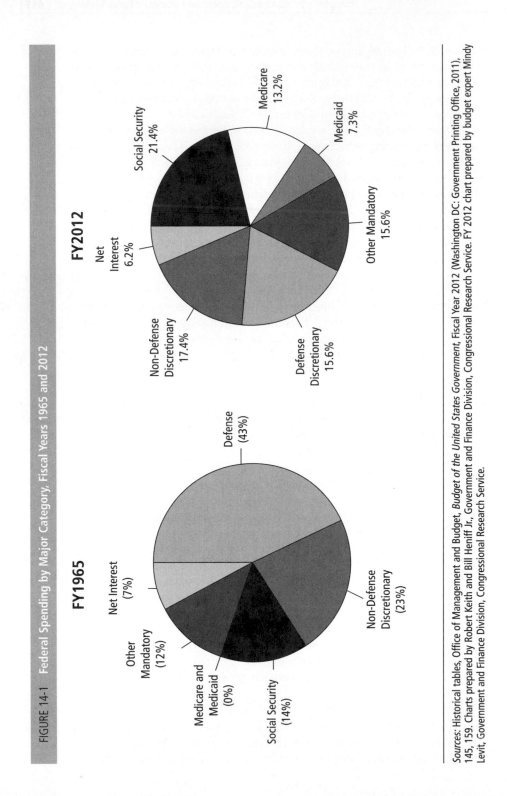

FIGURE 14-1 Federal Spending by Major Category, Fiscal Years 1965 and 2012

FY1965

- Defense (43%)
- Non-Defense Discretionary (23%)
- Social Security (14%)
- Medicare and Medicaid (0%)
- Other Mandatory (12%)
- Net Interest (7%)

FY2012

- Medicare 13.2%
- Medicaid 7.3%
- Other Mandatory 15.6%
- Defense Discretionary 15.6%
- Non-Defense Discretionary 17.4%
- Net Interest 6.2%
- Social Security 21.4%

Sources: Historical tables, Office of Management and Budget, *Budget of the United States Government,* Fiscal Year 2012 (Washington DC: Government Printing Office, 2011), 145, 159. Charts prepared by Robert Keith and Bill Heniff Jr., Government and Finance Division, Congressional Research Service. FY 2012 chart prepared by budget expert Mindy Levit, Government and Finance Division, Congressional Research Service.

discretionary (determined through yearly appropriations) to mandatory spending represents a dramatic reversal from that of a half-century ago. Unlike defense or domestic discretionary programs—for which the Appropriations panels recommend annual amounts and on which all lawmakers may vote—entitlement spending occurs automatically under the terms outlined in the statute.

Congress has done a reasonable job of containing discretionary spending, but reining in costly entitlements has proved to be a much more difficult task. In 1996 Congress passed legislation ending a decades-old national welfare entitlement program, Aid to Families with Dependent Children.[60] However, the recipients of the largest share of entitlement spending—senior citizens— are highly protective of these programs and also very likely to vote. A classic example of how hard it is to revamp entitlements occurred in the second term of President George W. Bush. He launched an intense lobbying drive to win public and congressional support for replacing Social Security with individual retirement accounts, but his reform effort failed to gain any traction. Even many Republicans opposed the plan's reliance on private accounts. "Social Security [is] the bedrock of support for seniors," said Sen. Olympia J. Snowe, R-Maine, "precisely because it's defined and guaranteed. What cost and what risk is it worth to erode the guaranteed benefit [through variable stock or bond investments]?"[61]

President Obama also faces the challenge posed by the escalating costs of the big three entitlement programs—Medicare, Medicaid, and Social Security. But this is hardly news. Public officials and analysts have been warning for years—without too much effect—that the projected expenditures of entitlement programs are unsustainable. For example, Medicare faces a prospective funding gap of at least $36 trillion; the Medicare fund is expected to run out of money in 2024.[62] Social Security is slated to pay full benefits to the elderly until 2033, after which seniors would receive 75–80 percent of their promised benefits unless changes are made to the existing laws.[63]

The long-term demographic challenge confronting Social Security and Medicare is that the United States is an aging society with a population that is living longer, thanks in part to advances in often-expensive medical technology. The nation is already witnessing the gradual retirement of the seventy-six million members of the "baby boom" generation (those born between 1946 and 1964), creating a pool of the largest number of retirees in the history of the country. This development will lead to huge retirement and medical expenditures for those who are eligible to receive Social Security and Medicare benefits. But, according to the projections, fewer workers (a "birth dearth") will be paying taxes to support the retirement and medical expenditures that will make up retirees' expected benefits. As a chair of the Senate Budget Committee pointed out,

> In 1950 there were about 16 Americans working for every 1 American retired. That meant programs such as Social Security . . . not only generated money to support those who were retired, they actually generated more money than needed to support the people who

retired. That is happening today even. But the number of people retiring compared to the number of people working has been changing. It has gone from 16 in 1950 down to about 3 and a half today. And further into this century, as the baby boom generation retires, it will drop to 2 people working for every 1 person retired. . . . It becomes pretty obvious, if you have only two people working to pay for one person retired, those two people are going to have to pay a lot more in taxes to support that one person. . . . So this creates a huge . . . unfunded liability [in future years as more money is taken out of Social Security than is paid in]. We do not know how we are going to pay for [Social Security and Medicare] in the out years.[64]

Many proposals have been advanced to deal with the long-term funding challenge, but each is controversial. For Social Security, the proposed changes include raising the retirement age, reducing benefits for future retirees, increasing the payroll tax rate, requiring affluent retirees to pay taxes on their benefits, and raising the amount of income subject to Social Security payroll taxes.[65]

Politically, there are risks for any lawmaker or political party that advocates such recommendations. In the 112th Congress, Rep. Paul Ryan, R-Wis., the chair of the Budget Committee, was one of many members of the fiscally conservative GOP-controlled House willing to take that risk. Representative Ryan has suggested overhauling Medicare and partially privatizing Social Security and cutting benefits. Many Democrats strongly oppose such proposals, arguing in Social Security's case that it will have no effect on escalating deficits ($1.5 trillion in 2012) until 2037. "Blaming Social Security for our deficit is nothing but an ideological attempt to slash benefits and privatize the program," declared Sen. Charles Schumer, D-N.Y.[66]

Why would congressional Republicans hand Democrats a political weapon that could erode GOP support among elderly voters in the next election? A Republican pollster suggested an answer. "It may be hard to understand why someone would try to jump off a cliff" to resolve a long-term entitlement spending issue, he said, "unless you understand that they are being chased by a tiger, and that tiger is the Tea Party."[67] Other GOP strategists disagree. They underscore that because of crushing budget realities the time is right politically for entitlement reform, provided the party does not move so fast as to "outstrip public opinion."[68]

Many analysts and public officials contend that the real entitlement budget buster of the future is not Social Security but the soaring costs of Medicare and health care in general: "The long-term fiscal problem truly is fundamentally one involving the rate at which healthcare costs grow. . . . Social Security and aging are important, but it is not where the money is," explained President Obama's former budget director.[69] Representative Ryan's 2012 budget plan proposed a major overhaul of Medicare—federally subsidized vouchers for seniors so they can purchase health insurance in the private sector—and Medicaid—block grants to the states to care for low-income individuals and families. Mitt Romney's selection of Ryan as his running mate reflected the popularity of the Wisconsin representative's approach among many Republicans, but the GOP ticket's defeat makes it unlikely that the Ryan budget will be enacted over the next few years.

With health care costs rising faster than inflation, with the graying of society, and with the advent of costly new medical technologies, Medicare is already paying out more in benefits than it is receiving in taxes. President Obama's landmark health care law, the Patient Protection and Affordable Care Act, aims to slow rising health care costs, but the outcome is unclear. Medicare's actuaries wonder whether the savings expected from the law's provisions will be enough "to reduce the perverse economic incentives [such as defensive medicine] and costs built into the health care system."[70] In short, citizens want Lexus health services on a Chevrolet budget.

Elected officials often focus first on Social Security because there is a rough consensus on the solutions to constrain its soaring cost. Not so with Medicare. Setting aside the president's health care law and Representative Ryan's health proposals, the other steps "Congress could take now to restrain Medicare's growth are politically perilous. Deny end-of-life care? Restrict eligibility? Reduce treatments? Raise costs?"[71] Even more frightening from a budget perspective is the prospect of providing long-term nursing home or other care for the elderly. Long-term care, said former representative Earl Pomeroy, D-N.D., is "the elephant in the living room that no one's talking about."[72] And Medicaid, a federal entitlement program for indigent and low-income persons that is jointly funded by the national and state governments, has "now surged past Medicare to become the nation's largest health care program."[73]

In short, an entitlement revolution is under way as the government today transfers more than half of federal monies to eligible families and individuals. "Call it government by ATM," remarked an analyst. "You walk up, hit the buttons, and the cash to which you're entitled pops out."[74] This transformation in the federal budget—away from discretionary to direct (or mandatory) spending—raises the question of whether this funding ratio is sustainable. Congress and the president face at least a dual fiscal challenge: the battle for scarce resources between entitlements and discretionary spending, and the struggle within the discretionary category between domestic versus defense and homeland security spending.

Two other major components of the budget merit separate mention as well: tax expenditures and interest on the national debt.

Tax Expenditures. An estimated $1 trillion is consumed by indirect spending, also called tax expenditures or tax preferences. This is the revenue that is forgone through various tax credits, subsidies, or deductions such as the home mortgage interest deduction. Rep. Jim Cooper, D-Tenn., declared that if "there is anything more out of control than entitlement spending," it is tax expenditures.[75] Compared with mandatory or discretionary spending, these expenditures receive scant public attention. One study noted that "much like entitlement programs, [tax expenditures] are on automatic pilot and do not receive sufficient scrutiny as part of the budget process."[76] Significantly, the total value of all tax preferences is virtually equal to the total value of all discretionary spending.

Negotiations between the White House and congressional leaders on deficit reduction in 2012–2013 have focused on ways to cap or otherwise limit deductions and other tax expenditures.[77] Like other government programs, tax expenditures have their own political constituencies that will fight attempts to eliminate or reduce this conglomeration of tax breaks and subsidies. Of the some 250 tax expenditures, most "disproportionately benefit those at the top of the economic ladder."[78] Scholars who study tax expenditures sometimes refer to this form of federal largess as "the submerged state" or the "hidden welfare state."[79]

Interest on the Debt. "There is a cancer eating away at the budget from within," wrote a journalist, and it is the ever-increasing interest that must be paid to service the national debt.[80] In 2013 interest payments on the national debt exceeded $300 billion, and in 2021 they are projected to be over $925 billion. This development further compounds the difficulty of resolving the long-term deficit. In 2014 interest payments are projected to "surpass the amount spent on education, transportation, energy, and all other discretionary programs outside of defense." In 2018 interest payments will surpass Medicare spending.[81] The options for Congress to slow the growth of interest payments on the debt appear straightforward, but they are politically controversial and substantively complex: tax more, spend less, combine those two, and foster economic growth.

To focus greater attention on issues such as tax expenditures, the debt ceiling, interest on the debt, entitlements, and much more, Congress passed almost forty years ago a landmark budgetary measure, the Congressional Budget and Impoundment Control Act of 1974. The goals of that act included bringing greater coordination and coherence to legislative budgeting and strengthening Congress's power of the purse. However, the results have been mixed because it is no easy task to control and monitor federal budgeting.

THE 1974 BUDGET ACT

Congress refocused its budgetary attention in the 1970s after its loose control of the purse strings gave rise to charges of financial irresponsibility. President Richard Nixon blamed Congress for annual deficits, consumer price hikes, high unemployment, and inflation. He also refused to spend monies duly appropriated by Congress, a practice called impoundment. Even though his administration lost every court challenge to the impoundments, Nixon held the political high ground. These diverse pressures prompted Congress to tighten its budget procedures.

The Budget and Impoundment Control Act of 1974 was landmark legislation. Among its principal features was the creation of House and Senate Budget Committees, as well as the CBO. The nonpartisan CBO prepares economic forecasts for Congress, estimates the costs of proposed legislation, and issues fiscal, monetary, and policy reports. The 1974 act also limited presidential use of impoundments and established a timetable for action on authorization, appropriation, and tax measures. The timetable has been changed periodically, and Congress commonly misses some of the target dates (see Box 14-2 for the timetable).

Of the many complex features of the 1974 act, two are central components of Congress's current budget process: the concurrent budget resolution and reconciliation. These two elements compel much of the time-consuming work, attract the attention of many interests and participants clamoring for fiscal resources, and influence policy decisions and outcomes.

Concurrent Budget Resolution

The core of Congress's annual budget process is adoption of a concurrent budget resolution. This measure is formulated by the House and Senate Budget Committees, which consider the views and estimates of numerous committees and witnesses.

The resolution consists of five basic parts. First, the budget resolution estimates what the federal government will spend in a fiscal year and for at least

---

BOX 14-2   The Congressional Budget Timetable

Deadline	Action to be completed
First Monday in February	President submits budget to Congress
February 15	Congressional Budget Office submits economic and budget outlook report to Budget Committees
Six weeks after president submits budget	Committees submit views and estimates to Budget Committees
April 1	Senate Budget Committee reports budget resolution
April 15	Congress completes action on budget resolution
May 15	Annual appropriations bills may be considered in the House, even if action on budget resolution has not been completed
June 10	House Appropriations Committee reports last annual appropriations bill
June 15	House completes action on reconciliation legislation (if required by budget resolution)
June 30	House completes action on annual appropriations bills
July 15	President submits mid-session review of his budget to Congress
October 1	Fiscal year begins

Source: Bill Heniff Jr., *The Congressional Budget Process Timetable*, Congressional Research Service Report 98–472 GOV, March 20, 2008.

the four following fiscal years. For each fiscal year covered by the resolution, the spending is expressed in terms of both budget authority and budget outlays. Second, the total aggregate spending is then subdivided among twenty functional categories such as defense, agriculture, or energy. For each category, the target indicates what Congress expects to spend in those substantive areas. Third, the budget resolution stipulates the recommended levels of federal revenues needed to pay for the projected spending during each of the fiscal years. Fourth, the budget resolution identifies the estimated deficits (or surpluses should they occur, which is infrequent). Fifth, the total outstanding public debt (savings bonds, Treasury securities, and other government obligations) permitted by law is also specified for at least the five-year period. In effect, the budget resolution sets the overall level of discretionary spending for each fiscal year.

The budget resolution is Congress's fiscal blueprint. It establishes the context of congressional budgeting; guides the budgetary actions of the authorizing, appropriating, and taxing committees; and reflects Congress's spending priorities. A senator described the purposes of the budget resolution: "[The budget] resolution would be analogous to an architect's set of plans for constructing a building. It gives the general direction, framework, and prioritization of Federal fiscal policy each year. Those priorities then drive the individual appropriations and tax measures which will support that architectural plan."[82]

In a period of polarized politics, partisan issues dominate debate on these resolutions as Democrats and Republicans battle over spending levels for their competing priorities. Since Republicans took over the House in 2010, House Budget Committee chair Paul Ryan has pushed a bold, politically risky budget blueprint that would slash nearly $6 trillion in federal spending over ten years, including, as noted earlier, the two health care entitlement programs (Medicare and Medicaid). Ryan called his budget blueprint the "path to prosperity." House Democratic leader Nancy Pelosi dubbed it a "path to poverty."[83] It is not unusual for minority party members in both chambers to vote as a bloc against the majority party's budget resolution.

The House and Senate each consider a budget resolution. In the House, budget resolutions are typically considered under special rules from the Rules Committee, which limit debate and impose restrictions on the number and types of amendments. In the Senate, the 1974 budget act sets a fifty-hour limitation for consideration of the budget resolution, unless members accept a unanimous consent agreement imposing other time restrictions. Amendments can be taken up and voted on after the fifty hours, but without debate. This circumstance often leads to "vote-a-ramas" over several days, when senators may "cast back-to-back votes on a dizzying array of dozens of amendments," often with the two Congresses in mind. As national policy makers, members of Congress may have to cast tough, but responsible, votes, which will "serve as valuable campaign fodder" for opponents in the next election.[84]

When the chambers pass budget resolutions with different aggregate and functional spending levels, as is normal practice, House and Senate members usually meet in conference to resolve their disagreements. The conference report is then submitted to both chambers for final action. Because Congress's budget resolution is not submitted to the president, it has no binding legal effect. Instead, it outlines a fiscal framework that enables Congress, through its Budget Committees, CBO, and other entities, to monitor all budget-related actions taken during the course of a year. When the House and Senate are late or unable to adopt a concurrent budget resolution, each chamber usually adopts a resolution (H. Res. or S. Res.) reflecting the budget levels and enforcement procedures contained in the resolution adopted by one chamber but not the other. The failure to pass a budget has become far more common in recent years amid the fierce partisan warfare over spending and taxes. The Democratic Senate did not pass a budget from 2010–2012, prompting severe criticism from Republicans. When Congress passed a bill temporarily increasing the debt limit in January 2013, House Republicans insisted on a provision that would dock the pay of members of either chamber if it failed to pass a budget. Although some observers doubted the legality of the provision, it highlighted the breakdown in the budget resolution process.

Reconciliation

The 1974 budget act established a special procedure called reconciliation, which is an optional process authorized when Congress adopts the budget resolution. Its basic purpose is to bring revenue and direct spending (entitlement) legislation into conformity (or reconciliation) with the fiscal targets established in the concurrent budget resolution.[85] Its basic objective is to make changes in federal policies that result in budgetary savings. First used in 1980, reconciliation has been employed over twenty times since. It is a controversial process that "forces committees that might not want to reduce spending for entitlements under their jurisdiction to act and report legislation."[86]

Reconciliation is a two-step process. In the first step, Congress adopts a budget resolution containing a provision that usually instructs two or more House and Senate committees to report legislation that changes existing law. The instructions name the committees required to report legislation; they give each committee a dollar figure for mandated savings but do not specify the policies to achieve those goals; and they establish a deadline for reporting legislation to achieve the savings. In the second step, the House and Senate Budget Committees compile into an omnibus reconciliation bill the legislative changes in revenue or direct (entitlement) spending programs recommended by the named committees. If the instructions involve only one committee in each chamber, then those panels would bypass the Budget Committee and report their recommendations to the full House or Senate. On several occasions, reconciliation directives have provided for the maximum of three reconciliation bills during each fiscal year: one involving taxes, another on spending, and a third on raising the statutory debt limit.

Reconciliation in the House is considered under the terms of a rule from the Rules Committee. Procedurally, however, reconciliation is focused on the

Senate, because measures governed by that optional process are treated differently from other bills or amendments. Reconciliation bills cannot be filibustered (a statutory time limit of twenty hours is placed on debate); passage requires a simple majority instead of the supermajority (sixty votes) needed to stop a talkathon; and amendments must be germane (the Senate has no general germaneness rule) and deficit-neutral (tax cuts or spending increases must be offset by equivalent revenue increases or spending reductions). There is little surprise that measures likely to arouse controversy in the Senate, such as tax bills, are attached to filibuster-proof reconciliation measures that could pass by majority votes. Democratic senator Robert Byrd lamented that reconciliation "can be used by a determined majority to circumvent the regular rules of the Senate in order to advance partisan legislation. We have seen one party, and then the other, use this process to limit debate and amendments on non-budgetary provisions that otherwise may not have passed under the regular rules."[87]

To prevent just such a usage of reconciliation bills, senators adopted the so-called Byrd Rule (named after Senator Byrd) in the mid-1980s. Under this complex rule, measures cannot be included in the Senate reconciliation package if they are viewed as extraneous provisions that are not primarily budget-related. When the parliamentarian rules that a provision violates the Byrd Rule, it is dropped from the bill unless sixty senators vote to waive the Byrd Rule. [88] Such provisions have been called "Byrd droppings."

The Byrd Rule played an important role in the 2009–2010 fight over health care reform. Some Democrats hoped to pass the massive overhaul through reconciliation, but doing so would have resulted in numerous provisions being dropped due to Byrd Rule violations. Democrats passed the overhaul through the standard sixty-vote cloture process in December 2009. However, before the bill could go to conference, Democrats lost their filibuster-proof margin in the Senate when Republican Scott Brown pulled off a dramatic upset in a January 2010 special election in Massachusetts.[89] To enact reform, Democrats had to resort to a complicated procedure in which the House adopted the previously passed Senate bill without any amendments, and the two chambers subsequently approved a set of minor changes to the legislation through reconciliation. The latter changes, however, were limited to budget-related adjustments that could pass muster with the Byrd Rule.

In summary, reconciliation offers a powerful procedure for fiscal policy. In a classic case, President Ronald Reagan and GOP congressional leaders used it for the first time on a grand scale in 1981. A reconciliation bill dictated deep, multiyear reductions (about $130 billion over three years) in domestic spending. Not long afterward, Congress also agreed to Reagan's tax legislation, the Economic Recovery Tax Act of 1981, which sharply cut tax rates for individuals and businesses. The revenue losses caused by the tax cut, combined with increased defense and entitlement expenditures and insufficient spending reductions in other areas, soon pushed annual budget deficits to levels unprecedented in peacetime, from double- to triple-digit shortfalls. Since the 1980s,

Congress has been grappling with large deficits, with only a brief interlude of surpluses during the Clinton presidency.

A Revised Budget Process

The growth of budget deficits after 1981 became the prime congressional issue as lawmakers and presidents adapted to a new world: the politics of deficit reduction. Numerous proposals were put forth to deal with the problem. A prominent approach has been to set binding deficit or spending targets, which would be enforced through across-the-board cuts—known as "sequestration"—if the targets were not met. One difficulty with sequestration, however, was that it could always be forestalled by adoption of a new budget law delaying the pain. An additional strategy, embodied in the Budget Enforcement Act of 1990 (BEA), was to subject tax and entitlement programs to a new pay-as-you-go (PAYGO) procedure, which required that any tax reductions or any increases in mandatory (entitlement) spending be offset by tax hikes or reductions in other entitlement programs. As the chief counsel of the Senate Budget Committee explained, "The 'pay-as-you-go' label implies that Congress and the President may cut taxes or create [new entitlement spending] programs— that is 'go'—if they also agree to provide offsetting increased revenues or spending reductions—that is 'pay.' "[90]

Throughout much of the 1990s, the GOP-controlled Congress and President Clinton waged fierce battles over deficit reduction. As part of their political game plan, Republicans sent Clinton appropriations and reconciliation bills making deep cuts in federal programs. The president vetoed the measures, forcing two partial shutdowns of the government—the longest in congressional history. A fiscal breakthrough soon emerged, however. Indeed, much to the surprise of most observers, an era of budget surpluses arrived in the late 1990s. The robust economy and booming stock market led to much higher federal revenues, while presidential and congressional budgetary decisions during the first George Bush administration, such as passage of the Budget Enforcement Act (BEA) of 1990, as well as President Clinton's 1993 economic package, encouraged fiscal restraint and led to budgetary savings. The end of the Cold War also led to reductions in defense expenditures. "Just about everything broke right that could have broken right," said Robert Reischauer, a former CBO director.[91] Not everyone believed that the politics of plenty had arrived or, if it had, that it would last indefinitely. Some lawmakers suggested to their colleagues that budget surpluses stood for "BS." Another economic recession, they said, could be around the corner. "The truth is there is no surplus," exclaimed a senator, citing a national debt at the time of $5.7 trillion.[92] Nevertheless, on January 30, 2001, the CBO revised its surplus projections over the next decade upward to $5.6 trillion. Shortly after President George W. Bush entered office, he and congressional Democrats began to argue about what to do with the huge projected surplus. Although many lawmakers and pundits recognized that the ten-year projection might never materialize—a slowing economy, international crises, or other reasons could intervene—politicians of both parties had their own ideas on how the surplus should be spent. It was a case of fiscal projections driving policy making, even though the money was not yet in the bank.

President Bush's top priority when he took office was a sizable tax cut. And on June 7, 2001, he signed into law the largest tax cut ($1.35 trillion) since Reagan's twenty years earlier. A little more than three months later, terrorists attacked the United States, and new demands and challenges confronted the country. The brief era (1998–2002) of surpluses came to a quick end.

What happened to the surplus? It disappeared because the factors that produced it reversed themselves. Instead of defense and intelligence cutbacks, the nation was paying for military conflicts in Afghanistan and Iraq, reconstruction of those countries, and enhanced homeland security. A record ten years of uninterrupted economic growth ended and the stock market performed poorly, shrinking federal revenues. The large tax cuts pushed by the Bush administration also contributed to the growing revenue shortfalls. Moreover, Congress's statutory fiscal constraints—spending caps and PAYGO— expired on September 30, 2002. Thus policy makers were now free to let the deficit increase without worrying about how to pay for tax cuts or spending hikes. While PAYGO had been effective when it was in place, it clashed with Republicans' goal of cutting taxes since it required finding savings to pay for lost revenues. When Republicans took control of the House in the 112th Congress, they put in place a "cut-as-you-go rule" (CUTGO), which focused on spending cuts to mandatory (entitlement) programs. Thus increases in entitlement spending must be offset only by spending reductions in other mandatory programs. However, tax initiatives are exempt from the CUTGO rule. House Republicans could thus cut taxes without finding offsets for the lost revenue.[93] The Senate, meanwhile, has adopted its own PAYGO rule, meaning that the two chambers are following different rules for paying for new programs. This means that tax hikes—off the table in the House—can be used in the Senate to offset new entitlement spending.[94]

Even as deficits have receded from the trillion-dollar levels observed during the Great Recession (2009–12), President Obama and Congress continue to confront a serious imbalance between spending and revenues. The CBO estimates that deficits will be in the $500-billion range over the next several years, before rising once again in the early 2020s as rising medical costs and retiree benefits increasingly stress the federal government's fiscal situation.[95]

If deficits remain high in the years ahead, the federal government faces a serious dilemma: how to fund competing priorities and commitments. As one budget analyst put it, "What we have done in the last several years is decide we can cut taxes, fight two wars, increase homeland security, expand government entitlement benefits, and leave the bill to future generations."[96]

The problem for Congress and the White House is determining what set of policies aimed at improving the nation's fiscal prospects can attract the necessary votes. As one analyst observed, on one side are people who stress the "national neglect" theory. Being competitive globally and flourishing at home require major government investments in areas such as education and transportation. On the other side are those who emphasize the "national gluttony" model, which holds that excessive federal spending must be curbed first, based on the theory that a nation cannot spend its way to prosperity.[97] Any attempt to reconcile these competing worldviews underscores the fact that federal budgeting is about more than numbers. It reflects the divergent views of the two political parties about what policies best serve the country's short- and long-term interests.

CONCLUSION

Today, lawmakers are preoccupied with scores of important policy issues: an ailing economy, defense and homeland security, joblessness, energy sources and usage, and the health of various domestic social programs. Former representative Barney Frank, D-Mass., has posed a question that crystallizes the debate over these various concerns: "What is the appropriate level of public activity in our society?"[98] Democrats and Republicans tend to answer that question differently. Governing, however, means making choices. Future decisions about budgeting and national priorities will surely reflect the values, goals, and interests that result from the confrontations and accommodations inherent in America's pluralist policy-making system.

"**H**ard" versus "Soft" Power for National Security. U.S. Army soldiers board a helicopter in south-central Afghanistan (top), as part of a surge against Taliban militants. Former Secretary of State Hillary Rodham Clinton testifies before the Senate Foreign Relations Committee in January 2013 concerning the deadly terrorist attack on the U.S. diplomatic mission in Benghazi, Libya (center left). Diplomacy is deployed as new Secretary of State John Kerry (bottom left) joins South Korean Foreign Minister Yun Byung-se in a news conference in Seoul in April 2013 concerning North Korea's bellicose threats. Likewise, the Agriculture Department's P.L. 480 program (bottom right) distributes surplus farm products abroad.

chapter

15

Congress and National Security Policies

O n March 19, 2011, the United States and its NATO allies launched an air campaign against the Libyan regime headed by the brutal dictator Muammar Gaddafi. The immediate goals were to eliminate Libya's air defense systems, establish a "no-fly" zone (preventing Libya's air force from bombing Gaddafi's opponents), and degrade the regime's military capabilities. The popular uprisings across the Middle East in countries such as Egypt and Tunisia had succeeded in ending their oppressive regimes, and so encouraged thousands of Libyans to take to the streets to end Gaddafi's tyrannical rule. Unlike the relatively nonviolent responses to the earlier uprisings in Egypt and Tunisia, Gaddafi ordered his military leaders to use their guns and bombs to slaughter the protestors, who had taken control of large portions of Libya. The protestors were a badly armed, untrained, ragtag rebel army of civilians who were no match for Gaddafi's army and air force.

To prevent a huge massacre, the United Nations Security Council adopted a resolution on March 17 authorizing "all necessary measures" to protect Libyan civilians. The Arab League also urged an international force to impose a no-fly zone over Libya. In response, the United States initially led a multilateral force in imposing the no-fly zone to help protect the rebel force from being crushed. Clandestine operatives of the Central Intelligence Agency (CIA) were also on the ground in Libya, gathering "intelligence for military airstrikes and to contact and vet the beleaguered rebels battling" Gaddafi's military.[1]

When President Barack Obama addressed the nation on March 28, 2011, to explain his decision on Libya, he emphasized the mission's humanitarian imperative and the United States' partnership with its allies. The president also dispatched his top cabinet officers to brief the House and Senate on the military campaign. One commentator noted the uniqueness of the Libyan situation: "using American military power to [participate in] a war, then dialing back to become more of an equal partner with international allies."[2] In the end, Libyan rebels took control of the country. To be sure, the transition has not been easy. As one account noted, top positions in the government are occupied by Islamic extremists, and democratic principles, such as a fair trial, are ignored.[3] Moreover, the country is rife with armed militias and terrorist groups, as demonstrated by the September 2012 attack on the U.S. diplomatic post in Benghazi that killed the American ambassador and three other U.S. personnel.

On the heels of Libya came Syria, where rebels have been trying for two years to topple the authoritarian regime of President Bashar Assad. Estimates are that over 70,000 people have been killed, mainly civilians; a million or more Syrians have fled their country to live in tents and squalor in refugee camps in neighboring countries; two million people inside Syria are homeless; feuding rebel forces fight one another; a civil war rages among sectarian groups; and, to stay in power, Assad has no qualms about ordering air strikes, artillery bombardments, or missile and chemical attacks on the populace.[4]

To date, the United States has provided food and other humanitarian aid, but the rebels want military weapons to combat the tanks, planes, and missiles used against them by the Assad forces. Unlike Libya, in this case President Obama has shown considerable reluctance to provide arms to the rebels—fearful that the weapons would fall into the hands of terrorists—or to provide military assistance to remove the Assad regime. Some administration officials and lawmakers advocate providing arms to rebel forces, as well as establishing no-fly zones over Syria as employed in Libya. Others urge caution in getting involved in another country's civil war. The United States, they argue, cannot be the global policeman and take on costly foreign entanglements. President Obama has made the case "for an America that can no longer do it all. It must pick its fights" based on a "mixture of realism and humanitarianism."[5] And if the United States does decide to get involved in other nations' conflicts, it prefers a multilateral approach rather than a unilateral undertaking.

International cooperation has not always marked U.S. foreign policy. Earlier generations of Americans tended to view themselves as special people set apart from the world's conflicts. Having forsaken Old World "wars and alarms," U.S. citizens—protected by two oceans—historically resolved to remain aloof from other nations' struggles. The most famous passage of President George Washington's 1796 Farewell Address counsels:

> The great rule of conduct for us, in regard to foreign nations is in extending our commercial relations to have with them as little political connection as possible. . . . 'Tis our true policy to steer clear of permanent alliances, with any portion of the foreign world. . . . Taking care to keep ourselves, by suitable establishments, on a respectable defensive posture, we may safely trust to temporary alliances for extraordinary emergencies.[6]

Although Washington's Farewell Address is dutifully read in the chambers of Congress every year on the first president's birthday, Washington's vision bears little resemblance to twenty-first century conditions. As a world power today with numerous alliances spanning the globe, the United States and its foreign policies would scarcely be recognized by the nation's founders.

Formulating and implementing U.S. foreign and national security policies are not episodic activities but continual obligations. Congress and the president share in these duties—just as in domestic and budgetary matters. Congress has broad constitutional authority to take part in foreign and domestic security decisions. Even the most decisive chief executives can find themselves constrained by active, informed, and determined policy makers on Capitol Hill.

CONSTITUTIONAL POWERS

The U.S. Constitution is, in Edward S. Corwin's classic words, "an invitation to struggle for the privilege of directing American foreign policy."[7] In other words, foreign and military powers are divided between the branches. "While the president is usually in a position to *propose,* the Senate and Congress are often in a technical position at least to *dispose.*"[8] The struggle over the proper role of each branch in shaping foreign policy involves conflict over policy as well as over process.

The President Proposes

The chief executive enjoys certain innate advantages in dealing with foreign affairs. As John Jay wrote in *Federalist* No. 64, the office's unity, its superior information sources, and its capacity for secrecy and dispatch give the president daily charge of foreign intercourse.[9] In Jay's time, Congress was not in session the whole year, whereas the president was always on hand to make decisions.

The president's explicit international powers are to negotiate treaties and appoint ambassadors (powers shared with the Senate), to receive ambassadors and other emissaries, and to serve as commander in chief of the armed forces. The latter power looms large over the interbranch politics of the modern period, during which presidents have at their disposal huge military, security, and intelligence capabilities. Presidents have claimed not only their explicit prerogatives but also others not spelled out in the Constitution. Whether they are called "implied," "inherent," or "emergency" powers, presidents increasingly invoke them in conducting foreign policy.

President George W. Bush, according to GOP senator Lindsey Graham, S.C., "came up with a pretty aggressive, bordering on bizarre, theory of inherent authority that had no boundaries. As [the Bush administration] saw it, the other two branches were basically neutered in the time of war."[10] President Obama's leadership style differs from Bush's; it is generally more deliberative, cautious, and pragmatic. But he was not reluctant to bypass Congress and claim that his Libyan actions were "consistent with his powers as the country's commander in chief."[11] Moreover, President Obama has embraced many of the national security approaches used by President Bush.[12]

The executive branch tends to be favored by foreign policy specialists, who often denigrate legislative involvement in foreign policy. Speaking to his fellow

Republicans just after they ascended to power on Capitol Hill in 1995, former secretary of state James Baker cautioned the new majority "not to meddle too much" in the (then Democratic) administration's foreign policy. U.S. leadership in the world, he declared, could be sustained only "if we understand that the president has primary responsibility for the conduct of the nation's foreign policy."[13] Many lawmakers and scholars take a perspective different from Baker's. Edward Corwin, the noted presidential and constitutional scholar, provided this balanced assessment of the legislative-executive relationship in foreign policy:

> What the Constitution does, *and all that it does,* is to confer on the President certain powers capable of affecting our foreign relations, and certain other powers of the same general kind on the Senate, and still other powers upon the Congress; but which of these organs shall have the decisive and final voice in determining the course of the American nation is left for events to resolve.[14]

The president's advantages are magnified in times of warfare or crisis. It was Congress's clumsy management of affairs during the Revolutionary War that, among other things, led the founders to champion an independent, energetic executive, and to designate the president as commander in chief. Authority tends to become more centralized during wars and crises, so presidential powers reach their zenith at such times. This held true during the Cold War between the United States and the Soviet Union (1947–1989) and the hot wars in Korea (1950–1953) and Vietnam (1964–1974). The same pattern was evident in the period following the terrorist attacks of September 11, 2001, on the United States. Heightened security fears and the wars in Afghanistan and Iraq brought new and sometimes unprecedented assertions of executive authority. Initially, at least, Congress's voice was muted.

Presidential powers usually contract and are subjected to sharper scrutiny from Capitol Hill when tensions ease or when the public tires of a prolonged conflict. Public opinion eventually came to oppose the Korean and Vietnam conflicts, a pattern that has repeated itself in the Iraq and Afghanistan wars. A 2011 poll found that nearly two-thirds of Americans agreed that "the war in Afghanistan is no longer worth fighting."[15] Divided control of the two policy-making branches spurs Congress to cast a more critical eye upon executive actions. Perhaps the most sensible statement of the separation of powers came from Justice Robert Jackson in *Youngstown Sheet and Tube Co. v. Sawyer* (1952). He wrote that "the president might act in external affairs without congressional authority," but he may not act "contrary to an act of Congress."[16]

Congress Reacts

Congress has an impressive arsenal of explicit constitutional duties, such as the power to declare war, to regulate foreign commerce, to raise and support military forces, and to make rules governing military forces, including for "captures on land and water" (Article I, section 8). Paramount is the power of the purse. According to Crabb, Antizzo, and Sarieddine, "It is within the power of Congress to determine the course of American diplomacy, by virtue of its control over expenditures by the federal government." [17]

From examining the historical record, Crabb and his colleagues identify three conditions for congressional activism in foreign and defense affairs: (1) periods of weak presidential leadership in foreign policy, (2) public groundswells of concern over America's international role, and (3) pressing domestic issues that impinge on foreign affairs. Their assessment of legislative activism in foreign affairs is pessimistic. They contend that legislative activism has been associated with "the least successful and impressive chapters in the annals of American diplomacy." [18]

Our own review of the historical record, however, yields a more positive assessment of legislative influence on foreign policy. Congress asserted itself following the Revolutionary War and at the outset of the other nineteenth-century wars. At the same time, it moved to rein in excessive presidential assertions of authority both before, during, and after those wars—an impulse that extends to the more recent wars: Korea, Vietnam, Afghanistan, and Iraq, as well as the later phases of the Cold War.

WHO SPEAKS FOR CONGRESS?

The wide-ranging subjects of foreign policy and military affairs fall within the purviews of some twenty-three congressional committees. Other House panels and Senate panels consider matters with a tangential bearing on foreign and military policy.

The foreign affairs and national security panels are among the most visible on Capitol Hill. The Senate Foreign Relations Committee considers treaties and the nominations of key foreign policy officials. It normally regards itself as a working partner and adviser to the president. In the late 1960s and early 1970s, during the height of dispute over the Vietnam War, the committee became a forum for antiwar debate under the leadership of its chair, J. William Fulbright, D-Ark. (1959–1974). A later chair, Jesse Helms, R-N.C. (1995–2001), attacked international agencies and thwarted many of the Clinton administration's diplomatic objectives. When Sen. (now Vice President) Joseph R. Biden Jr. chaired the panel, he and his Senate committee colleagues laid out alternatives to President George W. Bush's international policies.

Sen. John Kerry, D-Mass., chaired the panel for four years (2009–2013). At the age of twenty-seven, Kerry was the first Vietnam veteran to appear before the panel. On April 22, 1971, Kerry posed a now-famous question: "How do you ask a man to be the last man to die for a mistake?" [19] A senator steeped in international issues, Kerry was named Obama's second-term secretary of state in 2013. He was replaced as Foreign Relations chair by Sen. Robert Menendez, D-N.J. The son of Cuban immigrants, Senator Menendez is likely to take a harder line toward the Castro regime than has President Obama.

For most of its history, the House Foreign Affairs Committee worked in the shadow of its Senate counterpart. This situation changed after World War II, when foreign aid programs thrust the House—with its special powers of the purse—into virtual parity with the Senate.[20] Today, the House committee addresses nearly as wide a range of issues as the Senate committee. For example, Rep. Ed Royce, R-Calif., the chair of Foreign Affairs in the 113th Congress, advocates a number of issues, such as human rights, trade with Asia, a free market system, and the promotion of democracy in diverse regions of the world. As he said with respect to the troubled African nation of Mali, "We will assist the country in restoring democracy by focusing primarily on reconciliation, conflict prevention, and supporting the electoral process."[21] Foreign Affairs tends to attract members with a more global outlook than the House as a whole.

The Senate and House Armed Services Committees, which traditionally have a culture of bipartisanship, oversee the nation's military establishment. Annually, they authorize Pentagon spending for research, development, and procurement of weapons systems; construction of military facilities; and rules for civilian and uniformed personnel. The latter jurisdiction includes the Uniform Code of Military Conduct, which governs the lives of men and women in uniform and which has attracted congressional scrutiny of diverse matters such as sexual orientation, sexual harassment, treatment of enemy prisoners, overseas voting rights, and even the right of Jewish officers to wear yarmulkes while in uniform. Although global strategy and military readiness are important matters for the committees' members, what rivets their attention are issues closer to home such as force levels, military installations, and defense contracts. Thus constituency politics often drives military policy.

Because of their funding jurisdictions, House and Senate Appropriations subcommittees exert detailed control over foreign and defense policies. Tariffs and other trade regulations are the domains of the taxing committees (House Ways and Means, Senate Finance). Committees involved in banking handle international financial and monetary policies. And the commerce committees have jurisdiction over foreign commerce generally. With the creation of the Homeland Security Department, and despite the formation of homeland security committees in the House and Senate, scores of other panels assert jurisdiction linked in some way to local and national security.

The House and Senate Select Intelligence Committees were created in the late 1970s, following revelations of widespread abuses, illegalities, and misconduct on the part of intelligence agencies, particularly the Central Intelligence Agency (CIA) and the Federal Bureau of Investigation (FBI). After forty years, however, the two oversight panels are still hampered in conducting vigorous scrutiny of the intelligence community because, according to a scholar, they have "limited expertise and weak budgetary authority."[22]

Two other panels are important to note: the House Homeland Security Committee and the Senate Homeland Security and Governmental Affairs Committee. With respect to homeland security, both panels have roughly comparable responsibilities. Both, for example, have legislative and/or oversight jurisdiction over such matters as border security, threats to the United States, cybersecurity, the protection of the nation's critical infrastructure, and the Department of Homeland Security.

Faced with a profusion of congressional power centers, executive branch policy makers complain that they do not know whom to consult when crises arise, that they have to testify before too many committees, and that leaks of sensitive information are inevitable with so many players. But executive branch officials or their emissaries are often free to consult with as few or as many lawmakers as they choose—in some cases with only the joint party leaders, in others with chairs and ranking members of the relevant committees. And when Congress tries to step in to influence administration policies, executive officers predictably complain about "micromanagement."

TYPES OF FOREIGN AND NATIONAL SECURITY POLICIES

Foreign policy is the total of decisions and actions governing a nation's relations with other nations and consists of national goals to be achieved and resources for achieving them. Statecraft is the art of selecting preferred outcomes and marshaling the appropriate resources to attain them. As former secretary of state Henry A. Kissinger, a foreign policy pragmatist, put it, "Values are essential for defining objectives; strategy is what implements them by establishing priorities and defining timing."[23]

Defining a nation's goals is no simple matter. The subject has sparked intense conflict both between Congress and the president and within Congress itself. Momentous congressional debates have displayed widely diverging views on subjects such as ties to England and France during the nation's early decades, American expansion abroad, tariff rates, involvement in foreign wars, approaches to combating terrorists, and U.S. involvement in nation-building or forcible regime change.

Lee H. Hamilton, D-Ind., a former chair of the House Foreign Affairs Committee and an acknowledged authority on international relations, summarized in 1998 what he viewed as the major components of the national interest: (1) to preserve the territorial integrity of the United States and the safety and security of its people; (2) to sustain U.S. economic prosperity; (3) to promote democratic values; (4) to promote basic human rights; and (5) to protect the health and welfare of the American people.[24] Today, the national interest has been broadened to include a number of other components that affect the United States' security, such as soaring obesity rates which prevent many individuals from joining the military, and the "dysfunction" in Washington that raises questions, noted a defense secretary, "about the capacity of our democracy to respond to crisis."[25]

As for resources for meeting such goals, military strength and preparedness immediately come to mind. However, other assets such as wealth, productivity, creativity, political ideals, cultural values, and global credibility are even more potent in the long run. Former House member Jane Harman, D-Calif., an expert in national security policy making, emphasized the importance of assessing the nation's strategic interests: "It should be obvious that both our resources and our power are less than they have been in prior decades, and that requires a new assessment of how to deploy our scarce assets against the biggest threats to the U.S. homeland."[26]

In balancing national goals and national resources, policy makers confront several different and sometimes overlapping types of foreign and national security policies. Structural policies involve procuring and deploying resources or personnel; strategic policies advance the nation's objectives militarily or diplomatically; and crisis policies protect the nation from specific foreign or domestic threats.

STRUCTURAL POLICIES

National security programs involve millions of workers and the expenditure of billions of dollars annually. Decisions about deploying such vast resources are called structural policy decisions. Examples include choices of specific weapons systems, contracts with private suppliers, the location of military installations, sales of weapons and surplus goods to foreign countries, and trade policies that affect domestic industries and workers. Structural policy making on foreign and defense issues is virtually the same as distributive policy making in the domestic realm.

The last sixty years have seen a growing imbalance in the military versus nonmilitary elements of foreign policies. In fiscal year 2012, the U.S. military budget was larger than those of the next nineteen nations of the world combined.[27] But the singular military machine of the United States is, historically speaking, a fairly recent phenomenon. After earlier wars, the United States quickly "sent the boys home" and, under congressional pressure, shrank its armed forces—though each time to somewhat higher plateaus.[28] After World War II, however, the Cold War threat led to unprecedented levels of peacetime preparedness. By 1960, when retiring president Dwight D. Eisenhower, a career military officer, warned against the "military-industrial complex" (his speech draft said "military-industrial-congressional complex"), the new militarism was already deeply embedded in the nation's political and economic system.

Department of Defense (DOD) spending—about $650 billion in fiscal 2013—is the biggest discretionary portion of the federal budget. That amount is slated to drop as the March 1, 2013, sequester takes hold, with its requirement for automatic spending reductions in the Pentagon's programs, projects, and activities. As spending reductions occur in all the military services, the Obama administration's structural plan is to have a military that will be "smaller and leaner, but it will be agile, flexible, rapidly deployable and technologically advanced."[29] Even with cutbacks, the Pentagon remains the nation's largest employer, its largest customer, and its largest procurer of equipment and services. DOD controls a huge number of structural outlays, which attract a wide swath of political interests. As a venture capitalist put it, "The military is like a Fortune No. 1 company."[30]

The State Department, by contrast, makes relatively few such decisions. For every twenty-one federal dollars spent on the military, only about one dollar goes to international affairs—including not only diplomatic representation but also military assistance, foreign development, and humanitarian aid.[31] The State Department's services and achievements are largely intangible, and in any event it spends much of its energy and money overseas. It is little surprise, then, that it has few strong domestic clients and, compared with DOD, fewer champions on Capitol Hill. A surprising advocate for the State Department was Defense Secretary Robert Gates (2006–2011)— after all, State and Defense are typically rivals for resources and influence. Gates urged Congress to provide more money for State, and he stressed the importance of strengthening national security by better integrating diplomacy (soft power) with military action (hard power). "We must focus our energies beyond the guns and steel of the military," said Gates. "Success will be less a matter of imposing one's will and more a function of shaping [the] behavior of friends, adversaries and, most importantly, the people in between."[32] To be sure, there are tensions between the two departments, such as the Defense Department's large role in matters usually handled by the State Department: nation-building and economic development, for example.

The Military-Industrial-Congressional Complex

Defense dollars for projects, contracts, and bases, among other things, are sought by business firms, labor unions, and local communities. The Pentagon's ties to the business community are so cozy that an estimated 40 percent of its contracts are awarded without competitive bidding, according to an independent study of some 2.2 million contracts.[33] As champions of local interests, members of Congress are naturally drawn into the process. The impulse is wholly bipartisan. (Some observers have even suggested that a "surveillance-industrial complex" has emerged in the post-9/11 era, in which the government's interception of communications is contracted to private companies.[34])

Weapons Systems. Pentagon procurement officers anticipate congressional needs in planning and designing projects. The perfect weapons system, it is said, is one with a component manufactured in every congressional district in the nation. The Air Force's F-22 Raptor jet fighter, which has a price tag of nearly $300 million each, is assembled at Georgia and Texas factories from parts made by a thousand suppliers in forty-three states. "What it means to the company is the technology and the jobs," explained a factory manager.[35] When a defense secretary recommended significant reductions in the production of the F-22 fighter jet as evidence of "an outdated Cold-War mind-set," it set off howls of protest from lawmakers whose states and districts would lose jobs. In the end, the Obama administration prevailed, and further procurement of F-22s was limited in number, effectively ending their production.

An ostensible replacement for the F-22 is the F-35 Joint Strike Fighter, the largest and most expensive Pentagon weapons program in history. The acquisition and development costs of the weapons program have soared from $233 billion for 2,852 planes in 2011, when the program began, to $397 billion for 2,443 planes in 2012. Given design flaws and cost overruns, some Pentagon officials have indicated that in an era of spending cutbacks "the F-35s 30-year, $1 trillion operating bill is not affordable."[36] However, the prospect for serious spending reductions remains murky at best. Sequestration did little to trim the program. And Lockheed Martin, the F-35s designer and builder, engaged in what is called "political engineering." The company "supports about 133,000 jobs in 45 states and Puerto Rico," which in turn has "generated broad bipartisan support [for the F-35] on Capitol Hill."[37] (Worth noting: if the domestic use of drones, unmanned aerial systems, becomes widespread—setting aside their national security purposes—it could mean "millions of dollars in economic activity and tens of thousands of new jobs."[38])

Even when military planners decide to phase out a weapon, lawmakers may compel them to keep the item in production. One example is the Marines' V-22 Osprey, a tilt-rotor aircraft that flies like a conventional plane but takes off and lands like a helicopter. Conceived during the Cold War, the planes—now over $100 million apiece—were intended to change the way the Marines fight wars. But there were design problems: several planes crashed, claiming the lives of two dozen soldiers. Defense Secretary Richard B. "Dick" Cheney canceled the program in 1989, judging that it was too costly, but he was overruled by Congress and its fierce lobbying. The Tilt-Rotor Caucus, a group of representatives from regions in which the plane is manufactured, worked with contractors to keep the project alive.[39] In 2005, twenty years after the program was conceived, DOD's Defense Acquisition Board approved full-scale production of the Osprey. "It is the only major weapons system program that was canceled and then resurrected," claimed a member of the House Armed Services Committee.[40]

In March 2008, DOD signed a multiyear procurement contract through 2012 with the Boeing Company and Bell-Textron for the manufacture and delivery of V-22s.[41] Through 2009, 181 V-22s were procured. So the Ospreys fly on even though they occasionally crash. Military officials remain confident that the V-22 is operationally sound. "It is the hardest thing to do, to take a weapon out of the budget," a defense undersecretary noted. "It is just so easy to put one in."[42] Noteworthy is that the V-22 in coming years is expected to have a nonbattlefield job: "helping to transport VIPs to and from the White House," such as Secret Service agents, presidential aides, and members of the White House press corps.[43]

Military Base Closures. The proliferation and geographic dispersion of military installations is another example of distributive military policy making. L. Mendel Rivers, D-S.C., chair of the House Armed Services Committee from 1965 to 1971, kept defense money flowing to bases in Charleston, South Carolina, campaigning on the slogan "Rivers delivers!" More recently, Sen.

Trent Lott, R-Miss. (1989–2007), helped a Pascagoula, Mississippi, firm that builds ships for the Navy: "It's one of the most important shipyards in the country, and if I were not supportive of my hometown, that shipyard and the workers in that shipyard, I wouldn't deserve to be in Congress, now would I?"[44]

In the post–Cold War era, Congress tried to surmount the politically unpalatable problem of closing unneeded military installations. In 1988, it passed a law intended to insulate such decisions from congressional pressure by delegating them to bipartisan Base Realignment and Closing Commissions (BRACs). The BRACs were also intended to eliminate pressure on lawmakers to vote for an administration's programs in exchange for keeping open military bases in their districts. As Rep. Richard Armey, R-Texas, the champion of the BRAC legislation, stated: "The fact is, unfortunate as it is, that historically base closings have been used as a point of leverage by administrations, Democratic and Republican administrations, as political leverage over and above Members of Congress to encourage them to vote in a manner that the administration would like."[45]

Using the defense secretary's recommendations, a BRAC would draw up a list of installations targeted for closure. To make the decisions hard to overturn, the list had to be accepted or rejected as a whole by the president and Congress. Base closings were also part of Congress's wider effort to balance the budget.

Five rounds of BRACs (1988, 1991, 1993, 1995, and 2005) reduced or eliminated hundreds of defense installations. The political pressures were intense. One commission chair was greeted at base entrances by parents holding children who, they said, would starve if the base closed.[46] Lawmakers from affected areas fought the closure lists and nearly succeeded in overturning them. From the Pentagon's perspective, the closures of excess infrastructure meant that the savings could be spent on higher military priorities. Communities where bases were shuttered looked for new uses for the military facilities, such as the land and buildings, and in some cases requested federal assistance for the cleanup of environmental contamination at these installations.

The Pentagon in 2012 proposed another BRAC round to close unneeded military facilities as the armed forces are reduced because of the sequester and the post-Afghanistan drawdown of troops. However, many lawmakers are upset that the 2005 BRAC cost more to implement ($35 billion) than the savings ($15 billion) it produced by closing or consolidating facilities. "BRAC is a painful process with questionable cost savings," observed a senator.[47] Thus a new BRAC round is probably years away.

Trade Politics

Another arena for distributive politics is foreign trade. Since the First Congress (1789–1791), the legislative branch's constitutional power to "regulate commerce with foreign nations" and to "lay and collect taxes, duties, imposts, and excises" has been used to protect and enhance the competitive position of U.S. goods and industries, whether cotton, wheat, textiles, or computer software. Until the 1930s, tariff legislation—long the primary source of federal revenue—was contested on Capitol Hill by political parties and economic regions. Northern manufacturers, for example, wanted protectionist tariffs, and southern exporting states wanted low tariffs to avoid other nations' retaliatory tariffs against their agricultural products.

Starting with the Reciprocal Trade Agreements Act of 1934 (P.L. 73-316), however, Congress began to delegate the details of tariff negotiations to the executive branch. The 1974 Trade Act is a key statute that transfers trade negotiating authority to the president, subject to Congress's ability to approve or disapprove the agreements under expedited procedures (for example, limited floor debate and no amendments in either chamber). Expedited procedures provide assurances to trading partners that Congress will act on any negotiated agreements within a certain time period. Important to note is that the 1974 trade law specifically recognized the constitutional authority of either chamber to make or change its own rules regardless of any statutory provisions addressing the procedural operations of the House or Senate.

Divergent Views on Trade. Protectionist impulses have not waned, however; myriad trade interests are represented on Capitol Hill. One trade expert suggests that three groups largely shape the trade debate in Congress.[48] To varying degrees, the perspectives of all three groups are represented in both parties. Republicans are generally "trade liberalizers," which reflects the views of many in the business community, among others. They tend to favor lowering trade barriers at home and combating them abroad in order to open world markets for U.S. goods. After all, "95 percent of the world's consumers now live somewhere other than the United States."[49] The GOP chair of the House Rules Committee in the 112th Congress wrote: "Opening up new markets for U.S. producers, farmers, service providers and investors is essential for spurring growth and creating new job opportunities for both union and nonunion workers."[50]

Republicans' long-term commitments to free trade may be undergoing some change, however. As one account noted:

> While the modern GOP has traditionally been a bastion of support for free markets, times have changed. The public's embrace of trade has loosened considerably as American jobs have disappeared. That appears particularly true among grass-roots Tea Party activists, who often echo Democratic complaints about corporate outsourcing as well as popular concerns about the influence of global economic organizations that facilitate trade, such as the World Trade Organization (WTO) and the International Monetary Fund (IMF).[51]

Many Democrats are in the "fair trade" camp. They represent areas of union strength and favor barriers to curb the loss of jobs to low-wage countries. Fair traders argue that the poor labor, human rights, and environmental conditions in many countries enable them to undercut U.S. businesses through lower production costs. Fair traders want trade agreements—before they are entered into—to stipulate that nations must meet specific labor, environmental, and human rights standards.

The third group could be called "trade skeptics." They contend that trade agreements undermine U.S. sovereignty and largely benefit multinational corporations over small businesses, small farmers, and workers. Lawmakers who support labor unions and the Tea Party movement generally believe that trade has hurt the American economy by lowering wages and outsourcing jobs overseas.

The three different perspectives underscore the complexities and crosscurrents that suffuse trade policy and politics. Because both parties contain lawmakers in all three groups, it is too simple to identify one party (Republicans) as free trade and the other (Democrats) as protectionist.

A two-Congresses example illustrates the point. Republican senator Jeff Sessions of Alabama blocked a bipartisan trade bill supported by numerous business associations. His purpose was to prevent the duty-free import of sleeping bags from Bangladesh. Alabama is home to the only domestic manufacturer of inexpensive sleeping bags. As Senator Sessions explained:

> I do believe in trade. I think it's best for the world. But I would say to my colleagues we have got to have fair trade. And nations around the world ... have taken advantage of the United States and ... [think] that they can cheat on agreements and manipulate agreements and close down businesses ... and somehow we're just going to pass on by.[52]

From a bicameral perspective, the Senate generally leans toward free trade because export-minded agricultural interests are overrepresented. The House, with its constituency-attentive focus, has stronger protectionist leanings.

Other Pertinent Issues. In the debate over U.S.-China trade status, representatives splintered across the political spectrum. Christian conservatives allied with liberal, pro-labor Democrats in opposing a trade deal with China because of their concerns about Beijing's persecution of Christian and other religious leaders.[53] The lure of China's vast potential market for U.S. goods vied with doubts over China's unpredictable government and its poor human rights, worker safety, and environmental records. Trade policy and negotiations, asserts Rep. Sander M. Levin, D-Mich., "now involve virtually every area of what used to be considered U.S. domestic law—from antitrust and food safety to telecommunications."[54] Separating local from global issues is difficult. As President Obama has said, "We have learned that the success of the American economy is inextricably linked to the global economy."[55]

Having delegated most decisions to the executive, lawmakers who want to review specific trade deals must struggle to get back in the game. The Trade Act of 1974, as noted earlier, addressed this dilemma. The president, it said, must actively consult, notify, and involve Congress as he negotiates trade agreements. These agreements would take effect only after an implementing law is enacted, and such legislation would be handled under a fast-track procedure.

Most presidents since 1974 have been awarded fast-track (or trade promotion) authority to negotiate trade pacts subject to up-or-down votes in both houses of Congress within ninety days. However, that authority lapsed during the Clinton presidency and was not renewed by the Republican-led Congress. In 2002, after a vigorous lobbying effort, President Bush won a five-year renewal of the fast-track procedure. Even so, the House vote was close— 215 to 212 (the Senate margin was 64 to 34). To gain the needed House votes, numerous concessions were made to placate textile workers and citrus growers, among others. The measure also featured a Democratic-sponsored hike in aid for workers who had lost jobs to foreign competition.[56] The fast-track authority lapsed again in 2007 because of heightened national concern about the loss of U.S. jobs overseas, a trend toward economic nationalism, and sharper partisanship in Congress over trade deals.

Distributive politics underlie many other foreign and defense programs as well. For example, P.L. 480 (Food for Peace) dispenses food assistance to needy nations. This law, wrote former senators Richard Lugar, R-Ind., and Thomas Daschle, D-S.D., "provides vital humanitarian and emergency assistance to people facing famine, natural disasters or conflict." They add that the food produced by American farmers is a "key component of the U.S. national security strategy. Nations that struggle with severe poverty and hunger are at greater risk from terrorists and instability."[57]

The United States is the world's largest seller of arms to developing nations. The value of all arms transfer agreements with developing nations in 2009 was over $45 billion. Two years later, overseas weapons sales surged to $66.3 billion.[58] The Pentagon also trains military forces in numerous nations to use its weapons. Arms sales are a profitable enterprise for the government that—for good or ill—affects civil and military affairs in every corner of the globe.[59]

STRATEGIC POLICIES

To protect the nation's interests, decision makers design strategic policies on spending levels for international and defense programs; total military force levels; the basic mix of military forces and weapons systems; arms sales to foreign powers; foreign trade inducements or restrictions; allocation of economic, military, and technical aid to developing nations; treaty obligations to other nations; U.S. responses to human rights abuses abroad; and its stance toward international bodies such as the United Nations (UN), the North Atlantic Treaty Organization (NATO), and world financial agencies.

Strategic policies overlap and embrace most important foreign policy questions. They engage top-level executive decision makers as well as congressional committees and mid-level executive officers. Such debates can express citizens' ideological, ethnic, racial, or economic interests.[60] Strategic issues typically involve broad themes and invoke policy makers' long-term attitudes and beliefs. The key agencies for strategic decision making include the

State Department, the Office of the Secretary of Defense, the intelligence agencies, and the National Security Council—all advising the president.

The Power of the Purse

Congress uses its spending power to establish overall appropriations levels for foreign and defense purposes. Under those ceilings, priorities must be assigned among military services; among weapons systems; between uniformed personnel and military hardware; and to economic, cultural, or military aid—to name just a few of the choices. The president leads by presenting the annual budget, lobbying for the administration's priorities, and threatening to veto options deemed unacceptable. Yet if it chooses, Congress also can write its own budget down to the smallest detail. And the omnibus character of appropriations measures places pressure on the president to accede to the outcome of legislative bargaining on expenditures. To get the largest percent of the budget the administration wants, the president may have to swallow the smaller percent he opposes.

Post–Cold War Spending. Congress responds both to perceived levels of international tension and to shifting public views about global engagement. After the collapse of the Soviet Union, a bipartisan consensus in the Pentagon and in Congress agreed that defense funding and force levels could be cut gradually. That consensus arose either from the belief that a sizable "peace dividend" could be realized or from the hope that savings could be gained from smarter planning and trimming waste, fraud, and abuse. Downsizing the military establishment, however, is politically and economically disruptive. Defense Secretary Gates cautioned against cutting military expenditures significantly in the aftermath of the conflicts in Iraq and Afghanistan. In an address at the Naval War College in 2009, he argued:

> Every time we have come to an end of a conflict, somehow we have persuaded ourselves that the nature of mankind and the nature of the world have changed on an enduring basis and so we have dismantled our military and intelligence capabilities. My hope is that as we wind down in Iraq and whatever the level of our commitment in Afghanistan, that we not forget the basic nature of human kind has not changed.[61]

Footing the bill for combat operations poses dilemmas for Congress. How much money is needed, and how much freedom should the president have in spending it? President Lyndon B. Johnson gradually deepened U.S. involvement in Vietnam, but he hesitated to ask Congress to appropriate the needed funds. Thus the first supplemental funding bill was passed in February 1966, even though Congress had signed on to the war as early as August 1964 (with the Gulf of Tonkin Resolution). Johnson's effort to hide the escalating war costs while maintaining domestic programs elevated both inflation and the federal debt.

After the September 11, 2001, attacks on the United States, Congress acted swiftly to pass a $40 billion supplemental appropriations package, one-fourth of which was under the president's near-total control. After the U.S. invasion of Afghanistan in October 2001, Congress approved another $30 billion, again featuring flexibility. However, some lawmakers, especially on the funding committees, expressed their doubts. "All presidents want unlimited authority. In any time of conflict, there's a tendency to allow a little more leeway," said an Appropriations subcommittee chair. "We have a responsibility to maintain a balance . . . and we're struggling with that."[62]

The power of the purse is a blunt instrument in time of war. In the final analysis, no major foreign or military enterprise can be sustained unless Congress provides money and support. A president can conduct an operation for a time using existing funds and supplies, just as Johnson did at first in Vietnam and Obama in Libya, but sooner or later Congress must be asked for funding. The U.S. role in South Vietnam finally ended in 1974, when Congress simply refused to provide emergency aid funds.

Today because of the ballooning deficit and the intense focus on cutting federal spending, the size of the military budget makes it a prime target for spending reductions (after 9/11, the defense budget doubled in size). In the view of a defense specialist,

> we can't afford to keep policing a world in which many of our trading partners are growing faster and our military [missions] are contributing to national bankruptcy. The last thing America needs is a concept of its role in the world that is beyond the capacity of our economy and our political system to sustain, purchased with borrowed dollars that will make the emergence of new "peer competitors" more likely.[63]

Spending on Diplomacy. Unlike national defense, international affairs funding represents a relatively small expenditure (see Figure 15-1). For 2012, President Obama requested $47 billion for the State Department and the U.S. Agency for International Development (AID), but the 112th Congress reduced this amount by $6 billion from the 2011 level. Sen. Rand Paul, R-Ky., proposed cutting foreign aid entirely, and other lawmakers suggested reducing the State Department's budget to 2008 levels.[64] Historically, the nation's foreign operations required relatively small outlays. In the immediate post–World War II years of 1947–1951, however, programs to rebuild devastated Europe and Japan consumed as much as 16 percent of U.S. annual spending. Throughout the Cold War, the United States was a major provider of economic, military, and technical aid throughout the world.

In recent years, Department of State operations have accounted for about 1 percent of all expenditures. U.S. economic assistance to promote democracy, address poverty, and improve health and education is a fraction of that, and most of this aid goes to a handful of frontline states (Israel, Egypt, Afghanistan, and Iraq, most prominently). Yet foreign assistance, two lawmakers point out,

FIGURE 15-1   Defense and Foreign Policy Spending as Percentage of Total Budget Outlays, 1940–2012

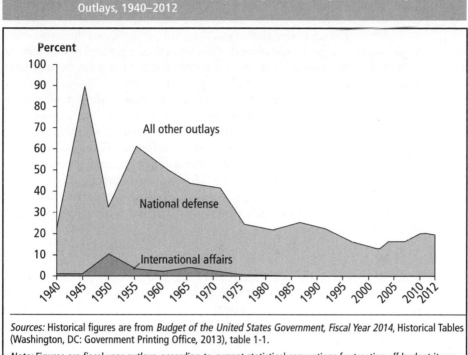

Sources: Historical figures are from *Budget of the United States Government, Fiscal Year 2014,* Historical Tables (Washington, DC: Government Printing Office, 2013), table 1-1.

Note: Figures are fiscal year outlays, according to current statistical conventions for treating off-budget items. The total budget in billions of dollars was $9.5 in 1940, $42.6 in 1950, $92.2 in 1960, $195.6 in 1970, $590.9 in 1980, $1,253.2 in 1990, $1,788.9 in 2000, and $3,537.1 in 2012, down from $3,603.0 in 2011.

is "a critical tool in the diplomatic toolkit. A great power must have the tools to act—beyond simply intervening militarily. A streamlined, effective foreign aid template can enhance U.S. values and influence in a dangerous world and help avoid the enormous costs in blood and treasure that inevitably result from military intervention."[65]

In opinion surveys, citizens indicate only lukewarm support for foreign aid spending, and they grossly overestimate how much is actually spent. In a 2010 University of Maryland poll, respondents said that 25 percent of the federal budget goes to foreign aid; a year earlier a Kaiser Foundation poll found that 45 percent believed that foreign aid is one of the largest categories of federal spending.[66] Perhaps that is the reason U.S. foreign aid, although high in pure dollar terms, ranks low among the world's wealthiest nations as a proportion of the gross domestic product.[67]

Some observers point to this imbalance between military and other aid as a weakness in the nation's ability to use diplomacy to prevent armed conflicts.

As Adm. Michael Mullen, former chair of the Joint Chiefs of Staff, pointed out, "Preventing wars is as important as winning them and far less costly."[68] Despite the funding imbalance between the Defense and State Departments, and the multitude of foreign policy challenges, the work of diplomacy fundamentally involves three categories of activities: defense, diplomacy, and development. As a defense secretary once said, "economic development is a lot cheaper than sending soldiers."[69]

One of former secretary of state Hillary Clinton's rather new tools in promoting democratic development was the social media, such as Facebook, Twitter, and YouTube. In 2011 social media websites were instrumental in mobilizing thousands of protestors to oust the dictators of Tunisia and Egypt, yet the Internet also can be used by authoritarian regimes to track down dissidents and put them in jail, or worse. The clash between Internet censorship and freedom, secrecy and openness, highlights the challenge of maintaining, as Clinton said, "an Internet that delivers the greatest possible good to the world."[70]

Treaties and Executive Agreements

The Constitution calls for Congress and the president to be partners in a key element of strategic policy: treaties with foreign powers. Under Article VI of the Constitution, all treaties "shall be the supreme Law of the Land" unless the treaty itself requires implementing legislation.

Although the president initiates them, treaties are made "by and with the advice and consent of the Senate." The Senate's consent is signified by the concurrence of two-thirds of the senators present and voting. Treaty approval by the Senate entails more than a simple up-or-down vote; it is conducted in two steps. First, the Senate takes up the treaty. If it must be amended, an infrequent occurrence, it must be renegotiated with the nations that were parties to it.

Second, the Senate considers a resolution of ratification. To this document can be added reservations, declarations, or understandings; their adoption by majority vote does not require renegotiation of the treaty. According to one scholar, the "three qualifiers demarcate future U.S. behavior, intent, or policy positions as a result of the treaty. . . . They can also specify U.S. policy on unrelated issues."[71] The Senate, of course, can simply refuse to consider a treaty. (Technically, ratification is a prerogative of the president and involves the exchange of pertinent documents between or among the nations who signed the treaty.)

Congress may or may not be taken into the president's confidence when treaties and executive agreements are negotiated. To avoid humiliation like that experienced by President Woodrow Wilson when the Senate rejected the Treaty of Versailles after World War I, modern chief executives typically inform key senators during the negotiation process. Rarely does the Senate reject a treaty outright. In fact, it has turned down only twenty treaties since 1789. One study found that the Senate had approved without change 69 percent of those treaties submitted to it.[72]

A different fate befell a major multilateral pact, the Comprehensive Test Ban Treaty (CTBT), in the fall of 1999. From the moment it reached the Senate two years earlier, the pact met fierce resistance from conservatives, who argued that it would jeopardize the nation's nuclear superiority and weaken deterrence against would-be nuclear powers. Senate Republicans realized from private consultations that they had the votes to kill the treaty. Normally, the Senate would have simply declined to act. But when pressed by President Clinton and Democratic leaders to bring the treaty to the floor, Republican leaders suddenly scheduled a flurry of hearings, quickly followed by floor debate. No bargaining was evident at either stage.[73] The treaty's foes seemed bent on humiliating the president and signaling their unilateralist approach to future arms control efforts. By the time the treaty's advocates realized they had fallen into a trap (partially of their own making), it was too late to turn back. After debate described as "nasty, brutish and short," the treaty failed by a 48–51 vote—short of a majority, much less the required two-thirds.[74] "While there was nothing improper or illegal in their parliamentary tactics," one commentator wrote, "it was nonetheless a nasty and contemptuous way of doing business quite out of character with the [Senate's] stately, sometimes ponderous way of doing business."[75]

A major success for President Obama was winning Senate approval of a major arms control treaty with Russia during the December 2010 lame-duck session of the 111th Congress (the legislative branch was convening after the November elections). Dubbed "New START" (Strategic Arms Reduction Treaty)—the original START treaty was negotiated in the late 1980s during the closing stages of the Cold War—the treaty received the Senate's consent on December 22, 2010, by a 71–26 vote. The president won the treaty approval battle after an intensive lobbying campaign:

> He mounted a five-week campaign that married public pressure and private suasion. He enlisted the likes of Henry Kissinger, asked Chancellor Angela Merkel of Germany to help and sent a team of officials to set up a war room of sorts on Capitol Hill. Vice President Joseph R. Biden, Jr. had at least 50 meetings or phone calls with Senators.[76]

Because of the hurdle of obtaining a two-thirds Senate vote, since World War II presidents have relied increasingly on executive agreements—international accords that are not submitted to the Senate for its advice and consent. As explained by two legal scholars:

> As a matter of historical practice, the president may also make international agreements if authorized to do so by a law passed by Congress. (These are called "congressional–executive" agreements; the North American Free Trade Agreement is a prominent example.) And in some narrow cases, the president may create an international agreement all by himself through his own constitutional powers. [All are] legally binding on the United States and future presidents.[77]

Executive agreements may also be made pursuant to an earlier treaty. "Narrow cases" often involve military matters.

According to a legal expert, between 1939 and 2009 the United States concluded about 16,500 executive agreements compared with some 1,100 treaties.[78] He described the subject matter of the agreements:

> The vast majority of executive agreements concern routine procedural matters such as postal agreements, mutual legal assistance, cooperation in the fields of science and technology, conservation, civil aviation agreements, and other relatively non-controversial issues. But the executive agreement has also been used to address important foreign policy issues, such as security and defense matters.[79]

Although the conventional wisdom typically attributes the rise of executive agreements to presidential evasion of the Senate's treaty confirmation role, political scientists Glen S. Krutz and Jeffrey S. Peake argue that executive agreements constitute "a rational response by the president and Congress to the challenges faced by the United States during the daunting complexity brought on by the emergence of its international leadership in the twentieth century" and beyond.[80] Executive agreements go into force more quickly than treaties and offer a much less cumbersome process for management of international affairs—efficiency gains that can benefit Congress as well as the president.

In federal court cases challenging whether such agreements should have been treaties, the justices have invoked the political questions doctrine and declined to rule on the merits. This doctrine holds that the issue is best left "to the discretion and expertise of the legislative and executive branches."[81]

Other Policy-Making Powers of Congress

In addition to its control of the purse strings, Congress employs an array of other techniques to shape or influence strategic policies. The most common tools of congressional policy leadership are informal advice, legislative prodding through nonbinding resolutions or policy statements, policy oversight, legislative directives or restrictions, and structural or procedural changes.[82]

Advising, Prodding. Congressional leaders and key members routinely provide the president and other executive officials with informal advice. Sometimes, this advice proves decisive. In 1954 President Eisenhower dispatched Secretary of State John Foster Dulles to meet with a small bipartisan group of congressional leaders to determine whether the United States should intervene militarily in Indochina (Vietnam). The leaders unanimously declined to sponsor a resolution favoring involvement until other nations indicated their support of military action. Lacking assurances from either Congress or foreign allies, Eisenhower decided against intervening.[83]

Congress engages in legislative prodding by proposing legislation or suggesting ideas to the administration. During the 111th Congress, for example, congressional Democrats urged President Obama to develop an exit strategy for Afghanistan and to devise benchmarks to measure the progress of the mission. As Sen. Carl Levin, D-Mich., the chair of the Armed Services Committee, explained, "We need metrics to measure progress to report to the American people and, importantly, to hold people accountable."[84] Prodding of the White House by various lawmakers no doubt contributed to President Obama's release of four secret Department of Justice legal opinions written during the George W. Bush administration detailing the harsh interrogation techniques that could be used to extract information from terrorist suspects.[85]

More frequently, Congress passes resolutions that are not legally binding or enforceable. Every recent Congress has approved numerous simple or concurrent resolutions. These measures may lend support to the executive branch, advance certain policies, or signal assurances or warnings to other nations. Occasionally, nonbinding resolutions put forward fresh policy ideas; at other times they are little more than posturing.

Congressional speeches are also important in framing media and public opinion. These speeches, two scholars note, can "shape media coverage of prospective uses of force, which in turn impacts public opinion about the war." They add: "All sorts of trouble, political or otherwise, await the president who loses public support for an ongoing military venture."[86] Another way for lawmakers to prod the administration is to use committee hearings. For example, Sen. Tom Coburn, R-Okla., testified at a hearing and criticized the Obama administration for not releasing on time a statutorily required report on the security of federal computer networks. "There's no reason for [the delay]," he said, "other than [the report] shows significant criticisms" of the government's performance in securing its computers from cyberattacks.[87]

Oversight. Congress shapes foreign policy through oversight of the executive branch's performance. Hearings and investigations often focus on foreign policy issues. Recurrent hearings on authorizing and funding State Department and Defense Department programs offer many opportunities for lawmakers to voice their concerns, large and small. Another device is to require that certain decisions or agreements be submitted to Congress before they go into effect. Congress and its committees may also require reports from the executive that "provide not only information for oversight but also a handle for action."[88] Hundreds of foreign and defense policy reporting requirements are embedded in current statutes.

Oversight in time of war or crisis is especially hazardous. The president resists intrusions, and lawmakers are reluctant to impede the action. "The trick is to rein in the White House but not seem unpatriotic," writes historian Bruce J. Schulman.[89] The boldest legislative foray into wartime oversight occurred during the Civil War. While Confederate guns were threatening Washington, D.C., the Joint Committee on the Conduct of the War (1861–1865), controlled by Radical Republicans, held hearings on Capitol Hill and published reports that questioned President Abraham Lincoln's war policies, criticized military operations, berated generals who failed to pursue the enemy, and exposed waste and fraud in military procurements.

During World War II, Missouri senator Harry S. Truman headed the Special Committee to Investigate the National Defense Program (1941–1948), which uncovered profiteering, contract abuses, and shoddy workmanship in wartime projects. The committee saved taxpayers billions of dollars and, not incidentally, boosted the career of its chair (it was the "Truman Committee," proclaimed its letterhead). The Senate Foreign Relations Committee hearings launched in 1966 raised doubts in the public's mind about the Vietnam War.

After the Vietnam War, Congress uncovered long-standing abuses by law enforcement and intelligence agencies. A Senate committee headed by Sen. Frank Church, D-Idaho (1957–1981), found that the FBI, CIA, and National Security Agency (NSA) had spied on politicians, protest groups, and civil rights activities; opened mail illegally; and sponsored scores of covert operations abroad. Oversight during the Cold War period had neglected these matters. As a result of the findings, Congress set up new permanent intelligence committees; required presidents to report covert operations; and in 1978 passed the Foreign Intelligence Surveillance Act (FISA, P.L. 95-511), which "squarely repudiated the idea of inherent executive power to spy on Americans without obtaining [judicial] warrants." "The United States must not adopt the tactics of the enemy," the Church committee declared, "for each time we do, each time the means we use are wrong, our inner strength, the strength that makes us free, is lessened."[90] After the burst of 1970s reforms, however, Congress reverted to a Cold War mode of acquiescence to executive leadership. Presidents of both parties exercised secret and unchecked powers and evaded or resisted legislative scrutiny.

Most observers of Congress agree that Republican Congresses (1995–2007) actively probed the Clinton administration's scandals, but "when George Bush became president, oversight [of issues that could embarrass the administration] largely disappeared. From homeland security to the conduct of the war in Iraq, from the torture issue uncovered by the Abu Ghraib revelations to the performance of the IRS, Congress has mostly ignored its responsibilities."[91] When Democrats took charge of the 110th Congress, they aggressively investigated the Bush administration. They continued to exercise vigorous oversight in the 111th Congress, even though their party was in charge of the executive establishment.

When the GOP took charge of the 112th House, Speaker John Boehner adopted intensive oversight of the Obama administration as a major theme. The topics included a host of national security issues such as cybersecurity, the withdrawal of troops from Iraq and Afghanistan, and the administration's 2011 handling of the "Arab Spring" in the Middle East. Of particular importance to the leadership was achieving fiscal savings in national security without jeopardizing the capacity of the military, intelligence, and homeland security agencies to deal with future terrorist threats.

Vigorous oversight of the Obama administration was evident in the 113th Congress concerning the president's nominations of Chuck Hagel to be defense secretary and John Brennan to head the Central Intelligence Agency. Senate Republicans aggressively used the confirmation process for oversight purposes. As GOP senator John McCain, Ariz., stated, "It's a time-honored practice. It's a way to get information." The leverage the Senate has is "to gauge our support for the confirmation of a nominee on whether they are forthcoming with information or not."[92] Consider the Brennan case for illustrative purposes. Senate Republicans demanded additional specific details on the administration's actions, including President Obama's, in the immediate aftermath of the terrorist attack on the U.S. consulate in Benghazi, Libya. Four Americans died in the attack, including the American ambassador to Libya. By holding Brennan's nomination hostage, the Senate succeeded in gaining additional information on the Benghazi tragedy. In the end, the Senate confirmed Brennan by a 63 to 34 vote, but not until after Sen. Rand Paul, R-Ky., conducted a thirteen-hour filibuster. Senator Paul wanted the administration to state that it would not use "aerial drones on U.S. soil to kill Americans suspected of terrorism."[93] (Paul's filibuster provoked further debate within and between the parties, as well as between Congress and the White House, over the administration's policy of targeted killings by drones—at home or abroad—of Americans suspected of terrorism.)

   Legislative Mandates. Congress sometimes makes foreign policy by legislative directives—to launch new programs, to authorize certain actions, or to set guidelines. A landmark enactment of the Cold War era was the Jackson-Vanik amendment to the Trade Act of 1974 (named for Sen. Henry M. "Scoop" Jackson, D-Wash., and Rep. Charles Vanik, D-Ohio). Prompted by concern over the Soviet Union's treatment of its Jewish minority, the amendment denied government credits and most-favored-nation trade status (now called "normal trade relations") to any communist country that restricted the free emigration of its citizens.

   Foreign policy statutes may include explicit legislative restrictions, which perhaps are Congress's most effective weapon. Often they are embedded in authorization or appropriations bills that the president is unlikely to veto. Throughout the Reagan presidency, for example, Congress passed many limits on military aid to Central American countries.

   Legislation also shapes the structures and procedures through which policies are carried out. "Congress changes the structure and procedures of decision making in the executive branch in order to influence the content of policy," writes James M. Lindsay.[94] When lawmakers wanted to reform military procurement, they restructured the Defense Department to clarify and streamline the process; when they wanted more say in trade negotiations, they wrote themselves into the process by enacting various trade laws.

CRISIS POLICIES: THE WAR POWERS

An international crisis endangering the nation's safety, security, or vital interests pushes aside other foreign policy goals. Examples range from Japan's attack on the U.S. naval fleet in Pearl Harbor in 1941 to the al-Qaeda attacks of September 11, 2001.

Crisis policies engage decision makers at the highest levels: the president, the secretaries of state and defense, the National Security Council, and the Joint Chiefs of Staff. Congressional leaders are sometimes brought into the picture. More rarely, congressional advice is sought out and heeded—as in President Eisenhower's 1954 decision against military intervention in Indochina. Often when executive decision makers fear congressional opposition, they simply neglect to inform Capitol Hill until the planned action is under way. A failed attempt in 1980 to rescue American hostages in Iran, for example, was planned in strictest secrecy, and no legislative consultations were undertaken by the Carter administration.

As long as a crisis lingers, policy makers keep a tight rein on information flowing upward from line officers. The attention of the media and the public is riveted on crisis events. Patriotism runs high. Citizens hasten to "rally 'round the flag" and support, at least initially, whatever course their leaders choose.[95]

Constitutional Powers

War powers are shared by the president and Congress. The president is the commander in chief of the military and naval forces of the United States (Article II, section 2), but Congress has the power to declare (authorize) war (Article I, section 8). The framers vested the power to declare war in Congress because they understood that monarchs and presidents often took their nations to war for diverse motives, such as ambition or military glory. As John Jay wrote in *Federalist* No. 4, "These and a variety of other motives, which affect only the mind of the sovereign, often lead him to engage in wars not sanctified by justice or the voices and interests of his people." The framers expected the commander in chief to defend the nation against sudden attacks, implying a limited military role for the president. Lawmakers and scholars have argued for decades about this division of the war powers.

Congress has declared war only five times: the War of 1812 (1812–1814), the Mexican War (1846–1848), the Spanish-American War (1898), World War I (1917–1918), and World War II (1941–1945). In four instances, Congress readily assented to the president's call for war, acknowledging in the declaration that a state of war already existed. Only once did Congress delve into the merits of waging war, and that was in 1812, when the vote was close. In two cases—the Mexican and Spanish-American conflicts—lawmakers later had reason to regret their haste.

In an age of undeclared wars, more problematic than formal declarations are the more than three hundred other instances in which U.S. military forces have been deployed abroad. (The number is uncertain because of quasi-engagements involving military or intelligence advisers.)[96] The examples range from an undeclared naval war with France (1798–1800) to the invasion of Iraq (2003). Since the end of the last declared war—World War II—in 1945, numerous military interventions have taken place abroad. Some were massive and prolonged wars: Korea (1950–1953), Vietnam (1964–1975), Afghanistan (2001–), and Iraq (1991, 2003–2011). Still others were short-lived actions (for example, military coordination of medical and disaster relief after the U.S. embassies in Kenya and Tanzania were bombed in 1998) and rescue or peacekeeping missions, some of which involved casualties (Lebanon, 1983; Somalia, 1992–1993).

Most of these interventions were authorized by the president as commander in chief on the stated grounds of protecting American lives, property, or interests abroad. Some were justified on the grounds of treaty obligations or "inherent powers" derived from a broad reading of executive prerogatives. Others were peacekeeping efforts under UN or NATO sponsorship.

A fundamental change has occurred in the division of war powers between Congress and the president. The change occurred in 1950 when President Truman took the nation to war against North Korea, without seeking a declaration of war or any formal congressional authorization. Instead, he received war-making authority from the Security Council of the United Nations. Since that time, explained scholar Andrew J. Bacevich, the "perceived imperative of waging the Cold War all but nullified [Congress's power to declare war]. When it comes to using force, presidents exercised wide discretion, ordering American troops into action and [often] notifying Congress after the fact."[97] Congress has an arsenal of tools to challenge the president (such as the purse strings, advice and consent, lawmaking, investigations, and debate), but it often defers to the chief executive rather than asserting its formidable constitutional prerogatives.

Members of Congress, though wary of armed interventions, are reluctant to halt them: "No one actually wants to cut off funds when American troops are in harm's way," a House leadership aide explained. "The preferred stand is to let the president make the decisions and, if it goes well, praise him, and if it doesn't, criticize him," observed former representative Lee Hamilton, who co-chaired the 9/11 Commission and the Iraq Study Group after he retired from Congress.[98] Interventions go well if they come to a swift, successful conclusion with few American lives lost. Actions that drag on without a satisfactory resolution or that cost many lives will eventually tax both lawmakers' and citizens' patience. As the sense of urgency subsides, competing information appears that may challenge the president's version of the event. Congressional critics thus are emboldened to voice their reservations. This reaction occurred as the undeclared wars in Korea and Vietnam dragged on and after U.S. troops suffered casualties in Lebanon and Somalia.

Although Congress has rarely used its power of the purse to withhold funds for executive war-making, it has many other indirect mechanisms to influence military policy. Tough congressional oversight, public criticism of the president in the news media, and resolutions of disapproval can all raise the political costs to presidents of continuing a military action. In a recent study, political scientist Douglas L. Kriner finds that the level of congressional opposition that presidents encounter to their military policies depends heavily on the share of Congress held by the opposition party.[99] Based on his analysis of all major U.S. military actions between 1877 and 2004, Kriner finds that presidents who encounter significant congressional opposition are more likely to limit the scope and duration of military engagements.

The War Powers Resolution

The Johnson and Nixon administrations' conduct of the war in Vietnam left many lawmakers skeptical of presidential war-making initiatives. In 1973 Congress passed the War Powers Resolution (WPR, P.L. 93-148) over President Richard Nixon's veto. This law requires the president to consult with Congress before introducing U.S. troops into hostilities; report to Congress any commitment of forces within forty-eight hours; and terminate the use of forces within sixty days—there is an additional thirty-day withdrawal period—if Congress does not declare war, does not extend the period by law, or is unable to meet.

Presidents commonly issue reports to Congress within forty-eight hours after troops have been deployed abroad. Congress, however, regularly abdicates its responsibility after the sixty-day period to pass legislation supporting U.S. military actions. For example, President Obama reported on March 21, 2011, "consistent with the War Powers Resolution" that he had deployed U.S. military forces "with the support of European allies and Arab partners, to prevent a humanitarian catastrophe and address the threat posed to international peace and security by the crisis in Libya."[100] However, the president missed the sixty-day deadline for securing congressional approval for military operations in Libya and thus was legally required to withdraw U.S. forces. Other presidents have also missed the sixty-day deadline, arguing that the WPR is unconstitutional, that the conflict or intervention is too small or limited to be called a "war," or that the United States is not really engaged in hostilities because NATO leaders are in command of the military operation, as in Libya.[101]

The WPR is an awkward compromise of executive and legislative authority, and presidents still intervene as they see fit. Members of Congress tend to sit on the sidelines and allow presidents to ignore the WPR because they are reluctant to interfere with ongoing military operations. There are, of course, lawmakers who challenge presidents for unilaterally authorizing military attacks without congressional consent. For example, the bloody conflict in Syria, where Assad forces target rebels and civilians alike, has caused a number of lawmakers to demand assurances from the Obama administration that Congress will be notified if and when U.S. military forces take action in Syria.[102]

Significantly, there is a new type of war evolving that has focused the attention of the elective branches. Call it cyberwar. U.S. intelligence agencies have determined that the Chinese military has an army unit that specializes in cyberattacks against American corporations, organizations, and governments.[103] As President Obama said in his 2013 State of the Union address, "Now our enemies are also seeking the ability to sabotage our power grid, our financial institutions and our air traffic control systems." The U.S. military has a Cyber

Command, which apparently launched a cyberattack against Iranian nuclear facilities. Cyberwar raises a number of questions, such as: What is the role of Congress in cyberwarfare? Can presidents order cyberattacks on any nation or group without congressional knowledge or approval? Are the enemies the president mentioned in his State of the Union message nations, terrorist groups, other nonstate actors, or a combination of all? As a noted law professor wrote, "stealth wars require rules, too." This implies a key role for Congress in defining "the scope of the new war, the authorities and limitations on presidential powers and the forms of review of the president's actions."[104]

Afghanistan, Iraq, and Changes in Warfare

Three days after the 9/11 terrorist attacks, with smoke still lingering above the damaged Pentagon building, both chambers passed S. J. Res. 23, authorizing the president "to use all necessary and appropriate force against those nations, organizations, or persons he determines planned, authorized, committed, or aided the terrorist attacks." The debate was scant, and all but one member in the two chambers voted for it. The measure included the assertion that "[n]othing in this resolution supersedes any requirement of the War Powers Resolution." But as Ivo H. Daalder and James M. Lindsay contend, "In effect, Congress declared war and left it up to the White House to decide who the enemy was."[105]

Some three weeks later, President George W. Bush notified Congress that he had launched an assault "designed to disrupt the use of Afghanistan as a terrorist base of operations." Once the operation had toppled Afghanistan's Taliban regime, however, the White House resumed its drumbeat of war threats against its preferred Middle East target: Saddam Hussein's Iraq regime. That regime had already survived the 1991 Gulf War, in which an international force led by the United States evicted the Iraqi military from Kuwait after it had invaded that country.

To sell the Iraq war to the American media and people, the White House framed the debate in three ways: (1) Saddam's weapons of mass destruction (WMD) posed an imminent threat (the WMD frame); (2) the Iraqi people should be freed from a cruel dictator (the liberation frame); and (3) Saddam collaborated with al-Qaeda (the terrorism frame).[106] The WMD argument prevailed until after the fighting began and no WMDs were found, and Americans learned that Saddam despised al-Qaeda. Thereafter, the liberation rationale dominated the administration's rhetoric.

In March 2003, the president launched the war. Even lawmakers with misgivings signed onto resolutions of "support for the troops." After no weapons of mass destruction were found in Iraq, the Bush administration found itself with a big problem. Moreover, soon public opinion began to turn against the war as the years of sectarian conflicts and suicide bombings in that nation were highlighted by the news media. By 2008, however, President Bush's "surge" strategy of sending more troops to Iraq (correcting the initial error of not deploying enough troops) was improving the security environment. Nonetheless, the American public was upset with President Bush's management of the war. One result: the 2008 November elections produced unified Democratic control of the government, with Barack Obama as president.

President Obama brought shifts in the nation's security policies. On Iraq, a war-weary nation welcomed President Obama's announcement that U.S. troops would end all combat operations by August 2010, with all American troops departing that country by the end of 2011. Those outcomes occurred, and the Iraq war is now officially over. (However, the CIA remains in Iraq, providing assistance to Iraqi units fighting terrorist groups.[107]) Many questions remain for Americans, and none are subject to easy answers. For example, was the war worth it in terms of the huge human and financial sacrifices? Is the Iraqi government strong enough to provide stability, a robust economy, and important services to its people? Will democratic practices and civil society take root and flourish in Iraq? As one account noted, "After the thousands of American lives lost and [more than $2 trillion] spent, it would be tragic if Iraq collapsed again into war or fell prey to Iran or other neighbors because of a security vacuum created by the U.S. withdrawal."[108] Iraq's future, in short, will be in the hands of the Iraqi people.

Obama's strategic focus shifted to shoring up a deteriorating situation in Afghanistan, as a renewed Taliban insurgency threatened the security and stability of the country. In 2009, emulating Bush's military "surge" in Iraq, President Obama dispatched thirty thousand more troops to Afghanistan to salvage a deteriorating war. His fundamental goals for Afghanistan: secure a stable nation that could defend itself and that could not, as under the Taliban, serve as a base of terrorist operations against the United States. However, after more than a decade of military battles in Afghanistan, polls show that nearly two-thirds of Americans believe the war is not worth fighting. Lawmakers and voters are also skeptical about the cost of nation-building in a feudal country, not to mention the direct cost of military operations (estimated to be $700 billion eleven years after the invasion) during a period of U.S. economic stress.[109]

President Obama plans to have all U.S. combat troops out of Afghanistan in 2014. Thus the current debate surrounding Afghanistan is about issues such as the size of any residual military force that might remain to train and advise the Afghan military, as well as to conduct counterterrorism operations against the Taliban and related groups. Whether Afghanistan can be a relatively secure and stable country post-2014 is fraught with uncertainty. For example, an Afghan lawmaker exclaimed that if U.S. troops leave, "Civil war will erupt, and the Taliban will once again control Afghanistan."[110] An Afghan general who is also a government official disagreed with that view. He contended that his country has enough troops to defeat the Taliban and other insurgents. "The important thing," he argued, "is a strong partnership [with the United States] and the existence of the U.S. as an ally."[111] These disparate views are reflected on Capitol Hill. Some lawmakers argue that the United States must have a successful outcome in Afghanistan, or it will have lost the gains it has made against the Taliban and other terrorist groups. Others argue that the United

States has done enough for Afghanistan, and it is time for Afghans to take charge of their country and its fate.[112]

Changes in Warfare. Just as the doctrines of war change, so too does the nature of warfare. The "spectrum of conflict," said Defense Secretary Gates, "ranging from unsophisticated insurgents or terrorists at the low end to sophisticated national armies at the high end, is becoming blurred." He further explained that "the black-and-white distinction between irregular war and conventional war is an outdated model. We must understand that we face a more complex future than that, a future where all conflict will range along a broad spectrum of operations and lethality."[113]

Increasingly, the future of warfare is being reshaped by at least five new developments. First, conventional warfighting between nations, while still possible as in the Iraq case, seems less likely today. Better international peacekeeping by the United Nations and productive trade agreements between nations (China and the United States, for example) and among nations may be factors that inhibit interstate warfare.[114] Instead, the past several decades have witnessed the rise of insurgent groups, terrorists, and various nonstate actors who are sometimes both hard to identify and difficult to defeat. There are no surrender ceremonies or peace treaties signed in counterinsurgency warfare.

Second, today's irregular warfare requires a complex of integrated activities. The United States' domestic and international intelligence-gathering agencies, since 9/11, are working together as multi-agency networks (for example, the CIA, the FBI, and the DEA [Drug Enforcement Agency]) to gather data and intelligence on insurgent groups and their leaders on a global scale. These networks "are collecting more and better intelligence at a faster pace, and turning it around to shooters in the field more rapidly than at any time in history."[115] This fusion of intelligence activities and military specialists is being conducted in large measure through "spies, special forces, and drone strikes," as well as in other ways (satellite surveillance and reconnaissance, for example).[116]

Third, technology has already reshaped warfare—pilotless drones, for example, can target individual terrorists with precision—and will continue to do so. Cyberattacks and cyberespionage are now a greater threat to U.S national security than al-Qaeda, according to top intelligence officials.[117] As a result, the Pentagon is creating an "offensive cyberforce" to protect the nation against major computer attacks.[118] The military is working on the technology to create war-fighting robots to replace humans on the battlefield. Small robots are in use in Afghanistan and "can be tossed over walls and through windows into homes allowing troops to look for bombs in areas they cannot see. The robots transmit images to troops waiting at a safe distance."[119] Researchers are devising "smart ammunition"—bullets that are programmed by computers in a rifle to explode and kill enemies hiding behind rocks or other cover.[120] The development of malicious software programs—a digital "guided missile"—can "emerge from cyberspace to destroy a physical target in the real world."[121] Even social media are employed by the United States and its enemies to win the propaganda war in countries such as Afghanistan.

Fourth, the scope of contemporary warfare is global. Terrorist groups, failed states, or insurgents can emerge anywhere on the planet. President Obama wants the military to pivot to Asia, but it is being "drawn into a string of messy wars in another, much poorer part of the world: Africa."[122] In fact, the U.S military in Africa is developing a counterterrorism model for a spending cut era: provide training, advice, and some money but let Africans do the fighting.[123] Some commentators are now worried about "mission creep" in Yemen, viewed as a hotbed of terrorist plots against the United States.

Fifth, there is concern in the United States that technology developed for the military—drones—can be used to spy and eavesdrop on Americans, arousing privacy fears among many people. On the other hand, drones have various domestic uses, such as in police work, and various organizations (universities, for example) have received permission to fly drones.[124] Another significant domestic concern, as noted earlier, is how to hold the president accountable for his secret decisions to target and kill individuals through drone strikes. Among the concerns in Congress is its weak oversight of a secret program that allows the president to authorize the killing of an American citizen, ostensibly active in a terrorist group, without any constitutional due process. As Sen. Angus King, I-Maine, put it: "Having the executive being the prosecutor, the judge, the jury and the executioner all in one is very contrary to the traditions and laws of this country."[125]

Congress's War Powers in Today's World

With each new crisis, the War Powers Resolution is attacked or defended, depending on the view held of the proposed intervention. Although presidents are encouraged to pause and consult before acting, experience since 1973 reveals that the WPR has not prevented them from boldly exercising military powers, including military responses to sudden threats.

For the record, every post-1973 president has challenged the WPR's legality, but few at either end of Pennsylvania Avenue are willing to risk having the Supreme Court resolve the question. Lawmakers strive vainly to be consulted, but they support the action as long as it is politically feasible. However, if the crisis persists and the president's actions backfire, Congress moves in and sometimes threatens or curtails the action by refusing funds. Congress unquestionably has the constitutional authority to end wars. As Brad Berenson, who served as an attorney in the Bush White House, has stated, "I am not aware of a serious dispute over whether it is constitutional for Congress to defund or otherwise terminate the war in Iraq. The big debate is over whether it is wise."[126] An outstanding issue, according to Andrew Bacevich, is whether a Congress that is often too compliant will recognize that its first responsibility "is not to support the commander in chief. It is to exercise independent judgment [about committing the nation to war], an obligation that transcends party."[127]

The WPR has few outright defenders, but lawmakers are not ready to repeal or replace it. Although it diminishes Congress's constitutional power of declaring war, the WPR has some practical virtues. It accommodates the rapid use of armed force without the traditional step of formally declaring war. In the current context, declaring war may not be a viable option. "You can't just go off and declare war when you don't know who you are declaring war against," remarked Sen. John B. Breaux, D-La., after the September 11, 2001, attacks.

The WPR gives at least a nodding respect to the framers' belief that Congress, the branch most representative of the people, is the sole source of legal and moral authority for major military enterprises. Presidents may succeed at short-lived actions without a legislative mandate and public support, but longer and more costly engagements will surely falter, as the Korean and Vietnam Wars did. For the time being, then, the enactment stands as a reminder of the ultimate need to gain congressional approval for major military deployments.

CONCLUSION

Three key developments enhance Congress's obligations in foreign policy. First, the United States continues to exert influence in every corner of the globe: militarily, diplomatically, and culturally. Second, global interdependence blurs the line that once demarked domestic policy from foreign policy. Insofar as the resulting issues trespass upon traditional domestic matters, they are bound to encourage congressional intervention and influence. Finally, the question of whether the nation is willing or able to underwrite its costly international projects is forcing Congress and the White House to reassess the nation's global commitments, relying more on multilateral rather than unilateral actions and policies.[128]

Members of Congress cannot avoid foreign and national security policies. As the world grows ever more interdependent, those policies impinge upon every citizen and every local community. An internationally minded electorate, sensitive to famines and plagues in Africa, deforestation in the Amazon, foreign competition for jobs and trade, earthquakes and tsunamis in Japan, and anti-Americanism and terrorism in various regions, draws fewer distinctions between domestic and global matters than in the past.

Today's legislators know that global developments touch their local constituencies, and they believe (rightly or wrongly) that they will be judged to some degree on their understanding of those subjects. It especially behooves lawmakers to debate, challenge, and question presidential war-making policies that could involve the blood and treasure of the nation. As West Virginia senator Robert C. Byrd once stated, "Two constitutional power centers—set up by the framers to check and balance one another—and do battle over politics, policies, and priorities—occupy their distinct ends of Pennsylvania Avenue. What makes it all work for the good of the nation is the character of the individuals who serve."[129]

Citizens and Congress. Tourists in the 1930s gawk at the Capitol's elaborately decorated rooms (left). Today's tourists (top right) can take a Segway tour of Capitol Hill, stopping at the Capitol's east front plaza. (Bottom), the $621 million Capitol Visitors Center, opened in 2008, informs people about Congress's duties and achievements, guides them toward tours of the building and its chambers, offers food, souvenirs, and restrooms, and treats citizens to an unusual underground view of the Capitol dome.

The Two Congresses and the American People

"That meeting was one of the most astounding experiences I've had in my 34 years in politics," remarked Sen. Charles E. Schumer, D-N.Y.[1] Schumer had just emerged from a summit with Treasury Secretary Henry M. Paulson Jr. and Federal Reserve chair Ben Bernanke. House and Senate leaders, along with a group of lawmakers responsible for oversight of financial markets, had assembled at 7:00 p.m. on September 18, 2008. Seated under a portrait of Abraham Lincoln, Bernanke somberly detailed the unfolding financial crisis and warned that the entire economy "was on the brink of a heart attack."[2]

Over the preceding ten days, the government had seized Fannie Mae and Freddie Mac, the investment bank Lehman Brothers had filed for bankruptcy, Merrill Lynch had been sold at a fire-sale price, and the giant insurance firm American International Group (AIG) had been pulled back from collapse by the federal government's $85 billion emergency loan. Credit markets were frozen, denying credit access to consumers and small businesses throughout the country. "I gulped," said Schumer. "We all realized we're not in normal times."[3]

To contain the crisis, the George W. Bush administration sought immediate congressional support for a plan that would allow the Treasury Department to buy up to $700 billion of the distressed assets weighing down the balance sheets of major financial institutions. To put this request in context, $700 billion is more than the Pentagon's annual budget.[4] The three-page proposal asked for unfettered authority to spend these vast sums, with nothing more than semiannual reports to Congress.

"Do you know what you are asking me to do?" said Senate majority leader Harry Reid, D-Nev. "It takes me 48 hours to get the Republicans to agree to flush the toilets around here."[5] The administration wanted Congress to act in a matter of days. "This is the United States Senate," said Reid. "We can't do it in that time frame."[6]

The 2008 financial crisis was so urgent that "the Capital almost had the feel of wartime."[7] Still, lawmakers understandably balked at authorizing so much taxpayer money with so little deliberation. "Just because God created the world in seven days doesn't mean we have to pass this bill in seven days," quipped Rep. Joe Barton, R-Texas.[8] Not all members were willing to trust the administration's claims of impending financial disaster. "Where have I heard this before? The Iraqis have weapons of mass destruction, and they're ready to use them," complained Rep. Gene Taylor, D-Miss. "I'm in no rush to do this."

The bailout proposal was extremely unpopular with constituents, who flooded members' offices with calls that ran as much as 30–1 against.[9] The first effort to pass the bill, on September 30, went down to defeat 228–205 in the House of Representatives.[10] The House's action caused a large-scale sell-off on Wall Street, with the Dow Jones stock index plunging 7 percent in one day.

As days unfolded without a congressional consensus, opinion leaders began to speak of "financial Armageddon" and a "credibility test for Congress."[11] Congress eventually acceded to the administration's $700 billion request, but lawmakers imposed some limits on the administration of the program. They amended the administration's proposal to restrict executive compensation, mandate program oversight, and require aid to Americans in danger of losing homes to foreclosure. The amended proposal was approved by Congress and signed into law on October 3, 2008.

In the end, however, Congress's efforts to assert more control over the bailout's implementation failed. In carrying out the program, the administration used the funds not to buy toxic assets but to recapitalize banks. It quickly became clear that the banks could not be held accountable for their use of these funds. Treasury also refused to act on mortgage relief. A Brookings Institution report concluded:

> Congress designed a financial package that allowed the Treasury to spend nearly $350 billion with no accountability for how the money was used, little transparency in how institutions were selected for infusions, no metrics for determining program effectiveness, and no mechanism for forcing the Treasury to comply with the terms of the law that required action to mitigate foreclosures.[12]

Congressional handling of the financial crisis was flawed in many respects. And long afterward, the bailout remained highly unpopular with voters.[13] Nevertheless, the program proved not nearly so expensive for taxpayers as had been expected: most of the funds disbursed to financial firms were paid back,[14] and the U.S. Treasury estimates that the program will turn a profit.[15] Many economists judged that the program helped to stabilize the financial system and forestall further damage.[16]

A crisis poses a severe challenge for legislative assemblies. The demand for immediate action runs counter to the deliberative processes that legislatures follow. The congressional process is inherently ponderous as different perspectives and interests are consulted and majorities are constructed. The United States is not, as some people have claimed, a "presidential nation"; it is a "separated system" marked by the ebb and flow of power among the policy-making branches of government.[17] As former Speaker Newt Gingrich, R-Ga.

(1995–1999), said of the nation's complex and frustrating governing arrangements,

> We have to get the country to understand that at the heart of the process of freedom is not the presidential press conference. It is the legislative process; it is the give and take of independently elected, free people coming together to try to create a better product by the friction of their passions and the friction of their ideas.[18]

The legislative "give and take" Gingrich described inevitably takes time. As a result, fast-moving crises—all too common in an interconnected world of complex financial and security relationships—often demand that Congress act quickly, frequently without due deliberation.

Anxious or fearful citizens need to keep in mind that the American system of government is one of deliberate interplay among institutions. Citizens' ambivalence toward the popular branch of government is yet another reminder of the dual character of Congress—the theme that has pervaded our explanations of how Congress and its members work. The two Congresses are manifest in public perceptions and assessments. Citizens evaluate Congress using standards and expectations that differ from those they use to assess their own senators and representatives.[19] This same duality appears in media coverage: the two Congresses are covered by different sets of reporters working for different kinds of media organizations.

CONGRESS-AS-POLITICIANS

Lawmakers' working conditions and schedules are far from ideal and beg for periodic examination.[20] The hours are killing, the pay comparatively modest, and the toll on family life heavy. A *Washington Post Magazine* profile of Rep. Joe Courtney, D-Conn., sketched his life as follows:

> Rising, going to hearings, meeting with lobbyists, fundraising, speaking on the House floor, taking more meetings, walking to the apartment, crashing, rising. . . . The [DCCC] continues to send him reminders about his fundraising goals: *Get off the Capitol grounds; get to the phone bank; make the call.* . . . Another knock. An aide pops in with a reminder: The fundraiser back home is that weekend. . . . "It just never stops. Never."[21]

"Your schedule is not your own," remarked Sen. Fred Thompson, R-Tenn. (1994–2003), on announcing his retirement.[22] Rep. Joe Scarborough, R-Fla. (1995–2001), complained that "the conflict between being a good congressman and full-time father has grown even greater in recent years."[23] "I'm basically single-parenting," said Courtney's wife.[24]

Members' Bonds with Constituents

The public places different expectations on individual members compared to Congress as a whole. From the institutional Congress, the public expects answers to the nation's problems developed in an open and fair policy process. By contrast, in assessing their own representatives, voters take into account far more than lawmakers' policy positions. They also weigh members' service to the state or district, their communication with constituents, and their home style. Put differently, Congress is viewed as a national policy-making institution, but individual members of Congress are only partly assessed in terms of their stances on national issues. Local representatives are also evaluated in light of the personal bonds they forge with constituents.

Members' high visibility in their states or districts reinforces their local ties. Constituents receive mail from their local representatives, read about them in newspapers and magazines, and see them on television. Large numbers of citizens report having contacts with their representatives. Incumbents miss few opportunities to do favors for constituents, gestures that are usually appreciated and remembered. It is no wonder, then, that constituents view their local representatives in more sympathetic, personal terms than they view the institution of Congress as a whole.

Senators and representatives present themselves to constituents largely on their own terms through advertising, self-promotion, and uncritical coverage by local or regional news media. Members devote countless hours to fund-raising to ensure that they have the money to purchase all the paid media they need. Reflecting on the hundreds of fund-raising calls he makes daily, Representative Courtney said, "You could be Abraham Lincoln, but if you don't have the heart of a telemarketer, you're not going to make it to Congress."[25]

Members and their staffs devote constant attention to generating publicity and local press. "I am never too busy to talk to local TV," said a prominent House member. "Period. Exclamation point."[26] A survey of House press secretaries showed virtually unanimous agreement: "We'd rather get in [the hometown paper] than on the front page of the *New York Times* any day."[27] Individual lawmakers tend to bask in the flattering light cast by their local media. Hometown reporters, especially for broadcast media, usually work on general assignment stories and are ill prepared to question the lawmaker in detail about issues or events. Often their primary goal is simply to get the legislator on video or audio. For politicians, this is an ideal situation. They can express their views in their own words with a minimum of editing and few challenges from reporters.

The importance of personal connections and public relations does not mean that constituents are uninterested in their representatives' issue stances. Lawmakers also forge bonds with voters out of mutual agreement on important national issues. At the same time, members' personal ties with voters can help insulate them from disapproval on the occasions when their issue positions diverge from local preferences.

Questions of Ethics

Congressional ethics, however, are perennially in doubt. In a 2012 survey, a mere 10 percent of respondents rated the honesty and ethical standards of Congress members as high or very high.[28] Voters, however, do view their own representatives as more ethical than the rest of Congress. In a 2006 poll, for example, although 69 percent of respondents assessed the honesty of members of Congress generally as either "not so good" or "poor," only 30 percent took such a negative view of their own representatives.[29]

Public assessments of congressional ethics stand at odds with the views of most political scientists and close observers of the institution. The conventional wisdom among experts is that the vast majority of lawmakers are dedicated and ethical in their behavior. "Members of Congress behave better than people think," declared former representative Lee H. Hamilton, D-Ind. (1965–1999).[30]

Despite public distrust, lawmakers' behavior today is more transparent and less corrupt than in the past. Members' rising qualifications, more intense media scrutiny, and reforms in campaign finance and ethics procedures have all helped to curtail corruption. Money used to flow freely under the table. "Back in the old days, it was a common occurrence that you walked around with envelopes of cash in your pocket" to hand out to powerful lawmakers, recalled a Washington lobbyist.[31] Today, campaign contributions and direct lobbying expenses are subject to considerably more scrutiny by reporters and civic groups. Although large loopholes remain, financial abuses today are rare by pre-1970s standards.

Why, then, do citizens and commentators remain so contemptuous of lawmakers' ethics? A variety of factors, some of which are beyond members' control, drive public skepticism

Unethical Behavior. One reason the public distrusts members' ethics is that, unfortunately, unethical behavior persists despite the network of laws and rules intended to restrain it. In 2010, for example, the House summoned veteran lawmaker Charlie Rangel, D-N.Y., to stand in the well of the House to receive formal censure for ethics violations.[32] The House of Representatives took this action after an internal House investigation concluded that Rangel had failed to pay taxes he owed, neglected to disclose several sources of income, and improperly solicited funds from corporations and lobbyists for a Charles B. Rangel Center for Public Service at City College of New York. Doubts stemming from congressional ethics investigations played a key role in the defeat of at least three House members in 2012.[33]

Scandals, even when they are uncovered and punished, weaken public confidence. Most notable was the mega-scandal centered on lobbyist Jack Abramoff, who advanced the interests of the gambling industry by means of donations, luxury trips, and favors for some half-dozen lawmakers. "I don't think we have had something of this scope, arrogance, and sheer venality in our lifetimes," observed Norman J. Ornstein, longtime analyst of the Hill scene.[34] Abramoff pleaded guilty in 2006 to fraud, tax evasion, and conspiracy to bribe public officials.[35] Association with the Abramoff case ended the political careers of at least six members of Congress, along with those of many congressional staffers and lobbyists. One member was sentenced to jail for bribery.[36]

Ethics Rules and Processes. Congress's internal processes to police members' ethical violations fail to inspire public confidence. Members typically cringe at passing judgment on their peers. "The House Ethics Committee and the Senate Ethics Committee are structured in a way to protect incumbents rather than to discipline them," observed an ethics lobbyist for Public Citizen. "Members are overseeing each other, and they make sure that nothing comes back to haunt them."[37] But even energetic ethics enforcement does not improve public perceptions. The House Ethics Committee was far more active in the 111th Congress (2009–2011) than it had been in recent years, conducting 111 inquiries into members' activities. Despite all this enforcement activity, a poll of likely voters in twelve competitive congressional districts in November 2010 revealed that only 7 percent believed congressional ethics had improved; 57 percent said that congressional ethics had deteriorated.[38]

Paradoxically, the intensified regulation of public life actually fuels public distrust. So many rules govern the public activities of lawmakers that they can run afoul of them unintentionally. "High-level public officials are particularly good targets for investigation," explains law professor Cass R. Sunstein, "if only because of the complex network of statutes that regulate their behavior."[39] Elected officials are scrutinized by the Federal Election Commission, the House and Senate ethics committees, the Office of Congressional Ethics, and occasionally by the Justice Department and federal prosecutors (see Box 16-1 on congressional ethics). A number of "watchdog" groups such as Citizens for Responsibility and Ethics in Washington and Public Citizen also closely monitor ethics issues and publicize the results of their investigations.

Changing Standards of Personal Behavior. Politicians today are held to higher standards of personal habits and conduct than were politicians in the past. The contemporary news media exert great enterprise and energy investigating personal indiscretions and ethical violations, a shift from the journalistic norms of earlier eras. The effect on public perceptions is to heighten awareness of congressional shortcomings, regardless of how atypical such failings might be. The diligent work of law-abiding members attracts little attention, while an ethical lapse—or even a rumor of one—makes headlines.

In particular, sexual misconduct and substance abuse are far less tolerated today than they were a generation ago. In 2011 alone, two House members and one senator were caught up in scandals related to extramarital activities. In June, Rep. Anthony Weiner, D-N.Y., resigned after conservative activists revealed that the married representative had "sexted" provocative photos of himself to several women.[40] In March, Sen. John Ensign, R-Nev., announced that he would not run for reelection, citing "consequences to sin" after admitting an affair with the wife of a top campaign staffer.[41] And in February, Rep. Chris Lee, R-N.Y., resigned from office after a gossip website revealed that

BOX 16-1 **Congressional Ethics**

Members of Congress are bound by the U.S. Constitution, federal laws, party provisions, and House and Senate rules and conduct codes. Although many observers criticize loopholes, the panoply of regulations is extensive.

- ▶ **Constitution.** Each chamber has the power to punish its members for "disorderly behavior" and, by a two-thirds vote, to expel a member. Members are immune from arrest during attendance at congressional sessions (except for treason, felony, or breach of peace) and "for any speech or debate in either house, they shall not be questioned in any other place" (Article I, section 6). This latter provision protects lawmakers from any reprisals for expressing their legislative views.
- ▶ **Criminal Laws.** Federal laws make it a crime to solicit or accept a bribe; to solicit or receive "anything of value" for performing any official act or service, or for using influence in any proceeding involving the federal government; to enter into or benefit from any contracts with the government; or to commit any fraud against the United States.
- ▶ **Ethics Codes.** Adopted in 1968 and substantially tightened in 1977, 1989, 1995, 1997, and 2007, the House and Senate ethics codes apply to members and key staff aides. The codes require extensive financial disclosure; restrict members' outside earned income (to 15 percent of salaries); prohibit unofficial office accounts that many members used to supplement official allowances; impose stricter standards for using the frank for mailings; and ban lawmakers from accepting most meals and gifts from lobbyists. The House Committee on Standards of Official Conduct and the Senate Select Ethics Committee implement the codes, hear charges against members, issue advisory opinions, and recommend disciplinary actions.
- ▶ **Party Rules.** Congressional parties can discipline members who run afoul of ethics requirements. House Democratic and Republican rules require a committee leader who is indicted to step aside temporarily; a leader who is censured or convicted is automatically replaced.
- ▶ **Federal Election Campaign Act Amendments of 1974.** As amended again in 1976 and 1979, the Federal Election Campaign Act imposes extensive requirements on congressional incumbents as well as challengers. Additional rules and penalties were set in the Bipartisan Campaign Reform Act of 2002.
- ▶ **Office of Congressional Ethics.** Established by the House of Representatives in 2008, the Office of Congressional Ethics is an independent, nonpartisan board of eight private citizens charged with reviewing allegations of misconduct against House members and staff and, when appropriate, referring matters to the Committee on Standards of Official Conduct.

he, a married man, had been seeking dates from women on the website Craigslist.[42] Reports of adulterous affairs have ended the careers of several other members in recent years.[43]

Opposition Research. Many scandals are driven by political opponents of the accused. Members of Congress, challengers, and party operatives all opportunistically seize on any ethical miscue, real or manufactured, for political advantage. In the early weeks of the 110th Congress (2007–2009), some media outlets ran stories criticizing the new Speaker, Nancy Pelosi, for apparently demanding a larger jet for trips home than the one used by her predecessor. It later surfaced that the request for a larger jet came not from the Speaker herself but from the House sergeant at arms because of security concerns and the added distance (Pelosi lived in California, her predecessor in Illinois).[44] That did not, however, prevent Speaker Pelosi's detractors from using the story to push a media narrative that she was abusing the privileges of her office.

In his study of the impact of what he calls the "ethics culture" on federal appointments, G. Calvin Mackenzie writes:

> Instead of getting out of the way so the winners can govern, the losers begin guerrilla operations that never cease, using every weapon and every opportunity to attack, harass, embarrass, and otherwise weaken those who hold office. If you cannot beat them in an election, current practice now suggests, then do everything in your power to keep the winners from governing and implementing their policy priorities.[45]

In other words, ethics charges and countercharges are often nothing more than "politics by other means."[46] Nevertheless, the political uses of ethics charges ensure that they are continually in the public eye, undercutting perceptions of lawmakers generally.

"A Small Class of People." Do these hazards of public life deter "the best and the brightest" from seeking elective office? It is hard to answer that question. Young people, for example, show lamentably scant interest in government careers, and yet their idealism often leads them to pursue other paths of public service.[47] The difficulties of balancing a parental or care-giving role with the round-the-clock demands of the lawmaker's life do appear to fall especially hard on women. Research suggests that the relentless schedule is an important reason why so few women run for political office.[48] The poor esteem in which the public holds Congress is another deterrent for potential candidates.[49]

American democracy requires that ambitious people put themselves forward as candidates. But many of the ablest individuals—especially in one-party areas—decide to sit on the sidelines. Although open seats seem to have little shortage of claimants, the unwillingness of talented, experienced politicians to challenge sitting incumbents raises the specter of unaccountability. Parties frequently have great difficulty recruiting good challengers to run against officeholders. Indeed, the absence of strong challengers, especially for House seats, is a major factor in the persistently high incumbent reelection rates. Meanwhile, the outcomes of congressional elections almost always reveal at least a few underperforming incumbents who would have been vulnerable to defeat, had they only drawn a credible opponent.[50] Congressional elections would be more competitive and voters would have better choices if greater numbers of talented individuals were willing to enter the fray.

The rising demands and costs of congressional life probably lie beyond the reach or interest of average men and women. Reflecting on the multiplicity of presidential duties, Woodrow Wilson once remarked that Americans might be forced to pick their leaders from among "wise and prudent athletes—a small class of people."[51] The same might now be said of senators and representatives.

CONGRESS-AS-INSTITUTION

Americans expect Congress to be active and productive. Opinion surveys have consistently found that people prefer that Congress play a strong, independent policy-making role. They want Congress to check the president's initiatives and to examine the president's proposals carefully.[52] Related to that desire, they often endorse the notion of divided government—that is, the White House controlled by one party and Capitol Hill controlled by the other.

Policy Success and Stalemate

Americans are often unaware of the specific ways in which Congress affects their daily lives. Lee Hamilton tells the following story:

> [A] group of [young people] visiting my Indiana office told me that Congress was irrelevant. So I asked them a few questions. How had they gotten to my office? On the interstate highway, they said. Had any of them gone to the local university? Yes, they said, admitting they'd got some help from federal student loans. Did any of them have grandparents on Social Security and Medicare? Well sure, they replied, picking up on where I was headed. Their lives had been profoundly affected by Congress. They just hadn't focused on all of the connections before.[53]

Nevertheless, most citizens do believe that Congress is an important institution that should share power equally with the president. When Indiana University's Center for Congress asked in the fall of 2012 how much of an impact Congress had on citizens' lives, 50 percent of respondents said "a great deal" and another 38 percent said "some." Most respondents also said it was easy to express their views to their senators and representatives.[54]

Its poor public reputation notwithstanding, Congress has produced many innovative and effective policies. In an intriguing experiment, Paul C. Light of the Brookings Institution set out to identify the federal government's most influential actions over a fifty-year period.[55] A survey of historians and political scientists served to winnow a preliminary roster of 588 items to a list of fifty "greatest achievements." For the record, the top three successes were judged to be rebuilding Europe after World War II (the Marshall Plan, 1947), expanding the right to vote (Voting Rights Act of 1965), and promoting equal access to public accommodations (Civil Rights Act of 1964).

In every case Light uncovered, Congress played a vital role in the policy's inception, ratification, or implementation. Although Congress was not always the initiator, many programs associated with given presidents—for example, the Marshall Plan (Harry S. Truman) and Medicare (Lyndon B. Johnson)—began as proposals on Capitol Hill. "No one party, Congress, or president can be credited with any single achievement. . . . Rather, achievement appears to be the direct product of endurance, consensus, and patience."[56]

Despite its past achievements, most observers could compile a must-do legislative agenda that would include many items left unaddressed by recent Congresses. According to a recent survey, the American public is concerned that Congress fails to debate and take leadership on important matters. Citizens are worried that Congress pays too little attention to long-term problems such as the cost of entitlements, the mushrooming public debt, energy issues, and infrastructure maintenance. The study concluded: "What we found is there is tremendous demand for answers. [The citizens] may not know exactly what to do, but they're very, very worried."[57]

Assessing the Congressional Process

Congress's institutional shortcomings are numerous and obvious. Beyond its structural and procedural complexities, the quality of its deliberations often falls short of democratic ideals. Lack of comity and bipartisanship, the growth of Senate roadblocks, and questions surrounding transparency contribute as well to Congress's muddied reputation. Are reforms possible?

Deliberation. Legislative assemblies are primarily designed to foster deliberation. "The assembly makes possible a deliberation in which conflicting judgments about the public good . . . can be examined, debated, and resolved," writes Richard Hall. "And through such a process the actions of government achieve legitimacy."[58] Recent developments have significantly undermined the quality and quantity of congressional deliberation. In order to cope with the pressures of lawmaking in a highly polarized and partisan environment, leaders of both parties tend to "short-circuit regular deliberative procedures in committee, on the floor, and in conference."[59]

The legislative process has morphed into a wide variety of highly centralized improvisations—what Barbara Sinclair has termed "unorthodox lawmaking."[60] Leaders package together disparate policies into omnibus vehicles so bulky that only a small number of staff aides and members know what provisions have been inserted or left out. Outcomes are normally predetermined, especially in the House, where majority party leaders oversee the pre-floor negotiations and craft the rules for debate. Most important House measures are considered under restrictive or closed rules permitting few or no amendments.[61] Floor deliberations are just a series of desultory recitations—public speaking in this country has become something of a lost art. Under such circumstances, lawmakers are often embarrassed by provisions they have voted into law.

Committee deliberation has been similarly weakened. Committee meetings are poorly attended, with the outcomes laid out by the chair and the chair's majority party colleagues. Leaders frequently bypass committee consideration altogether, bringing unreported bills directly to the floor. Staff resources for House and Senate committees were cut by more than a third between 1979 and

2005.[62] Committee budgets remain under downward pressure. The House imposed further cuts in 2012, ranging from a 10.1 percent cut for the Committee on Science, Space and Technology to a 2 percent cut for Armed Services. Interestingly, only the House Ethics Committee received an increase (11.5 percent) in its budget.[63] According to two analysts, "Committees have been marginalized in myriad ways, from central party direction to ad hoc groups to omnibus bills."[64] As committees become less consequential policy-making arenas, members have less incentive to develop policy expertise in the matters before their committees.

Even House-Senate interactions are less deliberative in character. Today's congressional leaders frequently avoid the conference process altogether, convening "pro forma" conferences to ratify deals worked out in leadership offices or exchanging bills back and forth between the chambers. On occasion, House-Senate negotiations have even excluded minority party conferees. Such tactics streamline the legislative process but forfeit the benefits of deliberation.

Another factor weakening congressional deliberation is Congress's frantic stop-and-go work schedule. Although earlier members did not live in the nation's capital, most of them stayed in town for weeks at a stretch, their days dominated by extended hearings or deliberations. By the mid-twentieth century, a minority of members—mostly from the eastern corridor—constituted a "Tuesday–Thursday club," spending long weekends at home. Nowadays, nearly all members follow such a schedule, which often shrinks to Tuesday night to Thursday afternoon. And extended nonlegislative or "district work periods" surround all the major holidays.

Thirty-four-year House veteran Hamilton has offered a blunt assessment of the situation:

> Congress doesn't work enough at its true job. Members of Congress spend too much of their week campaigning, and not enough of it doing the hard work of governing. Building a consensus behind an approach to a national problem is tough; it takes negotiation, extended discussion, and hard study. This is impossible when you spend three days on Capitol Hill and then rush home for an extended weekend of appearances.[65]

One remedy would seem simple: longer sessions (two weeks at least), alternating with periods for constituency work or official travel. Because of the pressures of campaigning in today's highly competitive environment, it is unlikely that the congressional calendar will become any more favorable to extended deliberation. Indeed, in the first session of the 112th Congress (2011), Majority Leader Eric Cantor, R-Va., announced a calendar in which the House would be in session only 123 days, "the lightest House schedule in a non-election year since 2005 and, before that, 1983."[66] Workweeks were to be no longer than four consecutive days, and votes were to be scheduled before 7:00 p.m. The goal, stated Cantor, was to stress "quality over quantity."[67]

Comity and Bipartisanship. Another institutional malady is the decline of interpersonal comity. This decline is the product of several converging factors, most notably the escalating cohesion within, and polarization between, the two parties. Nelson W. Polsby aptly termed the contemporary period an "era of ill feeling" in Congress.[68]

Critics have persuasively faulted the contemporary Congress for engaging in a "destructive form of partisanship" that prevents bipartisan give and take.[69] Party conflict has been the norm in American history. But during periods when the parties were more divided internally, there was greater potential for cross-party coalitions and minority party input. "Oh, those were frustrating years," recalled former Republican leader Robert Michel of Illinois, who served in the minority for all of his thirty-eight years in the House (1957–1995):

> But . . . I never really felt I was out of the game or that I had no part to play. Under the rules of the House, the traditions of the House . . . there is a role to play for the minority. . . . We struck a deal, we made a bargain [and worked at] bringing dissident factions together . . . to craft good legislation for the country. That was the joy of it![70]

As leaders centralize power, minority party members are less likely to be heard. Observing the failure to address major policy challenges in the mid-twentieth-century, many political scientists lamented the absence of "party government." They preferred a democratic politics in which parties would run on coherent platforms and command the leadership and unity to enact their programs into law. Key elements of the party government model have now come to pass. The parties are far more internally cohesive; the caucuses meet regularly to decide policy; members' party-line voting presents clear alternatives to voters. But no analyst has contended that these changes have lifted the quality of policy making. Instead, partisanship has been blamed for escalating the level of rancor and stalemate. Former representative and deputy GOP whip Mickey Edwards of Oklahoma (1977–1993) decries "partisanship in the extreme," which extends beyond policy or ideological differences:

> Instead of morphing from candidates to members of Congress on the day they are sworn in, today's legislators engage in permanent campaigning. Neither party is willing to allow the other to gain credit for an achievement that might help it in the next election, so the center aisle that divides Democrats from Republicans in the House has become a wall.[71]

Intense and pervasive partisan conflict undermines the public's trust in government. Congressional partisanship has a direct, negative effect on Americans' assessment of the institution.[72] According to one study's author,

> Citizens appear to equate partisan conflict with partisan biases and the notion that members of Congress are avoiding the facts—whatever they may be—when formulating policy. . . . [T]he public

perceives partisan conflict as a waste of time and resources that could be spent trying to solve the nation's problems.[73]

Senate Roadblocks. Nowhere has the rise of partisanship created more obstacles for policy making than in the Senate. For much of the Senate's history, filibusters were rare, employed for matters of great constituency or regional importance. Today, they have become a partisan tool. The partisan filibuster—in which most or all of the Senate majority party's agenda is systematically blocked by an organized minority party filibuster—is a recent innovation. Barbara Sinclair's research dates the partisan filibuster to the first two years of the Clinton presidency (the 103d Congress, 1993–1995), in which Republican-led filibusters obstructed half of all major measures.[74] The practice has escalated since the 1990s. "As long as I've served," remarked Vice President Joe Biden, "this is the first time every single solitary decision has required 60 senators."[75]

Because of the partisan filibuster, the Senate has evolved into an institution that is encountering exceptional difficulty in governing. "Requiring a supermajority to pass legislation that is at all controversial makes the coalition-building process much more difficult and increases a status quo–oriented system's tendency toward gridlock," writes Sinclair. "The costs of gridlock can be severe: a government that cannot act, that cannot respond satisfactorily to its citizens' demands, loses its legitimacy."[76]

The widespread use of delaying tactics in the Senate has effects that extend far beyond the highly controversial issues. It is not merely that the Senate's majority party faces great obstacles to passing a partisan agenda. The delays also impede the Senate's ability to manage the rest of its workload. As Scott Lilly, senior fellow at the Center for American Progress, explains, "The legislative calendar is so consumed by extended debate" that there is not enough time for the Senate to reauthorize expiring programs; nearly half of the funds appropriated for nondefense discretionary spending in fiscal year 2010 "had to be appropriated without legal authority."[77] In addition, appropriations bills almost never pass on time, denying federal agencies the information they need to plan budgets, evaluate competing contract proposals, and maximize value for taxpayers. Many uncontroversial matters that pass the House never receive Senate consideration simply because of the lack of floor time.

Transparency. Another important issue in evaluating Congress is transparency, the ability of the public to monitor and understand congressional proceedings. Questions of transparency present difficult trade-offs for legislative assemblies. On the one hand, a lack of transparency is a major source of public mistrust. People fear that a lack of public access will allow special interests to dominate the legislative process in secret. The Sunlight Foundation, a nonprofit group founded to champion congressional transparency, has pushed popular initiatives such as the online availability of members' financial statements and lobbying expenses, among other reforms. Generally speaking, the public does not trust legislators to act in the public interest in the absence of public scrutiny and accountability.

On the other hand, transparency can hamper internal legislative bargaining and compromise. It is more difficult for members to accept trade-offs that impose costs on their constituencies when those decisions are made in full public view.[78] Instead, lawmakers have a greater incentive to play to their external constituencies and refuse to engage in meaningful negotiations. One of the most significant transparency reforms ever adopted was to permit C-SPAN to telecast congressional proceedings.[79] This reform gave Americans much more access to the lawmaking process. But, just as opponents of televising Congress feared, it may have hindered congressional work. Television "has probably done more to make the Senate a more partisan place," points out veteran senator Orrin G. Hatch, R-Utah. "There's a lot of posturing before the camera."[80]

The Perils of Reform. Reforming Congress is often touted as a solution to its organizational or procedural faults. The House and Senate themselves periodically engage in self-examination (the last broad-scale inquiry took place in 1993). But such efforts are often impeded by the two-Congresses dilemma—that is, structural reforms can threaten members' electoral interests. E. Scott Adler warns, for example, that "any widespread change in the established order of policy deliberation—particularly in its centerpiece, the committee system—would create far too much uncertainty in members' electoral strategies."[81]

Congress's history nevertheless includes some major planned innovations affecting deliberation as well as electoral arrangements. At key moments, reformers with different and often conflicting goals—enhancing legislative power and efficiency, gaining partisan or policy advantage, or augmenting individual lawmakers' perquisites—have coalesced around significant changes. Because of the variety of goals involved, however, the results achieved are often different from those anticipated.

Reformers typically find that they must build upon preexisting institutions, rather than sweep away current practices and start afresh. An example was the series of new budget procedures piled like so many building blocks on top of the existing authorization-appropriations process. Little wonder that such reforms typically fall short of their sponsors' objectives. Based on a survey of forty-two major institutional innovations over the last century, one author concludes that instead of achieving stable, effective arrangements, congressional reforms result in "a set of institutions that often work at cross-purposes."[82]

Media Coverage

The most open and accessible of the three branches of government, Congress is covered by a large press corps populated by some of the nation's most skilled journalists. Long-time CBS News anchor Bob Schieffer claimed that Capitol Hill was the best news beat in Washington.[83] Paradoxically, however, neither reporters nor their editors are able to convey the internal subtleties or the external pressures that shape lawmaking. Moreover, the very media best suited to reporting on Congress—serious daily newspapers and magazines—are suffering long-term declines in circulation.[84] In response, newspapers have curtailed their coverage of Congress and national and global politics in general.

Pressrooms have been downsized; most foreign bureaus have been closed. Bottom-line pressures on the media threaten the nation's democratic processes by leaving people less informed.

The decline has been equally drastic in television (including the so-called all-news channels). "Apart from technology," says journalist Bill Moyers, "the biggest change in my thirty years in broadcasting has been the shift of content from news about government to consumer-driven information and celebrity features."[85]

Political news has changed in content as well as coverage. Fewer stories appear on policy issues and more on scandal, wrongdoing, or corruption. Following the canons of investigative journalism, reporters play the role of suspicious adversaries on the lookout for good guys and bad guys, winners and losers. Ethical problems, congressional pay and perquisites, campaign war chests, and foreign junkets are frequent targets. Generally speaking, political radio and TV talk shows are ill-informed, combative, and contemptuous of politicians and their work.[86]

As mentioned earlier, divergent press coverage—local versus national media—widens the gap between the two Congresses' distinct images: it is more positive for individual members than for the institution. Congress as an institution is covered by the national press with lots of skepticism and cynicism, while individual lawmakers are covered respectfully by the local media.

Citizens' Attitudes toward Congress

Individual members of Congress may receive respectable marks, but people often seem ready to flunk Congress as a whole (see Table 16-1). The institutional Congress usually ranks well below respondents' own representatives in public esteem. Citizens' ratings of the job Congress is doing fluctuate with economic conditions, wars and crises, scandals, trust in government overall, and levels of partisan conflict (see Figure 16-1). Approval of Congress surged briefly after it handled the Watergate affair in 1974, after the Republican takeover twenty years later, and after the terrorist attacks of September 11. The overall trend has been markedly downward since 2002, however, with Congress plumbing historic depths of public dissatisfaction. Congressional approval (in Gallup's poll) has not reached 25 percent since December 2009 and has averaged 17 percent since January 2010. In August 2012, only 10 percent of respondents approved of the way Congress was handling its job. Congressional approval increased from that historic low, standing at 18 percent after the 2012 elections.[87]

Congress is not well understood by the average citizen. Partly to blame are the institution's size and complexity, not to mention the arcane twists and turns of the legislative process. But many citizens simply find the whole legislative process distasteful.

Dissension is on display on Capitol Hill to a greater extent than in other branches of government. The president speaks with one voice: even though there is fierce competition for the president's ear, a statement from the president defines the administration's position. As for the judiciary, opinions are frequently divided or unclear as judges and justices disagree about law and

TABLE 16-1 **High Approval for Members, Low Approval for Congress**

Individual members	Congress as an institution
Serve constituents	Resolves national issues only with difficulty or not at all
Run against Congress	Has few defenders
Emphasize personal style and outreach to constituents	Operates as collegial body that is difficult for citizens to understand
Are covered by local media in generally positive terms	Is covered by national media, often negatively (with focus on scandals and conflicts)
Respond quickly to most constituent needs and inquiries	Moves slowly with cumbersome processes that inhibit rapid responses
Are able to highlight personal goals and accomplishments	Has many voices, but none can speak clearly for Congress as a whole

Sources: Timothy E. Cook, "Legislature vs. Legislator: A Note on the Paradox of Congressional Support," *Legislative Studies Quarterly* 4 (February 1979): 43–52; Glenn R. Parker and Roger H. Davidson, "Why Do Americans Love Their Congressmen So Much More Than Their Congress?" *Legislative Studies Quarterly* 4 (February 1979): 53–61; Richard Born, "The Shared Fortunes of Congress and Congressmen: Members May Run from Congress but They Can't Hide," *Journal of Politics* 52 (November 1990): 1223–1241.

policy, but their decisions are usually accepted as law. By contrast, no single member—not even the institution's top leaders—speaks for Congress.

The public's ambivalence toward Congress goes far deeper than unhappiness with specific policies or disgust with scandals, according to the sobering conclusions of John R. Hibbing and Elizabeth Theiss-Morse:

> People do not wish to see uncertainty, conflicting opinions, long debate, competing interests, confusion, bargaining, and compromised, imperfect solutions. They want government to do its job quietly and efficiently, sans conflict and sans fuss. In short . . . they often seek a patently unrealistic form of democracy.[88]

In other words, people seem to abhor the very attributes that are the hallmarks of robust representative assemblies. As Hibbing and Theiss-Morse observe, Congress "is structured to embody what we dislike about modern democratic government, which is almost everything."[89]

TWENTY-FIRST-CENTURY CHALLENGES

The U.S. Congress is now in its third century. Survival for more than two centuries is no mean feat. Congress has withstood repeated stress and

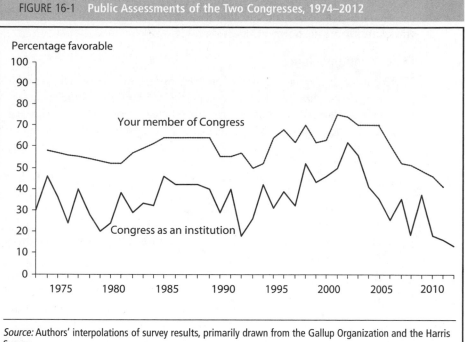

FIGURE 16-1   Public Assessments of the Two Congresses, 1974–2012

Percentage favorable

Source: Authors' interpolations of survey results, primarily drawn from the Gallup Organization and the Harris Survey.

Note: The Gallup Organization's questions are "Do you approve of the way the U.S. Congress is handling its job? Do you approve or disapprove of the way the representative from your own congressional district is handling his/her job?" The Harris Survey's question is "How would you rate the job done this past year by [Congress] [your member of Congress]—excellent, pretty good, only fair, or poor?" Responses are dichotomized as favorable ("excellent," "pretty good") or unfavorable ("only fair," "poor"). The plotted points in the figures indicate respondents having opinions who approve of or are favorable toward congressional performance. Polling data for 2010 and 2011 are from ABC News/*Washington Post* polls.

turbulence, including a civil war, political assassinations, terrorist attacks, domestic scandals, and contentious foreign involvement. The U.S. constitutional system is far older than most of the world's existing governments.

Security

The physical setting of the U.S. Capitol now exhibits the stepped-up security arrangements prevalent elsewhere since the September 11, 2001, terrorist attacks. Just over a decade ago, visitors and Hill personnel moved freely in and out of the Capitol and surrounding office buildings. Members of the public may still visit most Capitol Hill facilities, but they now encounter uniformed officers, metal detectors, and concrete barriers. In the wake of the shooting of Rep. Gabrielle Giffords, D-Ariz., in Tucson in January 2011, congressional leaders and members have considered additional security precautions.[90] One welcome development, however, is the long-needed U.S. Capitol Visitors Center—constructed under the east front that enhances the building's safety while introducing visitors to Congress and its work.

Checks and Imbalances?

The constitutional system of divided powers and competing branches does not yield a stable equilibrium. Powers ebb and flow among the branches. Crises tend to empower the executive branch, whereas more peaceful times are friendlier to congressional power. An activist bench can drive the judiciary into political thickets; at other times the bench defers to the other branches.

Executive Hubris. Executive branch encroachments upon legislative prerogatives are neither new nor confined to crisis periods. Most modern presidents have fought for broader leeway in spending appropriated funds and freedom to reorganize agencies and redeploy their personnel. Presidents and their appointees naturally seek to control information about what they are doing. There is no question that recent presidents have pushed the boundaries of presidential authority in ways that threaten to eclipse Congress.

Executive dominance is most apparent in military affairs. Throughout the post–World War II era, presidents have regularly embroiled the United States in military conflicts without seeking congressional support. In fact, since President Truman single-handedly intervened in the Korean War in 1950 without asking for congressional support, none of the United States' military actions has been accompanied by a congressional declaration of war.[91] Truman asserted the power to act without Congress under the United Nations Charter, UN Security Council resolutions, and NATO treaties; Congress did not contest those claims. Although Presidents George H. W. Bush and George W. Bush both asked for congressional authorizations of the use of force in Iraq, they—along with all other contemporary presidents—contended that they did not need congressional approval to act. President Bill Clinton did not ask for any kind of congressional support before launching cruise missiles against the Iraqi intelligence services in 1993, nor did he seek congressional authority before launching air strikes against the Serbs in 1994 and 1995.

The pattern continues in the Obama administration. When President Obama decided at a contentious White House meeting in March 2011 to support military action against the Gaddafi regime in Libya, he did so without broadly consulting with Congress or seeking any kind of congressional authorization.[92]

Presidents have also become more assertive in denying information to Congress. The George W. Bush administration made secrecy a watchword. The White House refused to share documents with Congress, permit certain executive officials to testify before congressional committees, or otherwise cooperate with investigative hearings.[93] Republican committee chairs Charles E. Grassley of Iowa (Senate Finance), Henry J. Hyde of Illinois (House International Relations), and F. James Sensenbrenner Jr. of Wisconsin (House Judiciary) repeatedly protested the executive's failure to provide information.[94]

Despite such complaints, it is also clear that Congress has been complicit in its loss of power. In its haste to respond to the terrorist attacks of 9/11, for example, Congress gave scant attention to details of the vast grants of power it ceded to the president and the executive branch by approving open-ended military action, the USA Patriot Act, and the 180,000-employee Homeland Security Department. "Congress has ceded its war power to the president," concluded former representative Hamilton.[95]

Party polarization may also have contributed to Congress's refusal to assert its prerogatives more vigorously during recent episodes of unified government. Reflecting on the relationship between the Republican Congress and President George W. Bush, Rep. Ray LaHood, R-Ill., conceded the point: "Our party controls the levers of government. We're not about to go out and look beneath a bunch of rocks and try and cause heartburn."[96] Loyalty to a president should be no excuse for congressional timidity. Partisan loyalties did not immunize past presidents, from Franklin D. Roosevelt, to Ronald Reagan, to Bill Clinton, against probing oversight and sometimes fierce opposition led by their party's leaders on Capitol Hill—even in wartime. If lawmakers do not fiercely defend their prerogatives, they have only themselves to blame when executives ignore them.

Judicial Lawmaking. Congress also faces attacks upon its powers from an activist federal judiciary, which has invalidated federal enactments in more than thirty cases since 1995. Since the 1990s, the courts have overturned federal laws in areas such as interstate commerce and civil rights, raising questions that were last litigated in the 1930s. By narrow majorities, for example, the U.S. Supreme Court curbed the 1990 Americans with Disabilities Act on the grounds it had not dared to apply to earlier civil rights statutes. Other recent Court rulings have progressively restricted Congress's ability to impose any meaningful regulations on campaign finance. The Court came within one vote of striking down Obamacare in the summer of 2012.

Members of Congress regularly criticize the courts for "judicial activism," by which they typically mean decisions on a handful of ideological issues, principally involving abortion and religious establishment clause jurisprudence. Meanwhile, relatively few seem troubled by rulings regarding fundamental state and federal authority. Senior federal circuit court judge John T. Noonan Jr., a Reagan appointee, argues that the Supreme Court has "invented criteria for Congress that invaded the legislative domain."[97] The judiciary retains the capacity to constrict legislative powers in much the same way that late-nineteenth-century courts gutted the Civil War constitutional amendments. As Noonan explains, "If five members of the Supreme Court are in agreement on an agenda, they are mightier than five hundred members of Congress with unmobilized or warring constituencies."[98]

Is Congress Permanently Damaged? Following the Vietnam War and the Watergate scandal, Congress sought to reclaim prerogatives that had slipped away during the Cold War period. In his detailed account of congressional initiatives, James L. Sundquist sums up that era:

The 1970s were a period of upheaval, of change so rapid and so radical as to transform the pattern of relationships that had evolved and settled into place over the span of half a century or more. But by the end of the decade the spirit of resurgence . . . had waned.[99]

The reform fervor was short lived. Reflecting on the period since the 1970s, Andrew Rudalevige revisits the question: Is there an imperial presidency? His short answer is yes: "Presidents have regained freedom of unilateral action in a variety of areas, from executive privilege to war powers to covert operations to campaign spending. . . . The default position between presidents and Congress has moved toward the presidential end of the inter-branch spectrum—and irreversibly so."[100]

Is this trend irreversible? As defenders of the constitutional system, we remain cautiously hopeful of the future. After all, partisans of all stripes have a long-term stake in an active, robust legislative branch. Executive initiatives, as popular as they may seem, demand critical review; executive programs must be overseen and evaluated.

What does the future hold? Much depends on a series of questions: Will members of Congress resolve partisan conflicts to make needed progress on pressing problems? Can Congress assert itself to protect its constitutional prerogatives against power-seeking presidents and judges? Unfortunately, no advocate of the framers' constitutional design can offer confident answers.

We conclude with a question for the twenty-first century: Are the two Congresses ultimately compatible, or are they diverging, each detrimental to the other? The burdens placed on both Congresses become increasingly heavy from an ever-growing and diverse nation in an increasingly complex world. Congress-as-institution is expected to resolve all kinds of problems. Meanwhile, members are pulled away from their legislative duties by the constant press of fund-raising, party competition, constituency expectations, and short legislative workweeks. Legislators struggle to keep abreast of conflicting demands.

Recent events are not encouraging, but the question remains whether representative democracy will in the end be a winning or losing effort. History is only mildly reassuring, and the future poses new and difficult challenges for which the margin of error may be narrower than ever before. And yet representative democracy itself is a gamble. The proposition that representation can yield wise policy making remains a daring one. As always, it is an article of faith whose proof lies inevitably in the future.

Reference Materials

APPENDIX A Party Control: Presidency, Senate, House, 1901–2013

Congress	Years	President	Senate			House		
			D	R	Other	D	R	Other
57th	1901–1903	William McKinley/ Theodore Roosevelt	31	55	4	151	197	9
58th	1903–1905	T. Roosevelt	33	57	—	178	208	—
59th	1905–1907	T. Roosevelt	33	57	—	136	250	—
60th	1907–1909	T. Roosevelt	31	61	—	164	222	—
61st	1909–1911	William Howard Taft	32	61	—	172	219	—
62d	1911–1913	Taft	41	51	—	228	161	1
63d	1913–1915	Woodrow Wilson	51	44	1	291	127	17
64th	1915–1917	Wilson	56	40	—	230	196	9
65th	1917–1919	Wilson	53	42	—	216	210	6
66th	1919–1921	Wilson	47	49	—	190	240	3
67th	1921–1923	Warren G. Harding	37	59	—	131	301	1
68th	1923–1925	Calvin Coolidge	43	51	2	205	225	5
69th	1925–1927	Coolidge	39	56	1	183	247	4
70th	1927–1929	Coolidge	46	49	1	195	237	3
71st	1929–1931	Herbert Hoover	39	56	1	167	267	1
72d	1931–1933	Hoover	47	48	1	220	214	1
73d	1933–1935	Franklin D. Roosevelt	60	35	1	313	117	5
74th	1935–1937	F. D. Roosevelt	69	25	2	319	103	10
75th	1937–1939	F. D. Roosevelt	76	16	4	331	89	13
76th	1939–1941	F. D. Roosevelt	69	23	4	261	164	4
77th	1941–1943	F. D. Roosevelt	66	28	2	268	162	5
78th	1943–1945	F. D. Roosevelt	58	37	1	218	208	4
79th	1945–1947	Harry S. Truman	56	38	1	242	190	2
80th	1947–1949	Truman	45	51	—	188	245	1
81st	1949–1951	Truman	54	42	—	263	171	1
82d	1951–1953	Truman	49	47	—	234	199	1
83d	1953–1955	Dwight D. Eisenhower	47	48	1	211	221	1
84th	1955–1957	Eisenhower	48	47	1	232	203	—
85th	1957–1959	Eisenhower	49	47	—	233	200	—
86th[a]	1959–1961	Eisenhower	65	35	—	284	153	—
87th[a]	1961–1963	John F. Kennedy	65	35	—	263	174	—
88th	1963–1965	Kennedy/ Lyndon B. Johnson	67	33	—	258	177	—

Congress	Years	President	Senate			House		
			D	R	Other	D	R	Other
89th	1965–1967	Johnson	68	32	—	295	140	—
90th	1967–1969	Johnson	64	36	—	247	187	—
91st	1969–1971	Richard M. Nixon	57	43	—	243	192	—
92d	1971–1973	Nixon	54	44	2	254	180	—
93d	1973–1975	Nixon/ Gerald R. Ford	56	42	2w	239	192	1
94th	1975–1977	Ford	60	37	2	291	144	—
95th	1977–1979	Jimmy Carter	61	38	1	292	143	—
96th	1979–1981	Carter	58	41	1	276	157	—
97th	1981–1983	Ronald Reagan	46	53	1	243	192	—
98th	1983–1985	Reagan	45	55	—	267	168	—
99th	1985–1987	Reagan	47	53	—	252	183	—
100th	1987–1989	Reagan	55	45	—	258	177	—
101st	1989–1991	George H. W. Bush	55	45	—	260	175	—
102d	1991–1993	Bush	57	43	—	268	166	1
103d	1993–1995	Bill Clinton	56	44	—	258	176	1
104th	1995–1997	Clinton	47	53	—	204	230	1
105th	1997–1999	Clinton	45	55	—	207	227	1
106th	1999–2001	Clinton	45	55	—	211	223	1
107th	2001–2003	George W. Bush	50	49	1	210	222	3
108th	2003–2005	Bush	48	51	1	205	229	1
109th	2005–2007	Bush	44	55	1	202	232	1
110th[b]	2007–2009	Bush	49	49	2	233	202	—
111th[c]	2009–2011	Barack Obama	58	40	2	257	178	—
112th	2011-2013	Obama	51	47	2	193	242	—
113th	2013-2015	Obama	53	45	2	200	233	—

☐ Republican control   ☐ Democratic control

Sources: Encyclopedia of the United States Congress, ed. Donald C. Bacon, Roger H. Davidson, and Morton Keller (New York: Simon and Schuster, 1995), 1556–1558; data compiled by authors for 103d through 112th Congresses.

Note: Figures are for the beginning of the first session of each Congress and do not include vacancies, subsequent shifts, or changes in party affiliation.

[a] The House in the 86th and 87th Congresses had 437 members because of an at-large representative given to both Alaska (January 3, 1959) and Hawaii (August 21, 1959) prior to redistricting in 1962.

[b] The two Senate independents caucused with the Democrats, giving them a 51–49 majority for the purpose of organizing the chamber.

[c] For the Senate, we have counted as Democrats Arlen Specter, who shifted parties in April 2009, and Al Franken of Minnesota, who was sworn in on July 7, 2009.

Capitol Hill is an excellent place to obtain first-hand experience with the U.S. government. With 541 lawmakers (representatives, senators, delegates, and resident commissioners); hundreds of committees and subcommittees; scores of informal caucuses; and three congressional support agencies (the Congressional Research Service, Government Accountability Office, and Congressional Budget Office), intern opportunities abound for students interested in experiencing Congress and its members up close and personal.

Undergraduates will find useful information about landing an internship on Capitol Hill in several sources. One of the best is published under the auspices of the American Political Science Association and is titled *Studying in Washington: Academic Internships in the Nation's Capital.* Political scientist Stephen E. Frantzich discusses how to get a good internship, make the most of the experience, and find a place to live in Washington, D.C.

From our own years of "soaking and poking" around Capitol Hill, we offer five observations about getting congressional experience. First, no central clearinghouse exists for internships. Every congressional office, committee, caucus, and support agency manages its own internship program. Contact information and intern applications may be found on member and committee websites (www.house.gov and www.senate.gov). Many intern opportunities are available for minority students, such as through the Congressional Hispanic Caucus Institute (www.chci.org) or the minority access internship program (www.minorityaccess.org). You must be persistent, patient, and determined to find a position that will be a rewarding learning experience. Not only should you find out what duties and functions will be assigned to you as a volunteer intern (it is sometimes possible to secure paid internships), but you also need to remember that you have something useful to offer. Most congressional offices and committees are understaffed and subject to high staff turnover. Although the market for interns is competitive, congressional lawmakers, committees, and staffers want and need your talent.

Second, develop some notion as to where you would like to intern. Do research on the committee, lawmaker, support agency, or caucus that interests you. Remember that every office has its own personality. Senate offices, for example, are often large enterprises with many staff aides, while House offices are generally smaller. Interns thus will have more opportunities for personal, day-to-day contact with House members than with senators. The best way to determine the office environment is by interviewing people who have worked in a particular office, talking with the internship coordinators at your college or university, or visiting the office yourself.

Third, target your own representative and senators. Many congressional members prefer interns from their own state or district, who are likely to be familiar with the geography and concerns of that area. In addition, potential interns probably will have family and friends who are constituents of the law-maker. Do not hesitate to use your contacts. You might also volunteer to work in a state or district office of the lawmaker. Before accepting an internship, consider your own views and ideals. If your views are conservative, working for a lawmaker who espouses liberal causes may be difficult. However, if you are tactful and open-minded, working for someone whose views differ from yours may be instructive. Because you are a student, an internship with someone who holds divergent ideological views probably will not be held against you later in landing a position.

Fourth, intern placement opportunities are plentiful. Many colleges and universities sponsor semester programs in Washington, D.C. Several schools, including American University, Boston University, Hamilton College, Georgetown University, State University of New York, University of Southern California, University of Illinois, and University of California run programs in Washington, D.C. Some accept students from other accredited colleges and universities. The Washington Center for Internships and Academic Seminars, in existence since 1975, has placed thousands of students from hundreds of colleges. To be sure, students can Google "congressional internships" and find numerous intern listings to peruse.

Finally, Congress needs and welcomes the influx of new ideas and experiences that interns bring with them. The work at times may be drudgery—answering mail and telephones, entering information into computers, and running errands—but the opportunity to learn about Congress and to pick up political smarts not easily available from textbooks is nearly without equal. You may even want to keep a private journal of your experiences: what you have done and what you have learned. In sum, an internship on Capitol Hill is likely to be rewarding intellectually and in other ways that are impossible to predict.

RESOURCES

The Congressional Intern Handbook. Washington, DC: Congressional Management Foundation, 2006.

Fleishman, Sandra. "The Annual Scramble: Washington Interns Line Up for Their First Lesson—in Housing Supply and Demand." *Washington Post,* May 29, 2004, F1.

Frantzich, Stephen E. *Studying in Washington: Academic Internships in the Nation's Capital.* 5th ed. Washington, DC: American Political Science Association, 2002.

Lee, Jennifer. "Crucial Unpaid Internships Increasingly Separate the Haves from the Have-Nots." *New York Times,* August 10, 2004, 16.

Manning, Jennifer E. "Internships, Fellowships, and Other Work Experience in the Federal Government," CRS Report 98-654, January 30, 2012. Provides useful listings and bibliographies of internships.

Maxwell, Bruce. *Insider's Guide to Finding a Job in Washington: Contacts and Strategies to Build Your Career in Public Policy.* Washington, DC: CQ Press, 1999.

Mershon, Erin. "Hill Internships 101: What You Need to Know," *Roll Call,* June 1, 2011 (online version).

Peterson's Internships. Princeton, NJ: Peterson's Guides. Annual.

Reeher, Grant, and Mack Mariani, eds. *The Insider's Guide to Political Internships: What to Do Once You're in the Door.* Boulder, CO: Westview Press, 2002.

Strand, Mark, Michael S. Johnson, and Jerome F. Climer. *Surviving Inside Congress.* Washington, DC: Congressional Institute, 2009.

Washington Center for Internships and Academic Seminars. Address: 2301 M Street N.W., Washington, DC 20037. Telephone: (202) 336-7600 or (800) 486-8921. Website: www.twc. edu/internships/index.htm.

Washington Information Directory. Washington, DC: Congressional Quarterly. Annual publication that provides information about governmental and nongovernmental groups as well as addresses and phone numbers for congressional offices and committees.

CHAPTER 1

Bianco, William, ed. *Congress on Display, Congress at Work.* Ann Arbor: University of Michigan Press, 2000.

Hamilton, Lee H. *How Congress Works, and Why You Should Care.* Bloomington: Indiana University Press, 2004.

Hibbing, John R., and Elizabeth Theiss-Morse. *Congress as Public Enemy.* Cambridge: Cambridge University Press, 1995.

———. *Stealth Democracy: Americans' Beliefs about How Government Should Work.* Cambridge: Cambridge University Press, 2002.

Mayhew, David R. *Congress: The Electoral Connection.* 2d ed. New Haven, CT: Yale University Press, 2004.

CHAPTER 2

Binder, Sarah A. *Minority Rights, Majority Rule: Partisanship and the Development of Congress.* Cambridge: Cambridge University Press, 1997.

Jenkins, Jeffery A., and Charles Stewart III. *Fighting for the Speakership: The House and the Rise of Party Government.* Princeton, NJ: Princeton University Press, 2013.

Polsby, Nelson W. *How Congress Evolves: Social Bases of Institutional Change.* New York: Oxford University Press, 2004.

Rakove, Jack N. *Original Meanings: Politics and Ideas in the Making of the Constitution.* New York: Vintage, 1997.

Schickler, Eric. *Disjointed Pluralism: Institutional Innovation and the Development of the U.S. Congress.* Princeton, NJ: Princeton University Press, 2001.

Swift, Elaine K. *The Making of an American Senate: Reconstitutive Change in Congress, 1787–1841.* Ann Arbor: University of Michigan Press, 1996.

Wirls, Daniel, and Stephen Wirls. *The Invention of the United States Senate.* Baltimore: Johns Hopkins University Press, 2004.

CHAPTER 3

Canon, David T. *Race, Redistricting, and Representation.* Chicago: University of Chicago Press, 1999.

Ehrenhalt, Alan. *The United States of Ambition.* New York: Random House, 1991.

Fowler, Linda L., and Robert D. McClure. *Political Ambition: Who Decides to Run for Congress.* New Haven, CT: Yale University Press, 1989.

Jacobson, Gary C. *The Politics of Congressional Elections.* 8th ed. New York: Pearson Longman, 2013.

Jacobson, Gary C., and Samuel Kernell. *Strategy and Choice in Congressional Elections.* New Haven, CT: Yale University Press, 1981.

CHAPTER 4

Abramowitz, Alan I. *The Disappearing Center: Engaged Citizens, Polarization, and American Democracy.* New Haven, CT: Yale University Press, 2010.

Dolan, Kathleen A. *Voting for Women: How the Public Evaluates Women Candidates.* Boulder, CO: Westview Press, 2003.

Fiorina, Morris P., Samuel J. Abrams, and Jeremy C. Pope. *Culture War? The Myth of Polarized America*. 2d ed. New York: Pearson Longman, 2005.

Herrnson, Paul S. *Congressional Elections: Campaigning at Home and in Washington*. 6th ed. Washington, DC: CQ Press, 2013.

Jacobson, Gary C. *The Politics of Congressional Elections*. 8th ed. New York: Pearson Longman, 2013.

Thurber, James A., ed. *The Battle for Congress: Consultants, Candidates, and Voters*. Washington, DC: Brookings, 2001.

Wattenburg, Martin. *Is Voting for Young People?* New York: Pearson Longman, 2007.

CHAPTER 5

Arnold, R. Douglas. *Congress, the Press, and Political Accountability*. Princeton, NJ: Princeton University Press, 2004.

Baker, Ross K. *House and Senate*. 4th ed. New York: Norton, 2008.

Burden, Barry C. *Personal Roots of Representation*. Princeton, NJ: Princeton University Press, 2007.

Davidson, Roger H. *The Role of the Congressman*. Indianapolis: Bobbs-Merrill, 1969.

Fenno, Richard F., Jr. *Home Style: House Members in Their Districts*. Boston: Little, Brown, 1978.

Fiorina, Morris P. *Congress: Keystone of the Washington Establishment*. 2d ed. New Haven, CT: Yale University Press, 1989.

Price, David E. *The Congressional Experience: A View from the Hill*. 3d ed. Boulder, CO: Westview Press, 2004.

Sellers, Patrick. *Cycles of Spin: Strategic Communication in the U.S. Congress*. New York: Cambridge University Press, 2010.

Swers, Michele L. *The Difference Women Make: The Policy Impact of Women in Congress*. Chicago: University of Chicago Press, 2002.

CHAPTER 6

Aldrich, John H. *Why Parties? The Origins and Transformation of Party Politics in America*. Chicago: University of Chicago Press, 1995.

Baker, Richard A., and Roger H. Davidson, eds. *First among Equals: Outstanding Senate Leaders of the Twentieth Century*. Washington, DC: Congressional Quarterly, 1991.

Cox, Gary W., and Mathew D. McCubbins. *Setting the Agenda: Responsible Party Government in the U.S. House of Representatives*. New York: Cambridge University Press, 2005.

Davidson, Roger H., Susan Webb Hammond, and Raymond W. Smock, eds. *Masters of the House: Congressional Leaders over Two Centuries*. Boulder, CO: Westview Press, 1998.

Green, Matthew N. *The Speaker of the House: A Study of Leadership*. New Haven, CT: Yale University Press, 2010.

Lee, Frances E. *Beyond Ideology: Politics, Principles, and Partisanship in the U.S. Senate*. Chicago: University of Chicago Press, 2009.

Rohde, David W. *Parties and Leaders in the Postreform House*. Chicago: University of Chicago Press, 1991.

Sinclair, Barbara. *Legislators, Leaders, and Lawmaking: The U.S. House of Representatives in the Postreform Era*. Baltimore: Johns Hopkins University Press, 1995.

———. *The Transformation of the U.S. Senate*. Baltimore: Johns Hopkins University Press, 1989.

Strahan, Randall. *Leading Representatives: The Agency of Leaders in the Politics of the U.S. House*. Baltimore: Johns Hopkins University Press, 2007.

Theriault, Sean M. *The Gingrich Senators: The Roots of Partisan Warfare in Congress*. New York: Oxford University Press, 2013.

CHAPTER 7

Deering, Christopher J., and Steven S. Smith. *Committees in Congress.* 3d ed. Washington, DC: CQ Press, 1997.

Evans, C. Lawrence. *Leadership in Committee: A Comparative Analysis of Leadership Behavior in the U.S. Senate.* Ann Arbor: University of Michigan Press, 1991.

Fenno, Richard F., Jr. *Congressmen in Committees.* Boston: Little, Brown, 1973.

Frisch, Scott A., and Sean Q. Kelly. *Committee Assignment Politics in the U.S. House of Representatives.* Norman, OK: University of Oklahoma Press, 2006.

Hall, Richard L. *Participation in Congress.* New Haven, CT: Yale University Press, 1998.

King, David C. *Turf Wars: How Congressional Committees Claim Jurisdiction.* Chicago: University of Chicago Press, 1997.

Krehbiel, Keith. *Information and Legislative Organization.* Ann Arbor: University of Michigan Press, 1991.

Maltzman, Forrest. *Competing Principals: Committees, Parties, and the Organization of Congress.* Ann Arbor: University of Michigan Press, 1997.

Wilson, Woodrow. *Congressional Government.* Reprint of 1885 ed. Baltimore: Johns Hopkins University Press, 1981.

CHAPTER 8

Arenberg, Richard A., and Robert B. Dove. *Defending the Filibuster.* Bloomington, IN: Indiana University Press, 2012.

Binder, Sarah A. *Stalemate: Causes and Consequences of Legislative Gridlock.* Washington, DC: Brookings, 2003.

Binder, Sarah A., and Steven S. Smith. *Politics or Principle? Filibustering in the United States Senate.* Washington, DC: Brookings, 1996.

Cox, Gary W., and Matthew D. McCubbins. *Setting the Agenda: Responsible Party Government in the U.S. House of Representatives.* New York: Cambridge University Press, 2005.

Evans, Diana. *Greasing the Wheels: Using Pork Barrel Projects to Build Majority Coalitions in Congress.* New York: Cambridge University Press, 2004.

Koger, Gregory. *Filibustering: A Political History of Obstruction in the House and Senate.* Chicago: University of Chicago Press, 2010.

Krehbiel, Keith. *Pivotal Politics: A Theory of U.S. Lawmaking.* Chicago: University of Chicago Press, 1998.

Longley, Lawrence D., and Walter J. Oleszek. *Bicameral Politics: Conference Committees in Congress.* New Haven, CT: Yale University Press, 1989.

Loomis, Burdett, ed. *Esteemed Colleagues: Civility and Deliberation in the U.S. Senate.* Washington, DC: Brookings, 2000.

McKay, William, and Charles W. Johnson. *Parliament and Congress: Representation and Scrutiny in the Twenty-First Century.* New York: Oxford University Press, 2010.

Oleszek, Walter J. *Congressional Procedures and the Policy Process.* 9th ed. Washington, DC: CQ Press, 2014.

Schickler, Eric, and Frances E. Lee. *The Oxford Handbook of Congress.* New York: Oxford University Press, 2011.

Sinclair, Barbara. *Unorthodox Lawmaking: New Legislative Processes in the U.S. Congress.* 3d ed. Washington, DC: CQ Press, 2007.

Smith, Steven S. *Call to Order: Floor Politics in the House and Senate.* Washington, DC: Brookings, 1989.

Taylor, Andrew J. *The Floor in Congressional Life.* Ann Arbor, MI: University of Michigan Press, 2012.

CHAPTER 9

Arnold, R. Douglas. *The Logic of Congressional Action.* New Haven, CT: Yale University Press, 1990.

Binder, Sarah A. *Stalemate: Causes and Consequences of Legislative Gridlock.* Washington, DC: Brookings, 2003.

Brownstein, Ronald. *The Second Civil War: How Extreme Partisanship Has Paralyzed Washington and Polarized America.* New York: Penguin Press, 2007.

Edwards, George C. *At the Margins: Presidential Leadership of Congress.* New Haven, CT: Yale University Press, 1989.

Kingdon, John W. *Congressmen's Voting Decisions.* 3d ed. Ann Arbor: University of Michigan Press, 1989.

Mucchiaroni, Gary, and Paul J. Quirk. *Deliberative Choices: Debating Public Policy in Congress.* Chicago: University of Chicago Press, 2006.

Sulkin, Tracy. *Issue Politics in Congress.* New York: Cambridge University Press, 2005.

Theriault, Sean M. *Party Polarization in Congress.* New York: Cambridge University Press, 2008.

CHAPTER 10

Binkley, Wilfred. *President and Congress.* New York: Knopf, 1947.

Bond, Jon R., and Richard Fleisher, eds. *Polarized Politics: Congress and the President in a Partisan Era.* Washington, DC: CQ Press, 2000.

Canes-Wrone, Brandice. *Who Leads Whom? Presidents, Policy, and the Public.* Chicago: University of Chicago Press, 2006.

Edwards, George C., III. *On Deaf Ears: The Limits of the Bully Pulpit.* New Haven, CT: Yale University Press, 2006.

Fisher, Louis. *Constitutional Conflicts between Congress and the President.* 4th ed. Lawrence: University Press of Kansas, 1997.

Gilmour, John B. *Strategic Disagreement: Stalemate in American Politics.* Pittsburgh: University of Pittsburgh Press, 1995.

Howell, William G. *Power without Persuasion: The Politics of Direct Presidential Action.* Princeton, NJ: Princeton University Press, 2003.

Mayhew, David R. *Divided We Govern: Party Control, Lawmaking, and Investigations, 1946–2002.* New Haven, CT: Yale University Press, 2005.

McNamara, Carol, and Melanie M. Marlowe, eds. *The Obama Presidency in the Constitutional Order.* Lanham, MD: Rowman and Littlefield, 2012.

Rudalevige, Andrew. *The New Imperial Presidency.* Ann Arbor: University of Michigan Press, 2005.

Thurber, James, ed. *Rivals for Power: Presidential-Congressional Relations,* 5th ed. Lanham, MD: Rowman and Littlefield, 2013.

CHAPTER 11

Aberbach, Joel D. *Keeping a Watchful Eye: The Politics of Congressional Oversight.* Washington, DC: Brookings, 1990.

Arnold, R. Douglas. *Congress and the Bureaucracy: A Theory of Influence.* New Haven, CT: Yale University Press, 1979.

Foreman, Christopher J., Jr. *Signals from the Hill: Congressional Oversight and the Challenge of Social Regulation.* New Haven, CT: Yale University Press, 1988.

Jenkins, Jeffrey, and Eric Patashnik, eds. *Living Legislation: Durability, Change, and the Politics of American Lawmaking.* Chicago: University of Chicago Press, 2012.

Light, Paul C. *A Government Ill Executed: The Decline of the Federal Service and How to Reverse It.* Cambridge, MA: Harvard University Press, 2008.

————. *The New Public Service.* Washington, DC: Brookings, 1999.

————. *The True Size of Government.* Washington, DC: Brookings, 1999.

Rosenbloom, David. *Building a Legislative-Centered Public Administration: Congress and the Administrative State, 1946–1999.* Tuscaloosa: University of Alabama Press, 2000.

Wilson, James Q. *Bureaucracy: What Government Agencies Do and Why They Do it.* New York: Basic Books, 2000.

CHAPTER 12

Berger, Raoul. *Congress v. The Supreme Court.* Cambridge, MA: Harvard University Press, 1969.

Binder, Sarah A., and Forrest Maltzman. *Advice and Dissent: The Struggle to Shape the Federal Judiciary.* Washington, DC: Brookings, 2009.

Fisher, Louis. *Constitutional Dialogues.* Princeton, NJ: Princeton University Press, 1988.

Geyh, Charles Gardner. *When Congress and Courts Collide.* Ann Arbor: University of Michigan Press, 2006.

Katzmann, Robert A. *Courts and Congress.* Washington, DC: Brookings, 1997.

Noonan, John T., Jr. *Narrowing the Nation's Power: The Supreme Court Sides with the States.* Berkeley: University of California Press, 2002.

Wittes, Benjamin. *Confirmation Wars: Preserving Independent Courts in Angry Times.* Lanham, MD: Rowman and Littlefield, 2006.

CHAPTER 13

Andres, Gary. *Lobbying Reconsidered.* New York: Pearson Education, Inc. 2009

Baumgartner, Frank R., Jeffrey M. Berry, Marie Hojnacki, David C. Kimball, and Beth L. Leech. *Lobbying and Policy Change: Who Wins, Who Loses and Why.* Chicago: University of Chicago Press, 2009.

Birnbaum, Jeffrey H., and Alan S. Murray. *Showdown at Gucci Gulch: Lawmakers, Lobbyists, and the Unlikely Triumph of Tax Reform.* New York: Random House, 1987.

Hall, Richard L., and Alan V. Deardorff. "Lobbying as Legislative Subsidy." *American Political Science Review* 100 (February 2006): 69–84.

Hojnacki, Marie, and David Kimball. "Organized Interests and the Decision of Whom to Lobby in Congress." *American Political Science Review* 92 (December 1998): 775–790.

Loomis, Burdett A., Peter L. Francia, and Dara Z. Strolovich, eds. *Guide to Interest Groups and Lobbying in the United States.* Washington, DC: CQ Press, 2011.

Rozell, Mark, Clyde Wilcox, and David Madland. *Interest Groups in American Campaigns: The New Face of Electioneering.* 2d ed. Washington, DC: CQ Press, 2005.

Truman, David B. *The Governmental Process, Political Interests, and Public Opinion.* 2d ed. New York: Knopf, 1971.

CHAPTER 14

Elving, Ronald D. *Conflict and Compromise: How Congress Makes the Law.* New York: Simon and Schuster, 1995.

Hilley, John L. *The Challenge of Legislation.* Washington, DC: Brookings, 2008.

Kelman, Steven. *Making Public Policy.* New York: Basic Books, 1987.

Kingdon, John W. *Agendas, Alternatives, and Public Policies.* Boston: Little, Brown, 1984.

Mettler, Suzanne. *The Submerged State: How Invisible Government Policies Undermine Democracy.* Chicago: University of Chicago Press, 2011.

Schick, Allen. *Congress and Money: Budgeting, Spending, and Taxing.* Washington, DC: Urban Institute, 1980.

————. *The Federal Budget: Politics, Policy, Process.* Rev. ed. Washington, DC: Brookings, 2007.

CHAPTER 15

Auerswald, David P., and Colton C. Campbell, eds. *Congress and National Security.* New York: Cambridge University Press, 2012.

Crabb, Cecil V., Jr., Glenn J. Antizzo, and Leila E. Sarieddine. *Congress and the Foreign Policy Process.* Baton Rouge: Louisiana State University Press, 2000.

Fisher, Louis. *Constitutional Conflicts between Congress and the President.* Lawrence: University Press of Kansas, 2007.

————. *The Constitution and 9/11.* Lawrence: University Press of Kansas, 2008.

Goldsmith, Jack. *The Terror Presidency: Law and Judgment inside the Bush Administration.* New York: Norton, 2007.

Hinckley, Barbara. *Less Than Meets the Eye: Foreign Policy Making and the Myth of the Assertive Congress.* Chicago: University of Chicago Press, 1994.

Howell, William G., and Jon C. Pevehouse. *While Dangers Gather: Congressional Checks on Presidential War Powers.* Chicago: University of Chicago Press, 2007.

Kriner, Douglas L. *After the Rubicon: Congress, Presidents, and the Politics of Waging War.* Chicago: University of Chicago Press, 2010.

Lindsay, James M. *Congress and the Politics of U.S. Foreign Policy.* Baltimore: Johns Hopkins University Press, 1994.

CHAPTER 16

Adler, E. Scott. *Why Congressional Reforms Fail: Reelection and the House Committee System.* Chicago: University of Chicago Press, 2002.

Cook, Timothy E. *Making Laws and Making News: Media Strategies in the U.S. House of Representatives.* Washington, DC: Brookings, 1989.

Hamilton, Lee H. *How Congress Works, and Why You Should Care.* Bloomington: Indiana University Press, 2004.

Hibbing, John R., and Elizabeth Theiss-Morse. *Stealth Democracy: Americans' Beliefs about How Government Should Work.* Cambridge: Cambridge University Press, 2002.

Mackenzie, G. Calvin, with Michael Hafken. *Scandal Proof: Do Ethics Laws Make Government Ethical?* Washington, DC: Brookings, 2002.

Mann, Thomas E., and Norman J. Ornstein. *The Broken Branch: How Congress Is Failing America and How to Get It Back on Track.* New York: Oxford University Press, 2006.

————. *It's Even Worse Than It Looks: How the American Constitutional System Collided with the New Politics of Extremism.* New York: Basic Books, 2012.

Taylor, Andrew J. *Congress: A Performance Appraisal.* Boulder, CO: Westview Press, 2013.

Wolfensberger, Donald. *Congress and the People: Deliberative Democracy on Trial.* Washington, DC: Woodrow Wilson Center Press, 2000.

CHAPTER 1

1. Quoted in Dakota Smith, "Brad Sherman's Decisive Win Raises Questions About Need to Reach Out to Howard Berman Supporters," *Los Angeles Daily News*, November 7, 2012, www.dailynews.com/ci_21953169/brad-shermans-decisive-win-raises-questions-about-need.

2. Editorial, "Howard Berman in the 30th Congressional District," *Los Angeles Times*, September 23, 2012.

3. Quoted in Ian Lovett, "2 Democrats, 2 Incumbents, and One Tough House Race," *New York Times*, September 26, 2012.

4. Quoted in Dakota Smith, "30th Congressional District: Sherman vs. Berman a Bruising Battle—Literally," *Los Angeles Times*, October 27, 2012, www.dailynews.com/ci_21870350/30th-congressional-district-sherman-vs-berman-bruising-battle.

5. John Bicknel and David Meyers, eds., *Politics in America 2012 (the 112th Congress)* (Washington, DC: CQ–Roll Call, Inc., 2012), http://library.cqpress.com/pia/OEpia112_116.

6. Quoted in Lovett, "2 Democrats, 2 Incumbents."

7. Michael Barone and Chuck McCutcheon, *The Almanac of American Politics, 2012* (Chicago: University of Chicago Press, 2011).

8. Michelle Quinn, "Brad Sherman Defeats Howard Berman after Bitter Fight," *Politico*, November 7, 2012.

9. Jean Merl, "Berman's Only Election Loss in Long Career Costs Him House Seat," *Los Angeles Times*, November 7, 2012.

10. John Bresnehan, "Brad Sherman Bows Out of House Foreign Affairs Committee Race," *Politico*, November 16, 2012.

11. Paul S. Herrnson, *Congressional Elections: Campaigning at Home and in Washington*, 5th ed. (Washington, DC: CQ Press, 2008), 272.

12. Sam Rayburn, *Speak, Mr. Speaker*, ed. H. G. Dulaney and Edward Hake Phillips (Bonham, TX: Sam Rayburn Foundation, 1978), 263–264. Rayburn was Speaker from 1940 to 1947, 1949 to 1953, and 1955 to 1961.

13. Quoted in Marin Cogan, "Allen West Gets Brushback from Veteran Bishop," *Politico*'s *On Congress: Congressional News and Analysis Blog*, December 21, 2010, www.politico.com/blogs/glenthrush.

14. Frank E. Smith, *Congressman from Mississippi* (New York: Random House, 1964), 127.

15. David R. Mayhew, *Congress: The Electoral Connection* (New Haven, CT: Yale University Press, 1974), 16.

16. Alan Abramowitz, "A Comparison of Voting for U.S. Senator and Representative in 1978," *American Political Science Review* 74 (September 1980): 633–640; Richard F. Fenno Jr., *The United States Senate: A Bicameral Perspective* (Washington, DC: American Enterprise Institute, 1982), 29ff; Frances E. Lee and Bruce I. Oppenheimer, *Sizing Up the Senate: The Unequal Consequences of Equal Representation* (Chicago: University of Chicago Press, 1999), 111–113.

17. U.S. Congress, Joint Committee on the Organization of Congress, *Organization of the Congress, Final Report*, 2 vols., H. Rep. 103–14, 103d Cong., 1st sess., December 1993, 2: 275–287. Also see Table 5-1 in this book.

18. Glenn R. Parker and Roger H. Davidson, "Why Do Americans Love Their Congressmen So Much More Than Their Congress?" *Legislative Studies Quarterly* 4 (February 1979): 53–61; Kelly D. Patterson and David B. Magleby, "Public Support for Congress," *Public Opinion Quarterly* 56 (Winter 1992): 539–540; and Randall B. Ripley, Samuel C. Patterson, Lynn M. Mauer, and Stephen V. Quinlan, "Constituents' Evaluations of U.S. House Members," *American Politics Quarterly* 20 (October 1992): 442–456.

19. On how the public's perceptions of the policy process affect Congress's institutional image, see John R. Hibbing and Elizabeth Theiss-Morse, *Congress as Public Enemy: Public Attitudes toward American Political Institutions* (New York: Cambridge University Press, 1995).

20. Alexander Hamilton, James Madison, and John Jay, *The Federalist Papers,* No. 51, ed. Clinton Rossiter (New York: Mentor, 1961), 322.

21. *Federalist Papers,* No. 52, 327.

22. Edmund Burke, "Speech to Electors at Bristol," in *Burke's Politics,* ed. Ross J. S. Hoffman and Paul Levack (New York: Knopf, 1949), 116.

23. Ibid.

24. Quoted in *Roll Call,* September 9, 1993, 16.

25. *U.S. Term Limits v. Thornton,* 115 S.Ct. 1842 (1995).

26. Quoted in Mark Carl Rom, "Why Not Assume That Public Officials Seek to Promote the Public Interest?" *Public Affairs Report* 37 (July 1996): 12.

27. For an accessible discussion of different voting systems, see Douglas J. Amy, *Behind the Ballot Box: A Citizen's Guide to Voting Systems* (Westport, CT: Praeger, 2000), 65.

28. For an analysis of members facing this representational difficulty, see Richard F. Fenno Jr., *Home Style: House Members in Their Districts* (Boston: Little, Brown, 1978), especially pages 91–99 and 102–114.

29. Alan I. Abramowitz, *The Disappearing Center: Engaged Citizens, Polarization, and American Democracy* (New Haven, CT: Yale University Press, 2010), 37.

30. Morris P. Fiorina, with Samuel J. Abrams, *Disconnect: The Breakdown of Representation in American Politics* (Norman: University of Oklahoma Press, 2009).

31. Fenno, *Home Style,* 168.

32. Matt Taibbi, "The Worst Congress Ever: How Our National Legislature Has Become a Stable of Thieves and Perverts—in Five Easy Steps," *Rolling Stone,* November 2, 2006, 46.

33. Woodrow Wilson, *Congressional Government* (1885; reprint, Baltimore: Johns Hopkins University Press, 1981), 210.

34. Thomas E. Mann and Norman J. Ornstein, *The Broken Branch: How Congress Is Failing America and How to Get It Back on Track* (New York: Oxford University Press, 2006), 141–191.

CHAPTER 2

1. Joseph J. Ellis, *His Excellency George Washington* (New York: Knopf, 2006), 184–186.

2. Alvin M. Josephy Jr., *On the Hill: A History of the American Congress* (New York: Simon and Schuster, 1980), 41–48.

3. Charles A. Beard and John P. Lewis, "Representative Government in Evolution," *American Political Science Review* (April 1932): 223–240.

4. Jack P. Green, ed., *Great Britain and the American Colonies, 1606–1763* (New York: Harper Torch Books, 1970), xxxix.

5. Edmund C. Burnett, *Continental Congress* (New York: Norton, 1964).

6. *Congressional Quarterly's Guide to Congress,* 5th ed., vol. 1 (Washington, DC: CQ Press, 2000), 9.

7. Burnett, *Continental Congress,* 171. The authors use modern capitalization when quoting the Declaration of Independence (as here) or the Constitution in this volume.

8. Jack N. Rakove, *The Beginnings of National Politics: An Interpretive History of the Continental Congress* (New York: Knopf, 1979), 43.

9. Charles C. Thach Jr., *The Creation of the Presidency, 1775–1789: A Study in Constitutional History* (Baltimore: Johns Hopkins University Press, 1969), 34.

10. James Sterling Young, "America's First Hundred Days," *Miller Center Journal* 1 (Winter 1994): 57.

11. On the framers' general consensus on the need for a stronger national government, see Lance Banning, "The Constitutional Convention," in *The Framing and Ratification of the*

Constitution, ed. Leonard W. Levy and Dennis J. Mahoney (New York: Macmillan, 1987); and John P. Roche, "The Founding Fathers: A Reform Caucus in Action," *American Political Science Review* 55 (1961): 799–816.

12. John Locke, *Two Tracts on Government,* ed. Philip Abrams (New York: Cambridge University Press, 1967), 374.

13. *National Federation of Small Business v. Sebelius,* 132 S. Ct. 2566, 2587 (2012).

14. Alexander Hamilton, James Madison, and John Jay, *The Federalist Papers,* No. 48, ed. Clinton Rossiter (New York: Mentor, 1961), 322.

15. Ibid., 308.

16. Joseph Story, *Commentaries on the Constitution of the United States,* 5th ed., vol. 1 (Boston: Little, Brown, 1905), 396. For Justice Robert Jackson's comments, see *Youngstown Sheet and Tube Co. v. Sawyer,* 343 U.S. 579, 635 (1952).

17. Mark A. Peterson, "The Three Branches of Government: Powers, Relationships and Checks," in *A Republic Divided,* ed. Annenberg Democracy Project (New York: Oxford University Press, 2007), 105. From his own survey, David R. Mayhew finds the same six out of ten success rate for presidential initiatives in *Partisan Balance: Why Political Parties Don't Kill the U.S. Constitutional System* (Princeton, NJ: Princeton University Press, 2011, 58).

18. Not all executive nominees require Senate approval. According to the Constitution, "inferior officers" need not be confirmed by the Senate, and Congress can vest the power to appoint inferior officers "in the President alone."

19. William Howell and Jon Pevehouse, "When Congress Stops Wars," *Foreign Affairs* (September/October 2007).

20. In *Nixon v. United States,* 506 U.S. 224 (1993), the Supreme Court refused to review the Senate's procedures. A former federal judge, Walter L. Nixon Jr. objected that although he had been convicted by a vote of the full Senate, the evidence in his case had been taken by one of the chamber's committees.

21. *Federalist Papers,* No. 65, 396.

22. Emily Field, Van Tassel, and Paul Finkelman, *Impeachable Offenses: A Documentary History from 1787 to the Present* (Washington, DC: Congressional Quarterly, 1999). The only Senate impeachment trial since 1999 was that of Judge G. Thomas Porteous Jr. of the federal district court in Louisiana. See Jennifer Steinhauer, "Senate, for Just the 8th Time, Votes to Oust a Federal Judge," *New York Times,* December 8, 2010.

23. *U.S. v. Rayburn House Office Bldg., Room 2113,* Washington, DC, 20515, 497 F.3d 654 (D.C. Cir. 2007).

24. *Marbury v. Madison,* 1 Cranch 137 (1803).

25. *The Constitution of the United States of America: Analysis and Interpretation,* S. Doc. 111-39 111th Congress, 2d sess., 199–201. Recent figures are courtesy of Kenneth Thomas, legislative attorney, American Law Division, Congressional Research Service.

26. The figures cited here are from J. Mitchell Pickerill, "Congressional Responses to Judicial Review," in *Congress and the Constitution,* ed. Neal Devins and Keith E. Whittington (Durham, NC, and London: Duke University Press, 2005), 159.

27. *Dred Scott v. Sandford,* 60 U.S. 393 (1856).

28. *Citizens United v. Federal Election Commission,* 130 S.Ct. 876 (2010).

29. *Immigration and Naturalization Service v. Chadha,* 463 U.S. 919 (1983).

30. William N. Eskridge Jr., "Overriding Supreme Court Statutory Interpretation Decisions," *Yale Law Journal* 101 (November 1991): 331–455. Also see R. Shep Melnick, *Between the Lines: Interpreting Welfare Rights* (Washington, DC: Brookings, 1994).

31. Louis Fisher, *Constitutional Dialogues: Interpretation as Political Process* (Princeton, NJ: Princeton University Press, 1988), 275.

32. Quoted in Charles Warren, *The Making of the Constitution* (Boston: Little, Brown, 1928), 162.

33. Quoted in Charles Warren, *The Supreme Court in United States History* (Boston: Little, Brown, 1919), 195.

34. Wendy J. Schiller, "Building Careers and Courting Constituents: U.S. Senate Representation: 1889–1924," *Studies in American Political Development* 20 (Fall 2006): 185–197.

35. See Charles Stewart III, "Responsiveness in the Upper Chamber: The Constitution and the Institutional Development of the Senate," in *The Constitution and American Political Development*, ed. Peter F. Nardulli (Urbana: University of Illinois Press, 1992), 63–96; and Gregory J. Wawro and Eric Schickler, *Filibuster: Obstruction and Lawmaking in the U.S. Senate* (Princeton, NJ: Princeton University Press, 2006).

36. Elaine K. Swift, *The Making of an American Senate* (Ann Arbor: University of Michigan Press, 1996), 5.

37. Joel H. Silbey, *The Partisan Imperative: The Dynamics of American Politics before the Civil War* (New York: Oxford University Press).

38. Sarah A. Binder, *Minority Rights, Majority Rule* (New York: Cambridge University Press, 1997), 49.

39. Norman J. Ornstein, Thomas E. Mann, and Michael J. Malbin, *Vital Statistics on Congress 2008* (Washington, DC: Brookings, 2002), 110–111.

40. See *Jefferson's Manual, and Rules of the House of Representatives*, Section XI, H. Doc. 105–358, 105th Cong., 2d sess., 1999, 145–148.

41. Nelson W. Polsby, "The Institutionalization of the House of Representatives," *American Political Science Review* 62 (March 1968): 146–147.

42. Ornstein, Mann, and Malbin, 127.

43. Eric Schickler, "Institutional Development of Congress," in *The Legislative Branch*, ed. Paul J. Quirk and Sarah A. Binder (New York: Oxford University Press), 40; Ornstein, Mann, and Malbin, *Vital Statistics on Congress, 2001–2002*, 149.

44. George B. Galloway, *History of the House of Representatives* (New York: Crowell, 1961), 67.

45. Joseph Cooper and Cheryl D. Young, "Bill Introduction in the Nineteenth Century: A Study of Institutional Change," *Legislative Studies Quarterly* 14: 67–105.

46. Ronald Brownstein, "Bold is Beautiful: The Super Committee Offers a Glimmer of Hope," *National Journal*, August 5, 2011.

47. Barbara Sinclair, *Unorthodox Lawmaking: New Legislative Processes in the U.S. Congress* (Washington, DC: CQ Press, 2005).

48. Andrew J. Taylor, "Size, Power, and Electoral Determinants: Exogenous Determinants of Legislative Procedural Choice," *Legislative Studies Quarterly* 31 (August 2006): 338.

49. Schickler, "Institutional Development of Congress," 40.

50. Roger H. Davidson and Walter J. Oleszek, *Congress against Itself* (Bloomington: Indiana University Press, 1977), 14.

51. Quoted in Eric Schickler, *Disjointed Pluralism: Institutional Innovation and the Development of the U.S. Congress* (Princeton, NJ: Princeton University Press, 2001), 142.

52. James L. Sundquist, *The Decline and Resurgence of Congress* (Washington, DC: Brookings, 1982).

53. Julian E. Zelizer, *On Capitol Hill: The Struggle to Reform Congress and Its Consequences, 1948–2000* (New York: Cambridge University Press, 2004), 153.

54. Roy Swanstrom, *The United States Senate, 1787–1801*, S. Doc. 99–19, 99th Cong., 1st sess., 1985, 283.

55. Jeffery A. Jenkins and Charles Stewart III, *Fighting for the Speakership: The House and the Rise of Party Government* (Princeton, NJ: Princeton University Press, 2013).

56. Ibid.

57. Binder, *Minority Rights, Majority Rule*, 17.

58. Gregory Koger, *Filibustering: A Political History of Obstruction in the House and Senate* (Chicago, University of Chicago Press, 2010).

59. Ibid., 84.

60. David R. Mayhew, *Congress: The Electoral Connection* (New Haven, CT: Yale University Press, 1974), 95.

61. See David W. Rohde, *Parties and Leaders in the Postreform House* (Chicago: University of Chicago Press, 1991); and Nelson W. Polsby, *How Congress Evolves: Social Bases of Institutional Change* (New York: Oxford University Press, 2004).

62. See Sarah A. Binder and Steven S. Smith, *Politics or Principle? Filibustering in the United States Senate* (Washington, DC: Brookings, 1997); Gregory J. Wawro and Eric Schickler, *Filibuster: Obstruction and Lawmaking in the U.S. Senate* (Princeton, NJ: Princeton University Press, 2006); and Sarah A. Binder, Anthony J. Madonna, and Steven S. Smith, "Going Nuclear, Senate Style," *Perspectives on Politics* 5(4): 729–740.

63. Schickler, *Disjointed Pluralism*, 13.

64. Ibid., 141–146.

65. Ibid., 213–217.

66. Ibid., 267.

67. Ibid.

68. James Sterling Young, *The Washington Community, 1800–1828* (New York: Harcourt Brace Jovanovich, 1966), 89.

69. Noble Cunningham Jr., ed., *Circular Letters of Congressmen, 1789–1839,* 3 vols. (Chapel Hill: University of North Carolina Press, 1978), 57.

70. Swanstrom, *United States Senate*, 80.

71. Mildred Amer, "Average Years of Service for Members of the Senate and the House of Representatives, First–109th Congresses," Congressional Research Service Report RL32648, November 9, 2005. Earlier studies include Nelson W. Polsby, "The Institutionalization of the House of Representatives," *American Political Science Review* 62 (March 1968): 146–147; and Randall B. Ripley, *Power in the Senate* (New York: St. Martin's Press, 1969), 42–43.

72. Sam Goldfarb, "Term Limits Win Out in Chairmen Picks," *CQ Weekly,* December 13, 2010, 2868.

73. Joe Martin, as told to Robert J. Donovan, *My First Fifty Years in Politics* (New York: McGraw-Hill, 1960), 49–50.

74. Robert H. Salisbury and Kenneth A. Shepsle, "U.S. Congressman as Enterprise" *Legislative Studies Quarterly* 6 (Nov. 1981): 559-576.

75. Curtis W. Copeland, "The Federal Workforce: Characteristics and Trends," Congressional Research Service Report No. RL34685, April 19, 2011, Table 2.

76. Cunningham, *Circular Letters of Congressmen.*

77. Martin, *My First Fifty Years*, 101.

78. Colleen J. Shogan, "Blackberries, Tweets, and YouTube: Technology and the Future of Communicating with Congress," *P.S.* 42 (April 2010): 231.

CHAPTER 3

1. *U.S. Term Limits v. Thornton*, 514 U.S. 779 (1995).

2. Arend Lijphart, *Democracies: Patterns of Majoritarian and Consensus Government in Twenty-one Countries* (New Haven, CT: Yale University Press, 1984), 174.

3. David Samuels and Richard Snyder, "The Value of a Vote: Malapportionment in Comparative Perspective," *British Journal of Political Science* 31, no. 4 (2001): 651–671.

4. See Daniel H. Pink, "Givers and Takers," *New York Times,* January 30, 2004, A21.

5. John D. Griffin, "Senate Apportionment as a Source of Political Inequality," *Legislative Studies Quarterly* 31 (August 2006): 425.

6. The idea is that proportional differences in the number of persons per representative for any pair of states should be kept to a minimum. The first fifty House seats are taken because the Constitution ensures that each state has at least one representative. The question then becomes, which state deserves the fifty-first seat, the fifty-second, and so forth? The mathematical formula yields a priority value for each seat, up to any desired number. The bottom line is to ensure that states are "entitled to a percentage of representatives equal to [their] portion of the national population."

7. Jeffrey W. Ladewig and Mathew P. Jasinski, "On the Causes and Consequences of and Remedies for Interstate Malapportionment of the U.S. House of Representatives," *Perspectives on Politics* 6 (2008): 90.

8. In 1960 the size of the House was temporarily increased from 435 to 437 members to accommodate the admission of Alaska and Hawaii as states. Three years later, after the 1960 reapportionment, the House reverted back to 435 members.

9. On the role of the Prohibition issue in the congressional failure to reapportion House seats in 1920, see Daniel Okrent, *Last Call: The Rise and Fall of Prohibition* (New York: Scribner, 2010), 239–241, 327–328.

10. *Congressional Quarterly's Guide to Congress,* vol. 2 (Washington, DC: CQ Press, 2000), 898.

11. Clark Bensen, "The Political Impact of Katrina: Apportionment in 2010," POLIDATA Press Release, December 22, 2006, 2.

12. Haya El Nasser, "For 2010 Census, the Counting Gets Tougher," *USA Today,* October 8, 2008, 1A.

13. Kathleen Hunter, "Minority Lawmakers to Ask Leadership to Address U.S. Census Undercounts," *CQ Today,* October 29, 2007, 6.

14. Sandy Hume, "GOP Fears 2000 Census Plan Will Overestimate Minorities," *The Hill,* May 7, 1997, 1.

15. *Department of Commerce et al. v. U.S. House of Representatives,* 525 U.S. 316 (1999).

16. Quoted in Charles Mathesian, "Dollars and Census," *Government Executive,* December 2007, 50.

17. *Lepak v. City of Irving,* 453 Fed. Appx. 522 (5th Cir. 2011).

18. For a more detailed discussion of districting than is provided here, see Thomas S. Arrington, "Redistricting in the U.S.: A Review of Scholarship and Plan for Future Research," *The Forum* 8 (2010): art. 7.

19. Arizona, California, Hawaii, Idaho, Montana, New Jersey, and Washington have established commissions for drawing congressional district lines.

20. Juliet Eilperin, "The Gerrymander That Ate America," *Slate,* April 17, 2006. Quoted from her book *Fight Club Politics: How Partisanship Is Poisoning the House of Representatives* (Lanham, MD: Rowman and Littlefield, 2006).

21. The classic study is still Gordon E. Baker, *The Reapportionment Revolution: Representation, Political Power, and the Supreme Court* (New York: Random House, 1966).

22. In 2001 Georgia Democrats produced a state legislature redistricting plan that tested the notion that a population deviation of plus or minus 5 percent would be acceptable at the state level. A circuit court panel invalidated the scheme and eventually drew up its own plan, which was ultimately affirmed by the Supreme Court. See *Larios v. Cox,* 300 F. Supp. 2d 1320 (N.D. Ga. 2004).

23. Alan Ehrenhalt, "Redistricting and the Erosion of Community," *Governing* (June 1992): 10.

24. The University of Southern California's Annenberg Center has created the ReDistricting Game, a Web application to illustrate how redistricting can be manipulated to achieve political goals; see www.redistrictinggame.org/.

25. *League of United Latin American Citizens v. Perry,* 548 U.S. 399 (2006).

26. *Davis v. Bandemer,* 478 U.S. 109 (1986).

27. See also *Vieth v. Jubelirer,* 541 U.S. 267 (2004), for another example of the Court grappling with issues of partisan gerrymandering but unable to articulate a definitive judicial standard to guide mapmakers.

28. Aaron Blake, "GOP Can Draw Nearly Half of New House Districts," The Fix, *Washington Post* weblog, November 4, 2010, http://voices.washingtonpost.com/thefix/redistricting/gop-can-draw-nearly-half-of-ne.html.

29. Griff Palmer and Michael Cooper, "How Maps Helped Republicans Keep an Edge in the House," *New York Times,* December 14, 2012, A10.

30. Sundeep Iyer, "Redistricting and Congressional Control Following the 2012 Election," Analysis, Brennan Center for Justice, New York University School of Law, November 28, 2012, www.brennancenter.org/content/resource/redistricting_and_congressional_control_following_the_2012_election/.

31. *Congressional Record,* 110th Cong., 2d sess., July 29, 2008, H7285.

32. Sean M. Theriault, *Party Polarization in Congress* (New York: Cambridge University Press, 2008), 83.

33. Nolan McCarty, Keith T. Poole, and Howard Rosenthal, "Does Gerrymandering Cause Polarization?" *American Journal of Political Science* 53 (2009): 678.

34. Rhodes Cook, "Do the Math, and the Result Is: Not Much of a Contest," *Washington Post,* October 6, 2002, B3.

35. The sole incumbent defeated in California between 2002 and 2010 was Republican Richard Pombo, who served from 1993 to 2007.

36. Charles Backstrom, Samuel Krislov, and Leonard Robins, "Desperately Seeking Standards: The Court's Frustrating Attempts to Limit Political Gerrymandering," *PS* (July 2006): 409.

37. See Andrew Gelman and Gary King, "Enhancing Democracy through Legislative Redistricting," *American Political Science Review* 88 (1994): 541–559.

38. Aaron Blake, "Breaking Down the Florida GOP's Redistricting Map," The Fix, *Washington Post* weblog, January 1, 2012, www.washingtonpost.com/blogs/the-fix/post/breaking-down-the-florida-gops-redistricting-map/2012/01/26/gIQAdCFYTQ_blog.html.

39. Steven Hill, "Schwarzenegger versus Gerrymander," *New York Times,* February 19, 2005, A29. See also Steve Lawrence, "Experts Question Redistricting Plan," *Santa Barbara News-Press,* February 20, 2005, A7.

40. Quoted in Bill Bishop, "You Can't Compete with Voters' Feet," *Washington Post,* May 15, 2005, B2. Also see James G. Gimpel and Jason E. Schucknect, *Patchwork Nation: Sectionalism and Political Change in American Politics* (Ann Arbor: University of Michigan Press, 2003); and Bill Bishop, *The Big Sort: Why the Clustering of Like-Minded America Is Tearing Us Apart* (Boston: Houghton Mifflin, 2008).

41. Ibid.

42. Quoted in Tricia Miller, "Redistricting Reform Is Tough Task Every Time," *Roll Call,* December 14, 2010.

43. Definition is from *Shaw v. Reno,* 509 U.S. 630 (1993), quoting *Davis v. Bandemer,* 478 U.S. 109 (1986).

44. Eric Foner, *Reconstruction: America's Unfinished Revolution, 1863–1877* (New York: Harper and Row, 1988), 590.

45. The "retrogression" standard was established in *Beer v. U.S.,* 425 U.S. 130 (1976). The 2006 amendments to the VRA clarified that the congressional intent behind Section 5 of the VRA was to "protect the ability of racial minorities to elect their candidates of choice" (P.L. 109–246).

46. National Conference of State Legislatures, *Redistricting Law 2010* (Washington, DC: National Conference of State Legislatures, 2009), 3.

47. *Shaw v. Reno*, 509 U.S. 630 (1993).

48. *Miller v. Johnson*, 515 U.S. 900 (1995).

49. Ibid.

50. The Court's interpretation of Section 2 of the VRA was laid out most clearly in *Thornburg v. Gingles*, 478 U.S. 30 (1986).

51. *Shaw v. Hunt*, 517 U.S. 899 (1996).

52. *Beer v. U.S.*, 425 U.S. 130 (1976). In *Shaw v. Reno* (509 U.S. 630, 655 [1993]), the Court stated, "A reapportionment plan would not be narrowly tailored to the goal of avoiding retrogression if the State went beyond what was reasonably necessary to avoid retrogression."

53. *Shaw v. Reno*, 509 U.S. 630 (1993); *Miller v. Johnson*, 515 U.S. 900 (1995); *Bush v. Vera*, 517 U.S. 952 (1996); *Shaw v. Hunt*, 517 U.S. 899 (1996).

54. *Miller v. Johnson*, 515 U.S. 900 (1995).

55. *Easley v. Cromartie*, 532 U.S. 234 (2001).

56. *Hunt v. Cromartie*, 526 U.S. 541 (1999).

57. Mara Caputo and Ragan Narash, "Despite Series of Court Rulings, State Officials Are Left Guessing," *CQ Weekly*, August 11, 2001, 1970.

58. Lani Guinier, "What Color Is Your Gerrymander?" *Washington Post*, March 27, 1994, C3.

59. David Lublin, Thomas L. Brunell, Bernard Grofman, and Lisa Handley, "Has the Voting Rights Act Outlived Its Usefulness? In a Word, 'No,'" *Legislative Studies Quarterly* 34 (2009): 547.

60. Scott Bland, "More Minorities, Less Clout?" *National Journal*, April 19, 2012.

61. Ehrenhalt, "Redistricting and the Erosion of Community," 10.

62. Kevin A. Hill, "Does the Creation of Majority Black Districts Aid Republicans? An Analysis of the 1992 Congressional Elections in Eight Southern States," *Journal of Politics* 57 (1995): 384–401. See also Seth C. McKee, *Republican Ascendancy in Southern U.S. House Elections* (Boulder, CO: Westview Press, 2010).

63. Carol M. Swain, *Black Faces, Black Interests: The Representation of African Americans in Congress* (Cambridge, MA: Harvard University Press, 1995), 205. But see Desmond S. King and Rogers S. Smith, "Strange Bedfellows? Polarized Politics? The Quest for Racial Equity in Contemporary America," *Political Research Quarterly* 64 (2008): 686–703. King and Smith argue, "Republicans benefited from the new districts but not via an unholy alliance" (p. 698).

64. David Lublin, *The Paradox of Representation: Racial Gerrymandering and Minority Interests in Congress* (Princeton, NJ: Princeton University Press, 1997).

65. Carol M. Swain, "The Voting Rights Act: Some Unintended Consequences," *Brookings Review* 10 (Winter 1992): 51. See also Lublin, *Paradox of Representation*.

66. Alexander Bolton, "Dems Seek to 'Unpack' Minority Districts," *The Hill*, May 9, 2001, 4.

67. Louis Sandy Maisel, *From Obscurity to Oblivion: Running in the Congressional Primary* (Knoxville: University of Tennessee Press, 1982), 34.

68. Quoted in Jon Margolis, "The Disappearing Candidates," *American Prospect*, January 31, 2000, 32.

69. Alan Ehrenhalt, *The United States of Ambition* (New York: Random House, 1991), 17.

70. The four Capitol Hill campaign committees are the National Republican Senatorial Committee (NRSC), Democratic Senatorial Campaign Committee (DSCC), National Republican Congressional Committee (NRCC), and Democratic Congressional Campaign Committee (DCCC). See Paul S. Herrson, *Congressional Elections: Campaigning at Home and in Washington*, 4th ed. (Washington, DC: CQ Press, 2004), 90–94.

71. Jennifer L. Lawless, *Becoming a Candidate: Political Ambition and the Decision to Run for Office* (New York: Cambridge University Press, 2012), 137.

72. Edward Walsh, "To Every Campaign, There Is a Recruiting Season," *Washington Post*, November 12, 1985, A1.

73. C. Douglas Swearingen and Walt Jatkowski III, "Is Timing Everything? Retirement and Seat Maintenance in the U.S. House of Representatives," *Legislative Studies Quarterly* 36 (May 2011): 309–330.

74. Alice A. Love, "Small Business Group Helps Grow Its Own Grassroots Candidates at Meeting Next Week," *Roll Call*, October 16, 1995, 22.

75. David T. Canon, *Actors, Athletes, and Astronauts: Political Amateurs in the United States Congress* (Chicago: University of Chicago Press, 1990), 2–3, 25–31.

76. David T. Canon, "The Year of the Outsider: Political Amateurs in the U.S. Congress," *The Forum* 8 (2010): art. 6, www.bepress.com/forum/v018/iss4/art6.

77. Michael Janofsky, "Two Congressional Candidates Know They'll Lose, But It's Still Fun," *New York Times*, October 31, 1992, 27.

78. Maisel, *From Obscurity to Oblivion*, 23.

79. This conceptualization is a combination of insights derived from a broad-based, pioneering study of House candidate recruitment by a team of scholars: Cherie D. Maestas, Sara Fulton, L. Sandy Maisel, and Walter J. Stone, "When to Risk It? Institutions, Ambitions, and the Decision to Run for the U.S. House," *American Political Science Review* 100 (May 2006): 195–208; and Stone and Maisel, "The Not-So-Simple Calculus of Winning: U.S. House Candidates' Nomination and General Election Prospects," *Journal of Politics* 65 (November 2003): 951–977.

80. The seminal work on strategic politician theory is Gary C. Jacobson and Samuel Kernell, *Strategy and Choice in Congressional Elections*, 2d ed. (New Haven, CT: Yale University Press, 1983).

81. Shira Toeplitz, "Ohio's Limits Tip Races," *Roll Call*, November 20, 2008, 15.

82. Jacobson and Kernell, *Strategy and Choice in Congressional Elections*, chap. 3.

83. L. Sandy Maisel, Cherie D. Maestas, and Walter J. Stone, "The Party Role in Congressional Competition," in *The Parties Respond*, ed. Paul S. Herrnson (Boulder, CO: Westview Press, 2002), 129.

84. Brian D. Feinstein, "The Dynasty Advantage: Family Ties in Congressional Elections," *Legislative Studies Quarterly* 35 (November 2010): 571–598.

85. Linda L. Fowler and Robert D. McClure, *Political Ambition: Who Decides to Run for Congress* (New Haven, CT: Yale University Press, 1989).

86. Quoted in Burt Solomon, "A Daunting Task: Running for House," *National Journal*, March 21, 1992, 712.

87. Jacobson, *Politics of Congressional Elections*, 23.

88. Catalina Camia, "Tenn. Democrats Disavow Party's Senate Nominee," On Politics, *USA Today*, August 4, 2012, http://content.usatoday.com/communities/onpolitics/post/2012/08/mark-clayton-tennessee-senate-bob-corker-hate-group/1#.UOYpoKzjNGo.

89. Jacobson, *Politics of Congressional Elections*, 38.

90. See Walter J. Stone, Sarah A. Fulton, Cherie D. Maestas, and L. Sandy Maisel, "Incumbency Reconsidered: Prospects, Strategic Retirement, and Incumbent Quality in U.S. House Elections," *Journal of Politics* 72 (January 2010): 178–190.

91. Ibid.

92. Maisel, Maestas, and Stone, "Party Role in Congressional Competition," 129.

93. Lawless, *Becoming a Candidate*, 171–172.

94. Jennifer L. Lawless and Richard L. Fox, *It Still Takes a Candidate: Why Women Don't Run for Office*, rev. ed. (New York: Cambridge University Press, 2010).

95. Jacobson, *Politics of Congressional Elections*, 19.

96. Stephen Ansolabehere, John Mark Hansen, Shigeo Hirano, and James M. Snyder Jr., "The Decline of Competition in U.S. Primary Elections, 1908–2004," in *The Marketplace of Democracy*, ed. Michael P. McDonald and John Samples (Washington, DC: Cato Institute and Brookings, 2006), 74–101.

97. Harvey L. Schantz, "Contested and Uncontested Primaries for the U.S. House," *Legislative Studies Quarterly* 5 (November 1980): 559. The linkage between interparty and intraparty competition is sometimes referred to as Key's Law. See V. O. Key Jr., *Parties, Politics, and Pressure Groups,* 5th ed. (New York: Crowell, 1964), 438, 447.

98. Ansolabehere et al., "Decline of Competition in U.S. Primary Elections," 81.

99. L. Sandy Maisel, Cary T. Gibson, and Elizabeth J. Ivry, "The Continuing Importance of the Rules of the Game: Subpresidential Nominations in 1994 and 1996," in *The Parties Respond: Changes in American Parties and Campaigns,* 3d ed., ed. L. Sandy Maisel (Boulder, CO: Westview Press, 1998), 162–164.

100. Maisel, Maestas, and Stone, "Party Role in Congressional Competition," 132.

101. Raymond Hernandez, "Rematches are Theme of Many House Races," *New York Times,* April 30, 2012, A22.

102. Austin Ranney, "Parties in State Politics," in *Politics in the American States,* ed. Herbert Jacob and Kenneth Vines (Boston: Little, Brown, 1976), 61–99.

103. John F. Bibby, "State Party Organizations," in *The Parties Respond,* 3d ed., ed. L. Sandy Maisel (Boulder, CO: Westview Press, 1998), 20.

CHAPTER 4

1. David Catanese, "Democrat Heidi Heitkamp Puts North Dakota Senate Seat in Play," October 7, 2012, www.politico.com/news/stories/1012/82106.html.

2. Jonathan Weisman, "'North Dakota Nice' Plays Well in Senate Race," *New York Times,* September 30, 2012, A1.

3. Quoted in ibid.

4. Quoted in Catanese, ibid.

5. Ibid.

6. Froma Harrop, "In Politics, Hate Can Backfire," *Real Clear Politics,* October 2, 2012, www.realclearpolitics.c./articles/2012/10/02/in_politics_hate_can_backfire_115634-comments.html.

7. See Richard G. Niemi, Lynda W. Powell, and Patricia L. Bickell, "The Effects of Congruity between Community and District on Salience of U.S. House Candidates," *Legislative Studies Quarterly* 11 (May 1986): 187–201; and Dena Levy and Peverill Squire, "Television Markets and the Competitiveness of U.S. House Elections," *Legislative Studies Quarterly* 25 (May 2000): 313–325.

8. Theodore E. Jackson Jr., "Brand Marketing in Today's Cluttered Political Marketplace," *Campaigns and Elections* 24 (April 2003): 30.

9. Allison Stevens, "House Candidates in Maryland Striving to Hone Their Messages," *The Hill,* May 8, 2002, 31–32.

10. Quoted in Robin Toner, "In a Cynical Election Season, the Ads Tell an Angry Tale," *New York Times,* October 24, 1994, A1.

11. Parke Skelton, quoted in Mary Clare Jalonick, "How to 'Primary' an Incumbent," *Campaigns and Elections* 22 (May 2001): 35.

12. See Paul S. Herrnson, *Congressional Elections: Campaigning at Home and in Washington,* 6th ed. (Washington, DC: CQ Press, 2012), 174.

13. The figures cited in this chapter for the 2011–2012 cycle were taken from the website of the Center for Responsive Politics, www.opensecrets.org.

14. Norman J. Ornstein, Thomas E. Mann, and Michael J. Malbin, *Vital Statistics on Congress, 2008* (Washington, DC: American Enterprise Institute, 2008), 75–76.

15. Quoted in Ryan Grim and Sabrina Siddiqui, "Call Time for Congress Shows How Fundraising Dominates Bleak Work," *Huffington Post,* politics blog, January 8, 2013,

www.huffingtonpost.com/2013/01/08/call-time-congressional-fundraising_n_2427291. html?ncid=edlinkusaolp00000003.

16. *Buckley v. Valeo,* 424 U.S. 1 (1976).

17. *Citizens United v.,* 558 U.S. __ (2010), slip op. at 44.

18. *Speechnow.org v. Federal Election Commission,* 99 F.3d 686 (2010).

19. Ibid., at 55.

20. David G. Savage, "Corporate Campaign Ads Haven't Followed Supreme Court's Prediction," *Los Angeles Times,* October 27, 2010 (online edition).

21. Michael Luo and Stephanie Strom, "Donor Names Remain Secret as Rules Shift," *New York Times,* September 20, 2010 (online edition).

22. Ray LaRaja, "Why Super PACs: How the American Party System Outgrew the Campaign Finance System," *The Forum* 10, no. 4 (2012): 91–104.

23. Michael M. Franz, "Interest Groups in Electoral Politics: 2012 in Context," *The Forum* 10, no. 4 (2012): 62–79.

24. Under the BCRA, individuals could donate $30,400 to national party committees per calendar year during the 2012 election cycle and $10,000 as a combined limit on contributions to state, district, and local party committees. These amounts are adjusted annually for inflation.

25. Quoted in Luo and Strom, "Donor Names Remain Secret as Rules Shift."

26. Campaign data are drawn from the Federal Elections Commission data compiled by the Center for Responsive Politics, www.opensecrets.org/overview/incumbs.php.

27. Gary C. Jacobson, *The Politics of Congressional Elections,* 8th ed. (New York: Pearson Education, 2013), 54.

28. For a recent study documenting the fund-raising advantage of majority party members, see Erik J. Engstrom and William Ewell, "The Impact of Unified Party Government on Campaign Contributions," *Legislative Studies Quarterly* 35 (2010): 543-569.

29. Thomas B. Edsall, "In Tight Races, Early Cash Means Staying Competitive," *Washington Post,* July 14, 1998, A6.

30. Gary C. Jacobson, "The Effects of Campaign Spending on Congressional Elections," *American Political Science Review* 72 (June 1978): 469–491.

31. Gary C. Jacobson, "Money in the 1980 and 1982 Congressional Elections," In *Money and Politics in the United States: Financing Elections in the 1980s,* ed. Michael J. Malbin (Chatham, NJ: Chatham House, 1984), 57.

32. Gary C. Jacobson, *The Politics of Congressional Elections,* 6th ed. (New York: Pearson Longman, 2004), 98.

33. Carl Hulse and Adam Nagourney, "Specter Switches Parties: More Heft for Democrats," *New York Times,* April 29, 2009, A1; Kathleen Hunder and Bart Jansen, "Specter's Defection Has Consequences for Balance of Power on Committees," *CQ Today,* April 30, 2009, 8, 12.

34. Alana Semuels, "Television Viewing at All-Time High," *Los Angeles Times,* February 24, 2009, http://articles.latimes.com/2009/feb/24/business/fi-tvwatching24.

35. Erika Franklin Fowler and Travis N. Ridout, "Negative, Angry, and Ubiquitous: Political Advertising in 2012," *The Forum,* 10, no. 4 (2012): 51–61.

36. Robin Toner, "In Final Rounds, Both Sides Whip Out Bare-Knuckle Ads," *New York Times,* October 21, 1996, B7.

37. James A. Thurber and Carolyn Long, "Brian Baird's 'Ring of Fire': The Quest for Funds and Votes in Washington's Third District," in *The Battle for Congress,* ed. James A. Thurber (Washington, DC: Brookings, 2001), 188.

38. Howard Fineman and Paul Blumenthal, "Political Consultants Rake It In, $266 Million and Counting in 2012 Cycle," *Huffington Post,* politics blog, May 8, 2012, www.huffingtonpost. com/2012/06/05/political-consultants-2012-campaign-big-money_n_1570157.html.

39. Tom Rosenstiel and Amy Mitchell, "As General Election Nears, Internet Gains Most as Campaign News Source but Cable TV Still Leads," Pew Research Center's Project for Excellence in Journalism, October 25, 2012, www.journalism.org/commentary_backgrounder/social_media_doubles_remains_limited.

40. University of Southern California, Annenberg School of Communications, Norman Lear Center, "Local TV News Largely Ignores Local Political Races," press release, February 15, 2005.

41. Larry J. Sabato and Glenn R. Simpson, *Dirty Little Secrets: The Persistence of Corruption in American Politics* (New York: Times Books, 1996), 156.

42. Joshua Miller, "Three Takeaways for 2014 from the RNC Autopsy Report," *Roll Call*, March 19, 2013, 11.

43. Quoted in Janet Hook, "Negative Ads a Positive in GOP Strategy," *Los Angeles Times*, September 26, 2006, A10.

44. Stephen Ansolabehere and Shanto Iyengar, *Going Negative: How Attack Ads Shrink and Polarize the Electorate* (New York: Free Press, 1996), 128.

45. Quoted in David S. Broder, "Death by Negative Ads," *Washington Post*, November 3, 2002, B7.

46. Katharine Q. Seelye, "Kentucky G.O.P. Candidate, Livid over Opponent's Ad, Lashes Out," *New York Times*, October 22, 2010, www.nytimes.com/2010/10/23/us/politics/23kentucky.html.

47. Frank Newport, "State of the States: Importance of Religion," Gallup press release, January 28, 2009, www.gallup.com/poll/114022/State-States-Importance-Religion.aspx.

48. Manu Raju, "'Aqua Buddha' Ad Backfires on Jack Conway," *Politico*, October 26, 2010, www.politico.com/news/stories/1010/44222.html.

49. See Howard Kurtz, "Hearing 'Foul,' Stations Pull Political Ads," *Washington Post*, September 20, 2002, A14.

50. Pew Research Center for the People and the Press, "In Changing News Landscape, Even Television Is Vulnerable," September 27, 2012, www.pcople-press.org/files/legacy-pdf/2012%20News%20Consumption%20Report.pdf.

51. Rosenstiel and Mitchell, "As General Election Nears."

52. Dan Morain, "Undercover Campaigning on the Web," *Los Angeles Times*, March 21, 2007, A11.

53. Ibid.

54. Merle Miller, *Lyndon: An Oral Biography* (New York: Putnam, 1980), 120.

55. "Lessons from Recent GOTV Experiments," GOTV, Yale University, Institution for Social and Policy Studies, http://gotv.research.yale.edu/?q=node/10.

56. Donald P. Green and Alan S. Gerber, *Get Out the Vote!* (Washington, DC: Brookings, 2004), 93–96.

57. Ibid., 40.

58. Dan Glickman, as told to Amy Zipkin, "Landing the Job He Wanted," *New York Times*, April 17, 2005, C10.

59. Paul Houston, "TV and High Tech Send Campaign Costs Soaring," *Los Angeles Times*, October 2, 1986, 121.

60. Jamie Stiehm, "Ben and Jerry's State Offers a Choice of Three Flavors," *The Hill*, November 22, 1995, 26.

61. Glenn R. Simpson, "In Rhode Island, Everyone Goes to Bristol Parade," *Roll Call*, July 9, 1990, 1; Glenn R. Simpson, "Judging from July 4th Bristol Parade in R.I., Chafee Looks Well-Positioned for November," *Roll Call*, July 11, 1994, 21.

62. Leslie Wayne, "Democrats Take Page from Their Rival's Playbook," *New York Times*, November 1, 2008, A15.

63. Jonathan E. Kaplan, "Large Voter Turnout Was Key to GOP Victory," *The Hill*, November 7, 2002, 17.

64. Reid Wilson, "Candidates Become Partisan Stereotypes in Super PAC Era," *National Journal*, November 4, 2012.

65. Michael P. McDonald, "Voter Turnout in the 2010 Midterm Election," *The Forum* 8 (2010): art. 8.

66. Michael P. McDonald, "2012 General Election Turnout Rates," *United States Elections Project*, George Mason University, accessed February 2, 2013, http://elections.gmu.edu/Turnout_2012G.html.

67. M. Margaret Conway, "Political Participation in Midterm Congressional Elections," *American Politics Quarterly* 9 (April 1981): 221–244.

68. International turnout figures from the Institute for Social Research, University of Michigan, reported in Pippa Norris, *Electoral Engineering: Voting Rules and Political Behavior* (Cambridge, U.K.: Cambridge University Press, 2004). A sensible review of the question is found in Martin P. Wattenberg, *Where Have All the Voters Gone?* (Cambridge, MA: Harvard University Press, 2002).

69. Pew Research Center for the People and the Press, "Who Votes, Who Doesn't, and Why," October 18, 2006, 4.

70. "Youth Turnout about 20%, Comparable to Recent Midterm Years," CIRCLE: The Center for Information and Research on Civic Learning and Engagement, Jonathan M. Tisch College of Citizenship and Public Service, Tufts University, November 3, 2010, www.civicyouth.org/youth-turnout-about-20-comparable-to-recent-midterm-years/.

71. Data on the results of the act are distressingly incomplete. See Raymond E. Wolfinger and Jonathan Hoffman, "Registering and Voting with Motor Voter," *PS* 34 (March 2001): 85–92.

72. Nina Totenberg, "Supreme Court Weighs Voter ID Requirements," *Morning Edition*, January 9, 2008, www.npr.org/templates/story/story.php?storyId=17942818.

73. Joseph D. Rich, "Playing Politics with Justice," *Los Angeles Times*, March 29, 2007, A23. Rich is former chief (1999–2005) of the voting section in the Department of Justice's Civil Rights Division.

74. *Crawford v. Marion County Election Board*, 553 U.S. ___ (2008).

75. David Damron and Scott Powers, "Researcher: Long Lines at Polls Caused 49,000 Not to Vote," *Orlando Sentinel*, December 29, 2012, http://articles.orlandosentinel.com/2012-12-29/news/os-discouraged-voters-20121229_1_long-lines-higher-turnout-election-day.

76. Richard Morin and Claudia Deane, "As Turnout Falls, Apathy Emerges as Driving Force," *Washington Post*, November 4, 2000, A1; Michael Waldman and Justin Levin, "The Myth of Voter Fraud," *Washington Post*, March 29, 2007, A19.

77. Samuel L. Popkin and Michael P. McDonald, "Turnout's Not as Bad as You Think," *Washington Post*, November 5, 2000, B1.

78. Sidney Verba, Kay Lehman Schlozman, and Henry E. Brady, *Voice and Equality: Civic Voluntarism in American Politics* (Cambridge, MA: Harvard University Press, 1995).

79. Samuel L. Popkin, *The Reasoning Voter* (Chicago: University of Chicago Press, 1994), 7.

80. Exit polls, November 2, 2004, and November 7, 2006, reported in *New York Times*, November 9, 2006, P7; and by Ronald Brownstein, "Democrats' Losses Go Far beyond One Defeat," *Los Angeles Times*, November 4, 2004, A1, A17.

81. National House exit poll, Election Center, CNN Politics, November 24, 2010, www.cnn.com/ELECTION/2010/results/polls.main/.

82. Quoted in Richard Morin and Claudia Deane, "How Independent Are Independents?" *Washington Post*, August 2, 2002, A1.

83. Gary C. Jacobson, *The Politics of Congressional Elections*, 5th ed. (New York: Addison, Wesley, Longman, 2001), 108.

84. Martin P. Wattenberg, *The Rise of Candidate-Centered Politics* (Cambridge, MA: Harvard University Press, 1991), 36–39.

85. See Bernard Grofman, William Koetzle, Michael P. McDonald, and Thomas L. Brunell, "A New Look at Split-Ticket Outcomes for House and President: The Comparative Midpoints Model," *Journal of Politics* 62 (February 2000): 34–50.

86. Cited in Jeffrey McMurray, "Conservative Southern Dems Disappearing," *Washington Post*, April 25, 2005, A1.

87. Jacobson, *Politics of Congressional Elections*, 8th ed., 176.

88. Ibid., 175.

89. James E. Campbell, "The Midterm Landslide of 2010: A Triple Wave Election," *The Forum* 8 (2010): art. 3.

90. Angus Campbell, "Surge and Decline: A Study of Electoral Change," in *Elections and the Political Order*, ed. Angus Campbell, Phillip E. Converse, Warren E. Miller, and Donald E. Stokes (New York: Wiley, 1966), 40–62; Raymond E. Wolfinger, Steven J. Rosenstone, and Richard A. McIntosh, "Presidential and Congressional Voters Compared," *American Politics Quarterly* 9 (April 1981): 245–255.

91. Eric M. Uslaner and M. Margaret Conway, "The Responsible Electorate: Watergate, the Economy, and Vote Choice in 1974," *American Political Science Review* 79 (September 1985): 788–803; Samuel Kernell, "Presidential Popularity and Negative Voting: An Alternative Explanation of the Midterm Congressional Decline of the President's Party," *American Political Science Review* 71 (March 1977): 44–46.

92. Roberto Alesina and Howard Rosenthal, *Partisan Politics, Divided Government, and the Economy* (New York: Cambridge University Press, 1995).

93. Joseph Bafumi, Robert S. Erikson, and Christopher Wlezien, "Balancing, Generic Polls and Midterm Congressional Elections," *Journal of Politics* 72 (2010): 705–719.

94. Quoted in Dale Russakoff, "In Tight Arkansas Senate Race, Family Matters," *Washington Post*, August 3, 2002, A1.

95. Jacobson, *Politics of Congressional Elections*, 8th ed., 35.

96. Ibid., 27–28.

97. David R. Mayhew, *Congress: The Electoral Connection*, 2d ed. (New Haven, CT: Yale University Press, 2004).

98. National Election Studies (now called the American National Election Studies, or ANES), 1980–2002, summarized in Jacobson, *Politics of Congressional Elections*, 122–126; Thomas E. Mann and Raymond E. Wolfinger, "Candidates and Parties in Congressional Elections," *American Political Science Review* 74 (September 1980): 623.

99. On the first view mentioned in this paragraph, see Morris P. Fiorina, *Congress: Keystone of the Washington Establishment*, 2d ed. (New Haven, CT: Yale University Press, 1989); and Bruce Cain, John Ferejohn, and Morris Fiorina, *The Personal Vote: Constituency Service and Electoral Independence* (Cambridge, MA: Harvard University Press, 1987), esp. chaps. 6–7. For more on the second view, see Glenn R. Parker and Roger H. Davidson, "Why Do Americans Love Their Congressmen So Much More Than Their Congress?" *Legislative Studies Quarterly* 4 (February 1979): 53–61. On the question of whether incumbents' resources are directly tied to votes, see John R. Johannes, *To Serve the People: Congress and Constituency Service* (Lincoln: University of Nebraska Press, 1984), esp. chap. 8.

100. Michael J. Robinson, "Three Faces of Congressional Media," in *The New Congress*, ed. Thomas E. Mann and Norman J. Ornstein (Washington, DC: American Enterprise Institute, 1981), 91.

101. Frances E. Lee and Bruce I. Oppenheimer, *Sizing Up the Senate: The Unequal Consequences of Equal Representation* (Chicago: University of Chicago Press, 1999), chap. 4.

102. Gary C. Jacobson, "Incumbents' Advantages in the 1978 U.S. Congressional Elections," *Legislative Studies Quarterly* 6 (May 1981): 198.

103. Owen G. Abbe, Jay Goodliffe, Paul S. Herrnson, and Kelly D. Patterson, "Agenda Setting in Congressional Elections: The Impact of Issues and Campaigns on Voting Behavior," *Political Research Quarterly* 56 (December 2003): 419.

104. John B. Bader, *Taking the Initiative: Leadership Agendas in Congress and the "Contract with America"* (Washington, DC: Georgetown University Press, 1996).

105. Edward Epstein, "The Search Is On for a Takeover Manifesto," *CQ Weekly,* February 8, 2010, 318.

106. Quoted in Judy Newman, "Do Women Vote for Women?" *Public Perspective* 7 (February–March 1996): 10.

107. Karen M. Kaufmann and John R. Petrocik, "The Changing Politics of American Men: Understanding the Sources of the Gender Gap," *American Journal of Political Science* 43 (July 1999): 864–887.

108. Quoted in Barbara Vobejda, "Fragmentation of Society Formidable Challenge to Candidates, Report Says," *Washington Post,* March 7, 1996, A15.

109. For a discussion of these reversals, see Gary Miller and Norman Schofield, "Activists and Partisan Realignment in the United States," *American Political Science Review* 97 (May 2003): 245–260.

110. Jacobson, *Politics of Congressional Elections,* 6th ed., 249–253.

111. Delegates to the parties' national conventions were analyzed in a classic study by Herbert McCloskey, Paul Hoffman, and Rosemary O'Hara, "Issue Conflict and Consensus among Party Leaders and Followers," *American Political Science Review* 54 (1950): 406–427.

112. The "middlingness" of the citizenry is vigorously argued in Morris P. Fiorina, with Samuel J. Abrams and Jeremy C. Pope, *Culture War? The Myth of a Polarized America* (New York: Pearson-Longman, 2005).

113. Alan I. Abramowitz, *The Disappearing Center: Engaged Citizens, Polarization, and American Democracy* (New Haven, CT: Yale University Press, 2010). See also Pew Research Center for the People and the Press, "The 2004 Political Landscape: Evenly Divided and Increasingly Polarized," survey report, November 5, 2003, www.people-press.org/reports/.

114. David W. Brady, "Electoral Realignments in the U.S. House of Representatives," in *Congress and Policy Change,* ed. Gerald C. Wright Jr., Leroy N. Reiselbach, and Lawrence C. Dodd (New York: Agathon Press, 1986), 46–69.

115. Campbell, "Midterm Landslide of 2010."

116. Jennifer E. Manning, "Membership of the 113th Congress: A Profile," Congressional Research Service, February 2013.

117. Warren E. Miller and Donald E. Stokes, "Constituency Influence in Congress," *American Political Science Review* 57 (March 1963): 45–57.

118. Tracy Sulkin, *Issue Politics in Congress* (New York: Cambridge University Press, 2005), 2.

119. Ibid., 177.

CHAPTER 5

1. Mike Dennison, "Baucus Urges Working Together," *The Montana Standard,* January 11, 2013.

2. Ben Geman, "Reid: Dems Won't Cave on Keystone," *The Hill,* April 25, 2012, 1.

3. Quoted in Juliet Eilperin, "For Montana, Pipeline a 'No-Brainer,'" *Washington Post,* July 9, 2012, A7.

4. Quoted in ibid.

5. Staff of Congressional Quarterly, *CQ's Politics in America 2008: The 110th Congress,* ed. Jackie Koszczuk and Martha Angle (Washington, DC: CQ Press, 2007), 597.

6. John K. Inglehart, "The New Medicare Prescription-Drug Benefit—A Pure Power Play," *New England Journal of Medicine* 350 (2004): 826–833.

7. "High Plains Grifters: A Misguided Senate Plan Repackages Agricultural Welfare as Disaster Relief" (editorial), *Washington Post,* October 28, 2007, B6.

8. Rachel Van Dongen, "110th Senate Committees: Finance," *CQ Weekly,* November 13, 2006, 3029.

9. Amy Goldstein, "Hill Supports Medicare Boost to Rural Areas," *Washington Post,* October 20, 2003, A1.

10. Ida Brudnick, "Congressional Salaries and Allowances" Congressional Research Service Report No. RL30064, January 15, 2013.

11. Open Secrets Blog, Center for Responsive Politics, January 16, 2013, www.opensecrets.org/news/2013/01/new-congress-new-and-more-wealth.html.

12. John Stuart Mill, *Considerations on Representative Government* (London: Longmans, Green, 1967 [1861]), quoted in Lisa Schwindt-Bayer and William Mishler, "An Integrated Model of Women's Representation," *Journal of Politics* 67 (2005): 413.

13. Hannah Finichel Pitkin, *The Concept of Representation* (Berkeley: University of California Press, 1967), 166.

14. See David T. Canon, *Race, Redistricting, and Representation: The Unintended Consequences of Black Majority Districts* (Chicago: University of Chicago Press, 1999); Brinck Kerr and Will Miller, "Latino Representation, It's Direct and Indirect," *American Journal of Political Science* 41 (1997): 1066–1071; Michele L. Swers, *The Difference Women Make* (Chicago: University of Chicago Press, 2002); and Sue Thomas, *How Women Legislate* (New York: Oxford University Press, 1994).

15. See Claudine Gay, "Spirals of Trust? The Effect of Descriptive Representation on the Relationship between Citizens and Their Government," *American Journal of Political Science* 46 (2002): 717–732; John D. Griffin and Michael Keane, "Descriptive Representation and the Composition of African American Turnout," *American Journal of Political Science* 50 (2006): 998–1012; and Katherine Tate, "The Political Representation of Blacks in Congress: Does Race Matter?" *Legislative Studies Quarterly* 26 (2001): 623–638.

16. Data on characteristics of members are found in Jennifer E. Manning, "Membership of the 113th Congress: A Profile," Congressional Research Service Report No. R41647, 2013.

17. Alan Ehrenhalt, *The United States of Ambition: Politicians, Power, and the Pursuit of Office* (New York: Times Books, 1992), 16.

18. William T. Bianco, "Last Post for 'The Greatest Generation': The Policy Implications of the Decline of Military Experience in the U.S. Congress," *Legislative Studies Quarterly* 30 (February 2005): 85–102.

19. Nicholas Carnes, "Does the Numerical Underrepresentation of the Working Class in Congress Matter?" *Legislative Studies Quarterly* 37, no. 1 (2012): 5–34.

20. Betsy Rothstein, "Congresswomen Press Women's Health Issues," *The Hill,* February 24, 1999, 19; Maureen Dowd, "Growing Sorority in Congress Edges into the Ol' Boys' Club," *New York Times,* March 5, 1993, A1, A18.

21. Kerry L. Haynie, "African Americans and the New Politics of Inclusion: A Representational Dilemma?" In *Congress Reconsidered,* 8th ed., ed. Lawrence C. Dodd and Bruce I. Oppenheimer (Washington, DC: CQ Press, 2005).

22. Thomas L. Brunell, Christopher J. Anderson, and Rachel K. Cremona, "Descriptive Representation, District Demography, and Attitudes toward Congress among African Americans," *Legislative Studies Quarterly* 33 (2008): 223–242.

23. Katherine Tate, "The Political Representation of Blacks in Congress: Does Race Matter?" *Legislative Studies Quarterly* 26 (November 2001): 631.

24. Janet M. Box-Steffensmeier, David C. Kimball, Scott R. Meinke, and Katherine Tate, "The Effects of Political Representation on the Electoral Advantages of Incumbents," *Political Research Quarterly* 56 (September 2003): 264.
25. See Canon, *Race, Redistricting, and Representation*; and Kerry L. Haynie, *African American Legislators in the American States* (New York: Columbia University Press, 2001).
26. Katrina L. Gamble, "Black Political Representation: An Examination of Legislative Activity within U.S. House Committees," *Legislative Studies Quarterly* 32 (2007): 421–448; Michael D. Minta, "Legislative Oversight and the Substantive Representation of Black and Latino Interests in Congress," *Legislative Studies Quarterly* 34 (2009): 193–218.
27. Inter-Parliamentary Union, "Women in National Parliaments," December 31, 2012, www.ipu.org/wmn-e/classif.htm.
28. The pioneering study of this subject is Irwin N. Gertzog, *Congressional Women: Their Recruitment, Treatment, and Behavior* (New York: Praeger, 1984). Two more recent studies are Barbara C. Burrell, *A Woman's Place Is in the House* (Ann Arbor: University of Michigan Press, 1994); and Richard Logan Fox, *Gender Dynamics in Congressional Elections* (Thousand Oaks, CA: Sage, 1997).
29. Quoted in Sheryl Gay Stolberg, "Working Mothers Swaying Senate Debate, as Senators," *New York Times,* June 7, 2003, A3.
30. Jamie Stiehm, "In Senate, Sisterhood Can Override Party," *The Hill,* November 22, 1995, 16.
31. Arturo Vega and Juanita Firestone, "The Effects of Gender on Congressional Behavior and the Substantive Representation of Women," *Legislative Studies Quarterly* 20 (May 1995): 213–222.
32. Kris Kitto, "Moms in Congress, Part I," *The Hill,* May 3, 2011.
33. Quoted in ibid., 19.
34. Kirk Victor, "Still an Old Boys' Club?" *National Journal,* March 12, 2005, 750, 752.
35. See Kathleen A. Dolan, *Voting for Women: How the Public Evaluates Women Candidates* (Boulder, CO: Westview Press, 2003); Leonie Huddy and Nayda Terkildsen, "Gender Stereotypes and the Perception of Male and Female Candidates," *American Journal of Political Science* 37 (1993): 119–147.
36. Michele Swers, "Building a Reputation on National Security: The Impact of Stereotypes Related to Gender and Military Experience," *Legislative Studies Quarterly* 32 (2007): 559–595.
37. Peter O'Dowd, "Sinema, First Openly Bisexual Member of Congress, Represents 'Changing Arizona,'" National Public Radio, January 1, 2013, www.npr.org/blogs/itsallpolitics/2013/01/08/168362011/sinema-first-openly-bisexual-member-of-congress-represents-changing-arizona.
38. Donald P. Haider-Markel, Mark R. Joslyn, and Chad J. Kniss, "Minority Group Interests and Political Representation: Gay Elected Officials in the Policy Process," *Journal of Politics* 62 (2000): 568–577.
39. Quoted in Erika Niedowski, "Four Walk Out of the Closet and toward the House," *CQ Weekly,* April 25, 1998, 1051.
40. Pew Forum on Religion and Public Life, *U.S. Religious Landscapes Survey,* February 2008, http://religions.pewforum.org/reports.
41. The Pew Charitable Trusts, Religion and Public Life, "Religious Composition of the 113th Congress," January 7, 2013, www.pewtrusts.org/our_work_report_detail.aspx?id=85899440886&category=326.
42. Manning, "Membership of the 113th Congress," 1–2.
43. Ibid., 6. For tenure figures, see Table 2-1.
44. Charles S. Bullock and Burdett A. Loomis, "The Changing Congressional Career," in *Congress Reconsidered,* 3d ed., ed. Lawrence C. Dodd and Bruce I. Oppenheimer (Washington, DC: CQ Press, 1985), 66–69, 80–82.

45. Jennifer Wolak, "Strategic Retirements: The Influence of Public Preferences on Voluntary Departures from Congress," *Legislative Studies Quarterly* 32 (May 2007): 285–308.

46. Quoted in Shailagh Murray, "GOP Lawmakers Gird for Rowdy Tea Party," *Washington Post,* July 18, 2010, A3.

47. Frances E. Lee and Bruce I. Oppenheimer, *Sizing Up the Senate: The Unequal Consequences of Equal Representation* (Chicago: University of Chicago Press, 1999), 20–23. Also see Robert A. Dahl, *A Preface to Democratic Theory* (New Haven, CT: Yale University Press, 1956).

48. John D. Griffin, "Senate Apportionment as a Source of Political Inequality," *Legislative Studies Quarterly* 31 (2006): 405–432.

49. Bruce I. Oppenheimer, "The Representational Experience: The Effect of State Population on Senator-Constituency Linkages," *American Journal of Political Science* 40 (1996): 1280–1299.

50. Frances E. Lee, "Representation and Public Policy: The Consequences of Senate Apportionment for the Geographic Distribution of Federal Funds," *Journal of Politics* 60 (1998): 34–64. Also see Stephen Ansolabehere, Alan Gerber, and James M. Snyder Jr., "Equal Votes: Equal Money: Court-Ordered Redistricting and the Distribution of Public Expenditures in the American States," *American Political Science Review* 96 (2002): 767–777; Cary M. Atlas, Thomas W. Gilligan, Robert J. Hendershott, and Mark A. Zupan, "Slicing the Federal Government Net Spending Pie: Who Wins, Who Loses, and Why," *American Economic Review* 85 (1995): 624–629.

51. Robert Weissberg, "Collective vs. Dyadic Representation in Congress," *American Political Science Review* 72 (1978): 535–547.

52. Jane Mansbridge, "Rethinking Representation," *American Political Science Review* 97 (November 2003): 515–528.

53. Barry C. Burden, *Personal Roots of Representation* (Princeton, NJ: Princeton University Press, 2007).

54. Richard F. Fenno Jr., *The Making of a Senator: Dan Quayle* (Washington, DC: CQ Press, 1989), 119.

55. Quoted in Adam Nagourney, "Upbeat Schumer Battles Polls, Low Turnouts, and His Image," *New York Times,* May 16, 1998, A14.

56. Frank E. Smith, *Congressman from Mississippi* (New York: Pantheon, 1964), 129–130.

57. Donald R. Matthews, *U.S. Senators and Their World* (Chapel Hill: University of North Carolina Press, 1960), chap. 5; Ross K. Baker, *House and Senate,* 3d ed. (New York: Norton, 2001), chap. 2.

58. Barbara Sinclair, *The Transformation of the U.S. Senate* (Baltimore: Johns Hopkins University Press, 1989).

59. Herbert B. Asher, "The Learning of Legislative Norms," *American Political Science Review* 67 (June 1973): 499–513.

60. "Political Incivility: A Weekend of Ugly Discourse Preceded Historic Health Vote," *Cleveland Plain Dealer,* March 22, 2010, www.cleveland.com/nation/index.ssf/2010/03/political_incivility_a_weekend.html.

61. Quoted in Thomas E. Cavanagh, "The Two Arenas of Congress," in *The House at Work,* ed. Joseph Cooper and G. Calvin Mackenzie (Austin: University of Texas Press, 1981), 65.

62. Daniel M. Butler, Christopher F. Karpowitz, and Jeremy C. Pope, "A Field Experiment on Legislators' Home Styles: Service versus Policy," *Journal of Politics* 74 (April 2012): 474-486.

63. David C. W. Parker and Craig Goodman, "Making a Good Impression: Resource Allocation, Home Styles, and Washington Work," *Legislative Studies Quarterly* 34 (November 2009): 493–524.

64. Box-Steffensmeier et al., "Effects of Political Representation," 266.

65. Kenneth M. Bickers and Robert M. Stein, "The Electoral Dynamics of the Federal Pork Barrel," *American Journal of Political Science* 40 (November 1996): 1300–1326.

66. Robert M. Stein and Kenneth M. Bickers, "Congressional Elections and the Pork Barrel," *Journal of Politics* 56 (May 1994): 377–399.

67. Quoted in Louis Jacobson, "For Arkansas, No Abundance of Clout," *National Journal,* February 20, 1999, 475.

68. Quoted in Scott MacKay, "Chafee's New Book Is Tough on Pro-War Democrats, Republicans, President Bush," *Providence Journal,* January 27, 2008.

69. Marian Currinder, *Money in the House: Campaign Funds and Congressional Party Politics* (Boulder, CO: Westview Press, 2009); Eric S. Heberlig, "Congressional Parties, Fundraising, and Committee Ambition," *Political Research Quarterly* 56 (2003): 151–161; Anne H. Bedlington and Michael J. Malbin, "The Party as Extended Network: Members Giving to Each Other and to Their Parties," in *Life after Reform,* ed. Michael J. Malbin (Lanham, MD: Rowman and Littlefield, 2003), 121–140.

70. Patrick Sellers, *Cycles of Spin: Strategic Communication in the U.S. Congress* (New York: Cambridge University Press, 2010).

71. Davidson, *Role of the Congressman,* 98; U.S. Congress, Senate Commission on the Operation of the Senate, *Toward a Modern Senate,* S. Doc. 94–278, 94th Cong., 2d sess., committee print, 1997, 27; U.S. Congress, House Commission on Administrative Review, *Final Report,* 2 vols., H. Doc. 95–272, 95th Cong., 1st sess., December 31, 1977, 2: 874–875.

72. Richard L. Hall, *Participation in Congress* (New Haven, CT: Yale University Press, 1998).

73. Ross A. Webber, "U.S. Senators: See How They Run," *Wharton Magazine* (Winter 1980–1981): 38.

74. Quoted in Richard E. Cohen, "Member Moms," *National Journal,* April 7, 2007, 17, 21.

75. U.S. Congress, Senate Commission on the Operation of the Senate, *Toward a Modern Senate.*

76. Quoted in Lindsay Sobel, "Former Lawmakers Find Trade Association Gold," *The Hill,* November 26, 1997, 14.

77. Center for Responsive Politics, *Congressional Operations: Congress Speaks—A Survey of the 100th Congress* (Washington, DC: Center for Responsive Politics, 1988), 47–49.

78. Quoted in *Washington Post,* October 18, 1994, B3.

79. U.S. Congress, Joint Committee on the Organization of Congress, *Organization of Congress,* December 1993 2:281–287; Luke Rosiak, "AWOL on Hill: Fundraising Trumps Voting," *Washington Times,* February 20, 2013, A1.

80. Quoted in Vernon Louviere, "For Retiring Congressmen, Enough Is Enough," *Nation's Business,* May 1980, 32.

81. John R. Hibbing, *Congressional Careers: Contours of Life in the U.S. House of Representatives* (Chapel Hill: University of North Carolina Press, 1991), 117.

82. Ibid., 126, 128.

83. Gerard Padro I. Miquel and James M. Snyder Jr., "Legislative Effectiveness and Legislative Careers," *Legislative Studies Quarterly* 31 (August 2006): 348.

84. Ibid.

85. Gary W. Cox and William C. Terry, "Legislative Productivity in the 93rd–105th Congresses," *Legislative Studies Quarterly* 33 (2008): 613.

86. William H. Riker, *The Theory of Political Coalitions* (New Haven, CT: Yale University Press, 1962), 24–38.

87. Pitkin, *Concept of Representation,* 166.

88. Steven Kull, *Expecting More Say: The American Public on Its Role in Government Decisionmaking* (Washington, DC: Center on Policy Attitudes, 1999), 13–14.

89. Henry J. Hyde, "Advice to Freshmen: 'There Are Things Worth Losing For,'" *Roll Call,* December 3, 1990, 5.

90. Quoted in Jamie Stiehm, "Ex-Rep Mike Synar, Who Fought Lobbyists, Succumbs to Brain Tumor," *The Hill,* January 10, 1996, 5.

91. Thomas E. Cavanagh, "The Calculus of Representation: A Congressional Perspective," *Western Political Quarterly* 35 (March 1982): 120–129.

92. John W. Kingdon, *Congressmen's Voting Decisions*, 3d ed. (Ann Arbor: University of Michigan Press, 1989), 47–54.

93. Lawrence N. Hansen, *Our Turn: Politicians Talk about Themselves, Politics, the Public, the Press, and Reform*, part 2 (Washington, DC: Centel Public Accountability Project, 1992), 9.

94. Richard F. Fenno Jr., *Home Style: House Members in Their Districts* (New York: Pearson Longman, 2003), 1.

95. See the discussion of senators' varied constituencies in Lee and Oppenheimer, *Sizing Up the Senate,* chap. 3.

96. Fenno, *Home Style,* 4–8.

97. John F. Bibby and Thomas M. Holbrook, "Parties and Elections," in *Politics in the American States: A Comparative Analysis,* 7th ed., ed. Virginia Gray, Russell L. Hanson, and Herbert Jacob (Washington, DC: CQ Press, 1999), 66–112. Also see Thomas L. Brunell, *Redistricting and Representation: Why Competitive Elections Are Bad for America* (New York: Routledge, 2008).

98. James L. Payne, "The Personal Electoral Advantage of House Incumbents, 1936–1976," *American Politics Quarterly* 8 (October 1980): 465–482; Robert S. Erikson, "Is There Such a Thing as a Safe Seat?" *Polity* 8 (Summer 1976): 623–632.

99. Thomas E. Mann, *Unsafe at Any Margin: Interpreting Congressional Elections* (Washington, DC: American Enterprise Institute, 1978).

100. Fenno, *Home Style,* 8–27.

101. Thomas P. O'Neill Jr., with William Novak, *Man of the House* (New York: St. Martin's Press, 1987), 25.

102. Nancy Bocskor, "Fundraising Lessons Candidates Can Learn from Tom Sawyer . . . and Other Great American Salesmen," *Campaigns and Elections* 24 (April 2003): 33.

103. Richard F. Fenno Jr., *Senators on the Campaign Trail* (Norman: University of Oklahoma Press, 1996), 131–132.

104. David E. Price, *The Congressional Experience,* 3d ed. (Boulder, CO: Westview Press, 2004), 10.

105. Fenno, *Home Style,* 153.

106. Ibid., 56.

107. Anthony Champagne, *Congressman Sam Rayburn* (New Brunswick, NJ: Rutgers University Press, 1984), 28.

108. Parker and Goodman, "Making a Good Impression," 517.

109. Kingdon, *Congressmen's Voting Decisions.*

110. Brian J. Fogarty, "The Strategy of the Story: Media Monitoring Legislative Activity," *Legislative Studies Quarterly* 33 (August 2008): 445–469.

111. Quoted in Jim Wright, *You and Your Congressman* (New York: Coward-McCann, 1965), 35.

112. Betsy Rothstein, "Hey, Congressman! Someone Is Blocking My Driveway!" *The Hill,* June 9, 2004, 18–19.

113. Lee and Oppenheimer, *Sizing Up the Senate,* 56.

114. The National Election Study is now the American National Election Study (ANES). Warren E. Miller, Donald R. Kinder, Steven J. Rosenstone, and the National Election Study, *American National Election Study, 1990: Post-Election Survey,* 2d ed. (Ann Arbor, MI: Inter-University Consortium for Political and Social Research, January 1992), 166–170.

115. Ida A. Brudnick, "Congressional Salaries and Allowances," Congressional Research Service Report RL30064, January 15, 2013. Also see Congressional Management Foundation, *1999 Senate Staff Employment Study* (Washington, DC: Congressional Management Foundation, 1999), 82ff; and Congressional Management Foundation, *2000 House Staff Employment Study* (Washington, DC: Congressional Management Foundation, 2000), 48–49.

116. Congressional Management Foundation, *1999 Senate Staff Employment Study,* 88–89; and Congressional Management Foundation, *2000 House Staff Employment Study,* 1–2.

117. Cited in C. Simon Davidson, "Congressional Office Off-Limits for Members' Campaigns," *Roll Call,* April 16, 2007, 8.

118. Brian Wingfield, "The Latest Initiative in Congress: Blogging," *New York Times,* February 24, 2005, E4; Jennifer Bendery, "Social Media Goes Viral on Capitol Hill," *Roll Call,* February 7, 2011, 1; Michael D. Shear, "G.O.P. to Open House to Electronic Devices," *New York Times,* December 25, 2010, A16.

119. E. Scott Adler, Chariti E. Gent, and Cary B. Overmeyer, "The Home Style Homepage: Legislator Use of the World Wide Web for Constituency Contact," *Legislative Studies Quarterly* 23 (November 1998): 585–595.

120. Dana Milbank, "A Tale of 140 Characters, Plus the Ones in Congress," *Washington Post,* February 25, 2009, A3; Jacob R. Strauss, Matthew Eric Glassman, Colleen J. Shogan, and Susan Navarro Smelcer, "Communicating in 140 Characters or Less: Congressional Adoption of Twitter in the 111th Congress," *PS, Political Science & Politics,* January 2013, 60–66, and Emily Cahn, "More Members Are Using Social Media to Interact with Their Constituents," *Roll Call,* January 4, 2013, 7.

121. Charles Bosley, "Senate Communications with the Public," in U.S. Senate, Commission on the Operation of the Senate, *Senate Communications with the Public,* 94th Cong., 2d sess., 1977, 17.

122. For descriptions of the studios, see Michael J. Robinson, "Three Faces of Congressional Media," in *The New Congress,* ed. Thomas E. Mann and Norman J. Ornstein (Washington, DC: American Enterprise Institute, 1981), 62–63; and Martin Tolchin, "TV Studio Serves Congress," *New York Times,* March 7, 1984, C22.

123. Tolchin, "TV Studio Serves Congress."

124. R. Douglas Arnold, *Congress, the Press, and Political Accountability* (Princeton, NJ: Princeton University Press, 2004).

125. Brian F. Schaffner, "Local News Coverage and the Incumbency Advantage in the U.S. House," *Legislative Studies Quarterly* 31 (November 2006): 491–511.

126. Robinson, "Three Faces of Congressional Media," 80–81.

127. Peter Clarke and Susan H. Evans, *Covering Campaigns: Journalism in Congressional Elections* (Stanford, CA: Stanford University Press, 1983). See also Charles M. Tidmarch and Brad S. Karp, "The Missing Beat: Press Coverage of Congressional Elections in Eight Metropolitan Areas," *Congress and the Presidency* 10 (Spring 1983): 47–61.

128. Robinson, "Three Faces of Congressional Media," 84.

129. Cokie Roberts, "Leadership and the Media in the 101st Congress," in *Leading Congress: New Styles, New Strategies,* ed. John J. Kornacki (Washington, DC: CQ Press, 1990), 94.

130. Markus Prior, "The Incumbent in the Living Room: The Rise of Television and the Incumbency Advantage in U.S. House Elections," *Journal of Politics* 68 (August 2006): 657–673.

131. Bob Benenson and Jonathan Allen, "It's Looking Like Blue Skies All Over Again," *CQ Weekly Report,* November 26, 2007, 3541.

132. Fenno, *Home Style,* 99.

CHAPTER 6

1. Quoted in David M. Herszenhorn, "Before Family and Friends, Passing a Gavel Heavy with Symbolism," *New York Times,* January 6, 2011, A16.

2. Rosalind S. Helderman, "House GOP Agrees to 2-Month Extension of Payroll Tax Cut," *Washington Post,* December 22, 2011, www.washingtonpost.com/politics/boehner-2-month-tax-cut-would-hurt-small-businesses/2011/12/22/gIQA5C1ZBP_story.html.

3. See, for example, the *Wall Street Journal* editorial of December 22, 2011, "The GOP's Payroll Tax Fiasco: How Did Republicans Manage to Lose the Tax Issue to Obama?"

4. Jake Sherman and John Bresnahan, "Behind the Scenes of a GOP Meltdown," *Politico*, December 20, 2012.

5. Peter Roff, "The Republicans' New House Rules," *U.S. News and World Report*, December 23, 2010 (online edition).

6. Quoted in Peter J. Boyer, "House Rule: Will John Boehner Control the Tea Party Caucus?" *The New Yorker*, December 13, 2010, 59.

7. Howard Fineman, "The Man Who Would Be Speaker: John Boehner's Improbable Cool," *Newsweek*, September 6, 2010, 17.

8. Quoted in Boyer, "House Rule."

9. *Wall Street Journal*, January 30, 1985, 5.

10. The seminal work on the collective action problem is by Mancur Olson, *The Logic of Collective Action, Public Goods, and the Theory of Groups* (Cambridge, MA: Harvard University Press, 1965).

11. Quoted in Kerry Kantin, "Rep. Rob Portman," *The Hill*, April 10, 2002, 12.

12. Matthew N. Green, *The Speaker of the House: A Study of Leadership* (New Haven, CT: Yale University Press, 2010), 4.

13. Michael Teitelbaum, "You're Off to a Great Start, but Can You Keep It Up," *CQ Today*, February 2, 2007, 1.

14. See Graeme Browning, "The Steward," *National Journal*, August 5, 1995, 2004–2007.

15. For an excellent discussion of this era, see Gregory Koger, *Filibustering: A Political History of Obstruction in the House and Senate* (Chicago: University of Chicago Press, 2010).

16. Quoted in *U.S. News and World Report*, October 13, 1950, 30.

17. See, for example, Barbara Sinclair, *Majority Leadership in the U.S. House* (Baltimore: Johns Hopkins University Press, 1983).

18. Tom Kenworthy, "House GOP Signals It's in a Fighting Mood," *Washington Post*, December 26, 1988, A8.

19. See Barbara Sinclair, *Unorthodox Lawmaking: New Legislative Processes in the U.S. Congress*, 3d ed. (Washington, DC: CQ Press, 2007), table 6.4, 123.

20. The GOP had wandered in the "wilderness of the minority" for forty years. A. B. Stoddard, "Rejuvenated Gingrich Mounts Media Offensive," *The Hill*, July 10, 1996, 24.

21. Ibid., 165–176.

22. Quoted in Cannon Centenary Conference, *The Changing Nature of the Speakership*, H. Doc. 108–204 (Washington, DC: Government Printing Office, 2004), 62.

23. Quoted in Eric Pianin and Helen Dewar, "GOP Leaders on Hill Find Unity Elusive," *Washington Post*, September 30, 2000, A10.

24. Ben Pershing, "Smith Spars with Leaders," *Roll Call*, March 26, 2003, 13.

25. Ibid.

26. Sarah A. Binder, Thomas E. Mann, Norman J. Ornstein, and Molly Reynolds, *Mending the Broken Branch: Assessing the 110th Congress, Anticipating the 111th*, Brookings, January 2009, www.brookings.edu/papers/2009/0108_broken_branch_binder_mann.aspx.

27. Edward Epstein, "Boehner Cracks the Whip on Errant Colleagues," *CQ Weekly*, June 21, 2010, 14–89.

28. Major Garrett, "A Politician's Politician," *National Journal*, January 7, 2011.

29. Jonathan Allen, "The A—hole Factor," *Politico*, December 13, 2012.

30. "Boehner's First Remarks as House Speaker," *New York Times*, January 5, 2011, www.nytimes.com/2011/01/06/us/politics/06cong-text.html?pagewanted=all.

31. See, for example, John H. Aldrich and David W. Rohde, "The Transition to Republican Rule in the House: Implications for Theories of Congressional Politics," *Political Science Quarterly* 112 (Winter 1997–1998): 541–567.

32. John H. Aldrich and David Rohde, "The Logic of Conditional Party Government: Revisiting the Electoral Connection," in *Congress Reconsidered*, 7th ed., ed. Lawrence Dodd and Bruce Oppenheimer (Washington, DC: CQ Press, 2001), 275–276.

33. See "The House in Sam Rayburn's Time," in Nelson W. Polsby, *How Congress Evolves: Social Bases of Institutional Change* (New York: Oxford University Press, 2003).

34. See Keith Krehbiel, *Pivotal Politics: A Theory of U.S. Lawmaking* (Chicago: University of Chicago Press, 1998).

35. Randall Strahan, *Leading Representatives: The Agency of Leaders in the Politics of the U.S. House* (Baltimore: Johns Hopkins University Press, 2007), xii.

36. See, for example, Green, *Speaker of the House;* Ronald M. Peters Jr., *The American Speakership: The Office in Historical Perspective*, 2d ed. (Baltimore: Johns Hopkins University Press, 1997); and D. B. Hardeman and Donald C. Bacon, *Rayburn: A Biography* (Austin: Texas Monthly Press, 1987).

37. Quoted in Jonathan Kaplan, "Hastert, DeLay: Political Pros Get Along to Go Along," *The Hill*, July 22, 2003, 8.

38. Alan K. Ota, "New Team Repackages the Right's Thinking," *CQ Weekly*, February 16, 2009, 340.

39. Sometimes exceptions are made to the general norm that top party leaders do not chair committees. During the 107th Congress (2001–2003), Majority Leader Dick Armey, R-Texas, chaired the Select Committee on Homeland Security, which reported the bill signed into law by President George W. Bush creating the Department of Homeland Security.

40. Christopher Madison, "Message Bearer," *National Journal*, December 1, 1990, 2906.

41. Floyd M. Riddick, *Congressional Procedure* (Boston: Chapman and Grimes, 1941), 345–346.

42. Philip Rucker and Paul Kane, "No Looking Back for Pelosi in House," *Washington Post*, December 22, 2010, A3.

43. Mike Lillis, "Pelosi to Stay on as House Dem Leader," *The Hill*, November 14, 2012.

44. Carl Hulse, "Fractured Democrats Keep Pelosi as Leader," *New York Times*, November 18, 2010, A22.

45. Richard E. Cohen, "GOP's Dilemma: Substance Versus Spin," *National Journal*, March 7, 2009.

46. See Charles O. Jones, *The Minority Party in Congress* (Boston: Little, Brown, 1970), 23.

47. Quoted in Jackie Kucinich, "New Whips Work in Tag Team," *Roll Call*, December 6, 2010.

48. Quoted in Jennifer Yachnin, "No 'Sharp Elbows' for Whip Clyburn," *Roll Call*, December 11, 2006, 36. Also see Richard Cohen, "A Different Kind of Whip," *National Journal*, January 20, 2007, 42–44.

49. Eric Cantor, Paul Ryan, and Kevin McCarthy, *Young Guns: A New Generation of Conservative Leaders* (New York: Threshold Editions, 2010).

50. Quoted in Michelle Cottle, "McCarthyism," *New Republic*, October 26, 2010, 17.

51. Jonathan Kaplan, "New GOP Whip, Roy Blunt Offers Different Style," *The Hill*, November 20, 2002, 4.

52. Michael Doyle, "House GOP's Vote-Getter Off to a Rough Start," McClatchy Washington Bureau, February 11, 2011.

53. Woodrow Wilson, *Congressional Government* (Boston: Houghton Mifflin, 1885), 223.

54. David J. Rothman, *Politics and Power: The United States Senate, 1869–1901* (Cambridge, MA: Harvard University Press, 1966), 5–7.

55. Margaret Munk, "Origin and Development of the Party Floor Leadership in the United States Senate," *Capital Studies* 2 (Winter 1974): 23–41; Richard A. Baker and Roger H. Davidson, eds., *First among Equals: Outstanding Senate Leaders of the Twentieth Century* (Washington, DC: Congressional Quarterly, 1991).

56. See Robert Caro, *Master of the Senate* (New York: Random House, 2002).

57. Rowland Evans and Robert Novak, *Lyndon B. Johnson: The Exercise of Power* (New York: New American Library, 1966), 104.

58. See John G. Stewart, "Two Strategies of Leadership: Johnson and Mansfield," in *Congressional Behavior,* ed. Nelson W. Polsby (New York: Random House, 1971), 61–92; William S. White, *Citadel: The Story of the United States Senate* (New York: Harper and Bros., 1956); Joseph S. Clark, *The Senate Establishment* (New York: Hill and Wang, 1963); and Randall B. Ripley, *Power in the Senate* (New York: St. Martin's Press, 1969).

59. *Congressional Record,* 96th Cong., 2d sess., April 18, 1980, S3294.

60. Quoted in Kathleen Hunter, "Zen and the Art of Walking Softly," *CQ Weekly,* June 29, 2009, 1504.

61. David S. Broder, "Don't Bet on Bipartisan Niceties," *Washington Post,* January 1, 2003, A19.

62. Quoted in Kathy Kiely and Wendy Koch, "Committee Shaped by Party Ties," *USA Today,* October 5, 1998, 2A.

63. See Frances E. Lee, *Beyond Ideology: Politics, Principles and Partisanship in the U.S. Senate* (Chicago: University of Chicago Press, 2009).

64

65. Quoted in William Welch, "In Reid, Bush Faces a Tenacious Force in the Senate," *USA Today,* December 12, 2006, 13A.

66. Quoted in Kirk Victor, "Getting to 60," *National Journal,* January 13, 2007, 37.

67. Kate Ackley and John Stanton, "Reid Keeps a Short List of Trusted Confidants," *Roll Call,* January 22, 2007, B-16.

68. Karen Tumulty, "Inside Man," *Time,* January 22, 2007, 29.

69. Quoted in ibid.

70. Quoted in Erin Billings, "McConnell Takes the Inside Track," *Roll Call,* January 31, 2007, 18.

71. Quoted in Carl Hulse, "Senate G.O.P. Leader Adapts to an Unexpected Role," *New York Times,* November 30, 2006, A20.

72. Quoted in Carl Hulse and Adam Nagourney, "Senate G.O.P. Leader Finds Weapon in Unity," *New York Times,* March 16, 2010.

73. Kirk Victor, "Short on Surprises," *National Journal,* October 28, 2006, 37.

74. Quoted in Jill Zuckman, "Dick Durbin's Passion Ignites Foes' Ire," *Chicago Tribune,* June 17, 2005 (online edition).

75. Carrie Mihalcik, "Most Conservative Members of Congress," *National Journal,* February 25, 2011, www.nationaljournal.com/magazine/most-conservatove-members-of-congress-20110224.

76. Susan Davis, "'Draft Cantor' Move Pondered," *Roll Call,* November 14, 2006, 18.

77. *New York Times,* December 6, 1988, B13.

78. David Truman, *The Congressional Party* (New York: Wiley, 1959).

79. Stephen Jessee and Neil Malholtra, "Are Congressional Leaders Middlepersons or Extremists? Yes." *Legislative Studies Quarterly* 35 (2010): 361–392.

80. David Grant, "Women Step Up in House GOP Leadership. Why That's Just a Start," DC Decoder Wire, *Christian Science Monitor,* November 15, 2012, www.csmonitor.com/USA/DC-Decoder/Decoder-Wire/2012/1115/Women-step-up-in-House-GOP-leadership.-Why-that-s-just-a-start.

81. Sinclair, *Majority Leadership in the U.S. House.*

82. *Congressional Record,* 98th Cong., 1st sess., November 15, 1983, H9856.

83. Quoted in Thomas B. Rosenstiel and Edith Stanley, "For Gingrich, It's 'Mr. Speaker!'" *Los Angeles Times,* November 9, 1994, A2.

84. *Congressional Record,* 94th Cong., 1st sess., January 26, 1973, S2301.

85. Richard E. Cohen, Jake Sherman, and Simmi Aujla, "GOP Taps Freshmen for Prime Spots," *Politico,* December 9, 2010, www.politico.com/news/stories/1210/46216.html.

86. Kirk Victor, "Reid's Smooth Start," *National Journal,* December 9, 2006, 47.

87. Neil MacNeil, *Dirksen: Portrait of a Public Man* (New York: World, 1970), 168–169.

88. Mark Preston, "Daschle May Write Book Chronicling His Times as Leader," *Roll Call Daily Issue E-newsletter,* May 20, 2002, 3.

89. Sidney Waldman, "Majority Leadership in the House of Representatives," *Political Science Quarterly* 95 (Fall 1980): 377.

90. Patrick Sellers, *Cycles of Spin: Strategic Communication in the U.S. Congress* (New York: Cambridge University Press, 2010).

91. *New York Times,* June 7, 1984, B16.

92. Noelle Straub and Melanie Fonder, "GOP Shifts Strategy for New Minority Status," *The Hill,* July 18, 2001, 6.

93. Mark Preston, "Lott Showcases Senators Facing Re-election," *Roll Call,* March 15, 2001, 3.

94. Eric Heberlig, Marc Hetherington, and Bruce Larson, "The Price of Leadership: Campaign Money and the Polarization of Congressional Parties," *Journal of Politics* 68 (2006): 992–1005.

95. Stephen Gettinger, "Potential Senate Leaders Flex Money Muscles," *Congressional Quarterly Weekly Report,* October 8, 1988, 2776.

96. Sinclair, *Majority Leadership in the U.S. House,* 96–97.

97. Gail Russell Chaddock, "Two House Health Care Reform Votes," *Christian Science Monitor,* March 20, 2010.

98. House Democrats disbanded their policy committee at Pelosi's direction. In its place, she established a revamped Steering Committee, which has a policy component (headed by George Miller of California) and a committee assignment component (chaired by Rosa DeLauro of Connecticut). See Erin Billings, "Pelosi Revamps the Steering Committee," *Roll Call,* March 13, 2003, 3.

99. Sen. Byron Dorgan, "Senate's DPC Role Expands as It Begins New Decade," *Roll Call,* January 30, 2007, 4.

100. Quoted in Fred Barnes, "Raging Representatives," *New Republic,* June 3, 1985, 9.

101. Jim Hoagland, "The Price of Polarization," *Washington Post,* May 5, 2005, A25.

102. Gail Russell Chaddock, "Obama Wins His Economic Stimulus Package, but without the Bipartisanship He Sought," *Christian Science Monitor,* February 14, 2009.

103. Erin Billings, "All Together Now, Senate," *Roll Call,* January 4, 2007, 1.

104. Shailagh Murray and Jonathan Weisman, "Iraq Resolution Typifies Rift in Senate," *Washington Post,* February 11, 2007, A3.

105. Quoted in Elizabeth Shogren, "Will Welfare Go Way of Health Reform?" *Los Angeles Times,* August 10, 1995, A18.

106. See V. O. Key Jr., *Politics, Parties, and Pressure Groups,* 5th ed. (New York: Crowell, 1964); and Austin Ranney and Willmoore Kendall, *Democracy and the American Party System* (New York: Harcourt Brace, 1956).

107. See Harold W. Stanley and Richard G. Niemi, *Vital Statistics on American Politics, 2007–2008* (Washington, DC: CQ Press, 2007), tables 1-10 and 1-11.

108. Quoted in Jackie Kucinich and Anna Palmer, "House GOP Bulks Up Outreach Operation," *Roll Call,* January 7, 2009.

109. *Congressional Record,* 104th Cong., 1st sess., October 11, 1995, E1926. Rep. Lee H. Hamilton, D-Ind., who made the comment, strongly opposed the overuse of omnibus bills.

110. Lee H. Hamilton, with Jordan Tama, *A Creative Tension: The Foreign Policy Roles of the President and Congress* (Washington, DC: Woodrow Wilson Center Press, 2002), 33.

111. Quoted in Richard E. Cohen, "Byrd of West Virginia: A New Job, a New Image," *National Journal,* August 20, 1977, 1294.

CHAPTER 7

1. *Washington Post,* May 14, 1987, A23.
2. *Congressional Record,* 100th Cong., 1st sess., June 25, 1987, H5564.
3. Woodrow Wilson coined the term *little legislatures* in *Congressional Government* (Boston: Houghton Mifflin, 1885), 79.
4. The House has five delegates (American Samoa, District of Columbia, Guam, Northern Mariana Islands, and Virgin Islands) and one resident commissioner (Puerto Rico).
5. Quoted in *New York Times,* July 11, 1988, A14.
6. See, for example, Kenneth A. Shepsle and Barry R. Weingast, "The Institutional Foundations of Committee Power," *American Political Science Review* (March 1987): 85–104.
7. See Keith Krehbiel, *Information and Legislative Organization* (Ann Arbor: University of Michigan Press, 1991); and Bruce Bimber, "Information as a Factor in Congressional Politics," *Legislative Studies Quarterly* (1991): 585–606.
8. John W. Ellwood, "The Great Exception: The Congressional Budget Process in an Age of Decentralization," in *Congress Reconsidered,* 3d ed., ed. Lawrence C. Dodd and Bruce I. Oppenheimer (Washington, DC: CQ Press, 1985), 329. For the classic discussion of committee and member roles, see Richard F. Fenno Jr., *Congressmen in Committees* (Boston: Little, Brown, 1973).
9. Roy Swanstrom, *The United States Senate, 1787–1801,* S. Doc. 87–64, 87th Cong., 1st sess., 1962, 224.
10. Lauros G. McConachie, *Congressional Committees* (New York: Crowell, 1898), 124.
11. DeAlva Stanwood Alexander, *History and Procedure of the House* of *Representatives* (Boston: Houghton Mifflin, 1916), 228; George H. Haynes, *The Senate of the United States: Its History and Practice,* vol. 1 (Boston: Houghton Mifflin, 1938), 272; Ralph V. Harlow, *The History of Legislative Methods in the Period before 1825* (New Haven, CT: Yale University Press, 1917), 157–158.
12. *Cannon's Procedures in the House of Representatives,* H. Doc. 80–122, 80th Cong., 1st sess., 1959, 83.
13. Quoted in *Wall Street Journal,* May 3, 1979, 1.
14. Alan K. Ota, "Reid's New Panel Ratios Meet GOP Resistance," *Roll Call,* November 14, 2012 (online edition). Sens. Angus King of Maine and Bernard Sanders of Vermont, neither of whom ran as Democrats, are considered Democrats because they caucus with that party.
15. Ibid.
16. Sam Goldfarb, "Trimming of House Panels Eliminates 73 Committee Slots," *CQ Today,* January 24, 2011, 6.
17. Jessica Brady, "Waxman Reduces Number of Subcommittees; Lineup Set," *National Journal's CongressDaily PM,* December 12, 2006, 10.
18. *Congressional Record,* 104th Cong., 1st sess., January 4, 1995, H33.
19. Theo Emery, "Controversial King Denied Top Immigration Slot," *CQ Today,* January 10, 2011, 5.
20. Emma Dumain, "Issa Elevates D.C. Affairs to Full Committee," *Roll Call,* January 3, 2013, 3.
21. Sean Lengell, "Democrats Lament Demise of a Committee," *Washington Times,* December 6, 2010, A3.
22. Lawrence D. Longley and Walter J. Oleszek, *Bicameral Politics: Conference Committees in Congress* (New Haven, CT: Yale University Press, 1989), 196.
23. Keith Krehbiel, Kenneth A. Shepsle, and Barry R. Weingast, "Why Are Congressional Committees Powerful?" *American Political Science Review* 81 (September 1987): 935.
24. Roderick Kiewiet and Mathew McCubbins, *The Logic of Delegation: Congressional Parties and the Appropriations Process* (Chicago: University of Chicago Press, 1991).

25. Humberto Sanchez and Niels Lesniewski, "Spending Panel Loses Its Luster," *Roll Call,* December 21, 2012, 1.

26. Brian Faier, "Appropriations Loses Allure in Tight-Budget Congress," *The Washington Examiner,* January 31, 2011, 13.

27. Carl Hulse, "3 Republicans in Race to Lead Appropriations Committee," *New York Times,* December 7, 2010, A5.

28. Alex Isenstadt, "The Lucre of Landing a Key Committee," *Politico,* January 19, 2011, 20.

29. James Bornemeier, "Berman Accepts Seat on House Ethics Panel," *Los Angeles Times,* February 5, 1997, B1; *CQ Daily Monitor,* December 11, 1999, 1.

30. Sonni Efron and Janet Hook, "Lugar Now the Man in the Middle," *Los Angeles Times,* December 23, 2002, A7. Also see Shailagh Murray, "Foreign Relations at Center Stage," *Washington Post,* March 28, 2007, A13.

31. Dan Friedman, "The End of Foreign Relations," *National Journal Daily,* May 14, 2012, 3.

32. Fenno, *Congressmen in Committees.* Also see Heinz Eulau, "Legislative Committee Assignments," *Legislative Studies Quarterly* (November 1984): 587–633.

33. Christopher J. Deering and Steven S. Smith, *Committees in Congress,* 3d ed. (Washington, DC: CQ Press, 1997), 61–62, 78.

34. Shirley Chisholm, *Unbought and Unbossed* (Boston: Houghton Mifflin, 1970), 84, 86.

35. Quoted in Ethan Wallison, "Freshman Democrats Get Panel Waivers," *Roll Call,* June 21, 1999, 20.

36. Reid Wilson, "McConnell Promises Boozman Ag Seat," *National Journal Hotline,* July 7, 2010 (online version).

37. Alexander Jaffe, "Powerful Committee Seats Rewarded to Dems Who Survived Tough Races," *The Hill,* December 12, 2012 (online edition).

38. Andrew Beadle, "First Lady's Résumé Won't Impress Seniority System," *CQ Daily Monitor,* November 20, 2000, 9.

39. Quoted in Peter Kaplan and David Mark, "With Election Day Over, the Campaigns Begin in the House," *CQ Daily Monitor,* November 20, 2000, 3.

40. Jim VandeHei, "Would-Be Chairmen Hit Money Trail," *Roll Call,* July 12, 1999, 1.

41. Jonathan Strong, "Speak Softly or Carry a Big Stick," *CQ Weekly,* January 24, 2013, 63.

42. Jonathan Allen, "The A—Hole Factor," *Politico,* December 13, 2012 (online edition).

43. Paul Gigot, "Mack Uses Knife on Old Senate Order," *Wall Street Journal,* July 14, 1995, A12.

44. Margaret Kriz, "Gavels Turn Green," *National Journal,* November 18, 2006, 62.

45. Jonathan Broder, "A New Obstacle to Any Shift toward Cuba," *CQ Weekly* January 13, 2013, 16.

46. Chris Frates, "Trust Fall," *National Journal,* February 2, 2013, 35.

47. Quoted in *Washington Post,* November 20, 1983, A9.

48. Amy Fagan, "Thomas Takes Reins on Social Security," *Washington Times,* February 6, 2005, A3.

49. Anna Palmer, "Cummings Bypasses Issa in Fight over Access to Letters," *Roll Call,* January 31, 2011 (online edition).

50. See David King, *Turf Wars* (Chicago: University of Chicago Press, 1997).

51. Allison Stevens, "No Ordinary Power Grab: Chairman Complains of 'Bold' Power Grab," *CQ Today,* June 23, 2004, 1, 9.

52. Darren Samuelsohn and Robin Bravender, "GOP Takeover Prompts Committee Turf Wars," *Politico,* November 11, 2010, 21.

53. Rep. Fred Upton, "Don't Dilute Energy and Commerce Clout," *Roll Call,* November 3, 2010, 5.

54. Samuelsohn and Bravender, "GOP Takeover Prompts Committee Turf Wars," 21.

55. *CQ Today,* December 10, 2010, 10.

56. Quoted in Bob Pool, "Survivors Take Stock of Gains against Cancer," *Los Angeles Times,* May 30, 1997, B1.

57. Ralph Vartabedian, "Senate Panel Is Ready to Take IRS to Task," *Los Angeles Times*, September 22, 1997, A1.

58. "Dodd-Frank" refers to Sen. Christopher Dodd, D-Conn., who chaired the Banking, Housing, and Urban Affairs Committee, and Rep. Barney Frank, D-Mass., who headed the Financial Services Committee. Senator Dodd retired at the end of the 111th Congress. Frank served as the ranking member on Financial Services because of GOP control of the House in the 112th Congress; he retired at the end of that Congress.

59. Jane Norman, "Harkin Plans Hearings on Health Law to Counter GOP," *CQ Today*, January 7, 2011, 2.

60. Darlene Superville, "Congressional Panels Seek 'Real People,'" *Los Angeles Times*, March 25, 2007 (online edition).

61. Elizabeth Brotherton, "Webcasting Goes Mainstream among House Committees," *Roll Call*, March 7, 2007, 3.

62. Sean Piccoli, "Hill Samples 'Third Wave,'" *Washington Times*, June 13, 1995, A8.

63. Warren Leary, "When Astronauts Brief Congress, a Little Levity Goes a Long Way," *New York Times*, June 15, 2005, A16.

64. *Congressional Record*, 107th Cong., 2d sess., July 16, 2002, S6849.

65. Quoted in *Washington Post*, November 25, 1985, A4. Also see Richard L. Hall, *Participation in Congress* (New Haven, CT: Yale University Press, 1998).

66. Quoted in "CQ Midday Update Email," December 14, 2004, 1, www.cq.com.

67. Eric Redman, *The Dance of Legislation* (New York: Simon and Schuster, 1973), 140.

68. Hugh Heclo, "Issue Networks in the Executive Establishment," in *The New American Political System*, ed. Anthony King (Washington, DC: American Enterprise Institute, 1978), 87–124. Also see David E. Price, "Policy Making in Congressional Committees: The Impact of 'Environmental Factors,'" *American Political Science Review* (Fall 1978): 548–574.

69. Molly Hopper, "House Judiciary Committee Seeks Bipartisan Touch," *The Hill*, January 18, 2011, 8.

70. Norris Cotton, *In the Senate* (New York: Dodd, Mead, 1978), 65.

71. *Washington Post*, March 20, 1977, E9.

72. David Whiteman, *Communication in Congress: Members, Staff, and the Search for Information* (Lawrence: University Press of Kansas, 1995). A good article on the role of staff is Steven T. Dennis, "Nabors Is the 'Glue' Between WH, Congress," *Roll Call*, May 10, 2012, 1.

73. Siobhan Gorman and Richard Cohen, "Hurtling toward an Intelligence Overhaul," *National Journal*, September 18, 2004, 2808.

74. Quoted in *Washington Post*, November 20, 1983, A13.

75. Brett Pulley, "Black Clerics Criticize Torricelli on Minority Hiring for His Staff," *New York Times*, March 21, 1997, A25.

76. Josephine Hearn, "House Staffers Follow Bosses' Footsteps on the Campaign Trail," *The Hill*, October 18, 2006, 4.

77. Quoted in Andrew Taylor, "Security Plan Changes Committee Name, Little Else," *CQ Today*, October 8, 2004, 1.

78. Ibid., 4.

79. *Congressional Record*, 109th Cong., 1st sess., January 4, 2005, H25–H26.

80. *CQ Weekly*, December 27, 2010, 2901.

81. Emily Ethridge, "Republicans Push for New Health Committee," *Roll Call*, November 15, 2012, 10.

82. Tim Starks, "Plan to Eliminate House Panel Raises Budgetary Oversight Questions," *CQ Today*, January 5, 2011, 9.

83. Chris Strohm, "House Dems Want Oversight Panel Reinstated," *National Journal CongressDaily PM*, January 19, 2011, 2.

84. *Congressional Record*, September 23, 2008, S9268.
85. Quoted in Roger H. Davidson and Walter J. Oleszek, *Congress against Itself* (Bloomington: Indiana University Press, 1977), 263.
86. E. Scott Adler, *Why Congressional Reforms Fail* (Chicago: University of Chicago Press, 2002), 11.
87. Richard Cohen and Marilyn Serfina, "Taxing Times," *National Journal*, December 23, 2000, 39–61.
88. David Firestone, "G.O.P.'s 'Cardinals of Spending' Are Reined In by House Leaders," *New York Times*, December 2, 2002, A16.
89. Alexander Bolton, "House GOP Puts Taylor on Warning," *The Hill*, February 15, 2005, 1.
90. Quoted in Josephine Hearn, "Pelosi Riles Old Guard Chairmen," *Politico*, January 23, 2007, 4.
91. John Boehner, "What the Next Speaker Must Do," *Wall Street Journal*, November 5, 2010, A19.
92. Stacy Kaper, Nancy Cook, and Jim Tankersley, "Congressional Committees, RIP: 1789–2011," *National Journal Daily*, December 19, 2011, 1.
93. David Drucker and Emily Pierce, "Reid to Baucus: Stop Chasing GOP Votes on Health Care," *Roll Call*, July 7, 2009 (online edition).
94. David Nather, "Daschle's Soft Touch Lost in Tough Senate Arena," *CQ Weekly*, July 20, 2002, 1922.
95. Noelle Straub, "Senate Finance Panel Faces July 15 Deadline," *The Hill*, July 3, 2002, 6.
96. Manu Raju, "How Hill Leaders Sow Dysfunction," *Politico*, December 20, 2011, 1, 10.
97. Frates, "Trust Fall," 35.
98. Susan Davis, "Pelosi, Boehner Name Eight Members to Ethics Task Force," *Roll Call*, February 1, 2007, 3.
99. Jonathan Weisman, "House Creates New Panel on Ethics," *Washington Post*, March 12, 2008, A1.
100. Alan Ota, "Republicans Look for Input from House High-Tech Team," *CQ Today*, January 25, 2011, 1.
101. *National Journal*'s *CongressDaily AM*, January 30, 2007, 15.
102. *Congressional Record*, 108th Cong., 2d sess., February 14, 2004, S1496.
103. *Congressional Record*, 112th Cong., 1st sess., January 5, 2011, S17.
104. Nather, "Daschle's Soft Touch Lost."
105. Paul Kane, "Committee Chairs Seek to Reassert Power in Congress," *Washington Post*, February 17, 2013, A4.
106. *Committee Structure*, Hearings before the Joint Committee on the Organization of Congress (Washington, DC: Government Printing Office, 1993), 779.
107. Curt Suplee, "The Science Chairman's Unpredictable Approach," *Washington Post*, October 15, 1991, A21.

CHAPTER 8

1. *Constitution, Jefferson's Manual, and Rules of the House of Representatives*, H. Doc. 111–157, 111th Cong., 2011, 129. The rules of the Senate are contained in *Senate Manual*, S. Doc. 107–1, 107th Cong., 2002.
2. Donald R. Matthews, *U.S. Senators and Their World* (Chapel Hill: University of North Carolina Press, 1960), chap. 5.
3. See Daniel Newhauser, "Authority Statements Are Often Vague," *Roll Call*, April 10, 2012, 11.
4. See Barry C. Burden, *Personal Roots of Representation* (Princeton, NJ: Princeton University Press, 2007).
5. Quoted in John Solomon, "Family Crisis Shifts Politics," *USA Today*, August 16, 2001, 15A.
6. Deborah Sontag, "When Politics Is Personal," *New York Times Magazine*, September 15, 2002, 92.
7. *National Journal*, April 10, 1982, 632.

8. Reid Wilson, "Partisan Roles Don't Keep Van Hollen, Sessions from Reaching across the Aisle," *The Hill*, March 12, 2009, 3.

9. Quoted in Julie Rovner, "Senate Committee Approves Health Warnings on Alcohol," *Congressional Quarterly Weekly Report*, May 24, 1986, 1175.

10. Woodrow Wilson, *Congressional Government* (Boston: Houghton Mifflin, 1885), 320.

11. Theodore Sorensen, *Kennedy* (New York: Harper and Row, 1965), 184.

12. *Wall Street Journal*, June 2, 1988, 56.

13. *Congressional Record*, 95th Cong., 1st sess., May 17, 1977, E3076.

14. Richard Simon, "Congress Turns Bill Titles into Acts of Exaggeration," *Los Angeles Times*, June 19, 2011 (online edition).

15. Quoted in Chuck Todd, "So Many Bills of Rights, So Little Time," *National Journal's CongressDaily PM*, August 1, 2001, 1.

16. Peter Baker, "White House Finds 'Fast Track' Too Slippery," *Washington Post*, September 14, 1997, A4. Also see *Congressional Record*, 105th Cong., 2d sess., September 29, 1998, S11133; *Congressional Record*, 106th Cong., 1st sess., January 25, 1999, S979; and Ceci Connolly, "Consultant Offers GOP a Language for the Future," *Washington Post*, September 4, 1997, A1.

17. For information on the drafting process, see Lawrence E. Filson, *The Legislative Drafter's Desk Reference* (Washington, DC: Congressional Quarterly, 1992).

18. *CQ Monitor*, July 24, 1998, 5.

19. Lawrence J. Haas, "Unauthorized Action," *National Journal*, January 2, 1988, 20.

20. Rep. John Boehner, "What the Next Speaker Must Do," *Wall Street Journal*, November 5, 2010, A19.

21. Michael Gerson, "In Victory, Obama Failed," *Washington Post*, October 30, 2012, A19.

22. Alex Wayne, "Fight the Curse of the Big Bill," *CQ Weekly*, March 8, 2010, 558.

23. Stacy Kaper, "Bob Corker Charts Leadership Course," *National Journal Daily*, April 13, 2013, 5.

24. T. R. Reid, *Congressional Odyssey: The Saga of a Senate Bill* (San Francisco: W. H. Freeman, 1980), 17.

25. Paul Singer, "More Bills, More Lawyers for Leg. Offices," *Roll Call*, March 28, 2007, 22.

26. Carroll J. Doherty, "Lots of Inertia, Little Lawmaking as Election '98 Approaches," *CQ Weekly*, July 18, 1998, 1925.

27. Quoted in Margaret Kriz, "Still Charging," *National Journal*, December 6, 1997, 2462.

28. Jackie Kucinich, "GOP Surveys Itself on New Agenda," *Los Angeles Times*, July 6, 2010 (online edition).

29. Pete Kasperowicz, "House Sked Too Light, Say Democrats," *The Hill*, October 28, 2011, 8.

30. Jonathan Nicholson, "Congress on Pace to Enact Fewest Laws In Post-War Era," *Daily Report for Executives*, April 16, 2012, B-1.

31. Donald R. Wolfensberger, "Suspended Partisanship in the House: How Most Laws Are Really Made" (paper prepared for the annual meeting of the American Political Science Association, Boston, August 29–September 1, 2002), 11.

32. Martin Gold et al., *The Book on Congress* (Washington, DC: Big Eagle Publishing, 1992), 124.

33. *Congressional Record*, 112th Cong., 1st sess., January 5, 2011, H29.

34. Quoted in Jonathan Salant, "Under Open Rules, Discord Rules," *Congressional Quarterly Weekly Report*, January 28, 1995, 277.

35. *National Journal*, January 21, 1995, 183.

36. Lizette Alvarez, "Campaign Finance Measure Soundly Rejected by House," *New York Times*, June 18, 1998, A26.

37. Stanley Bach and Steven Smith, *Managing Uncertainty in the House of Representatives: Adaptation and Innovation in Special Rules* (Washington, DC: Brookings, 1988), 87.

38. *Congresssional Record*, 110th Cong., 1st sess., March 20, 2007, H2682.

39. Don Wolfensberger, "Leadership Control Is Faulted for House Ills," *Roll Call*, December 14, 2010, 15.

40. Quoted in S. A. Miller, "Democrats Hedge on Bipartisan Pledge," *Washington Times*, January 25, 2007, A9.

41. *Congressional Record*, 112th Cong., 1st sess., January 5, 2011, H5.

42. Ibid., January 15, 2011, H805.

43. "Switched Votes for Gas Bill," *Congressional Quarterly Weekly Report*, February 14, 1976, 313.

44. Mary Lynn F. Jones, "The Republican Railroad," *American Prospect*, April 2003, 16.

45. Molly Hooper, "Leaders Push Back on Farm Bill Vote," *The Hill*, September 19, 2012, 8.

46. Lindsay Sobel, "Democrats Weigh Discharge Petition Barrage," *The Hill*, July 1, 1998, 2.

47. Emily Ethridge, "House GOP Leaders Join Effort to Force Vote on Repeal of Health Care Law," *CQ Today*, July 1, 2010, 13.

48. Alexander Bolton, "House Leaders Tighten Grip, Anger Centrists," *The Hill*, January 15, 2003, 23.

49. Information courtesy of Richard Beth, specialist in legislative process, Congressional Research Service, Library of Congress.

50. Molly Hooper, "Two Weeks On, One Week Off in 2011 House Schedule," *The Hill*, December 9, 2010, 6.

51. Sam Goldfarb, "House's Two-Weeks-On, One-Week-Off Plan Diverges from Senate, Tradition," *CQ Today*, December 9, 2010, 23.

52. *National Journal*'s *CongressDaily PM*, January 13, 1995, 4.

53. Robert S. Walker, "Why House Republicans Need a Watchdog," *Roll Call*, January 19, 1987, 10.

54. John F. Bibby, ed., *Congress Off the Record* (Washington, DC: American Enterprise Institute, 1983), 2.

55. *Congressional Record*, 111th Cong., 2d sess., May 20, 2010, H3683.

56. Sen. J. Bennett Johnston, D-La. (1972–1997), quoted in *New York Times*, November 22, 1985, B8.

57. Quoted in "Democrats to Forgo Control in Brief Edge," *Washington Times*, November 29, 2000, A4.

58. *Congressional Record*, 101st Cong., 2d sess., July 20, 1990, S10183.

59. Susan F. Rasky, "With Few Bills Passed or Ready for Action, Congress Seems Sluggish," *New York Times*, May 14, 1989, 24.

60. *Congressional Record*, 98th Cong., 2d sess., January 27, 1984, S328–S329.

61. Walter J. Oleszek, *Congressional Procedures and the Policy Process*, 9th ed. (Washington, DC: CQ Press, 2014), 319–325. Also see Lewis A. Froman Jr., *The Congressional Process* (Boston: Little, Brown, 1967); and Terry Sullivan, *Procedural Structure: Success and Influence in Congress* (New York: Praeger, 1984).

62. *Congressional Record*, 111th Cong., 2d sess., September 21, 2010, S7251.

63. Elizabeth Drew, *Senator* (New York: Simon and Schuster, 1979), 158.

64. *Congressional Record*, 97th Cong., 2d sess., May 20, 1982, S5648.

65. Mary Dalrymple, "Democrats Say They Are Unified in Opposition Platform," *CQ Today*, January 29, 2002, 5.

66. Christopher M. Davis, "Filling the Amendment Tree in the Senate," *CRS Report* RS22854, February 2, 2011, 2.

67. Gail Russell Chaddock, "Limits on Filibusters Are Already Pervasive," *Christian Science Monitor*, May 24, 2005, 2.

68. *Congressional Record*, 107th Cong., 2d sess., April 17, 2002, S2850.

69. Helen Dewar, "'Hold' Likely for IRS Pick, Daschle Says," *Washington Post*, October 30, 1997, A11.

70. Meredith Shiner and Humberto Sanchez, "Senators Shy from Obama Filibuster Reform," *Roll Call*, January 26, 2012, 10.

71. See comments by Alan Cranston of California, then Senate Democratic whip, in *New York Times*, July 17, 1986, A3.

72. Quoted in Sean Piccoli, "Byrd Still Senate Caesar Despite GOP Takeover," *Washington Times*, February 14, 1995, A11.

73. David Herszenhorn, "Thrust and Parry on the Senate Floor," *New York Times*, November 22, 2009, E3.

74. U.S. Congress, *Operations of the Congress: Testimony of House and Senate Leaders*, hearing before the Joint Committee on the Organization of Congress (Washington, DC: Government Printing Office, 1993), 50.

75. Doug Obey, "Alaska," *The Hill*, July 10, 1996, 27.

76. Sixteen additional cloture motions were filed but not voted upon. Two of the sixteen, however, were agreed to by unanimous consent. Information for the 109th Congress compiled by the U.S. Senate Library.

77. Eve Fairbanks, "Tough Reid," *New Republic*, April 15, 2009, 14.

78. Josh Smith, "Majority Does Not Rule in Filibuster-Filled 111th Senate," *National Journal*, December 17, 2010, 4.

79. Humberto Sanchez, "Harry Reid Beats Back Majority of Filibusters in 2011," *Roll Call*, January 2, 2012 (online version).

80. Martin P. Paone, "Senate Rule Changes Come with Risk," *The Hill*, May 15, 2012, 29.

81. *Congressional Record*, 111th Cong., 2d sess., September 15, 2010, S7120.

82. *Congressional Record*, 112th Cong., 1st sess., January 27, 2011, S322.

83. Some analysts associate the nuclear option with a 2005 plan by Majority Leader Bill Frist, R-Tenn., to end filibusters on a specific matter—judicial nominations.

84. See, for example, Steven Dennis, "Rocky Road for Senate Comity," *Roll Call*, June 16, 2011, 1; Humberto Sanchez, "Gentlemen's Agreement Showing Signs of Wear," *The Hill*, October 12, 2011, 20; and Humberto Sanchez, "Filibuster Tests Senate Agreement," *The Hill*, December 7, 2011, 3.

85. *Congressional Record*, October 6, 2011, S6314-S6315.

86. "Reid Sets Procedural Precedent; Senate Minority Rights at Stake," *CQ Weekly*, October 10, 2011, 2103.

87. Testimony of Steven S. Smith, University of Minnesota, before the Joint Committee on the Organization of Congress, 103d Cong., 1st sess., May 20, 1993, 14.

88. See Barbara Sinclair, "Ping Pong and Other Congressional Pursuits: Party Leaders and Post-Passage Procedural Choice," in Jacob Strauss, ed., *Party and Procedure in the United States Congress* (Lanham, MD: Rowman & Littlefield Publishers, 2012), 231–252.

89. Carl Hulse and Robert Pear, "Feeling Left Out on Major Bills, Democrats Turn to Stalling Others," *New York Times*, May 3, 2004, A18.

90. Jonathan Allen and John Cochran, "The Might of the Right," *CQ Weekly*, November 8, 2003, 2762.

91. Randall B. Ripley, *Power in the Senate* (New York: St. Martin's Press, 1969), 128.

92. Barbara Sinclair, *Unorthodox Lawmaking: New Legislative Processes in the U.S. Congress*, 4th ed. (Washington, DC: CQ Press, 2012).

93. Barber B. Conable, "Weaving Webs: Lobbying by Charities," *Tax Notes*, November 10, 1975, 27–28.

CHAPTER 9

1. David M. Herszenhorn, "In Senate, Republicans Block Spending Measure," *New York Times*, March 6, 2009, A16.

2. Quoted in ibid.

3. Humberto Sanchez and Christian Bourge, "Reid Sees Senate Action on Omnibus by March 6 Deadline," *National Journal CongressDaily PM*, February 24, 2009.

4. Gail Russell Chaddock, "Omnibus Bill's Hidden Item: A Democratic Rift," *Christian Science Monitor*, March 12, 2009 (online edition).

5. Robert Pear, "House Passes Spending Bill, and Critics Are Quick to Point Out Pork," *New York Times*, February 26, 2009, A20.

6. Evan Bayh, "Deficits and Fiscal Credibility," *Wall Street Journal*, March 4, 2009.

7. Shailagh Murray, "Democrats Stung by Dissenters: Unity on Agenda Eludes Party Leaders," *Washington Post*, March 10, 2009, A1.

8. Quoted in Jill Smallen and Jason Dick, "The Week on the Hill: Obama Signs Omnibus Package," *National Journal*, March 14, 2009 (online edition).

9. Dan Friedman, "Despite Threat, Appointed Senators Hold Firm against Vitter," *National Journal CongressDaily AM*, March 11, 2009 (online edition).

10. Quoted in Ibid.

11. Quoted in Ibid.

12. Quoted in Emily Pierce, "Omnibus' Fate Not Accompli," *Roll Call*, March 5, 2009.

13. Quoted in Ibid.

14. Emily Pierce, "Menendez Feels the Heat; Senators Fume over Omnibus," *Roll Call*, March 11, 2009 (online edition).

15. Quoted in Ibid.

16. Paul Kane and Scott Wilson, "Obama Signs Spending Bill, Vowing to Battle Earmarks," *Washington Post*, March 12, 2009, A01.

17. Richard L. Hall, *Participation in Congress* (New Haven, CT: Yale University Press, 1998), 27–30.

18. Lauren Whittington, "Obscure Caucus: Members Allergic to the Spotlight Find a Home," *Roll Call*, September 10, 2007. The listing omits senators: "Senators are by definition not obscure, although there are several who seem to strive for it." To be listed in the Obscure Caucus, House members must have served at least two full terms.

19. Quoted in *The Hill*, November 15, 2000, 16.

20. David Price, *Who Makes the Laws?* (Cambridge, MA: Schenkman Publishing, 1972), 297; David E. Price, *The Congressional Experience*, 3d ed. (Boulder, CO: Westview Press, 2004), chap. 6.

21. Quoted in Bernard Asbell, *The Senate Nobody Knows* (Garden City, NY: Doubleday, 1978), 210.

22. Richard F. Fenno Jr., "Observation, Context, and Sequence in the Study of Politics," *American Political Science Review* 80 (March 1976): 3–15.

23. Lindsay Sobel, "Early Fast-Track Support Cost Members Leverage," *The Hill*, November 12, 1997, 33.

24. Matthew Daly, "Indians Benefited in 111th Congress," *Washington Times*, December 30, 2010, A4.

25. Cited in Philippe Shepnick, "Moynihan Is Champion Bill Writer," *The Hill*, March 10, 1999, 6.

26. Rick K. Wilson and Cheryl D. Young, "Cosponsorship in the U.S. Congress," *Legislative Studies Quarterly* 22 (February 1997): 25–43.

27. Jacob R. Straus, "Dear Colleague Letters in the House of Representatives: The Tracking of Internal House Communications" (paper presented at the annual meeting of the Midwest Political Science Association, Chicago, April 2–5, 2009), fig. 1.

28. T. R. Reid, *Congressional Odyssey: The Saga of a Senate Bill* (San Francisco: W. H. Freeman, 1980), 15.

29. Hall, *Participation in Congress*, 139; also see 119.

30. Ibid., 126–127.

31. Ibid., 102.

32. Gary Mucchiaroni and Paul J. Quirk, *Deliberative Choices: Debating Public Policy in Congress* (Chicago: University of Chicago Press, 2006), 197.

33. "Final Word," NationalJournal.com, June 5, 2012, 4.

34. *Congressional Record*, August 2, 2012, H5660, H5662.

35. *Congressional Record*, 103d Cong., 1st sess., June 23, 1993, H3941–H3973.

36. John D. Wilkerson, "'Killer' Amendments in Congress," *American Political Science Review* 93 (September 1999): 535–552.

37. Quoted in Peter Gosselin, "Paulson Will Have No Peer under Bailout Deal," *Los Angeles Times*, September 29, 2008 (online edition).

38. Dave Cook, "'Brutal Vote' Ahead on Whether to Raise the National Debt Ceiling," *Christian Science Monitor*, November 19, 2010 (online edition).

39. Ryan Kelly, "On the Record," *CQ Weekly*, January 16, 2012, 122; and Ryan Kelly, "Still Showing Up," *CQ Weekly*, January 21, 2013, 142.

40. Niels Lesniewski and Stacey Skotzko, "Members Go to Great Lengths for Voting Stats," *Roll Call*, July 16, 2012, 5.

41. Paul Kane, "Partisanship Is No Longer Something to Hide on Hill," *Washington Post*, December 8, 2011, A6.

42. Dan Friedman, "A Rare 'Present' Vote for Schumer," NationalJournal.com, July 16, 2012 (online edition).

43. John B. Gilmour, *Strategic Disagreement: Stalemate in American Politics* (Pittsburgh: University of Pittsburgh Press, 1995), 41.

44. Quoted in Ramesh Ponnuru, "Division on the Right," *National Review*, November 21, 2003.

45. David C. King and Richard J. Zeckhauser, "Congressional Vote Options," *Legislative Studies Quarterly* 28 (August 2003): 400–401.

46. Quoted in Eric Schmitt, "House Votes to Bar Religious Abuse Abroad," *New York Times*, May 15, 1998, A1.

47. Albert R. Hunt, "Balanced-Budget Measure Is Likely to Pass Senate Next Week, Faces Battle in House," *Wall Street Journal*, July 30, 1982, 2.

48. Humberto Sanchez, "Fight for Control Shows in Votes," *CQ Weekly*, January 21, 2013, 132. The quote following this note in the text is also from this article.

49. Emily Ethride, "Ever More Polarized, Parties Set Records," *CQ Weekly*, January 6, 2012, 112.

50. Sanchez, "Fight for Control Shows in Votes," 132.

51. Ibid., 134.

52. Ibid., 136.

53. Shankar Vedantam, "My Team vs. Your Team: The Political Arena Lives Up to Its Name," *Washington Post*, September 29, 2008, A6.

54. For an extended analysis of partisan interests as a source of party cohesion and conflict, see Frances E. Lee, *Beyond Ideology: Politics, Principles, and Partisanship in the U.S. Senate* (Chicago: University of Chicago Press, 2009).

55. Gary C. Jacobson, *The Politics of Congressional Elections*, 7th ed. (New York: Pearson Longman, 2009), 135–144.

56. Tom Hamburger, "Missouri Clergy Join Akin in Battle for GOP's 'Soul,'" *Washington Post*, October 9, 2012, A8.

57. John Breaux, "Congress's Lost Art of Compromise," *Roll Call*, April 19, 2005, 17.

58. Quoted in Ibid.

59. Gary W. Cox and Mathew D. McCubbins, *Setting the Agenda: Responsible Party Government in the U.S. House of Representatives* (New York: Cambridge University Press, 2005), 18.

60. See John W. Kingdon, *Congressmen's Voting Decisions* (New York: Harper and Row, 1981); and Randall B. Ripley, *Party Leaders in the House of Representatives* (Washington, DC: Brookings, 1967), 139–159.

61. Donald R. Matthews and James A. Stimson, *Yeas and Nays: Normal Decisionmaking in the U.S. House of Representatives* (New York: John Wiley, 1975), 95.

62. Quoted in Morton Kondracke, "Who's Running the House? GOP Freshmen or Newt?" *Roll Call,* December 18, 1995, 5.

63. See Gary W. Cox and Mathew D. McCubbins, *Legislative Leviathan: Party Government in the House* (Berkeley: University of California Press, 1993); Gary W. Cox and Keith T. Poole, "On Measuring Partisanship in Roll-Call Voting: The U.S. House of Representatives, 1877–1999," *American Journal of Political Science* 46 (3): 477–489; and Sean M. Theriault, *Party Polarization in Congress* (New York: Cambridge University Press, 2008).

64. *Congressional Record,* 100th Cong., 1st sess., June 23, 1987, S8438.

65. David Fahrenthold, "In Political Gamble, Reid Holds Senate Votes He Knows He'll Lose," *Washington Post,* December 9, 2010, A3.

66. Helmut Norpoth, "Explaining Party Cohesion in Congress: The Case of Shared Policy Attitudes," *American Political Science Review* 70 (December 1976): 1171.

67. Major Garrett, "The $100 Billion Cave," *National Journal,* February 19, 2011, 48.

68. Seung Min Kim, "New Democrats Try to Redefine 'Moderate,'" *Politico,* May 11, 2012, 15.

69. For discussion of the "creative class," see Richard Florida, "The Rise of the Creative Class," *Washington Monthly,* May 2002. For extended treatment of these different sources of electoral support for the Democratic Party, see John B. Judis and Ruy Teixeira, *The Emerging Democratic Majority* (New York: Simon and Schuster, 2004).

70. John F. Manley, "The Conservative Coalition in Congress," *American Behavioral Scientist* 17 (December 1973): 223–247; Barbara Sinclair, *Congressional Realignment: 1925–1978* (Austin: University of Texas Press, 1982); Mack C. Shelley, *The Permanent Majority: The Conservative Coalition in the United States Congress* (Tuscaloosa: University of Alabama Press, 1983).

71. See, for example, William A. Galston, "Can a Polarized American Party System Be 'Healthy'?" *Issues in Governance Studies* (Brookings), April 20, 2010, 1; and Thomas E. Mann and Norman J. Ornstein, *It's Even Worse Than It Looks, How the American Constitutional System Collided with the New Politics of Extremism* (New York: Basic Books, 2012), 51–58.

72. Stephen Gettinger, "R.I.P. to a Conservative Force," *CQ Weekly,* January 9, 1999, 82–83.

73. Sarah A. Binder, "The Disappearing Political Center," *Brookings Review* 15 (Fall 1996): 36–39. An extended analysis of the problem and its results is found in Sarah A. Binder, *Stalemate: Causes and Consequences of Legislative Gridlock* (Washington, DC: Brookings, 2003).

74. Keith T. Poole and Howard Rosenthal, "Patterns of Congressional Voting," *American Journal of Political Science* 35 (February 1991): 228–278; Keith T. Poole and Howard Rosenthal, *Congress: A Political-Economic History of Roll-Call Voting* (New York: Oxford University Press, 1997). See Norman J. Ornstein, Thomas F. Mann, and Michael J. Malbin, *Vital Statistics on Congress, 2008* (Washington, DC: Brookings, 2008), 160–161.

75. Using different measures of similar data, the same point is made in Morris P. Fiorina, with Samuel J. Adams and Jeremy C. Pope, *Culture War? The Myth of a Polarized America,* 2d ed. (New York: Pearson Longman, 2006), 16–21 and fig. 2-2.

76. Sean M. Theriault, "The Case of the Vanishing Moderates: Party Polarization in the Modern Congress" (paper presented at the 2003 annual meeting of the Western Political Science Association, Denver), fig. 1. Ideology scores from similar years (1969–1970 and 1999–2000) yield virtually the same results. Binder, *Stalemate,* 23–26.

77. Quoted by E. J. Dionne Jr., "The Real Pelosi," *Washington Post,* April 9, 2009, A17.

78. Binder, "Disappearing Political Center," 37. Binder defines centrists as those members who are closer to the ideological midpoint between the two parties than to the ideological center of their own party.

79. These estimates are based on Prof. Keith Poole's DW-NOMINATE scores for senators and House members provided on his website, http://voteview.com/dwnomin.htm.

80. The South includes the eleven states of the Confederacy.

81. David W. Rohde, "Electoral Forces," in "Parties and Leaders in the Postreform House (Chicago: University of Chicago Press, 1991), esp. 34–40.

82. Jeffrey M. Stonecash, Mark D. Brewer, and Mack Mariani, *Diverging Parties* (Boulder, CO: Westview Press, 2002).

83. David Wasserman, "The Bittersweet Mosaic," *National Journal,* April 14, 2012, 27.

84. Ibid., 30. Also see Naftali Bendavid, "Southern White Democrats Face End of Era in Congress," *Wall Street Journal,* August 9, 2012, A1; and Ed O'Keefe, "White Democratic Congressmen in the South Are Becoming an Endangered Species," *Washington Post,* September 7, 2012, A9.

85. R. Douglas Arnold, *The Logic of Congressional Action* (New Haven, CT: Yale University Press, 1990).

86. Ibid., 68.

87. Ibid., 84.

88. It is worth noting that recent presidents have taken stands on fewer issues. See Ornstein, Mann, and Malbin, *Vital Statistics on Congress, 2008,* 144–145.

89. Joseph Schatz, "Legislative Success, Political Peril," *CQ Weekly,* January 3, 2011 19.

90. Shawn Zeller, "Victory from Defeat," *CQ Weekly*, January 21, 2013, 120.

91. Ibid.

92. Roger H. Davidson, *The Role of the Congressman* (Indianapolis: Bobbs-Merrill, 1969), 22–23.

93. Robert L. Peabody, "Organization Theory and Legislative Behavior: Bargaining, Hierarchy, and Change in the U.S. House of Representatives" (paper presented at the 1963 annual meeting of the American Political Science Association, New York).

94. Carl J. Friedrich, *Constitutional Government and Democracy,* 4th ed. (Waltham, MA: Blaisdell Publishing, 1967), 269–270.

95. John W. Kingdon, *Congressmen's Voting Decisions,* 3d ed. (Ann Arbor: University of Michigan Press, 1989).

96. Quoted in John F. Bibby, ed., *Congress Off the Record* (Washington, DC: American Enterprise Institute, 1983), 22.

97. Quoted in Claudia Dreifus, "Exit Reasonable Right," *New York Times Magazine,* June 2, 1996, 26.

98. It is worth noting that a fall 2010 poll found that nearly "half of America—including nearly two-thirds of Republicans and 53 percent of independents—admires political leaders who refuse to compromise." But governing means bargaining. If half of Americans "admire political leaders who stick to their positions without compromising," then they are endorsing a formula for policy gridlock and polarized partisanship. Major Garrett, "Poll: Americans Want Their Leaders to Stand and Fight," *National Journal CongressDaily AM,* September 21, 2010, 1.

99. Meredith Shiner, "The Speaker of the Unruly," *CQ Weekly,* September 10, 2012, 1834.

100. Edward J. Derwinski, "The Art of Negotiation within the Congress," in *International Negotiation: Art and Science,* ed. Diane B. Bendahmane and John W. McDonald Jr. (Washington, DC: U.S. Department of State, Foreign Service Institute, 1984), 11.

101. Elliott Abrams, "Unforgettable Scoop Jackson," *Reader's Digest,* February 1985. Quotation cited in *Congressional Record,* 99th Cong., 1st sess., February 20, 1985, E478.

102. Quoted in David E. Rosenbaum, "The Favors of Rostenkowski: Tax Revision's Quid Pro Quo," *New York Times,* November 27, 1985, B6.

103. Quoted in John Sawyer, "Prescription Drug Vote Came Down to Emerson, Push for Reimportation; Missouri Republican Believes Measure Could Save Billions in Drug Costs," *St. Louis Post-Dispatch,* June 29, 2003, A5.

104. Ibid.

105. Lynn Sweet, "House OKs Foreign Drug Imports," *Chicago Sun-Times,* July 26, 2003, 3.

106. Quotes from Jonathan Allen, "Effective House Leadership Makes the Most of Majority," *CQ Weekly,* March 29, 2003, 751.

107. See, for example, Chris Frates, "Payoffs for States Get Reid to 60," *Politico,* December 19, 2010, (online edition).

108. Gilmour, *Strategic Disagreement,* 4.

109. Gary W. Cox and Jonathan N. Katz, "Gerrymandering Roll Calls in Congress, 1879–2000," *American Journal of Political Science* 51 (January 2007): 117.

110. See William H. Riker, *The Theory of Political Coalitions* (New Haven, CT: Yale University Press, 1962), 32. Theorists define legislative bargaining situations formally as *n*-person, zero-sum games in which side payments are permitted— that is, a sizable number of participants are involved; when some participants win, others must lose; and participants can trade items outside the substantive issues under consideration.

111. John G. Stewart, "Two Strategies of Leadership: Johnson and Mansfield," in *Congressional Behavior,* ed. Nelson W. Polsby (New York: Random House, 1971), 67.

112. Russell Hardin, "Hollow Victory: The Minimum Winning Coalition," *American Political Science Review* 79 (December 1976): 1202–1214.

113. Breaux, "Congress's Lost Art of Compromise," 17.

114. Binder, *Stalemate,* 127.

115. Robert J. Dole, quoting Dirksen, in remarks to the Senate, March 29, 2000. Dole quoted in *The Hill,* April 5, 2000, 32.

116. Clinton T. Brass, "Shutdown of the Federal Government: Causes, Processes, and Effects," Congressional Research Service Report RL34680, September 27, 2011. Note that "funding gaps" occur when there is a lag between the expiration of a continuing resolution (CR) and the enactment of a new one. In the absence of a CR, agencies begin their shutdown, even if it is only for a few days. For further information about funding gaps, see Jessica Tollestrup, "Federal Funding Gaps: A Brief Overview," Congressional Research Service Report RS20348, January 19, 2012. A summary of the controversial 1995–1996 shutdowns can be found in the *Congressional Quarterly Almanac, 1995* (Washington, DC: Congressional Quarterly, 1996), 11-3–11-6.

CHAPTER 10

1. Steven T. Dennis, "A Preview of Cliffs to Come," *CQ Weekly,* December 3, 2012, 2414.

2. Lori Montgomery and Zachary A. Goldfarb, "Hill Leaders and Obama Show Unity on 'Cliff,'" *Washington Post,* November 17, 2012, A12.

3. Jake Sherman and Carrie Budoff Brown, "Little Movement in GOP Cliff Offer," *Politico,* December 4, 2012, 4.

4. Michael Grunwald, "The Party of No," *Time,* September 13, 2012, 4. The McConnell quote is also from this article.

5. Ben Smith, "Health Reform Foes Plan Obama's 'Waterloo,'" *Politico,* July 17, 2009, 1.

6. Charlie Cook, "An Insular Obama," *National Journal,* November 10, 2012, 68.

7. Bob Woodward, *The Price of Politics* (New York: Simon & Schuster, 2012), 58.

8. Manu Raju, "Debt Talks Test McConnell, Obama," *Politico,* July 1, 2011, 10. It is interesting to note that at the start of the 111th Congress, Senator McConnell extended President Obama "an open invitation to attend the weekly GOP caucus luncheons." Senator McConnell's

reported purpose was to "develop working ties to a president he never got to know particularly well during the previous four years, when Obama was the junior senator from Illinois." See Alan K. Ota, "Collaboration or Collision?" *CQ Weekly*, January 26, 2009, 178.

9. Aaron Lorenzo, "Rep. Bachus Leads Assault on What GOP Labels Regulatory Overreach of Dodd-Frank," *Daily Report for Executives*, January 27, 2011, EE7.

10. Quoted in Michael Memoli, "Mitch McConnell's Remarks on 2012 Draw White House Ire," *Los Angeles Times*, October 27, 2012 (online edition).

11. Amie Parnes, "Raring for a Fight, President Obama Heads into His Second Term Swinging," *The Hill*, January 9, 2013, 6. Also see Jacob Weisberg, "A New-Model President in No Mood to Compromise," *Financial Times,* January 11, 2013, 9.

12. Rosalind S. Helderman, "Outgoing Congress Remains Unproductive to the End," *Washington Post*, December 30, 2012, A11.

13. Ross K. Baker, "Democrats, Not So Fast," *USA Today,* June 19, 2008, 11A.

14. Jim VandeHei and Mike Allen, "Lesson: Communication Is More Than Eloquence," *Politico*, March 20, 2009, 7.

15. See Stephen Wayne, *The Legislative Presidency* (New York: Harper and Row, 1978).

16. Charles O. Jones, *Separate but Equal Branches: Congress and the Presidency* (Chatham, NJ: Chatham House, 1995), 138–157.

17. See Norman J. Ornstein, "Theories of the Presidency," in *Encyclopedia of the American Presidency,* vol. 4, ed. Leonard Levy and Louis Fisher (New York: Simon and Schuster, 1994), 1458–1462.

18. Richard E. Neustadt, *Presidential Power* (New York: John Wiley, 1960), 23.

19. Ibid., 16.

20. Leonard D. White, *The Federalists* (New York: Macmillan, 1948), 55.

21. Leonard D. White, *The Jeffersonians* (New York: Macmillan, 1951), 35.

22. Paul C. Light, *The President's Agenda* (Baltimore: Johns Hopkins University Press, 1982), 230–231.

23. John A. Farrell, *Tip O'Neill and the Democratic Century* (Boston: Little, Brown, 2001), 553.

24. Susan Page and Mimi Hall, "Will Doing 'Big Things' Wind Up Costing Obama?" *USA Today,* May 12, 2010, 2A.

25. Michael Gerson, "In Victory, Obama Failed," *Washington Post*, October 30, 2012, AS19.

26. Michael Scherer, "Mr. Unpopular," *Time*, September 13, 2010, 31.

27. Susan Davis, "Go Big and Go Home," *National Journal*, December 18, 2010, 39.

28. Mark Wegner, "Hastert: GOP to Take Political Offensive," *CongressDaily AM*, March 15, 2004, 5. National Journal, Inc., publishes this legislative bulletin.

29. Linda Feldmann, "Bold Moves, Then a Backlash," *Christian Science Monitor,* July 19, 2010, 17.

30. Jennifer Steinhauer and Robert Pear, "G.O.P. Newcomers Set Out to Undo Obama Victories," *New York Times,* January 3, 2011, A1.

31. Zachary A. Goldfarb, "Obama, Congress May Get Breather on Debt Limit," *Washington Post*, April 26, 2013, A10.

32. "Taking the Fight Outside," *Economist*, November 17, 2012, 30.

33. Lyndon B. Johnson, *The Vantage Point* (New York: Popular Library, 1971), 448.

34. Jack Valenti, "Some Advice on the Care and Feeding of Congressional Egos," *Los Angeles Times,* April 23, 1978, 3.

35. Richard Berke, "Courting Congress Nonstop, Clinton Looks for an Alliance," *New York Times,* March 8, 1993, A1.

36. Roy P. Basler, ed., *The Collected Works of Abraham Lincoln,* vol. 3 (New Brunswick: Rutgers University Press, 1953), 27.

37. Samuel Kernell, *Going Public: New Strategies of Presidential Leadership,* 3d ed. (Washington, DC: CQ Press, 1997), 2. Also see James Ceaser et al., "The Rise of the Rhetorical Presidency," *Presidential Studies Quarterly* 21 (Spring 1981): 158–171.

38. Richard M. Pious, *The American Presidency* (New York: Basic Books, 1979), 194. Also see George C. Edwards III, *The Public Presidency* (New York: St. Martin's Press, 1983).

39. George C. Edwards III, *On Deaf Ears: The Limits of the Bully Pulpit* (New Haven, CT: Yale University Press, 2003); *Governing by Campaigning: The Politics of the Bush Presidency* (New York: Pearson Longman, 2008); and *The Strategic President: Persuasion and Opportunity in Presidential Leadership* (Princeton, NJ: Princeton University Press, 2009).

40. Farrell, *Tip O'Neill and the Democratic Century,* 553.

41. *Wall Street Journal,* December 4, 1987, 8D.

42. George Hager, "For GOP, a New Song—Same Ending," *Congressional Quarterly Weekly Report,* June 14, 1997, 1406.

43. Paul Bedard, "Living, Dying by the Polls," *Washington Times,* April 30, 1993, A1.

44. David S. Broder, "The Reticent President," *Washington Post,* April 22, 2001, B7. Also see Mike Allen, "Bush on Stage: Deft or Just Lacking Depth?" *Washington Post,* February 19, 2001, A8–A9.

45. Ibid., A20.

46. Quoted in Jeff Eller, "It's Time to Rewrite the Bully Pulpit," *Politico,* November 18, 2008, 29.

47. Peter Baker, "President Sticks to the Script, with a Little Help," *New York Times,* March 6, 2009, A16. President Obama uses a teleprompter regularly for both major addresses and routine announcements.

48. Christi Parsona and Mark Z. Barabak, "Obama to Sit Down with Leno on *The Tonight Show,*" *Los Angeles Times,* March 17, 2009 (online edition).

49. Jonathan Martin, "Obama Wants Filter-Free News," *Politico,* March 24, 2009, 17.

50. Sheryl Gay Stolberg, "Obama Makes History in Live Internet Video Chat," *New York Times,* March 27, 2009, A15.

51. Cecilia Kang, "Obama to Hold First Twitter Town Hall," *Washington Post,* July 6, 2011, A4; and Hayley Peterson, "Obama to Field 'Tweets' On Jobs, Economy," *Washington Examiner,* July 6, 2011, 12.

52. Darlene Superville, "Obama Sets Up Web Page for Citizen Petitions," *Washington Times,* September 2, 2011, A4.

53. Chris Cillizza, "Three Lessons for Obama from His First Four Years," *Washington Post,* January 21, 2013, A2.

54. Michael Gerson, "The Lost Communicator," *Washington Post,* September 10, 2010, A27.

55. John Stanton, "Kaufman: Democrats Muffed Their Message," *Roll Call,* September 30, 2010 (online edition).

56. John Harwood, "After 15 Months in Office, Policy vs. Politics for Obama," *New York Times,* April 26, 2010, A13.

57. The figures for both the informal and formal press sessions are cited in Donovan Slack, "Obama Lags in First-Term Press Conferences," *Politico,* January 16, 2013, 11. On the other hand, the president has given numerous TV interviews. See George E. Condon Jr., "Tuned Out," *National Journal,* November 5, 2011, 26–33.

58. Gary Lee Malecha and Daniel J. Reagan, *The Public Congress, Congressional Deliberation in a New Media Age* (New York: Routledge, 2012), 137.

59. Quoted in Walter Pincus, "More from Nixon the Political Scientist," *Washington Post,* January 26, 2010, A13.

60. See, for example, Richard P. Nathan, *The Administrative Presidency* (New York: John Wiley, 1983); and Robert R. Durant, *The Administrative Presidency Revisited* (Albany: State University of New York Press, 1992).

61. William G. Howell and David E. Lewis, "Agencies by Presidential Design," *Journal of Politics,* November 2002, 1096.

62. Ibid., 1100.

63. William G. Howell, *Power without Persuasion: The Politics of Direct Presidential Action*

(Princeton, NJ: Princeton University Press, 2003). The Obama administration has abandoned the term *enemy combatant* for those held at Guantánamo Bay, Cuba. See David Savage, "No More 'Enemy Combatants' at Guantánamo Bay," *Los Angeles Times,* March 14, 2009 (online edition).

64. Josh Gerstein, "Obama Unveils Gun Proposals," *Politico,* January 17, 2013, 1.

65. Joel Achenbach, Scott Higham, and Sari Horwitz, "No Compromise, No Gun Legislation," *Washington Post,* January 13, 2013, A7.

66. See Kenneth Mayer, *With the Stroke of a Pen: Executive Orders and Presidential Power* (Princeton, NJ: Princeton University Press, 2001).

67. Elizabeth Shogren, "President Plans Blitz of Executive Orders Soon," *Los Angeles Times,* July 5, 1998, A11.

68. Linda Feldmann, "Faith-Based Initiatives Quietly Lunge Forward," *Christian Science Monitor,* February 6, 2003, 2.

69. Gregg Carlstrom, "Midnight Rule-Making Bonanza," *Federal Times,* November 3, 2008, 19.

70. Ceci Connolly and R. Jeffrey Smith, "Obama Positioned to Quickly Reverse Bush Actions," *Washington Post,* November 9, 2008, A16.

71. Charlie Savage, "Shift on Executive Power Lets Obama Bypass Rivals," *New York Times,* April 23, 2012, A1. See Andrew Rudalevige, "Executive Orders and Presidential Unilateralism," *Presidential Studies Quarterly,* March 2012, 138–160.

72. Lyndsey Layton, "Education Overhaul Largely Bypasses Congress," *Washington Post,* September 21, 2012, A1.

73. David Harrison, "Bypassing Congress, White House Grants Temporary Legal Status to Thousands," *CQ Today,* June 18, 2012, 3.

74. Aaron Wildavsky, "The Two Presidencies Thesis Revisited at a Time of Political Dissensus," in *The Beleaguered Presidency,* ed. Aaron Wildavsky (Brunswick, NJ: Transaction Publishers, 1991), 29. Wildavsky's article originally appeared in the December 1966 issue of *Transaction* magazine.

75. Ibid., 47–65.

76. Dan Balz, "Bush Lays out Ambitious Plan for Long Term," *Washington Post,* May 6, 2001, A10.

77. Ronald Brownstein, "Strategies Shift as Bush Drops in Polls," *Los Angeles Times,* July 5, 2001, A9.

78. John Harwood and Jeanne Cummings, "Bush's Approval Rating Slips to 50%, a 5-Year Presidential Low," *Wall Street Journal,* June 28, 2001, A18.

79. Ron Faucheux, "Presidential Popularity: A History of Highs and Lows," *CQ Daily Monitor,* February 7, 2002, 14.

80. Editorial, "Bush's Big Regret," *Los Angeles Times,* December 4, 2008 (online edition).

81. Woodrow Wilson, *Congressional Government* (Boston: Houghton Mifflin, 1885), 52.

82. Kevin R. Kosar, "Regular Vetoes and Pocket Vetoes: An Overview," Congressional Research Service Report RS22188, January 26, 2009, 1.

83. Kara Rowland, "Obama's Veto Pen Likely to See More Action in 112th Congress," *Washington Times,* January 12, 2011, A4.

84. Alexis Simendinger, "The Veto-Free Zone," *National Journal,* December 17, 2005, 3888.

85. Ethan Wallison, "Can President Bush Stay Veto-Free for Four More Years?" *Roll Call,* January 24, 2005, 10.

86. Jill Barshay, "Popularity Not Required," *CQ Weekly,* January 1, 2007, 45.

87. Nancy Ognanovich, "Obama Veto Threat Said to Doom Spending Earmarks for Next Two Years," *Daily Report for Executives,* January 27, 2011, A-22. Also see Sam Youngman, "Obama Promises That He'll Veto All Earmarks," *The Hill,* January 26, 2011, 1.

88. Dave Boyer, "For Obama, Veto Isn't Overriding Concern," *Washington Times,* December 26, 2012, A1.

89. Dave Boyer, "Republicans Question Obama's Use of Autopen to Sign 'Cliff' Bill," *Washington Times,* January 4, 2013, A3.

90. *Los Angeles Times,* March 18, 1988, part I, 4.

91. See T. J. Halstead, "Presidential Signing Statements: Constitutional and Institutional Implications," Congressional Research Service Report RL33667, April 13, 2007.

92. Ibid., 9.

93. Charles Savage, "Bush Challenges Hundreds of Laws; President Cites Powers of His Office," *Boston Globe,* April 30, 2006, A1. Also see Phillip J. Cooper, "George W. Bush, Edgar Allan Poe, and the Use and Abuse of Presidential Signing Statements," *Presidential Studies Quarterly* (September 2005): 515–532.

94. Dan Friedman, "On the Other Hand," *National Journal,* March 28, 2009, 54.

95. Michael D. Shear, "Obama Pledges to Limit Use of Signing Statements," *Washington Post,* March 10, 2009, A4.

96. Charlie Savage, "Obama Says He Can Ignore Some Parts of Spending Bill," *New York Times,* March 12, 2009, A18.

97. David Nather, "Grassley Blows Whistle on Obama for Signing Statement," *CQ Today,* March 16, 2009, 10.

98. Aaron Lorenzo, "Obama Review of Past Signing Statements Does Not Signal End of Presidential Practice," *Daily Report for Executives,* March 10, 2009, A-25.

99. Charlie Savage, "Obama Disputes Detainee Limits in Defense Bill," *New York Times,* January 4, 2013, A14.

100. Laura Meckler, "Obama Shifts View of Executive Power," *Wall Street Journal,* March 30, 2012, A12.

101. *Congressional Record,* 110th Cong., 2d sess., October 2, 2008, E2197.

102. Louis Fisher, "The Pocket Veto: Its Current Status," Congressional Research Service Report RL30909, March 30, 2001, summary.

103. Erika Niedowski, "GOP to Skirt Line-Item Veto," *The Hill,* February 12, 1997, 24.

104. John Broder, "Clinton Vetoes Eight Projects, Two in States of Leadership," *New York Times,* October 18, 1997, A10.

105. Helen Dewar and Joan Biskupic, "Line-Item Vote Struck Down: Backers Push for Alternative," *Washington Post,* June 26, 1998, A1.

106. Neustadt, *Presidential Power,* 187.

107. Glenn Thrush, "With the 111th, the Age of Pelosi Dawns," *Politico,* January 6, 2009, 16.

108. Doyle McManus, "The Death of the Moderate Republican," *Los Angeles Times,* November 18, 2012 (online edition).

109. James B. Stewart, "In Budget Talks, Getting To 'Yes,'" *New York Times,* January 19, 2013 B1.

110. Johnson, *Vantage Point,* 448.

111. Niels Lesniewski and Steven T. Dennis, "Schmoozer in Chief Helps to Save the Day," *CQ Weekly,* January 7, 2013, 14.

112. Peter Baker, "Washington Worries about Its New Power Couple," *New York Times,* November 10, 2010, A18.

113. See Joseph P. Harris, *The Advice and Consent of the Senate* (Berkeley: University of California Press, 1953); and G. Calvin Mackenzie, *The Politics of Presidential Appointments* (New York: Free Press, 1981).

114. James MacGregor Burns, *Presidential Government* (Boston: Houghton Mifflin, 1966), 284.

115. See, for example, Stephen J. Wayne, "Great Expectations: What People Want from Presidents," in *Rethinking the Presidency,* ed. Thomas E. Cronin (Boston: Little, Brown, 1982), 185–199.

116. Dean Scott, "Next President Likely to Have Limited Chance for Passage of Emission Caps, Senator Says," *Daily Report for Executives,* August 4, 2008, A-15.

117. Arthur M. Schlesinger Jr. and Alfred De Grazia, *Congress and the Presidency: Their Role in Modern Times* (Washington, DC: American Enterprise Institute, 1967), 1.

118. Wilson, *Congressional Government;* Burns, *Presidential Government.*

119. See Joseph S. Clark, *Congress: The Sapless Branch* (New York: Harper and Row, 1964); and Arthur Schlesinger Jr., *The Imperial Presidency* (Boston: Houghton Mifflin, 1973).

120. Andrew Restuccia, "Cantor Assails Obama's 'Imperial Presidency,'" *Politico*, October 24, 2012, 28.

121. David Mayhew, *Divided We Govern* (New Haven, CT: Yale University Press, 1991), 198.

CHAPTER 11

1. A Pew Research Center poll in 2013 "found that 53 percent of adults feel that the federal government poses a threat to their personal rights and freedoms," compared to 36 percent in 1995. See "Majority of Voters Say Government Threatens Their Liberties," *The Hill*, February 4, 2013, 9.

2. Bill Bishop, "Don't Trust Government? It's a Global Phenomenon," *Politico*, April 29, 2010, 26. Also see James A. Barnes, "The Great Distrust," *National Journal*, March 26, 2011, 24–28.

3. Michael Walzer, "The Popular Patron," *New Republic*, April 9, 1984, 35.

4. David S. Broder, "So, Now Bigger Is Better?" *Washington Post*, January 12, 2003, B1.

5. Janet Hook, "Obama's Budget Is the End of an Era," *Los Angeles Times*, February 27, 2009 (online edition).

6. Donald F. Kettl, "Heading for Disaster," *Government Executive*, February 2009, 22. "Governmentalizing the economy" is Professor Kettl's phrase.

7. Nancy Cook, "The 51 Percent," *National Journal*, February 11, 2012, 14.

8. "Transcript: Obama on Taxes, Economy, and START," interview, National Public Radio, December 10, 2010, 5.

9. Lee H. Hamilton, "We'll Never Agree on the Role of Government . . . And That's Fine," *Newsletter,* Center on Congress, Indiana University, September 12, 2012, 2–3.

10. Quoted in E. J. Dionne Jr., "Back from the Dead: Neoprogressivism in the '90s," *American Prospect*, September–October 1996, 25.

11. Kate Zerkike, "Proposed Amendment Would Enable States to Repeal Federal Law," *New York Times*, December 19, 2010, A13.

12. Sean Wilentz, "States of Anarchy," *New Republic*, April 29, 2010, 5.

13. Jonathan Walters, "Preempting Washington," *Governing*, September 2004, 12.

14. *Congressional Record,* 106th Cong., 1st sess., November 5, 1997, S11737.

15. Richard E. Neustadt, "Politicians and Bureaucrats," in *The Congress and America's Future,* 2d ed., ed. David B. Truman (Englewood Cliffs, NJ: Prentice-Hall, 1973), 199. See also Louis Fisher, *The Politics of Shared Power: Congress and the Executive,* 3d ed. (Washington, DC: CQ Press, 1993).

16. See Harold Relyea, "Executive Branch Reorganization and Management Initiatives: A Brief Overview," Congressional Research Service Report RL33441, May 30, 2006.

17. *Congressional Record,* 109th Cong., 1st sess., February 15, 2005, S1437.

18. Keith Koffler, "Confirmation Wars Could Be Thing of the Past," *Roll Call,* November 21, 2008, 10.

19. Steven V. Roberts, "In Confirmation Process, Hearings Offer a Stage," *New York Times,* February 8, 1989, B7.

20. "*Noel Canning* Would Have Nixed Hundreds," *Daily Report for Executives,* February 6, 2013, A-10.

21. Robert Barnes and Steven Mufson, "Obama Recess Picks Invalid," *Washington Post,* January 26, 2013, A1.

22. Charlie Savage and Steven Greenhouse, "Court Rejects Obama Move to Fill Posts," *New York Times*, January 26, 2013, A1.

23. Norman Ornstein, "Court Ruling on Recess Appointments Is an Exercise of Judicial Overreach," *Roll Call*, February 7, 2013, 12. Also see Sally Katzen, "What about the Filibuster?" *Washington Post*, February 4, 2013, A15.

24. Brian Friel, "Senate to Block Recess Appointments," *CQ Today*, September 30, 2010, 20; Ezra Klein, "Same Old Senate Employs a New Maneuver," *Washington Post*, October 1, 2010, A15.

25. See Henry Hogue, *Temporarily Filling Presidentially Appointed, Senate-Confirmed Positions*, Congressional Research Service Report RS21412, January 25, 2008.

26. See, for example, Will Englund, "Czar Wars," *National Journal*, February 14, 2009, 16–24.

27. Jim Puzzanghera and Peter Nicholas, "Obama Decision to Avoid Confirmation Battle for Elizabeth Warren Is Hailed and Criticized," *Los Angeles Times*, September 18, 2010 (online edition). Also see John Maggs, "Warring over Warren," *National Journal*, July 1, 2010, 41–42.

28. Mark J. Rozell and Mitchel A. Sollenberger, "Congress Should Deal with Unchecked Czars," *Roll Call*, February 1, 2011, 14.

29. Bruce Ackerman, "A Role for Congress to Reclaim," *Washington Post*, March 11, 2009, A15.

30. Ibid.; William Schneider, "New Rules for the Game of Politics," *National Journal*, April 1, 1989, 830.

31. See Dennis Thompson, *Ethics in Congress* (Washington, DC: Brookings, 1995).

32. Anne Kornblut and Michael Shear, "Obama Says He Erred in Nominations," *Washington Post*, February 4, 2009, A1.

33. Norman Ornstein, "Confirmation Process Leaves Government in Serious Gridlock," *Roll Call*, March 25, 2009, 6.

34. Edward Luce and Krishna Guha, "Appointments Bottleneck at Treasury Tightens," *Financial Times*, March 19, 2009, 4.

35. Philip Rucker, "Potential Obama Appointees Face Extensive Vetting," *Washington Post*, November 18, 2008, A12.

36. Nancy Kassebaum Baker and Franklin Raines, "Uncle Sam Wants a Few Good Appointees," *Los Angeles Times*, April 5, 2001, A17. Baker and Raines were cochairs of the Presidential Appointee Initiative Advisory Board, a project of the Brookings Institution. Its basic goal was to propose improvements in the presidential appointment process. See *To Form a Government: A Bipartisan Plan to Improve the Presidential Appointments Process* (Washington, DC: Brookings, April 2001).

37. G. Calvin Mackenzie, "Hung Out to Dry," *Washington Post*, April 1, 2001, B5.

38. Alan K. Ota, "A Capital's Empty Chairs," *CQ Weekly*, July 5, 2010, 1604.

39. Brady Dennis and Scott Wilson, "Warren Takes Post; Liberals Cheer," *Washington Post*, September 18, 2010, A8.

40. See Clay Johnson and Mack McLarty, "A Better Way to Govern," *The Aspen Idea* (Summer 2012): 64–66.

41. For a detailed review of these nomination changes—statutory and Senate standing order—see Maeve P. Carey, "Presidential Appointments, the Senate's Confirmation Process, and Changes Made in the 112th Congress," Congressional Research Service Report R41872, October 9, 2012, 1–25.

42. Paul C. Light, *Thickening Government* (Washington, DC: Brookings and Governance Institute, 1995), esp. 111–116.

43. Paul C. Light, "Big Bureaucracy," *Washington Times*, May 10, 2001, A17.

44. Christopher Lee, "Agencies Getting Heavier on Top," *Washington Times*, July 23, 2004, A27.

45. Stephen Barr, "Title Creep Reported at Agencies," *Washington Post*, March 8, 1999, A17.

46. Fareed Zakaria, "Be More Like Ike," *Newsweek*, August 28 and 30, 2010, 18.

47. Paul C. Light, *A Government Ill Executed* (Cambridge, MA: Harvard University Press, 2008), 53.

48. Lee, "Agencies Getting Heavier on Top," A27.

49. G. Calvin Mackenzie, ed., *Innocent until Nominated* (Washington, DC: Brookings, 2001), 30.

50. Jim Rutenberg, "Secret Donors Finance Fight against Hagel," *New York Times*, January 27, 2013, 1.

51. Doyle McManus and Robert Shogun, "Acrid Tone Reflects Long-Term Trend for Nominations," *Los Angeles Times*, March 9, 1997, A6.

52. Peter Grier, "Why Senate Roughs Up Some Cabinet Nominees," *Christian Science Monitor*, March 19, 1997, 3.

53. Stephen Barr, "Plum Book Counts Political Jobs in Executive, Legislative Branches," *Washington Post*, December 15, 2004, B2.

54. See Henry Hogue, "Statutory Qualifications for Executive Branch Positions," Congressional Research Service Report RL33886, February 20, 2007.

55. *Congressional Record*, 105th Cong., 1st sess., September 12, 1996, S10367.

56. Shankar Vedantam, "Who Are the Better Managers—Political Appointees or Career Bureaucrats?" *Washington Post*, November 24, 2008, A6.

57. Alyssa Rosenberg, "Minding the Hatch Act," *Government Executive*, October 2008, 76.

58. Joe Davidson, "Guidelines on Hatch Act and Social Media Are 'Rules of the Road' for Upcoming Elections," *Washington Post*, August 24, 2010, B3.

59. Bart Jansen, "Details of the Lobbying Rules Law," *CQ Weekly*, September 17, 2007, 2693.

60. Zachary A. Goldfarb, "Regulators See Chance to Cash In," *Washington Post*, December 30, 2010, A11.

61. Kenneth P. Vogel, "Not Even Obama Can Halt the Hill's Revolving Door," *Politico*, January 18, 2011, 6.

62. See the three-part series on the post-9/11 explosion of the intelligence community in Dana Priest and William Arkin, "A Hidden World, Growing Beyond Control," *Washington Post*, July 19, 2010, A1; "National Security, Inc.," July 20, 2010, A1; and "The Secrets Next Door," July 21, 2010, A1.

63. Jackie Calmes, "Cuts to Achieve Goal for Deficit, but Toll Is High," *New York Times*, March 3, 2013, 26.

64. Craig Whitlock, "Thousands of Defense Jobs to Be Eliminated," *Washington Post*, August 10, 2010, A4.

65. Ellen Nakashima, "Pentagon Hires Out More Than In," *Washington Post*, April 3, 2001, A19.

66. Ibid.

67. Paul C. Light, "The True Size of Government," *Government Executive*, January 1999, 20. Also see Light, *The True Size of Government* (Washington, DC: Brookings, 1990). Periodically, Light updates the number of contract workers. In his August 2006 revision, he compares the number of contract workers in 1999 (6.968 million) to 2005 (10.526 million), a 51.1 percent increase.

68. Joe Davidson, "Defining 'Inherently Governmental' and Role of Contractors in War," *Washington Post*, June 22, 2010, B3.

69. *Congressional Record*, 100th Cong., 1st sess., July 29, 1987, S10850.

70. Richard S. Beth, "The Congressional Review Act and Possible Consolidation into a Single Measure of Resolutions Disapproving Regulations," Congressional Research Service Report R40163, January 26, 2009, 8.

71. Rebecca Adams, "Republicans Dust Off a Little-Used Tool to Go after Overhaul Rules," *CQ Today*, November 29, 2010, 3.

72. Billy House, "House Republicans Are Dusting Off an Old Weapon to Target Obama Laws," *National Journal CongressDaily PM Update*, January 11, 2011, 12.

73. Stephen Losey, "Rule-Making's New Mass Appeal," *Federal Times*, June 15, 2009, 1, 22.

74. Matthew Wald, "Court Voids a Bush Move on Energy," *New York Times,* January 14, 2004, A12.

75. Cyril Zaneski, "Escape Artist," *Government Executive,* March 2001, 29.

76. Susan Dudley, "Government Regulations: Rhetoric vs. Reality," *Politico,* September 13, 2012, 28. Also see Jia Lynn Yang, "Do Federal Regulations Really Kill Jobs?" *Washington Post,* November 14, 2011, A1.

77. The quotations are found in Cheryl Bolen, "Federal Agencies Told to Take into Account Cumulative Costs of Rules on Businesses," *Daily Report for Executives,* March 21, 2012, A-14; and Aaron Lorenzo, "OIRA Touts $10 Billion in Savings from Finalized Regulatory Reforms," *Daily Report for Executives,* August 24, 2011, AA-1.

78. Larry Margasak, "GOP Agenda: Major Impact May Be on 2012 Election," *The Washington Examiner,* January 3, 2011, 13.

79. Editorial, "A Coming Assault on the E.P.A.," *New York Times,* December 25, 2010, A20.

80. Amy Harder, "House GOP Push on EPA Running out of Steam," *National Journal Daily,* December 6, 2012, 8.

81. Dudley, "Government Regulations: Rhetoric vs. Reality," 28.

82. Frank Ackerman, Lisa Heinzerling, James K. Hammitt, and Milton C. Weinstein, "Balancing Lives against Lucre," *Los Angeles Times,* February 25, 2004, A17. Ackerman and Heinzerling are economists, and Hammitt and Weinstein are risk analysis experts.

83. *Congressional Record,* 104th Cong., 1st sess., July 11, 1995, S9705.

84. Ibid., S9697.

85. Joseph S. Clark, *Congress: The Sapless Branch* (New York: Harper and Row, 1964), 63–64.

86. David B. Frohnmayer, "The Separation of Powers: An Essay on the Vitality of a Constitutional Idea," *Oregon Law Review* (Spring 1973): 330.

87. David B. Truman, *The Governmental Process,* rev. ed. (New York: Knopf, 1971), 439.

88. Woodrow Wilson, *Congressional Government* (Boston: Houghton Mifflin, 1885), 297.

89. Lisa Rein, "Conversations: Gene L. Dorado," *Washington Post,* December 30, 2010, B3.

90. David Rogers, "Sen. Lott Becomes GOP's New Standard-bearer, but His Style Will Be Tested in the Next Congress," *Wall Street Journal,* November 15, 1996, A16.

91. Wilson, *Congressional Government,* 303.

92. Rochelle Stanfield, "Plotting Every Move," *National Journal,* March 26, 1988, 796.

93. *Watkins v. United States,* 354 U.S. 178 (1957). See also James Hamilton, *The Power to Probe* (New York: Vantage Books, 1976).

94. William S. Cohen and George J. Mitchell, *Men of Zeal: A Candid Inside Story of the Iran-Contra Hearings* (New York: Viking Penguin, 1988), 305.

95. *Immigration and Naturalization Service v. Chadha,* 462 U.S. 919 (1983).

96. Louis Fisher, in *Extensions* (Carl Albert Congressional Research and Studies Center newsletter) (Spring 1984): 2.

97. John R. Johannes, "Study and Recommend: Statutory Reporting Requirements as a Technique of Legislative Initiative—A Research Note," *Western Political Quarterly* (December 1976): 589–596.

98. Guy Gugliotta, "Reporting on a Practice That's Ripe for Reform," *Washington Post,* February 11, 1997, A19.

99. John T. Bennett, "Fewer Reports to Congress? DoD Move Could Backfire, Experts Warn," *Federal Times,* October 18, 2010, 11.

100. Ibid.

101. Michael W. Kirst, *Government without Passing Laws* (Chapel Hill: University of North Carolina Press, 1969).

102. Joseph A. Davis, "War Declared over Report-Language Issue," *Congressional Quarterly Weekly Report,* June 25, 1988, 1752–1753; David Rapp, "OMB's Miller Backs Away from Report-Language Battle," *Congressional Quarterly Weekly Report,* July 9, 1988, 1928.

103. Sen. Chuck Grassley, "The Federal Government Needs an IG in Chief," *Politico*, July 22, 2009, 30. Also see Charles S. Clark, "Into the Limelight," *Government Executive*, March 2011, 17–24.

104. R. Jeffrey Smith, "Initiative on Worker Safety Gets Poor Marks," *Washington Post*, April 2, 2009, A6.

105. Otto Kreisher, "Pentagon IG Details Waste in Military Contractor Spending," *National Journal CongressDaily AM*, February 27, 2009, 8.

106. Jared Allen, "'Personal Pain' Is Teed Up for Head of HUD," *The Hill*, July 30, 2010, 8.

107. Greta Wodele, "DHS Facing Appropriators' Wrath for Missing Deadlines," *National Journal CongressDaily PM*, February 17, 2005, 2.

108. Slade Gorton and Larry Craig, "Congress's Call to Accounting," *Washington Post*, July 27, 1998, A23.

109. Jason A. MacDonald, "Limitation Riders and Congressional Influence over Bureaucratic Policy Decisions," *American Political Science Review*, November 2010, 781. Also see Jessica Tollestrup, "The Appropriations Process and Limitation Amendments: A Case Study of Party Politics on the House Floor," in Jacob Strauss, ed., *Party and Procedure in the United States Congress* (Lanham, MD.: Rowan & Littlefield, 2012), 61–99.

110. *Congressional Record,* 95th Cong., 1st sess., April 30, 1975, E2080.

111. Alan Baron and Michael Gerhardt, "Porteous Impeachment: A First," *National Law Journal,* January 17, 2011, 34.

112. See Peter Baker, *The Breach: Inside the Impeachment and Trial of William Jefferson Clinton* (New York: Scribner, 2000).

113. See Joel D. Aberbach, *Keeping a Watchful Eye: The Politics of Congressional Oversight* (Washington, DC: Brookings, 1990); and James Q. Wilson, *Bureaucracy: What Governmental Agencies Do and Why They Do It* (New York: Basic Books, 1991).

114. Richard Cohen, "King of Oversight," *Government Executive*, September 1988, 17.

115. David Nather, "Congress as Watchdog: Asleep on the Job?" *CQ Weekly*, May 22, 2004, 1190.

116. *Congressional Record,* 111th Cong., 2d sess., September 29, 2010, S7705.

117. Larry Margasak, "Biden Makes Peace Offering to Rising House Republican," *Washington Times*, December 14, 2010, A4.

118. Susan Crabtree and Michael Gleeson, "Issa Surveys Broad Spectrum of Businesses on Obama Regs," *The Hill*, January 6, 2011, 4.

119. Joel D. Aberbach, "The Congressional Committee Intelligence System: Information, Oversight, and Change," *Congress and the Presidency* 14 (Spring 1987): 51–76; Mathew McCubbins and Thomas Schwartz, "Congressional Oversight Overlooked: Police Patrol versus Fire Alarm," *American Journal of Political Science* (February 1984): 165–177.

120. Bill Myers, "'Google Your Government' Database Bill Signed into Law," *Examiner*, September 29, 2006, 17.

121. Jennifer Martinez, "GOP to Public: We Want to Know What You'd Cut," *Politico*, January 20, 2011, 6.

122. Lyndsey Layton, "'Citizen Regulators' Take Toy Safety Testing into Their Own Hands," *Washington Post*, December 26, 2010, A3.

123. Louis Fisher, "Micromanagement by Congress: Reality and Mythology" (paper presented at a conference sponsored by the American Enterprise Institute, Washington, DC, April 8–9, 1988), 8. See also David S. Broder and Stephen Barr, "Hill's Micromanagement of Cabinet Blurs Separation of Powers," *Washington Post*, July 25, 1993, A1.

CHAPTER 12

1. Alexis de Tocqueville, *Democracy in America* (New York: American Library, 1956), 72.

2. *Marbury v. Madison,* 5 U.S. (1 Cranch) 137 (1803).

3. *United States v. Nixon,* 418 U.S. 683 (1974).

4. See Dexter Perkins and Glyndon Van Deusen, *The United States of America: A History,* vol. 2 (New York: Macmillan, 1962), 560–566.

5. Alexander Bickel, *The Least Dangerous Branch* (Indianapolis, IN: Bobbs-Merrill, 1962), 1.

6. *National Federation of Independent Business v. Sebelius,* 527 U.S. ____(2012).

7. Jamin Raskin, "Courts v. Citizens," *American Prospect* 14 (March 2003): A25.

8. Charles Gardner Geyh, *When Courts and Congress Collide: The Struggle for Control of America's Judicial System* (Ann Arbor: University of Michigan Press, 2006), 229.

9. *District of Columbia v. Heller,* 554 U.S. 570 (2008).

10. See, for example, Robert Schlesinger, "Sotomayor Hearings Remind Us the Republicans Can Be Judicial Activists, Too," *U.S. News and World Report,* July 22, 2009, www.usnews.com.

11. *Kelo v. City of New London,* 545 U.S. 469 (2005). See, for example, an editorial in the July 11, 2005, *New Republic* praising the *Kelo* decision as one that "defenders of judicial constraint, particularly liberals, should applaud" (p. 7).

12. For example, Sen. John McCain singled out *Kelo* as an example of judicial activism in a speech at Wake Forest University on May 6, 2008. Sen. Jeff Sessions made the same point in a *Washington Post* op-ed on May 7, 2010, A25.

13. Sandra Day O'Connor, "The Threat to Judicial Independence," *Wall Street Journal,* September 27, 2006, A18.

14. See, for example, the House debate on the Lilly Ledbetter case, *Congressional Record,* 111th Cong., 1st sess., January 9, 2009, H113–H138.

15. Louis Fisher, "The Law: Litigating the War Power with *Campbell v. Clinton,*" *Presidential Studies Quarterly* (September 2000): 568.

16. *National Federation of Independent Business v. Sebelius,* 527 U.S. ____(2012).

17. *Carr v. United States,* 130 S. Ct. 2229, 2236 (2010).

18. See Robert A. Katzmann, ed., *Judges and Legislators* (Washington, DC: Brookings, 1988); and Robert A. Katzmann, *Courts and Congress* (Washington, DC: Brookings, 1997).

19. *New York Times,* May 12, 1983, B8.

20. Dan Eggen, "Record Shows Senators' 'Debate' That Wasn't," *Washington Post,* March 29, 2006, A6.

21. Emily Bazelon, "Invisible Men: Did Lindsey Graham and Jon Kyl Mislead the Supreme Court?" *Slate,* March 27, 2006.

22. Eggen, "Record Shows Senators' 'Debate' That Wasn't," A6.

23. See, for example, Antonin Scalia, *A Matter of Interpretation* (Princeton, NJ: Princeton University Press, 1997).

24. Quoted in Joan Biskupic, "Scalia Sees No Justice in Trying to Judge Intent of Congress on a Law," *Washington Post,* May 11, 1993, A4.

25. Jonathan Kaplan, "High Court to Congress," *The Hill,* February 5, 2003, 21.

26. Stanley I. Kutler, *Judicial Power and Reconstruction Politics* (Chicago: University of Chicago Press, 1968).

27. Howard Gillman, "How Political Parties Can Use the Courts to Advance Their Agendas: Federal Courts in the United States, 1875–1891," *American Political Science Review* 96 (September 2002): 511–524.

28. Quoted in Stephen Dinan, "DeLay Threatens to Curb Courts' Jurisdiction," *Washington Times,* March 6, 2003, A4.

29. Tom S. Clark, "The Separation of Powers, Court Curbing, and Judicial Legitimacy," *American Journal of Political Science* 53 (October 2009): 971–989.

30. Joan Biskupic and Elder Witt, *Guide to the U.S. Supreme Court,* 3d ed., vol. 2 (Washington, DC: CQ Press, 1997), 720.

31. William H. Rehnquist, *Grand Inquests: The Historic Impeachment of Justice Samuel Chase and President Andrew Johnson* (New York: William Morrow, 1992), 132.

32. Russell R. Wheeler and Robert A. Katzmann, "A Primer on Interbranch Relations," *Georgetown Law Journal* (April 2007): 1172.

33. Rehnquist, *Grand Inquests,* 114.

34. "History of the Federal Judiciary: Impeachments of Federal Judges," Federal Judicial Center, www.fjc.gov/history/home.nsf/page/judges_impeachments.html.

35. Biskupic and Witt, *Guide to the U.S. Supreme Court,* 717.

36. Ibid., 718.

37. Carol Leonning, "New Rules for Judges Are Weaker, Critics Say," *Washington Post,* December 17, 2004, A31; David Von Drehle, "Scalia Rejects Pleas for Recusal in Cheney Case," *Washington Post,* February 12, 2004, A35; Eileen Sullivan, "Courts Order Review of Judges' Security," *Federal Times,* March 21, 2005, 12.

38. Tony Mauro, "Kennedy Talks Tough on Salaries, Cameras," *Legal Times,* February 19, 2007, 14.

39. Nathan Koppel, "Kagan Says 'Yes' to Cameras in the Courtroom," *WSJ Law Blog,* June 29, 2010, http://blogs.wsj.com/law/.

40. Seth Stern, "A Career as Federal Judge Isn't What It Used to Be," *Christian Science Monitor,* January 22, 2002, 1.

41. American Bar Association, "Federal Judicial Pay, an Update on the Urgent Need for Action," May 2003, 4.

42. Mark Sherman, "Big Money Depletes Judges' Ranks," *Washington Times,* December 30, 2008, B3. Also see Adam Liptak, "The State of Courts, and a Plea for a Raise," *New York Times,* January 1, 2009, A13.

43. Linda Greenhouse, "Chief Justice Advocates Higher Pay for Judiciary," A14. Also see editorial, "There Oughta Be a Law," *USA Today,* January 9, 2007, 12A.

44. Adam Liptak, "On the Subject of Judicial Salaries, a Sharp Difference of Opinion," *New York Times,* January 20, 2009, A14.

45. *Chisholm v. Georgia,* 2 U.S. 419 (1793).

46. *Dred Scott v. Sandford,* 60 U.S. 393 (1857).

47. See Louis Fisher, *American Constitutional Law,* 6th ed. (Durham, NC: Carolina Academic Press, 2005), 1072.

48. Jennifer Dlouhy, "Congress Reluctant to Change Constitution," *CQ Today,* February 11, 2003, 9.

49. Norman Ornstein, "To Break the Stalemate, Give Judges Less Than Life," *Washington Post,* November 28, 2004, B3.

50. Tony Mauro, "Profs Pitch Plan for Limits on Supreme Court Service," *Legal Times,* January 3, 2005, 1. Also see Robert Barnes, "Legal Experts Propose Limiting Justices' Powers, Terms," *Washington Post,* February 23, 2009, A15.

51. Jeff Zeleny, "A Premium on Secrecy in Vetting of Court Pick," *New York Times,* May 13, 2009.

52. Alpheus Thomas Mason, *Harlan Fiske Stone: Pillar of the Law* (New York: Viking, 1959), chap. 12.

53. Dennis Steven Rutkus and Lorraine H. Tong, "The Chief Justice of the United States: Responsibilities of the Office and Process for Appointment," Congressional Research Service Report RL32831, September 12, 2005, 30.

54. Ibid., 37.

55. Ibid., 34.

56. Brannon Denning, "The 'Blue Slip': Enforcing the Norms of the Judicial Confirmation Process," *William and Mary Bill of Rights Journal* 10 (December 2001): 92.

57. Sheldon Goldman, Elliot Slotnick, and Sara Schiavoni, "Obama's Judiciary at Midterm," *Judicature* 94 , no. 6 (2011): 267.

58. Quoted in ibid., 268.

59. Josiah Ryan, "Senate Ends Practice of Secret Holds," *The Hill,* January 27, 2011.

60. Ibid.

61. Quoted in Keith Perine, "As Judiciary Battles Loom, Leahy Revives Senate 'Blue Slip' Tradition," *CQ Today,* January 4, 2007, 3.

62. Ralph Neas, "United States Needs More Discussion of Judicial Philosophy," *Roll Call,* May 9, 2002, 10.

63. Seth Stern, "Senate Shows Supreme Decline in Deference," *CQ Weekly,* July 12, 2010, 1635.

64. Quoted in ibid.

65. Terri L. Peretti, "Where Have All the Politicians Gone? Recruiting for the Modern Supreme Court," *Judicature* (November–December 2007): 120. Also see Paul A. Sracic, "Politician on Court Isn't a Bad Thing," *USA Today,* March 30, 2005, 13A.

66. Charles E. Schumer, "Judging by Ideology," *New York Times,* June 26, 2001.

67. Lee Epstein, René Lindstädt, Jeffrey A. Segal, and Chad Westerland, "The Changing Dynamics of Senate Voting on Supreme Court Nominees," *Journal of Politics* 68 (May 2006): 306.

68. James Robertson, "A Cure for What Ails the Judiciary," *Washington Post,* May 27, 2003, A19.

69. Ronald Brownstein, "To End Battle over Judicial Picks, Each Side Must Lay Down Arms," *Los Angeles Times,* February 21, 2005, A8.

70. Linda Greenhouse, "Case of the Dwindling Docket Mystifies the Supreme Court," *New York Times,* December 7, 2006, A1.

71. Warren Richey, "Conservatives Near Lock on U.S. Courts," *Christian Science Monitor,* April 14, 2005, 10.

72. Elizabeth Palmer, "Appellate Courts at Center of Fight for Control of Judiciary," *CQ Weekly,* February 23, 2002, 534.

73. Ibid.

74. John Stanton, "GOP Begins Judge Blockade," *Roll Call,* June 14, 2012.

75. See, for example, Sen. Mike Lee in the *Congressional Record,* June 25, 2012, S4438.

76. Sarah Binder, "Advice and Consent for Judicial Nominations," (Paper prepared for delivery at the seminar "Presidential Nominations and the Senate Confirmation Process," Woodrow Wilson International Center for Scholars, Washington, DC, March 16, 2009), 16.

77. Neil A. Lewis, "New Democratic Majority Throws Bush's Judicial Nominations into Uncertainty," *New York Times,* November 12, 2006, 22.

78. R. Jeffrey Smith, "Judge's Fate Could Turn on 1994 Case," *Washington Post,* May 27, 2003, A8.

79. E. J. Dionne Jr., "They Started It," *Washington Post,* February 21, 2003, A27.

80. Charlie Savage, "Obama Lags on Judicial Picks, Limiting His Mark on Courts," *New York Times,* August 17, 2012.

81. Goldman et al., "Obama's Judiciary at Midterm," 263.

82. Ibid., 265.

83. Ibid.

84. Quoted in ibid.

85. Information available at www.uscourts.gov/JudgesAndJudgeships/JudicialVacancies.aspx (last accessed October 25, 2012).

86. Sarah A. Binder and Forrest Maltzman, *Advice and Dissent: The Struggle to Shape the Federal Judiciary* (Washington, DC: Brookings, 2009), 75.

87. Jerry Markon and Shailagh Murray, "Federal Judicial Vacancies Reaching Crisis Point," *Washington Post,* February 8, 2011, A1.

88. Louis Fisher, "Congressional Checks on the Judiciary," in *Congress Confronts the Court,* ed. Colton C. Campbell and John F. Stack Jr. (Lanham, MD: Rowman and Littlefield, 2001), 35.

CHAPTER 13

1. Peter Dreier, "Lessons from the Health-Care Wars," *American Prospect* (May 2010): 29.
2. Dan Eggen, "Interest Groups Rally for a Big Finish on Health-Care Reform," *Washington Post*, February 28, 2010, A3.
3. Michael D. Shear, "Health Bill Foes Solicit Funds for Economic Study," *Washington Post*, November 16, 2001, A1.
4. Bennett Roth and Alex Knott, "Medical Interests Spend $876 Million on Reform," *Roll Call*, May 3, 2010, 6. For an analysis of the battle over President Clinton's health care plan, see Haynes Johnson and David S. Broder, *The System* (Boston: Little, Brown, 1996).
5. See John R. Hibbing and Elizabeth Theiss-Morse, *Congress as Public Enemy: Public Attitudes toward American Political Institutions* (New York: Cambridge University Press, 1995).
6. Joel Jankowsky and Thomas Goldstein, "In Defense of Lobbying," *Wall Street Journal*, September 4, 2009, A15.
7. Kate Ackley, "'Kick the Lobbyist' Is Still a Favorite Pastime," *Roll Call*, May 10, 2010, 10.
8. Data are from James A. Thurber, American University.
9. Bill Swindell, "Industry's Increased D.C. Presence Reflects New Reality," *National Journal CongressDaily AM*, July 28, 2010, 1, 14. *CongressDaily* is published by *National Journal*, a Washington-based journal.
10. M. B. Pell and Joe Eaton, "K Street Cashes In on Bill," *Politico*, May 21, 2010.
11. Swindell, "Industry's Increased D.C. Presence Reflects New Reality," 14.
12. Baa Vaida, "Brisk Business for K Street in 2010," *National Journal*, July 24, 2010, 44. Many lobbying groups have their offices on K Street in the District of Columbia.
13. Kenneth P. Doyle, "Reported Spending on Federal Lobbying Up 5% in 2009 to $3.47 Billion, Study Finds," *Daily Report for Executives*, February 16, 2010, A-12.
14. Kate Ackley, "K Streeters Counteract Losses by Diversifying," *Roll Call*, January 25, 2013, 7.
15. Anna Palmer, "K Street's Continuing Slump," *Politico*, July 23, 2012, 4.
16. Kate Ackey and Aaron Guerrero, "K Street's Largest Firms Saw Some Dips in 2011 Business," *Roll Call*, January 23, 2013, A-4.
17. Alexis de Tocqueville, *Democracy in America*, ed. Phillips Bradley (New York: Knopf, 1951), 119. See also Richard A. Smith, "Interest Group Influence in the U.S. Congress," *Legislative Studies Quarterly* 20 (February 1995): 89–139.
18. Janny Scott, "Medicine's Big Dose of Politics," *Los Angeles Times*, September 25, 1991, A15.
19. Robert Putnam, "The Strange Disappearance of Civic America," *American Prospect* (Winter 1996): 35.
20. Quoted in Suzi Parker, "Civic Clubs: Elks, Lions May Go Way of the Dodo," *Christian Science Monitor*, August 24, 1998, 1.
21. Seth Stern, "No More Bowling Alone," *Christian Science Monitor*, September 4, 2003, 17.
22. Everett Carll Ladd, "The American Way—Civic Engagement—Thrives," *Christian Science Monitor*, March 1, 1999, 9. See Theda Skocpol, *Diminished Democracy: From Membership to Management in American Civic Life* (Norman: University of Oklahoma Press, 2003). Professor Skocpol argues that the decline of broad membership organizations such as the Elks or Moose, which encouraged civic and political participation, occurred in part because many middle-class citizens chose to rely on professionally run advocacy groups to speak on their behalf.
23. Ladd, "American Way."
24. Doyle McManus, "Great Recession's Psychological Fallout," *Los Angeles Times*, July 15, 2010 (online edition).
25. Mancur Olson Jr., *The Logic of Collective Action: Public Goods and the Theory of Groups* (Cambridge, MA: Harvard University Press, 1965).

26. Kay L. Schlozman and John T. Tierney, *Organized Interests and American Democracy* (New York: Harper and Row, 1986).

27. E. E. Schattschneider, *The Semi-Sovereign People* (New York: Holt, Rinehart and Winston, 1960), 35.

28. Melinda Burns, "K Street and the Status Quo," *Miller-McCune,* September–October 2010, 65. Also see Frank R. Baumgartner et al., *Lobbying and Policy Change: Who Wins, Who Loses and Why* (Chicago: University of Chicago Press, 2009).

29. Kristina C. Miler, "The View from the Hill: Legislative Perceptions of the District," *Legislative Studies Quarterly* 32 (November 2007): 597–628.

30. Sidney Verba, Kay Lehman Schlozman, and Henry Brady, "The Big Tilt: Participatory Inequality in America," *American Prospect* (May/June 1997): 78.

31. Greg Sargent, "Democrats' Sequester Conundrum," *Washington Post,* April 30, 2013, A13. Also see Darren Samuelsohn, "Sequester Exemptions as Earmarks," *Politico,* April 23, 2013, 1.

32. Elise D. Garcia, "Money in Politics," *Common Cause,* February 1981, 11.

33. Jeffrey H. Birnbaum, "Lobbyists: Why the Bad Rap?" *American Enterprise,* November/ December 1992, 74. Also see also Jeffrey H. Birnbaum, *The Lobbyists* (New York: Times Books, 1992).

34. Norman J. Ornstein and Shirley Elder, *Interest Groups, Lobbying, and Policymaking* (Washington, DC: Congressional Quarterly, 1978), 224.

35. Tory Newmyer, "Majority Formalizes K St. Ties," *Roll Call,* February 15, 2007, 23.

36. Alexander Bolton, "Dems Enlist Help to Push Their Agenda," *The Hill,* February 14, 2007, 1.

37. Anna Palmer, "K Street Prepares for Televised Rendezvous with GOP Leaders," *Roll Call,* July 15, 2010 (online edition).

38. Jeffrey Birnbaum, "The Thursday Group," *Time,* March 27, 1995, 30–31.

39. Emily Pierce, "GOP Taps Thune to Get Cozy with K St.," *Roll Call,* January 22, 2009.

40. Quoted in Hedrick Smith, *The Power Game* (New York: Random House, 1988), 232.

41. Fredreka Schouten, "Private Citizens Take Troubles to Lobbyists," *USA Today,* June 1, 2010, 6A.

42. See, for example, David S. Fallis and Dan Keating, "Lobbyists Can Try to Influence Bills That Go before Relatives," *Washington Post,* December 30, 2012, A1.

43. Quoted in Alan K. Ota, "Democratic Foot in Revolving Door," *CQ Weekly,* June 25, 2007, 1900.

44. Ronald J. Hrebenar and Ruth K. Scott, *Interest Group Politics in America* (Englewood Cliffs, NJ: Prentice-Hall, 1982), 63.

45. Dave Levinthal, "Ex-Members Really *Do* Get Special Access," *Politico,* April 20, 2012, 1, 10.

46. Chris Frates, "Hill Experience Gives Lobbyists a Leg Up," *Politico,* May 17, 2007.

47. R. Jeffrey Smith and Dan Eggen, "More Former Lobbyists Flocking to Jobs on Hill," *Washington Post,* March 18, 2011, A1.

48. Mark Preston, "Ex-GOP Senators Get Special Access," *Roll Call,* April 3, 2003, 1, 24.

49. Quoted in Alan K. Ota, "Democratic Foot in the Revolving Door," *CQ Weekly,* June 25, 2007, 1900.

50. Anna Palmer, "Help Wanted: Lobbyists Who Can Raise Cash," *Politico,* May 21, 2012, 15.

51. Sarah Pekkanen, "How Lobbyists Are Changing the Lobbying Game," *The Hill,* February 12, 1997, 21.

52. *National Journal CongressDaily PM,* May 30, 1997, 6.

53. Quoted in Sam Walker, "Who's In and Who's Out among Capitol Lobbyists," *Christian Science Monitor,* November 8, 1995, 3.

54. Quoted in *National Journal CongressDaily PM,* March 15, 2002, 8.

55. Steven Brill, "On Sale: Your Government," *Time,* July 12, 2010, 32.

56. Bertram J. Levine, *The Art of Lobbying: Building Trust and Selling Policy* (Washington, DC: CQ Press, 2008).

57. *New York Times,* January 20, 1981, B3.

58. Adam Graham-Silverman, "Travel Decreases as Ethics Rules Complicate Privately Funded Trips," *CQ Weekly,* December 1, 2008, 3178.

59. John Cochran and Martin Kady II, "The New Laws of the Lobby," *CQ Weekly,* February 26, 2007, 594.

60. Amanda Becker, "Outside Groups Spent Big on Congressional Travel," *Roll Call,* January 15, 2013, 4. See also Amanda Becker, "Traveling on Whose Dime?" *Outlook: A CQ Roll Call Special Publication,* June 2012, 10–11.

61. Eliza Newlin Carney and Bara Vaida, "Shifting Ground," *National Journal,* March 31, 2007, 27.

62. Quoted in Cochran and Kady, "New Laws of the Lobby," 594.

63. Joseph Curl, "Big Money Buys Seats at Lawmakers' Dinner Tables," *Washington Times,* November 3, 2009, A1.

64. David Kirkpatrick, "Congress Finds Ways of Avoiding Lobbyist Limit," *New York Times,* February 11, 2007, 1. The political action committee of Finance chair Max Baucus, D-Mont., often sponsors fund-raising events at the Big Sky Resort in Montana that feature "fly-fishing and golf in the summer and skiing in the winter." See Kate Ackley, "Baucus' Network in High Demand," *Roll Call,* June 19, 2012, 21.

65. Ibid.

66. Carol Matlack, "Getting around the Rules," *National Journal,* May 12, 1990, 1139.

67. Eric Lipton, "Congressional Charities Pulling in Corporate Cash," *New York Times,* September 5, 2010, A1.

68. Ibid., A10.

69. Eric Lipton, "Lawmakers Linked to Centers Endowed by Corporate Money," *New York Times,* August 6, 2010, A3.

70. Ibid.

71. John Breaux, "Effective Coalitions for Coalitions," *The Hill,* March 21, 2007, 18.

72. Kate Ackley, "Defense, Other Sectors Band Together to Fight Sequester," *Roll Call,* February 8, 2013 (online edition).

73. Dan Eggen, "Investments Can Yield More on K Street, Study Indicates," *Washington Post,* April 12, 2009, A8.

74. Ernest Wittenberg, "How Lobbying Helps Make Democracy Work," *Vital Speeches of the Day,* November 1, 1982, 47.

75. Robert Pear, "In Divide over Health Care Overhaul, 2 Major Unions Withdraw from a Coalition," *New York Times,* March 7, 2009, A12.

76. Jeff Patch, "Farm Bill Renewal Sows Fresh Alliances on Subsidies," *Politico,* May 8, 2007, www.politico.com.

77. Ellyn Ferguson, "An Unexpected Alliance Fights Ethanol Expansion," *CQ Today,* July 26, 2010, 7. Also see Anna Palmer, "Lobbying Coalition Calls for Congressional Hearing on Ethanol," *Roll Call,* August 25, 2010 (online edition).

78. Martin Kady II, "Keeping Grass-Roots Lobbying under Wraps," *CQ Weekly,* March 26, 2007, 877.

79. Shawn Zeller, "SEIU Spreads Its Wings, Ruffles Some Feathers," *CQ Weekly,* May 12, 2008, 1233.

80. John T. Tierney and Kay Lehman Schlozman, "Congress and Organized Interests," in *Congressional Politics,* ed. Christopher J. Deering (Chicago: Dorsey, 1989), 212.

81. *Washington Star,* December 31, 1980, C2.

82. Kady, "Keeping Grass-Roots Lobbying under Wraps," 877.

83. Ibid.
84. Juliet Eilperin, "Police Track Down Telecom Telegraphs," *Roll Call,* August 7, 1995, 1.
85. Lisa Caruso, "Turf Battle," *National Journal,* March 31, 2007, 34.
86. Cited in Jack Maskell, "Grassroots Lobbying: Constitutionality of Disclosure Requirements," Congressional Research Service Report RL33794, January 12, 2007, 3. Also see, for example, John Cochran, "A New Medium for the Message," *CQ Weekly,* March 13, 2006, 652–658; and Kady, "Keeping Grass-Roots Lobbying under Wraps," 877–878.
87. Alison Mitchell, "A New Form of Lobbying Puts Public Face on Private Interest," *New York Times,* September 30, 1998, A14. Also see Ken Kollman, *Outside Lobbying: Public Opinion and Interest Group Strategies* (Princeton, NJ: Princeton University Press, 1998).
88. Sara Fritz and Dan Morain, "Stealth Lobby Drives Fuel-Additive War," *Los Angeles Times,* June 16, 1997, A6.
89. Dave Levinthal, "K Street Says 'Let's Meet,' Hill Staffers Say 'Text Me,'" *Politico,* June 12, 2012, 1.
90. Bennett Roth, "Interest Groups Log On for Fight over Kagan," *Roll Call,* May 24, 2010, 10.
91. Justin Cox, "Trading Bullhorns for Blog Posts," *The Hill,* June 23, 2010, 42.
92. Cecilia Kane, "Twitter: A Live Megaphone for Lobbying Groups, Firms," *Washington Post,* February 14, 2013, A12.
93. Mitchell, "New Form of Lobbying Puts Public Face on Private Interest."
94. "Trends in Grassroots Lobbying: Consultant Q&A," *Campaigns and Elections,* February 1999, 22.
95. *New York Times,* January 24, 1980, A16.
96. David Gelles, "Lobbying Scuttles US Piracy Laws," *Financial Times,* January 21–22, 2012, 1.
97. Keach Hagey, "Komen Flap Fueled by the Firepower of Facebook, Twitter," *Politico,* February 6, 2012, 3. Also see Janie Lorber, "New Power for the People," *Outlook: A CQ Roll Special Publication,* June 2012, 22–23.
98. Quoted in Jeffrey Birnbaum, "Advocacy Groups Blur Media Lines," *Washington Post,* December 6, 2004, A1.
99. Ibid., A7.
100. Eric Litchtblau, "Beyond Guns: N.R.A. Expands Political Agenda," *New York Times,* July 13, 2010, A3.
101. Matea Gold, Joseph Tanfani, and Lisa Mascaro, "NRA Clout Rooted More in Its Tactics Than Its Election Spending," *Los Angeles Times,* July 29, 2012 (online edition).
102. Fawn Johnson, "Pro-Gun Lobby in Safe Zone," *National Journal Daily,* July 20, 2012 (online edition).
103. Jeffrey Birnbaum, "The Forces That Set the Agenda," *Washington Post,* April 24, 2005, B5.
104. Tom Hamburger, "U.S. Chamber of Commerce Grows into a Political Force," *Los Angeles Times,* March 8, 2010 (online edition).
105. Paul S. Herrnson, "Party Organizations, Party-Connected Committees, Party Allies, and the Financing of Federal Elections," *Journal of Politics* (November 2009).
106. Brody Mullins, "Growing Role for Lobbyists: Raising Funds for Lawmakers," *Wall Street Journal,* January 27, 2006, A1.
107. Philip M. Stern, "The Tin Cup Congress," *Washington Monthly,* May 1988, 24.
108. *Congressional Record,* 100th Cong., 1st sess., August 5, 1987, S11292.
109. "Fundamentals of Fund-raising," *Washington Post,* December 5, 1990, A23.
110. Fredreka Schouten, "Polled PAC Donations Add $33M Punch to Races," *USA Today,* August 17, 2010, 5A.
111. Manu Raju, "Members Get Bundles of Lobbyist Cash," *Politico,* February 16, 2010, 1.
112. Jack Maskell, "Lobbying Law and Ethics Rules Changes in the 110th Congress," Congressional Research Service Report RL 33836, September 18, 2007.

113. Tom McGinty and Brody Mullins, "Political Spending by Unions Far Exceeds Direct Donations," *Wall Street Journal*, July 10, 2012, A1, A7.

114. Shane Goldmacher, "House GOP Leaders Court Conservatives," *National Journal Daily*, February 14, 2013, 1.

115. John Brinkley, "Members of Congress Perform under Judging Eyes of Lobbyists," *Washington Times*, March 16, 1994, A16. See John Cochran, "Interest Groups Make Sure Lawmakers Know the 'Score,'" *CQ Weekly*, April 19, 2003, 924–929.

116. See Robert L. Reynolds, "A Pledge to End All Pledges," *Wall Street Journal*, December 24, 2012, A13; and Grover Norquist, "The Case for the Tax Pledge: Political Accountability," *USA Today*, December 13, 2012, 8A.

117. Bill Whalen, "Rating Lawmakers' Politics by Looking into Their Eyes," *Insight*, October 20, 1986, 21. See Cochran, "Interest Groups Make Sure Lawmakers Know the 'Score.'"

118. *New York Times*, May 13, 1986, A24.

119. Eliza Newlin Carney, "Keeping Score," *CQ Weekly*, January 21, 2013, 118–119.

120. *CQ Monitor*, April 13, 1998, 4.

121. "Environment," *National Journal CongressDaily PM*, February 21, 2006, 10.

122. Hibbing and Theiss-Morse, *Congress as Public Enemy*, 63–65.

123. Frank R. Baumgartner and Beth L. Leech, *Basic Interests: The Importance of Groups in Politics and in Political Science* (Princeton, NJ: Princeton University Press, 1998), 13.

124. Burns, "K Street and the Status Quo," 64. To be sure, some studies find that "corporations that poured money into Congress typically got the votes they wanted." See Leslie Wayne, "Lobbyists' Gift to Politicians Reap Benefits, Study Shows," *New York Times*, January 23, 1997, B11.

125. Interview with Prof. Marie Elizabeth Hojnacki, *CQ Weekly*, September 6, 2010, 2005.

126. Janet M. Gretzke, "PACs and the Congressional Supermarket: The Currency Is Complex," *American Journal of Political Science* 33 (1989): 1–24; Lawrence S. Rothenberg, *Linking Citizens to Government: Interest Group Politics at Common Cause* (New York: Cambridge University Press, 1992); John R. Wright, "Contributions, Lobbying, and Committee Voting in the U.S. House of Representatives," *American Political Science Review* 84 (1990): 417–438.

127. Gary J. Andres, *Lobbying Reconsidered* (New York: Pearson Longman, 2009), 159. Worth noting is that the House Office of Congressional Ethics has investigated the "propriety of [lawmakers] using a vote as a fundraising opportunity by hosting events in close proximity to a major vote." See Edward Epstein, "Outside Panel in for Insider Criticism," *CQ Weekly*, August 9, 2010, 1911.

128. See the labor union profile at the Center for Responsive Politics, www.opensecrets.org/. The center is a nonprofit research organization that tracks the role of money in politics.

129. See the oil and gas industry's profile at the Center for Responsive Politics, www.opensecrets. org.

130. Richard L. Hall and Frank W. Wayman, "Buying Time: Moneyed Interests and the Mobilization of Bias in Congressional Committees," *American Political Science Review* 84 (September 1990): 800. See also their review of the literature on patterns in campaign contributions on pages 799–800.

131. Quoted in Claudia Dreifus, "And Then There Was Frank," *New York Times Magazine*, February 4, 1996, 25.

132. Don Van Natta Jr., "$250,000 Buys Donors 'Best Access to Congress,'" *New York Times*, January 27, 1997, A1.

133. See Richard A. Smith, "Advocacy, Interpretation, and Influence in the U.S. Congress," *American Political Science Review* 78 (1984): 44–63; and Hall and Wayman, "Buying Time."

Also see Eric Lipton and Kevin Sack, "Fiscal Footnote: Big Senate Gift to Drug Maker," *New York Times*, January 20, 2013, A1.

134. Marie Hojnacki and David C. Kimball, "Organized Interests and the Decision of Whom to Lobby in Congress," *American Political Science Review* (December 1998): 775–790.

135. *Washington Star*, May 22, 1978, A1.

136. Elizabeth Brotherton, "A Recycled Idea," *Roll Call*, June 13, 2006, 3.

137. See Eric Lipton and Eric Lichtblau, "In Black Caucus, a Fund-Raising Powerhouse," *New York Times*, February 14, 2010, 1; Paul Singer, "The Tax-Payer-Funded Caucus Is Still Thriving," *Roll Call*, May 18, 2010, 4; Fredreka Schouten, "Lobbyists Get Power Access Via Caucuses," *USA Today*, July 24–26, 2009, 1A.

138. Richard L. Hall and Alan V. Deardorff, "Lobbying as Legislative Subsidy," *American Political Science Review* (February 2006): 69–84.

139. *Wall Street Journal*, October 5, 1987, 54.

140. Thomas Hale Boggs Jr., "All Interests Are Special," *New York Times*, February 16, 1993, A17.

141. Mary Lynn Jones, "Survey Says Lobbyists Find Information Rules the Hill," *The Hill*, November 18, 1998, 8. A recent study of congressional lobbying suggests that lobbyists' political connections to lawmakers are more important than their issue expertise. The president of the American League of Lobbyists, however, disputes this judgment. See Jeremy Hainsworth, "Study Finds Who You Know Counts Most Among Congressional Lobbyists," *Daily Report for Executives*, March 25, 2011, A-8.

142. Kirk Victor, "New Kids on the Block," *National Journal*, October 31, 1987, 2727.

143. Burns, "K Street and the Status Quo," 66. As an example, see Patrice Hill, "Facts Spin on Small-Business Tax," *Washington Times*, August 31, 2010, A1.

144. *Congressional Record*, December 15, 2011, S8629.

145. Ibid.

146. The "Guide to the Lobbying Disclosure Act" can be found on the website of the clerk of the U.S. House of Representatives: http://clerk.house.gov.

147. William Luneburg and Thomas Susman, *The Lobbying Manual*, 3d ed. (Washington, DC: American Bar Association, 2005), 7.

148. U.S. Congress, *Organization of the Congress*, H. Rept. 1675, 79th Cong., 2d sess., 1946, 26.

149. *United States v. Harriss*, 347 U.S. 612 (1954).

150. Francesca Contiguaglia, "GAO Finds That Lobbyist Registration Has Soared," *Roll Call*, May 14, 1998, 14.

151. Sam Fulwood, "Lobbying Reform Passes House on Unanimous Vote," *Los Angeles Times*, November 30, 1995, A9.

152. Alex Knott, *Special Report: Industry of Influence Nets Almost $13 Billion* (Washington, DC: Center for Public Integrity, 2005), 1–4.

153. Lee H. Hamilton, "Lobbying Murkiness Undermines Our Trust in Congress," Center on Congress at Indiana University, April 11, 2005, 2, http://congress.indiana.edu.

154. Deirdre Shesgreen, "Shining a Dim Light," *Legal Times*, December 21 and 28, 1998, 26, 27.

155. Editorial, "Scandal? What Scandal? Congress Ducks Ethics Reform," *USA Today*, September 6, 2006, 12A.

156. Michael Crowley and Jay Newton-Small, "Cleaning the People's House," *Time*, August 16, 2010, 24.

157. See John D. McKinnon and Brody Mullins, "Lawmakers Face Ethics Probe," *Wall Street Journal*, September 1, 2010, A4.

158. Dan Eggen, "Success of Lobbying Crackdown Questioned," *Washington Post*, February 14, 2010, A3.

159. Josh Rogin, "Committee Needs Waiver to Act on Lynn Nomination for Defense Deputy," *CQ Today*, January 23, 2009, 11.

160. T. W. Farnam, "At White House, No Scarcity of Lobbyists," *Washington Lobbyist*, May 21, 2012, A1.

161. Kenneth Doyle, "Lobbyists Urged to Disclose Contributions after GAO Reported Thousands Fail to Do So," *Daily Report for Executives*, June 17, 2010, A-2.

162. Andrew Ramonas, "No Retribution, No Fear," *Legal Times*, April 16, 2012, 11, 14.

163. See Kenneth P. Doyle, "$45,000 Settlement Revealed in First Case in Years Enforcing the Lobbying Disclosure Act," *Daily Report for Executives*, December 7, 2011, A-24; and press release, U.S. Attorney's Office, District of Columbia, September 21, 2012.

164. David D. Kirkpatrick, "Intended to Rein In Lobbyists, Law Sends Them Underground," *New York Times*, January 18, 2010, A1.

165. Kate Ackley, "Unlobbyists Give Real Lobbyists a Bad Name," *Roll Call*, February 13, 2012, 1.

166. Chris Frates, "When a Lobbyist Isn't a Lobbyist," *Politico*, July 26, 2010, 1, 12.

167. Eric Lichtblau, "Tired of 'Tainted' Image, Lobbyists Try Makeover," *New York Times*, May 4, 2012, A17.

168. Janie Lorber and Kate Ackley, "Tracking Lobbyists for Other Countries," *Roll Call*, October 2, 2012, 3. Also see Arnd Jurgensen and Renan Levine, "Foreign Lobbying," in Burdett Loomis, ed., *Guide to Interest Groups and Lobbying in the United States* (Washington, DC: CQ Press, 2012), 321–332.

169. T. W. Farnam, "Trips Fly through Hole in Rules," *Washington Post*, February 18, 2013, A6. The material in this paragraph is drawn from the detailed analysis of these cultural exchange trips conducted by the *Post*.

170. Kevin Bogardus, "Korea Bulks Up on K Street as Obama Presses Trade Deal," *The Hill*, July 16, 2010, 9.

171. Kevin Bogardus, "First DC Firm to Sign with Libyan Rebels Is Rewarded with Contract," *The Hill*, April 4, 2012, 20.

172. See Ken Silverstein, "Oil Adds Sheen to Kazakh Regime," *Los Angeles Times*, May 12, 2004, A1.

173. Ibid.

174. See Adam Hochschild, "Into the Light from the Heart of Darkness," *Los Angeles Times*, December 6, 1998, M1; and Katharine Seeyle, "National Rifle Association Is Turning to World Stage to Fight Gun Control," *New York Times*, April 2, 1997, A12.

175. Julian Pecquet, "NRA Draws Red Line on Civilian Weapons in UN's Arms Treaty," *The Hill*, July 12, 2012, 9.

176. Alan Ohnsman and Gopal Ratnam, "Toyota to Boost Lobbying Efforts as U.S. Operations Expand," *The Washington Examiner*, March 7, 2007, 21.

177. Edgar Lane, *Lobbying and the Law* (Berkeley: University of California Press, 1964), 18.

178. Brill, "On Sale: Your Government," 32.

CHAPTER 14

1. Lori Montgomery, "Treasury Chief Issues Dire Warning to Hill to Raise Debt Ceiling," *Washington Post*, January 7, 2011, p. A4.

2. Ibid.

3. William McQuillien, "Goolsbee Says Failure to Raise U.S. Debt Ceiling Would Be 'Catastrophic,'" *Bloomberg News*, January 2, 2011, www.bloomberg.com/news/2011-01-02/goolsbee-says-failure-to-raise-u-s-debt-ceiling-would-be-catastrophic-.html.

4. Matt Bai, "Obama vs. Bochner: Who Killed the Debt Deal?" *New York Times Magazine*, March 28, 2012.

5. James Oliphant, "Obama: Debt-Limit Impasse Could Halt Social Security Checks," *Los Angeles Times*, July 12, 2011, http://articles.latimes.com/2011/jul/12/news/la-pn-obama-social-security-20110712.

6. John Cranford and Joseph Schatz, "Debt Ceiling: In Whose Hands?" *CQ Weekly*, January 18, 2011, 1546–1550.

7. "Default Avoided at Eleventh Hour," *CQ Almanac*, 2011.

8. Michael Cooper and Megan Thee-Brenan, "Congress Seen as Top Culprit in Debt Debate," *New York Times*, August 5, 2011, 1.

9. Randall B. Ripley and Grace A. Franklin, *Congress, the Bureaucracy, and Public Policy*, 5th ed. (Pacific Grove, CA: Brooks/Cole, 1991).

10. John W. Kingdon, *Agendas, Alternatives, and Public Policies* (Boston: Little, Brown, 1984), 3.

11. Ibid., 17–19.

12. Ibid., chap. 2.

13. Fareed Zakaria, "Free at Last," *Newsweek*, April 13, 2009, 42.

14. Ben Wolfgang, "U.S. Poised to Overtake Saudi Oil Production," *Washington Times*, November 13, 2012, A1.

15. Steven Chu, "Pulling the Plug on Oil," *Newsweek*, April 13, 2009, 44.

16. Nelson W. Polsby, "Strengthening Congress in National Policymaking," *Yale Review* (Summer 1970): 481–497.

17. James L. Sundquist, *Politics and Policy: The Eisenhower, Kennedy, and Johnson Years* (Washington, DC: Brookings, 1968).

18. Elizabeth Wehr, "Numerous Factors Favoring Good Relationship between Reagan and New Congress," *Congressional Quarterly Weekly Report*, January 24, 1981, 173.

19. Kingdon, *Agendas, Alternatives, and Public Policies*, 148–149.

20. American Enterprise Institute, *The State of the Congress: Tomorrow's Challenges?* (Washington, DC: AEI, 1981), 8.

21. Theodore Lowi, "American Business, Public Policy, Case Studies, and Political Theory," *World Politics* (July 1964): 677–715; Theodore Lowi, "Four Systems of Policy, Politics, and Choice," *Public Administration Review* (July–August 1972): 298–310; Samuel P. Huntington, *The Common Defense* (New York: Columbia University Press, 1961); Ripley and Franklin, *Congress, the Bureaucracy, and Public Policy*.

22. Mary Russell, "'Park-Barrel Bill' Clears House Panel," *Washington Post*, June 22, 1978, A3.

23. George E. Condon Jr., "Bending Congress's Ear(marks)," *National Journal CongressDaily*, February 11, 2011, 5.

24. Stephen Dinan, "Earmarks End for One Year, but Perk Still Potent on Hill," *Washington Times*, February 10, 2011, A6.

25. Ibid.

26. *Congressional Record*, 111th Cong., 1st sess., May 6, 2009, H5279.

27. Frank Oliveri, "McKeon Lays Out Rules for Keeping Earmarks Out of Defense Authorization Bill," *CQ Today*, March 28, 2011, 2.

28. Raymond Hernandez, "A House District Liked Its Earmarks, and Then Elected Someone Who Didn't," *New York Times*, February 5, 2011, A16.

29. Humberto Sanchez, "Senators Line Up to Endorse Earmark Moratorium," *National Journal CongressDaily*, February 2, 2011, 7.

30. Kerry Young, "McCaskill, Toomey Seek Permanent Ban on Earmarks," *CQ News*, January 23, 2013 (online edition).

31. Eliza Newlin Carney, "The Earmarks Paradox," *National Journal CongressDaily*, February 14, 2011, 5.

32. Humberto Sanchez, "Senators Want to Clarify What Makes an Earmark," *National Journal CongressDaily*, March 3, 2011, 11.

33. Ron Nixon, "Earmarks Ban May Loom, but Lawmakers Find Ways to Finance Pet Projects," *New York Times*, December 28, 2010, A11.

34. Kevin Bogardus, "Keep the Earmark Requests Coming, Says Some Lawmakers to Constituents," *The Hill*, March 17, 2011, 12.

35. Condon, "Bending Congress's Ear(marks)," 5.

36. See, for example, Margaret Kriz, "Heavy Breathing," *National Journal*, January 4, 1997, 8–12.

37. Joby Warrick, "White House Taking a Hands-on Role in Writing New Clean Air Standards," *Washington Post*, May 22, 1997, A10.

38. Chris Frates, "Rule-Writing a Second Stimulus for K Street," *Politico*, March 17, 2011, 1.

39. Alan Charles Raul, "Obama Review of Regulatory Burden to Be Weighed in Cost-Benefit Analysis," *Daily Report for Executives*, February 9, 2011, B-1.

40. See, for example, Kenneth A. Shepsle, Robert P. Van Houweling, Samuel J. Abrams, and Peter C. Hanson, "The Senate Electoral Cycle and Bicameral Appropriation Politics," *American Journal of Political Science* 53 (2009): 343–359; Jeffrey Lazarus and Amy Steigerwalt, "Different Houses: The Distribution of Earmarks in the U.S. House and Senate," *Legislative Studies Quarterly* 34 (2009): 347–373; and Robert A. Bernstein, Gerald C. Wright Jr., and Michael B. Berkman, "Do U.S. Senators Moderate Strategically?" *American Political Science Review* 82 (1988): 237–245.

41. Donald Lambro, "Steady GOP Rebound Strategy," *Washington Times*, June 7, 2001, A17.

42. Judy Sarasohn, "Money for Lat. 40 N, Long. 73 W," *Congressional Quarterly Weekly Report*, May 12, 1979, 916.

43. Paula Drummond, "Unfunded Mandates Bill Becomes Law," *Kansas Government Journal*, May 1995, 122.

44. "Don't Just Do Something, Sit There," *Economist*, December 23, 1995–January 5, 1996, 11–12.

45. Editorial, "Feel-good Legislation: Congress's Symbolic Energy Bills," *Houston Chronicle*, May 15, 2008, www.chron.com/opinion/editorials/article/Feel-good-legislation-Congress-symbolic-energy-1772616.php.

46. Barber Conable, "Government Is Working," *Roll Call*, April 19, 1984, 3. Congress has initiated change many times. A classic example is the Thirty-seventh Congress (1861–1863), which drafted "the blueprint for modern America" by enacting measures to finance the Civil War, build the transcontinental railroad, eradicate slavery, promote the land-grant college movement, provide settlers with homestead land, and create the Department of Agriculture. See James M. McPherson, *Battle Cry of Freedom: The Civil War Era* (New York: Ballantine, 1988), 452.

47. *Congressional Record*, 110th Cong., 2d sess., September 22, 2008, S9173.

48. Robert Luce, *Legislative Problems* (Boston: Houghton Mifflin, 1935), 426. Also see Louis Fisher, "The Authorization-Appropriation Process in Congress: Formal Rules and Informal Practices," *Catholic University Law Review* (Fall 1979): 51–105; Richard F. Fenno Jr., *The Power of the Purse* (Boston: Little, Brown, 1966).

49. John Cranford, "Just Say Maybe," *CQ Weekly*, March 7, 2011, 542.

50. Richard Munson, *The Cardinals of Capitol Hill* (New York: Grove Press, 1993), 6.

51. See Louis Fisher, "Annual Authorizations: Durable Roadblocks to Biennial Budgeting," *Public Budgeting and Finance* (Spring 1983): 23–40.

52. Chris Strohm, "Tensions Arise over Revised Intel Measure," *National Journal CongressDaily*, March 16, 2011, 16.

53. Quoted in Alan Ota, "Spending Bills May Be Democrats' Plan B," *CQ Today*, April 27, 2007, 8.

54. *Congressional Record*, 109th Cong., 1st sess., May 10, 2005, S4847.

55. See Elana Shor and Jackie Kucinich, "GOP Plots Blue-Slip Attack," *The Hill,* May 30, 2007, 1.

56. Major Garrett, "Extreme Makeover," *National Journal,* March 12, 2011, 20.

57. Ibid., 18.

58. Susan Davis, "Yellow Lights," *National Journal,* February 5, 2011, 47.

59. Sarah Barr, "House Republicans Plan Legislation to Make Defunding Reform Law Easier," *Daily Report for Executives,* March 4, 2011, A-15.

60. Jason DeParle, "U.S. Welfare System Dies as State Programs Emerge," *New York Times,* June 30, 1997, A1.

61. Quoted in Jonathan Weisman and Michael Fletcher, "GOP May Be Splintering on Social Security," *Washington Post,* April 27, 2005, A4.

62. Social Security Administration, "A Summary of the 2012 Annual Reports," www.ssa.gov/oact/trsum/index.html.

63. Ibid.

64. *Congressional Record,* 109th Cong., 1st sess., February 28, 2005, S1784.

65. David R. Francis, "Social Security: A Contrarian View," *Christian Science Monitor,* February 26, 2007, 17.

66. Billy House, "Dems Ramp Up Criticism of GOP on Social Security Cuts," *National Journal CongressDaily,* March 10, 2011, 12.

67. Neil King Jr. and Scott Greenberg, "Poll Shows Budget-Cuts Dilemma," *Wall Street Journal,* March 3, 2011, A5.

68. Alex Roarty, "Senior Moment," *National Journal,* February 26, 2001, 76.

69. David Cook, "Rising Healthcare Costs Pose Fundamental Risk to U.S.," *Christian Science Monitor,* September 18, 2007 (online edition).

70. Tim Fernholz, "Mind the Gap," *National Journal,* February 19, 2011, 50.

71. William Welch, "Medicare: The Next Riddle for the Ages," *USA Today,* March 17, 2005, 10A.

72. Quoted in Julie Rovner, "The Real Budget Buster," *National Journal's CongressDaily AM,* April 5, 2001, 5.

73. Donald Kettl, "Looking for a Real Crisis: Try Medicaid," *Governing,* April 2005, 20.

74. Matthew Miller, "The Big Federal Freeze," *New York Times Magazine,* October 15, 2000, 94.

75. Jonathan Nicholson, "Do Tax Expenditures Really Work? Experts Say Not Enough Data to Tell," *Daily Report for Executives,* October 25, 2010, J-1.

76. Ibid.

77. Robert A. Green, "Limiting Deductions Could Be the New Tax Hike in Fiscal Cliff Avoidance," *Forbes,* November, 12, 2012.

78. N. Gregory Mankiw, "The Blur between Spending and Taxes," *New York Times,* November 21, 2010, B5. Also see Nicholson, "Do Tax Expenditures Really Work?" J-1.

79. Gregory Rodriguez, "Hidden Federal Benefits," *Los Angeles Times,* February 28, 2011 (online edition). See Suzanne Mettler, *The Submerged State: How Invisible Government Policies Undermine American Democracy* (Chicago: University of Chicago Press, 2011); and Christopher Howard, *The Hidden Welfare State: Tax Expenditures and Social Policy in the United States* (Princeton, NJ: Princeton University Press, 1997).

80. Gerald F. Seib, "As Budget Battle Rages On, a Quiet Cancer Grows," *Wall Street Journal,* March 8, 2011, A4.

81. Steven Mufson, "On National Debt, Interest Is the Monster," *Washington Post,* February 17, 2011, A1.

82. *Congressional Record,* 106th Cong., 2d sess., March 2, 2000, S1050.

83. Stephanie Kirchgaessner, "Republicans' Rising Start Takes Risk on Medicare," *Financial Times,* April 6, 2011, 4. See Paul D. Ryan, "The GOP Path to Prosperity," *Wall Street Journal,* April 5, 2011, A15.

84. Mark Preston, "'Vote-a-Rama' Keeps Wearing Senate Down," *Roll Call,* March 26, 2003, 1.

85. *Congressional Record,* 107th Cong., 1st sess., February 15, 2001, S1532.

86. John Ellwood, "Budget Control in a Redistributive Environment," in *Making Economic Policy in Congress,* ed. Allen Schick (Washington, DC: American Enterprise Institute, 1983), 93. Data on the number of times reconciliation has been employed were provided by budget expert Robert Keith, Congressional Research Service.

87. Testimony of Sen. Robert C. Byrd, Senate Budget Committee, *Senate Procedures for Consideration of the Budget Resolution/Reconciliation,* February 12, 2009, 3.

88. David Rosenbaum, "Democratic Filibuster Hopes Fade," *New York Times,* November 18, 2002, A15; David Baumann, "The Octopus That Might Eat Congress," *National Journal,* May 14, 2005, 1470–1475.

89. The election was to fill the vacancy due to the death of Democrat Ted Kennedy.

90. William Dauster, "Budget Process Issues for 1993," *Journal of Law and Politics* 9 (1992): 26.

91. Quoted in ibid., 27.

92. *Congressional Record,* 107th Cong., 1st sess., January 4, 2001, S19.

93. Lori Montgomery, "House GOP Passes New Rules on Tax and Spending Legislation," *Washington Post,* January 6, 2011, A7.

94. Paul Krawzak, "House Conservatives Seek Big Cuts," *CQ Weekly,* January 24, 2011, 211.

95. Congressional Budget Office, "Budget Projections, May 2013," http://www.cbo.gov/publication/44195

96. Gail Russell Chaddock, "GOP's Family Feud over Spending," *Christian Science Monitor,* May 22, 2006, 10.

97. Matt Bai, "Sure Recipe for Decline: Neglect and Gluttony," *New York Times,* February 17, 2011, A17.

98. *Congressional Record,* 107th Cong., 2d sess., July 16, 2002, H4749.

CHAPTER 15

1. Mark Mazzetti and Eric Schmitt, "C.I.A. Spies Aiding Airstrikes and Assessing Quaddafi's Foes," *New York Times,* March 31, 2011, A1.

2. Philip Ewing, "Partisan Battle Lines Blur on Libya," *Politico,* March 31, 2011, 13.

3. Abigail Hauslohner, "Libyan Prison Symbolizes Role Reversal after Gaddafi," *Washington Post,* March 4, 2013, A8.

4. Dave Boyer, "Obama Backs Off Syria 'Red Line,'" *Washington Times,* May 1, 2013, A1.

5. Robert W. Merry, "The Obama Doctrine," *The New York Times Book Review,* July 15, 2012, 11. The quote is from Merry's review of David E. Sanger's book: *Confront and Conceal.* "Mixture of realism and humanitarianism" are the words of Merry.

6. Quoted in Samuel Eliot Morison, *The Oxford History of the American People* (New York: Oxford University Press, 1965), 346.

7. Edward S. Corwin, *The President: Office and Powers, 1787–1957,* 4th ed. (New York: New York University Press, 1957), 171. Also see Cecil V. Crabb Jr. and Pat M. Holt, *Invitation to Struggle: Congress, the President, and Foreign Policy,* 4th ed. (Washington, DC: CQ Press, 1992).

8. Corwin, *The President,* 171 (emphasis in the original).

9. Alexander Hamilton, James Madison, and John Jay, *The Federalist Papers,* ed. Clinton Rossiter (New York: Mentor Books, 1961), 391–393.

10. Jonathan Mahler, "After the Imperial Presidency," *New York Times Magazine,* November 9, 2008, 45.

11. Jonathan Broder and Emily Cadei, "A Question of Authority," *CQ Weekly,* March 28, 2011, 670. Obama did consult with a small number of congressional leaders before the air war campaign began.

12. See Peter Baker, "Obama's Turn in Bush's Bind," *New York Times*, February 10, 2013, 1; Craig Whitlock, "Under Obama, Continued Renditions," *Washington Post*, January 2, 2013, A1; and Lara Seligman, "Voters: Obama Is No Better Than Bush on Security vs. Civil Liberties," *The Hill*, February 11, 2013, 10.

13. Testimony before the House International Relations Committee, January 12, 1995. Reported by Maureen Dowd, *New York Times*, January 13, 1995, A1.

14. Corwin, *The President*, 171 (emphasis in the original).

15. Rajiv Chandrasekaran, "Battle Looms over Pace of Afghanistan Pullout," *Washington Post*, March 31, 2011, A11.

16. *Youngstown Sheet and Tube Co. v. Sawyer*, 343 U.S. 636 (1952).

17. Cecil V. Crabb Jr., Glenn J. Antizzo, and Leila E. Sarieddine, *Congress and the Foreign Policy Process* (Baton Rouge: Louisiana State University Press, 2000), 4.

18. Ibid., 163.

19. Bryan Bender, "Kerry Poised to Cap Long Journey," *Boston Globe*, November 20, 2008 (online edition).

20. Holbert N. Carroll, *The House of Representatives and Foreign Affairs*, rev. ed. (Boston: Little, Brown, 1966), 20.

21. "Royce: al-Qaida Armed to the Teeth," *United Press International*, February 12, 2013 (online edition).

22. Amy B. Zegart, "The Domestic Politics of Irrational Intelligence Oversight, *Political Science Quarterly* (Spring 2011): 25.

23. Henry A. Kissinger, "Implementing Bush's Vision," *Washington Post*, May 16, 2005, A17.

24. *Congressional Record*, 105th Cong., 2d sess., March 2, 1998, E252.

25. Kevin Baron, "Panetta Says Washington 'Dysfunction' Now a Security Threat," *NationalJournal. com*, June 22, 2012 (online edition).

26. Chris Strohm, "A Secure Role," *National Journal's CongressDaily*, February 28, 2011, 3.

27. Information provided by Congressional Research Service defense expert Pat Towell.

28. Christopher J. Deering, "Congress, the President, and Military Policy," in *Congress and the Presidency: Invitation to Struggle*, ed. Roger H. Davidson, *The Annals* 499 (September 1988): 136–147.

29. Walter Pincus, "The Military's New Metrics: Smaller, Leaner, More Agile," *Washington Post*, February 7, 2012, A25.

30. Quoted in Matt Richtel, "Trade Investors Cull Start-Ups for Pentagon," *New York Times*, May 7, 2007, C8.

31. *Budget of the United States Government, Fiscal Year 2006, Historical Tables* (Washington, DC: Government Printing Office, 2005), table 3.2.

32. Quoted in Thomas Shanker, "Defense Secretary Urges More Spending for U.S. Diplomacy," *New York Times*, November 27, 2007, A6.

33. Leslie Wayne, "Pentagon Spends without Bids, a Study Finds," *New York Times*, September 30, 2004, C1.

34. Christopher Dickey, "The Surveillance-Industrial Complex," *New York Times Book Review*, January 11, 2009, 11.

35. Tim Smart, "Getting the F-22 off the Ground," *Washington Post*, April 20, 1998, 12; Tim Weiner, "Air Superiority at $258 Million a Pop," *New York Times*, October 27, 2004, C1.

36. Rowan Scarborough, "Prices Soar, Enthusiasm Dives for F-35 Lightning," *Washington Times*, March 7, 2013, A1. The items quoted in this paragraph are taken from this source.

37. Rajiv Chandrasekaran, "Too Big to Bail," *Washington Post*, March 10, 2013, A8, A9.

38. Ben Wolfgang, "Drones As Economic Engines," *Washington Times*, March 13, 2013, A6.

39. Tim Weiner, "For Military Plane in Crash, a History of Political Conflict," *New York Times,* April 11, 2000, A1.

40. Quoted in Roxana Tiron, "Marines, Weldon Score Victory on Osprey," *The Hill,* October 6, 2005, 16.

41. Christopher Bolkcom, "V-22 Osprey Tilt-Rotor Aircraft," Congressional Research Service Report RL31384, January 2, 2009, 11.

42. Quoted in Vernon Loeb, "Weapon Systems Die Hard, Especially on Capitol Hill," *Washington Post,* May 6, 2002, A4. See Richard Lardner, "Army, Congress Battle over Tanks," *Washington Times,* April 29, 2013, A3.

43. Carlo Munoz, "Crash Won't Alter V-22 Purchase Plans," *The Hill,* April 12, 2012, 12.

44. Quoted in Kevin Sack, "For the South, GOP Secures Defense Bounty," *New York Times,* November 18, 1997, A1.

45. *Congressional Record,* 100th Cong., 2d sess., July 7, 1988, 17072.

46. Karl Viox, "It's Closing Time for Base Commission," *Washington Post,* December 29, 1995, A21. Scholars regard this as an intriguing example of blame-avoidance politics. See, for example, Christopher J. Deering, "Congress, the President, and Automatic Government: The Case of Military Base Closures," in *Rivals for Power: Presidential-Congressional Relations,* ed. James A. Thurber (Washington, DC: CQ Press, 1996).

47. Megan Scully, "Military Plan Hits BRAC Wall," *CQ Weekly,* February 6, 2012, 235.

48. William H. Cooper, "The Future of U.S. Trade Policy: An Analysis of Issues and Options for the 112th Congress," Congressional Research Service Report R41145, January 4, 2011.

49. U.S. Trade Representative Ron Kirk, "The Monitor Breakfast," *Christian Science Monitor,* March 28, 2011, 19.

50. Rep. David Dreier, "Parties Can Work Together to Revive Trade Agenda," *Politico,* January 5, 2011, 35.

51. Joseph J. Schartz, "Trade Pacts No Longer an Easy Sell in GOP," *CQ Weekly,* December 13, 2010, 2848.

52. Quoted in John Stanton, "Sessions Continues Blockade of Trade Bill over Sleeping Bags," *Roll Call,* February 9, 2011 (online edition).

53. John E. Yang, "House Backs Clinton on China Trade Privileges," *Washington Post,* June 25, 1997, A1.

54. Sander Levin, "Derailing a Consensus on Trade," *Washington Post,* December 5, 2001, A29.

55. Barack Obama, "Making the World Work Again," *Los Angeles Times,* March 24, 2009 (online edition).

56. Richard Simon and Nancy Cleeland, "Senate OKs Fast-Track Trade Bill," *Los Angeles Times,* August 2, 2002, A1.

57. Richard G. Lugar and Thomas A. Daschle, "Defeating a Global Enemy—Hunger," *Washington Times,* May 1, 2013, B4.

58. Thom Shanker, "U.S. Arms Sales Make Up Most of Global Market," *New York Times,* August 27, 2012, A6.

59. Leslie Wayne, "Foreign Sales by U.S. Arms Makers Doubled in a Year," *New York Times,* November 11, 2006, B3.

60. Charles McC. Mathias Jr., "Ethnic Groups and Foreign Policy," *Foreign Affairs* 59 (Summer 1981): 975–998.

61. Megan Scully, "Gates Warns against Big Cuts in Future Defense Spending," *National Journal's CongressDaily PM,* April 17, 2009, 4.

62. Joseph J. Schatz, "Has Congress Given Bush Too Free a Spending Hand?" *CQ Weekly,* April 12, 2002, 859.

63. James Kitfield, "The Indispensable, Unaffordable Nation," *National Journal,* September 11, 2010, 35.

64. Micah Zenko and Rebecca R. Friedman, "A Soft Power Bargain," *Los Angeles Times*, February 16, 2011 (online edition).

65. Reps. Howard I. Berman and Gerald E. Connolly, "Overhaul of US Foreign Aid Is Overdue," *The Hill*, December 21, 2012, 16.

66. Zenko and Friedman, "Soft Power Bargain."

67. Robin Wright, "Don't Just Fund the War, Shell Out for Peace," *Washington Post*, March 10, 2001, B5; and Stephen Kinzer, "Why They Don't Know Us," *New York Times*, November 11, 2001, D5.

68. Ibid.

69. Berman and Connolly, "Overhaul of US Foreign Aid Is Overdue," 16.

70. Josh Smith, "Global Reach," *National Journal Daily*, March 2, 2011, 5. Also see Sen. Dick Durbin, "Tyrants Can Use Facebook, Too," *Politico*, March 7, 2011, 21; and Mark Preifle, "Web's Identity Crisis: Tool of Freedom or Repression," *Christian Science Monitor*, March 14, 2011, 34.

71. David P. Auerswald, "Advice and Consent: The Forgotten Power," in *Congress and the Politics of Foreign Policy*, ed. Colton C. Campbell, Nicol C. Rae, and John Stack (Upper Saddle River, NJ: Prentice Hall, 2003), 47–48.

72. Loch Johnson and James M. McCormick, "Foreign Policy by Executive Fiat," *Foreign Policy* 28 (Fall 1977): 118–124.

73. Roger H. Davidson, "Senate Floor Deliberation: A Preliminary Inquiry," in *The Contentious Senate*, ed. Colton C. Campbell and Nicol C. Rae (Lanham, MD: Rowman and Littlefield, 2001), 22–29.

74. David Silverberg, "Nasty, Brutish and Short: The CTBT Debates," *The Hill*, December 8, 1999, 16.

75. Ibid.

76. Peter Baker, "Gamble by Obama Pays Off with Final Approval of Arms Control Pact," *New York Times*, December 23, 2010, A6.

77. Quoted in Gail Russell Chaddock, "Off-Radar Tax Breaks Draw New Scrutiny," *Christian Science Monitor*, March 9, 2005, 11.

78. Michael John Garcia, "International Law and Agreements: Their Effect Upon U.S. Law," Congressional Research Service Report RL32528, January 26, 2010, 3.

79. Ibid., 21.

80. Glen S. Krutz and Jeffrey S. Peake, *Treaty Politics and the Rise of Executive Agreements: International Commitments in a System of Shared Powers* (Ann Arbor: University of Michigan Press, 2009), 10.

81. Jeanne J. Grimmett, "Why Certain Trade Agreements Are Approved as Congressional-Executive Agreements Rather Than as Treaties," Congressional Research Service Report 97–896, February 17, 2009, 5.

82. This section draws on the invaluable summary of congressional policy initiation in Ellen C. Collier, "Foreign Policy Roles of the President and Congress," Congressional Research Service Report 93–20F, January 6, 1993, 11–17.

83. The classic account of this incident is Chalmers M. Roberts, "The Day We Didn't Go to War," *Reporter*, September 14, 1954, 31–35.

84. Alexander Bolton, "Dems Want Clearer Benchmarks from Obama on Afghanistan," *The Hill*, April 15, 2009, 3.

85. See Thomas R. Pickering, "The Truth about Torture," *Washington Post*, April 19, 2013, A23.

86. William G. Howell and Jon C. Pevehouse, *When Danger Lurks: Congressional Checks on Presidential War Powers* (Princeton, NJ: Princeton University Press, 2007), 223.

87. Shaun Waterman, "Report on Networks' Security Is on Hold," *Washington Times*, March 8, 2013, A4.

88. Ellen C. Collier, "Foreign Policy by Reporting Requirement," *Washington Quarterly* 11 (Winter 1988): 75.

89. Bruce J. Schulman, "Congress' Wartime Quandary," *Los Angeles Times*, April 27, 2003, M2.

90. Cited in Frederick A. O. Schwarz Jr. and Aziz Huq, "Where's Congress in This Power Play?" *Washington Post*, April 1, 2007, B1.

91. Thomas E. Mann and Norman J. Ornstein, *The Broken Branch* (New York: Oxford University Press, 2006), 151–152.

92. Stacy Kaper, "Hold on Nominees Useful Leverage for Senate Hawks," *National Journal Daily*, January 15, 2013, 8.

93. Peter Finn and Aaron Blake, "CIA Chief Confirmed after Debate over Drones," *Washington Post*, March 8, 2013, A4.

94. James M. Lindsay, "Congress, Foreign Policy, and the New Institutionalism," *International Studies Quarterly* 38 (June 1994): 281–304.

95. An early influential analysis of this phenomenon is John E. Mueller, *War, Presidents, and Public Opinion* (New York: Wiley, 1973), 208–213.

96. Richard F. Grimmett, "Instances of Use of United States Armed Forces Abroad, 1798–2006," Congressional Research Service Report RL32170, January 8, 2007.

97. Andrew J. Bacevich, "War Powers in the Age of Terror," *New York Times*, October 31, 2005, A21.

98. Quotes from Helen Dewar, "Congress's Reaction to TV Coverage Shows Ambivalence on Foreign Policy," *Washington Post*, October 9, 1993, A14; and Helen Dewar, "Clinton, Congress at Brink of Foreign Policy Dispute," *Washington Post*, May 16, 1994, A1.

99. Douglas L. Kriner, *After the Rubicon: Congress, Presidents, and the Politics of Waging War* (Chicago: University of Chicago Press, 2010).

100. Richard F. Grimmett, "War Powers Resolution: Presidential Compliance," Congressional Research Service Report RL33532, March 25, 2011. Also see Richard Grimmett, "The War Powers Resolution: After Thirty-Six Years," Congressional Research Service Report R4119, April 22, 2010.

101. See David A. Fahrenthold, "Obama Misses Deadline for Approval of Libya Operations," *Washington Post*, May 21, 2011, A3; and John C. Yoo and Robert J. Delahunty, "Libya and the War Powers Resolution," *Wall Street Journal*, May 20, 2011, A15.

102. Carlos Munoz and Jeremy Herb, "House GOP Challenges Pentagon on War Powers for Action in Syria," *The Hill*, April 20, 2012, 12.

103. David E. Sanger, David Barboza, and Nicole Perlroth, "China's Army Seen as Tied to Hacking Against U.S.," *New York Times*, February 19, 2013, A1.

104. Jack Goldsmith, "Stealth Wars Require Rules, Too," *Washington Post*, February 6, 2013, A17. Goldsmith also includes covert action, special forces, drone surveillance and targeting, and other stealthy means within his call for new rules for a new type of war. Also see David E. Sanger, "In Cyberspace, New Cold War," *New York Times*, February 25, 2013 A1.

105. Ivo H. Daalder and James M. Lindsay, *America Unbound: The Bush Revolution in Foreign Policy* (New York: Brookings, 2003), 90.

106. Caroline Heldman, "Presidential Persuasion and Press Coverage of the War in Iraq," in *Understanding the Presidency*, 4th ed., ed. James P. Pfiffner and Roger H. Davidson (New York: Pearson Longman, 2007), 199–200.

107. Adam Entous, Julian E Barnes, and Siobhan Gorman, "CIA Ramps Up Role in Iraq," *Wall Street Journal*, March 12, 2013, A1.

108. Editorial, "Iraq's Ticking Clock," *Washington Post*, April 3, 2011, A20. See Daniel Dombey and Funja Guler, "Iraq, 10 Years On, the US Won the War, Iran Won the Peace and Turkey Won the Contracts," *Financial Times*, March 13, 2013, 1; and Daniel Trotta, "Iraq War Costs U.S.

More Than $2 Trillion," *Reuters*, March 14, 2013 (online edition). Trotta's article is based on a study by Brown University.

109. Joseph Stiglitz and Linda Blimes, "There Will Be No Peace Dividend after Afghanistan," *Financial Times*, January 24, 2013, 11.

110. Ashisn Kumar Sen, "Afghans Fear a Civil War If All U.S. Troops Depart," *Washington Times*, January 15, 2013, A1.

111. Scott Peterson, "Afghanistan in 2015," *Christian Science Monitor Weekly*, January 21, 2013, 10.

112. See Frank Oliveri, "Deciding America's Role in Afghanistan after 2014," *CQ Weekly*, December 17, 2012, 2516–2517; Mark Landler and Michael R. Gordon, "U.S. Is Open to Withdraw Afghan Force after 2014," *New York Times*, January 9, 2013, A8; and Emily Cadei, "Avoiding History in Afghanistan," *CQ Weekly*, March 4, 2013, 408–412.

113. Quoted in Stephen Daggett, "Quadrennial Defense Review 2010: Overview and Implications for National Security Planning," Congressional Research Service Report R41250, May 17, 2010, 2–3.

114. Joshua S. Goldstein and Steven Pinker, "War Really Is Going Out of Style," *New York Times*, December 18, 2011, SR4.

115. James Kitfield, "Patterns of Death," *National Journal*, March 10, 2012, 24.

116. Daniel Dombey, James Blitz, and Peter Spiegel, "An Advancing Front," May 20, 2011, 9.

117. Ken Dilanian, "Cyber-Attacks a Bigger Threat Than Al Qaeda, Officials Say," *Los Angeles Times*, March 12, 2013 (online edition).

118. Kristina Wong, "Offensive Cyberforce Being Built," *Washington Times*, March 13, 2013, A4; and Ellen Nakashima, "Pentagon Plans to Add 40 Teams to Combat Growing Online Threat," *Washington Post*, March 13, 2013, A2.

119. Tom Vanden Brook and Gregg Zoroya, "Robot to Aid Troop Patrols," *USA Today*, October 17, 2011, 1A. Also see Tom Malinowski, "A Dangerous Future of Robots," *Washington Post*, November 23, 2012, A23.

120. "Magic Bullets," *Economist*, January 14, 2012, 76–77.

121. Mark Clayton, "Warning of a New Kind of War," *Christian Science Monitor*, October 17, 2011, 18.

122. Craig Whitlock, "For Pentagon, Pivot to Asia Becomes Shift toward Africa," *Washington Post*, February 15, 2013, A8.

123. James Kitfield, "Leading from the Shadows," *National Journal*, March 9, 2013, 18–24. Also see Jonathan Broder, "The Battlefield Grows Larger," *CQ Weekly*, January 28, 2013, 204–211.

124. See Ben Wolfgang, "With Rise of Drones, Neutralizers Come into Fashion," *Washington Times*, May 1, 2013, A1.

125. Scott Shane, "A Court to Vet Kill Lists," *New York Times*, February 9, 2011, A1. Also see "Here's Looking at You," *Economist*, February 16, 2013, 31; Somini Sengupta, "Lawmakers Set Limits on Police in Using Drones," *New York Times*, February 16, 2013, A1; Sara Sorcher, "The Case for Drones at Home," *National Journal*, March 9, 2013, 27; Vicki Divoll, "Drone Strikes: What's the Law?" *Los Angeles Times*, February 17, 2013 (online edition); and Michael B. Mukasey, "How to Untangle an Incoherent Drone Policy," *Wall Street Journal*, February 19, 2013, A15.

126. Michael Abramowitz, "Bush, Congress Could Face Confrontation on Issue of War Powers," *Washington Post*, February 16, 2007, A5.

127. Bacevich, "War Powers in the Age of Terror," A21.

128. James M. Lindsay, "Congress and Foreign Policy: Why the Hill Matters," *Political Science Quarterly* 107 (Winter 1992–1993): 626–627.

129. Robert C. Byrd, *Losing America* (New York: Norton, 2005), 23

CHAPTER 16

1. Quoted in Carl Hulse and David M. Herszenhorn, "Behind Closed Doors, Warnings of Calamity," *New York Times*, September 20, 2008, C5.
2. Jonathan Weisman, David Cho, and Paul Kane, "With No Plan B, House Reluctantly Passes Politically Risky Measure," *Washington Post*, October 4, 2008, A1.
3. Quoted in ibid.
4. David M. Herszenhorn, "Administration Is Seeking $700 Billion for Wall Street in Possible Record Bailout," *New York Times*, September 21, 2008, A1.
5. Quoted in Hulse and Herszenhorn, "Behind Closed Doors," C5.
6. Quoted in Joe Nocera, "36 Hours of Alarm and Action as Crisis Spread," *New York Times*, October 2, 2008, A1.
7. Jackie Calmes, "Dazed Capital Feels Its Way, Eyes on Nov. 4," *Washington Post*, September 20, 2008, A1.
8. Quoted in Lori Montgomery, Paul Kane, and Neil Irwin, "Bailout Proposal Meets Bipartisan Outrage; Lawmakers Balk as Officials Press Case for Quick Action," *Washington Post*, September 24, 2008, A1.
9. David M. Herszenhorn, "Word Reaches Congress: As the Market Goes Down, So Goes the Electorate," *New York Times*, October 2, 2008, C10.
10. Jonathan Weisman, "House Rejects Financial Rescue, Sending Stocks Plummeting," *Washington Post*, September 30, 2008, A1.
11. Editorial, "Bailout Breakdown," *New York Times*, September 25, 2008, A18; David S. Broder, "Credibility Test for Congress," September 25, 2008, A19.
12. Sarah A. Binder, Thomas E. Mann, Norman J. Ornstein, and Molly Reynolds, "Mending the Broken Branch: Assessing the 110th Congress, Anticipating the 111th," Brookings Institution Report, January 2009, www.brookings.edu/papers/2009/0108_broken_branch_binder_mann.aspx, 33.
13. Andrew Kohut, "Pessimistic Public Doubts Effectiveness of Stimulus, TARP," Pew Research Center for the People and the Press, April 28, 2010, http://people-press.org/reports/pdf/608.pdf.
14. Considering both repayment and investment gains, the program has cost the government approximately $29 billion, as of November 2012. Paul Kiel and Dan Nguyen, "Bailout Tracker," ProPublica (updated November 26, 2012), projects.propublica.org/bailout/main/summary.
15. Tim Massad, "The Response to the Financial Crisis—In Charts," *Treasury Notes*, U.S. Department of the Treasury, April 13, 2012, www.treasury.gov/connect/blog/Pages/financial-crisis-response-in-charts.aspx.
16. Steven Pearlstein, "Unfairly Rewarding Greedy Bankers, and Why It Works," *Washington Post*, January 14, 2009, D1.
17. See Charles O. Jones, *The Presidency in a Separated System* (Washington, DC: Brookings, 1994).
18. *Congressional Record*, 105th Cong., 1st sess., May 21, 1997, H3072.
19. Glenn R. Parker and Roger H. Davidson, "Why Do Americans Love Their Congressmen So Much More Than Their Congress?" *Legislative Studies Quarterly* 4 (February 1979): 53–61.
20. See Roger H. Davidson, "The House of Representatives: Managing Legislative Complexity," in *Workways of Governance: Monitoring Our Government's Health*, ed. Roger H. Davidson (Washington, DC: Governance Institute and Brookings, 2003), 24–46; and Sarah A. Binder, "The Senate: Does It Deliberate? Can It Act?" in Davidson, *Workways of Governance*, 47–64.
21. Michael Leahy, "House Rules: Freshman Congressman Joe Courtney, Elected by a Margin of 83 Votes, Is Learning That the First Requirement of Power Is Self-Preservation," *Washington Post Magazine*, June 10, 2007, W12.
22. Quoted in Mary Lynn F. Jones, "Family Concerns Prompt Early Hill Retirements," *The Hill*, March 20, 2002, 12.

23. Quoted in ibid.

24. Quoted in Leahy, "House Rules," W12.

25. Quoted in ibid.

26. Bob Benenson, "Savvy 'Stars' Making Local TV a Potent Tool," *Congressional Quarterly Weekly Report,* July 18, 1987, 1551–1555.

27. Timothy Cook, *Making Laws and Making News: Media Strategies in the U.S. House of Representatives* (Washington, DC: Brookings, 1989), 82–83.

28. Frank Newport, "Congress Retains Low Honesty Rating," News Release, Gallup Politics, December 3, 2012, www.gallup.com/poll/159035/congress-retains-low-honesty-rating.aspx.

29. Jeffrey M. Jones, "Nurses Top Honesty and Ethics List for 11th Year: Lobbyists, Car Salespeople, Members of Congress Get the Lowest Ratings," Gallup, Inc., News Release, December 3, 2010, www.gallup.com/poll/145043/nurses-top-honesty-ethics-list-11-year.aspx.

30. Lee H. Hamilton, "Ten Things I Wish Political Scientists Would Teach about Congress," Pi Sigma Alpha Lecture, American Political Science Association, August 31, 2000, 7. Also see Hamilton's thoughtful book, *How Congress Works and Why You Should Care* (Bloomington: Indiana University Press, 2004).

31. Quoted in T. R. Goldman, "The Influence Industry's Senior Class," *Legal Times,* June 16, 1997, 4.

32. John Bresnehan and Jonathan Allen, "House Censures a Defiant Charles Rangel by Overwhelming Vote," *Politico,* December 2, 2010, www,politico.com/news/stories/1210/ 45883.html.

33. Amanda Becker, "Congressional Ethics Inquiries Helped Sweep Some Lawmakers Out of Office," *Roll Call,* November 13, 2012.

34. Norman J. Ornstein, "The Abramoff Saga: The Worst Hill Scandal in Our Lifetime?" *Roll Call,* October 19, 2005, 5–6.

35. Susan Schmidt and James V. Grimaldi, "Abramoff Pleads Guilty to 3 Counts," *Washington Post,* January 4, 2006, A1.

36. Paul Blumenthal, "Abramoff Investigation Continues Apace," Sunlight Foundation weblog, February 2, 2009, http://sunlightfoundation.com/blog/2009/02/02/abramoff-investigation-continues-apace/.

37. Scott Higham, "Congressional Ethics Committees Protect Legislators, Critics Say," *Washington Post,* October 7, 2012, www.washingtonpost.com/investigations/congressional-ethics-committees-protect-legislators-critics-say/2012/10/07/a313e59c-c251-11e1-ae7f-d2a13e249eb2_story.html.

38. Bob Cusack, "Speaker Nancy Pelosi Did Not Drain Swamp, Key Voters Believe," *The Hill,* October 7, 2010.

39. Cass R. Sunstein, "Unchecked and Unbalanced," *American Prospect* 38 (May–June 1998): 23. Sunstein served as the head of the Office of Information and Regulatory Affairs in the Office of Management and Budget during President Obama's first term.

40. Amanda Muñoz-Temple, "The Man behind Weiner's Resignation," *National Journal,* June 16, 2011, /www.nationaljournal.com/the-man-behind-weiner-s-resignation-20110616.

41. David Catanese, "John Ensign, Citing 'Consequences to Sin,' Announces Retirement," *Politico,* March 7, 2011, www.politico.com/news/stories/0311/50799.html.

42. David A. Fahrenthold and Aaron Blake, "Rep. Chris Lee Resigns after Reports of Craigslist Flirtation," *Washington Post,* February 10, 2011.

43. This list includes would-be Speaker Bob Livingston, R-La. (1977–1999), Rep. Gary A. Condit, D-Calif. (1989–2003), Rep. Mark Foley, R-Fla. (1995–2006), Rep. Tim Mahoney, D-Fla. (2007–2008), and Rep. Mark Souder, R-Ind. (1995–2010).

44. Edward Epstein, "GOP Makes Much Ado about the Size of Pelosi's Plane; the House Speaker Has Had the Use of a Government Jet since the September 11 Attacks," *San Francisco Chronicle,* February 8, 2007, A3.

45. G. Calvin Mackenzie with Michael Hafken, *Scandal Proof: Do Ethics Laws Make Government Ethical?* (Washington, DC: Brookings, 2002), 158.

46. Benjamin Ginsberg and Martin Shefter, *Politics by Other Means: Politicians, Prosecutors, and the Press from Watergate to Whitewater*, 3d ed. (New York: Norton, 2002).

47. Paul C. Light, "Measuring the Health of the Public Service," in Davidson, *Workways of Governance*, 96–97.

48. Jennifer L. Lawless and Richard Logan Fox, *It Still Takes a Candidate: Why Women Don't Run For Office* (New York: Cambridge University Press, 2010).

49. Jennifer L. Lawless, *Becoming a Candidate: Political Ambition and the Decision to Run for Office* (New York: Cambridge University Press), 166–170.

50. Gary C. Jacobson, "The Misallocation of Resources in House Campaigns," *Congress Reconsidered*, 5th ed., ed. Lawrence C. Dodd and Bruce I. Oppenheimer (Washington, DC: CQ Press, 1993), 153–182.

51. Woodrow Wilson, *Constitutional Government in the United States* (New York: Columbia University Press, 1908), 79–80.

52. Diane Hollern Harvey, "Who Should Govern? Public Preferences for Congressional and Presidential Power," Ph.D. dissertation, University of Maryland, 1998.

53. Hamilton, "Ten Things I Wish Political Scientists Would Teach about Congress," 3.

54. Center on Congress, Indiana University, November 2012 Public Opinion Survey, http://congress.indiana.edu/november-2012-public-opinion-survey (accessed December 9, 2012).

55. Paul C. Light, *Government's Greatest Achievements: From Civil Rights to Homeland Security* (Washington, DC: Brookings, 2002).

56. Ibid., 63.

57. Devlin Barrett, "Most in U.S. Say Congress Short-Sighted," *Washington Post,* September 29, 2006.

58. Richard Hall, *Participation in Congress* (New Haven, CT: Yale University Press, 1996), 2.

59. Binder et al., "Mending the Broken Branch," 7.

60. Barbara Sinclair, *Unorthodox Lawmaking: New Legislative Processes in the U.S. Congress*, 4th ed. (Washington, DC: CQ Press, 2011).

61. Ibid.

62. Norman J. Ornstein, Thomas E. Mann, and Michael J. Malbin, *Vital Statistics on Congress, 2008* (Washington, DC: Brookings, 2008), 110.

63. Debbie Siegelbaum, "House Is Cutting Committee Budgets—Some More Than Others," *The Hill,* February 1, 2012, http://thehill.com/blogs/blog-briefing-room/news/208051-house-cutting-committee-budgets-some-more-than-others-.

64. Thomas E. Mann and Norman J. Ornstein, *The Broken Branch: How Congress Is Failing America and How to Get It Back on Track* (New York: Oxford University Press, 2006), 216.

65. Lee Hamilton, "We Can't Wait Much Longer to Fix Congress," *Comments on Congress,* December 15, 2005.

66. "Efficiency Up against Precedent," *CQ Weekly,* December 13, 2010: 2841.

67. Paul Bedard, "House to Work Just 32 Weeks in 2011," *U.S. News and World Report,* Weblog, December 8, 2010, www.usnews.com/news/washington-whispers/articles/2010/12/08/house-to-work-just-32-weeks-in-2011.

68. Nelson W. Polsby, *How Congress Evolves: Social Bases of Institutional Change* (New York: Oxford University Press, 2004), 130–137.

69. Binder et al., "Mending the Broken Branch," 7.

70. Quoted by David S. Broder, "Role Models, Now More Than Ever," *Washington Post,* July 13, 2003, B7.

71. Mickey Edwards, "Wanted: A Congress with a Backbone," *Los Angeles Times,* August 29, 2006, B13.

72. Laurel Harbridge and Neil Malhotra, "Electoral Incentives and Partisan Conflict in Congress: Evidence from Survey Experiments," *American Journal of Political Science* 55 (July 2011): 494–510.

73. Mark D. Ramirez, "The Dynamics of Partisan Conflict on Congressional Approval," *American Journal of Political Science* 53 (July 2009): 683.

74. Sinclair, *Unorthodox Lawmaking*.

75. Alexander Burns, "VP: Constitution 'On Its Head,'" Weblog, 44: A Living Diary of the Obama Presidency, *Politico*, January 18, 2010, www.politico.com/politico44/perm/0110/biden_slams_filibuster_fe40df44-9045-4c26-a715-51c427035eae.html.

76. Sinclair, *Unorthodox Lawmaking*, 282.

77. Ian Millhiser, "The Tyranny of the Timepiece: Senate Rules Obstruct Voting to a Degree That Wounds Our Government," Center for American Progress Report, September 28, 2010, www.americanprogress.org/issues/2010/09/tyranny_of_the_timepiece.html.

78. For an extended analysis of these dilemmas, see John B. Gilmour, *Strategic Disagreement: Stalemate in American Politics* (Pittsburgh: University of Pittsburgh Press, 1995).

79. C-SPAN began gavel-to-gavel telecasting of House proceedings in 1979 and Senate proceedings in 1986.

80. Joseph J. Schatz, "Tune a New Channel into the Senate," *CQ Weekly*, April 19, 2010, 956.

81. E. Scott Adler, *Why Congressional Reforms Fail: Reelection and the House Committee System* (Chicago: University of Chicago Press, 2002), 11.

82. Eric Schickler, *Disjointed Pluralism: Institutional Innovation and the Development of the U.S. Congress* (Princeton, NJ: Princeton University Press, 2001), 268.Ibid., 267.

83. Bob Schieffer, *This Just In: What I Couldn't Tell You on TV* (New York: Putnam, 2003).

84. See Martin P. Wattenberg, *Is Voting for Young People?* 2d ed. (New York: Pearson Longman, 2007), esp. chaps. 1–2.

85. Bill Moyers, "Journalism and Democracy," *Nation*, May 7, 2001, 12.

86. Media critic Neal Gabler's commentaries are especially incisive. See "The Media Bias Myth," *Los Angeles Times*, December 22, 2002, M1.

87. Lydia Saad, "Congress Approval at 18%, Stuck in Long-Term Low Streak," Gallup, Inc., News Release, November 26, 2012, www.gallup.com/poll/158948/congress-approval-stuck-long-term-low-streak.aspx.

88. John R. Hibbing and Elizabeth Theiss-Morse, *Congress as Public Enemy* (Cambridge: Cambridge University Press, 1995), 147.

89. Ibid., 158.

90. Alan K. Ota, "Finding Solutions to Secure Events," *CQ Weekly*, January 17, 2011, 164.

91. See Louis Fisher, *Presidential War Power*, 2d ed. (Lawrence: University Press of Kansas, 2004).

92. Josh Rogin, "How Obama Turned on a Dime toward War," The Cable, *Foreign Policy* Weblog, March 18, 2011, http://thecable.foreignpolicy.com/posts/2011/03/18/how_obama_turned_on_a_dime_toward_war.

93. Quoted in Kirk Victor, "Congress in Eclipse," *National Journal*, April 5, 2003, 1068.

94. Ibid., 1069.

95. Hamilton, "We Can't Wait Much Longer to Fix Congress."

96. David Nather, "Congress as Watchdog: Asleep on the Job?" *CQ Weekly*, May 22, 2004, 1190.

97. John T. Noonan Jr., *Narrowing the Nation's Power* (Berkeley: University of California Press, 2002), 11.

98. Ibid., 139.

99. James L. Sundquist, *The Decline and Resurgence of Congress* (Washington, DC: Brookings, 1981), 482–483.

100. Andrew Rudalevige, *The New Imperial Presidency: Renewing Presidential Power after Watergate* (Ann Arbor: University of Michigan Press, 2005), 261.

Boxes, figures, tables, and notes are indicated by *b, f, t,* and *n.*
Appendix page numbers start with A, and note page numbers start with N.

Frontispiece, page xviii: Library of Congress (top left and top right); *The New York Times* (center); AP Images (bottom).

Chapter 1, page 2: Roll Call/Getty Images (top); John McCoy/*Los Angeles Daily News* (center); Roll Call/Getty Images (bottom).

Chapter 2, page 14: Library of Congress (top and center); Fang Zhe/Xinhua Press/Corbis (bottom).

Chapter 3, page 40: U.S. Census Bureau (top left); Bob Daemmrich/Bob Daemmrich Photography, Inc./Corbis (top right); Getty Images (center); Michael Dwyer/AP/Corbis (bottom left); MCT via Getty Images (bottom right).

Chapter 4, page 64: Will Kincaid/AP/Corbis (top); Associated Press (center); Brooks Kraft/Corbis (bottom).

Chapter 5, page 102: Cliff Owen/AP/Corbis (top left); AP Images (top right, bottom left, and bottom right).

Chapter 6, page 130: Xinhua/Yuri Gripas/Xinhua Press/Corbis (top right); Joshua Roberts/Reuters/Corbis (top left); Michael Reynolds/epa/Corbis (bottom left); Jim Young/Reuters (bottom right).

Chapter 7, page 162: Alex Wong/Getty Images (top left); CQ Roll Call (top right); Roll Call/Getty Images (center); Congressional Quarterly/Newscom (bottom).

Chapter 8, page 204: Bettmann/Corbis/AP Images (top); Brendan Hoffman/Getty Images (center); Congressional Quarterly/Newscom (bottom).

Chapter 9, page 244: AP Photo/TV/CSPAN (top left); Brendan Hoffman/Getty Images; AP Photo/CSPAN (bottom left); The Humane Society of the United States, reprinted with permission (bottom right).

Chapter 10, page 274: Pool/Getty Images (top); Associated Press (center); Joshua Roberts/Bloomberg/Getty Images (bottom).

Chapter 11, page 308: Associated Press (top left); Tim Sloan/AFP/Getty Images (top right); Michael Reynolds/epa/Corbis (bottom left); Jack Kurtz/ZUMA Press/Corbis (center right); John David Mercer/Pool/epa/Corbis (bottom right).

Chapter 12, page 340: Christy Bowe/Corbis (top); Chip Somodevilla/Getty Images (center); Associated Press (bottom).

Chapter 13, page 366: Associated Press (top); Roll Call/Getty Images (center left); Getty Images (bottom left); Michael Reynolds/epa/Corbis (bottom right).

Chapter 14, page 398: Nikki Kahn/*The Washington Post* (top); Associated Press (center); AFP/Getty Images (bottom).

Chapter 15, page 430: Alex Wong/Getty Images (top); Associated Press (center left); Lee Jae-Won/Reuters/Corbis (bottom left); Associated Press (bottom right).

Chapter 16, page 462: Margaret Bourke-White/Time & Life Pictures/Getty Images (left); Tom Williams/Roll Call/Getty Images (top right); Alex Wong/Getty Images (bottom).

CONGRESSIONAL TIME LINE: **1789–1932**

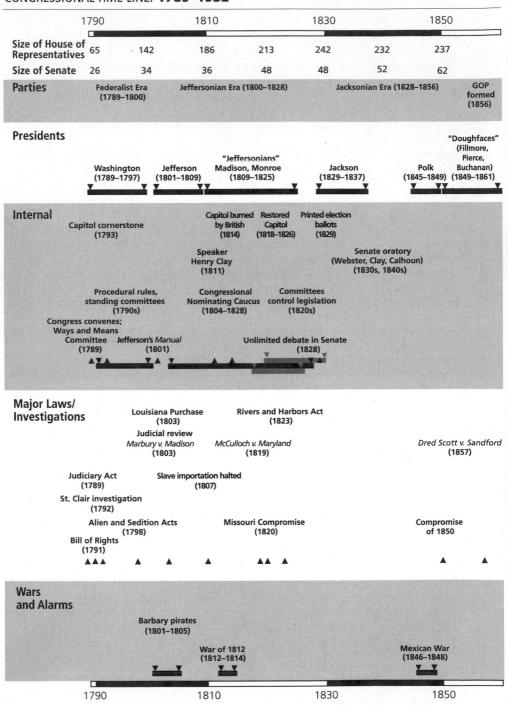

	1790		1810		1830		1850	
Size of House of Representatives	65	142	186	213	242	232	237	
Size of Senate	26	34	36	48	48	52	62	

Parties
Federalist Era (1789–1800) · Jeffersonian Era (1800–1828) · Jacksonian Era (1828–1856) · GOP formed (1856)

Presidents
"Doughfaces" (Fillmore, Pierce, Buchanan) (1849–1861)
Washington (1789–1797) · Jefferson (1801–1809) · "Jeffersonians" Madison, Monroe (1809–1825) · Jackson (1829–1837) · Polk (1845–1849)

Internal
Capitol cornerstone (1793)
Capitol burned by British (1814) · Restored Capitol (1818–1826) · Printed election ballots (1829)
Speaker Henry Clay (1811)
Senate oratory (Webster, Clay, Calhoun) (1830s, 1840s)
Procedural rules, standing committees (1790s) · Congressional Nominating Caucus (1804–1828) · Committees control legislation (1820s)
Congress convenes; Ways and Means Committee (1789) · Jefferson's *Manual* (1801) · Unlimited debate in Senate (1828)

Major Laws/ Investigations
Louisiana Purchase (1803) · Rivers and Harbors Act (1823)
Judicial review *Marbury v. Madison* (1803) · *McCulloch v. Maryland* (1819) · *Dred Scott v. Sandford* (1857)
Judiciary Act (1789) · Slave importation halted (1807)
St. Clair investigation (1792)
Alien and Sedition Acts (1798) · Missouri Compromise (1820) · Compromise of 1850
Bill of Rights (1791)

Wars and Alarms
Barbary pirates (1801–1805)
War of 1812 (1812–1814)
Mexican War (1846–1848)

1790	1810	1830	1850